Examining Multiple Intelligences and Digital Technologies for Enhanced Learning Opportunities

Robert Z. Zheng
University of Utah, USA

A volume in the Advances in Educational Technologies and Instructional Design (AETID) Book Series

Published in the United States of America by
IGI Global
Information Science Reference (an imprint of IGI Global)
701 E. Chocolate Avenue
Hershey PA, USA 17033
Tel: 717-533-8845
Fax: 717-533-8661
E-mail: cust@igi-global.com
Web site: http://www.igi-global.com

Copyright © 2020 by IGI Global. All rights reserved. No part of this publication may be reproduced, stored or distributed in any form or by any means, electronic or mechanical, including photocopying, without written permission from the publisher. Product or company names used in this set are for identification purposes only. Inclusion of the names of the products or companies does not indicate a claim of ownership by IGI Global of the trademark or registered trademark.

Library of Congress Cataloging-in-Publication Data

Names: Zheng, Robert Z., editor.
Title: Examining multiple intelligences and digital technologies for
  enhanced learning opportunities / Robert Z. Zheng, editor.
Description: Hershey, PA : Information Science Reference, 2020. | Includes
  bibliographical references. | Summary: ""This book examines the
  relationship between multiple intelligences and information and
  communication technology in formal and informal learning
  settings"--Provided by publisher"-- Provided by publisher.
Identifiers: LCCN 2019019332 | ISBN 9781799802495 (hardcover) | ISBN
  9781799802501 (paperback) | ISBN 9781799802518 (ebook)
Subjects: LCSH: Cognitive learning. | Cognitive styles. | Multiple
  intelligences. | Educational technology--Psychologicial aspects. |
  Education--Effect of technological innovations on.
Classification: LCC LB1062 .E93 2020 | DDC 370.15/2--dc23
LC record available at https://lccn.loc.gov/2019019332

This book is published in the IGI Global book series Advances in Educational Technologies and Instructional Design (AETID) (ISSN: 2326-8905; eISSN: 2326-8913)

British Cataloguing in Publication Data
A Cataloguing in Publication record for this book is available from the British Library.

All work contributed to this book is new, previously-unpublished material. The views expressed in this book are those of the authors, but not necessarily of the publisher.

For electronic access to this publication, please contact: eresources@igi-global.com.

Advances in Educational Technologies and Instructional Design (AETID) Book Series

Lawrence A. Tomei
Robert Morris University, USA

ISSN:2326-8905
EISSN:2326-8913

Mission

Education has undergone, and continues to undergo, immense changes in the way it is enacted and distributed to both child and adult learners. In modern education, the traditional classroom learning experience has evolved to include technological resources and to provide online classroom opportunities to students of all ages regardless of their geographical locations. From distance education, Massive-Open-Online-Courses (MOOCs), and electronic tablets in the classroom, technology is now an integral part of learning and is also affecting the way educators communicate information to students.

The **Advances in Educational Technologies & Instructional Design (AETID) Book Series** explores new research and theories for facilitating learning and improving educational performance utilizing technological processes and resources. The series examines technologies that can be integrated into K-12 classrooms to improve skills and learning abilities in all subjects including STEM education and language learning. Additionally, it studies the emergence of fully online classrooms for young and adult learners alike, and the communication and accountability challenges that can arise. Trending topics that are covered include adaptive learning, game-based learning, virtual school environments, and social media effects. School administrators, educators, academicians, researchers, and students will find this series to be an excellent resource for the effective design and implementation of learning technologies in their classes.

Coverage

- E-Learning
- Classroom Response Systems
- Higher Education Technologies
- Online Media in Classrooms
- Instructional Design
- Adaptive Learning
- Collaboration Tools
- Instructional Design Models
- Virtual School Environments
- Web 2.0 and Education

> IGI Global is currently accepting manuscripts for publication within this series. To submit a proposal for a volume in this series, please contact our Acquisition Editors at Acquisitions@igi-global.com or visit: http://www.igi-global.com/publish/.

The Advances in Educational Technologies and Instructional Design (AETID) Book Series (ISSN 2326-8905) is published by IGI Global, 701 E. Chocolate Avenue, Hershey, PA 17033-1240, USA, www.igi-global.com. This series is composed of titles available for purchase individually; each title is edited to be contextually exclusive from any other title within the series. For pricing and ordering information please visit http://www.igi-global.com/book-series/advances-educational-technologies-instructional-design/73678. Postmaster: Send all address changes to above address. ©© 2020 IGI Global. All rights, including translation in other languages reserved by the publisher. No part of this series may be reproduced or used in any form or by any means – graphics, electronic, or mechanical, including photocopying, recording, taping, or information and retrieval systems – without written permission from the publisher, except for non commercial, educational use, including classroom teaching purposes. The views expressed in this series are those of the authors, but not necessarily of IGI Global.

Titles in this Series
For a list of additional titles in this series, please visit: www.igi-global.com/book-series

Blended Online Learning and Instructional Design for TPACK Emerging Research and Opportunities
Margaret L. Niess (Oregon State University, USA)
Information Science Reference • ©2019 • 213pp • H/C (ISBN: 9781522588795) • US $145.00

Handbook of Research on Assessment Practices and Pedagogical Models for Immigrant Students
Jared Keengwe (University of North Dakota, USA) and Grace Onchwari (University of North Dakota, USA)
Information Science Reference • ©2019 • 454pp • H/C (ISBN: 9781522593485) • US $255.00

Recent Advances in Applying Identity and Society Awareness to Virtual Learning
Andrew G. Stricker (The Air University, USA) Cynthia Calongne (Colorado Technical University, USA) Barbara Truman (University of Central Florida, USA) and Fil J. Arenas (The Air University, USA)
Information Science Reference • ©2019 • 370pp • H/C (ISBN: 9781522596790) • US $195.00

Handbook of Research on Faculty Development for Digital Teaching and Learning
Alev Elçi (Aksaray University, Turkey) Linda L. Beith (Roger Williams University, USA) and Atilla Elçi (Aksaray University, Turkey)
Information Science Reference • ©2019 • 624pp • H/C (ISBN: 9781522584766) • US $285.00

Evidence-Based Approaches to Becoming a Culturally Responsive Educator Emerging Research and Opportunities
Anthony Broughton (Claflin University, USA)
Information Science Reference • ©2019 • 178pp • H/C (ISBN: 9781522588672) • US $155.00

Cognitive Computing in Technology-Enhanced Learning
Miltiadis D. Lytras (Deree – The American College of Greece, Greece & Effat University, Saudi Arabia) Naif Aljohani (King Abdulaziz University, Saudi Arabia) Linda Daniela (University of Latvia, Latvia) and Anna Visvizi (Deree – The American College of Greece, Greece & Effat University, Saudi Arabia)
Information Science Reference • ©2019 • 345pp • H/C (ISBN: 9781522590316) • US $195.00

Innovative Trends in Flipped Teaching and Adaptive Learning
María Luisa Sein-Echaluce (University of Zaragoza, Spain) Ángel Fidalgo-Blanco (Technical University of Madrid, Spain) and Francisco José García-Peñalvo (University of Salamanca, Spain)
Information Science Reference • ©2019 • 306pp • H/C (ISBN: 9781522581420) • US $185.00

701 East Chocolate Avenue, Hershey, PA 17033, USA
Tel: 717-533-8845 x100 • Fax: 717-533-8661
E-Mail: cust@igi-global.com • www.igi-global.com

Editorial Advisory Board

Larianne Collins, *University of North Carolina at Charlotte, USA*
Anne Cook, *University of Utah, USA*
Michael K. Gardner, *University of Utah, USA*
Monika Lahani, *University of Utah, USA*
Emma O'Brien, *University of Limerick, Ireland*
Eric Poitras, *University of Utah, USA*
Ke Zhang, *Wayne State University, USA*

Table of Contents

Preface xv

Acknowledgment xxi

Section 1
Theoretical and Methodological Aspects in Digital Technology and MI Research

Chapter 1
Multiple Intelligence Theory in the Digital Age of Learning 1
    Aubrey L. C. Statti, The Chicago School of Professional Psychology, USA
    Kelly M. Torres, The Chicago School of Professional Psychology, USA

Chapter 2
Enhancing 21st Century Learning Using Digital Learning Objects and Multiple Intelligence
Theory: A Conceptual Model 19
    Emma O Brien, Mary Immaculate College, Ireland

Chapter 3
Multiple Intelligences and Digital Learning Game Design: How to Consider the Intelligences of
Players? 41
    Pejman Sajjadi, Pennsylvania State University, USA
    Olga De Troyer, Vrije Universiteit, Brussels, Belgium

Chapter 4
Understanding the Role of Digital Technology in Multiple Intelligence Education: A Meta-Analysis 65
    Kevin Greenberg, University of Utah, USA
    Robert Z. Zheng, University of Utah, USA
    Isabelle Maloy, University of Utah, USA

Chapter 5
An Educational Data Mining Application by Using Multiple Intelligences 93
    Esra Aksoy, Dokuz Eylül University, Turkey
    Serkan Narli, Dokuz Eylül University, Turkey
    Mehmet Akif Aksoy, Dokuz Eylül University, Turkey

Section 2
Integrating Digital Technology in Multiple Intelligences-Based Teaching and Learning: Visual-Spatial Intelligence

Chapter 6
Creating Geospatial Thinkers 112
Larianne Collins, University of North Carolina at Charlotte, USA

Chapter 7
Stimulating Multiple Intelligences in Infant Education From an Augmented Didactic Itinerary 124
María del Rosario Neira-Piñeiro, University of Oviedo, Spain
M. Esther Del-Moral, University of Oviedo, Spain
Inés Fombella-Coto, University of Oviedo, Spain

Chapter 8
Geolocation for the Improvement of Spatial and Naturalist Intelligence in Primary Education 141
Lourdes Villalustre Martínez, University of Oviedo, Spain
María Belén San Pedro-Veledo, University of Oviedo, Spain
Inés López-Manrique, University of Oviedo, Spain

Section 3
Integrating Digital Technology in Multiple Intelligences-Based Teaching and Learning: Verbal-Linguistic Intelligence

Chapter 9
Influence of Multimedia and Cognitive Strategies in Deep and Surface Verbal Processing: A Verbal-Linguistic Intelligence Perspective 162
Robert Z. Zheng, University of Utah, USA

Chapter 10
Concepts of Propaganda: Educating Responsible Citizens by Integrating Multiple Intelligences and Learning Styles Into a Smart Learning Environment 184
Anastasia D. Vakaloudi, Greek Ministry of Education, Greece

Section 4
Integrating Digital Technology in Multiple Intelligences-Based Teaching and Learning: Logical-Mathematical Intelligence

Chapter 11
How Can Digital Technology Enhance Mathematics Teaching and Learning? 216
Monika Dockendorff, Pontificia Universidad Católica de Chile, Chile

Chapter 12
Game Development-Based Learning: A New Paradigm for Teaching Computer and Object-Oriented Programming 244
    Alaa Khalaf Al-Makhzoomy, Yarmouk University, Jordan
    Ke Zhang, Wayne State University, USA
    Timothy Spannaus, Wayne State University, USA

Section 5
Integrating Digital Technology in Multiple Intelligences-Based Teaching and Learning: Intra- and Inter-Personal Intelligences

Chapter 13
Multiple Intelligences Analysis and Emotional Implications in STEM Education for Students up to K-12 261
    Esperanza Rosiña, University of Extremadura, Spain
    M. Luisa Bermejo, University of Extremadura, Spain
    Miriam del Barco, University of Extremadura, Spain
    Florentina Cañada, University of Extremadura, Spain
    Jesus Sanchez-Martin, University of Extremadura, Spain

Chapter 14
A Framework for Human-Technology Social Systems: The Role of Inter-Personal Interactions 281
    Monika Lohani, University of Utah, USA
    Eric G. Poitras, University of Utah, USA
    Charlene Stokes, The MITRE Corporation, USA

Compilation of References 310

About the Contributors 363

Index 369

Detailed Table of Contents

Preface xv

Acknowledgment xxi

Section 1
Theoretical and Methodological Aspects in Digital Technology and MI Research

Chapter 1
Multiple Intelligence Theory in the Digital Age of Learning 1
Aubrey L. C. Statti, The Chicago School of Professional Psychology, USA
Kelly M. Torres, The Chicago School of Professional Psychology, USA

The understanding of how individuals learn is continually changing. With the tremendous influence of technology in the classroom, it is vital that educators integrate the use of technology with specific attention and profound thought with respect to the needs of learners, including the role of multiple intelligences. Moreover, learning environments are now customizable due to new communication and information technology tools that are revolutionizing education. Research indicates the need to coordinate the use of technology with the style in which students learn. With the tremendous options and continual transformations available, educators must appraise instructional techniques, specifically the use of technology, with consideration to various learning styles and intelligences in order to engage students in their learning and also to reinforce learning in various ways. This article seeks to explore the concepts of multiple intelligence theory through technology applications.

Chapter 2
Enhancing 21st Century Learning Using Digital Learning Objects and Multiple Intelligence
Theory: A Conceptual Model 19
Emma O Brien, Mary Immaculate College, Ireland

The educational system is undergoing radical pressure to change. The increased need for individuals to learn and adapt has resulted in a huge demand for higher education. However, higher educational institutes are failing to keep pace with learner and societal needs. Firstly, the skills profile required for individuals to succeed is changing; there is a change in emphasis from discipline-specific to transversal skills due to the dynamic labor market. Secondly, the learner profile has changed with individuals from diverse backgrounds, cultures, abilities, and contexts, and catering for such a diverse range of students is challenging. Technology is a key enabler in providing HEIs with the means to address such issues.

This chapter explores a conceptual model which integrates pedagogical approaches such as multiple intelligence theory, learning styles, competency-based education with digital technologies to offer a solution to some of the concerns facing higher education in the 21st century.

Chapter 3
Multiple Intelligences and Digital Learning Game Design: How to Consider the Intelligences of Players? 41
    Pejman Sajjadi, Pennsylvania State University, USA
    Olga De Troyer, Vrije Universiteit, Brussels, Belgium

Empirical research that draws a framework on how the theory of MI could be incorporated in (learning) games is non-existent. Furthermore, the theory of MI fits well into the concept of individualization, as it distinguishes between individuals in terms of their abilities. In light of this, the chapter reports on the first evidence-based set of mappings between this theory and fundamental constructs of games known as mechanics. These mappings can be utilized by designers in the individualization paradigm of player-centered game design as guidelines on what mechanics to include in their design when targeting an audience with specific MI profiles. Such individualization can potentially positively affect the game experience of players while establishing the proper frame for affecting learning. As such, these mappings, available in form of a recommendation tool, act as guidelines on how to design (learning) games while considering the intelligences of the target audience.

Chapter 4
Understanding the Role of Digital Technology in Multiple Intelligence Education: A Meta-Analysis 65
    Kevin Greenberg, University of Utah, USA
    Robert Z. Zheng, University of Utah, USA
    Isabelle Maloy, University of Utah, USA

The theory of multiple intelligences has been embraced by the education and research communities worldwide. Substantial research has been conducted to understand multiple intelligences and learning. However, studies that examine how various types of technology affect across the board the different types of intelligences in learning is lacking. This chapter reviews the multiple intelligence (MI) theory and how emergent technologies can be used to support MI learning in education using a meta-analysis method. The results reveal that bodily-kinesthetic is most responsive to technology-based intervention compared to other types of intelligences and that immersive and visual images are effective in improving verbal linguistic and bodily-kinesthetic intelligences. Discussion of the findings are made along with their implications in educational practices. Suggestions for future research and practice are made in regard to multiple intelligence and emergent digital technology.

Chapter 5
An Educational Data Mining Application by Using Multiple Intelligences 93
    Esra Aksoy, Dokuz Eylül University, Turkey
    Serkan Narli, Dokuz Eylül University, Turkey
    Mehmet Akif Aksoy, Dokuz Eylül University, Turkey

The aim of this chapter is to illustrate both uses of data mining methods and the way of these methods can be applied in education by using students' multiple intelligences. Data mining is a data analysis methodology that has been successfully used in different areas including the educational domain. In this context, in this study, an application of EDM will be illustrated by using multiple intelligence and some other variables (e.g., learning styles and personality types). The decision tree model was implemented using students' learning styles, multiple intelligences, and personality types to identify gifted students. The sample size was 735 middle school students. The constructed decision tree model with 70% validity revealed that examination of mathematically gifted students using data mining techniques may be possible if specific characteristics are included.

Section 2
Integrating Digital Technology in Multiple Intelligences-Based Teaching and Learning: Visual-Spatial Intelligence

Chapter 6
Creating Geospatial Thinkers 112
Larianne Collins, University of North Carolina at Charlotte, USA

In today's contemporary digital world, where geospatial technologies are an integral part of society, it is imperative that students learn to think spatially. The ability to think spatially is crucial for making well-informed decisions, and these skills are rapidly becoming exponentially more important. This chapter will explore the complexity of spatial thinking, and multiple spatial thinking skills will be identified. Methods best suited for delivering content that fosters the improvement of these spatial thinking skills will also be discussed. The chapter concludes with an exploration of some of the necessary elements required for the sustained use of geospatial technologies in the classroom and offers recommendations for transformation in teacher practice such as pre-service intervention, continuous follow-up and coaching, and curriculum modifications, which include the direct instruction of both spatial thinking and geospatial technologies.

Chapter 7
Stimulating Multiple Intelligences in Infant Education From an Augmented Didactic Itinerary 124
María del Rosario Neira-Piñeiro, University of Oviedo, Spain
M. Esther Del-Moral, University of Oviedo, Spain
Inés Fombella-Coto, University of Oviedo, Spain

This chapter investigates the contributions made by augmented reality (AR) to develop multiple intelligences in infant education, along with the opportunities offered by augmented didactic itineraries (ADI) as a suitable formula for the global activation of different intelligences by means of AR resources. The methodological guidelines followed to prepare an ADI are explained, and the case study method is adopted for the purpose of describing a model aimed at infant education schoolchildren—used in teacher training—in which are specified the activities included, together with the AR resources and applications that it comprises. More precisely, this ADI takes children's literature as a starting point and especially activates naturalistic, spatial, and bodily kinesthetic intelligence. Likewise, its training potential is analyzed from a didactic, digital and creative dimension so that it can serve as a model for future teachers to design their own aids.

Chapter 8
Geolocation for the Improvement of Spatial and Naturalist Intelligence in Primary Education 141
    Lourdes Villalustre Martínez, University of Oviedo, Spain
    María Belén San Pedro-Veledo, University of Oviedo, Spain
    Inés López-Manrique, University of Oviedo, Spain

Geolocation provides a new learning model by combining physical and digital content, creating an enriched and interactive universe. This mobile technology offers new opportunities for the promotion of learning inside and outside the classroom, linked to multiple intelligences, in particular, to the spatial and naturalistic intelligences. Taking these premises into account, an analysis of several geolocation applications (N=20) is carried out in order to determine their potential to develop spatial and naturalistic intelligences. To this end, case study methodology is adopted, and an analysis instrument is proposed consisting of 15 indicators grouped into three dimensions: 1) geolocation, 2) spatial intelligence (spatial orientation and spatial representation), and 3) naturalistic intelligence (physical geography and environment). Although the geolocation applications analyzed boost spatial intelligence through the different options they incorporate, the same cannot be said of the naturalist one. It is considered relevant that they include contents oriented to environmental awareness.

Section 3
Integrating Digital Technology in Multiple Intelligences-Based Teaching and Learning:
Verbal-Linguistic Intelligence

Chapter 9
Influence of Multimedia and Cognitive Strategies in Deep and Surface Verbal Processing: A
Verbal-Linguistic Intelligence Perspective 162
    Robert Z. Zheng, University of Utah, USA

The traditional view of linguistic-verbal intelligences focuses on individual linguistic abilities at the levels of phonology, syntax, and semantics. This chapter discusses the individual linguistic abilities from a text-comprehension perspective. The chapter examines the roles of multimedia and cognitive prompts in deep and surface verbal processing. Drawn from research in working memory, multimedia learning, and deep processing, a theoretical framework is proposed to promote learners' deep and surface learning in reading. Evidence from empirical studies are reviewed to support the underlying theoretical assumptions of the framework. The theoretical and practical significance of the theoretical framework is discussed with suggestions for future research.

Chapter 10
Concepts of Propaganda: Educating Responsible Citizens by Integrating Multiple Intelligences
and Learning Styles Into a Smart Learning Environment 184
    Anastasia D. Vakaloudi, Greek Ministry of Education, Greece

Propaganda represents the communication of information or ideas aimed to influence the audience's view and position on subjects. Forms of propaganda have permeated society for centuries and have evolved to become a common tool of warfare. Through the study of propagandistic posters from the two World Wars-era in the proposed project, students assess the powers of words and images in communication and learn to evaluate the messages they encounter, particularly when those messages urge action. The project is designed as a smart learning environment with the use of open educational resources that focuses on the strengths of all types of learners and the improvement of their weaknesses by integrating learner-centered theories and multiple intelligences and learning styles strategies with various combinations and by enhancing the efforts for self-discovery. This aims to promote students' cognitive engagement, which enables them to immerse themselves in in-depth reflective learning processes that are situated in realistic problem-solving tasks.

Section 4
Integrating Digital Technology in Multiple Intelligences-Based Teaching and Learning: Logical-Mathematical Intelligence

Chapter 11
How Can Digital Technology Enhance Mathematics Teaching and Learning? 216
Monika Dockendorff, Pontificia Universidad Católica de Chile, Chile

As digital technology becomes more ubiquitous in society and education, mathematics teachers are expected to design and integrate technology-enriched learning environments effectively. This task encompasses many challenges, but primarily, it entails the identification of how technology may produce insights. This study examines several categories of core mathematical processes that can be enhanced by the integration of dynamic interactive software such as identifying properties, connecting multiple representations, and solving problems, among others. The process of visualization appears at the center of dynamic and interactive mathematics learning environments. Evidence of its functionality and the benefits it reports to the teaching and learning process for each category is presented. Further discussion on the challenges that mathematics teacher education programs and teachers face—not only in their digital competences but also in the role they play—are outlined.

Chapter 12
Game Development-Based Learning: A New Paradigm for Teaching Computer and Object-Oriented Programming 244
Alaa Khalaf Al-Makhzoomy, Yarmouk University, Jordan
Ke Zhang, Wayne State University, USA
Timothy Spannaus, Wayne State University, USA

This chapter presents the findings from a quasi-experimental study analyzing the effect of Game Development-Based Learning on students' academic performance in programming courses in Jordan. The study tested an argument proposing a positive significant association between GDBL instruction and students' performance. The analysis of variance results investigating the effect of enrollment and completion of a concurrent GDBL course to normal courses found that the treatment group outperformed two other groups: the control and the comparison group. The positive gains in the post-assessment scores, were consistent across the two programming courses: C++ and Object-Oriented Programming. This finding confirms the earlier results across countries and contexts documenting the salubrious effect of GDBL on students' academic performance in Computer Science and Information Technology courses. Findings also support the overarching constructionist approach where the use of scaffolding and technology in instruction and assessment yield better academic outcomes for learners.

Section 5
Integrating Digital Technology in Multiple Intelligences-Based Teaching and Learning: Intra- and Inter-Personal Intelligences

Chapter 13
Multiple Intelligences Analysis and Emotional Implications in STEM Education for Students up to K-12 261
    Esperanza Rosiña, University of Extremadura, Spain
    M. Luisa Bermejo, University of Extremadura, Spain
    Miriam del Barco, University of Extremadura, Spain
    Florentina Cañada, University of Extremadura, Spain
    Jesus Sanchez-Martin, University of Extremadura, Spain

This chapter investigates whether there is a relationship between emotional management and the prevailing intelligence profile of a sample of pupils in the last year of primary education and two years of lower secondary education with respect to their learning in STEM subjects. A questionnaire was designed to collect information on multiple intelligences and the emotional factor. The sample comprised 143 pupils from the 6th of primary education and 2nd and 4th of secondary education classes in a state school. It was found that the pupils with a predominantly logical-mathematical and/or visual-spatial intelligence also scored better on the items related to the emotional and adaptation factor in science classes.

Chapter 14
A Framework for Human-Technology Social Systems: The Role of Inter-Personal Interactions 281
    Monika Lohani, University of Utah, USA
    Eric G. Poitras, University of Utah, USA
    Charlene Stokes, The MITRE Corporation, USA

Advancements in semi- and fully-autonomous systems have made human-technology interaction a dynamic and social process. In this chapter, the authors highlight the importance of interpersonal interactions between human and technology and how they can be modeled, tracked, and fostered in the context of adaptive instructional systems. They will first introduce a human-technology social systems framework, which integrates individual factors (human and technology), situational factors (e.g., stress), and team interaction-relevant factors (e.g., communication and team cognition) that contribute to various team-related outcomes (e.g., learning and performance). Using examples from interactive virtual agents and educational technology, they discuss attributes of technology that should be considered to optimize joint learning and performance in applied contexts. The proposed framework points to novel research directions and is likely to offer an understanding of mechanisms that could enhance learning opportunities in diverse socioemotional contexts.

Compilation of References 310

About the Contributors 363

Index 369

Preface

Howard Gardner in his *Frames of Mind: The Theory of Multiple Intelligences* (1983) redefines human intelligence as a multi-dimensional construct by differentiating human intelligence into multiple traits, rather than a single general intelligence. Since its inception, the theory of multiple intelligences (MI) has changed people's perception of how humans learn in terms of their abilities in content acquisition and application. As a cognitive psychology theory, MI has significantly changed the landscape in education by showing all learners are different and each of them merits special attention given his/her unique intellectual ability or a combination of abilities in learning. Research has demonstrated a strong association between individual intelligences and their cognitive processes in learning (Batdi, 2017; Lowrie, Logan, & Ramful, 2017). Lowrie et al. (2017) implemented a training program focusing on visual-spatial intelligence in mathematics thinking. They found that classroom-based visuospatial training improved students' spatial reasoning and mathematics performance. Similar arguments have been made by the authors in this edited volume who claim that visual spatial intelligence is significantly correlated with learner domain performance such as geology and mathematics (See Collins in Chapter 6; Dokendorff in Chapter 11; Martínez, Pedro-Veledo, & López-Manrique in Chapter 8).

While the literature has evinced a plethora of research on multiple intelligences, it remains unknown how each of or a combination of these intelligences can be effectively optimized through instructional intervention, particularly through the use of emerging learning technology. Initial evidence from empirical studies has suggested that information and communication technologies (ICTs) can significantly influenced learners' information processing in the context of multiple intelligences (Chen, Chiang, & Lin, 2013; Martin-Monje, Castrillo, & Manana-Rodriguez, 2018). Chen and colleagues incorporated interactive technology (e.g., whiteboard) in classroom teaching. They discovered that those who studied with whiteboard demonstrated a significant improvement in performance, especially for those with low logical-mathematical intelligence. Albeit the efforts in unveiling the relationship between ICTs and its potential for improving individual intelligences, a knowledge in how MI theory may guide the use of ICTs to enhance the learning opportunities for student with ICTs is lacking. The discrepancy in practice and lack of knowledge in the relationship between MI theory and ICTs can significantly hamper the practice of teaching and learning in schools and training settings given that learners in the 21st century are exposed to a wide range of technologies from visuals, to interactive multimedia, and from 3D learning to educational gaming, to virtual reality, etc., all of which activate and bring forth learners' multiple intelligences in play, that is, learners' abilities in visual-spatial processing, kinesthetic manipulation, abstract thinking, and so forth. Evidently, the knowledge of and an understanding of how these factors interact with each other is critical for teachers and learners. As such, this book steps up to fill a critical need that has significant implications for the research and practice of MI and ICTs in education.

THE CONTRIBUTION OF THIS BOOK

This edited volume is marked by its unique contributions to the educational and research communities. First, it brings together multiple perspectives on multiple intelligences and the use of digital technology in MI education. Scholars of this book present through their newest research the unique roles of digital technology in MI education, which include gaming, multimedia, visual images, etc. to support language, geology, mathematics, and STEM related learning. Second, the edited book contributes to the research community the understanding of the relationship between digital technology and MI education through its theoretical frameworks. These frameworks, proposed by the authors in this book, focus on various aspects in MI education by illuminating how digital technology may both facilitate and benefit from the integration of multiple intelligences theory in teaching and learning. Meanwhile, the book offers a range of strategies and approaches in MI education, which makes it practically significant as teachers and professional educators may find the book useful as they deploy MI educational strategies in their classroom. Finally, the book reflects a collective effort by scholars at the international level to bring together research on digital technology and multiple intelligences. It includes researchers from a broad range of academic institutions and organizations: from teaching colleges to research intensive universities, from education-focused industry to government, and from K-12 schools to high education.

This volume is appropriate for use as a text in graduate and undergraduate courses in programs like teacher education, instructional design, educational technology, and pedagogy. The text is also appropriate as a supplementary reading for general education, cognition, and methods courses. Professionals in applied areas, such as K through 12 teachers, university instructors in teacher education programs, and corporate trainers, may find the book helpful in their professional teaching and training. For researchers, university faculty and graduate students who pursue research the relevant areas, this text provides a current sampling of research and theory in the field, and presents this information in an integrated way. We hope you will enjoy reading this book as much as we have enjoyed making it.

ORGANIZATION OF THIS BOOK

This book is divided into two sections with first section focusing on the theoretical and methodological aspects of digital technology in multiple intelligences research. The second section highlights the aspects of digital technology in specific intelligences in terms of teaching and learning. Specifically, four types of intelligences are covered in this section. They include visual-spatial, verbal-linguistic, logical-mathematical, and intra- and interpersonal intelligences. The authors in this section provide unique perspectives on the role of digital technology in multiple intelligences development.

Section 1 consists of five chapters focusing on the theoretical and methodological aspects related to MI and digital technology. The theoretical framework and methodology introduced in this section point toward the new directions in MI and digital technology research.

Chapter 1 presents a theoretical perspective on MI and digital technology. In this chapter, Drs. Aubrey Statti and Kelly Torres (The Chicago School of Professional Psychology, USA) argue that educators should integrate the use of technology with specific attention and profound thought with respect to the needs of learners. Given that learning environments are now customizable due to new communication and information technology tools, educators need to coordinate the use of technology with the style in which students learn. With the tremendous options and continual transformations available, educators

Preface

must appraise instructional techniques, specifically the use of technology, with consideration to various learning styles and intelligences in order to engage students in their learning. The chapter evaluates each multiple intelligence (verbal-linguistic, mathematical-logical, musical-rhythmic, bodily-kinesthetic, interpersonal, intrapersonal, visual-spatial, naturalist and the existential) and their appropriate and specific uses with technology in the digital age of learning.

Chapter 2 focuses on enhancing 21st century learning using digital learning objects and Multiple Intelligence theory. Emma O'Brien of Mary Immaculate College, Ireland, points out that the educational system is undergoing radical pressure to change. However higher educational institutes are failing to keep pace with learner and societal needs. This chapter explores a conceptual model that integrates pedagogical approaches such as Multiple Intelligence Theory, Learning Styles, Competency Based education with digital technologies to offer a solution to some of the concerns facing higher education in the twenty first century.

Chapter 3 examines the relationship between MI and the design of educational games by mapping between the traits of MI theory and fundamental constructs of games. Pejman Sajjadi and Olga De Troyer of Bielefeld University, Belgium, discussed a novel approach to analyzing the variables related to MI and digital technology. The authors reported the findings of a study by mapping the relationship between MI and game design factors. The authors suggested that the mappings can be utilized by designers as guidelines on what mechanics to include in their design when targeting an audience with specific MI profiles. Such individualization can potentially positively affect the game experience of players, while establishing the proper frame for effective learning.

Chapter 4 aims to understand the role of digital technology in multiple intelligence education by conducting a meta-analysis based on 210 cases from 96 studies. Kevin Greenberg, Robert Zheng, and Isabelle Maloy of University of Utah, USA, reviewed the multiple intelligence (MI) theory and how emergent technologies can be used to support MI learning in education. The results of meta-analysis revealed that bodily-kinesthetic is most responsive to technology based intervention compared to other types of intelligences and that immersive and visual images are effective in improving verbal linguistic and bodily-kinesthetic intelligences. Discussion of the findings are made along with their implications in educational practices. Suggestions for future research and practice are proposed in regard to multiple intelligence and emergent digital technology use.

Chapter 5 illustrates both uses of data mining methods and the way of these methods can be applied in education by using students' multiple intelligences. Data mining is a data analysis methodology that has been successfully used in different areas including the educational domain. Esra Aksoy, Serkan Narlı, and Mehmet Akif Aksoy of Dokuz Eylül University, Turky, showed that educational datamining (EDM) technique can be effectively applied to understanding multiple intelligence and some other variables (e.g., learning styles and personality types) in education. The decision tree model was implemented using students' learning styles, multiple intelligences and personality types to identify gifted students. The sample size was 735 middle school students. The constructed decision tree model with 70% validity revealed that examination of mathematically gifted students using data mining techniques may be possible if specific characteristics are included.

The following sections offer an array of essays on MI and digital technology in terms of teaching and learning. Section is organized around four types of intelligences: visual-spatial (Chapters 6-8), verbal-linguistic (Chapters 9-10), logical-mathematical (Chapters 11-12), and intra- and interpersonal (Chapters 13-14) by focusing on the facilitating role of digital technology in multiple intelligence support and development. Chapters in this section represent the cutting-edge research in MI and digital technology. The technologies covered in this section include educational gaming, multimedia, and augmented reality (AR) for enhancing multiple intelligences in learning.

Chapter 6 examines the underlying factors affecting geospatial creative thinking. Larianne Collins of University of North Carolina-Charlotte, USA, argues that in today's contemporary, digital world where geospatial technologies are an integral part of society, it is imperative that students learn to think spatially. The ability to think spatially is crucial for making well-informed decisions and these skills are rapidly becoming exponentially more important. In this chapter the author explores the complexity of spatial thinking and identifies multiple spatial thinking skills in relation to geospatial learning. The chapter concludes with an exploration of some of the necessary elements required for the sustained use of geospatial technologies in the classroom and offers recommendations for transformation in teacher practice such as pre-service intervention, continuous follow-up and coaching, and curriculum modifications which include the direct instruction of both spatial thinking and geospatial technologies.

Chapter 7 investigates the contributions of augmented reality (AR) to developing multiple intelligences (e.g., visual-spatial) in infant education. The authors (María del Rosario Neira-Piñeiro, M. Esther del-Moral-Pérez, and Inés Fombella-Coto of University of Oviedo, Spain) studied augmented didactic itineraries (ADIS) as a suitable approach to global activation of different intelligences via AR resources. The methodological guidelines to preparing an ADI are explained, along with a case study describing a model in infant education using AR resources. The authors noted the relation between ADI and activation of naturalistic, spatial and bodily-kinesthetic intelligence in the acquisition of literature by young children.

Chapter 8 also focuses on geospatial related topic by looking at the role of digital technology in visual-spatial intelligence, but leans more toward practical aspects. Lourdes Villalustre Martínez, María Belén San Pedro-Veledo, and Inés López-Manrique of University of Oviedo, Spain, investigated the affordances of mobile technology in geolocation study in terms of promoting learning inside and outside the classroom as well as its connection to multiple intelligences, in particular, spatial and naturalistic intelligences. The authors studied geolocation applications (N=20) to determine their potential to develop spatial and naturalistic intelligences. The method of case-study is used with an analysis instrument consisting of 15 indicators grouped into three dimensions: 1) Geolocation, 2) Spatial Intelligence (Spatial Orientation, and Spatial Representation), and 3) Naturalistic Intelligence (Physical Geography and Environment). Results revealed that although the geolocation applications improved spatial intelligence through different options incorporated in the applications, the same cannot be said of the naturalist one. The authors suggest that content relating to environmental awareness should be built into future applications to improve learners' naturalist intelligence.

Chapter 9 discusses the influence of multimedia and cognitive strategies in deep and surface verbal processing. Drawn from research in working memory, multimedia learning and deep processing, Robert Zheng (University of Utah, USA) examines the roles of multimedia and cognitive prompts in deep and surface verbal processing. A theoretical framework is proposed to promote learners' deep and surface learning in reading. Evidences from empirical studies are reviewed to support the underlying theoretical assumptions of the framework. The theoretical and practical significance of the theoretical framework is discussed with suggestions for future research.

In Chapter 10 Anastasia Vakaloudi who is affiliated with Greek Ministry of Education, Greece, discussed educating responsible citizens by integrating learning styles and multiple intelligences. Vakaloudi examined the role and forms of propaganda as a communication tool in developing civil responsibilities

Preface

in students. Through the study of propagandistic posters from the two World Wars-era in the proposed project, students assess the power of words and images in communication and learn to evaluate the messages they encounter, particularly when those messages urge action. The multiple intelligence strategies are incorporated to focus on the strengths of all types of learners and encourage self-awareness and self-discovery in learning.

Chapter 11 reflects a theoretical endeavor by the author (Monika Dockendorff of Pontificia Universidad Católica de Chile, Chile) who queries how digital technology can enhance mathematics teaching and learning. The author noted that as digital technology becomes more ubiquitous in society and education, mathematics teachers are expected to design and integrate technology-enriched learning environments effectively. This task encompasses many challenges, but primarily, it entails the identification of how technology may produce insights. In this chapter, the author studied categories of core mathematical processes that can be enhanced by the integration of dynamic interactive software to facilitate the process of visualization – an indicator of visual-spatial intelligence – in interactive mathematics learning environments.

Chapter 12 by Alaa Khalaf Al-Makhzoomy of Yarmouk University, Jordan, Drs. Ke Zhang and Timothy Spannaus of Wayne State University, USA, presents the findings from a quasi-experimental study analyzing the effect of Game Development-Based Learning on students' academic performance in programming courses in Jordan. The study tested an argument proposing a positive significant association between GDBL instruction and students' performance. The finding of the study demonstrate the connection between logical-mathematical thinking and programming, it also supports the overarching constructionist approach where the use of scaffolding and technology in instruction and assessment yield better academic outcomes for learners.

Chapter 13 written by Esperanza Rosiña, M. Luisa Bermejo, Miriam Hernandez, Florentina Cañada, and Jesus Sanchez-Martin of University of Extremadura, Spain, focuses on multiple intelligences and emotional implications in STEM education. The chapter presents a study that investigates whether there is a relationship between emotional management and the prevailing intelligence profile of a sample of pupils in the last year of primary education and two years of lower secondary education with respect to their learning in STEM subjects (Science Technology Engineering Mathematics). A questionnaire was designed to collect information on multiple intelligences and the emotional factor. The sample comprised 143 pupils from the 6th of primary education and 2nd and 4th of secondary education classes in a state school. It was found that the pupils with a predominantly logical-mathematical and/or visual-spatial intelligence also scored better on the items related to the emotional and adaptation factor in science classes.

In Chapter 14 Drs. Monika Lahani, Eric Poitras of University of Utah and Charlene Stokes of The MITRE Corporation, USA, argue that human-technology relationships can be improved by integrating the literatures on inter-personal interactions from the fields of social cognition, human-computer interaction, and affective computing. The authors propose a human-technology social systems framework, which integrates individual factors (human and technology), situational factors (e.g., stress), and team interaction-relevant factors (e.g., communication and team cognition) that contribute to various team-related outcomes (e.g., learning and performance). Using examples from specific technologies, interactive virtual agents, and educational technology, the authors discuss attributes of technology that could be considered to optimize joint learning and performance in applied contexts. The proposed framework points to novel research directions and is likely to offer an understanding of mechanisms that could enhance learning opportunities in diverse socioemotional contexts.

CONCLUSION

The current book focuses on the role of digital technology in promoting MI in education with a wide range of coverage from geoscience to mathematics, to language learning; and from theoretical framework to practice in digital-based multiple intelligences education. *Examining Multiple Intelligences and the Use of Digital Technologies for Enhanced Learning Opportunities* is the first book of its kind that explores the relationship between digital technology and MI. The studies in this book unveil the unique roles of digital technology (e.g., gaming, multimedia, visuals, augmented reality, etc.) in facilitating and developing individual intelligences in learning that include visual-spatial, logical-mathematics, verbal-linguistics, naturalistic, inter- and intra- personal intelligences. The theoretical frameworks provide informative guidance to teachers, educators, administrators, and policy makers with respect to how to effectively integrate digital technologies in MI curricula and education.

With the advancement of digital technology, digital technology-based strategies and approaches have been widely integrated into educational settings to support various learning activities and performance including MI education. Yet, a book that systematically examines various roles of digital technology and their relation to MI learning is lacking. The current book provides a much-needed resource for those who are interested in applying digital technology to MI education.

Robert Z. Zheng
University of Utah, USA

REFERENCES

Batdi, V. (2017). The effects of multiple intelligences on academic achievement: A meta-analytic and thematic study. *Educational Sciences: Theory and Practice*, *17*(6), 2057–2092. doi:10.12738/estp.2017.6.0104

Chen, H.-R., Chiang, C.-H., & Lin, W.-S. (2013). Learning effects of interactive whiteboard pedagogy for students in Taiwan from the perspective of multiple intelligences. *Journal of Educational Computing Research*, *49*(2), 173–187. doi:10.2190/EC.49.2.c

Gardner, H. (1983a). *Frames of Mind: The Theory of Multiple Intelligences*. New York: Basic Books.

Lowrie, T., Logan, T., & Ramful, A. (2017). Visuospatial training improves elementary students' mathematics performance. *The British Journal of Educational Psychology*, *87*(2), 170–186. doi:10.1111/bjep.12142 PMID:28097646

Martin-Monje, E., Castrillo, M. D., & Manana-Rodriguez, J. (2018). Understanding online interaction in language MOOCs through learning analytics. *Computer Assisted Language Learning*, *31*(3), 251–272. doi:10.1080/09588221.2017.1378237

Acknowledgment

This book would not have been possible if it were not for the hard work of many individuals who have written chapters for it. As a group, they voluntarily spent hundreds of hours putting together a collection of essays that provide readers with an overview of the theoretical and practical perspectives on the use of digital technology in multiple intelligences education. I would like to thank our authors for their outstanding contributions.

My appreciation also goes to our reviewers for their expertise assistance, who provided insightful comments and suggestions which have made this book up to highest standard and quality. I would like to thank IGI development team whose guidance and support have made the process a smooth and pleasant journey.

And last, but not the least, I would like to thank my family, Sharon, Joanna and Henry, for their encouragement, support, and warm reception they give to my work and for their allowance for my work schedules. I could not have done this without them! Finally, I would like to thank my mother who has always been the source of inspiration in my life.

Robert Z. Zheng
University of Utah, USA

Section 1
Theoretical and Methodological Aspects in Digital Technology and MI Research

Chapter 1
Multiple Intelligence Theory in the Digital Age of Learning

Aubrey L. C. Statti
The Chicago School of Professional Psychology, USA

Kelly M. Torres
The Chicago School of Professional Psychology, USA

ABSTRACT

The understanding of how individuals learn is continually changing. With the tremendous influence of technology in the classroom, it is vital that educators integrate the use of technology with specific attention and profound thought with respect to the needs of learners, including the role of multiple intelligences. Moreover, learning environments are now customizable due to new communication and information technology tools that are revolutionizing education. Research indicates the need to coordinate the use of technology with the style in which students learn. With the tremendous options and continual transformations available, educators must appraise instructional techniques, specifically the use of technology, with consideration to various learning styles and intelligences in order to engage students in their learning and also to reinforce learning in various ways. This article seeks to explore the concepts of multiple intelligence theory through technology applications.

INTRODUCTION

The understanding of how individuals learn is continually changing (Jackson, Gaudet, McDaniel, & Brammer, 2009). With the tremendous influence of technology in the classroom, it is vital that educators integrate the use of technology with specific attention and profound thought with respect to the needs of learners. Moreover, learning environments are now customizable due to new communication and information technology tools that are revolutionizing education, primarily due to the rapid changes with the Internet (Nelson, 1998) and technology's role in society. Research indicates the need to coordinate the use of technology with the style in which students learn (Arce, 2006; Eris Fose, 2005; Jackson, et al., 2009; Prensky, 2001; Sanchez-Martinez, Alvarez-Gragera, Davila-Acedo, & Mellado, 2017; Tamilselvi & Geetha, 2015).

DOI: 10.4018/978-1-7998-0249-5.ch001

In addition to the revolution of technology's role in education, cognitive psychologists are continually developing new theories and researching innovative findings regarding the individual differences in human thinking and learning (Nelson, 1998). Intelligence can be defined as "the ability to perceive information and retain it as knowledge for applying to itself or other instances of knowledge or information" (Tamilselvi & Geetha, 2015, p. 1). The concept of intelligence plays a significant role in an individual's social status, educational opportunities, and career choices (Zahedi & Moghaddam, 2016). However, not all learners acquire intelligence in the same manner. Education professor Howard Gardner, of Harvard University, originally introduced the idea of different learning styles through his theory of Multiple Intelligences (MIT) in 1983. Gardner (1983) defined intelligence as "the ability to solve problems, or create products, that are valued within one or more cultural settings" and as "the capacity to respond successfully to new situations...to tackle a task demanded by life" (p. 8). Gardner posited that intelligence should not be limited to purely cognitive facets but rather should consider the affective and emotional sides of intelligence (Gardner 1983 a,b & Gardner 1995 as cited in Sanchez-Martinez, et al., 2017). Specifically, as the theory itself developed, MIT expanded the concept of intelligence to include verbal-linguistic, mathematical-logical, musical-rhythmic, bodily-kinesthetic, interpersonal, intrapersonal, visual-spatial, naturalist and the existential (Gardner, 1999).

Though not immediately embraced in the educational community, the notion that students who were not naturally gifted with traditional logical or linguistic skills still possess cognitive abilities did become a more accepted idea in educational assessments (Jackson, et al., 2009). Over the past three decades, MIT has been further built upon and relied on and remains relevant in today's culture of education. As Eris Fose (2005) explained, all students possess every single intelligence, however, the manner and degree to which they use each intelligence is as individualized as their fingerprint. Moreover, by "making use of these intelligence areas, individuals may solve a problem which can be regarded within one or more than one cultural frameworks and may have a skill of creating a product" (Saban, 2011, p. 1643).

Additionally, in the modern classroom, technology has become a viable means for students to "attain information, reconstruct knowledge, and demonstrate learning" (Marquez Chisholm & Beckett, 2003, p. 262). The influence of the Internet as well as the evolving capabilities of technology have created a teaching environment with the potential to capitalize on a student's individual strength (Macedo, 2013; Nelson, 1998). Further, Jackson, et al. (2009) posited that it is the educator's "responsibility to stay abreast of technology by discovering new and innovative ways to develop and present curriculum" (p. 75). Instructional tools that are technology based allowed for "collaborative learning, classroom presentation, discovery, exploration, synchronous and asynchronous communication, remote and distance learning, ...memorization, direct instruction, deduction, drill and practice projects, peer teaching, discussion, teaching games, independent study, programmed instruction, lecture and stimulation" (Nelson, 1998, p. 90). With the tremendous options and continual transformations available, educators must appraise instructional techniques, specifically the use of technology, with consideration to various learning styles and intelligences in order to engage students in their learning and also to reinforce learning in various ways (Eris Fose, 2005; Jackson, et al., 2009; Tamilselvi & Geetha, 2015).

THEORETICAL APPROACH OF MULTIPLE INTELLIGENCE THEORY

Gardner's theory of multiple intelligences is a continuation of John Dewey's theory of education, in that "both authors claim that the subject matters should provide links with real-life situations in order [for] students' knowledge to be useful. [Also,] the starting point of both authors is the child's nature and the need to adjunct curriculum to its individual features" (Leshkovska & Spaseva, 2016, p. 61). Supported by studies in child development, psychometrics, changes in cognition within different cultures and throughout history, cognitive skills under conditions of brain damage, and psychological transfer and generalization, Gardner's intelligence theory is backed by an extensive research base that integrates physiology, anthropology, and personal and cultural history (Silver, Strong, & Perini, 1998). As Silver, et al. (1998), claimed "this theoretical depth is sadly lacking in most learning-style models" (para. 13).

Gardner (2011) postulated that past theories such as the IQ, the Piagetian, and the information-processing approaches primarily focus on a specific kind of linguistic or logical problem-solving yet ignore the impact of biology and are insensitive to higher levels of creativity. Additionally, according to Gardner (2011), these theories lack an understanding "to the range of roles highlighted in human society. Consequently, these facts have engendered an alternative point of view that focuses precisely on these neglected areas" (p. 25-26). According to MIT, students can approach learning a specific subject matter in more than just one or two basic ways and that by only considering linguistic and logical-mathematical intelligence, educators are limiting a great number of an individual's mental abilities (Zahedi & Moghaddam, 2016).

Further, Saban (2011) explained that according to MIT, in learning environments utilizing multiple intelligences both the right and left hemispheres of the brain are active. Therefore, the usage percentage of the human brain increases. Thus, students are provided learning opportunities to develop higher thinking skills, enrich their imagination, and increase their learning activity in various environments. Of note, Gardner himself did not significantly focus on the use of MIT within the educational context and instead focused more on the psychological aspect of his research. However, his work has been explored in the educational context by researchers and practitioners for several decades (Leshkovska & Spaseva, 2016).

According to MIT, there is a specific criterion for being included on the list of multiple intelligences. First, the brain must contain a specific location for the thought, creating in what results as an isolation of the specific brain function. Second, there must be a presence of the intelligence in exceptional individuals. In other words, savants or prodigies must demonstrate characteristics of the specific intelligences. Thirdly, the intelligence must include a set core of operations. Next, the intelligence must have a developmental component that undergoes stages in both an individual's life and human history as a whole. Additionally, the intelligence must be a supported by psychological tasks that can be carried out, observed, and measured. Further, MIT supports psychometric testing in order to identify and quantify true unique intelligences. Lastly, the intelligence is required to be encoded into a system of symbols (Gardner, 1983a,b, 2011; McCoog, 2010; McKenzie, 2004).

LEARNING IN THE MILLENNIAL AGE

When exploring the use of MIT and technology integration, it is important to consider current trends impacting students and modern educational environments. Millennial learners, generally characterized as those born after 1990, have been exposed to technology more than any other generation before them (Dorfeld, 2016). Students as young as the preschool level and reaching into the collegiate levels, have spent their entire lives inundated with digital media through the use of computers, cell phones, video games, digital music players, tablets, and other digital tools and toys (Prensky, 2011). Interestingly, Prensky (2001) who referred to these students as digital natives, posited that millennial learner's brains have physically changed due to these influences of technology and digital media. For example, Jones and Shao (2011) indicated that current generations of learners are able to receive information more quickly, be more adept at multitasking, and have higher preferences for active learning activities rather than passively receiving information. Also, researchers have theorized that technology has an impact on millennial learners' mental well-being and social relationships (Kardefelf-Winther, 2017). Further, research demonstrates that these learners often disregard black-and-white text and find this traditional format of reading to be tedious and uninteresting. Millennial students respond up to 90% better through visuals, auditory clips, class discussion, and layouts spanning from the top to bottom versus left to right (Mall, 2012).

Additionally, school districts in the United States are beginning to invest largely in tablets over computers due to the cost savings, ease of teacher and student use, and the availability and assortment of applications designed to run on the devices that are of low-cost or free (Bano, Zowghi, Kearney, Schuck, & Aubusson, 2018; Pappas, Giannakos, and Sampson, 2017; Webster, 2011). However, veteran teachers, who Prensky (2001) referred to as digital immigrants, are often underprepared or overwhelmed in teaching through the use of technology in the classroom. Prensky stated that "immigrant teachers assume that learners are the same as they have always been, and that the same methods that worked for the teacher when they were students will work for their students now. But that assumption is no longer valid. Today's learners are different" (2001, p. 2). In order to address these differences, it is posited that both technology and digital learning is effectively integrated into the educational environment at all levels and ages of learning.

DIGITAL LEARNING OPPORTUNITIES FOR SPECIFIC INTELLIGENCES

The following chapter will begin with an outline of each unique intelligence: verbal-linguistic, mathematical-logical, musical-rhythmic, bodily-kinesthetic, interpersonal, intrapersonal, visual-spatial, naturalist and the existential (Gardner, 1999) and the description of digital influences and opportunities for student learning in this unique format.

Verbal-Linguistic

Silver, Strong, and Perini (1997) defined this intelligence as the capacity to use language to describe events and sequence activities, the aptitude of using language to build rapport and trust with others, the ability of developing logical arguments and using rhetoric, and apt to use metaphoric and expressive language. The verbal-linguistic learner is strong in areas of reading, writing, and speaking. This type of learner is characterized by effectively using language to express thought (Eris Fose, 2005).

Possibly the intelligence most immediately impacted through the use of technology is the verbal-linguistic intelligence (Zahedi & Ghabanchi, 2014). Jackson, et al. (2009) reasoned that "as we enter into the 21st century, students with verbal linguistic intelligences can easily access a multitude of information through worldwide databases and computer networks" (p. 72). Moreover, Dickinson (1998) stated that "the development of linguistic skills for all populations can be catalyzed by remarkable new electronic tools for accessing and managing information and communicating, learning, and developing intelligence in unpresented ways" (p. 2). Dickinson further explained the value of the computer in verbal-linguistic development as it allows educators the opportunity to provide written feedback to learners to revise and rework their writing promptly in order to develop greater fluency and a stronger writing style and approach. Additionally, Eris Fose (2005) recommended educators use Microsoft PowerPoint in order to create classroom group games such as *Jeopardy* or *Who Wants to be a Millionaire*. Other suggestions for group activities that cater to the verbal-linguistic learner include *American Idol or Wheel of Fortune* for English language learners. Furthermore, educators are encouraged to utilize the discussion format, which can easily be accomplished through online discussion forums or Internet based meetings, in order to create interaction among students. This "interaction makes a text [or concept] more palpable because multiple viewpoints are being shared" Dorfeld, 2016, p. 68).

English Language Learning Through MIT Principles

Furthermore, the principles of MIT integrated with technology use has been demonstrated as an effective approach to teaching the English language and providing equitable education to English language learners (Han & Wang, 2013; Marquez Chisholm & Beckett, 2003; Zahedi & Moghaddam, 2016). Han and Wang (2013) argued that the college English network teaching style, which is teaching college-level students the English language with support from the student's network such as peer tutors, student centers, roommates, and co-workers, combined with multimedia technology "is the most advanced teaching mode, which features a multi-faced and three-dimensional effect" (p. 2739). They explained that a learner's multiple intelligence, with a focus language intelligence, is enhanced through this attention to both learner network and multimedia technology. Han and Wang (2013) described multimedia technology as providing the English language learner with pictures, words, sounds, and videos, etc. to deliver a comprehensive stimulation from all senses.

Mathematical-Logical

The most well documented and discussed cognitive processing expertise is the logical-mathematical intelligence (Jackson, et al., 2009). Silver, Strong, and Perini (1997) defined this intelligence as the ability to use mathematical concepts to produce conjectures, establish proofs, and apply mathematics and mathematical data to situations and to construct arguments. Additionally, it is the attention to patterns, symmetry, logic, and aesthetics of mathematics in order to solve design and modeling problems as well as the ability to utilize mathematics in personal and daily life. Additionally, they characterized the mastery level of mathematical-logical intelligence as the ability of numbers to compute, describe, and document such as those in the accounting, bookkeeping, and statistics career fields.

Technology is effective in providing opportunities for scaffolded learning and increased development of the mathematical-logical intelligence (Dickinson, 1998). Specifically, computer programs in the gaming format are particularly applicable to reaching this type of learner as students can develop their logic and creative thinking skills through this learning design (Jackson, et al., 2009). Computer or mobile games offer students drill and practice and provide immediate feedback on correct and incorrect answers, helping students to engage with the material and improve their understanding of the learning concepts (Dickinson, 1998). Eris Fose (2005) suggested that logical demonstrations, such as that of a spirograph java applet (Garg, n.d.), is appealing to students strong in the logical-mathematical intelligence in teaching students the basic concepts of circle radius, circle offset, and revolutions. She further suggested the use of Qarbon's Viewlet (https://www.qarbon.com/presentation-software/viewlet/viewlet_gallery.php, 2018) software as a tool in teaching more difficult mathematical concepts through visual demonstrations, such as probability, numerical methods, quadratic functions, differentiation, and complex numbers.

Musical-Rhythmic

Musical-rhythmic intelligence includes the ability to produce creative and expressive compositions and performances, to interpret musical forms and ideas, to respond emotionally to music, to work collaboratively to create music in order to meet the needs of others, and at the mastery level, to understand and develop musical technique (Silver, Strong, & Perini, 1997). Additionally, of all the gifts an individual may be created with, none develops earlier than the gift of musical talent, though it remains uncertain as to why this is (Gardner, 2011). However, Jackson, et al., (2009) explained, "when it comes to musical intelligence, there is limited evidence that a bridge between musical activities and musical growth exists when working with young learners" (p. 74). Moreover, the research is divided regarding the impact of digital technology on music education (Macedo, 2013).

Still, in certain educational settings, such as through the use of technology, musical intelligence can be related to learning, learning enjoyment, and enrichment of the multiple intelligences (Silver, Strong, & Perini, 1997). For example, some scholars in the field of music are concerned that the use of "artificial" music in education removes the need for students to learn about and understand harmony, notation, scoring, and reading music. However, Dickinson, (1998) posited that students may be so motivated by what they learn and create through musical technology that they are stimulated to explore these areas further. Additionally, as Macedo (2013) noted, "since its inception towards the end of the nineteenth century, music technology brought radical changes in the creative and technical aspects of music making and in the way it is performed, transmitted and received by the listener, leading to the development of new music styles and genres and to the emergence of new agents and institutions related to its commercial, industrial, institutional, educational, and scientific aspects" (p. 211). Further, Webster (2011) explained that technology has historically influenced music through the physics of sound as well as the manner in which music is consumed and distributed globally.

Moreover, digital technology, which combines digital audio with visual input, provides a learning opportunity for beginner students to the field of music to learn and experience concepts often thought too complicated for novice learners. Further, interactive multimedia experiences allow the student to explore pieces musically, historically, culturally, and politically (Dickinson, 1998). Also, Hunt (2009) explored the development of musical intelligence through the use of centers and included a specific technology center where students completed pre-selected lessons and games through the software *Music Ace Maestro*. At the listening center, students listened to assigned pieces of music through headphones and completed listening logs appropriate to their grade-level. These logs can be created through Microsoft Excel or other computer programs, which will further allow the integration of technology into the center learning environment. Likewise, the recent developments of video conferences have created a high-quality sound available for e-meetings (Webster, 2011), thus providing further opportunities for students to hear, produce, enjoy, value, and explore music through technology.

Bodily-Kinesthetic

Gardner (2011) posited that the modern American culture often promotes a "divorce between the mental and the physical" and views "what we do with our bodies is somehow less privileged, less special, than those problem-solving routines carried out chiefly through the use of language, logic, or some other relatively abstract symbolic system" (p. 219-220). However, as Gardner continued on to explain, this distinction is not drawn in many other cultures. Gardner's theory attempted to highlight the value of bodily-kinesthetic intelligence, exploration, learning, and performance.

Silver, Strong, and Perini (1997) characterized bodily-kinesthetic intelligence as the appreciation of the aesthetics of the body, the creation of new forms of expression with the body, planning strategically, and critiquing the actions of the body. Additionally, they noted that on the interpersonal level, bodily-kinesthetic learners utilize the body to build rapport with, persuade, console, and support others and at the mastery level they use the body and tools to construct, repair or take affective action. A student with a high bodily-kinesthetic intelligence learns best through doing. This learner is much more efficient at tasks after viewing a demonstration and then mimicking the actions of the teacher. Additionally, bodily-kinesthetic learners may find it difficult to sit still for lengthy periods of time or may become easily bored or distracted if not given the opportunity to be actively involved in a hands-on lesson (Eris Fose, 2005). Further, bodily-kinesthetic proficiency requires the use of the whole body to express feelings and ideas, and includes the use of one's hands to create or transform things during the learning process. Moreover, the bodily-kinesthetic intelligence includes tangible skills, such as balance, flexibility, coordination, power, dexterity, and speed (Jackson, et al., 2009). Gardner (2011) noted examples of individuals who have reached a mastery level of bodily-kinesthetic intelligence as those who have a sense of master over their bodies, such as runners, dancers and swimmers, and those who are able to manipulate objects with finesse such as ball players, skiers, ice skaters, artisans, and instrumentalists. Professionals strong in this intelligence may find success as a coach, trainer, mechanic, contractor, physical educator, sports analyst, or professional athlete, among others (Silver, Strong, & Perini, 1997).

Because computers and tables rely on hand-eye coordination for use of their operation, technology can be used to reinforce learning and encourage the student to become active in the learning process through their engagement with the mouse, keyboard, and touch screen (Dickinson, 1998). Additionally, Eris Fose (2005) recommended that teachers assign students a building project of a 3D object that requires the use of a digital still camera or camcorder to document the progress of the object's development. She also suggested the use of WebQuest activities, which were developed by San Diego State University professors Bernie Dodge and Thomas March as a means to create inquiry-oriented activities that require students utilize the Internet to explore and complete. These WebQuests include teamwork, role-playing, and higher-level thinking such as synthesis and problem solving. Furthermore, Eris Fose (2005) suggested that teachers utilize "scavenger hunts" on various topics that encourage students to search the Web or other computer applications. Moreover, innovations in technology have made it possible to teach physical activity such as dance or athletic skills. For example, augmented reality, computer-generated slide images or a camera operated videotape can allow the performance to be viewed and edited in a collaborative approach from students or teammates (Dickinson, 1998).

Interpersonal

Mastery of the interpersonal intelligence is the ability to organize people and groups and to communicate clearly the needed steps to complete a process. These skills are often found in politicians, managers, and administrators. This intelligence involves the ability to empathize with and help others, to solve problems, to identify and interpret among differing interpersonal clues, habits, and behaviors, as well as the ability to influence and inspire others towards the completion of a common goal. Interpersonal intelligence relies on personal interactions with others as a learning tool (Silver, Strong, & Perini, 1997). Students with strong interpersonal intelligence enjoy team activities, are generally sensitive to others' feelings, are adept at conflict resolution and mediation, and are skilled at drawing others out in group discussions (Eris Fose, 2005).

However, not all students are naturally highly skilled in this area. Therefore, because of the daily reliance on interpersonal skills in the workplace, school environment, and personal and professional relationships, interpersonal skills must be continually taught and developed with students of all learning capabilities. Indeed, as Baker, Parks-Savage, and Rehfuss (2009) stated, "technology has become a force so powerful in everyday life that its impact on daily interpersonal interactions is nearly impossible to ignore" (p. 210). In addition to the traditional interpersonal skills needed face-to-face, students now must learn and develop effective interpersonal communications through technology such as email, cell phones, texting, blogging, and instant messaging. Technology can be used to develop both types of interpersonal skills by providing an area of practice to lessen the anxiety of social situations and reduce potential confusion of "real world" multi-source inputs (Baker, Parks-Savage, & Rehfuss, 2009; Moore, 1998). Baker, Parks-Savage, and Rehfuss (2009) further touted the ability of a multi-user virtual environment (MUVE) to develop the interpersonal intelligence of children in small groups through interactive educational quests and social gatherings through various websites and computer games.

Autism Spectrum Disorder and Emotional and Behavioral Disability

Current research indicates that mobile technology can produce positive outcomes for students with autism spectrum disorder (ASD), specifically for teaching interpersonal and social skills (Haydon, Musti-Rao, McCune, Clouse, McCoy, Kalra, & Hawkins, 2017). Further, students who are diagnosed with an emotional and behavioral disability (EBD) suffer from "an inability to build or maintain satisfactory interpersonal relationships with teachers, caregivers, and peers" (Henriccson & Rydell, 2004; Koback, Little, Race, & Acosta, 2001 as cited in Haydon, et al., 2017, p. 154). Students with EBD often display aggressive and impulsive behavior (Morgan, Higgins, Miller, Pierce, Boone, & Tandy, 2016). With a growing number of students with EBD spending the majority of their day in the general education classroom, these students need to receive ongoing social skills training and support in order for successful inclusion in the classroom to occur. With the significant influence of various online social environments and social medias, students with EBD also need the guidance and practice in appropriate online behaviors in order to (a) protect themselves against online victimization, and (b) to guard against becoming the victimizer (Morgan, et al., 2016).

Technology, specifically video self-modeling, has been found effective in allowing students to repeatedly video appropriate target behavior and additionally to practice and observe themselves completing a behavior or skills appropriately (Haydon, et al., 2017). In order to effectively use video monitoring and mobile technology, such as smart phones and tablet computers, to teach and support EBD students with interpersonal intelligence, Haydon, et al., (2017) suggested that teachers "(a) consider prerequisite skills, (b) identify the target behavior, (c) identify the skill components and setting for instruction, (d) record a video of the student or model engaging in target behavior, (e) edit the video, and (f) develop a system to monitor behavior" (p. 155).

Intrapersonal

In contrast to the interpersonal learner, the intrapersonal learner focuses more on inward feelings, beliefs, and values and desires knowledge about the meaning, purpose, and significance of things (Eris Fose, 2005). Individuals strong in this intelligence are able to assess their own talents, interests, strengths and weaknesses and use these areas to set personal goals. They also employ their understanding of themselves in order to help and assist others, such as professionals in the counseling and social work fields. Additionally, they demonstrate the aptitude to create and develop concepts, ideas, and theories based on an examination and understanding of oneself, such as that of a psychologist. Further, individuals stronger in the area of intrapersonal intelligence are apt to reflect on their inner moods, temperaments, attitudes, behaviors, and intuitions and then use these feelings to create and express a personal vision (Silver, Strong, & Perini, 1997). Self-esteem, self-worth, and self-discipline are indicators of strong intrapersonal intelligence (Mettetal, Jordan, & Harpers, 1997).

Jackson et al. (2009) postulated that traditional education has for the most part overlooked interpersonal intelligence. However, new educational approaches, such as student-centered learning and digital learning, consider and value this unique intelligence. Moreover, technology can be used to encourage and develop this intelligence through the exploration and expansion of the human mind. As Dickinson (1998), explained "technology offers the means to pursue a line of thought in great depth as well as to have random access to divergent ideas" (p. 12). Dickinson suggested the use of computer programs such as Ceres' "Inspiration", which is a thought processor that can be utilized to facilitate individual brainstorming and cluster ideas into mindmaps or traditional outlines as the ideas are generated by the student. The program uses graphics and tests to provide a visual representation of the student's ideas and relationships between the ideas.

In addition to computer games and graphic capabilities, teachers and students can develop individual student learning or personal growth plans and goals through computer programs (Dickinson, 1998). Technology can also be used to encourage students to maintain a personal journal or blog to practice self-reflection and to then share their thoughts, ideas, and experiences with their teacher or classmates. Eris Fose (2005) vouched for the effectiveness of blogging based on the constructivist ideas that students learn better through interactions with others and therefore are able to develop a sense of self as a creator of knowledge through the blogging process. Further, Eris Fose suggested the use of Blogger.com or Blog Wave Studio to help students establish a free blog account.

Visual-Spatial

Gardner (2011) described spatial intelligence as "the capacities to perceive the visual world accurately, to perform transformations and modifications upon one's initial perceptions, and to be able to re-create aspects of one's visual experience, even in the absence of relevant physical stimuli" (p 182). However, he was quick to point out at that the visual component is not required for spatial intelligence, though they are often termed together. He noted that an individual who is blind and has no direct access to the visual world, can still develop and demonstrate spatial intelligence. Still, the term "visual-spatial" is often used in current research (Jackson, et al., 2009).

Silver, Strong, and Perini (1997) characterized this learner as one who is apt to transform visual and spatial ideas into imaginative and expressive creations. Further, they are generally able to interpret and graphically model visual or spatial ideas, such as an architect or computer graphics designer, and have the keen sense to arrange color, shape, line, form, and space in order to meet the needs and desires of others, such as that of an interior decorator, clothing designer, or painter. Moreover, individuals strong in the visual-spatial intelligence perceive and represent the visual-spatial world accurately.

Further, Jackson, et al., (2009) explained that "learning for visual-spatial students takes place all at once, with large chunks of information grasped in intuitive leaps, rather than in the gradual addition of isolated facts, such as small steps or habit patterns gained through practice" (p. 73). Visual-spatial learners are able to envision the spatial world in their own mind and are often strong with a visual memory but challenged with auditory memory. Students strong in this intelligence are often artistic and creative, yet easily distracted in the traditional classroom setting (Jackson, et al., 2009). Therefore, technology can be an effective means of reaching this unique demographic of students. Eris Fose (2005) suggested the use of MacroMedia Flash or SnapzPro for students to create visually rich digital media in order to learn and explore various topics. Additionally, as visual-spatial learners often enjoy reading maps, the educational software tool, *Inspiration*, can be effective in allowing students to use mindmaps to explore ideas and information.

Naturalist

An intelligence not included in Gardner's original list, and not as widely researched, is the naturalist intelligence. Individuals strong in this intelligence enjoy being outside, have keen sensory skills, possess an ability to observe and categorize, demonstrate an interest in caring for plants and animals, show an acute sense of observation, possess an interest in books or movies about nature, have a heightened sense of awareness and a protective sense for conserving species or places, and demonstrate the ability to learn names, categories or other details about species or plants (Covacevich, 2013). Essentially, individuals who possess this type of intelligence have an interest in living things, plants, animals, and the planet and they have an ability to recognize and categorize these objects in nature. Eris Fose (2005) suggested the following options for utilizing technology to develop and encourage the naturalists intelligence: (a) allow student to record their experiences in nature through camcorder videos and then teach students to edit their movie with iMovie; encourage students to share their videos with the class through a "virtual field trip"; (b) teach students to use Microsoft Excel to create spreadsheets that will catalogue collections and classifications; (c) instruct students to create a PowerPoint to research and present information on a specific science or nature related topic of the student's choice; (d) provide opportunities for mobile learning outside so that students can collect field data in their nature experiences; and (e) encourage students to complete a virtual science fair project. More currently, educators can also consider the use of cell phones, tablets, augmented reality, virtual reality, or mixed realities in order to record movies or complete virtual field trips and can use Prezi, VoiceThread, or digital storytelling software to complete these activities. Further, students are able to utilize technology to research naturalistic settings and organize community projects (e.g., park clean-up, recycle drive).

Existential

Jarvis (2006) defined existential learning where an individual's mind, body, and social situational experiences are "transformed cognitively, emotively, or practically" resulting in a "continually changing (or more experienced) person" (p. 134). McCoog (2010) also described the existential learner as one who can see "the big picture" and make connections between similar and dissimilar concepts. The nature of existentialism includes both personal and subjective inquiry (Roberts, 2010). Existential learners excel when asked "why" and "what if" questions and desire "the freedom to ponder, conceptualize, and hypothesize about the content presented in class" (McCoog, 2010, p. 127). Further, individuals with a strong existential intelligence are highly introspective and recognize that they must first be aware of their own feelings and self in order to fully understand the world around them. Thus, learners who excel in existential activities generally also have a dominant intrapersonal intelligence as well (McCoog, 2010). Gardner (1998) himself defined existential intelligence as "the human proclivity to raise and ponder fundamental questions about existence, life, [and] death" (p. 21). Interestingly, children begin raising these types of existential questions from a young age in order to understand the world through their cognitive and emotional development (McCoog, 2010). Noteworthy, because of the narrow manner in which Gardner defined the 9th intelligence in his theory, its development has been restricted (Roberts, 2010).

However, today's modern use of technology is an extremely effective manner in teaching to the existentialist. Charteris, Quinn, Parkes, Fletcher, and Reyes (2016) noted that existentialism can be experienced through relational interactions in online communities, social media outlets such as Facebook and ephemeral media like Snapchat. In order to further develop the existential intelligence, Eris Fose (2005) recommended the use of Socratic-type questioning through a real-time chat tool. Examples of this tool can include: BlackBoard's Virtual Classroom, Canvas's Virtual Classroom, and Edmodo Backchannel Chat. Additionally, Charteris, et al. (2016) suggested that students utilize automated feedback from online quizzes, an option often available in online higher education courses, in order to diagnose their own gaps in knowledge.

THE IMPACT OF MIT ON STUDENT-CENTERED LEARNING

In addition to the drastic increase in technology use, the modern, digital-age classroom has also transitioned from the traditional teacher approach reliant on lecture and a primary course textbook to now being pointedly more student-centered (Oprescu, Craciun, & Banaduc, 2011). Gardner, like John Dewey before him, argued that the American education system needed to move towards a student-centered teaching style (Leshkovska & Spaseva, 2016). Meaning, as Saban (2011) explained, "the teacher teaches, the students learns, [has been replaced] with the understanding [that] the teacher provides the learning, and the teaching and student learn and share together" (p. 16642). Therefore, students are no longer passive receptors of information and instead should be guided toward a more active approach in knowledge acquisition through skills such as thinking, questioning, researching, constructing, and producing (Saban, 2011).

Jackson, et al. (2009) further posited that it is essential for educators to offer students learning activities that allow for the practice of formulating and solving real-life problems. Moreover, because research indicates that students learn best through various approaches including seeing, hearing, doing, listening to or playing music, analyzing, and discussing, it is important to evaluate instructional approaches, specifically approaches using technology, in order to assess the effectiveness of the practice in relation to student learning (Tamilselvi & Geetha, 2015). Robert's (2010) research supported this notion by explaining that educators need to balance method and meaning, process, and content, which "requires a delicate and rather artful approach to sound pedagogy and imagination for educators today" (p. 243).

Further, Sanchez-Martinez, et al. (2017) postulated that educators must consider emotions and feelings in the teaching-learning process. Further, while a positive emotional state can produce learning and learning enjoyment, a negative emotional state can severely hinder a student's ability and desire to learn (Vazquez & Manassero, 2007). In addition, the use of technology, specifically social networking communities, allows students to not only explore and develop multiple intelligences, but it also allows students to discover how other cultures and societies address the various intelligences in their respective learning process and customs (Webster, 2011). Additionally, the formatting of testing should also be considered through the lens of MIT. As Zahedi & Moghaddam (2016) found, students may have a significant variation in success levels of multiple-choice testing, depending upon their multiple intelligence. They recommend that teachers utilize a variety of testing formats in order to provide a fairer and more balanced evaluation approach.

As Prensky (2001) claimed, even at the turn of the century, "students have changed radically. Today's students are no longer the people our educational system was designed to teach" (p. 1). Therefore, in order to reach a more student-centered approach to teaching and learning, educational considerations must reflect these changes and consider both the use of digital technology preferred by students and the importance of multiple intelligences exhibited by students.

HIGHER EDUCATION AND THE ONLINE LEARNING ENVIRONMENT

The learning process of all levels including higher education and the influence of online learning should be considered in regards to MIT. As Jackson et al. (2009) explained, multiple intelligence teaching approaches (MITA) "offer realistic approaches to the enrichment of learning opportunities for a greater population of post-secondary learners" (p. 76). They further posited that the typical trends in college and university instruction does not provide a high level of engagement or active role for students and fails to prioritize the diversity of learning styles in higher education classrooms. Additionally, Macedo (2013) postulated that in order for academic degrees to serve a meaningful and relevant place in students' lives, the degree programs and faculty should move beyond the strictly technical component of study and instead aid the students in developing critical and perceptual skills that will produce quality work and engagement in their future career paths. Therefore, technology, a common ground in higher education, should be utilized to further address and develop the multiple learning intelligences of students at the post-secondary levels.

Using MIT for Adult Learners

MIT has proven an effective means to reach and develop the learning in both adult students and employees (Arce, 2006). Arce (2006) further posited that due to the increase in adults returning to school as well as the ever more competitive environment in the business world, that attention multiple intelligence is necessary in developing adults potential learning and workplace production. Adults who were unsuccessful in their educational pursuits in the past may now be more likely to succeed due to the attention placed on specific learning intelligences.

Additionally, Coil (1998, as cited in Arce, 2006) found that the use of computer tutorials and hypermedia instructional materials combined with MI-based activities resulted in positive attitudes toward learning and achievement gains in the classroom. More specifically, Eris Fose (2005) suggested the use of online discussion forums, which are currently commonly found in online education, to develop and foster learning through the verbal-linguistic intelligence. She also recommended that professors step back from leading these discussions and instead assign specific students, on a rotating basis, the opportunity to lead the discussion as a means of taking ownership and leadership in their own learning and coursework.

Challenges in Teaching to Multiple Intelligences in the Digital Age

Despite the benefits of teaching through the lens of MIT in the digital age, educators still report a difficulty in trying to cover all learning intelligences in the classroom. Teachers in primary grades also note that a lack of training, funding, and materials as well as the refusal of some students or parents to participate provide further challenges in the difficulty of teaching with MIT (Oprescu, Craciun, & Banaduc, 2011). Faculty in higher education describe feelings of incompetence or lack of knowledge in how to apply MIT principles and technology into their instructional style. Additionally, the integration of technology into the classroom requires a significant investment in time, yet teachers and faculty reward systems do not often acknowledge the value and impact of this effort (Marquez Chisholm & Beckett, 2003). Marquez Chisholm and Beckett (2003) suggested that this is the most difficult hurdle for the integration of technology and MIT principles is administrator and educator buy-in. In addition, Mettetal, Jordan, and Harpers's (1997) research indicated that while parents were generally supportive of the principles of MIT, parents also questioned the importance of activity rooms or enrichment clusters during the day, wondering if these activities should be completed through optional afterschool programs.

In addition to the challenges of providing attention to MIT and practice, challenges with using technology in learning must also be addressed. As Nelson (1998) explained, the sheer volume of information available on the Internet can be overwhelming and time consuming for students trying to find specific information. Additionally, some learners may be confused by the branching capabilities with hypertext and hypermedia. Further, "there is also the problem of content and legitimacy of information accessible on the Internet/Web. Anyone can post anything including erroneous, false or misleading information, hate and violence-inciting rants and hard-core pornography" (Nelson, 1998, p. 90). Lastly, challenges in using technology in addition to MIT learning may move beyond the learners themselves and impact the teacher. Research indicates that educators may feel intimated and overwhelmed by the use of technology in the classroom (Prensky, 2001).

Further, Silver, et al. (1998) posited that despite its many strengths, MIT is lacking in its attention to the individualized process of learning due to its focus on the content of learning and its relation to the specific disciplines. Additionally, there is fear that students may be incorrectly labeled as a certain type of learner from a young age, preventing them from expressing other intelligences and reaching full development in their true intelligences (Groff, 2013). Moreover, Groff (2013) claimed that the field of arts education has been hindered due to its reliance primarily on multiple intelligences theory because of the theory's misunderstanding of the relationship between the arts, human development, and learning. She posited that a new theory of mind, *whole-mindedness*, should be explored and valued in order to redefine and justify the importance of arts education in schools, specifically "the digitally and visually rich world" (p. 15).

CLOSING THOUGHTS AND RECOMMENDATIONS FOR FUTURE LEARNING

In closing, the intent of this chapter was to further explicate the positive impacts of MIT concepts and technology use in classroom instruction in a modern age of education in order to advance the acceptance of these ideas in the digital age of learning. Research indicates that the importance of MIT inclusion in the education setting is equally as important today, as when it was first presented (Adcock, 2014). As Arce (2006) stated, "MI is a critical tool that educators and business leaders need to help more people become more successful today than ever before" (p. 89). However, the age range of learners may impact how MI is integrated by educators into their classroom settings.

Additionally, educators are encouraged to utilize not only Gardener's theory of multiple intelligences in student interactions, curriculum design decisions, and technology integration, but also Daniel Goleman's (1995) theory of social and emotional intelligence (Adcock, 2014). Goleman (1995, 2006) posited that a person's behavior and decision making is driven by their feelings and passions. As well, he stressed the importance that individuals enhance their ability to recognize and control their emotions. Further, he noted the value in an individual's ability to recognize and work well with the emotions of others (Adcock, 2014). Moreover, by developing emotional intelligence, an individual may be more successful in their own endeavors and those of others (Serrat, 2017). Future learning strategies, teaching-learning approaches, and specifically the use of technology in the classroom would be served well through the consideration of these additional intelligences in developing a generation of introspective, empathetic, and successful generation of learners and workers.

REFERENCES

Adcock, P. (2014). The longevity of multiple intelligence theory in education. *The Delta Kappa Gamma Bulletin*, 50-57.

Arce, P. (2006). Learning futures: Using multiple intelligence theory for adult learners. *Futurics*, *30*(3/4), 89–90.

Bano, M., Zowghi, D., Kearney, M., Schuck, S., & Aubusson, P. (2018). Mobile learning for science and mathematics school education: A systematic review of empirical evidence. *Computers & Education*, *121*, 30–58. doi:10.1016/j.compedu.2018.02.006

Charteris, J., Quinn, F., Parkes, M., Fletcher, P., & Reyes, V. (2016). e-Assessement for learning. *Australasian Journal of Educational Technology*, *32*(3), 112–122.

Coil, R. A. (1998). *Multiple intelligences and computer assisted learning with adult learners* (Ph.D. diss.). Union Institute. Retrieved from Dissertation Abstracts International, 58, no. 12, 4523A, UMI. (No. AAT 98-17952)

Covacevich, J. A. (2013). A naturalist born, made or both? *Queensland Naturalist, 51*(1/2/3), 3-4.

Dickinson, D. (1998). *How Technology Enhances Howard Gardner's Eight Intelligences*. New Horizons for Learning and America Tomorrow. Retrieved from https://www.yumpu.com/en/document/view/44874093/how-technology-enhances-howard-gardners-eight-intelligences

Dorfeld, N. M. (2016). Being heard: Motivating millennials through multiple intelligences. *Journal on Excellence in College Teaching*, *27*(4), 65–75.

Eris Fose, L. (2005). *Exploring technology to address student multiple intelligences & learning styles*. Retrieved from https://www.calpoly.edu/~lfose/articles/Exploring_Technology.pdf

Gardner, H. (1983a). *Frames of Mind: The Theory of Multiple Intelligences*. New York: Basic Books.

Gardner, H. (1983b). *Multiple Intelligences: The Theory in Practice*. New York: Basic Books.

Gardner, H. (1995). Reflections on multiple Intelligences: Myths and Messages. *Phi Delta Capan*, *77*, 200–209.

Gardner, H. (1998). A multiplicity of intelligences. *Scientific American Presents: Exploring Intelligence*, *9*(4), 18–23.

Gardner, H. (1999). *Intelligence Reframed: Multiple Intelligences for the 21st Century*. New York: Basic Books.

Gardner, H. (2011). *Frames of Mind: The Theory of Multiple Intelligences*. New York: Basic Books.

Garg, A. (n.d.). *Spirograph*. Retrieved from http://www.wordsmith.org/~anu/java/spirograph.html

Groff, J. (2013). Expanding our "frames" of mind for education and the arts. *Harvard Educational Review*, *83*(1), 15–39. doi:10.17763/haer.83.1.kk34802147665819

Haydon, T., Musti-Rao, S., McCune, A., Clouse, D., McCoy, D., Kalra, H., & Hawkins, R. (2017). Using video modeling and mobile technology to teach social skills. *Intervention in School and Clinic*, *52*(3), 154–162. doi:10.1177/1053451216644828

Henriccson, L., & Rydell, A. M. (2004). Elementary school children with behavior problems: Teacher-child relations and self-perception: A prospective study. *Merrill-Palmer Quarterly*, *50*(2), 111–138. doi:10.1353/mpq.2004.0012

Hunt, B. (2009). Teaching and learning through music centers. *Musicien Educateur AU Canada*, *50*(4), 51–53.

Jackson, A., Gaudet, L., McDaniel, L., & Brammer, D. (2009). Curriculum integration: The use of technology to support learning. *Journal of College Teaching and Learning*, *6*(7), 71–78.

Jarvis, P. (2006). *Towards a comprehensive theory of human learning*. London: Routledge.

Jones, C., & Shao, B. (2011). The net generation and digital natives. *Higher Education Academy*. Retrieved from https://www.heacademy.ac.uk/system/files/next-generation-and-digital-natives.pdf

Kardefelf-Winther, D. (2017). How does the time children spend using digital technology impact their mental well-being, social relationships and physical activity? *UNICEF*. Retrieved from https://www.unicef-irc.org/publications/pdf/Children-digital-technology-wellbeing.pdf

Koback, R., Little, M., Race, E., & Acosta, M. C. (2001). Attachment disruptions in seriously emotionally disturbed children: Implications for treatment. *Attachment & Human Development*, *3*(3), 243–258. doi:10.1080/14616730110096861 PMID:11885812

Leshkovska, E. A., & Spaseva, S. M. (2016). John Dewey's educational theory and educational implications of Howard Gardner's multiple intelligence theory. *International Journal of Cognitive Research in Science, Engineering and Education, 4*(2), 57–66.

Macedo, F. (2013). Teaching creative music technology in higher education: A phenomenological approach. *Journal of Music, Technology & Education, 6*(2), 207–219.

Mall, K. (2012). *Are you reaching your digital natives?* Scholastic. Retrieved from https://www.scholastic.com/teachers/blog-posts/kristy-mall/are-you-reaching-your-digital-natives/

Marquesz Chisholm, I., & Beckett, E. D. (2003). Teacher preparation for equitable access through the integration of TESOL standards, multiple intelligences and technology. *Technology, Pedagogy and Education, 12*(2), 249–276. doi:10.1080/14759390300200157

McCoog, I. (2010). The existential learner. *The Clearing House: A Journal of Educational Strategies, Issues and Ideas, 83*(4), 126–128. doi:10.1080/00098651003774828

McKenzie, W. (2004). *Gardner's eight criteria for identifying an intelligence.* Retrieved January 3, 2018 from http://surfaquarium.com/MI/criteria.htm

Mettetal, G., Jordan, C., & Harper, S. (1997). Attitudes toward a multiple intelligences curriculum. *The Journal of Educational Research, 91*(2), 115–122. doi:10.1080/00220679709597529

Moore, D. J. (1998). Computers and people with autism/Asperger syndrome. *Communication*, 20-21.

Morgan, J., Higgins, K., Miller, S., Pierce, T., Boone, R., & Tandy, R. (2016). Teaching online social skills to students with emotional and behavioral disorders. *Journal of Special Education Technology, 31*(2), 109–120. doi:10.1177/0162643416651725

Nelson, G. (1998). Internet/Web-based instruction and multiple intelligences. *Educational Media International, 35*(2), 90–94. doi:10.1080/0952398980350206

Oprescu, M., Cracium, D., & Banaduc, I. (2011). Multiple intelligences in conventional and student-centered school. *Journal of Educational Sciences & Psychology, 1*(1), 86–94.

Pappas, I., Giannakos, M., & Sampson, D. (2017). Fuzzy set analysis as a means to understand users of 21st-century learning systems: The case of mobile learning and reflections on learning analytics research. *Computers in Human Behavior*, 1–14.

Prensky. (2001). Digital natives, digital immigrants. *On the Horizon, 9*(5). Retrieved from http://marcprensky.com/writing/Prensky%20%20Digital%20Natives%20Digital%20Immigrants%20-%20Part1.pdf

Qarbon Viewlet. (2018). *Viewlet Gallery.* Retrieved January 5, 2018 from https://www.qarbon.com/presentation-software/viewlet/viewlet_gallery.php

Roberts, M. (2010). Encounters with existential intelligence: Possibilities for today's effective educator. *The International Journal of Interdisciplinary Social Sciences: Annual Review, 5*(7), 241–253. doi:10.18848/1833-1882/CGP/v05i07/51794

Saban, A. I. (2011). An evaluation of the teaching activities implemented in the elementary science and technology courses in terms of multiple intelligence theory: A sample from Adana. *Educational Sciences: Theory and Practice, 11*(3), 1641–1649.

Sanchez-Martin, J., Alvaez-Gragera, G. J., Davila-Acedo, M. A., & Mellado, V. (2017). Teaching technology: From knowing to feeling enhancing emotional and content acquisition performance through Gardner's multiple intelligences theory in technology and design lesson. *Journal of Technology and Science Education, 7*(1), 58–79. doi:10.3926/jotse.238

Serrat, O. (2017). *Knowledge Solutions*. Singapore: Springer. doi:10.1007/978-981-10-0983-9

Silver, H., Strong, R., & Perini, M. (1997). Integrating learning styles and multiple intelligences. *Educational Leadership, 55*(1), 22–27. Retrieved from http://www.ascd.org/publications/educational-leadership/sept97/vol55/num01/Integrating-Learning-Styles-and-Multiple-Intelligences.aspx

Tamilselvi, T. & Geetha, D. (2015). Efficacy in teaching through "multiple intelligence" instructional strategies. *i-Manager's Journal on School Educational Technology, 11*(2), 1-11.

Vazquez, A., & Manassero, M. A. (2007). In defense of attitudes and emotions in the scientific Education (I): Evidences and general arguments (En defensa de las actitudes y emociones en la educacion cientifica (I): Evidencias y argumentos generales). *Eureka Journal of Science Education and Divulgation, 4*(2), 247–271.

Webster, P. R. (2011). Key research in music technology and music teaching and learning. Journal of Music. *Technology and Education, 4*(2 & 3), 115–130.

Zahedi, S., & Moghaddam, E. M. (2016). The relationship between multiple intelligence and performance of EFL students in different forms of reading comprehension tests. *Theory and Practice in Language Studies, 6*(10), 1929–2939. doi:10.17507/tpls.0610.06

Zahedi, Z., & Ghabanchi, Z. (2014). The relationship between logical, naturalist intelligences and learning grammar for EFL learners at elementary level. *Theory and Practice in Language Studies, 4*(2), 403–410. doi:10.4304/tpls.4.2.403-410

ADDITIONAL READING

Armstrong, T. (2009). *Multiple intelligence in the classroom*. Alexandria, VA: Association for Supervision and Curriculum Development.

Arnold, E. (2007). *MI strategy bank: 800 + multiple intelligence ides for the elementary classroom*. Chicago, IL: Zephyr Press.

Chen, J., Moran, S., & Gardner, H. (2009). *Multiple intelligences around the world*. San Francisco, CA: Jossey-Bass.

Eysenck, H. (2018). *Intelligence*. New York, NY: Routledge.

Gardner, H. (1999). *Intelligence reframed: Multiple intelligences for the 21st century*. New York, NY: Basic Books.

Gunduz, N., & Ozcan, D. (2016). The development of multiple intelligence with storytelling. *International Journal of Educational Sciences*, *15*(1-2), 242–251. doi:10.1080/09751122.2016.11890533

Illeris, K. (2018). *Contemporary theories of learning*. London, UK: Routledge. doi:10.4324/9781315147277

Keane, T., Keane, W., & Blicblau, A. (2016). Beyond traditional literacy: Learning and transformative practices using ICT. *Education and Information Technologies*, *21*(4), 769–781. doi:10.100710639-014-9353-5

Keengwe, J., & Bhargava, M. (2014). Mobile learning and integration of mobile technologies in education. *Education and Information Technologies*, *19*(4), 737–746. doi:10.100710639-013-9250-3

Pratiwi, W. N., Rochintaniawati, D., & Agustin, R. R. (2018). The effect of multiple intelligence-based learning towards students' concept mastery and interest in matter. *Journal of Science Learning*, *1*(2), 49–52. doi:10.17509/jsl.v1i2.8739

Sajjadi, P., Vlieghe, J., & De Troyer, O. (2017). Exploring the relation between the Theory of Multiple Intelligences and games for the purpose of player-centered game design. *Electronic Journal of e-Learning*, *15*(4), 320-334.

Wlodkowski, R., & Ginsberg, M. (2017). *Enhancing adult motivation to learn: A comprehensive guide for teaching all adults* (4th ed.). San Francisco, CA: Jossey-Bass.

KEY TERMS AND DEFINITIONS

Constructivist Teaching Strategies: Strategies used in the classroom that are based on the constructivist learning theory which posits that students learn better through interactions with others and when they are actively involved in the learning process, as opposed to passively receiving the information that is taught.

Digital Age: The digital age refers to the time-period in which personal computers and other subsequent technologies were introduced to provide users the ability to easily and rapidly transfer information.

Multiple Intelligences Theory: The Theory of Multiple Intelligences postulates that individuals learn and understand information differently and that educators should present and assess content in a variety of ways to capture the eight types of intelligences: 1) linguistic, 2) logical-mathematical, 3) spatial, 4) bodily-kinesthetic, 5) musical, 6) interpersonal, 7) intrapersonal, and 8) naturalist.

Online Learning: Online learning comprises student learning through the internet and a personal computer.

Student-Centered Learning: Student-centered learning involves learners being active rather than passive recipients of knowledge that is driven by individual academic needs and abilities.

Chapter 2
Enhancing 21st Century Learning Using Digital Learning Objects and Multiple Intelligence Theory:
A Conceptual Model

Emma O Brien
Mary Immaculate College, Ireland

ABSTRACT

The educational system is undergoing radical pressure to change. The increased need for individuals to learn and adapt has resulted in a huge demand for higher education. However, higher educational institutes are failing to keep pace with learner and societal needs. Firstly, the skills profile required for individuals to succeed is changing; there is a change in emphasis from discipline-specific to transversal skills due to the dynamic labor market. Secondly, the learner profile has changed with individuals from diverse backgrounds, cultures, abilities, and contexts, and catering for such a diverse range of students is challenging. Technology is a key enabler in providing HEIs with the means to address such issues. This chapter explores a conceptual model which integrates pedagogical approaches such as multiple intelligence theory, learning styles, competency-based education with digital technologies to offer a solution to some of the concerns facing higher education in the 21st century.

INTRODUCTION

Today we live in a fast-paced society that requires citizens to be proactive and responsive. (Chai & Kong, 2017) Many of the jobs that exist currently will phase out over the next decade, leading to new skills which are required for emerging job roles. (Kirschner & Stoyanov, 2018) In light of this it is difficult to prepare individuals for a future workforce. With the advent of new technologies multimedia literacies are gaining traction as a 21st century skill. Multimodal literacies advocate the need for students to curate and

DOI: 10.4018/978-1-7998-0249-5.ch002

critically consume materials of all forms of material (Sinclar, 2010). Furthermore, skills that empower individuals to become self-directed, autonomous learners are necessary to adapt to change

Fuelled by this uncertainty the education sector is experiencing a significant transition. The learner profile is diversifying with students from a variety of backgrounds, abilities and needs (Digitalisierung, 2017) This provides potential to offer to a richer learning environment where peers can learn from each other., However often such learners must juggle multiple personal and professional demands with educational commitments. Ensuring these learners are fully engaged in the learning experience allowing them to both benefit and contribute to the learning environment is a challenge.

Given the heterogeneity and complexity of the learner profile a one size fits all, mass education system is no longer appropriate. (Digitalisierung, 2017) Policies are criticising the one to many teaching approaches and advocating more flexible, personalised approaches to learning, which motivates and engages learners (Beetham and Sharpe, 2013) However the current educational system is under resourced and educators have limited capacity to tailor their approaches for different learners. Leveraging from technology can provide the capacity to offer tailored personalised learning to students. (Union, 2014). ICT can provide the potential to facilitate the provision of timely, relevant content to learners in formats or through medium that align to their preferred modality and preference of learning

This chapter will explore a conceptual model which integrates Multiple Intelligence Theory, Learning styles, Competence Based education and digital learning objects to offer personalised approaches to learning in the 21st Century. It will examine how technology can facilitate personalised learning approaches by enabling learners to develop a learner profile by self-assessing their competence level, multiple intelligence and learning style. Using this profile and algorithms based on instructional design principles a Personalised Learning Environment, can automatically search for relevant digital learning outcomes.

PERSONALISED LEARNING PEDAGOGIES

The concept of personalised or individualised learning is not a new phenomenon. The concept is strongly rooted in the constructivism pedagogical paradigm. Theorists back as far as Socrates have recognised the importance of identifying the individuals *'ability and natural disposition'* (Lawrence, 1970, p. 4). This was later reinforced by Rosseau in his theory of well-regulated freedom in which students are given choice to support their natural capacity to learn. (Dishon, 2017) and was advocated by Dewey in his criticism of the traditional didactic model.

Theory of Multiple Intelligences (MI)

Later this was expanded by Gardner in his theory of multiple intelligences. Gardner highlights that contrary to traditional perceptions which identify one dimension of intelligence, several types of intelligences exist and are developed differently in each individual. (Gardner 1993) He argues that these intelligences can develop over time and are not static. The capacity to develop different intelligences may depend on the developmental stage a learner is at (in line with Paget's developmental theory), their natural disposition, their experiences and background. It is important to note that MI theory does not identify if a student will to learn in a particular way, it is a measure of the student's level of ability in each intelligence. In total Gardner has identified eight intelligences these are (Gardner 1993)

- Verbal/Linguistic
- Logical/Mathematical
- Visual/Spatial
- Bodily/Kinesthetics
- Musical
- Interpersonal
- Intra Personal
- Naturalist

MI theory has undergone several criticisms both by Gardner himself and other researchers, it is said it lacks robust experimental research (Denig, 2004)

Since then, there have been several studies into the impact of application of MI theory on student achievement. In a study conducted by Baş & Beyhab (2017) with fifty primary students it was found that there was a significant increase in student performance using the MI methods in comparison to traditional teaching methods. Many other studies have found positive correlations between academic achievement and MI, in a meta-analysis conducted by Bas (2016), it was found that 97% of studies indicated the positive impact of MI (Saban, 2009; Shearer, 2004). Furthermore, MI has raised awareness amongst educators of different learning modalities and preferences.

Many theorists have argued that Multiple intelligences is difficult to measure (Saban, 2004). Gardner advocated strongly against quantitatively measuring the intelligences in favour of more qualitative contextualised approaches such as observation (Gardner, 2004). However, this method can be very time consuming particularly in the distributed mass educational system we live in today. Furthermore observation, if not conducted rigorously can be subject to bias. To address such issues several quantitative methods for measuring dominant forms of MI have been developed.

The Teele inventory of Multiple Intelligence is questionnaire that identifies the most dominant forms of Intelligence of the eight MI identified by Gardner. Students are presented with 56 questions and are asked to identify the choice which they identify most with (Ucak, Bag, Usak, & Esra Ucak, 2006). Armstrong (2009) developed a MI inventory checklist in which they check the items that relate to them. It is a guide to inform learners of their dominant forms of intelligences, so they can make informed choices regarding their natural learning disposition and choose learning activities that relate to their individual needs. MI theory has informed many other pedagogical approaches including learning styles, multimodal teaching and Universal Design for Learning.

Learning Styles Theories

Around the same time as Gardner's MI theory the concept of learning styles and preferences gained traction. Myers Briggs, Kolb's learning styles inventory, Honey and Mumford and Dunn and Dunn Learning Styles are just some of the many learning styles that emerged during this period. Coffield, Moseley, Hall, and Ecclestone (2004) classified the many learning styles models into those based on

- Modalities of learning which are closely aligned to MI theory however in contrast to MI theory they feel these are influenced by genetic characteristics more than the learning environment e.g. Dunn and Dunn learning styles questionnaire
- Cognitive ability which are largely hereditary e.g. Riding

- Individuals personality which are not subject to change
- Learning preferences which identify which learning activities an individual has preference for, these are flexible yet stable e.g. Honey and Mumford
- Learning approaches which can be modified by the students learning environment e.g. Endwhistle

In recent years learning styles theories have undergone severe criticism and several studies have found that MI has a positive impact on academic achievement. However, learning styles fail to generate the similar outcomes (Husmann & O'loughlin, 2019). The research conducted into the impact of learning styles on student learning has been deemed as unreliable due to the complexity of learning (Coffield et al., 2004). However, it is seen to be useful to increase self-awareness and forming a dialogue for learning.

Vermunts learning styles inventory examines four aspects of learning cognitive processing, learning orientation, mental modelling and learning regulation on eighteen subscales. From the questionnaire the learners orientation is categorised as meaning orientated, application orientated, reproduction orientated or undirected (Vermunt, 1998). By identifying the learner orientation the way learning material should be sequenced can be determined, for example if a person is application orientated they should be presented with an activity requires to apply what is learned and then they reflect and derive meaning from this.

Multimodal Teaching and Learning

Many of the learning styles theories are centred around modality of learning and in recent years there has been significant emphasis on multimodal teaching approaches. These approaches appeal to all types of learners by combining different modes of learning to make meaning, learners can then choose the most relevant resources to their individual needs (Jewitt, 2006). Learning resources are representative in multiple ways that appeal to all senses, learning preferences, approaches and contexts. With the transition from print based to multimedia-based teaching this has been made possible (Papageorgiou & Lameras, 2017). However, the pedagogical underpinnings of this approach are not clearly defined. It is being widely adopted in language learning (Erfanian Mohammadi, Elahi Shirvan, & Akbari, 2018) and more recently as one of the main principles of Universal Design for Learning (UDL)

Universal Design for Learning

Universal Design for Learning (UDL) is a multimodal pedagogy which advocates the use of technology to offer flexibility to learners. UDL ensures all learning caters for students with diverse needs, while at the same time developing expert learners or 'learn to learn' skills (Hayden, 2011)

UDL originated in the construction sector to provide consumers with solutions that are accessible to the widest possible audience and uses (McCarthy & Butler, 2013). This was later adapted to the educational sector in light of the massification of education, and the increase in diversity of learners. (Meyer & Rose, 2006). The UDL model has three primary principles

- **Multiple Means of Representation:** This is the what. It provides learner choice in what they learn and in what way. The principle considers how information of knowledge should be represented and advocates
- **Multiple Means of Action and Expression:** This is the how of learning. How the learner can interact with the learning material.

Enhancing 21st Century Learning Using Digital Learning Objects

- **Multiple Means of Engagement** Why of learning. Motivating learners and providing them with opportunities to apply their learning.

These principles are underpinned by neuroscience, aligning to three cognitive functions known as recognition networks, strategic networks and affective networks. How each person applies these cognitive functions and how they work together differs for each individual.

McCarthy and Butler (2013) highlighted the synergies between MI ad UDL highlighting that *'both focus on the differentiated classroom and reaching out to all students.* However rather than personalising learning UDL focuses on making learning Universal for all. Choice is a key facet of UDL as the learner has choice in every piece of material, assessment and way they engage in learning (Rose, Harbour, Johnston, Daley, & Abarbanell, 2006). This aligns to Manwaring's research findings on the positive correlation between emotional engagement and choice in online environments (Manwaring, Larsen, Graham, Henrie, & Halverson, 2017).

Technology can impact all three principles, in particular how knowledge is represented, multimedia can be used to represent learning in different ways to provide learner choice and flexibility. In today's educational environment it is even more important to adapt teaching and learning to the individual intelligence profile of each student is quite laborious to implement in the traditional classroom environment, both Gardner and Dewey realised this limitation. In particular, identifying learner preferences and profiling students is extremely difficult. Furthermore, preparing learning content to address the needs of multiple learner profiles can be time consuming. However, with the advent of technology this can be simplified.

Theories such as MI, UDL and Multimodal teaching advocate personalising learning by providing choice to ensure the learning environment is relevant to an individual need. However, we live in a culture where individuals are inundated with information and choice. Learners are often overwhelmed and find it difficult to navigate through the volume of information to support learners it is important to provide informed choice.

Combining theories such as learning styles with MI inventory testing can provide informed choice to learners in which recommends a ranked index of learning resources and activities relevant to an individual's learning profile. However, it is also essential to consider what the learner might need to learn. The next section looks at models that can inform the choice of learning material.

PERSONALISING LEARNING CONTENT

To ensure the learner is provided with content and learning activities relevant to their individual learning needs it is important to

1. Identify the learner's preferences and modalities.
2. Identify the content they need to learn

The last section looked at pedagogies that can support the identification of the learner's preferences and modalities. It is important to consider how to identify the content the learners need to learn.

Traditional educational approaches involves identifying a specific programme in which the educator designs a series of modules which the student is required to undertake. For each module learning outcomes are identified and the educator provides the content the student needs to learn and dedicated specific timelines for completing predefined assessments. However, this model is no longer seen as adequate for three reasons 1) The diversity of the learner profile demands an educational system that can be tailored for all learners, 2) Often the skills are taught in educational programmes are narrow and can become outdated quite quickly. Therefore, there is a need to broaden the skills base to incorporate skills which can be applied to multiple contexts, and 3) Often the formal didactic teaching undertaken in formal educational institutes is far removed from the contexts in which they are applied, it is therefore necessary to advocate models which extend the boundaries of formal education into areas in learners can demonstrate the application of such skills.

Competency based education (CBE) is a flexible model of learning which has gained popularity in the US over the past ten years. First introduced in the 1960s in the US (Nodine, 2016) it is experiencing a revival in the past ten years. The competency-based approach has been identified as a way of addressing the emerging 21st century skills deficit (Le, Wolfe, & Steinberg, 2014; Surr & Redding, 2016). By offering a broad set of core competencies comprising of several skills students demonstrate a wide range of discipline specific and transversal skills. Emphasis is not on seat time or didactic hours but on the application of learning (Kelchen, 2015). CBE is seen as a flexible form of learning as it allows learners to become autonomous learners, they decide how they would like to acquire and demonstrate the application of the learning associated with each competence. Learners do not move to the next competency unless they have demonstrated mastery. Therefore, it offers a personalised self-paced methodology (Surr & Rasumussen, 2015). It not only offers flexibility in delivery of content but also the learning activities and assessment the learner engages in. Therefore, it aligns closely with all three UDL principles discussed in the previous section. Furthermore, it emphasises the multimodality of learning recommending a combination of instruction, peer learning, evidence based, applied and self-regulated learning (DeLorenzo, Battino, Schreiber, & Carrio, 2009).

Redding (2016) highlights the rigour associated with CBE and its potential to guide learner choice. *"A competency is defined as a cluster of related capabilities (skills and knowledge) with methods and criteria to determine the degree to which a person demonstrates mastery in them…………….the competency would be further defined by itemising the measurable or observable skills and knowledge that constituted……..it would include criteria and methods of determining the mastery of the competency's constituent skills and knowledge, and the assessment would include demonstration or application"* (p. 6). The competency framework provides a guide to allow the learner to self-assess their mastery at a specific competency and make choices about the content which they learn and how to apply it.

Providing competency models for learners, can offer a structure to provided informed choice to learners of what they need to learn and how can apply Furthermore, Digitalisierung, (2017) highlights that digital competency tests and follow up preparatory courses can identify gaps in knowledge among prospective students before the course begins and help the to close these gaps.

The next section will look at the types of technology that can facilitate the identification of the relevant learning material and activities that can provided informed choice to the learners in terms of modality, content and preference of learning.

TECHNOLOGY FOR PERSONALISING LEARNING

Contemporary pedagogies such as UDL emphasise the role of technology in providing inclusive learning environments which foster self-directed, expert learners. This section will explore some of the technologies that can facilitate this, in particular personalised learning environments and learning objects which can form the foundation of digital personalised learning.

Personalised Learning Environments

Technology has been identified as a key enabler in personalising learning and providing non-traditional learners with access to education. One of the main technologies which is used to allow the bricks and mortar walls of educational institutes to extend to non-traditional learners is the Virtual Learning Environment (VLE). The VLE provides the opportunity for academic staff to provide educational resources, learning activities and spaces for students to reflect outside of class time. (Wilson et al, 2007) It can manage assessment provide opportunities for student engagement and interaction. However, it is largely driven by the educator. The educator decides what information the learner needs to engage with, how they are assessed, when they submit assessments and for the provision of learning activities (Atwell, 2007)

In recent times in an effort to ensure learning becomes learner focused and driven personalised learning environments (PLE) are being explored (Patterson, Stephens, Chiang, Price, Work, & Snelgrove-Clarke, 2017). PLEs offer students more ownership of their learning and are aligned to learner centred pedagogies such as constructivism, MI and UDL. They offer multimodal learning. (Wilson, Liber, Johnson, Beauvoir, Sharples, Milligan, 2007). However, in traditional learning environments educators make choices on behalf of the learners therefore the shift to a learning environment which is student driven can be difficult for some individuals (Dabbagh & Kitansas, 2012). Therefore guided choice becomes even more important to assist learners in the transition from teacher to learner driven educational environments.

To date PLEs have largely been commercially driven by Microsoft through solutions linked in learning and Microsoft educator community. These solutions provide video based learning material and learning activities for students to engage with and are largely concerned with the provision of high-quality learning content through video. To date, they do not integrate different modalities of learning or learning preferences.

Patterson et al. (2007) suggest adapting PLEs to form Personally Significant Learning Environments which focus on the interplay of modalities, interpersonal, intrapersonal, learning environment and learning styles. However, they argue that challenge is integrating the various technologies to do this. Kurilovas, Kurilova, and Andruskevic (2016) suggest developing personalised learning packages consisting of learning objects, learning activities and environments, such as the VLE. They examined the adoption of Fielder-Silverman's learning styles model to produce an algorithm which identifies the suitability index of a personalised learning package. They suggest such technologies should be thoughtfully integrated with standards such as IEEE LOM. However, they do not consider the limitations posed by learning styles, modalities of learning and how to determine suitable content for the given learner profile. By extending this concept learning objects can provide blocks to offer personalised informed choice for learners. The next section will examine learning objects in more detail.

Digital Learning Objects

The concept of Learning Objects was first introduced by Wayne Hodgins in 1994 when he considered breaking courses into pieces like Lego blocks allowing them to be reused to form other courses. Since then many definitions of learning objects have been stated, some of which are quiet broad, the most comprehensive however, is the definition adopted by Wiley:

"A Learning Object is any digital resource that can be reused to support learning" (Wiley, 2000)

As mentioned in section 2 creating learning resources that meet the needs of each learner modality, preference and style is a laborious task. Therefore, maximising the use of these resources is key. Learning objects are granular pieces of learning which can be easily be combined with other learning objects or activities to personalise learning. It provides opportunities for focused, timely, relevant learning and when combined with learning activities students can apply their learning to different contexts.

Ensuring the reusability and relevance of the learning object is key. Returning to the example of Lego, to be able to compose different pieces together it is necessary that all the blocks are of a certain width, otherwise they will not fit together. There are similar issues with learning objects, certain requirements that need to be considered to maximise reusability:

Granularity. It refers to the size of the learning object. This is an important consideration for reusability. Obviously the smaller the learning object the more reusable it is. For example a picture of a fire extinguisher could be used in many more contexts than a labelled diagram of a fire extinguisher. However, returning to Wiley's definition of a learning object it is important that a learning object can support learning. A picture does not contain any instructional design and has limited teaching capability. Therefore, a learning object must be larger than a single item such as a picture. Ideally a Learning Object should be standalone and should be capable of teaching a single learning objective (Longmire, 2000). These present guidelines for the granularity a learning object without specifying rigid, quantitative terms.

Accessibility. It refers to the availability of Learning Objects. For LOs to be reusable it is important that they can be easily searched for and found. To make learning objects accessible they must be placed in a repository where they can be searched, however as LO's are objects which may not always be text they may be difficult to search therefore they need information attached to them about their content. For example, if your LO teaches the components of a fire extinguisher, data needs to be attached to this Learning object that states, this learning object teaches the components of a fire extinguisher. When an individual goes to search for such a learning object it can be easily found based on this data.

Interoperability. This requires the Learning Object to be independent of the technical requirements of the system. As Learning Objects are digital, it is important that they can be used on any technical the IEEE defines interoperability as being *"the ability of two or more systems or components to exchange information and to use the information that has been exchanged"* (IEEE, 1990). If this is not the case, then learning objects are not truly reusable as they can only be reused in certain contexts.

To ensure complete accessibility and interoperability of learning objects and ensure all LOs are of the same granularity it is necessary to implement standards, so they can be searched for and operate together in a seamless manner. For example, in the electrical industry, there are three different plug standards to allow electrical goods to operate regardless of what supplier they are bought from. This eliminates the need for customers to have to purchase electrical goods off the same supplier or from having to install different plug types for different goods. Furthermore, there are adapters available that allow these three plug standards to interface with each other. In the e-learning industry standards are necessary for similar reasons, standards allow LOs to interoperate with other software easily. There are a number of standard bodies conducting research in the e-learning industry, however these do co-operate to some extent, so they are compatible. The standard bodies provide criteria on aggregation level, metadata and interoperability (Fallon and Brown, 2000).

Aggregation Level

As specified previously Wiley's definition of a learning object allows for different levels of granularity of a learning object. Learning Content Object Models address this problem by specifying different aggregation levels for Learning Objects (i.e. specifying what size learning objects can be). The two most well-known Learning Content Object Models are those developed by SCORM and CISCO standard bodies.

SCORM's content aggregation model defines the following types of learning content (SCORM, 2004)

- Assets – these are electronic representations of media for example a graphic, text, audio or other data that can be put on a web client. They are the most basic representation of a learning resource
- SCO – Shareable Content Object – this is a file with one or more assets combined
- Content Aggregations – this is a combination of SCOs and assets to produce a unit of education e.g. lesson, unit, topic etc (Verbert and Duval, 2004)

Metadata

Metadata is data about data. It provides information to describe the learning objects. To describe an LOs it is necessary to define a set of elements that can best outline its description, this is known as a metadata set. There are three main bodies that oversee and collate to create metadata sets.

Dublin Core Metadata Initiative (DCMI) is an organisation that is dedicated to promoting widespread adoption of interoperable metadata standards. Its metadata element set is a standard to describe any information. The standard includes two levels simple which consists of fifteen elements (sample of these in Table 1) and qualified which includes an additional element called Audience and also a group of elements refinements. Each element known as a term in Dublin Core has a set of attributes which helps to clarify its meaning. (DCMI, 2014)

Learning Object Metadata is a metadata set developed by the IEEE standards committee. For this standard "a metadata instance for a learning object describes relevant characteristics of the learning object

Table 1. Sample of Dublin core simple metadata elements and the definition attribute (sample from DCMI, 2005)

Term /Element	Definition Attribute
Creator	The person who created the content
Date	The Date the content was created/updated
Description	An account of the content of the resource
Format	The physical manifestation of the resource
Language	The language of intellectual content of the resource

to which it applies" (IEEE, 2002). The characteristics may be categorised into nine different categories. Each category then has a number of data elements associated with it that can be used to describe the learning object similar to the Dublin Core's terms. Each data element has a set schema used to define the data element similar to the Dublin Core's attributes (IEEE, 2002)

- **General:** This category outlines the general information that describes the learning object as a whole. Examples of data elements that it may contain would be title, language, description, and aggregation level.
- **Lifecycle:** This category outlines the history and current state of the LO. Examples of data elements would be version and status.
- **Meta-Metadata:** This category gives information about the metadata itself such as how it can be identified, who created the metadata, when it was created. Examples of data elements include identifier, date, and language.
- **Technical:** This category describes the technical requirements of the learning object. Examples of data elements are format, size, location, and requirements.
- **Educational:** This category describes the pedagogic characteristics of the learning object. Examples interactivity type, interactivity level, context, difficulty
- **Rights:** This category describes the intellectual property rights of the learning objects. Examples cost and copyright
- **Relation:** This category describes the relationship between the learning object and other learning objects. Examples kind, description.
- **Annotation:** This category comments on the educational use of the learning object
- **Classification:** This category describes where the learning object falls within a particular classification system

Some of the above data elements overlap with the Dublin Core metadata set. However, the LOM is more suitable for e-learning development as it is specifically tailored for this area whereas the Dublin Core model is more general for any online content regardless of its educational value.

Instructional Management Systems (IMS) was a project set up to eliminate obstacles that existed preventing a global education marketplace. As part of this a metadata set was created which built on the Dublin Core model adding on additional fields which learning content may require. The IMS have also collaborated with the IEEE LOM standard committee so the metadata sets are quite similar. Similar to LOM the IMS standard consists of nine classification types. Each classification has a set of data elements. Five attributes can be used to define each data element. The categories are (IMS, 2001):

- **Base Scheme:** Similar to the general category in LOM examples of data elements include title, description, language
- **Lifecycle**: Identical to the same category in LOM
- **Meta-Metadata:** Similar to LOM except one additional data element, catalogue entry
- **Technical:** Similar to LOM except IMS has removed the data element or Composite
- **Educational**: Identical to the same category in LOM
- **Rights:** Identical to the same category in LOM
- **Relation:** Similar to LOM except one additional data element, catalogue entry
- **Annotation:** Similar to LOM except entity is known as person in IMS

- **Classification:** Identical to the same category in LOM

The IMS metadata set is very similar to that of the IEEE LOM, illustrates that standard bodies are co-operating to ensure easy accessibility to repositories of digital learning objects. Moreover, other standard bodies are opting to use such metadata sets developed by SCORM, IMS and IEEE LOM, for example the SCORM standard body uses the IEEE LOM metadata sets to describe its learning objects

Interoperability

Further to the other standards outlined there are bodies which specify how LOs should be launched and how they should interface with each other and other systems. Two of the main standard bodies addressing the issue of interoperability are SCORM and IMS. SCORM has produced a run time environment model and the IMS a content packaging information model which addresses the above issues if interoperability.

Prior to introducing the SCORM runtime model it is first necessary to explain what a Learning Management System (LMS) is. An LMS is a piece of software that hosts learning material. Students can access the material by logging into the system and searching for it or by going to their individual profile and launching the course material from there.

It is important however that learning objects and activities ranked by adopting best practice in instructional design. The next section will explore instructional design models which can facilitate this.

INSTRUCTIONAL DESIGN MODELS

Learning Objectives identify the performance level you wish the learner to attain at a specific task and are used as an indication that learning has been accomplished (Gagne, Briggs, & Wager, 1992). For example, if an employee requires training in market research techniques at the end of taking a course you may wish them to list the types of market research, identify the steps involved in conducting a market research and demonstrate how to conduct a market research. They form a key part of both traditional and competence-based education.

Once high-level competences are identified, these must be translated into learning objectives i.e. desired learning outcomes. Instructional Design theories can assist this by specifying ideal outcomes depending on the content type of the competence.

An Instructional Design theory can be defined as "A theory that offers guidance on how to better help people learn and develop" (Reigeluth, 1999). Furthermore, Reigeluth gives an example of what an instructional theory is like using Perkins "Theory One". Perkins stated that any instruction should have the following components:

1. **Clear Information:** Identify the knowledge and performances you expect your learners to acquire and give examples and descriptions of these goals (learning objectives)
2. **Thoughtful Practice:** An opportunity to engage the learner in activities relevant to the learning objectives
3. **Informative Feedback:** Inform learners of their performance in achieving the learning objectives
4. **Strong Intrinsic or Extrinsic Motivation:** A method of rewarding learners if they achieve their learning goals.

Most Instructional Design theories identify methods of how best to help people to learn however they do not specify how to determine learner's performance. Two Instructional design theories that do assist the construction of learning objectives are blooms taxonomy and Merrill's component display theory (CDT)

Blooms Taxonomy of Educational Objectives

Bloom created a taxonomy of that allowed the classification of different educational outcomes. There are six major classes in the taxonomy, these can represent six levels of learning ranging from least to most complex (Bloom, 1956)

1. **Knowledge:** The learner is required to recall what they have learned. For example: The learner will be able to define market research
2. **Comprehension:** The learner is required to explain what they have learned. For example: The learner will be able to explain the two types of market research
3. **Application**: The learner is required to apply what they have learned to a situation. For example, the learner will be able to conduct a market research
4. **Analysis:** The learner is required to breakdown material and detect the relationships between the material. For example, the learner will be able to choose the appropriate type of market research depending on the situation
5. **Synthesis**: The learner is required to piece together elements and parts to form a whole. For example, the learner will be able to conduct the appropriate market research depending on the situation
6. **Evaluation:** The learner is required to make judgements about the value, for some purpose of ideas, works, solutions, methods or material. For example, the learner will be able to develop a market strategy based on the market research

Bloom provides an ideal generic framework to assist trainers to identify educational objectives. However, he does not prescribe situations in which to use each level of the taxonomy. A theory is required that will allow the selection of the most appropriate educational objectives associated with the learner's requirements.

Merrill's Component Display theory

Merrill's Component Display Theory (CDT) is an instructional design theory that indicates what set of components are most likely to achieve the desired learning outcomes under certain conditions (Reigheluth, 1983). The CDT classifies learning objectives on two dimensions:

1. The type of content
2. Performance level

Therefore, a learning object may require the learner to remember the steps in the procedure, conduct the procedure or find a new way of using the procedure (Reigheluth, 1983)

Merrill outlined a performance-content matrix based on content and performance level based on the type of content different levels of performances are expected from the learner:

Firstly, a piece of content is defined as:

- **Fact:** "Facts are arbitrarily associated pieces of information" (Merrill, 1983). Examples may be Dublin is the capital of Ireland, George Bush is the president of the US
- **Concepts:** "Concepts are groups of objects, events or symbols that all share common characteristics and are identified by the same name" (Merrill, 1983) Examples include a mammal is an animal who gives birth to live young, is warm blooded and has body hair, a reptile is an animal which is cold blooded, has scaled flesh and lays eggs rather than giving birth to young.
- **Procedure**: "Procedures are an ordered sequence of steps necessary to accomplish some goal, solve a particular class of problem or produce some product" (Merrill, 1983) Examples of procedures would be the steps to write an if statement, a recipe, or a production process
- **Principle:** "Principles are explanations or predictions of why things happen in the world" (Merrill, 1983) Example if you increase the temperature the ice will melt and if you decrease the temperature the ice will harden. If you have more than one line in an if statement in Java programming, you need to use curly brackets if you only have one line you do not need these.

Then the performance level is identified:

- **Remember:** Simply asks the user to remember a fact, concept, procedure or principle
  - **Remember Fact – Example:** Define the capital of Ireland
  - **Remember Concept – Example:** Outline the characteristics of a mammal
  - **Remember Procedure – Example:** List the steps to write an if statement
  - **Remember Principle – Example:** What factor affects the composition of ice
- **Use** – Requires the learner to use the piece of information learned. A piece of content that is classified as a fact does not require the learner to perform at the use level:
  - **Use Concept – Example:** From the above description is this animal a mammal
  - **Use Procedure – Example:** Write an if statement for the above problem
  - **Use Principle – Example:** If you increase the temperature what happens to the ice
- **Find**: Requires the learner to use the information in a different scenario A piece of content that is classified as a fact does not require the learner to perform at the find level
  - **Find Concept – Example:** Identify the characteristics common to the below set of animals
  - **Find Procedure – Example:** Write a program that checks if a temperature is in Celsius and if not changes it to this format
  - **Find Principle – Example:** What would happen to the ice if you increased the temperature to 100c

Once the content type is specified learning objectives can be generated by attaching a desired performance outcome to the content. The content then can be developed to teach this learning objective. For example, if a training need is market research techniques this could be classified as a concept as there are different types of market research and it could also be classified as a procedure as market research is carried out in steps. Therefore, the learning objectives for this may be:

- Identify the types of market research
- List the characteristics of these types of market research
- List the steps involved in market research
- Demonstrate how a market research is conducted

Once these are created the CDT identifies a presentation form for presenting the content to teach the learning objective to the student. Merrill states that all subject matter can be represented on two dimensions (Merrill, 1983):

1. Generalities - These are general statements of definition. For example, a generality for a fact may be define, a generality for a procedure may be list the steps, a generality for a concept may be outline the characteristics
2. Instances – These are specific cases of concepts, procedures and principles. This is usually an example. E.g. Give an example of a mammal, demonstrate/give an example of how to write an if statement, demonstrate to the student how temperature affects ice

Moreover, material is presented in an expository and inquisitory manner. A generality can be presented to the learner in an expository way which means that it will be explained to the student. Or it can be presented in an Inquisitory manner by questioning the student. A combination of these presentation types ensures optimum learning for the student.

The above consists of primary presentation forms, there are also secondary presentation forms which are not core for optimum learning but may be of interest to the student. These are:

- **Context:** Information regarding the context or historical background of the lesson
- **Pre-Requisite:** Prior knowledge the student may be required to know
- **Mnemonics:** These are attention focus devices such as arrows, colours etc
- **Help:** Provides additional assistance for the students
- **Feedback:** When a student is asked a question, provide a response to the answer it terms of whether it was right or wrong and why.

The Component Display Theory provides an ideal instructional design theory for creating learning objectives from the content to be taught and an optimum presentation format for these objectives. Furthermore, to this it describes an instructional design method to teach these objectives in an optimum format.

Moreover, this theory classifies content according to Squires theory. Squire, a neuroscientist stated that there are two basic memory processes (Squire, 1997):

1. **Declarative Memory**: Which is memory for the processing of facts and concepts
2. **Procedural or non-Declarative Memory**: Which are for other more complex cognitive operations such as procedural or action of techniques and skills (which could correspond to procedures and principles in the CDT)

Based on these arguments it can be concluded that the CDT provides an ideal method to construct learning objectives to assess the performance of learners within the proposed Competence based framework. It conextualises learning outcomes based on performance and content, competences can be categorised by defining the content type and the performance you wish to achieve and is based on the application of context. Furthermore, the presentation formats consider the modality of the learning object. This can allow the learning object to be sequenced according to the competence being taught and the preferred modality identified in the learner profile.

Enhancing 21st Century Learning Using Digital Learning Objects

The following section will explore how to integrate all of these elements to a personalised framework for 21st Century learning.

THE STUDY: A CONCEPTUAL MODEL FOR INTEGRATING DIGITAL LEARNING OBJECTS WITH MI THEORY TO PERSONALISE LEARNING

This chapter will provide a case study of how digital learning objects (Los) can be exploited to provide personalised informed learner choice based on instructional design principles and an individual's learning preferences profile. The model in Figure 1 considers the role of three agents in using MI theory and digital learning objects to enhance 21st century learning. The learner, the educator and the technology (VLE/PLE).

The learner is responsible for completing an assessment of their modalities of learning, learner preferences and competence level, they undertake the relevant learning objects and activities relevant to their desired competence, learning preference and motility from a recommended choice list. They monitor their progression to 'expert learner' by self-assessing their competence level.

Figure 1. Agent roles in a personalised learning environment.

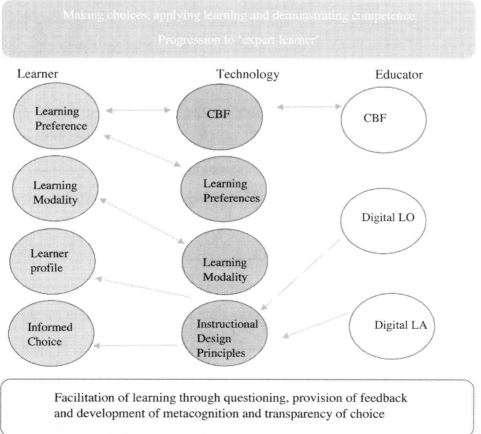

The educator is responsible for providing the competency-based framework (CBF), high quality digital learning objects and activities. They categorise the Los according to their modality of learning, preference of learning and the competency the teach as well as the type of activity they focused on. This will be done by extending the IEE meta data schema. They act as a faciliatory of learning providing questioning, feedback and encouraging metacognition in learning and informed choice

Technology through the VLE or PLE is responsible for hosting the digital learning objects and sequencing them in a manner that complies with the CBF, modality, learning preferences and instructional design principles.

To implement this model, five steps are proposed:

Step 1: Identifying the content needs
Step 2: Packaging the digital learning objects
Step 3: Identifying the learner profile
Step 4: Ranked learner choice

Step 1: Identifying the Content Needs

The educator needs first to identify the competency framework (CBF) for the material they are teaching and the contexts and disciplines in which they can be applied. There are many international and national examples of competency frameworks which can be considered. For examine competency frameworks are widely used in the medical domain for doctors and psychologists. However, they need to be explored for other domains to ensure a flexible learner driven model to 21st century learning. Educators play a key role in considering the application of what they teach. To do this it is necessary that CBF are informed by evidence-based practice. Once a CPF is in place this can be modelled on the VLE/PLE. The learner then completes a self assessment rating their competency level for each component in the CBF. An which the algorithm outlines learning outcomes for each competency using a Merrill's CDT.

Step 2: Packaging the Digital Learning Object

The educator designs and packages various the digital learning objects for each component of the competency mode. Correct packaging is required so they can be easily identified to meet the learner needs. The conceptual model suggests updating the current IMS content packaging metadata schema needs to be extended to add three elements:

1. Competency this element details be the skill(s) or knowledge in the competency framework the LO is focused on developing, it can address more than one.
2. Learning modality: this element details what mode of learning the object is focused aligning to the multiple intelligences identified by Gardner on e.g. verbal, kinaesthetic, interpersonal et
3. Learning activity: this element details what activities the learner is focused on. The learning activities are classified according to Laurillard's (2002) learning activities developed in her conversational framework and can be easily aligned to the multiple modes of representation, engagement and action in UDL as well as the modalities of learning aligned to MI theory. These are:
   a. Acquisition activities are those which are passive, the learner is reading, listening, watching, observing.

      b. Investigation activities are those which are active, the learner explores and reflects on what is being taught. The learner can do this through kinaesthetic methods by physically considering concrete objects and reflecting on these or through verbal or written means by reading and exploring texts.
      c. Collaboration activities are those which require the learner to interact with peers or their tutor. Again, the learner can do this through kinaesthetic methods by meeting with their peers or written means
      d. Discussion activities are those which require the learner to articulate their ideas. This can be done through physical expression by role play or simulating or by verbal means through written discussion posts.
      e. Practice activities require the learner to apply their learning and reflect on the implications or impact through reflection. This can be done through the physical application of skills through action or through written practice and prose.
      f. Production activities require the learner to apply the content and generate new understanding
4. Classification: The LO must be classified according to Merrill's CDT as a fact, concept, procedure or principle to allow Instructional design principles to inform the recommended sequence of learning activities.

Step 3: Identifying the Learner Profile

The third step is concerned with identifying the profile of the learner. This involves the learner completing a self-assessment questionnaire consisting of three elements

1. The preference for modality of learning is identified using Armstrong's inventory checklist.
2. The preferred learning approach of the individual adopting Vermunt's Inventory of Learning Styles which has been identified as one of the more reliable learning styles theories (Coffield et al., 2004)
3. The competency level of the learner in which the learner self-assesses their level of skill for each competence component. Where a competence is in deficit a learner content need is identified.

    The PLE/VLE hosts both questionnaires and the learner completes these electronically. From the learner reponses an algorithm generates a learner profile is developed which informs the learner of their preferred modality, approach and competency requirements.

Step 4: Ranked Learner Choice

Once the learner profile has been generated the VLE/PLE provides a ranked learner choice of Los and LAs that meet their preferred learning approach, modality and competency needs. This is informed by instructional design principles. This provides the learner with an informed choice that they can choose to navigate or adapt.
    In this case study the IMS metadata was extended classify the learning outcome of a learning object using Merrill's CDT and allow the learning objects to be tagged or defined by learning modality and preferred approach. The Los were packaged using the IMS content packaging and stored in a learning management system The Vermnut learning styles inventory was disseminated to learners via an online

form which also asked the learner to identify their skills needs. This was used to automatically tailor a course that related both to the learning style of the individual and their individual skills needs

This chapter discusses this concept in the context of 21st century skills and how it may be extended to take account of Multiple intelligence inventory personalised learning systems. However, there are a number of limitations with the model which will be explored in the next section.

FUTURE RESEARCH AND CONCLUSION

This model has been successfully applied in commercial contexts where there is predefined roles and contexts for learning. However, the extension of this model into mainstream education and training provides some constraints

Firstly, competency-based education is not widely used and adopted in higher education, with the exception of traditional professions such as medicine, psychology, accounting and engineering CBE is not common place. Furthermore, in these contexts CBE is adopted more as a model of continuous professional development rather than being applied in formal third level programmes.

Secondly is the creation of high-quality learning resources. Although digital education is widespread, the availability of high-quality learning resources is relatively scarce. Commercial organisations such as Microsoft are making efforts to produce such however as mentioned these are limited to video and also are not underpinned by academic credit systems. A number of initiatives to encourage academic staff to share learning resources have been unsuccessful e.g. NDLR in Ireland. Significant amounts of research is being conducted into open educational resources and motivating academic staff to share and engage.

The proposed model is based on static models which require the learner to complete questionnaires to self-assess their competency level, modality and learning approaches. Algorithms which facilitate adaptive learning allowing the ranked choice to changed based on the student's integration with Los and progression through LAs would enhance personalisation and provide a more dynamic approach.

REFERENCES

Armstrong, T. (2009). *Multiple intelligences in the classroom*. Alexander, VA: ASCD.

Attwell, G. (2007). The personal learning environments - the future of eLearning? *eLearn. Pap., 2*(1).

Bas, G. (2016). The Effect of Multiple Intelligences Theory-Based Education on Academic Achievement: A Meta-Analytic Review. *Educational Sciences: Theory and Practice, 16*(6), 1833–1864. doi:10.12738/estp.2016.6.0015

Baş, G., & Beyhab, Ö. (2017). Effects of multiple intelligences supported project-based learning on students' achievement levels and attitudes towards English lesson. *International Electronic Journal of Elementary Education, 2*(3), 365–386.

Beetham, H., & Sharpe, R. (Eds.). (2013). *Rethinking pedagogy for a digital age: Designing for 21st century learning*. Routledge.

Bloom, B. S. (1956). Taxonomy of Educational Objectives. New York: Academic Press.

Chai, C. S., & Kong, S. C. (2017). Professional learning for 21st century education. *Journal of Computers in Education*, *4*(1), 1–4. doi:10.100740692-016-0069-y

Coffield, F., Moseley, D., Hall, E., & Ecclestone, K. (2004). *Learning styles and pedagogy in post-16 learning: A systematic and critical review*. Academic Press.

Dabbagh, N., & Kitsantas, A. (2012). Personal Learning Environments, social media, and self regulated learning: A natural formula for connecting formal and informal learning. *Internet High. Educ.*, *15*(1), 3–8. doi:10.1016/j.iheduc.2011.06.002

DCMI. (2014). *Dublin Core Metadata Initiative*. Retrieved from http://www.dublincore.org/documents/dcmi-terms/

DeLorenzo, R. A., Battino, W., Schreiber, R., & Carrio, B. (2009). *Delivering on the promise*. Solution Tree Press.

Denig, S. J. (2004). Multiple intelligences and learning styles: Two complementary dimensions. *Teachers College Record*, *106*(1), 96–111. doi:10.1111/j.1467-9620.2004.00322.x

Digitalisierung, H. (2017). *The digital turn À pathways for higher education in the digital age*. Hochschulforum Digitalisierung, Arbeitspap.

Dishon, G. (2017). New data, old tensions: Big data, personalized learning, and the challenges of progressive education. *Theory and Research in Education*, *15*(3), 272–289. doi:10.1177/1477878517735233

Erfanian Mohammadi, J., Elahi Shirvan, M., & Akbari, O. (2018). Systemic functional multimodal discourse analysis of teaching students developing classroom materials. *Teaching in Higher Education*, 1–23. doi:10.1080/13562517.2018.1527763

Fallon, C., & Brown, S. (2000). e-Learning Standards: A Guide to Purchasing, Developing and Deploying Standards-Conformant E-Learning. St Lucie Press.

Gagne, R., Briggs, L., & Wager, W. (1992). *Principles of instructional design*. Fort Worth, TX: Harcourt Brace Jovanovich College Publishers.

Gardner, H. (1993). *Frames of mind: The theory of multiple intelligences* (2nd ed.). London: Fontana Press.

Gardner, H. (1999). Are there additional intelligences? The case for naturalist, spiritual, and existential intelligences. In Education, information and transformation. Englewood Cliffs, NJ: Prentice Hall.

Hayden, S. (2011). *Enabling Curricula: The Development of a Teaching Observation Protocol to Address Students' Diverse Learning Needs*. ProQuest LLC.

Husmann, P. R., & O'loughlin, V. D. (2019). Another nail in the coffin for learning styles? disparities among undergraduate anatomy students' study strategies, class performance, and reported vark learning styles. *Anatomical Sciences Education*, *12*(1), 6–19. doi:10.1002/ase.1777 PMID:29533532

IEEE. (1990). *IEEE Standard computer dictionary: A compilation of IEEE standard computer glossaries*. New York: IEEE.

IEEE. (2002). *Learning Object Metadata*. Retrieved from https://standards.ieee.org/standard/1484_12_1-2002.html

IMS. (2001). *IMS Learning Resource Meta-Data Information Model*. Retrieved from https://www.imsglobal.org/metadata/imsmdv1p2p1/imsmd_infov1p2p1.html

Jewitt, C. (2006). *Technology, literacy and learning: A multimodal approach*. London: Routledge.

Kelchen, R. (2015). *The landscape of competency-based education*. Washington, DC: American Enterprise Institute.

Kirschner, P. A., & Stoyanov, S. (2018). Educating Youth for Nonexistent/Not Yet Existing Professions. *Educational Policy*.

Kurilovas, E., Kurilova, J., & Andruskevic, T. (2016). On suitability index to create optimal personalised learning packages. In *International Conference on Information and Software Technologies* (pp. 479-490). Springer. 10.1007/978-3-319-46254-7_38

Laurillard, D. (2002). *Rethinking university teaching: A conversational framework for the effective use of learning technologies*. New York: Routledge. doi:10.4324/9780203160329

Lawrence, E. (1970). *The Origins and Growth of Modern Education*. London: Penguin Books.

Le, C., Wolfe, R., & Steinberg, A. (2014). *The past and the promise: Today's competency education movement. Students at the Center: Competency Education Research Series*. Boston, MA: Jobs for the Future.

Longmire, W. (2000, March). A Primer on Learning Objects. *Learning Circuits*, 6.

Manwaring, K. C., Larsen, R., Graham, C. R., Henrie, C. R., & Halverson, L. R. (2017). Investigating student engagement in blended learning settings using experience sampling and structural equation modeling. *The Internet and Higher Education*, *35*, 21–33. doi:10.1016/j.iheduc.2017.06.002

McCarthy, M., & Butler, B. (2013). *Universal Design for Learning and Multiple Intelligences Theory and Practice as SoTL Levers*. Academic Press.

Merrill, D. (1983). Component Display Theory. In C. Reigeluth (Ed.), *Instructional-design theories and models: an overview of their current status*. Hillsdale, NJ: Lawrence Erlbaum Associates.

Meyer, A., & Rose, D. H. (2000). Universal Design for Individual Differences. *Educational Leadership*, *58*(3), 39–43.

Nodine, T. R. (2016). How did we get here? A brief history of competency-based higher education in the United States. *The Journal of Competency-Based Education*, *1*(1), 5–11. doi:10.1002/cbe2.1004

Papageorgiou, V., & Lameras, P. (2017). *Multimodal Teaching and Learning with the Use of Technology: Meanings, Practices and Discourses*. International Association for Development of the Information Society.

Patterson, C., Stephens, M., Chiang, V., Price, A. M., Work, F., & Snelgrove-Clarke, E. (2017). The significance of personal learning environments (PLEs) in nursing education: Extending current conceptualizations. *Nurse Education Today*, *48*, 99–105. doi:10.1016/j.nedt.2016.09.010 PMID:27744138

Redding, S. (2016). Competencies and personalized learning. In M. Murphy, S. Redding, & J. Twyman (Eds.), *Handbook on personalized learning for states, districts, and schools* (pp. 3–18). Philadelphia, PA: Temple University, Center on Innovations in Learning.

Reigeluth, C. (1999). The Elaboration Theory: Guidence for Scope and Sequence Decisions. In C. Reigeluth (Ed.), Instructional Design Theories and Models Volume 2: A new paradigm of Instructional Theory (pp. 428 – 453). Mahwah, NJ: Lawrence Erlbaum.

Rose, D. H., Harbour, W. S., Johnston, C. S., Daley, S. G., & Abarbanell, L. (2006). Universal design for learning in postsecondary education: Reflections on principles and their application. *Journal of postsecondary education and disability*, *19*(2), 135–151.

Saban, A. (2009). Content analysis of Turkish studies about the multiple intelligences theory. *Educational Sciences: Theory and Practice*, *9*, 859–876.

SCORM. (2004). *SCORM 1.2*. Retrieved on 13th May 2019 from https://scorm.com/scorm-explained/technical-scorm/scorm-12-overview-for-developers/

Shearer, C. B. (2004). Using a multiple intelligences assessment to promote teacher development and student achievement. *Teachers College Record*, *106*(1), 147–162. doi:10.1111/j.1467-9620.2004.00325.x

Sinclair, G. (2010). *Exploring Canada's digital future*. Paper presented at the Congress of the Humanities and Social Science, Concordia University, Montreal, Canada.

Surr, W., & Rasmussen, J. (2015). *Partners in crafting competency-based pathways to college and career readiness*. Washington, DC: Great Lakes and Midwest Regional Deeper Learning Initiative, American Institutes for Research. Retrieved from http://www.deeperlearning-cc.org/

Surr, W., & Redding, S. (2017). *Competency-based education: staying shallow or going deep?* Retrieved on June 17, 2019 from https://ccrscenter.org/sites/default/files/CBE_GoingDeep.pdf

Ucak, E., Bag, H., Usak, M., & Esra Ucak, H. B. (2006). Enhancing Learning through Multiple Intelligences in Elementary Education. *Journal of Baltic Science Education*, *2*(10), 61–69.

Union, I. (2014). *Communication from the Commission to the European Parliament, the Council, the European Economic and Social Committee and the Committee of the Regions*. Retrieved from http://www.xploit-eu.com/pdfs/Europe,202020,20

Verbert, K., & Duval, E. (2004). Towards a Global Component Architecture for Learning Objects: A Comparative Analysis of Learning Object Content Models. Edmedia 2004, Lugano, Switzerland.

Vermunt, J. D. (1998). The regulation of constructive learning processes. *The British Journal of Educational Psychology*, *68*(2), 149–171. doi:10.1111/j.2044-8279.1998.tb01281.x

Wiley, D. A. (2000). *Learning Object Design and Sequencing Theory*. Department of Instructional Psychology and Technology, Brigham Young University.

Wilson, S., Liber, O., Johnson, M., Beauvoir, P., Sharples, P., & Milligan, C. (2007). Personal learning environments: challenging the dominant design of educational systems. *Journal of e-Learn*, *3*, 27–38.

ADDITIONAL READING

Boyle, T., & Duval, E. (2017). Learning Objects. In *Technology Enhanced Learning* (pp. 137–144). Cham: Springer. doi:10.1007/978-3-319-02600-8_13

Imran, H., Belghis-Zadeh, M., Chang, T. W., & Graf, S. (2016). PLORS: A personalized learning object recommender system. *Vietnam Journal of Computer Science*, *3*(1), 3–13. doi:10.100740595-015-0049-6

Lane, I. F. (2010). Professional competencies in health sciences education: From multiple intelligences to the clinic floor. *Advances in Health Sciences Education: Theory and Practice*, *15*(1), 129–146. doi:10.100710459-009-9172-4 PMID:19585247

Şener, S., & Çokçalışkan, A. (2018). An Investigation between Multiple Intelligences and Learning Styles. *Journal of Education and Training Studies*, *6*(2), 125–132. doi:10.11114/jets.v6i2.2643

Truong, H. M. (2016). Integrating learning styles and adaptive e-learning system: Current developments, problems and opportunities. *Computers in Human Behavior*, *55*, 1185–1193. doi:10.1016/j.chb.2015.02.014

Worsley, M., & Blikstein, P. (2015, March). Leveraging multimodal learning analytics to differentiate student learning strategies. In *Proceedings of the Fifth International Conference on Learning Analytics And Knowledge* (pp. 360-367). ACM. 10.1145/2723576.2723624

KEY TERMS AND DEFINITIONS

21st Century Learning: Skills or attributes required to actively participate and add value in a changing society.

Competency: Attributes, skills, or behaviors of a person required to perform a specific role or task.

Digital Learning Object: A standalone piece of digital content that can be used and reused for learning purposes.

Multimodal Learning: Learning that offers multiple forms of engagement.

Multiple Intelligences: A theory that illustrates the capacity of individuals to develop and apply skills can occur in different ways and are represented differently in each individual. It acknowledges that all forms of intelligence given equal recognition to allow an individual to fully contribute and participate in meaningful learning.

Personalized: Tailored to an individual's needs.

Personalized Learning Environment: A digital space that is tailored to an individual's learning preferences and mode of learning to present the relevant learning content and learning activities in a sequence, format and engagement mode that meets their personal learning needs.

Chapter 3
Multiple Intelligences and Digital Learning Game Design:
How to Consider the Intelligences of Players?

Pejman Sajjadi
Pennsylvania State University, USA

Olga De Troyer
Vrije Universiteit, Brussels, Belgium

ABSTRACT

Empirical research that draws a framework on how the theory of MI could be incorporated in (learning) games is non-existent. Furthermore, the theory of MI fits well into the concept of individualization, as it distinguishes between individuals in terms of their abilities. In light of this, the chapter reports on the first evidence-based set of mappings between this theory and fundamental constructs of games known as mechanics. These mappings can be utilized by designers in the individualization paradigm of player-centered game design as guidelines on what mechanics to include in their design when targeting an audience with specific MI profiles. Such individualization can potentially positively affect the game experience of players while establishing the proper frame for affecting learning. As such, these mappings, available in form of a recommendation tool, act as guidelines on how to design (learning) games while considering the intelligences of the target audience.

INTRODUCTION

Since the advent of modern computers, technology has increasingly become an important part of learning environments (Garrison, 2011; Koehler & Mishra, 2009; Rosenberg, 2001). Over the past decades, prevalent computer-supported learning systems have emerged. These systems appeal to educators as they support rich content and have the potential to reach large populations while maintaining an individualized experience. In education, individualization is argued to be an effective way to positively affect the

DOI: 10.4018/978-1-7998-0249-5.ch003

learning outcomes of people (see e.g. (Tseng, Chu, Hwang, & Tsai, 2008; Yasir & Sharif, 2011)). Individualization is the opposite of the "one-size-fits-all" approach often used in classical learning environments. A variety of terms are used to refer to this principle: e.g. learner-centered design, personalization, adaptivity, and adaptation. In this chapter, the term individualization is used to refer to this principle.

In recent years, interest in the use of rich and sophisticated media forms, such as games for educational purposes has increased. Games have the potential to provide fun, engaging, and motivating learning environments to support players in learning new concepts or acquiring new skills and/or behaviors (Dondlinger, 2007; Gee, 2004; Paras & Bizzocchi, 2005; Wouters, van der Spek, & van Oostendorp, 2009). In the literature, a variety of terms are used to refer to games for learning. This includes terms like educational games, edutainment games, serious games, and learning games. The term learning games will be used throughout this chapter to refer to this concept.

Strategies such as learner-centered design (called player-centered design in the context of games), and individualization are already given due attention in the domain of learning games (e.g. (Chanel, Rebetez, Bétrancourt, & Pun, 2008; Lopes & Bidarra, 2011; Magerko, 2009; Muir & Conati, 2012; Yannakakis et al., 2010)). It is often argued that by considering the needs, abilities and preferences of players, one could create games that can positively influence both the gaming experience and learning outcomes (discussed further in section 2). Various conceptual frameworks on individualized learning through games have proposed different factors that could contribute to the process of individualization (see e.g. (Charles, Kerr, & McNeill, 2005; Kickmeier-Rust, Mattheiss, Steiner, & Albert, 2012; Lopes & Bidarra, 2011; Sajjadi, Broeckhoven, & Troyer, 2014)). These range from factors used to drive the individualization, such as different aspects of the player and how they can be measured, to aspects of the game that can be subject to individualization, over strategies for when and how to apply individualization. The research presented in this chapter and its contributions to the state of the art in the domain of learning games are directly related to one of the least explored aspects of the players to drive individualization, more precisely, the intelligences of players with respect to the "Theory of Multiple Intelligences" (MI) (Gardner, 2011). Furthermore, game mechanics are considered as the aspect of the game subject to the individualization based on players' intelligences (section 3). As such, this chapter presents the first evidence-based set of mappings between the different MI dimensions and fundamental constructs of games, i.e. game mechanics, which can be used to tailor the design of games based on the MI profile of the target audience. Moreover, this chapter takes a first step in demonstrating that such individualization could result in better game experiences as well as higher learning outcomes (section 4).

INDIVIDUALIZATION

Individualization in contemporary settings is defined as tailoring the digital learning environment to the individuals' needs, abilities and preferences (Beldagli & Adiguzel, 2010; Brusilovsky, 2001; Kickmeier-Rust & Albert, 2010). In the context of game-based learning, tailoring the learning environment to the individuals can be achieved in different ways and at different stages. Tailoring can be done in advance (during design, i.e. player-centered game design), at the start of playing the game/level (often called static adaptation or personalization), or completely dynamically while playing (often called dynamic adaptation or adaptivity). Numerous researchers have defined the terminology associated with individualization (e.g. (Beldagli & Adiguzel, 2010; Göbel, Hardy, & Wendel, 2010; Linssen, 2011; Lopes & Bidarra, 2011)). In the case of adaptation and personalization, a rather generic version of the game (learning system) is

Multiple Intelligences and Digital Learning Game Design

available, which will be either tailored based on static information about the player (stable information that is not prone to immediate change, e.g. playing style), or will dynamically change during the gameplay based on the player's performance or other dynamic factors (e.g. stress level, attention level, etc.). In player-centered game design however, the game is specially designed for a specific group of people (called the target audience). Note that the term player-centered game design has also been used in the literature with a different meaning. In (Charles & Black, 2004) for instance, player-centered game design is about catering adaptation for individual players. This may be a source of confusion. Therefore, it was decided to define the term as follows:

Player-Centered Game Design: A game design paradigm by which different aspects of the game (e.g. game mechanics, game narrative, interaction modality) are tailored to suit one or more groups of players that can be clustered based on certain characteristics (e.g. playing style, personality, intelligences).

As a consequence, individualization in light of player-centered game design is completely static because it focuses on designing a game for a specific group of players that have common characteristics (such as common playing style, learning style, personality, or intelligences). Furthermore, the customization choices based on these characteristics are made during the design of the game. Evidently, it is possible to augment a player-centered game design with more dynamic forms of individualization such as adaptation. For example, one could design a game targeting people who exhibit strength for the visual-spatial MI dimension, and on top provide dynamic difficulty adjustment based on their competency levels.

Individualization is a complex task and if studied systematically, composed of different facets. For instance, based on the work of (Karagiannidis & Sampson, 2004) and (Brusilovsky, 1996) the different involved facets can be defined as *motivations for using individualization*, the *aspects of the user that can be used for individualization* (e.g. playing style, gamer type), *the aspects of the system that can be individualized* (e.g. game objects and game world, narrative, music, game mechanics), and *how individualization can be realized*. Evidently, discussing each of these facets in relation to learning games demands their own chapters. Notwithstanding, the *motivation* facet will be briefly discussed, as it will help us understand why this is an important topic of study. Furthermore, the rest of this chapter will focus on a concrete case of individualization in light of player-centered game design, focusing on the intelligences of players with respect to the theory of MI as the *aspect of the users* to drive the individualization, mechanics of the learning game as the *aspects of the* system to adapt, and relationship between MI dimensions and game mechanics as *how* individualization can be realized.

Different scholars have argued that considering individual differences among players is an important factor for the success of learning games, e.g. as mentioned by Van Eck:

If we continue to preach only that games can be effective, we run the risk of creating the impression that all games are good for all learners and for all learning outcomes, which is categorically not the case (Van Eck, 2006) (Page 2).

In light of this, one of the most engaging question in the domain of learning games can be simply put as: beyond the obvious benefits of individualization in games (i.e. boosting game experience as done in entertainment games), what other benefits individualization can bring to learning games? It has been argued by many that taking individual differences into account can contribute to the improvement of the learning outcome as much as it can to game experience. Moreno and Mayer (2007) for instance, argue that a massive amount of information imposed by a game may overload the working memory capacity of players leading to weak or incorrect learning. Therefore, some players may benefit from a slower pace in the presentation of the information and instructions inside the game. On the other hand, if the pace is too slow, it may lead to cognitive underload, which can lead to boredom and disengagement and consequently detrition of performance (Paas, Renkl, & Sweller, 2004; Saxby, Matthews, Hitchcock, & Warm, 2007). This notion basically points to the "Flow state", introduced in the "Flow theory" (Csikszentmihalyi & Csikszentmihalyi, 1992). This state is defined as a state of absolute absorption to a task to a point of losing self-consciousness where the activity itself becomes rewarding in its own, and this enables an individual to function at his/her fullest capacity (Shernoff, Csikszentmihalyi, Shneider, & Shernoff, 2003). According to several researchers, this means that a game must provide a balance between challenges imposed by the game and the competence of the players (Cowley, Charles, Black, & Hickey, 2008; Sweetser & Wyeth, 2005). Furthermore, it has been argued that when experiencing the flow state, individuals work at their fullest capacity, including the capacity to learn (Kiili, 2005; Webster, Trevino, & Ryan, 1993). Therefore, flow is an important factor for effective learning in games. The state of flow is often used as a metric when describing the game experience of individuals and can be looked at as an argument in favor of incorporating individualization in learning games, as it addresses individual differences in terms of competence in relation to challenge.

Good game experience also often involves a high level of immersion. While having a strong entertainment value, immersion has also been claimed to positively affect learning. Witmer & Singer (1998) defined immersion as:

A psychological state characterized by perceiving oneself to be enveloped by, included in, and interacting with an environment that provides a continuous stream of stimuli and experiences (Page 3).

Dede (2009) has argued that there are three ways in which immersion can enhance learning. Firstly, immersive experiences give people:

The ability to change one's perspective or frame of reference [which] is a powerful means of understanding complex phenomenon (ibid, Page 2).

Secondly, immersion into authentic contexts and activities can foster forms of situated learning as the learner can gain and apply knowledge in an environment that closely resembles a real-world situation. This goes hand in hand with the third way mentioned by Dede, namely improving the transfer of the knowledge to a real-world situation based on accurate simulations of those situations. As such, these arguments appear to provide further support for the claim that good game experiences can positively influence learning outcomes and thus be a motivation for individualization.

On similar grounds, the necessity for incorporating individualization in learning games is motivated in (Charles et al., 2005) based on the fact that people learn in different ways, at different paces, and based on different learning styles. Additionally, people have different playing strategies and styles. Moreover, the range of gaming skills and capabilities among the players may vary. This justifies the need for principles that can individualize different aspects of the game based on the profile and preferences of the players. Furthermore, Lopes and Bidarra (Lopes & Bidarra, 2011) argue that the content of the game, the rules, the narrative, the environment, etc. are mostly static, while the player that interacts with them is dynamic. Constantly having static content throughout the game could lead to problems such as losing the motivation to continue playing, predictability, non-replayability, and repeatedly using a previously successful strategy. As Lopes and Bidarra point out, this problem is more severe in the case of learning games, due to the fact that not everyone learns in the same way.

RELATIONSHIP BETWEEN MI AND GAME MECHANICS

Despite its potential, one of the least explored opportunities for individualization is the "Theory of Multiple Intelligences" (MI), developed by Howard Gardner (2011). MI states that humans have eight different intellectual capabilities (referred to as *intelligence dimensions*). Furthermore, this theory suggests that individual differences between people are the result of the differences in strength of these intellectual capabilities and how they work together and affect each other. MI explicitly stresses individual differences in terms of the various abilities to solve problems and create products. Gardner suggests that people with different intelligences or intellectual strengths often exhibit clear preferences, abilities and competencies with respect to specific tasks (Gardner, 1983). This chapter explores whether this knowledge could be transferred to learning games and utilized for the purpose of individualization (i.e. in player-centered game design). If people with different intellectual strengths exhibit clear preferences for certain game constructs, and if game designers were aware of the MI profile of their target audience, they would be able to design their games accordingly. To do so, they could incorporate constructs such as game mechanics and interaction modalities that have been proven to support and improve game experience as well as learning outcome among their target audience. Such individualization could better facilitate knowledge gain in games and transfer from games to real-world contexts, and perhaps even develop the weaker intelligences of players.

Related Work

The potential relationship between MI and games has been pointed out by other researchers as well. Two of the most important works that suggest the existence of such relationship are the ones of Becker (Becker, 2007) and Starks (Starks, 2014). These two researchers have suggested theoretical mappings between each dimension of MI and certain characteristics of games. These suggestions are briefly explained in the next paragraphs.

Becker (2007) argues that there is a link between the written and spoken elements and instructions in games and the development of the linguistic intelligence. According to Becker:

This is one reason why children often experience success in learning to read through games like Pokémon (Page 371).

Similarly, she maps musical intelligence to a game's soundtrack and auditory feedback, referring to games such as *Karaoke Revolution*; logical-mathematical intelligence to in-game strategizing, arithmetic, management style and puzzle games such as *Pikmin*; visual-spatial intelligence to the graphical environment, visual elements of games and how they are perceived through the screen; bodily-kinesthetic intelligence to games that promote physical movement as well as the different physical states a player experiences while playing a game such as *Dance Dance Revolution*; intrapersonal intelligence to games that involve ethical dilemmas and moral decision making such as *Black & White*; interpersonal intelligence to multiplayer collaboration, communication and competition; and naturalistic intelligence to realistic portrayal of natural environments in games such as *Zoo Tycoon*.

Starks (2014) provides similar arguments, stating that in-game graphics engage a person's visual intelligence, while the way a player moves in the game environment engages their spatial intelligence. She also states that relationships inside and surrounding a game refer to the use of the interpersonal intelligence, like in MMO games; that empathy provoking situations inside a game, such as in *Darfur is Dying*, engages a person's intrapersonal intelligence; that music and sounds engage a player's musical intelligence; that narrative and language used inside the game engage the linguistic intelligence; that components like arithmetic, calculations and geometry, as well as pattern detection and logical deduction activate logical-mathematical intelligence; that in-game actions requiring actual physical movement engage bodily-kinesthetic intelligence; and that realistic representations and simulations of natural environments in a game engage a player's naturalistic intelligence.

It is important to note that the observations of both Becker and Starks are solely based on their theoretical analyses, and not sustained by any empirical evidence.

Apart from application of MI in more conventional contexts (i.e. classrooms), this theory has also been studied in relation to games as well. In (Crescenzi-Lanna & Grané-Oró, 2016) the importance of developing the intelligences of children at an early age is stressed. The study analyses 100 educational apps (including games) for children under the age of eight. The results indicate that most of the current apps focus on the visual-spatial and logical-mathematical dimensions. The results also show that other dimensions such as kinesthetic, interpersonal, intrapersonal or musical are neglected, even though they are developmentally essential for children at that age. Jing et al. (Jing, Sujuan, & Linqing, 2012), provide an overview of several educational games that can aid in the development of a player's logical-mathematical intelligence. Similarly, Chuang and Sheng-Hsiung (2012) claim that games can be used as a tool to enhance players' intelligences and learning outcomes. Li et al (2013) have investigated the effect of Role Playing Games on intrapersonal intelligence.

Despite the potential of applying MI in learning games, empirical correlations between MI dimensions and games are non-existent. However, such empirical evidence is crucial for effectively utilizing MI for individualization. To investigate the existence of such evidence, a survey study was used to explore the relationship between MI dimensions and preferences for games. Based on the results of this survey, evidence-based mappings between MI dimensions and fundamental constructs of games known as game mechanics were suggested. Such mappings can assist designers in making informed decisions when designing player-cantered games targeting specific dimension(s) of MI, on what mechanics to include in their design, in order to positively affect the game experience and learning outcomes of their audience.

SURVEY STUDY

Based on the results of an online survey study conducted among 308 avid gamers in July 2015, it was revealed that individual differences in terms of MI dimensions show significant correlations with preferences for certain games (Sajjadi, Vlieghe, & De Troyer, 2016). The study also revealed that these correlations

Multiple Intelligences and Digital Learning Game Design

could not be solely explained by the genres of the involved games. This highlighted the necessity for looking into more detailed characteristics of the games to be able to explain the correlations and identify the shared features among games preferred by players exhibiting strength for certain MI dimensions.

The methodology used for collecting the survey data as well as their analyses are explained in (Sajjadi, Vlieghe, et al., 2016; Sajjadi, Vlieghe, & Troyer, 2017). Notwithstanding, the main results of the survey study are briefly mentioned in this chapter as they will help in better understanding the proposed evidence-based mapping between the MI of players and game mechanics.

Firstly, using the technique of Principle Component Analysis (PCA), patterns between each MI score of the participants and their preferences for 47 game titles were identified. Secondly, a series of bivariate correlation analyses were used to unveil significant corrections that may exist between participants' MI scores and their preferences for the 47 game titles considered in the survey. 42 of the preselected game titles showed to be significantly correlate to one or more MI dimensions. Table 1 shows a summary of the found correlations.

As a final step, a bivariate correlation analysis was performed to investigate whether these correlations could be explained in in light of the genre(s) of the games. The results show that the observed correlations cannot be explained in terms of unique preferences for one or multiple game genres (see (Sajjadi et al., 2017) for more detail). As such, the used game titles were analyzed based on their game mechanics, to try to identify the shared characteristics among them. The rationale behind the selection of the game titles in that study, the used instrument for measuring the MI of participants, and details on the analysis can be found in (Sajjadi, Vlieghe, et al., 2016; Sajjadi et al., 2017).

Mapping Between MI Dimensions and Game Mechanics

Various definitions of the term game mechanic have been proposed (e.g. (Fabricatore, 2007; Järvinen, 2008b; Lundgren & Bjork, 2003; Sicart, 2008)). In this chapter, the definition of Sicart is used as: "Methods invoked by agents, designed for interaction with the game state" (Sicart, 2008, paragraph 25). Furthermore, a number of different classification schemes for game mechanics have been suggested (e.g. (Fabricatore, 2007; Järvinen, 2008a; Salen & Zimmerman, 2004; Sicart, 2008)). These classifications are based on the role a mechanic plays in a game. The proposed classification schemes include classes such as core versus satellite; primary versus secondary; sub and modifiers; global versus local; and enhancement, alternate, or opposition mechanics.

The categorization scheme used in this chapter is the one of Fabricatore (2007): *Core* and *Satellite*. This categorization helps in determining whether a game mechanic plays a dominant role in the game or not, and is an important factor to consider when deciding whether that game mechanic has a relationship with a specific dimensions of MI; i.e. a core mechanic is more decisive than a satellite mechanic. According to Fabricatore, a core mechanic is defined as:

The set of activities that the player will undertake more frequently during the game experience, and which are indispensable to win the game" (ibid, Page 12)

And a satellite mechanic is defined as:

… special kinds of mechanics, aimed at enhancing already existing activities. These are called satellite game mechanics since their design is functional to already existing core mechanics (ibid, Page 13).

Table 1. Summary of the bivariate correlation analyses. + (positive), - (negative), P < 0.01 ** or P < 0.05* (S represents a game series).

Game Genre	Game Title	Linguistics	Logical-Mathematical	Visual-Spatial	Bodily-Kinesthetic	Musical	Interpersonal	Intrapersonal	Naturalist
Puzzle	Portal[S]	+ *	+ **					+ **	
	Angry Birds	+ *			+ **		+ *		
	The Room[S]	+ *		+ **					
	2048	- *	+ **	+ *				- *	
	Tetris				+ **		+ *		
	Where's My Water?				+ **	+ **	+ *		
	Scribblenauts							+ *	
Word puzzle	Wordfeud								- *
	Wordament		- *					- *	
Puzzle/action	Braid	+ **	+ **				+ *		+ *
Action	Street Fighter	+ *				- *			+ *
Action/sandbox	Minecraft			+ *	+ *				
Action/adventure	L.A. Noire	+ *		+ *		+ *		+ *	
	Heavy Rain	+ **	- *					+ **	
	Infamous[S]				- *				
Action/shooter	DayZ			+ *	+ *		+ *		
Action/RPG/shooter	Mass Effect[S]				- *			+ *	
Music/dance/rhythm/action/platformer	Bit.Trip Runner					+ *			
Action/educational	The Typing of the Dead				- *	+ **			
Music/dance	Rock Band	+ *				+ *		+ **	+ *
	SingStar[S]	+ *		+ *		+ *	+ **		
	Just Dance[S]	+ *		+ *	+ **		+ **	+ **	+ **
	Fantasia: Music Evolved		+ *	+ *		+ *			
	Dance Central Spotlight[S]			+ *	+ *				+ *
	Dance Dance Revolution[S]				+ *	+ *	+ *		
	Guitar Hero[S]					+ **			
	Audiosurf							+ **	
Simulation	The Sims[S]	+ *	- **	+ **					
	Afrika		+ *	+ **					
Simulation/adventure	Endless Ocean	- *	- *		- *		- *		
	Spore			+ **		+ *		+ *	
Simulation/RPG	Second Life			+ **				+ **	
	Farmville[S]						+ **	+ **	
Adventure	Flower	+ *						+ **	
	Ace Attorney[S]			- **	- *				
	The Walking Dead	+ **						+ **	

continued on following page

Multiple Intelligences and Digital Learning Game Design

Table 1. Continued

Game Genre	Game Title	Linguistics	Logical-Mathematical	Visual-Spatial	Bodily-Kinesthetic	Musical	Interpersonal	Intrapersonal	Naturalist
RPG	Fable	+ *	+ **	+ *				+ *	
RPG	Fallout[s]	+ **	+ **	+ *			+ *		
RPG	World of Warcraft		- *	+ *				+ **	
Sports	Xbox Fitness		+ *					+ *	
Racing	Dirt[s]			+ **		+ *			- **
Strategy	Black & White[s]	+ **		+ **			+ *		

The purpose of the mapping between MI dimensions and game mechanics is to indicate which game mechanics suit which MI dimensions. First, a comprehensive list of game mechanics that covers different aspects of games belonging to different types and genres were created. This resulted in a repository[1] of 236 distinct game mechanics. Next, all 42 game titles from the survey that showed to be either negatively or positively correlated to one or more MI dimension on different levels of significance were analyzed in detail to discover which mechanics they were employing. Afterwards, a protocol was used to establish mappings between the different MI dimensions and the game mechanics.

During the analysis of the games, it was also important to consider the role a game mechanic was playing in a game in terms of core or satellite. Based on their definitions, core mechanics were assigned a higher weight than the satellite ones in our protocol that determines whether a game mechanic is related to an MI dimension. Furthermore, if such relation exists, the protocol considers the roles of the mechanics to decide about the nature of that relationship.

For each MI dimension, the games having a correlation with that dimension were clustered into two groups. The *positive* group contains the games that have a positive correlation with the MI dimension, and the *negative* group contains the games that have a negative correlation. Subsequently, the mechanics for all the games in both clusters were marked as either core (c) or satellite (s) depending on their role in that game. An excerpt of the tables constructed in this way is given in Table 2. The columns are used for the games, while the rows are used for the mechanics. The cells indicate whether the game mechanic is used in a game as core mechanics (indicated by "c") or as a satellite mechanics (indicated by "s") or not used at all (no value). The games colored in light grey are in the positive group and the ones colored in dark grey are in the negative group. The decision on the role of a game mechanic in a game was made based on our experience in playing the game, studying the design of the game based on the information available on the official website of the game, forums and in some cases Wiki pages of the game, as well as by analyzing hours of gameplay videos. Table 2 shows the results of this analysis for the Bodily-kinesthetic MI dimension. For example, in this dimension, the games "Angry Birds" and "Mass Effect" are respectively in the positive and negative groups. Evidently, the examples in Table 2 are only a small subset of the complete analysis on all 42 games. Each game was analyzed with respect to the 243 collected game mechanics. This process resulted in 8 tables, i.e. one table per MI dimension.

Our objective was to establish relationships between game mechanics and all MI dimensions. For example, it is desired to be able to state whether a game mechanic like "points" is preferred by and thus suitable for the bodily-kinesthetically intelligent people or not. Arriving at such relationships requires complementing the analysis with a protocol that determines the nature of this relationship.

Table 2. Example of the decision protocol for a relationship between the "Points" mechanic and the Bodily-kinesthetic dimension of MI

Mechanics	Angry Birds	Tetris	Where's My Water?	Minecraft	Dayz	Just Dance [series]	Dance Central Spotlight [series]	Dance Dance Revolution [series]	Total weight	Infamous [series]	Mass Effect [series]	The Typing of the Dead	Endless Ocean	Ace Attorney [series]	Total weight
Points	c (+2)	c (+2)	c (+2)			c (+2)	c (+2)	c (+2)	12	c (+2)		c (+2)		c (+2)	6
Tutorial / first run scenarios	s (+1)		s (+1)			c (+2)	c (+2)	s (+1)	7	c (+2)	c (+2)			c (+2)	6
Dialogue tree									0	s (+1)	c (+2)			c (+2)	5

The following rule was established to determine if a mechanic is related to an MI dimension: *the game mechanic should be utilized by at least half of the games correlated to that MI dimension in either the negative or the positive clusters.* This rule considers the fact that if more than half of the games correlated to a MI dimension in each cluster are not using a particular game mechanic, there is not sufficient evidence that this game mechanic plays an important role in the preference (or lack thereof) for these games. However, if the majority of the games in either of the clusters utilize the game mechanic, then it is reasonable to conclude that the game mechanic has an influence on the game preference (or lack thereof) of the players. The decisions for mappings between a few game mechanics and the bodily-kinesthetic MI dimension can be seen in Table 2.

The "Points" game mechanic for the Bodily-kinesthetic MI dimension is used in 6 out of 8 games in the positive cluster, and in 3 out of 5 games in the negative cluster. This means that at least half of the games in each cluster have utilized the game mechanic "Points", and therefore the mechanic is considered to be related to the dimension. The decision for the nature of the relationship is based on the comparison of the weights of the game mechanic for the positive and for the negative cluster (see Table 2). The weight for a cluster is calculated as follows: each time the game mechanic is used as a core mechanic in the cluster, a weight of +2 is added and when it is used as a satellite mechanic a weight of +1 is added.

Three types of possible relationships were devised: "positive", "dubious" (uncertain), and "negative". If the total weight in the positive cluster is larger than the one for the negative cluster by at least 2, that game mechanic is declared to have a "positive" relation with that dimension of MI. On the contrary, if the total weight for the negative cluster is larger than the one for the positive cluster by at least 2, the game mechanic is declared to have a "negative" relation with that dimension of MI. In the other case (i.e. the weights are equal or the difference between the weights is at most one) the relationship is "dubious". For example, the "Points" game mechanic plays 6 times the role of "core" in the positive cluster, giving it a total weight of 12 in this cluster, and 3 times the role of "core" in the negative cluster, giving it a total weight of 6 in this cluster. Therefore, this game mechanic is declared to have a positive relation with the Bodily-kinesthetic dimension of MI. Following this procedure, for each MI dimension relationships between that dimension and game mechanics were identified.

This analysis showed that within our games sample, the 8 different MI dimensions have relationships with 116 different game mechanics. Now, these relationships can be used to help game designers in designing games for a specific audience (i.e. player-centered game design) by selecting appropriate game mechanics that will provide a tailored gameplay experience and enhance the players' overall game experience. Positive relationships indicate that players with a particular MI intelligence will generally respond positively to the game mechanic. Therefore, it is *recommended* to use this game mechanic if designers aim to enhance the game experience of players who exhibit strength for this particular MI intelligence. Game mechanics with a negative relationship to a particular MI dimension evoke mostly negative responses and therefore it is *recommended not to use them* when targeting that MI dimension. Dubious relationships point towards a fairly equal mix of positive and negative responses. In our opinion, game mechanics with a dubious relationship can be used but require extra caution as they might results in both positive and negative responses among people within the targeted MI dimension. Furthermore, there are game mechanics that have a positive relationship with almost all MI dimensions, such as "quick feedback". These particular mechanics represent constructs that seem to be appealing to almost all gamers, regardless of their intelligences. Thus, they can be assumed to provide a good game experience for all players.

It should be note that the mappings were derived indirectly, based on the preferences of the participants for games, and were not explicitly verified with the participants. In addition, the decisions made throughout the process of establishing the mappings, both in terms of the role a game mechanic plays in a game, as well as the choice for the protocol used for determining the nature of the relationships, were made by the researchers and thus are subjective. Therefore, the recommendations should be considered as suggestions and not as hard and general rules, and further validation is desirable.

Validation

The applicability of the proposed evidence-based mappings between game mechanics and MI dimensions in the context of player-centered game design has been evaluated in two case studies. In each case study a specific dimension of MI is targeted. In both cases, the game experience of players exhibiting strength for the targeted MI dimension were compared against players who did not exhibit strength for that dimension of MI. In addition to game experience, in one of the case studies, also the learning outcome of the target audience was studied in a controlled experiment.

The first case study focused on a game called LeapBalancer specifically targeting the bodily-kinesthetic dimension of MI. Namely, mostly game mechanics that were shown to have a positive relation with this dimension of MI were included in the design of the game. The game was evaluated with 22 participants, of which 11 exhibited bodily-kinesthetic intelligences as one of their dominant intelligences, while the rest of the population did not. The details of the game and the methodology used for its evaluation, as well as the discussion of the results are available in full detail in (Sajjadi, Lo-A-Njoe, Vlieghe, & De Troyer, 2016). In short, the results of a pilot study demonstrated the advantage of considering the intelligences of the players during game design. For this particular case study, the proposed evidence-based mappings between MI dimensions and game mechanics have led to the design of a game that positively affects the game experience for players who exhibit the targeted MI dimension. More specifically, the bodily-kinesthetically intelligent players were experiencing significantly more competence, and immersion while experiencing significantly less amount of tension compared to players who did not exhibit this MI dimensions as one their dominant intelligences.

The second case study focused on a game called TrueBiters designed for practicing the truth tables of proposition logic, and specifically targeting the logical-mathematical dimension of MI. This game was evaluated on two levels in two pilot studies: one on learning outcome (with 4 participants), and another on game experience (with 11 participants). The details of the game and the methodology used for its evaluation, as well as the discussion of the results are available in full detail in (Sajjadi, El Sayed,

& De Troyer, 2016). In short, the results indicate that the logically-mathematically intelligent players performed better compared to the rest of the population in a pre- and post-test evaluation with respect to learning outcome. Moreover, it was observed that the game experience of the target audience was significantly better compared to the rest of the population in terms of immersion.

Although preliminary, both case studies provide promising results. It was observed that utilizing the proposed evidence-based mappings between the different dimensions of MI and fundamental constructs of games during the design of player-centered games can indeed yield successful individualized games. In both cases, the target audiences of the games were the ones benefitting most from the games in terms of game experience as well as learning outcome. Of course, the results of these case studies are only a partial and preliminary validation of the proposed mappings in terms of the effect they could have on game experience and learning outcome. As such, conclusions made in relation to validating the proposed mappings are limited to the MI dimensions under study, the games, and the population used in these case studies. In order to generalize the findings, more large-scale experiments should be conducted.

RECOMMENDATION TOOL[2]

To obtain an easy overview of the proposed mappings and to quickly find game mechanics for particular MI dimensions or to see the relationships of game mechanics with different MI dimensions, we developed an on-line tool. The tool also allows the game designers and developers to create a report of game mechanics they want to include in their game and how these are related to the different MI dimensions. With this report they can detect possible conflict is terms of suitable game mechanics when different MI dimensions are targeted.

The tool allows users to select one or more MI dimensions. Based on this selection, the system compiles and visualizes an overview of all game mechanics correlated with the selected MI dimensions. The system uses the "concept network" visualization technique to display the overview (see Figure 1).

In the overview, the 8 intelligence dimensions are positioned in the middle of the figure (Figure 1). All the related game mechanics are placed around them. Lines are used to represent the relationship between an MI dimension and game mechanics. The user can browse over the MI dimensions to see which game mechanics are related with each individual MI dimension. The selected MI dimension and the lines are highlighted in blue. To avoid burdening the user with too much information at once, a selection panel was added at the top of the screen (see Figure 2 (a)). The user can use this panel to select one or more MI dimensions on which to focus. In Figure 2 (a), the Bodily-Kinesthetic and Logical-Mathematical dimensions are selected. The selected dimensions and the related game mechanics will be shown on the screen, while the other dimensions and game mechanics are hidden.

The game mechanic nodes are grouped by color. The colors represent different classes of mechanics, e.g. blue is used for game mechanics in the "Challenge" class. The classes represent groups of mechanics that can be placed under the same umbrella and represent an important aspect of a game. There are 10 classes in total: "Involvement", "Challenge", "Motivation", "Competition", "Assistance", "Player movements", "Object manipulation", "Dialogue", "Game environment", and "Relatedness". Classes can be used as a filtering mechanism in the tool by selecting or deselecting the classes from the panel on the left hand side (Figure 2 (b)). The mechanics belonging to the deselected classes will be excluded from the visualization. This panel allows the game designers and developers to focus on different types of game mechanics one by one. The panel can be collapsed.

Multiple Intelligences and Digital Learning Game Design

Figure 1. Main visualization: Visualization of all MI dimensions and game mechanics

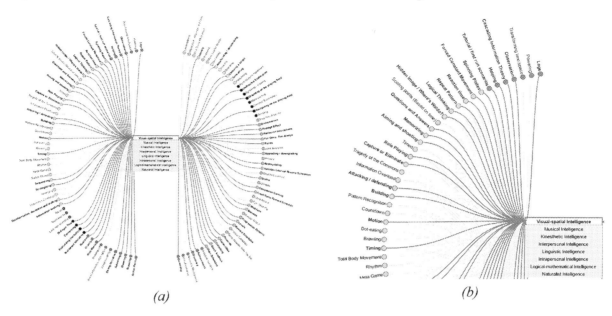

(a)　　　　　　　　　　　　　　　(b)

Figure 2. Classes of mechanics and relations to MI dimensions

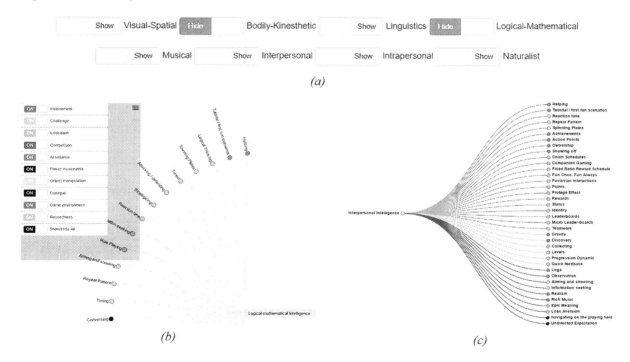

53

Multiple Intelligences and Digital Learning Game Design

To see the nature of the relations (i.e. positive, negative or dubious) between a MI dimension and the associated game mechanics, users can click on the MI dimension. The system will then display a different visualization that indicates the nature of the relationships by using 3 different colors for the relationships: green for positive, yellow for dubious, and red for negative (see Figure 2 (c) as well as the online tool for colors).

In this visualization, the classes of the different game mechanics are also denoted by means of their color. To reduce working memory load, a legend was added that explains the different colors (see Figure 3). The legend is hidden by default, but users can call up this legend at any time by clicking the 'help map' button.

The user can get quick access to the definition of a game mechanic by clicking on the label of a game mechanic. Doing so will result in a new visualization, in which the definition of that mechanic and the relationships it has with the dimensions of MI are shown (if any) (see Figure 4, which gives the definition of the game mechanic Logical Thinking and shows that this mechanic has a positive relationship with the logical-mathematical intelligence dimension, and negative relationships with the linguistic, intrapersonal, and visual-spatial intelligence dimension). As for the previous visualizations, the colors, green, red and yellow are used to indicate respectively positive, negative and dubious relationships.

Figure 3. MI dimension visualization with legend

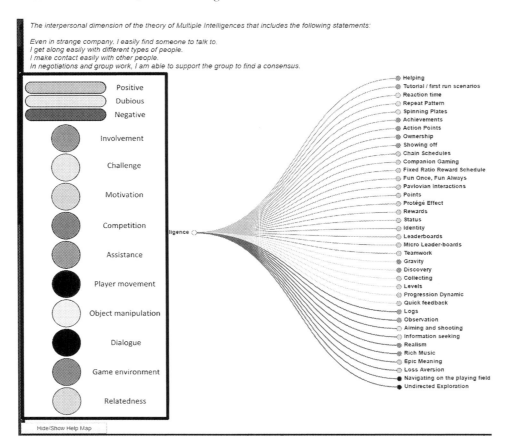

Multiple Intelligences and Digital Learning Game Design

Figure 4. Visualization of a game mechanic's relations

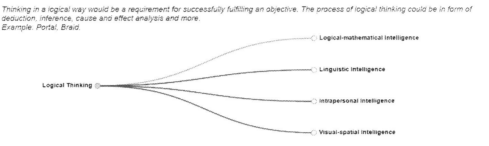

The game mechanic visualization functionality is also available in the main visualization screen (Figure 1), meaning that if the user clicks on a game mechanic in the main visualization, the visualization of that mechanic, as given in Figure 4, will be shown. Moreover, in the MI dimension visualization (Figure 5) hovering over a game mechanic will result in a pop-up window that contains the definition of that mechanic. This functionality is made available to ease the process of report generation that will be explained in the coming paragraphs.

To ease the process of searching for a particular game mechanic, a search functionality is provided using a combo box, which provides suggestions based on the input entered in the search field (see Figure 6).

As mentioned, the users can use the system to draw up some reports. Such a report contains the selected game mechanics, their relationship to the selected MI dimensions, as well as the nature of the relationships. For example, consider a scenario where a game designer is interested in designing a game for logically-mathematically intelligent players. She or he can use the tool to explore all the relations between this MI dimension and game mechanics. The game designer can use the MI dimension filter to focus only on the logically-mathematically dimension. She or he can then search or explore game mechanics and select the game mechanics she/he wants to incorporate in the game by clicking on the corresponding nodes. The selected game mechanics (nodes) are highlighted by a blue circle (see Figure

Figure 5. Game mechanic definition "Quickview"

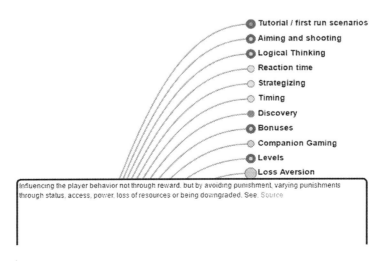

Figure 6. Autosuggest searching of game mechanics

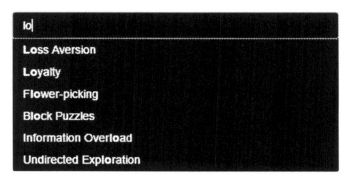

Figure 7. Report of the selected game mechanics

Mechanic(s)	Logical-mathematical Intelligence
Tutorial / first run scenarios	positive
Aiming and shooting	positive
Logical Thinking	positive
Bonuses	positive
Levels	positive
Quick feedback	positive
Spinning Plates	dubious
Action Points	dubious
Fixed Ratio Reward Schedule	dubious

5). Once the selection process is completed, the tool provides the "generate report" functionality. The result of this function is shown in Figure 7.

Obviously, the game designer can consider more than one MI dimension. Therefore, he can filter on more than one MI dimension in the visualization (e.g. logical-mathematical as well as bodily-kinesthetic). However, selecting particular game mechanics that have relations to both of these MI dimensions can raise conflicts, i.e. a game mechanic can be positive for one dimension and negative for another dimension. The color use in the report allows the designers and developers to quickly spot such conflicts (see Figure 8). Note that the system does not offer or suggest a final decision on what to do with the conflict. It is up to the designer to decide how to deal with it: to keep the mechanic or to replace it by another one.

Figure 8. Report of the selected mechanics for more than one MI dimension

Mechanic(s)	Logical-mathematical Intelligence	Kinesthetic Intelligence
Tutorial / first run scenarios	positive	dubious
Aiming and shooting	positive	negative
Logical Thinking	positive	
Bonuses	positive	positive
Levels	positive	negative
Quick feedback	positive	dubious
Spinning Plates	dubious	dubious
Action Points	dubious	
Fixed Ratio Reward Schedule	dubious	dubious

This decision will be dependent on the situation: sometimes a mechanic is essential for the gameplay; sometimes one MI dimension is more important than others; or sometimes a negative mechanic may be considered for a target audience to stimulate the development of a weaker MI dimension (further discussed in the next section).

DISCUSSION AND CONCLUSION

This chapter started by discussing the concept of individualization and how it can benefit learners. As the theory of MI can be used to differentiate between learners in light of their abilities, it was investigated as a potential aspect of players for driving the individualization of digital learning games. Based on the results of a survey, evidence-based mappings (i.e. positive, negative, and dubious) between MI dimensions and game mechanics were drawn. These evidence-based mappings can be used in the process of player-centered game design to customize the game mechanics to the MI dimensions of the targeted players. A first validation of these mappings in two case studies indicate that individualizing the mechanics of (learning) games based on the intelligences of the target audience can positively affect both the game experience and learning outcome of the players. To make these mappings available to game designers, a recommendation tool was developed. This recommendation tool visualizes the proposed mappings, while providing different ways for easily finding game mechanics and inspecting their definitions, selecting the desired mechanics to include in the design, and generating a report about the selection. The latter feature helps designers in identifying potential conflicts that may arise as a result of targeting more than one dimension of MI in their design.

Evidently, the presented work has some limitations. Firstly, the authors recognize that the selection of game titles used in the survey represents a snapshot of the current landscape of popular video games, and that this selection could have influenced the outcome of the study. However, to minimize any effect, a broad range of games was carefully selected. Secondly, although the suggested mappings are derived from the results of the survey study, they are based on our interpretations of the empirical data, and thus cannot yet be considered as hard rules, but rather as a first set of recommendations for the use of MI dimensions in the context of individualization. Lastly, the validation of the proposed mappings in form of two case studies, although an important first step, is partial and inconclusive. Several evaluations on a variety of player-centered games targeting different dimensions of MI should be performed to be able to draw definite conclusions regarding the applicability of the proposed mappings. Notwithstanding, the preliminary results indicate a promising direction this research is heading towards.

The focus of this chapter with respect to individualization has been on player-centered game design, but personalization and adaptation can also benefit from our mappings. In those cases, first a generic game can be designed and developed and then be personalized based on the MI intelligences of its player before each play session, or dynamically adapted in real-time and during gameplay, by including/excluding game mechanics. To automate the process of assessing the MI intelligences of the players and then performing personalization and/or adaptation accordingly, stealth measurement techniques (e.g. (Shute, 2011)) can be used. This means inferring the MI intelligences of the players based on the in-game decisions, actions, choices and other behaviors. This could be partially based on our mappings, as these mappings indicate preferences for certain game mechanics by people with certain MI intelligences. As such, players' attitude towards the different mechanics of a game can be monitored to assess whether there are indicators of their dominant intelligences.

Furthermore, as was explained in section 3, a few research works have focused on the use of games for the improvement of (one or more) of the MI intelligences of players. The research presented in this chapter could be utilized for this purposed. Namely, the knowledge regarding which game mechanics are negatively and which ones are positively related to certain MI dimensions, could be used to enable players practicing skills related to less dominant MI dimensions. As such, the proposed mappings presented in this research work can be applied in educational context in two ways: 1) to improve the game experience and learning outcome of players by employing game mechanics that are in accordance with their MI profiles, and 2) to develop the weaker intelligences of players by employing relevant game mechanics related to those dimensions of MI in the design of games. For example, if one wants to develop the bodily-kinesthetic intelligence of players, one could employ game mechanics such as: *motion, repeat pattern, forced constant movement,* and *timing* in the design of their game, which are all positively related to this MI dimension. This could be a rather important and quite interesting implication of the research presented in this chapter but needs further investigation.

REFERENCES

Becker, K. (2007). *Pedagogy in commercial video games. In Games and Simulations in Online Learning: Research and Development Frameworks*. Hershey, PA: Information Science Publishing.

Beldagli, B., & Adiguzel, T. (2010). Illustrating an ideal adaptive e-learning: A conceptual framework. *Procedia: Social and Behavioral Sciences*, 2(2), 5755–5761. doi:10.1016/j.sbspro.2010.03.939

Brusilovsky, P. (1996). Methods and Techniques of Adaptive Hypermedia. *User Modeling and User-Adapted Interaction: The Journal of Personalization Research*, 6(2–3), 87–129. doi:10.1007/BF00143964

Brusilovsky, P. (2001). *User Modeling and User-Adapted Interaction*. Kluwer Academic Publishers.

Chanel, G., Rebetez, C., Bétrancourt, M., & Pun, T. (2008). Boredom, engagement and anxiety as indicators for adaptation to difficulty in games. *Proceedings of the 12th International Conference on Entertainment and Media in the Ubiquitous Era - MindTrek '08*, 13. 10.1145/1457199.1457203

Charles, D., & Black, M. (2004). Dynamic Player Modelling: A Framework for Player-centred Digital Games. *Proceedings of 5th International Conference on Computer Games: Artificial Intelligence, Design and Education (CGAIDE'04), Microsoft*, 29–35.

Charles, D., Kerr, A., & McNeill, M. (2005). Player-centred game design: Player modelling and adaptive digital games. *Proceedings of the Digital Games Research Conference*, 285(6), 285–298.

Chuang, T.-Y., & Sheng-Hsiung, S. (2012). Using mobile console games for multiple intelligences and education. *International Journal of Mobile Learning and Organisation*, 6(3–4), 204–217. doi:10.1504/IJMLO.2012.050047

Cowley, B., Charles, D., Black, M., & Hickey, R. (2008). Toward an understanding of flow in video games. *Computers in Entertainment*, 6(2), 1. doi:10.1145/1371216.1371223

Crescenzi-Lanna, L., & Grané-Oró, M. (2016). An Analysis of the Interaction Design of the Best Educational Apps for Children Aged Zero to Eight. *Comunicar*, 24(46), 77–85. doi:10.3916/C46-2016-08

Csikszentmihalyi, M., & Csikszentmihalyi, I. S. (1992). *Optimal experience: Psychological studies of flow in consciousness*. Cambridge University Press.

Dede, C. (2009). Immersive Interfaces for Engagement and Learning. *Science*, 323(5910), 66–69. doi:10.1126cience.1167311 PMID:19119219

Dondlinger, M. J. (2007). Educational video game design: A review of the literature. *Journal of Applied Educational Technology*, 4(1), 21–31. doi:10.1108/10748120410540463

Fabricatore, C. (2007). Gameplay and game mechanics design: a key to quality in video games. *Proceedings of the OECD-CERI Expert Meeting on Videogames and Education*, 1–18. Retrieved from http://www.oecd.org/dataoecd/44/17/39414829.pdf

Gardner, H. (1983). *Frames of Mind: The Theory of Multiple Intelligences*. Basic Books.

Garrison, D. R. (2011). *E-learning in the 21st century: A framework for research and practice*. Taylor & Francis.

Gee, J. P. (2004). *Situated language and learning: A critique of traditional schooling*. Psychology Press. doi:10.1111/j.1467-9345.2006.02802_1.x

Göbel, S., Hardy, S., & Wendel, V. (2010). Serious Games for Health - Personalized Exergames. *Proceedings of the 18th ACM International Conference on Multimedia*, 1663–1666. 10.1145/1873951.1874316

Järvinen, A. (2008a). *Games without frontiers: Theories and methods for game studies and design. Game Studies.* Tampere University Press.

Järvinen, A. (2008b). *Games without Frontiers: Theories and Methods for Game Studies and Design.* Game Studies.

Jing, L., Sujuan, M., & Linqing, M. (2012). The Study on the Effect of Educational Games for the Development of Students' Logic-Mathematics of Multiple Intelligence. *Physics Procedia, 33,* 1749–1752. doi:10.1016/j.phpro.2012.05.280

Karagiannidis, C., & Sampson, D. (2004). Adaptation Rules Relating Learning Styles Research and Learning Objects Meta-data. *Workshop on Individual Differences in Adaptive Hypermedia. 3rd International Conference on Adaptive Hypermedia and Adaptive Web-based Systems (AH2004).*

Kickmeier-Rust, M. D., & Albert, D. (2010). Micro-adaptivity: Protecting immersion in didactically adaptive digital educational games. *Journal of Computer Assisted Learning, 26*(2), 95–105. doi:10.1111/j.1365-2729.2009.00332.x

Kickmeier-Rust, M. D., Mattheiss, E., Steiner, C., & Albert, D. (2012). A Psycho-Pedagogical Framework for Multi-Adaptive Educational Games. *International Journal of Game-Based Learning, 1*(1), 45–58. doi:10.4018/ijgbl.2011010104

Kiili, K. (2005). Digital game-based learning: Towards an experiential gaming model. *The Internet and Higher Education, 8*(1), 13–24. doi:10.1016/j.iheduc.2004.12.001

Koehler, M. J., & Mishra, P. (2009). What is Technological Pedagogical Content Knowledge (TPACK)? *Contemporary Issues in Technology & Teacher Education, 9*(1), 60–70. doi:10.1016/j.compedu.2010.07.009

Li, Q., Zhang, T., Wang, B., & Wang, N. (2013). Effects of RPG on middle school players intrapersonal intelligence. In *Transactions on Edutainment IX* (pp. 160–175). Springer. doi:10.1007/978-3-642-37042-7_10

Linssen, J. (2011). *Adaptive Learning in an Educational Game-Adapting Game Complexity to Gameplay Increases Efficiency of Learning.* Academic Press.

Lopes, R., & Bidarra, R. (2011). Adaptivity challenges in games and simulations: A survey. *IEEE Transactions on Computational Intelligence and AI in Games, 3*(2), 85–99. doi:10.1109/TCIAIG.2011.2152841

Lundgren, S., & Bjork, S. (2003). Game mechanics: Describing computer-augmented games in terms of interaction. *Proceedings of TIDSE.*

Magerko, B. (2009). The Future of Digital Game-Based Learning. Handbook of Research on Effective Electronic Gaming in Education, 3, 1274–1288. doi:10.4018/978-1-59904-808-6

Moreno, R., & Mayer, R. (2007). Interactive Multimodal Learning Environments. *Educational Psychology Review, 19*(3), 309–326. doi:10.100710648-007-9047-2

Muir, M., & Conati, C. (2012). An Analysis of Attention to Student–Adaptive Hints in an Educational Game. *Intelligent Tutoring Systems,* 112–122. Retrieved from http://www.springerlink.com/index/4L28G36M16605352.pdf

Paas, F., Renkl, A., & Sweller, J. (2004). Cognitive Load Theory : Instructional Implications of the Interaction between Information Structures and Cognitive Architecture. *Learning and Instruction*, *32*(1/2), 1–8. doi:10.1023/B:TRUC.0000021806.17516.d0

Paras, B., & Bizzocchi, J. (2005). *Game, Motivation, and Effective Learning: An Integrated Model for Educational Game Design*. Academic Press.

Rosenberg, M. J. (2001). *E-learning: Strategies for delivering knowledge in the digital age*. McGraw-Hill.

Sajjadi, P., El Sayed, E., & De Troyer, O. (2016). On the Impact of the Dominant Intelligences of Players on Learning Outcome and Game Experience in Educational Games: The TrueBiters Case. In R. Bottino, J. Jeuring, & R. C. Veltkamp (Eds.), *Games and Learning Alliance: 5th International Conference, GALA 2016, Utrecht, The Netherlands, December 5-7, 2016, Proceedings* (pp. 221–231). Cham: Springer International Publishing. 10.1007/978-3-319-50182-6_20

Sajjadi, P., Lo-A-Njoe, A., Vlieghe, J., & De Troyer, O. (2016). Exploring the Relation Between Game Experience and Game Mechanics for Bodily-Kinesthetic Players. In R. Bottino, J. Jeuring, & R. C. Veltkamp (Eds.), *Games and Learning Alliance: 5th International Conference, GALA 2016, Utrecht, The Netherlands, December 5-7, 2016, Proceedings* (pp. 354–364). Cham: Springer International Publishing. 10.1007/978-3-319-50182-6_32

Sajjadi, P., Van Broeckhoven, F., & De Troyer, O. (2014). Dynamically Adaptive Educational Games: A New Perspective. In Games for Training, Education, Health and Sports (pp. 71–76). Springer International Publishing. doi:10.1007/978-3-319-05972-3_8

Sajjadi, P., Vlieghe, J., & De Troyer, O. (2016). Relation Between Multiple Intelligences and Game Preferences: an Evidence-Based Approach. In *ECGBL2016-10th European Conference on Games Based Learning: ECGBL2016*.

Sajjadi, P., Vlieghe, J., & Troyer, O. (2017). *Exploring the Relation between the Theory of Multiple Intelligences and Games For the Purpose of Player-Centred Game Design*. Academic Press.

Salen, K., & Zimmerman, E. (2004). *Rules of Play: Game Design Fundamentals*. MIT Press.

Saxby, D., Matthews, G., Hitchcock, E., & Warm, J. (2007). Development of active and passive fatigue manipulations using a driving simulator. In *Proceedings of the Human Factors and Ergonomics Society Annual Meeting* (pp. 1237–1241). Sage Publications. 10.1177/154193120705101839

Shernoff, D. J., Csikszentmihalyi, M., Shneider, B., & Shernoff, E. S. (2003). Student engagement in high school classrooms from the perspective of flow theory. *School Psychology Quarterly*, *18*(2), 158–176. doi:10.1521cpq.18.2.158.21860

Shute, V. J. (2011). Stealth Assessment in Computer-Based Games To Support Learning. *Computer Games and Instruction*, 503–524. Retrieved from www.ncbi.nlm.nih.gov

Sicart, M. (2008). Defining game mechanics. *Game Studies*, *8*(2), 1–14.

Starks, K. (2014). Cognitive behavioral game design: A unified model for designing serious games. *Frontiers in Psychology*, *5*. doi:10.3389/fpsyg.2014.00028 PMID:24550858

Sweetser, P., & Wyeth, P. (2005). GameFlow: A model for evaluating player enjoyment in games. *Computers in Entertainment*, *3*(3), 1–24. doi:10.1145/1077246.1077253

Tseng, J. C. R., Chu, H. C., Hwang, G. J., & Tsai, C. C. (2008). Development of an adaptive learning system with two sources of personalization information. *Computers & Education*, *51*(2), 776–786. doi:10.1016/j.compedu.2007.08.002

Van Eck, R. (2006). Digital Game-Based Learning: It's Not Just the Digital Natives Who Are Restless. *EDUCAUSE Review*, *41*(2), 16–30. doi:10.1145/950566.950596

Webster, J., Trevino, L. K., & Ryan, L. (1993). The dimensionality and correlates of flow in human-computer interactions. *Computers in Human Behavior*, *9*(4), 411–426. doi:10.1016/0747-5632(93)90032-N

Witmer, B. G., & Singer, M. J. (1998). Measuring Presence in Virtual Environments: A Presence Questionnaire. *Presence: Teleoper. Virtual Environ.*, *7*(3), 225–240. doi:10.1162/105474698565686

Wouters, P., van der Spek, E. D., & van Oostendorp, H. (2009). Current practices in serious game research: A review from a learning outcomes perspective. *Effective Practices*, 232–250. doi:10.4018/978-1-60566-360-9

Yannakakis, G. N., Togelius, J., Khaled, R., Jhala, A., Karpouzis, K., Paiva, A., & Vasalou, A. (2010). Siren: Towards Adaptive Serious Games for Teaching Conflict Resolution. *4th Europeen Conference on Games Based Learning ECGBL2010, Copenhagen, Denmark*, 10. Retrieved from http://www.image.ntua.gr/papers/640.pdf

Yasir, M., & Sharif, S. (2011). An approach to Adaptive E-Learning Hypermedia System based on Learning Styles (AEHS-LS): Implementation and evaluation. *International Journal of Library and Information Science*, *3*(January), 15–28. Retrieved from http://www.academicjournals.org/journal/IJLIS/edition/January_2011

ADDITIONAL READING

Becker, K. (2007). *Pedagogy in commercial video games. Games and Simulations in Online Learning: Research and Development Frameworks*. Hershey, PA: Information Science Publishing.

Chuang, T.-Y., & Sheng-Hsiung, S. (2012). Using mobile console games for multiple intelligences and education. *International Journal of Mobile Learning and Organisation*, *6*(3–4), 204–217. doi:10.1504/IJMLO.2012.050047

Crescenzi-Lanna, L., & Grané-Oró, M. (2016). An Analysis of the Interaction Design of the Best Educational Apps for Children Aged Zero to Eight. *Comunicar*, *24*(46), 77–85. doi:10.3916/C46-2016-08

de Boer, A.-L., du Toit, P., & Bothma, T. (2015). Activating whole brain innovation: A means of nourishing multiple intelligence in higher education. *Td-the Journal for Transdisciplinary Research in Southern Africa*, *11*(2), 55–72.

Esther, M., Pérez, M., Duque, A. P. G., & García, L. C. F. (2018).. . *Game-Based Learning : Increasing the Logical-Mathematical, Naturalistic, and Linguistic Learning Levels of Primary School Students*, 7(1), 31–39. doi:10.7821/naer.2018.1.248

Jing, L., Sujuan, M., & Linqing, M. (2012). The Study on the Effect of Educational Games for the Development of Students' Logic-Mathematics of Multiple Intelligence. *Physics Procedia*, *33*, 1749–1752. doi:10.1016/j.phpro.2012.05.280

Li, Q., Zhang, T., Wang, B., & Wang, N. (2013). Effects of RPG on middle school players intrapersonal intelligence. In Transactions on Edutainment IX, 160–175 doi:10.1007/978-3-642-37042-7_10

McLellan, H. (1994). Virtual reality and multiple intelligences: Potentials for higher education. *Journal of Computing in Higher Education*, *5*(2), 33–66. doi:10.1007/BF02948570

Moran, S., & Gardner, H. (2006). *Multiple intelligences in the workplace. Multiple intelligences: New horizons*. New York: Basic Books.

Sajjadi, P., (2017). Individualizing Learning Games : Incorporating the Theory of Multiple Intelligences in Player-Centered Game Design.

Sajjadi, P., El Sayed, E., & De Troyer, O. (2016). On the Impact of the Dominant Intelligences of Players on Learning Outcome and Game Experience in Educational Games: The TrueBiters Case. In R. Bottino, J. Jeuring, & R. C. Veltkamp (Eds.), Games and Learning Alliance: 5th International Conference, GALA 2016, Utrecht, The Netherlands, December 5--7, 2016, Proceedings, 221–231, Cham: Springer International Publishing. 10.1007/978-3-319-50182-6_20

Sajjadi, P., Lo-A-Njoe, A., Vlieghe, J., & De Troyer, O. (2016). Exploring the Relation Between Game Experience and Game Mechanics for Bodily-Kinesthetic Players. In R. Bottino, J. Jeuring, & R. C. Veltkamp (Eds.), Games and Learning Alliance: 5th International Conference, GALA 2016, Utrecht, The Netherlands, December 5--7, 2016, Proceedings, 354–364, Cham: Springer International Publishing. 10.1007/978-3-319-50182-6_32

Sajjadi, P., Vlieghe, J., & De Troyer, O. (2016). Evidence-Based Mapping Between the Theory of Multiple Intelligences and Game Mechanics for the Purpose of Player-Centered Serious Game Design. In VS-Games 2016, 8th International Conference on Games and Virtual Worlds for Serious Applications, 1-8, IEEE. 10.1109/VS-GAMES.2016.7590348

Sajjadi, P., Vlieghe, J., & De Troyer, O. (2016b). Relation Between Multiple Intelligences and Game Preferences: an Evidence-Based Approach. In ECGBL2016-10th European Conference on Games Based Learning: ECGBL2016, (p. 565).

Sajjadi, P., Vlieghe, J., & Troyer, O. De. (2017). Exploring the Relation between the Theory of Multiple Intelligences and Games For the Purpose of Player-Centred Game Design, 15(4), 320–334.

Starks, K. (2014). Cognitive behavioral game design: A unified model for designing serious games. *Frontiers in Psychology*, 5. PMID:24550858

KEY TERMS AND DEFINITIONS

Digital Game-Based Learning: The use of digital games for any purpose beyond pure entertainment.

Game Experience: What the players experience as a consequence of interacting with a game. These experiences are generally studied in light of metrics such as flow, immersion, competence, challenge, tension, and negative/positive affect.

Game Mechanic: Fundamental game constructs of different levels, enabling players to interact with the game.

Individualization: Opposed to the one-size-fits-all approach. Focuses on utilizing the differences between individualizes in relation to gaming/learning activities.

Multiple Intelligences: A theory that views humans' intelligence to be multi-dimensional and defined as abilities to solve problems or create products deemed valuable in one or more cultural settings.

Player-Centered Game Design: A paradigm in which the game is tailored at design time to suit one or more groups of players that can be clustered based on certain common characteristics.

Recommendation Tool: A software that provides recommendations/suggestions to the users based on a series of determinants (user actions).

Stealth Assessment: The process of measuring different characteristics/preferences of players in an indirect way through inference.

ENDNOTES

[1] Available at: https://dl.dropboxusercontent.com/u/27597047/Complete%20list%20of%20game%20mechanics.xlsx

[2] https://wise.vub.ac.be/dpl

Chapter 4
Understanding the Role of Digital Technology in Multiple Intelligence Education:
A Meta-Analysis

Kevin Greenberg
University of Utah, USA

Robert Z. Zheng
University of Utah, USA

Isabelle Maloy
University of Utah, USA

ABSTRACT

The theory of multiple intelligences has been embraced by the education and research communities worldwide. Substantial research has been conducted to understand multiple intelligences and learning. However, studies that examine how various types of technology affect across the board the different types of intelligences in learning is lacking. This chapter reviews the multiple intelligence (MI) theory and how emergent technologies can be used to support MI learning in education using a meta-analysis method. The results reveal that bodily-kinesthetic is most responsive to technology-based intervention compared to other types of intelligences and that immersive and visual images are effective in improving verbal linguistic and bodily-kinesthetic intelligences. Discussion of the findings are made along with their implications in educational practices. Suggestions for future research and practice are made in regard to multiple intelligence and emergent digital technology.

DOI: 10.4018/978-1-7998-0249-5.ch004

INTRODUCTION

Humans' abilities to obtain and apply knowledge and skills can be largely influenced by factors like intelligence that involve logic thinking, reasoning, elaboration, planning, problem solving, and so forth. Traditionally, intelligence is defined as a general capacity for knowledge conceptualization and application that can be measured by IQ (Intelligence Quotients) (Bas, 2016; Visser, Ashton, & Vernon, 2006). This traditional definition of intelligence is challenged with the publication of Howard Gardner's seminal book *Frames of mind: The theory of multiple intelligences* in 1983. Instead of defining intelligence in terms of mental tests or IQs (Binet & Simon, 1916; Boring, 1950), Gardner argues that intelligence should be examined in a larger social and cultural context. According to Gardner (1983), there are at least seven types of intelligences: verbal-linguistic, logical-mathematical, musical-rhythmic, bodily-kinesthetic, visual-spatial, interpersonal, and intrapersonal. Later, he suggested naturalistic and existential intelligences are worthy of being included (Gardner, 1999).

Gardner's pluralistic view changes the traditional perception on intelligence. It embraces the notion that intelligence should be treated as a full range, rather than a single, construct and that learners should be assessed based on their own strengths. In other words, the pluralistic view of intelligence capitalizes on individual differences and strengths when assessing learners' performance in academic learning (Bars, 2016; Wilson, 2018). For example, a learner who is talented in art may not necessarily hold up to the same standard as those defined in IQ test. That is, he or she may not perform as desirably as others in mathematics and reasoning problems which are the major foci in IQ test. However, he or she has the talent or intelligence that could make them stand out and potentially becomes a successful artist. It is evident that the learner's artistic talent or intelligence can never be fully recognized by the standards identified in traditional IQ tests. Researchers point out that negligence of learners' intelligences in areas other than verbal linguistics and logical mathematics could in fact lead to disservices to our students (Armstrong, 1994; Denig, 2004; Kezar, 2001).

Research on multiple intelligences has gone in multiple directions and can be roughly defined in the areas of learning styles, self-efficacy, instruction and pedagogy, motivation, achievements, and technology. While previous research has revealed significant findings with regard to their relations with multiple intelligences, the focus of the current chapter, due to space constraints, will center on the technological aspects by investigating how different types of digital technology (e.g., gaming, multimedia, graphics, animation, etc.) may influence the learners' development of multiple intelligences in learning. The goal of the current chapter is to reveal the roles of digital technology in multiple intelligence education. To achieve this goal, we employ a meta-analysis approach to analyze the relationship and interactions between digital technologies and multiple intelligences. The chapter is divided into two sections: literature review and meta-analysis. The literature review has two purposes: (1) providing an overview on research pertaining to multiple intelligence education in the context of educational technology, and (2) developing a theoretical framework for meta-analysis based on the view of current research in multiple intelligences and digital technology. The meta-analysis section also includes two sub-sections: (1) methodological approaches (e.g., data sources, search criteria, data coding scheme, etc.) and (2) presentation of the results. The chapter ends with a discussion on the findings and recommendations for future research and practices. By reading the chapter, the readers will learn:

1. The relations between multiple intelligences and digital technologies,
2. The status of digital technologies in support of variety of intelligences,

3. The impact of digital technology on the development of multiple intelligences in schools,
4. The best practices in applying digital technologies to facilitating learners' multiple intelligences in learning.

LITERATURE REVIEW

Digital technology has increasingly found its presence in schools, corporation training and other professional training settings. The role of digital technologies in support of learning has been well documented (Mariano, Doolittle, & Hicks, 2009; Mayer, 2001; Zheng, 2018; Zheng & Truong, 2017). Studies have shown that digital technology supports learners' deep learning (Hacker & Niederhauser, 2000; Havard, 2018), self-regulation and motivation (Dabbagh & Kitsantas, 2018; Kitsantas, 2011; Nguyen & Ikeda, 2015), critical and creative thinking (Clark, Sampson, Weinberger, & Erkens, 2007), visualization (Scheiter, Wiebe, & Holsanova, 2009), and social communication skills (Ang et al., 2017; Zheng, Burrow-Sanchez, & Drew, 2010). The study by Havard (2018) indicates that the structure and techniques of web-based technology like Learning Management System (LMS) support learners' cognitive and metacogntive learning by scaffolding and promoting their deep thinking in learning. Dabbagh and Kitsantas (2018) point out that immersive and social-networking technologies like Web 2.0 embrace multilayered and multipurpose approaches that are well poised to develop learners' self-regulated skills and motivation. Research has demonstrated the role of technologies in critical and creative thinking. For example, Cook and colleagues (2009) investigated the impact of multimedia on critical reasoning and thinking. They noticed leaners' performance improved with multimedia support. In addition to its role in supporting learners' cognitive and metacognitive processes, digital technology is deemed to be well suited for developing learners' social skills such as interpersonal relationship. Zheng and associates (2010) studied the relationship between digital technology and social communication. They argued that human need for relatedness (i.e., the urge for social connection) leads to gregarious efforts in forming interpersonal relationships and group membership. Technologies like social networking, blogs, and online discussion forums provide an ideal environment for nurturing online social skills and interpersonal relationship.

The above discussion on digital technology has revealed important roles of digital technology in promoting learners' cognitive, social and metacognitive skills and knowledge in learning. Some researchers further point out that the research on digital technology should be grounded in a theoretical framework that defines digital technology in ways that are compatible and complementary with the cognitive and social processes (Kozma, 1994; Reed, 2006; Reiser, 1994; Zheng, 2007). They urge researchers and practitioners to understand the dynamic relationship between the characteristics of digital technology and learning, as well as the reciprocal interaction between the learners' cognitive processes and the unique features of digital technology. Zheng (2007; 2008) called attention to the cognitive functionality of digital technology in learning, arguing that certain features of media can benefit particular cognitive processes in terms of information encoding and retrieval.

Cognitive Functionality of Digital Technology

In early eighties, Clark (1983) challenged the educational community to reexamine its research design and results, claiming that most media research was confounded, and there were no significant differences among various media. He further pointed out that the research should focus on method, aptitude, and task variables of instruction rather than media themselves. Kozma (1994) countered that certain media attributes facilitate certain types of learning outcomes for particular types of learners (also see Reiser, 1994). Salomon (1979) observed that "something *within* the mediated stimulus ... makes the presented information more comprehensible or better memorized by learners of particular characteristics" (p. 6). Based on the dual coding theory (Paivio, 1986), Mayer and associates (1997, 2001; Mayer & Sims, 1994; Moreno & Mayer, 1999) investigated learners' information processing in both multimedia and non-multimedia learning environments and concluded that appropriately designed multimedia can significantly improve learners' mental representation in spatial learning as measured by comprehension and knowledge transfer. Given the evidence of relationship between digital technology and cognitive processes, the following sections discuss the cognitive functionality of digital technology in learning.

The Role of Digital Technology in Schema Activation

Schema is an essential component of learning. Learning is a cumulative process, building on the past and to make future understanding possible, thus developing schemas can be critical in rendering the process of learning meaningful and effective (Zheng & Gardner, 2019). Zheng, Yang, Garcia, and McCadden (2008) studied the role of interactive multimedia in schema activation pertaining to science learning. Learners were provided with an example of a water turbine supported by interactive multimedia, with which they studied the water flow, pump, and the turbine driven by the water. The goal was to first familiarize learners with the water system, then to activate their knowledge about how water-driven turbine works, followed by applying the knowledge to similar concepts in target content, in this case, an electric circuit (Figure 1). Results showed that learners who studied with interactive multimedia per-

Figure 1. Interactive multimedia for schema-induced analogical reasoning (Zheng et al., 2008. Used with permission)

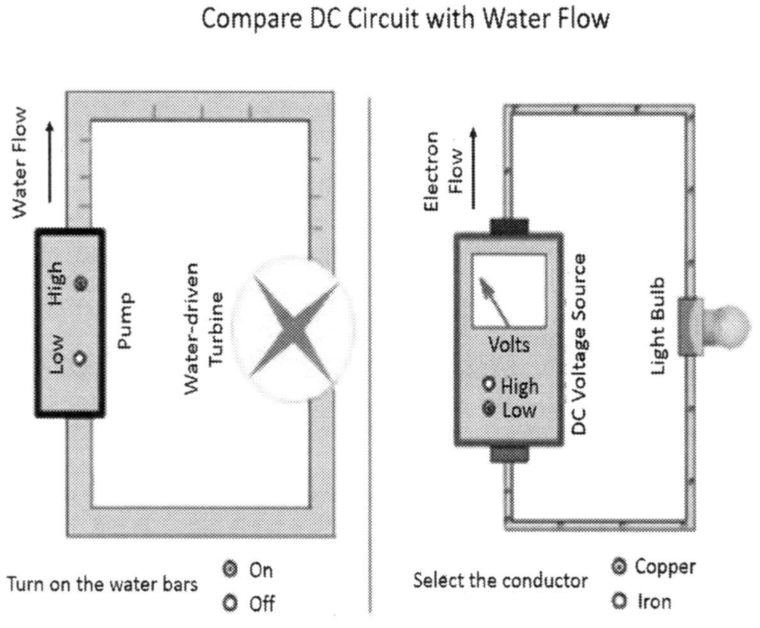

Understanding the Role of Digital Technology in Multiple Intelligence Education

formed better than those who studied without interactive multimedia. To revisit Clark's argument which states it was the instructional method that made learning happen, not the media, evidence from Zheng et al.'s study indicated that the instructional strategy like analogical reasoning would not be effective if the interactive multimedia were not used in the learning. Zheng et al. argued that it is possible that learners' understanding of the relationship between the resistance in the water and the power of pump would be compromised if it were not for the simulation they practiced. Consequently, they would not be able to transfer the knowledge of water system to the similar concepts in the electric circuit system.

The Role of Digital Technology in Spatial and Visual Learning

Learner's spatial and visual abilities are important for learning subjects that require spatial and visual processing such as geometry, physics, chemistry, biology, and so forth. It can be cognitively challenging for learners to solve a geometry problem without some kind of visual support. Consider the example in Figure 2. If the problem is presented with text only like the left side of Figure 2 or verbally presented without the diagram on the right, the learner will be confused, trying to figure out what lines are and what angles are, at the same time trying to visualize the figure and lines. If, however, the problem is presented with both text and diagram like Figure 2, the learner will have an easy time understanding the problem and its requirements. Evidently, adding visuals to content that requires visual and spatial processing can be beneficial to leaners. Visual media like diagrams facilitate cognitive visualization process by relating the text to the visual representation. The current example clearly demonstrates the cognitive function of digital technology in learning.

The Role of Digital Technology in Social Learning

The theory of social learning is one of the most important contributions to the field of psychology in the 20th century (Bahn, 2001). Social learning theory builds on the concepts that people learn through observing others' behavior, attitudes, and outcomes of those behaviors, and that human learning is a process of reciprocal interaction with others through cognitive, behavioral, and environmental influences (Bandura, 1977; Bandura & Walters, 1963). The notion that people learn from one another, via observation, imitation, and modeling (Bandura, 1977) has been shared by the distributed cognition theory

Figure 2. Graphics for visual and spatial learning

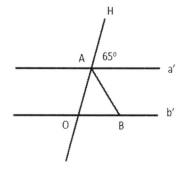

Instruction:

- a' and b' are two parallel lines intercepted by line H.
- Line AB goes from the intercept point of line H and line a' to the line b' to form a triangle AOB.
- Angle HAa' is 65°
- Angle a'AO is evenly divided by line AB
- Find the angle ABO

69

which posits human learning is a shared process in which cognitive resources are distributed among the members of social community in order to accomplish something that an individual learner may not be able to achieve alone (Hutchins, 1995). Within a social learning environment like collaborative learning, the cognitive process is off-loaded onto the group, that is, the cognition is distributed and processed collaboratively among the members of the group and the environment over space and time (Hutchins, 1995; Vasciliou, Loannou, Stylianou-Georgiou, & Zaphiris, 2017).

Several instructional strategies emerged in response to the research in social learning and distributed cognition. Among them are collaborative learning (Dillenbourg, 1999) and cooperative learning (Johnson & Johnson, 1989). The terms *collaborative learning* and *cooperative learning* are sometimes used interchangeably in many educational occasions. Some point out that they are actually different in regard to the strategies and implementation in education. Collaborative learning refers to situations where two or more people learn or work together to accomplish a task. It capitalizes on one another's resources and skills and is based on the notion that knowledge can be created with a social group where members actively interact with each other by sharing experiences and taking on asymmetric roles. Within the collaborative environment, the members of learning community depend on and are accountable to each other. Cooperative learning, while sharing many characteristics of collaborative learning such as structuring positive interdependence and accountability, focusing on positive goals in which learners learn how to (a) work cooperatively with others, (b) compete for fun and enjoyment, and (c) work autonomously on their own. Within cooperative situations, learners seek outcomes that are beneficial to themselves and beneficial to all other group members. In cooperative learning, student efforts are evaluated on a criteria-referenced basis as opposed to norm-referenced basis in competitive learning (Johnson & Johnson, 2009).

Collaborative and cooperative learning strategies are well accepted by the educational community to promote social learning and socially distributed cognition (Ghufron & Ermawati, 2018; Vogel et al., 2016). However, traditional practice in collaborative and cooperative learning approaches have shown some limitations. First, it is limited by space and time. Learner interaction is mostly limited to local, rather at a global, level. Next, there is a limitation in knowledge sharing and distribution, that is, learners' abilities to gain multiple perspectives on issues and problems are constrained by the geographical locations in traditional practice, primarily within classrooms and schools only. As such, the traditional practice has rendered the collaborative learning less effective as learners are not able to interact fully with larger learning communities beyond their physical boundaries.

The advancement of digital technology, especially Web 2.0 technologies like blogs and social media, has significantly improved the effectiveness of collaborative and cooperative learning with multiple benefits for cognitive health and social learning. With new digital technology like social media (Instagram, Facebook, Twitter, etc.), learners are able to access larger communities via online discussion forums and blogs. Knowledge construction becomes a dynamic process distributed and contributed at a global level. Studies have already demonstrated the benefits of digital technology on social and collaborative learning. For example, Raspopovic, Cvetanovic, Medan, and Ljubojevic (2017) studied the effect of social learning environment (SLE) which is a conglomerate of different media (e.g., LMS, blogs, Facebook, etc.) on learners' cognitive and affective performances in collaborative learning. Results showed that learners were satisfied with the SLE system commenting SLE is "an effective tool for group collaboration" (p. 154). The researchers concluded that SLE served as a connecting interactive learning space for increasing the communication between students and the teacher, and motivated students for active learning through collaborative problem solving tasks. A study conducted by Mondahl and Razmerita,

L. (2014) also reveals that the social media-enhanced collaborative learning environment facilitates social learning and collaborative process. The authors find that the social media-collaborative learning environment enables learners to engage in constructivist thinking through multiple perspectives and fosters collaborative knowledge construction, sharing and building.

Summary

The cognitive functionality of digital technology has been well studied with palpable evidences showing both cognitive and affective benefits in learning (Zheng, 2008). Evidence from empirical research reveals that digital technology when designed appropriately, is effective in supporting learner cognitive processes such as building schematic knowledge and coordinating visual and spatial information for deep understanding (Mayer, 2001; Zheng et al., 2008). The new generation of digital technology like social media and online virtual reality platforms (e.g., Second Life), supports well social learning based strategies regarding collaborative and cooperative learning.

The identification of the cognitive functionality of digital technology in its support of cognitive and affective learning leads to a new query in research which is central to this chapter: Does the cognitive functionality of digital technology support the development of multiple intelligences? The next section discusses the relations between digital technology and the development of multiple intelligences with a proposed theoretical framework for the current study.

Relations Between Digital Technology and Multiple Intelligences

As discussed in the previous paragraphs, digital technology has proven to be effective in facilitating many cognitive abilities in learning including spatial-visual ability and interpersonal skills (Mayer & Sims, 1994; Raspopovic et al., 2017). It also plays a key role in supporting schema construction (Zheng et al., 2008). There is an overlap between the cognitive abilities discussed earlier and the constructs in MI theory. For example, the construct of visual-spatial ability mentioned in the previous paragraph is synonymous to the visual-spatial intelligence construct in MI theory. The theoretical alignment between cognitive abilities in general psychology and intelligences in MI theory thus leads to the next step of our discussion: Does digital technology support multiple intelligence development as it does for the cognitive abilities?

Digital Technology to Support Multiple Intelligences

Research evidence has shown the role of digital technology in MI development. Sajjadi, Vlieghe, and De Troyer (2017) studied intelligence-game factor and found significant correlations between the game factors and multiple intelligences. Sajjadi et al.'s finding was well supported by earlier studies where game was found to facilitate learners' multiple intelligences including verbal-linguistic, logical-mathematic, visual-spatial, and interpersonal (Lin & Chen, 2016; Nachimuthu & Vijayakumari, 2011; Smith, 2012; Stark, 2014).

Studies have demonstrated the connection between the features of digital technology and multiple intelligences. Stark (2014) noted that some of the MI elements are inherent to games such as visuals and sound. Sajjadi et al. (2017) further demonstrated the mapping relationship between game mechanics and different MI dimensions. While Stark's and Sajjadi et al.'s studies center primarily on the role of game in MI development, research suggests that other types of technology like visual images, multimedia, social media, immersive technology (e.g., simulation, games, augmented reality), and computer application have equal important roles in influencing multiple intelligences (Gracious & Shyla, 2012). Therefore the following discussion will frame around these types of technology to illuminate their roles in MI development.

Immersive technology. Immersive technology refers to techniques that provide a learning experience to simulate the real world. It includes emerging technologies like virtual reality (VR), augmented reality (AR), artificial intelligence (AI), and 3D printing. Research has demonstrated the benefits of immersive technology in supporting various types of intelligences that include verbal-linguistic, logical-mathematical, visual-spatial, bodily-kinesthetic, interpersonal, and so forth.

Smith (2012) studied immersive experience with game-based digital books for young readers. It was found that game-based digital books significantly improved learners' abilities in reading which is related to verbal-linguistic intelligence. Immersive technology is also found to support logical-mathematical intelligence. Bottino, Ferlino, Ott, and Tavella (2007) implemented computer games in classrooms to foster students' strategic and logical reasoning in mathematics. They noticed a significant improvement in students' mathematical thinking with computer games. Visual-spatial intelligence is associated with cognitive processes involving space and dimensions. Wallet et al. (2011) found that virtual reality facilitated visual-spatial related cognitive processes. They reported a spatial transfer effect with virtual reality technology where learners successfully performed wayfinding, sketch mapping, and scene classification.

The benefits of immersive technology are also reported in bodily-kinesthetic abilities. Soltani and associates (2017) studied the effects of exergame in training swimming athletes. By playing the exergame, athletes showed an improvement in muscular activation and endurance in swimming. Immersive technology is also found to benefit interpersonal skills. Longman, O'Conner, and Obst (2009) investigated interpersonal skills by immersing learners in a game-based environment. Learners were engaged in WarCraft which is a massively multiplayer online game (MMOG). Results showed that learners developed better interpersonal skills by playing WarCraft where they collaborated with and provided cognitive and affective support to each other during the game.

Multimedia. Multimedia is defined as a technology with multiple modes of presentation. It has interactive and non-interactive forms. In interactive multimedia, learners are able to manipulate the content object, control the pace of learning, and adjust the learning level based on their needs. In non-interactive multimedia, learners are simply exposed to various modes of presentation, primarily sound and visuals, and are usually not able to manipulate the content. It is believed that multimedia can enhance learners' cognitive abilities, especially their multiple intelligences in learning.

Research on verbal-linguistic ability and multimedia is well documented. In a meta-analysis on vocabulary learning with multimedia, Kuder (2017) reported that with multimedia learners "had significant higher scores on vocabulary probes and learned the words faster than when they were taught using the standard approach" (p. 162). Like its role in verbal-linguistic intelligence development, multimedia is found to support logical-mathematical related cognitive processes like size and scale calculation (Magna, 2014), along with spatial-visual development through an enhanced understanding, for example, in the structure of cellular molecule in biology (Munzer, Suefert, & Brunken, 2009).

Evidence from empirical research has shown the relation between multimedia and bodily-kinesthetic performance. Paek, Hoffman, and Black (2016) studied the effect of multimedia on perceptual factors relating to bodily-kinesthetic manipulation. They found bodily-kinesthetic manipulation in multimedia significantly intervened learners' understanding and outcomes. In addition, multimedia is also found to foster musical intelligence (Thibeault, 2011), interpersonal skills in promoting social collaboration (Acuna, Lopez-Aymes, & Acuna-Castillo, 2018), and intrapersonal skills in developing self-reflection (Cheng & Chau, 2009).

Visual images. Visual images include photos, pictures, graphics and other visually related instructional materials that support learners' cognitive process in content acquisition. Studies have shown that visual images provide necessary cognitive and affective support for multiple intelligences. For example, O'Neill (2011) identified the benefits of visual images in supporting reading comprehension. Russo (2016) found the picture story book useful for students exploring the concept of equivalence in mathematics. Gyselinck, Meneghetti, De Beni, and Pazzaglia (2009) discovered the unique role of pictures in visual-spatial related learning. Treadwell and Taylor (2017) used voice activated pictures to help students self-reflect on their PE activities – an awareness in bodily-kinesthetic intelligence. Finally, Ganz, Simpson, and Lund (2012) implemented a picture exchange system to facilitate social communication skills of autism learners. They found pictures played a key role in supporting social skills including developing empathy during communication (Also see Salay, 2018).

Social media. Social media encompass various online communication platforms including blogs, discussion forum, social networking, and so forth. Like other types of technology, social media provides a positive learning environment for fostering multiple intelligences.

Reinhardt (2019) conducted a review of research published between 2009 and mid-2018 on the effects of social media in language learning. The author found that social media like Facebook, Twitter, Instagram, etc. increased intercultural awareness and aided the development of language competency. Ferrer (2004) also examined social media and logical-mathematical competencies. It was found that social media, characterized by its multiple perspectives and interactions, provides the necessary support to learners' logical-mathematical thinking. Social media is also reported to benefit intrapersonal development (Annamalai & Jaganathan, 2017). Annamalai and Jaganathan studied the Facebook platform for reflective writing. They reported that when studying with social media, students were more engaged in self-reflection and self-correction in essay writing. Social media is generally considered to be an effective venue for nurturing and developing interpersonal relationship and skills (Leow & Neo, 2015; Snethen & Zook, 2016). Leow and Neo (2015) identified the benefits associated with social media like Web 2.0 by showing that social media supports many interpersonal skills including group processing, social interaction, and collaboration.

Computer application. The concept of computer application refers to all digital technologies other than the ones discussed above. The computer application may include e-Book apps, computer software and hardware, online resources, and so forth. Since computer application encompasses a wide range of technologies, the discussion of its role in multiple intelligence development will take the approach of focusing on individual technologies while still subsuming it under the umbrella concept of computer application.

Putman (2005) implemented a technology-based reading program to study learners' self-efficacy and competencies in reading. The researcher noticed the effect of point system in the computer-based reading program on learners' self-efficacy and value of reading, suggesting features of the computer-based reading program may influence learners' affective aspect which consequently influences their cognitive performance in reading. Hansen and associates (2012) examined the role of laptops in students' abstract reasoning (e.g., analogies and categories). Results showed that laptops were effective in fostering students' logical abstract thinking with students in the laptop group significantly outperformed those in the control group in terms of analogy and category reasoning. Urban (2017) discussed the use of digital pen to support learning in a visually oriented subject like chemistry. Learning gains were found with the digital pen group where students became more interested and engaged, being able "to customize the learning environment to their own unique learning style" (p. 1058). Like social media, computer applications have been used to support interpersonal skill development. Chorianopoulos and Lekakos (2008) investigated the social TV to understand its role in support of interpersonal social skill development. The authors point out that the synchronous and asynchronous features in interactive social TV bridge the distance between social circles of people, provide motivation for learning, and facilitate cognitive information process.

Summary

Similar to its role in supporting cognitive processes in learning (see the discussion in the section of *Cognitive functionality of digital technology*), digital technology has displayed its multi-functionality in fostering multiple intelligence development. Specifically, we examined the roles of immersive technology, multimedia, visual images, social media, and computer application by looking their support for six types of intelligences, namely, verbal-linguistic, logical-mathematic, visual-spatial, bodily-kinesthetic, intrapersonal, and interpersonal. We did not include naturalist intelligence in our review due to a lack of literature in the pertinent area.

Overall, the literature shows the relations between the types of digital technology and multiple intelligences. We found immersive technology supports verbal-linguistic, logical-mathematic, visual-spatial, bodily-kinesthetic, and interpersonal intelligences. Multimedia is found to support all six types of intelligences included in this chapter. Visual images support verbal-linguistic, logical-mathematic, visual-spatial, bodily-kinesthetic, and interpersonal. Social media is shown to support verbal-linguistic, logical-mathematic, intrapersonal and interpersonal, failing to yield literature to support visual-spatial, bodily-kinesthetic, and music. Finally, computer application is found to support verbal-linguistic, logical-mathematic, visual-spatial, bodily-kinesthetic, music and interpersonal.

Based on above discussion, we develop a framework describing the relationship between the types of digital technology and multiple intelligences (Figure 3). The framework serves as a theoretical basis for the meta-analysis presented in the next section.

RELATIONSHIP BETWEEN DIGITAL TECHNOLOGY AND MI: A META-ANALYSIS

While there is a plethora of research on digital technology and multiple intelligences, the reported outcomes however remain uneven across the studies with some showing large effect sizes and others reporting small effect sizes. As such, it is difficult to assess how and which technologies may have played key roles in impacting the development of multiple intelligences. To address the issue, a meta-analysis was performed on the use of digital technology and multiple intelligences. A meta-analysis is a well-founded research method for examining the relationship between types of technology and multiple intelligence performance by synthesizing the results across studies while allowing the groups of studies with similar nature to compare outcomes such as the use of digital images on verbal learning and mathematical reasoning. In the current study, we specifically examined the types of digital technology in the context of changes in multiple intelligence performance.

Figure 3. Framework of MI and digital technology analysis

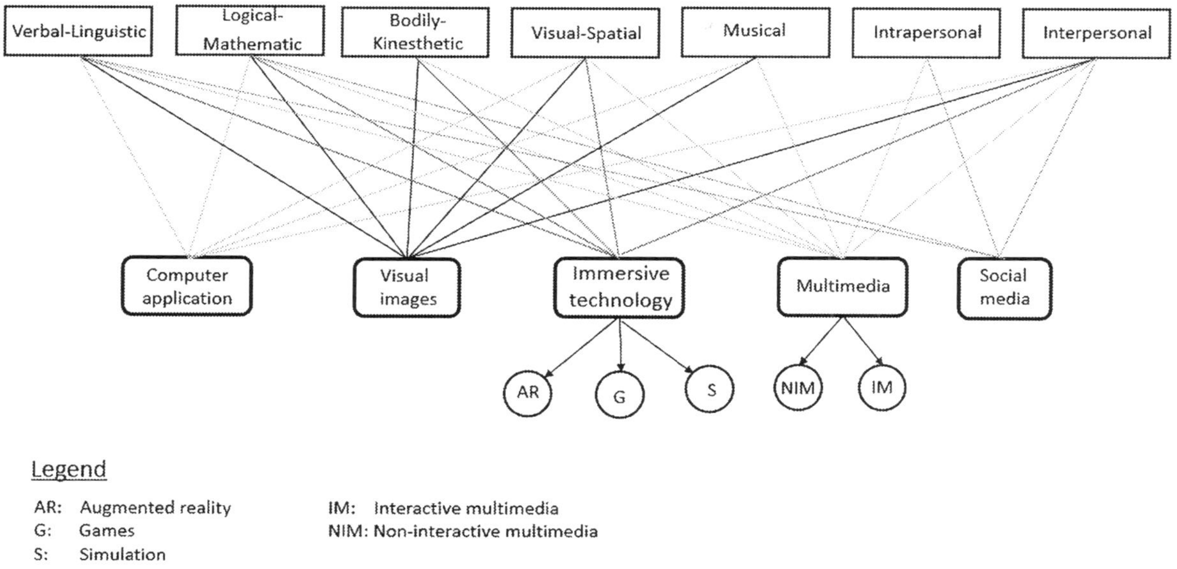

Legend
AR: Augmented reality
G: Games
S: Simulation
IM: Interactive multimedia
NIM: Non-interactive multimedia

METHOD

Selection of Studies

Six criteria were established to select the studies. Studies were include if they (a) reported on multiple intelligences and technology, (b) had a randomized experimental design, (c) were published in a peer-reviewed journal, (d) included mean and standard deviation, or relevant statistics (e.g., F-value) for calculating the Cohen's *d*, (e) contained two independent groups when reporting t-test results, and (f) were published between 1995 and 2019. The reason the 1995-2019 time period was chosen was that technology, such as computers, tablets, virtual reality, started to make its presence in education around mid-90s in last century.

To ensure that the articles selected met the criteria for meta-analysis, a set of exclusion criteria were also used. Studies were excluded if they (a) were conceptual, theoretical, descriptive, or non-experimental papers, (b) were unpublished dissertations, (c) contained insufficient data for effect size calculation such as reporting mean with standard deviation without sample size, (d) were experimental studies with only relational data, and (e) were experimental studies with paired group t-test results. The exclusion criteria helped assure the sample of studies contained the appropriate information for a meta-analysis study.

A search of ERIC, PsycArticles, PsycINFO, and Psychology and Behavioral Sciences Collection databases using the advanced search feature with two groups of search keywords yielded an initial result of 153 relevant publications published between 1995 and 2019. Table 1 reported the search databases and groups of search keywords. Using the inclusion and exclusion criteria, 96 studies were identified for final meta-analysis. A further examination of the studies revealed that the majority of the studies focus on verbal-linguistic, logical mathematical, bodily-kinesthetic, and visual-spatial intelligences. Due to the paucity of studies in other three types of intelligences (i.e., musical, interpersonal, intrapersonal

Table 1. Search keywords and databases

Description	Examples
Databases	ERIC, PsycArticles, PsycINFO, and Psychology and Behavioral Sciences Collection
Group 1 search keywords (multiple intelligences)	multiple intelligence, multiple intelligences, verbal learning, linguistic, mathematics, abstract thinking, logical, spatial, visual, social, interpersonal, intrapersonal, haptic, bodily-kinesthetic, musical-rhythmic, music.
Group 2 search keywords (technology)	digital technology, digital technology in education, learning technology, educational technology, instructional technology, technology, multimedia, gaming, educational gaming, virtual reality, animation, interactive multimedia, computer application.

intelligences), the current study included verbal-linguistic, logical-mathematics, bodily-kinesthetic, and visual-spatial intelligences in its final analysis.

Sample of Studies

Of 96 studies, some studies were considered influential cases as their effect sizes heavily moved the direction of the analysis. If an effect size confidence interval did not overlap with the overall confidence interval the effect size was considered an influential cases and removed from the data analysis (Viechtbauer & Cheung, 2010). The overall confidence interval ranged from 0.282 to 0.396, resulting in five effect sizes being classified as influential cases and being removed from the meta-analysis. In total there were 210 cases from 96 studies (Table 2).

Coding

Separate coding schemes were developed for multiple intelligence and digital technology. For multiple intelligences, keywords and phrases that were indicative of a particular type of intelligence were identified. For example, keywords like reading, writing, linguistics were used to code studies with verbal-linguistic intelligence. Table 3 shows the types of intelligences and their relevant keywords and phrases.

A similar coding scheme was developed for technology. Eleven types of technologies were initially identified which were then categorized into four types of technology based on their roles and functions. The categories of technology include computer application, multimedia, immersive technology, and visual images. Table 4 presents the coding scheme for digital technology.

Table 2. Frequency of cases for types of intelligences by technologies

Categories	Computer Application	Multimedia	Immersive	Visual Images	Total
Verbal-linguistics	11	28	9	8	56
Logical-mathematics	5	22	13	0	43
Body-Kinesthetic	1	14	22	10	47
Visual-spatial	12	15	37	3	67
Total	29	79	81	24	210

Table 3. Codes for intelligences

Verbal-Linguistics	Logical-Mathematics	Bodily-Kinesthetic	Visual-Spatial
1) Reading 2) Writing 3) Linguistics	1) Mathematic ability 2) Reasoning 3) Problem solving 4) Accuracy Score	1) Body manipulation 2) Physical activity 3) Physical reaction time 4) Physical movement accuracy	1) Spatial manipulation 2) Spatial ability 3) Spatial orientation 4) Visualization

Table 4. Codes for technologies

Computer Application	Multimedia	Immersive	Visual Images
1) Computers 2) Smartphones & tablets, etc.	1) Non-interactive multimedia 2) Interactive multimedia	1) Augmented reality 2) 3D technology 3) Gaming 4) Simulation 5) Artificial intelligences	1) Photos 2) Pictures 3) Graphics

Interrater Reliability

The interrater reliability for coding and data analysis was conducted by two researchers. A random sampling of twenty percent cases (*n*=42, out of total 210 cases), which came from 19 of the 96 studies, were selected for coding. After receiving training of the code book, both researchers independently coded the cases. The inter-rater reliability was analyzed using Cohen's Kappa, resulting in $\kappa = .757, p < .001$, suggesting substantial inter-rater reliability (McHugh, 2012).

DATA ANALYSES AND RESULTS

Publication Bias

Publication bias is one of the concerns in meta-analysis. Rothstein, Sutton, and Borenstein (2005) noted that studies with large effect sizes are more likely to be accepted and published. Thus, meta-analysis can be potentially affected by the file-draw problem or publication bias that may influence the generalizability of the results. One of the techniques in addressing the publication bias is to statistically graph the samples through a funnel plot. A symmetrical funnel plot indicates low publication bias.

The small-study effects method is also commonly used to analyze publication bias. This method by Borenstein, Hedges, Higgins, and Rothstein (2010) assumes studies with larger sample sizes are more likely to be published, studies with medium sample sizes are published with moderate effect sizes but with some studies missing, while studies with small sample sizes are most likely to be unpublished unless they have large effect sizes. The small-study method focuses on if studies with small samples sizes (e.g. studies with larger standard errors) and small effect sizes are missing. If publication bias exists, the funnel plot often appears to be asymmetrical, the trim and fill method will then indicate the number of studies that must be either added or removed to reduce publication bias.

With 210 cases a funnel plot was analyzed to determine if publication bias existed in sample studies. Following the assumptions of the small-study effects method, the results show the funnel plot is symmetrical (Figure 4) and the trim and fill method indicates no studies need to be added or removed, indicating there is not publication bias for the studies in the meta-analysis (Duval, & Tweedie, 2000).

Heterogeneity Tests

To ascertain that the variation was due to heterogeneity rather than chance, the heterogeneity tests were performed in meta-analysis. Cochran's Q, which is a weighted measure of the variation from the average effect size, is often performed. A significant Cochran's Q indicates the samples of studies are from the same population. Higgins and Thompson's I^2 is often used to analyze heterogeneity which provides a confidence interval of uncertainty and has an intuitive interpretation (i.e. percent of total variation due to heterogeneity rather than chance) (Higgins, Thompson, Deeks, & Altman, 2003). Borenstein et al. (2010) point out that when I^2 indicates either moderate or substantial heterogeneity (50% to 75%, respectively), a meta-analysis should examine moderators to analyze the dispersion of true effect sizes by means of a random-effects model.

Using a restricted maximum likelihood method, Cochran's Q was significant, $p < .001$. The weighted variation in effect size varied from the average, $\beta = .329$, with a 95% confidence interval of 0.276 to 0.382, indicating all the cases are measuring the same effect. The studies had moderate to substantial heterogeneity, with $I^2 = 63.96\%$ (95% $CI = 59.87\%, 75.95\%$) (Raudenbush & Bryk, 2002). As suggested by Borenstein et al. (2010) that when I^2 indicates either moderate or substantial heterogeneity (50% to 75%, respectively), a meta-analysis should examine moderators to analyze the dispersion of true effect sizes by means of a random-effects model. In the current analysis, the type of intelligence and the type of technology were used as moderators in random-effects models to determine what characteristics account for the true heterogeneity.

Figure 4. Funnel plot of standard error for the effect sizes of the studies

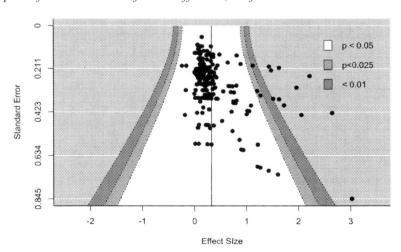

Random-Effects Model

In meta-analysis a random-effects model allows for effect sizes to vary in a normal distribution, meaning we do not assume all the factors (e.g., technologies) that influence the different types of intelligences are the same. The random-effects model is considered the more appropriate choice for meta-analysis (Fleiss & Gross, 1991; Field & Gillett, 2010), for it allows for random error within the studies and true error between studies, rather than limiting the studies to a single effect size (Borenstein et al., 2010). Based on the discussion above, a random-effects model with moderators were performed to analyze the cases.

Intelligence as Single Moderator

The analysis showed the random-effects model with intelligence as a moderator accounted for 9.00% of the variance as the single moderator model was significant, $X^2 (3, N = 210) = 9.60, p < .05$. Compared with other types of intelligences, body-kinesthetic intelligence had a significantly higher effect size, $\beta = .194, p < .05$, suggesting technology-based intervention has its largest impact on body-kinesthetic intelligence (Figure 5).

Technology as Single Moderator

The second single moderator random-effects model included the type of technology as the moderator. This model accounted for 10.91% of the variance, which was significant with the moderator, $X^2 (3, N = 210) = 12.30, p < .01$. The multimedia technology had a significantly smaller effect size, $\beta = -0.175, p < .05$, indicating multimedia technology may have the smallest effect on influencing different types of intelligences (Figure 6).

Figure 5. Effect sizes for the four types of intelligences

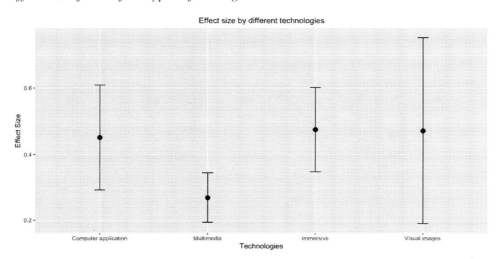

Figure 6. Effect sizes for the four types of technologies

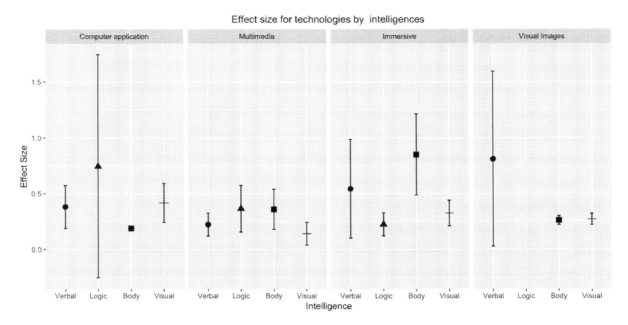

Two Moderator Variable Analysis

Given the results of above random-effects models with single moderators which account for significant true variance, exploring the potential relationship between two moderator variables aids our understanding in the effects of digital technology on multiple intelligences. Lipsey (2003) noted that ignoring this process can lead to inaccurate conclusions. Results showed that the moderators were significant, X^2 (6, $N = 210$) = 23.61, $p < .001$ within the random-effects model with the type of technology and type of intelligence as moderators. The random-effects model with both moderators accounted for 19.23% of the true variance. Comparing the types of intelligence, the results show body-kinesthetic intelligence studies had significantly larger effect sizes than other types of intelligences, $\beta = .166$, $p < .05$. In addition, multimedia technology had significantly smaller effect sizes than other types of technologies, $\beta = -.204$, $p < .01$. No interrelation between the type of intelligences and the type of technologies was found (Figure 7).

Based on the results of two moderate variable analysis, several post hoc analyses were conducted to examine how the different intelligences were influenced within technologies. In other words, does one type of technology have a larger effect on a specific intelligence, but not on others? The Scheffé Method was used for post hoc analysis as this method accounts for unequal sample sizes (see Tables 2 & 5). The post hoc analyses indicated that within the immersive technology studies, the bodily-kinesthetic intelligence had significantly larger effect sizes than the logical-mathematics intelligence ($p < .05$) and the visual-spatial intelligence $p < .01$). The post hoc analysis suggests that immersive technology may have the largest positive influence on bodily-kinesthetic intelligence. In addition, verbal-linguistics intelligence had a significantly larger effect size for visual images technology compared to multimedia

Figure 7. Effect sizes for the four types of intelligences by technologies

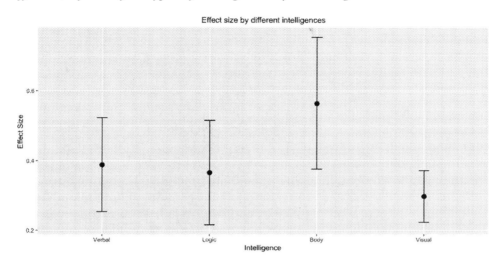

Table 5. Means, standard deviations, and standard errors of effect sizes by the moderators of technologies and types of intelligences

Type of Technology	Type of Intelligence	N	Effect Size	Standard Deviation	Standard Error
Computer application	Verbal-linguistics	11	0.380	0.287	0.087
	Logical-mathematics	5	0.744	0.804	0.359
	Bodily-kinesthetic	1	0.187	N/A	N/A
	Visual-spatial	12	0.416	0.276	0.080
Multimedia	Verbal-linguistics	28	0.221	0.266	0.050
	Logical-mathematics	22	0.363	0.472	0.101
	Bodily-kinesthetic	14	0.358	0.312	0.083
	Visual-spatial	15	0.140	0.183	0.047
Immersive	Verbal-linguistics	9	0.542	0.577	0.192
	Logical-mathematics	13	0.223	0.171	0.047
	Bodily-kinesthetic	22	0.850	0.820	0.175
	Visual-spatial	37	0.324	0.345	0.057
Visual Images	Verbal-linguistics	8	0.810	0.936	0.331
	Logical-mathematics	0	N/A	N/A	N/A
	Bodily-kinesthetic	10	0.261	0.056	0.018
	Visual-spatial	3	0.271	0.020	0.012

technology ($p < .05$). Also, the analysis on the types of technology and logical-mathematics revealed no significant difference for logical-mathematics intelligence by technology $F(2,37) = 2.383, p = .106$. Logical-mathematics intelligence with computer application is not significantly larger than multimedia and immersive technology ($p = .25$ & $p = .1064$, respectively).

DISCUSSION

The results of current study reveal that of four types of intelligences under study, bodily-kinesthetic appears to be most responsive to technology-based intervention since it has the largest effect size of all. The findings also show that of four types of technologies, multimedia appears to be least effective in promoting multiple intelligences given its small effect size among the technology-based interventions. There are several possible explanations to the above findings. First, since bodily-kinesthetic essentially involves multiple sensory processing (e.g., seeing, hearing, haptic, interaction), technologies that stimulate sensory processing like immersive technology can improve skill acquisition and application. Second, compared to bodily-kinesthetic, other types of intelligences seem to be less responsive to technology-based intervention which is counter-intuitive as visual-spatial, for example, is likely to benefit from visual images, multimedia, and other types of digital technology (Chen & Sun, 2012; Smith & Woody, 2000). The inconsistency between the finding of this study and the literature may be explained by the scale of the coding scheme of the intelligence, that is, the keywords and phrases under relevant intelligences may be expanded. Third, immersive technology is reported to have a larger effect on bodily-kinesthetic than on logical-mathematics. This findings are quite expected since immersive technology like virtual reality and augmented reality is pervasively used in bodily-kinesthetically related skill training whereas few immersive technologies have been found to support mathematic learning and training. Interestingly, it was found that none of the technology types (i.e., computer application, multimedia, immersive technologies) differed significantly on logical-mathematics intelligence, suggesting the development of logical-mathematics intelligence was equally influenced by technologies. Finally, visual images were found to have larger effect on verbal-linguistics intelligence than had multimedia. This finding is again in contrast to what the literature has found where studies reported ESL students, for example, have benefited from multimedia learning (Bava Harji & Gheitanchian, 2017; Shadiev, Hwang, & Liu, 2018).

In sum, the current study investigated the relationship between multiple intelligences and digital technology. The findings revealed digital technologies like immersive technology and visual images are found to support at various levels learners' abilities or their intelligences in learning. The current study revealed inconsistencies with the literature. For example, multimedia was found to be ineffective in supporting all types of intelligences. Visual images, compared to multimedia, were found to have a larger effect on verbal-linguistics intelligences, while four types of technology were found to equally influence logical-mathematics intelligence. Given the equivocal findings that pertain to types of technology and intelligences, more research is warranted to understand the functions and roles of various technology in multiple intelligence learning.

FUTURE RESEARCH

The current study investigated the relationship between types of technology and multiple intelligences. Several findings appear to be inconsistent with the literature, suggesting future research is needed to understand the level at which technology can be used to support multiple intelligences learning. For example, mathematics learning can be associated with spatial-visual related (e.g., geometry) and spatial-visual unrelated (algebra) content. With spatial-visual related content, visual technology like images, multimedia and 3D have shown to support learners' cognitive processing in mathematics (Milovanovic, Obradovic, & Milajic, 2013). It is suggested that future research for meta-analysis consider the match between variables such as visual- and non-visual content in mathematics and the role of technology. Future meta-analysis should be conducted to understand factors like pedagogy, other than technology, on learner multiple intelligences, as well as the interaction of pedagogy and technology on multiple intelligence development.

CONCLUSION

Since its first publication of *Frames of mind: The theory of multiple intelligences* (1983) by Howard Gardner, the theory of multiple intelligences has been accepted by the educational research and practice communities worldwide. It raises the awareness that learners are different and they are unique in their own way and that traditional perception about intelligence is a biased perspective that can hurt learners. Substantial research has been conducted to study multiple intelligences and learning, resulting findings that have enlightened our understanding of learning, learning behavior and outcomes. New digital technology in late 20th and early 21st centuries has advanced our knowledge about learners' cognitive, metacognitive and affective processes in learning which includes how technology benefits learners with multiple intelligences. Despite the research and practices in multiple intelligences with technology, there is a lack of understanding how various types of technology affect across the board the different types of intelligences in learning, hence the current study in response to the need in the research and practice fields.

The current study took a meta-analysis approach to understand the relationship between types of technology and multiple intelligences in learning. The initial search resulted 153 relevant publications, of which 96 were used in final analysis. Due to the paucity of publications in interpersonal, intrapersonal and music intelligences pertaining to technology use, the final dataset identified four types of intelligences for the analysis: verbal-linguistics, logical-mathematics, bodily-kinesthetic, and visual-spatial. In regard to technology, we initially identified 12 types of technologies. After a further examination of the nature, the role, and the function of the technologies identified, the technologies were categorized and subsumed under four categories: computer application, multimedia, immersive technology, and visual images. The study showed that among all the intelligences identified, bodily-kinesthetic intelligence was shown to be most responsive to technology-based intervention. In terms of the impact of technology on multiple intelligences, visual images and immersive technology were found to benefit verbal-linguistics and bodily-kinesthetic, respectively. Multimedia was found to have least impact on all types of intelligences. The findings are significant in that they inform the research and practice communities about (a) the types of intelligence and their responsiveness to technology, and (b) the role and function of types of technology in impacting types of intelligences. Nonetheless, some of the findings from the current study ran counter to what has been found in the literature. They accordingly warrant further investigation and verification. Future research in meta-analysis on multiple intelligences and technology should take a broader scope with more depth by including pedagogy, technology, human and social-cultural factors to better understand the relationship between multiple intelligences and related factors.

REFERENCES

Acuna, S. R., Lopez-Aymes, C., & Acuna-Castillo, S. T. (2018). How does the type of task influence the performance and social regulation of collaborative learning? *International Journal of Higher Education*, *7*(2), 28–29. doi:10.5430/ijhe.v7n2p28

Ang, R., Tan, J. L., Goh, D. H., Huan, V. S., Ooi, Y. P., Boon, J. S. T., & Fung, D. S. S. (2017). A game-based approach to teaching social problem-solving skills. In R. Zheng & M. Gardner (Eds.), *Serious game for educational applications* (pp. 168–195). Hershey, PA: IGI Publishing. doi:10.4018/978-1-5225-0513-6.ch008

Annamalai, N., & Jaganathan, P. (2017). Exploring students' reflective writing on Facebook. *The EUROCALL Review*, *25*(2), 3–17. doi:10.4995/eurocall.2017.7750

Armstrong, T. (1994). *Multiple intelligences in the classroom*. Alexandria, VA: Association for Supervision and Curriculum Development.

Bahn, D. (2001). Social learning theory: Its application in the context of nurse education. *Nurse Education Today*, *21*(2), 110–117. doi:10.1054/nedt.2000.0522 PMID:11170797

Bandura, A. (1977). *Social learning theory*. New York: General Learning Press.

Bandura, A., & Walters, R. (1963). *Social learning and personality development*. New York: Holt, Rinehart & Winston.

Bas, G. (2016). The effect of multiple intelligences theory-based education on academic achievement: A meta-analytic review. *Educational Sciences: Theory & Research*, *16*(6), 1833–1864.

Bava Harji, M., & Gheitanchian, M. (2017). Effects of multimedia task-based teaching and learning approach on EFL learners' accuracy, fluency and complexity of oral production. *Turkish Online Journal of Educational Technology*, *16*(2), 25–34.

Binet, A., & Simon, T. (1916). *The development of intelligence in children*. Baltimore, MD: Williams & Wilkins.

Borenstein, M., Hedges, L. V., Higgins, J. P., & Rothstein, H. R. (2010). A basic introduction to fixed-effect and random-effects models for meta-analysis. *Research Synthesis Methods*, *1*(2), 97–111. doi:10.1002/jrsm.12 PMID:26061376

Boring, E. G. (1950). *A history of experimental psychology*. New York, NY: Appleton-Century-Crofts.

Bottino, R. M., Ferlino, L., Ott, M., & Tavella, M. (2007). Developing strategies and reasoning abilities with computer games at primary school level. *Computers & Education*, *49*(4), 1272–1286. doi:10.1016/j.compedu.2006.02.003

Chen, C.-M., & Sun, Y.-C. (2012). Assessing the effects of different multimedia materials on emotions and learning performance for visual and verbal style learners. *Computers & Education*, *59*(4), 1273–1285. doi:10.1016/j.compedu.2012.05.006

Cheng, G., & Chau, J. (2009). Digital video for fostering self-reflection in an ePortfolio environment. *Learning, Media and Technology*, *34*(4), 337–350. doi:10.1080/17439880903338614

Chorianopoulos, K., & Lekakos, G. (2008). Introduction to social TV: Enhancing the shared experience with interactive TV. *International Journal of Human-Computer Interaction*, *24*(2), 113–120. doi:10.1080/10447310701821574

Clark, D. B., Sampson, V., Weinberger, A., & Erkens, G. (2007). Analytic frameworks for assessing dialogic argumentation in online learning environments. *Educational Psychology Review*, *19*(3), 343–374. doi:10.100710648-007-9050-7

Clark, R. (1983). Reconsidering research on learning from media. *Review of Educational Research*, *53*(4), 445–459. doi:10.3102/00346543053004445

Cook, A., Zheng, R., & Blaz, J. W. (2009). Measurement of cognitive load during multimedia learning activities. In R. Zheng (Ed.), *Cognitive effectives of multimedia learning* (pp. 34–50). Hershey, PA: Information Science Reference/IGI Global Publishing. doi:10.4018/978-1-60566-158-2.ch003

Dabbagh, N., & Kitsantas, A. (2018). Fostering self-regulated learning with digital technologies. In R. Zheng (Ed.), Strategies for deep learning with digital technology (pp. 51-69). New York, NY: Nova Science Publishers.

Denig, S. J. (2004). Multiple intelligences and learning styles: Two complementary dimensions. *Teachers College Record*, *106*(1), 96–111. doi:10.1111/j.1467-9620.2004.00322.x

Dillenbourg, P. (1999). *Collaborative learning: Cognitive and computational approaches*. New York, NY: Elsevier.

Duval, S., & Tweedie, R. (2000). Trim and fill: A simple funnel-plot–based method of testing and adjusting for publication bias in meta-analysis. *Biometrics*, *56*(2), 455–463. doi:10.1111/j.0006-341X.2000.00455.x PMID:10877304

Ferrer, L. M. (2004). Developing understanding and social skills through cooperative learning. *Journal of Science and Mathematics Education in Southeast Asia*, *27*(2), 45–61.

Field, A. P., & Gillett, R. (2010). How to do a meta-analysis. *British Journal of Mathematical & Statistical Psychology*, *63*(3), 665–694. doi:10.1348/000711010X502733 PMID:20497626

Fleiss, J. L., & Gross, A. J. (1991). Meta-analysis in epidemiology, with special reference to studies of the association between exposure to environmental tobacco smoke and lung cancer: A critique. *Journal of Clinical Epidemiology*, *44*(2), 127–139. doi:10.1016/0895-4356(91)90261-7 PMID:1995774

Ganz, J. B., Simpson, R. L., & Lund, E. M. (2012). The picture exchange communication system (PECS): A promising method for improving communication skills of learners with autism spectrum disorders. *Education and Training in Autism and Developmental Disabilities*, *47*(2), 176–186.

Gardner, H. (1983). *Frames of mind: The theory of multiple intelligences*. New York: Basic Books.

Gardner, H. (1999). *Intelligence Reframed. Multiple intelligences for the 21st century*. New York: Basic Books.

Ghufron, M. A., & Ermawati, S. (2018). The strengths and weaknesses of cooperative learning and problem-based learning in EFL writing class: Teachers' and students' perspectives. *International Journal of Instruction, 11*(4), 657–672. doi:10.12973/iji.2018.11441a

Gracious, F. L. A, & Shyla, F. L. J. A. (2012). Multiple intelligence and digital learning awareness of prospective B. Ed. teachers. *Turkish Online Journal of Distance Education, 3*.

Gyselinck, V., Meneghetti, G., De Beni, R., & Pazzaglia, F. (2009). The role of working memory in spatial text processing: What benefit of imagery strategy and visuospatial abilities? *Learning and Individual Differences, 19*(1), 12–20. doi:10.1016/j.lindif.2008.08.002

Hacker, D. J., & Niederhauser, D. S. (2000). Promoting deep and durable learning in the online classroom. *New Dimensions for Teaching and Learning, 84*(84), 53–63. doi:10.1002/tl.848

Hansen, N., Koudenburg, N., Hiersemann, R., Tellegen, P. J., Kocsev, M., & Postmes, T. (2012). Laptop usage affects abstract reasoning of children in the developing world. *Computers & Education, 59*(3), 989–1000. doi:10.1016/j.compedu.2012.04.013

Havard, B. (2018). Online discussion structure and instructor roles for the promotion of deep learning. In R. Zheng (Ed.), Strategies for deep learning with digital technology (pp. 71-89). New York, NY: Nova Science Publishers.

Higgins, J. P., Thompson, S. G., Deeks, J. J., & Altman, D. G. (2003). Measuring inconsistency in meta-analyses. *BMJ (Clinical Research Ed.), 327*(7414), 557–560. doi:10.1136/bmj.327.7414.557 PMID:12958120

Hutchins, E. (1995). *Cognition in the wild*. Cambridge, MA: MIT Press.

Johnson, D. W., & Johnson, R. (1989). *Cooperation and competition: Theory and research*. Edina, MN: Interaction Book Company.

Johnson, D. W., & Johnson, R. (2009). An educational psychology success story: Social interdependence theory and cooperative learning. *Educational Researcher, 38*(5), 365–379. doi:10.3102/0013189X09339057

Kezar, A. (2001). Theory of Multiple Intelligences: Implications for Higher Education. *Innovative Higher Education, 26*(2), 141–154. doi:10.1023/A:1012292522528

Kitsantas, A., & Dabbagh, N. (2011). The role of web 2.0 technologies in self-regulated learning. *New Directions for Teaching and Learning, 126*(126), 99–106. doi:10.1002/tl.448

Kozma, R. (1994). Will media influence learning? Reframing the debate. *Educational Technology Research and Development, 42*(2), 7–19. doi:10.1007/BF02299087

Kuder, J. S. (2017). Vocabulary instruction for secondary students with reading disabilities: An updated research review. *Learning Disability Quarterly, 40*(3), 155–164. doi:10.1177/0731948717690113

Leow, F. T., & Neo, M. (2015). Collaborative learning with Web 2.0 tools: Analyzing Malaysian students' perceptions and peer interaction. *Educational Media International, 52*(4), 308–327. doi:10.1080/09523987.2015.1100392

Lin, C.-H., & Chen, C.-M. (2016). Developing spatial visualization and mental rotation with a digital puzzle game at primary school level. *Computers in Human Behavior*, *57*, 23–30. doi:10.1016/j.chb.2015.12.026

Lipsey, M. W. (2003). Those confounded moderators in meta-analysis: Good, bad, and ugly. *The Annals of the American Academy of Political and Social Science*, *587*(1), 69–81. doi:10.1177/0002716202250791

Longman, H., O'Conner, E., & Obst, P. (2009). The effect of social support derived from World of Warcraft on negative psychological symptoms. *Cyberpsychology & Behavior*, *12*(5), 563–566. doi:10.1089/cpb.2009.0001 PMID:19817567

Magna, A. J. (2014). Learning strategies and multimedia techniques for scaffolding size and scale cognition. *Computers & Education*, *72*, 367–377. doi:10.1016/j.compedu.2013.11.012

Mariano, G. J., Doolittle, P., & Hicks, D. (2009). Fostering transfer in multimedia instructional materials. In R. Zheng (Ed.), *Cognitive effects of multimedia learning* (pp. 237–258). Hershey, PA: Information Science Reference/IGI Global. doi:10.4018/978-1-60566-158-2.ch013

Mayer, R. E. (1997). Multimedia learning: Are we asking the right questions? *Educational Psychologist*, *32*(1), 1–19. doi:10.120715326985ep3201_1

Mayer, R. E. (2001). *Multimedia learning*. Cambridge, UK: Cambridge University Press. doi:10.1017/CBO9781139164603

Mayer, R. E., & Sims, V. K. (1994). For whom is a picture worth a thousand words? Extensions of a dual-coding theory of multimedia learning. *Journal of Educational Psychology*, *86*(3), 389–401. doi:10.1037/0022-0663.86.3.389

Milovanovic, M., Obradovic, J., & Milajic, A. (2013). Application of interactive multimedia tools in teaching mathematics--examples of lessons from geometry. *Turkish Online Journal of Educational Technology*, *12*(1), 19–31.

Mondahl, M., & Razmerita, L. (2014). Social media, collaboration and social learning--A case-study of foreign language learning. *Electronic Journal of e-Learning*, *12*(4), 339-352.

Moreno, R., & Mayer, R. E. (1999). Cognitive principles of multimedia learning: The role of modality and contiguity. *Journal of Educational Psychology*, *91*(2), 358–368. doi:10.1037/0022-0663.91.2.358

Munzer, S., Suefert, T., & Brunken, R. (2009). Learning from multimedia presentations: Facilitation function of animations and spatial abilities. *Learning and Individual Differences*, *19*(4), 481–485. doi:10.1016/j.lindif.2009.05.001

Nachimuthu, K., & Vijayakumari, G. (2011). Role of educational games improves meaningful learning. *i-Manager's Journal of Educational Technology*, *8*(2).

Nguyen, L. T., & Ikeda, M. (2015). The effects of ePortfolio-based learning model on student self-regulated learning. *Active Learning in Higher Education*, *16*(3), 197–209. doi:10.1177/1469787415589532

O'Neill, K. E. (2011). Reading pictures: Developing visual literacy for greater comprehension. *The Reading Teacher*, *65*(3), 214–223. doi:10.1002/TRTR.01026

Paek, S., Hoffman, D. L., & Black, J. B. (2016). Perceptual factors and learning in digital environments. *Educational Technology Research and Development, 64*(3), 435–457. doi:10.100711423-016-9427-8

Paivio, A. (1986). *Mental representations: A dual coding approach.* Oxford, UK: Oxford University Press.

Putman, M. S. (2005). Computer-based reading technology in the classroom: The affective influence of performance contingent point accumulation on 4th grade students. *Reading Research and Instruction, 45*(1), 19–37. doi:10.1080/19388070509558440

Raspopovic, M., Cvetanovic, S., Medan, I., & Ljubojevic, D. (2017). The Effects of Integrating Social Learning Environment with Online Learning. *International Review of Research in Open and Distributed Learning, 18*(1), 141–160. doi:10.19173/irrodl.v18i1.2645

Raudenbush, S. W., & Bryk, A. S. (2002). *Hierarchical linear models: Applications and data analysis methods* (Vol. 1). Sage Publications, Inc.

Reed, S. K. (2006). Cognitive architectures for multimedia learning. *Educational Psychologist, 41*(2), 87–98. doi:10.120715326985ep4102_2

Reinhardt, J. (2019). Social Media in second and foreign language teaching and learning: Blogs, wikis, and social networking. *Language Teaching, 52*(1), 1–39. doi:10.1017/S0261444818000356

Reiser, R. (1994). Clark's invitation to the dance: An instructional designer's response. *Educational Technology Research and Development, 42*(2), 45–48. doi:10.1007/BF02299091

Rothstein, H. R., Sutton, A. J., & Borenstein, M. (2005). Publication bias in meta-analysis. In R. H. Rothestein, A. J. Sutton, & M. Borenstein (Eds.), Publication bias in meta-analysis (pp. 1-7). Hoboken, NJ: John Wiley & Sons Ltd.

Russo, J. (2016). Using picture story books to discover and explore the concept of equivalence. *Australian Primary Mathematics Classroom, 21*(2), 26–31.

Sajjadi, P., Vlieghe, J., & De Troyer, O. (2017). Exploring the relation between the theory of multiple intelligences and games for the purpose of play-centered game design. *The Electronic Journal of e-Learning, 15*(4), 320-334.

Salay, D. M. (2018). *Walk in their shoes: How picture books and critical literacy instruction can foster empathy in first grade students* (Unpublished Dissertation). Drexel University.

Salomon, G. (1979). *Interaction of media, cognition, and learning.* San Francisco: Jossey-Bass.

Scheiter, K., Wiebe, E., & Holsanova, J. (2009). Theoretical and instructional aspects of learning with visualizations. In R. Zheng (Ed.), Cognitive effects of multimedia learning (pp. 67-88). Hershey, PA: IGI Global. doi:10.4018/978-1-60566-158-2.ch005

Shadiev, R., Hwang, W.-Y., & Liu, T.-Y. (2018). Investigating the effectiveness of a learning activity supported by a mobile multimedia learning system to enhance autonomous EFL learning in authentic contexts. *Educational Technology Research and Development, 66*(4), 893–912. doi:10.100711423-018-9590-1

Smith, G. G. (2012). Compute game play as an imaginary stage for reading: Implicit spatial effects of computer games embedded in hard copy book. *Journal of Research in Reading, 35*(1), 1–19.

Smith, S. M., & Woody, P. C. (2000). Interactive effect of multimedia instruction and learning styles. *Teaching of Psychology, 27*(3), 220–223. doi:10.1207/S15328023TOP2703_10

Snethen, G., & Zook, P. (2016). Utilizing social media to support community integration. *American Journal of Psychiatric Rehabilitation, 19*(2), 160–174. doi:10.1080/15487768.2016.1171176

Soltani, P., Figueiredo, P., Fernandes, R. J., & Vilas-Boas, J. P. (2017). Muscle activation behavior in a swimming exergame: Differences by experience and gaming velocity. *Physiology & Behavior, 181*, 23–28. doi:10.1016/j.physbeh.2017.09.001 PMID:28882467

Stark, K. (2014). Cognitive behavior game design: A unified model for designing serious games. *Frontier in Psychology*. Retrieved on March 11, 2019 from https://www.frontiersin.org/articles/10.3389/fpsyg.2014.00028/full

Thibeault, M. D. (2011). Learning from looking at sound: Using multimedia spectrograms to explore world music. *General Music Today, 25*(1), 50–55. doi:10.1177/1048371311414050

Treadwell, S. M., & Taylor, N. (2017). PE in pictures: Using photovoice to promote middle school students' reflections on physical activity during free time. *Journal of Physical Education, Recreation & Dance, 88*(4), 26–33. doi:10.1080/07303084.2017.1280436

Urban, S. (2017). Pen-enabled, real-time student engagement for teaching in STEM subjects. *Journal of Chemical Education, 94*(8), 1051–1059. doi:10.1021/acs.jchemed.7b00127

Vasciliou, C., Loannou, A., Stylianou-Georgiou, A., & Zaphiris, P. (2017). A glance into social and evolutionary aspects of an artifact ecology for collaborative learning through the lens of distributed cognition. *International Journal of Human-Computer Interaction, 33*(8), 642–654. doi:10.1080/10447318.2016.1277638

Viechtbauer, W., & Cheung, M. W.-L. (2010). Outlier and influence diagnostics for meta-analysis. *Research Synthesis Methods, 1*(2), 112–125. doi:10.1002/jrsm.11 PMID:26061377

Visser, B. A., Ashton, M. C., & Vernon, P. A. (2006). Beyond g: Putting multiple intelligences theory to the test. *Intelligence, 34*(5), 487–501. doi:10.1016/j.intell.2006.02.004

Vogel, F., Kollar, I., Ufer, S., Reichersdorfer, E., Reiss, K., & Fischer, F. (2016). Developing argumentation skills in mathematics through computer-supported collaborative learning: The role of transactivity. *Instructional Science, 44*(5), 477–500. doi:10.100711251-016-9380-2

Wallet, G., Sauzeon, H., Pala, P. A., Larrue, F., Zheng, X., & N'Kaoua, B. (2011). Virtual/real transfer of spatial knowledge: Benefit from visual fidelity provided in a virtual environment and impact of active navigation. *Cyberpsychology, Behavior, and Social Networking, 14*(7-8), 417–423. doi:10.1089/cyber.2009.0187 PMID:21288136

Wilson, S. D. (2018). Implementing co-creation and multiple intelligence practices to transform the classroom experience. *Contemporary Issues in Education Research, 11*(4), 127–132. doi:10.19030/cier.v11i4.10206

Zheng, R. (2007). Cognitive functionality of multimedia in problem solving. In T. Kidd & H. Song (Eds.), *Handbook of Research on Instructional Systems and Technology* (pp. 230–246). Hershey, PA: Information Science Reference/IGI Global Publishing. doi:10.4018/978-1-59904-865-9.ch017

Zheng, R. (Ed.). (2008). *Cognitive effectives of multimedia learning*. Hershey, PA: Information Science Reference/IGI Global Publishing.

Zheng, R. (2018). Personalization with digital technology: A deep cognitive process perspective. In R. Zheng (Ed.), *Digital technologies and instructional design for personalized learning* (pp. 1–27). Hershey, PA: Information Science Reference/IGI Global Publishing. doi:10.4018/978-1-5225-3940-7.ch001

Zheng, R., Burrow-Sanchez, J., Donnelly, S., Call, M., & Drew, C. (2010). Toward an integrated conceptual framework of research in teen online communication. In R. Zheng, J. Burrow-Sanchez, & C. Drew (Eds.), *Adolescent Online Social Communication and Behavior: Relationship Formation on the Internet* (pp. 1–13). Hershey, PA: Information Science Reference/IGI Global Publishing. doi:10.4018/978-1-60566-926-7.ch001

Zheng, R., Burrow-Sanchez, J., & Drew, C. (Eds.). (2010). *Adolescent online social communication and behavior: Relationship formation on the Internet*. Hershey, PA: Information Science Reference/IGI Global Publishing. doi:10.4018/978-1-60566-926-7

Zheng, R., & Gardner, M. (2019). *Memory in education*. New York, NY: Routledge.

Zheng, R., & Truong, T. N. (2017). A framework for promoting knowledge transfer in SNS game-based learning. In R. Zheng & M. Gardner (Eds.), *Serious game for educational applications* (pp. 66–91). Hershey, PA: IGI Publishing. doi:10.4018/978-1-5225-0513-6.ch004

Zheng, R., Yang, W., Garcia, D., & McCadden, B. P. (2008). Effects of multimedia on schema induced analogical reasoning in science learning. *Journal of Computer Assisted Learning*, *24*(6), 474–482. doi:10.1111/j.1365-2729.2008.00282.x

ADDITIONAL READING

Armstrong, T. (2009). *Multiple intelligences in the classroom* (3rd ed.). Alexandria, VA: ASCD.

Baker, J., Parks-Savage, A., & Rehfuss, M. (2009). Teaching social skills in a virtual environment: An exploratory study. *Journal for Specialists in Group Work*, *34*(3), 209–226. doi:10.1080/01933920903039195

Bas, G. (2016). The effects of multiple intelligences theory-based education on academic achievement: A meta-analytic review. *Educational Sciences: Theory and Practice*, *16*(6), 1833–1864. doi:10.12738/estp.2016.6.0015

Chen, H.-R., Chiang, C.-H., & Lin, W.-S. (2013). Learning effects of interactive whiteboard pedagogy for students in Taiwan from the perspective of multiple intelligences. *Journal of Educational Computing Research*, *49*(2), 173–187. doi:10.2190/EC.49.2.c del Moral Pérez, M. E., Guzmán Duque, A. P., & Carlota Fernández, G. L. (2018). Game-based learning: Increasing the logical-mathematical, naturalistic, and linguistic learning levels of primary school students. *Journal of New Approaches in Educational Research, 7*(1), 31–39. doi:10.7821/naer.2018.1.248

Dinçer, S., & Doğanay, A. (2017). The effects of multiple-pedagogical agents on learners academic success, motivation, and cognitive load. *Computers & Education, 111*, 74–100. doi:10.1016/j.compedu.2017.04.005

Folkestad, J. E., & Anderson, S. K. (2009). Investigating the promise of mass-customized education: A content analysis self-reported descriptions of web 2.0-learning-tools based on multiple intelligence theory. *I-Manager's. Journal of Educational Psychology, 2*(3), 34–47.

Hajhashemi, K., Caltabiano, N., & Anderson, N. (2018). Multiple intelligences, motivations and learning experience regarding video-assisted subjects in a rural university. *International Journal of Instruction, 11*(1), 167–182. doi:10.12973/iji.2018.11112a

Perveen, A. (2018). Facilitating multiple intelligences through multimodal learning analytics. *Turkish Online Journal of Distance Education, 19*(1), 18–30. doi:10.17718/tojde.382655

Plass, J. L., Homer, B. D., Case, J., O'Keefe, P. A., & Hayward, E. O. (2013). The impact of individual, competitive, and collaborative mathematics game play on learning, performance, and motivation. *Journal of Educational Psychology, 105*(4), 1050–1066. doi:10.1037/a0032688

Sanchez-Martin, J., Alvarez-Gragera, G. J., Davila-Acedo, M. A., & Mellado, V. (2017). Teaching technology: From knowing to feeling enhancing emotional and content acquisition performance through Gardner's multiple intelligences theory in technology and design lessons. *Journal of Technology and Science Education, 7*(1), 58–79. doi:10.3926/jotse.238

Su, S.-C., & Liang, E. (2017). Action research of the multiple intelligence (MI), cooperative learning, and game-based teaching into summer intensive English classes for mixed-level and mixed-age students. *Universal Journal of Educational Research, 5*(11), 1977–1985. doi:10.13189/ujer.2017.051114

KEY TERMS AND DEFINITIONS

Bodily Kinesthetic Intelligence: This area of intelligence applies to an individual's ability for large gross body motion and fine skilled movement. It is commonly seen in athletics, dance, and craft-making.

Computer Application: This form of technology that aids in learning includes technologies such as computers (software and hardware), tablets, smartphones, e-Books, and online resources. Examples are laptops and e-readers.

Immersive Technology: Technology that is immersive refers to simulation, games, 3D printing augmented reality, such as virtual reality and artificial intelligence. A common example is a driving simulator.

Logical-Mathematic Intelligence: This form of intelligence is related to abilities such as logic, reasoning, (abstract, deductive, and inductive), numbers, problem-solving, and critical thinking. For instance, it is a form of intelligence used in solving the tower of Hanoi problem.

Multimedia: Multimedia refers to using more than one medium to concurrently present the content in teaching and learning. Examples of multimedia include a PowerPoint presentation that combines text, sound and/or motion video to deliver the content.

Verbal-Linguistic Intelligence: This intelligence is one's ability to generate and comprehend language in the forms of reading, writing, and spoken.

Visual Images: Visual images are a form of technology that include photos, pictures, graphics and other visually related instructional materials that aid in cognitive processing for learner's understanding.

Visual-Spatial Intelligence: This type of intelligence refers to one's spatial ability and judgement. It includes spatial manipulation and orientation, along with visualization. Wayfinding is an example.

Chapter 5
An Educational Data Mining Application by Using Multiple Intelligences

Esra Aksoy
Dokuz Eylül University, Turkey

Serkan Narli
https://orcid.org/0000-0001-8629-8722
Dokuz Eylül University, Turkey

Mehmet Akif Aksoy
Dokuz Eylül University, Turkey

ABSTRACT

The aim of this chapter is to illustrate both uses of data mining methods and the way of these methods can be applied in education by using students' multiple intelligences. Data mining is a data analysis methodology that has been successfully used in different areas including the educational domain. In this context, in this study, an application of EDM will be illustrated by using multiple intelligence and some other variables (e.g., learning styles and personality types). The decision tree model was implemented using students' learning styles, multiple intelligences, and personality types to identify gifted students. The sample size was 735 middle school students. The constructed decision tree model with 70% validity revealed that examination of mathematically gifted students using data mining techniques may be possible if specific characteristics are included.

INTRODUCTION

Data mining has been used in different areas such as Marketing, Banking, Insurance, Telecommunication, Health, Industry, Internet, Science and Engineering, and provided significant improvements in these areas. Recently, one of these areas is the educational environment. Educational data mining (EDM) literature has shown that it can represent new and significant contributions to educational research. Recently, various

DOI: 10.4018/978-1-7998-0249-5.ch005

data mining methods have been implemented to different educational environment such as traditional, e-learning, computer-based learning etc. In this context, this study aimed to illustrate both uses of data mining methods and to present a study that implemented data mining methods in traditional education. By using data mining techniques, Aksoy, Narli, and Aksoy (2018) aimed to examine mathematically gifted students in terms of their learning styles, multiple intelligences, personality types, genders and grade levels in order to help teachers and educators to determine potential gifted students. Educational data mining literature and a short review of the characteristics included in the study will be described in next sections.

THEORETICAL BACKGROUND

Educational Data Mining

Data mining can be defined as: applications of different algorithms, to identify patterns and relationships in a data set. It is similar to mining to obtain ore from the sand. That is, it can be considered that sand is data and ore is knowledge. Although it should be defined as knowledge mining, it is defined as 'data mining' to emphasize large amounts of data. "Data mining is an inductive, analytic, and exploratory approach, which is concerned with knowledge discovery through identification of patterns within large sets of data" (Angeli, Howard, Ma, Yang, & Kirschner, 2017, p. 226).

Data mining performs two functions: one is to identify regularities among data records (e.g., concept cluster, concept comparison, and discrimination), another to find relations among variables in the data that will predict unknown or future values of the variables. Unlike descriptive and inferential statistical analyses that rely on means and standard deviations, data mining uses both logical and mathematical (deterministic, and parametric and nonparametric statistical) reasoning to analyze data records (Liu & Ruiz, 2008).

As a result of the application of data mining techniques to educational data, the educational data mining (EDM) field has emerged. EDM is defined as "an emerging discipline, concerned with developing methods for exploring the unique types of data that come from educational settings, and using those methods to better understand students, and the settings in which they learn" by the International Educational Data Mining Society (2011, p. 601).

Data mining has attracted a great deal of attention in the information industry in recent years, due to the wide availability of huge amounts of data and the imminent need for turning such data into useful information and knowledge (Han & Kamber, 2006). The education sector also has huge amounts of data and needs such techniques. Therefore, many educators and scholars have begun to pay more attention to applying data mining techniques to educational data. Romero and Ventura (2007) summarized the role of data mining in the education sector as: "The application of knowledge extraction techniques to educational systems in order to improve learning can be viewed as a formative evaluation technique. Formative evaluation is the evaluation of an educational program while it is still in development, and for the purpose of continually improving the program. Data mining techniques can discover useful information that can be used in formative evaluation to assist educators establish a pedagogical basis for decisions when designing or modifying an environment or teaching approach."

An Educational Data Mining Application by Using Multiple Intelligences

Baker and Yacef (2009) described four objectives of EDM: (1) predicting students' characteristics of learning, (2) discovering or developing existing models, (3) investigating the effects of educational support, and (4) extracting knowledge concerning teaching and learning. Nithya, Umamaheswari, and Umadevi (2016) described some applications of DM in education sector such as predicting student performance, grouping students according to their characteristics, educational planning and scheduling, organizing syllabus, detecting cheating in online examination, identifying students profiling, and user modeling.

Data mining is a process that minimally has four stages (Nisbet, Elder & Miner, 2009): (1) data preparation that may involve data cleaning and data transformation, (2) initial preparation of the data, (3) model building or pattern identification, and (4) deployment, which means subjecting new data to the model to predict outcomes of cases found in the new data. Data mining techniques can be classified as below:

1. **Clustering:** A process of grouping physical or abstract objects into classes of similar objects (Romero &Ventura, 2007). Clustering is a type of analysis that divides data (cases or variables, depending on how specified) into groups such that members of each groups are as close as possible to each other, while different groups are as far apart from each other as possible (Nisbet et al, 2009).
2. **Classification and Regression:** In classification, the predicted variable is a binary or categorical variable. Some popular classification methods include decision trees, logistic regression and support vector machines. In regression, the predicted variable is a continuous variable. Some popular regression methods within educational data mining include linear regression, neural networks, and support vector machine regression. Classification techniques like decision trees and Bayesian networks can be used to predict the student's behaviour in an educational environment, his/her interest towards a subject or his outcome in the examination (Kumar & Vijayalakshmi, 2011). Classification techniques are predictive models. And predictive modelling compares the students behaviour with past similar students behaviours to predict what she will do in order to recommend how to proceed (Lee, 2007).
3. **Association Rules**: Associates one or more attributes of a dataset with another attribute, producing an if-then statement concerning attribute values (Romero & Ventura, 2007). Association rules are characteristic rules (it describes current situation), but classification rules are prediction rules for describing future situation (Tiwari, Singh & Vimal, 2013). This method can be used in various areas of education data to bring out the interesting rules about the learner's records. It can be used to bring out the hidden facts in understanding the behavior of the learner in a learning environment, learning style, examination pattern and assessment. Following issues and the suitable data mining techniques can be example for using data mining in education:
    a. Determining which factors have effect on misconceptions encountered in especially qualitative researches (classification techniques or association rules)
    b. Determining which misconceptions or mistakes occur together. (Association rules)
    c. Determining factors which are important to form compatible groups for collaborative learning (classification techniques or clustering)
    d. Determining factors that affect mathematical achievement (classification techniques)
    e. Predicting students' final performance at the beginning of the year and taking precautions (classification techniques)

f. To determine characteristics of special needs students (Clustering)
g. To investigate relationships among different theoretical perspectives used in education and to link them (association rules or classification techniques)
h. Finding out relationships in learners' behaviour patterns (Association rules)

There exist a great number of studies that applied these data mining methods to educational data. In order to highlight the data mining techniques applied in the educational data or to identify the main research trends at EDM, some papers performed literature review in EDM. Baker and Yacef (2009) discussed the trends in the EDM literature and illustrated the most influential papers in this context. The authors highlighted the increased emphasis on the prediction techniques in literature. Romero and Ventura (2010) performed a literature review that described a list of typical educational issues which use the EDM methods. Peña-Ayala (2014) reviewed EDM research with two goals; the first is to preserve and enhance the trends of recent EDM advances development; the second is to organize, analyze, and discuss the content of the review based on the outcomes gathered by a data mining techniques. Thus, as result of the selection and analysis of 240 EDM works, an EDM work profile was compiled. One of the key findings of this review was that most of the EDM papers focused on three kinds of educational systems (educational tasks, methods, and algorithms). Bakhshinategh, Zaiane, ElAtia, and Ipperciel (2018) conducted a review EDM research and illustrated the EDM applications with research examples related to each category of applications. the authors identified 13 kind of applications and grouped similar applications under three main categories based on their objectives, namely, student modeling, decision support systems and others. Rodrigues, Zárate, and Isotani (2018) performed a review of EDM research with the aim of identifying the perspectives and trends in EDM concerning e-learning domain. As a result of the review, the authors identified potential applications such as identifying patterns of student behavior during the learning process, investigating the cooperation between teacher and student during the educational activities, identifying the main factors that influence students, and identifying student's deficiencies during the learning process in order to improve student performance.

Students' performance prediction is one of the most popular application of EDM. Having been using data mining methods to investigate the performance of university students, Asif, Merceron, Ali, and Haider (2017) suggested that it is possible to provide timely warning for supporting low achieving students, and for advice and opportunities to high achieving students. Liu and Ruiz (2008) reported a study on using data mining to predict K–12 students' competence levels on test items related to energy. Data sources were the 1995 Third International Mathematics and Science Study (TIMSS), 1999 TIMSS-Repeat, 2003 TIMSS, and the National Assessment of Educational Progress (NAEP). Two data mining algorithms, C4.5 and M5, were used to construct a decision tree and a linear function to predict students' performance levels. A combination of factors related to content, context, and cognitive demand of items and students' grade levels were found to predict student population performances on test items.

Fernandes et al. (2019) conducted classification methods to predict students' academic performance. The authors collected the data containing variables obtained both prior to the start of the school year and two months after the beginning. They found that although *grades* and *absences* were the most relevant for predicting the end of the year academic outcomes of student performance, the analysis of demographic attributes reveals that neighborhood, school and age are also potential indicators of a student's academic success or failure. Costa, Fonseca, Santana, de Araújo, and Rego (2017) used four educational data mining techniques to early predict students likely to fail in courses and then evaluated the effectiveness of these four prediction techniques. They found that all of these techniques were successful to predict the students likely to fail, and the support vector machine technique outperforms the other ones in a statistically significant way. Burgos et al. (2018) used logistic regression models in order to predict whether a student will drop out of a course. Based on the obtained predictive models, the authors designed a tutoring action plan and reported reduces of the dropout rate after applying this plan. Narli, Özgen, and Alkan (2011) aimed to identify the relationship between individuals' multiple intelligences and learning styles using the rough sets. They identified potential learning styles that a student can have based on the learning style s/he already has, and constructed decision rules for multiple intelligences and learning styles. Núñez Cardenas, Camacho, Mariano and Redondo (2015) used clustering technique to bring together university students according to their multiple intelligences

The following studies demonstrate the constructive role of data mining techniques in gifted student research. Nokelainen, Tirri, and Merenti-Välimäki (2007) proposed a neural network model for identification of a gifted student. With a specially designed questionnaire, they measure implicit capabilities of giftedness and cluster the students with similar characteristics. They also applied data mining techniques to extract a type of giftedness and their characteristics. Data mining techniques such as clustering and classification is applied to extract the type of giftedness and their characteristics. The neural network was used to evaluate the similarity between characteristics of student and type of giftedness. They stated that in the future, they could refine their identification model using various data mining techniques and develop an intelligent learning guide system for "potential" gifted students. Gülen and Özdemir (2013) aimed to predict interest areas of gifted students and discover relationships between these areas by using educational data mining methods. By making use of the *a-priori* association algorithm, area pairs in which gifted students are frequently interested in are detected. They stated that results obtained from that study will provide many benefits to science and art centers, such as giving differentiated instruction by meeting individual needs and organizing course programs more effectively. Im, Kim, Bae, and Park (2005) examined the influence of attribution styles on the development of mathematical talent by using the data mining technique. The results of conducted Bayesian classification modelling show that items attributing success to effort and failure and to lack of effort are the best predictors for the level of mild mathematical giftedness and gender. Aksoy and Narlı (2015) aimed to examine mathematically gifted students' learning styles through data mining method. The construct decision tree was examined for predicting mathematically gifted students' learning styles according to their multiple intelligences and gender and grade level.

Learning Style

The term *learning style* has been used to describe an individual's natural, habitual, and preferred way of absorbing, processing, and retaining new information and skills (Oxford, 1998). Kolb (1984) defines learning style as a preferred way of gathering information, whereas for Dunn (1984), learning style is an individual way of absorbing and retaining information or skills. The growing interest in learning styles is in recognition of the fact that learners differ in ways that need to be taken into account when teachers make decisions about course content and teaching methodology (Wu & Alrabah, 2009). Identifying the learning styles of students facilitates their understanding of themselves and hence increases teaching performance. Focusing on different aspects, there are many kinds of models and theories which allow for determination of students' learning styles. In present study, due to widespread use, Kolb's learning style model was preferred. This model is based on experiential learning theory (ELT) which is based on theories of Dewey, Lewin and Piaget. Four learning style in this model can be summarized as follows (Kolb, 2005):

People with the diverging style are best at viewing concrete situations from many different points of view. (...) In formal learning situations, students with the diverging style prefer to work in groups, listening with an open mind to different points of view and receiving personalized feedback. (...) People with the assimilating style are best at understanding a wide range of information and putting it into concise, logical form. (...) In formal learning situations, students with this style prefer readings, lectures, exploring analytical models, and having time to think things through. (...) People with the converging style are best at finding practical uses for ideas and theories. (...) In formal learning situations, students with this style prefer to experiment with new ideas, simulations, laboratory assignments, and practical applications. (...) People with the accommodating style have the ability to learn from primarily "hands-on" experience. (...) In formal learning situations, students with the accommodating learning style prefer to work with others to get assignments done, to set goals, to do field work, and to test out different approaches to completing a project (p.5).

Multiple Intelligences

Gardner's theory of multiple intelligences (MI) has aroused more interest in the distinction of different human abilities than other theoretical framework (Chan, 2008, as cited in Hernández-Torrano et al., 2014). There is a growing awareness among teachers, however, that intelligence is a complex construct and that individuals have many kinds of abilities and strengths, not all of which can be measured by traditional IQ tests (Wu & Alrabah, 2009). Gardner's theory therefore provides a useful foundation for understanding individual differences (Gouws & Dicker, 2011).

Gardner has identified eight intelligences: verbal-linguistic, logical-mathematical, naturalistic, visual-spatial, musical, bodily-kinaesthetic, intrapersonal, and interpersonal (Gardner, 1993). Each person possesses all of these intelligences, but they typically differ in strength (Klein, 2003). These intelligences are briefly described below (Adapted from Gardner 1999; Gouws & Dicker, 2011; Wu & Alrabah, 2009, Chan, 2006):

Visual-spatial intelligence: the ability to perceive the visual-spatial world accurately and to perform transformations based on those perceptions. Musical intelligence: the ability to perceive and create pitch and rhythmic patterns, capacities such as the recognition of and use of rhythmic and tonal patterns and sensitivity to sounds from the environment, the human voice, and musical instruments, namely, the capacity to perceive, discriminate, transform, and express musical forms. Bodily-kinesthetic intelligence: fine motor movement, athletic prowess; the ability to use the body to express emotion, to play a game, and to create a new product. Interpersonal intelligence: the ability to work cooperatively with others in a small group, as well as the ability to communicate verbally and nonverbally with other people. Intrapersonal intelligence: self-knowledge and the ability to act adaptively on the basis of this knowledge. Verbal-linguistic intelligence: ability to use words effectively whether orally or in writing, and to use abstract reasoning, symbolic thinking and conceptual patterning. Naturalist intelligence: the ability to recognize patterns in nature and classify objects; the mastery of taxonomy; sensitivity to features of the natural world, and an understanding of different species. Mathematical-logical intelligence: the capacity to use numbers effectively and to reason well.

Personality Type

There are different approaches in the analysis of the personality. "One of them is Enneagram-a powerful and dynamic personality system that describes nine distinct and fundamentally different patterns of thinking, feeling and acting" (Daniels & Price, 2000; 2009). It is used for analyzing and comprehending the ego mechanisms (Palmer, 1991).

The word *Enneagram* derives from Greek words "ennea" (nine) and "grammos" (points) (Palmer, 1991). It is a circle enclosing nine points connected by nine intersecting lines. Enneagram advocates that there are nine fundamental personality types, and the Enneagram System of Personality was designed to assess the degree to which an individual resembles each of these types (Riso & Hudson, 1999). One of the potentially promising features of this typology is that it captures some of the changes in our personal characteristics when we are under stress. Each type is connected to another by an arrow. Under conditions of stress, an individual takes on some of the connected types with more negative characteristics. Conversely, in times of security or relaxation, an individual is inclined to take on positive characteristics of the type away from which the other arrow is pointing (Sutton, Allinson, & Williams, 2013). Key characteristics of these nine types have been highlighted below (adapted from Riso & Hudson, 1999; Sutten et al., 2013):

The Perfectionist (Type 1) is the principled, idealistic type, purposeful and self-controlled. They perceive the world as being judgmental and inclined towards punishing bad behavior and impulses. People of this type believe they can only gain love through being good, correcting error and meeting their own high internal standards. Their attention is directed towards identifying error. The Giver (Type 2) is the caring, interpersonal type, generous, demonstrative, people-pleasing, and possessive. They believe that in order to have their own needs met, they must give. This type tries to gain love and get their personal needs met by giving others what they need and expecting others to give in return. Attention is directed towards identifying the needs of others. The Achiever (Type 3) is the adaptable, success-oriented type, excelling, driven, and image-conscious. They perceive that the world only rewards people for what they do, rather than who they are. People of this type believe they can only gain love through success and portray this successful image to others and themselves. Attention naturally focuses on tasks and things to accomplish. The Romantic (Type 4) is the romantic, introspective type, expressive, dramatic, self-absorbed, and temperamental. They experience a world in which an idealized love is missing. They believe the real connection can be found in a unique, special love or situation and strive to make themselves as unique as possible. Attention is directed towards what is missing rather than what is present. The Observer (Type 5) is the intense, cerebral type, perceptive, innovative, secretive, and isolated. They experience a world which they consider to be too demanding and giving too little in return. They therefore come to believe they can gain protection from intrusion by learning self-sufficiency, limiting their own needs and gaining knowledge. Attention is given to detaching themselves from the world in order to observe it. The Loyal-sceptic (Type 6) is the committed, security-oriented type, engaging, responsible, anxious, and suspicious. They perceive the world as hazardous and unpredictable. To gain security and certainty, people of this type attempt to mitigate harm through vigilance and questioning. Attention is directed towards worst case scenarios. The Epicure (Type 7) is the busy, productive type, spontaneous, versatile, acquisitive, and scattered. They perceive the world as frustrating, limiting or painful. They believe that frustration and pain can be avoided and a good life can be assured by going into opportunities and adventures. Attention focuses on options and keeping life up. The Protector (Type 8) is the powerful, dominating type, self-confident, decisive, willful, and confrontational. They see the world as a hard and unjust place where the powerful take advantage of the weak. People of this type try to assure protection and gain respect by becoming strong and powerful and hiding their vulnerability. Attention goes towards injustices and to what needs control or assertiveness. The Mediator (Type 9) is the easy-going, self-effacing type, receptive, reassuring, complacent, and resigned. They perceive the world as considering them to be unimportant. They believe they can gain acceptance by attending to and merging with others, i.e. blending in with everyone else. Attention is directed towards others claims on them.

Purpose of the Study

This study aimed to illustrate both uses of data mining applications in EDM research and to present a study that implemented data mining methods in traditional education. The present paper can contribute both EDM researchers to illustrate an application with survey in traditional education, and educators to determine potential gifted students. Making this examination using different, useful and novel techniques is also one of the aims. So, unlike conventional methods, data mining techniques were applied to data collected from students. Compared to traditional statistical studies, data mining can (1) provide a more complete understanding of data by finding patterns previously not seen and (2) make models that predict, thus enabling people to make better decisions, take action, and therefore shape future events (Nisbet et al., 2009)

METHOD

Participants

The participants of this study consist of 501 (non-gifted) students from a rural and three urban middle schools and 234 mathematically gifted students from four different Sciences and Arts Centers in two different cities in Turkey by using convenience sampling and random selection. Sciences and Arts Training Centers serves for gifted students who could receive additional training in addition to their formal education. In order to be accepted into this center, students take tests which measure their gifted abilities. After removing incomplete or incorrect data, the last sample size is determined to be 735 students (353 female and 382 males). In areas where data mining is practiced, millions of data are usually used. However, it is difficult to reach these numbers when the survey is conducted in education. Besides the number of mathematically gifted students that can be reached is limited. Therefore, this sample size is deemed large for the survey studies in education. These 735 participants were in grades 5 to 8 and were aged 11 to 14. Distribution of the participants according to giftedness, grade and gender can be seen in Table 1.

An Educational Data Mining Application by Using Multiple Intelligences

Table 1. Demographic characteristic of gifted and non-gifted students

Mathematically Gifted or Non-Gifted		Grades				Total	
		5th	6th	7th	8th		
Mathematically non-gifted	Male	51	71	54	60	237	501
	Female	48	89	74	51	264	
Mathematically gifted	Male	43	54	34	15	145	234
	Female	37	29	16	7	89	
Total		179	243	178	135	735	

Instruments

All participants responded to a four-part questionnaire, including the 'Learning Style Inventory' (Kolb, 2005), 'Enneagram Personality Scale' (Daniels & Price, 2004), 'Multiple Intelligences Scale' (Selçuk, Kayılı & Okut, 2004), and a range of questions that elicited such demographic information as gender, age and grade level.

Learning Style: The Turkish version of Kolb's Learning Style Inventory (version 3.1) (Kolb, 2005), adapted by Gencel (2007), was used to assess individual learning styles. The twelve-point questionnaire had four choices for each prompt, which the student ranked by similarity to their learning style. Reliability has been proven, with Cronbach's alpha coefficients ranging from 0.73 to 0.81.

Personality Type: In determining the personality type of the students, the Enneagram Personality scale developed in the book (translated to Turkish) by Daniels and Price (2004) was used. The scale consists of nine paragraphs describing the features of each personality type. Students were asked to choose one of these paragraphs describing their personality best. For this scale, the authors reported high level of reliability using test-retest method (Kappa=0.589 p<0,0001).

Multiple Intelligences: Multiple Intelligences Scale (Selçuk et al., 2004) was used to assess students' MI. The Multiple Intelligence (MI) Inventory used in this study has 80 items. The instrument used a 5-point Likert-type scale ranging from 1 = strongly disagree to 5 = strongly agree. The items aim to measure students' multiple intelligence preferences. The inventory includes 10 items for each of the eight multiple intelligence fields, these fields are verbal/linguistic, logical/mathematical, visual/spatial, musical, bodily-kinesthetic, interpersonal, naturalistic, and intrapersonal. In this sample, Cronbach's α coefficients for the MI scores were .65, .78, .75, .73, .74, .84, .69 and .85, respectively.

Data Analysis

SPSS Clementine 10.1 was used to analyze collected data. Clementine is the SPSS enterprise-strength data mining workbench built by IBM. It has been used to build predictive models and conduct other analytic tasks. It has a visual interface which allows users to obtain statistical and data mining algorithms without programming. Its name has changed to the SPSS Modeller which is an extensive predictive analytics platform that is designed to bring predictive intelligence to decisions made by individuals, groups, systems and the enterprise. (IBM, n.d.). In present study, a data mining technique, decision tree, was implemented.

A decision tree is a flowchart-like tree structure, where each internal node (nonleaf node) denotes a test on an attribute. Each branch represents an outcome of the test, and each leaf node (or terminal node) holds a class label. The topmost node in a tree is the root node (Han & Kamber, 2006). During the construction of these trees, the data is split into smaller subsets iteratively. At each iteration, choosing the most suitable independent variable and branching the tree in terms of this variable is an important issue. Decision trees work by recursively partitioning the data based on input field values. The data partitions are called branches. The initial branch (sometimes called the root) encompasses all data records. The root is split into subsets, or child branches, based on the value of a particular input field. Each child branch can be further split into sub-branches, which can in turn be split again, and so on. At the lowest level of the tree are branches that have no more splits. Such branches are known as terminal branches (or leaves) (SPSS Clementine 10.1 Node Reference).

There are different types of algorithm that use different 'attribute selection measure' to construct decision tree (e.g. ID3 (Iterative Dichotomiser 3), CART (Classification and Regression Trees), C4.5, C5.0, CHAID (Chi-Squared Automatic Interaction Detector), QUEST (Quick, Unbiased, Efficient Statistical Tree) etc.). As for this study, C5.0 algorithm was used. C5.0 works by splitting the sample based on the field that provides the maximum information gain. It can also build both decision tree and rule set (SPSS Clementine 10.1 Node Reference).

RESULTS

The represented tree is so large that the image of tree is minimized. To interpret the decision tree, it was divided into two parts and these parts are enlarged to read easily. As it can be seen in Figure 1 and Figure 2, the parts are shown using decision tree map so you can understand which part of tree it is. In constructed decision tree, the target variable is mathematically giftedness. And independent variables are students' learning styles, dominant intelligences, personality types, genders and grade levels. Figure 1 shows the first part of the tree for mathematically giftedness, the top level is the root of tree containing all the records of sample (N=735) (Node 0).

Figure 1. Decision tree for examination of mathematically gifted students (left-hand side)

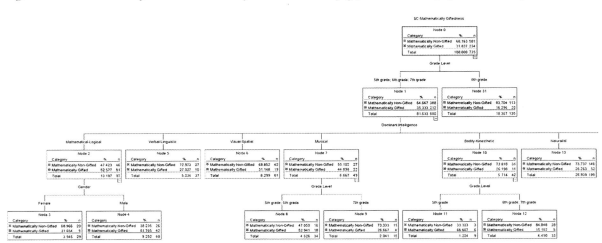

An Educational Data Mining Application by Using Multiple Intelligences

Figure 2. Decision tree for examination of mathematically gifted students (right-hand side)

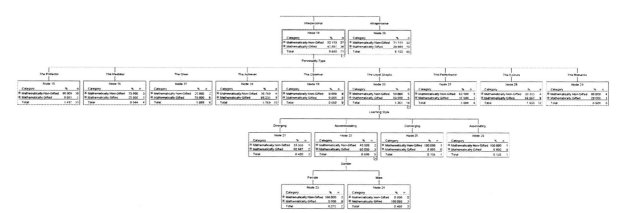

The first branch of the decision tree has been made with respect to grade level variable. The first branch of the decision tree shows the most influential variable in the formation of tree. Consequently, it can be said that grade level information should be examined first among a student's such data (gender, grade level, learning styles, multiple intelligences and personality type) to determine the probability of his/her mathematically giftedness. However, 5, 6, and 7th grade students were grouped together at first branch, and 8th grade students were classed separately. This situation can be due to the fact that 8th grade mathematically gifted student ratio (9.4%) is too low. Because of this reason, interpretation of the constructed tree will start with the nodes of dominant intelligences coming after grade level variable. It is likely to be said that the C5.0 tree indicated that all independent variables have some sort of effect on mathematically giftedness, but the most effective feature is found to be dominant intelligence.

The nodes which include students whose dominant intelligences are visual-spatial or verbal-linguistic (Node 5 and Node 6), did not divide into any child nodes and these nodes constructed terminal branches (leaves). At these nodes, 27 percent of the students with visual-spatial intelligence (Node 5) and 31.1 percent of the students with verbal-linguistic intelligence (Node 5) are mathematically gifted. Gender also seems to be tested at child nodes of Node 2 which contains the students whose dominant intelligence is logical-mathematical. As a result, it is likely to be said that 31 percent of girls and 61.7 percent of male students, in this node, are mathematically gifted.

The node which consists of students whose dominant intelligences are musical-rhythmic created terminal nodes after being tested with grade level variable. It can be said that 52.9 percent of these fifth or sixth grade students (Node 7) and 26.6 percent of these seventh-grade students (Node 9) are mathematically gifted. It can be seen that the personality type variable was tested in the next branch of the node with students whose dominant intelligences are interpersonal (Node 14). It means personality types of students with interpersonal intelligence have an effect on this decision. Child nodes of this node (Node 14) constructed terminal branches. Decision rules of these nodes are as follows:

- 9 percent of these students with protector personality type (Node 15),
- 25 percent of these students with mediator personality type (Node 16),
- 75 percent of these students with giver personality type (Node 17),
- 69.2 percent of these students with achiever personality type (Node 18) are mathematically gifted.

There is no student whose dominant intelligence is interpersonal and is observer (Node 19). Node 20, one of the child nodes of Node 14, contains loyal-sceptic students. And, this node is also separated into four by learning style input variable. That means if a student's dominant intelligence is interpersonal and he/she is a loyal-sceptic in Enneagram system then, learning style is a distinctive feature for him/her in terms of giftedness. As for child nodes of Node 20, Node 21 contains students with diverging style, Node 25 contains students with converging style and Node 26 contains students with assimilating style stopped branching and constructed terminal leaves. Percentages for mathematically giftedness of these nodes are 66 percent, 6 percent, 0 percent and 60 percent respectively.

The last division of the decision tree occurs in this level, Node 22. The terminal nodes Node 23 and Node 24 are generated by division with respect to gender of students. Students in Node 22 have accommodating learning style, and 60 percent of these students are mathematically gifted. Besides, all of male students in this node are also mathematically gifted. That is, in Node 24, male students whose dominant intelligences are interpersonal and who have loyal-sceptic personality types and who have accommodating learning style are mathematically gifted with 100 percent in this study (Node0, Node 14, Node 20, Node 22 and Node 24).

The knowledge represented by decision tree can be extracted and represented in the form of IF-THEN rules as shown in Table 2. Using C5.0, decision rules for mathematically giftedness are extracted. Thus, these rules can be searched to understand some characteristics of mathematically gifted students.

In the Table 2, the characteristics are written on the left side and the decision about the giftedness is on the right side. The first rule in the Table 2 was interpreted as follows, and the others can be interpreted similarly:

Table 2. Decision rules for mathematically gifted students

Rule	If;	Then,
1	Learning Style: Accommodating Dominant Intelligence: Interpersonal Personality Type: Loyal-sceptic (Type 6) Gender: Male	Mathematically gifted (with 83% probability)
2	Dominant Intelligence: Interpersonal Personality Type: Achiever (Type 3) Grade Level: 5., 6., 7.	Mathematically gifted (with 66% probability)
3	Dominant Intelligence: Interpersonal Personality Type: Epicure (Type 7) Grade Level: 5., 6., 7.	Mathematically gifted (with 64% probability)
4	Dominant Intelligence: Bodily-Kinesthetic Grade Level: 5.	Mathematically gifted (with 63% probability)
5	Dominant Intelligence: Mathematical-Logical Gender: Male Grade level: 5., 6., 7.	Mathematically gifted (with 61% probability)
6	Dominant Intelligence: Musical Grade Level: 5., 6.	Mathematically gifted (with 52% probability)
7	Dominant Intelligence: Mathematical-Logical Grade level: 5., 6., 7.	Mathematically gifted (with 52% probability)

- If a student is male, and his dominant intelligence is interpersonal, and his learning style is accommodating, and his personality type is loyal-sceptic, then he is mathematically gifted with eighty three percent probabilities.
- If a student is in 5th, 6th or 7th grade, and his dominant intelligence is interpersonal, and his personality type is achiever, then he is mathematically gifted with sixty six percent probabilities.

Evaluation of Created Decision Tree Model

To evaluate the created decision tree model for examination of mathematically gifted students, accuracy and validity of the model were examined. Accuracy of the model was found to be 73.33 percent. To determine validity of the model, cross-validation, which allows using all data, was used. A cross validation method is a preferred method when the amount of data is limited. Because mentioning large amounts of data in data mining applications, is relatively more difficult to reach in educational areas, this evaluation analysis was preferred.

Cross-Validation is a statistical method of evaluating and comparing learning algorithms by dividing data into two segments: one used to learn or train a model and the other used to validate the model (Refaeilzadeh, Tang, & Liu, 2009). After the validation rate of this model is calculated, the same process is repeated by changing the roles of testing and training sets. Consequently, the model's validation rate is calculated by the average value of two independent validation rates (Berthold & Hand, 2000). Results of cross validation analysis for the decision tree created in this study, were found to be 70.11 percent and 71.35 percent. Consequently, the average of these two ratios was determined to be 70.73 percent.

CONCLUSION

The application in this study was about investigating the characteristics that facilitate to recognize mathematically gifted students before formal identification stage. Thus, the error rate of teachers in the nomination process may be reduced. Although there are some specific characteristics that mathematically gifted students have, it should be investigated in terms of more general characteristics. After literature review, because of widespread use at both gifted education and non-gifted education we decided to use characteristics such as multiple intelligences, learning style and personality type. This result showed that if the specific characteristics are used, this method could become an effective tool that can be used in the process of identifying gifted students. And, examination of the relations between these features can also be provided. The results obtained from this study cannot be generalized but it can be mentioned that they are promising.

The knowledge represented by decision tree was extracted and represented in the form of IF-THEN rules. These rules can be used in education to understand some characteristics of mathematically giftedness. It should be accepted that these rules are not adequate to decide whether a student is mathematically gifted or not. But they are important to show its usefulness. Educators can develop these rules by increasing the sample size and using more attributes. Thus, the rules can be generalized and used in an educational environment. Teachers may use these rules to have an idea whether a student is mathematically gifted or not.

The created decision tree covers much information to be used for observing characteristic profiles of students. Constructed decision tree models with C5.0 algorithm revealed that all of variables used in this study have some sort of effect on the mathematically giftedness but the most affective attribute was found to be multiple intelligence. Analyzing the tree, factors effecting mathematically giftedness, can be listed respectively in decision tree as multiple intelligence, personality type, learning style and gender. The characteristics identified in this study should be searched for deeper understanding by experts. Because this study focused on using data mining techniques for the examination of gifted students, the results about these characteristics were not investigated.

The results of the survey can also be used to increase awareness of each group's strengths and abilities. Students can identify, analyze and use their strengths to succeed in their academic studies, to develop their social relationships, and to learn. It is thought that findings of this research will be able to give opinion to researchers, mathematics educators and parents, besides contributing to the literature. It would also help educators in selecting more appropriate learning opportunities for their students and to design teaching strategies and materials that accommodate their students' learning styles, multiple intelligences and personality types.

The decision tree model's validation rate is calculated as 70.73 percent. That means the possibility of being a gifted student, identified with the help of this model using the characteristics such as learning style, multiple intelligences, personality type, gender, and grade level, was calculated as 70.73 percent. This result is not enough but it can be discussed that it is promising for further research. By increasing the number and diversity of samples it is expected to reach more definitive conclusions.

LIMITATIONS AND FURTHER RESEARCH

This study certainly has many limitations. The sample size was an important limitation of this study. The number of the sample size may be quite acceptable for educational studies, but data mining is related to large amounts of data which includes millions in general. So, the results can be more generalized with increased amount of data. However, it is difficult to reach large amounts of data without using databases in educational studies.

Besides general characteristics, specific characteristics of mathematically gifted students should be used. Thus, this makes the study more comprehensive. So, this study is accepted as a step for this field by the authors. Another major limitation of this study was the complete reliance on self-report data on multiple intelligences, learning styles and personality types from students. Observations and interviews can contribute to better examination of students' characteristics. Future studies aim to test the structure of characteristics of gifted students obtaining these characteristics by multiple ways.

The algorithm which has the highest accuracy rate can be determined by establishing models with different decision tree algorithms and by comparing them. The model which has the highest accuracy rate can also be determined by establishing models with different classification techniques. Mathematically gifted students were selected for this study. Similar studies can be conducted selecting gifted students from other areas such as science or arts. A model created considering all these suggestions can be made into software and given to teachers. Teachers can examine the mentioned characteristics of students through this software and can have an idea whether that student may be mathematically gifted or not. Consequently, it is likely to be said the rate of false nomination could be reduced.

REFERENCES

Aksoy, E., & Narlı, S. (2015). An Examination of Mathematically Gifted Students' Learning Styles by Decision Trees. *Turkish Journal of Giftedness & Education*, 5(2).

Aksoy, E., Narli, S., & Aksoy, M. A. (2018). Examination of Mathematically Gifted Students Using Data Mining Techniques in Terms of Some Variables. *International Journal of Research in Education and Science*, 4(2), 471–485. doi:10.21890/ijres.428280

Angeli, C., Howard, S. K., Ma, J., Yang, J., & Kirschner, P. A. (2017). Data mining in educational technology classroom research: Can it make a contribution? *Computers & Education*, 113, 226–242. doi:10.1016/j.compedu.2017.05.021

Asif, R., Merceron, A., Ali, S. A., & Haider, N. G. (2017). Analyzing undergraduate students' performance using educational data mining. *Computers & Education*, 113, 177–194. doi:10.1016/j.compedu.2017.05.007

Baker, R. S., & Yacef, K. (2009). The state of educational data mining in 2009: A review and future visions. *Journal of Educational Data Mining*, 1(1), 3-17.

Bakhshinategh, B., Zaiane, O. R., ElAtia, S., & Ipperciel, D. (2018). Educational data mining applications and tasks: A survey of the last 10 years. *Education and Information Technologies*, 23(1), 537–553. doi:10.100710639-017-9616-z

Berthold, M., & Hand, D. I. (2000). Intelligent data analysis. *Technometrics*, 42(4), 442–442. doi:10.1080/00401706.2000.10485739

Burgos, C., Campanario, M. L., de la Pena, D., Lara, J. A., Lizcano, D., & Martínez, M. A. (2018). Data mining for modeling students' performance: A tutoring action plan to prevent academic dropout. *Computers & Electrical Engineering*, 66, 541–556. doi:10.1016/j.compeleceng.2017.03.005

Chan, D. W. (2006). Perceived multiple intelligences among male and female Chinese gifted students in Hong Kong: The structure of the student multiple intelligences profile. *Gifted Child Quarterly*, 50(4), 325–338. doi:10.1177/0016986206050000405

Chan, D. W. (2008). Giftedness of Chinese students in Hong Kong: Perspectives from different conceptions of intelligences. *Gifted Child Quarterly*, 52(1), 40–54. doi:10.1177/0016986207311058

Costa, E. B., Fonseca, B., Santana, M. A., de Araújo, F. F., & Rego, J. (2017). Evaluating the effectiveness of educational data mining techniques for early prediction of students' academic failure in introductory programming courses. *Computers in Human Behavior*, 73, 247–256. doi:10.1016/j.chb.2017.01.047

Daniels, D., & Price, V. (2000/2009). *The Essential Enneagram: The Definitive Personality Test and Self-Discovery Guide--Revised & Updated*. Harper Collins.

Daniels, D. & Price V. (2004). *Essential Enneagram the Definitive Personality Test and Self Discovery Guide* (S. Çiftçi, Trans.). İstanbul Kaknüs. (Original work published 2000)

Dunn, R. (1984). Learning style: State of the science. *Theory into Practice*, 23(1), 10–19. doi:10.1080/00405848409543084

Fernandes, E., Holanda, M., Victorino, M., Borges, V., Carvalho, R., & Van Erven, G. (2019). Educational data mining: Predictive analysis of academic performance of public school students in the capital of Brazil. *Journal of Business Research*, *94*, 335–343. doi:10.1016/j.jbusres.2018.02.012

Gardner, H. (1993). *Multiple intelligences: The theory in practice*. Basic books.

Gardner, H. (1999). *Intelligences reframed: Multiple intelligences for the 21st century*. New York: Basic Books.

Gencel, İ. E. (2007). Kolb'un Deneyimsel Öğrenme Kuramına Dayalı Öğrenme Stilleri Envanteri-III'ü Türkçeye Uyarlama Çalışması. *Dokuz Eylül Üniversitesi Sosyal Bilimler Enstitüsü Dergisi*, *9*(2), 120–139.

Gouws, E., & Dicker, A. M. (2011). Teaching mathematics that addresses learners' multiple intelligences. *Africa Education Review*, *8*(3), 568–587. doi:10.1080/18146627.2011.618721

Gülen, Ö., & Özdemir, S. (2013). Veri Madenciliği Teknikleri İle Üstün Yetenekli Öğrencilerin İlgi Alanlarının Analizi. *Journal of Gifted Education Research*, *1*(3), 215–226.

Han, J., & Kamber, M. (2006). *Data mining: concepts and techniques* (2nd ed.). Morgan Kaufmann.

Hernández-Torrano, D., Prieto, M. D., Ferrándiz, C., Bermejo, R., & Sáinz, M. (2013). Characteristics leading teachers to nominate secondary students as gifted in Spain. *Gifted Child Quarterly*, *57*(3), 181–196. doi:10.1177/0016986213490197

IBM. (n.d.). Retrieved from http://www-01.ibm.com/

Im, K. H., Kim, T. H., Bae, S., & Park, S. C. (2005). Conceptual modeling with neural network for giftedness identification and education. In *Advances in Natural Computation* (pp. 530–538). Springer Berlin Heidelberg. doi:10.1007/11539117_76

International Educational Data Mining Society. (2011). Available: http://www.educationaldatamining.org/

Klein, P. D. (2003). Rethinking the multiplicity of cognitive resources and curricular representations: Alternatives to 'learning styles' and 'multiple intelligences'. *Journal of Curriculum Studies*, *35*(1), 45–81. doi:10.1080/00220270210141891

Kolb, A. Y. (2005). *The Kolb Learning Style İnventory–Version 3.1 2005 Technical Specifications*. Boston, MA: Hay Resource Direct.

Kolb, D. A. (1984). *Experiential learning: Experience as the source of learning and development*. Prentice-Hall.

Kumar, S. A., & Vijayalakshmi, M. N. (2011, July). Efficiency of decision trees in predicting student's academic performance. *First International Conference On Computer Science*, Engineering And Applications, India.

Lee, C. S. (2007). Diagnostic, predictive and compositional modeling with data mining in integrated learning environments. *Computers & Education*, *49*(3), 562–580. doi:10.1016/j.compedu.2005.10.010

Liu, X., & Ruiz, M. E. (2008). Using data mining to predict K–12 students' performance on large-scale assessment items related to energy. *Journal of Research in Science Teaching*, *45*(5), 554–573. doi:10.1002/tea.20232

Narlı, S., Özgen, K., & Alkan, H. (2011). In the context of multiple intelligences theory, intelligent data analysis of learning styles was based on rough set theory. *Learning and Individual Differences*, *21*(5), 613–618. doi:10.1016/j.lindif.2011.07.012

Nisbet, R., Elder, J., & Miner, G. (2009). *Handbook of statistical analysis and data mining applications*. Academic Press.

Nithya, P., Umamaheswari, B., & Umadevi, A. (2016). A survey on educational data mining in field of education. *International Journal of Advanced Research in Computer Engineering & Technology*, *5*(1), 69–78.

Nokelainen, P., Tirri, K., & Merenti-Välimäki, H. L. (2007). Investigating the influence of attribution styles on the development of mathematical talent. *Gifted Child Quarterly*, *51*(1), 64–81. doi:10.1177/0016986206296659

Núñez Cardenas, F. D. J., Hernández Camacho, J., Mariano, T., Tomas, V., Redondo, F., & María, A. (2015). Application of Data Mining to describe Multiple Intelligences in University Students. *International Journal of Combinatorial Optimization Problems and Informatics*, *6*(1), 20–30.

Oxford, R. (1998). Style Analysis Survey (SAS): Assessing your own learning and working styles. In J. M. Reid (Ed.), *Understanding learning styles in the second language classroom* (pp. 179–186). Upper Saddle River, NJ: Prentice Hall Regents.

Palmer, H. (1991). *The Enneagram: Understanding yourself and the others in your life*. Harper San Francisco.

Peña-Ayala, A. (2014). Educational data mining: A survey and a data mining-based analysis of recent works. *Expert Systems with Applications*, *41*(4), 1432–1462. doi:10.1016/j.eswa.2013.08.042

Refaeilzadeh, P., Tang, L., & Liu, H. (2009). Cross-validation. In Encyclopedia of database systems (pp. 532-538). Springer US.

Riso, D. R., & Hudson, R. (1996). *Personality types: Using the Enneagram for self-discovery*. Houghton Mifflin Harcourt.

Riso, D. R., & Hudson, R. (1999). *The wisdom of the Enneagram: The complete guide to psychological and spiritual growth for the nine personality types*. New York: Bantam.

Rodrigues, M. W., Zárate, L. E., & Isotani, S. (2018). Educational Data Mining: A review of evaluation process in the e-learning. *Telematics and Informatics*, *35*(6), 1701–1717. doi:10.1016/j.tele.2018.04.015

Romero, C., & Ventura, S. (2007). Educational Data Mining: A Survey from 1995 to 2005. *Expert Systems with Applications*, *33*(1), 135–146. doi:10.1016/j.eswa.2006.04.005

Romero, C., & Ventura, S. (2010). Educational data mining: A review of the state of the art. *IEEE Transactions on Systems, Man and Cybernetics. Part C, Applications and Reviews, 40*(6), 601–618. doi:10.1109/TSMCC.2010.2053532

Selçuk, Z., Kayılı, H., & Okut, L. (2004). *Çoklu zeka uygulamaları*. Ankara: Nobel Yayın Dağıtım.

SPSS Inc. (2004). Clementine 10.1 Node Reference. Author.

Sutton, A., Allinson, C., & Williams, H. (2013). Personality type and work-related outcomes: An exploratory application of the Enneagram model. *European Management Journal, 31*(3), 234–249. doi:10.1016/j.emj.2012.12.004

Tiwari, M., Singh, R., & Vimal, N. (2013). An empirical study of application of dm techniques for predicting student performance. *International Journal of Computer Science and Mobile Computing IJCSMC, 2*(2), 53–57.

Wu, S. H., & Alrabah, S. (2009). A cross-cultural study of Taiwanese and Kuwaiti EFL students' learning styles and multiple intelligences. *Innovations in Education and Teaching International, 46*(4), 393–403. doi:10.1080/14703290903301826

ADDITIONAL READING

Allport, G. W. (1961). *Pattern and growth in personality*. New York: Holt, Rinehart and Winston.

Bilen, Ö., Hotaman, D., Aşkın, Ö. E., & Büyüklü, A. H. (2014). Analyzing the School Performances in terms of LYS Successes through using Educational Data Mining Techniques: İstanbul Sample, 2011. *Eğitim ve Bilim., 39*(172), 78–94.

Campagni, R., Merlini, D., Sprugnoli, R., & Verri, M. C. (2015). Data mining models for student careers. *Expert Systems with Applications, 42*(13), 5508–5521. doi:10.1016/j.eswa.2015.02.052

Narlı, S., Aksoy, E., & Ercire, Y. E. (2014). Investigation of Prospective Elementary Mathematics Teachers' Learning Styles and Relationships between Them Using Data Mining. *International Journal of Educational Studies in Mathematics, 1*(1), 37–57. doi:10.17278/ijesim.2014.01.004

Peña-Ayala, A. (Ed.). (2013). *Educational data mining: applications and trends* (Vol. 524). Springer.

Romero, C., Ventura, S., Pechenizkiy, M., & Baker, R. S. (Eds.). (2010). *Handbook of educational data mining*. CRC press. doi:10.1201/b10274

Slater, S., Joksimović, S., Kovanovic, V., Baker, R. S., & Gasevic, D. (2017). Tools for educational data mining: A review. *Journal of Educational and Behavioral Statistics, 42*(1), 85–106. doi:10.3102/1076998616666808

Xing, W., Guo, R., Petakovic, E., & Goggins, S. (2015). Participation-based student final performance prediction model through interpretable Genetic Programming: Integrating learning analytics, educational data mining and theory. *Computers in Human Behavior, 47*, 168–181. doi:10.1016/j.chb.2014.09.034

Section 2

Integrating Digital Technology in Multiple Intelligences–Based Teaching and Learning: Visual–Spatial Intelligence

Chapter 6
Creating Geospatial Thinkers

Larianne Collins
University of North Carolina at Charlotte, USA

ABSTRACT

In today's contemporary digital world, where geospatial technologies are an integral part of society, it is imperative that students learn to think spatially. The ability to think spatially is crucial for making well-informed decisions, and these skills are rapidly becoming exponentially more important. This chapter will explore the complexity of spatial thinking, and multiple spatial thinking skills will be identified. Methods best suited for delivering content that fosters the improvement of these spatial thinking skills will also be discussed. The chapter concludes with an exploration of some of the necessary elements required for the sustained use of geospatial technologies in the classroom and offers recommendations for transformation in teacher practice such as pre-service intervention, continuous follow-up and coaching, and curriculum modifications, which include the direct instruction of both spatial thinking and geospatial technologies.

INTRODUCTION

In today's contemporary, digital world where geospatial technologies are an integral part of society, it is imperative that students learn to think spatially. The ability to think spatially is crucial for making well-informed decisions and these skills are rapidly becoming exponentially more important. Having a population that is spatially literate and can reason geographically is critical for numerous workplace decisions in business, diplomatic relations, emergency preparedness, and intelligence to name a few. It is the concept of space that makes spatial thinking a distinctive form of thinking. It is a way of thinking that can be taught with multiple pathways to improvement. This chapter aims to situate spatial thinking as one type of universal intelligence that is used in everyday life as well as academic and workplace settings. The complexity of spatial thinking will be defined and multiple spatial thinking skills will be identified. The development of spatial knowledge and the direct teaching and learning of spatial thinking skills is severely underrepresented in the classroom. Methods best suited for delivering content that fosters the improvement of these spatial thinking skills will be discussed.

DOI: 10.4018/978-1-7998-0249-5.ch006

Creating Geospatial Thinkers

Over the past decade there have been a rapidly increasing number of digital technologies available, in large part a consequence of the substantial growth and accessibility of geospatial data, commonly referred to as the geospatial revolution. This chapter attempts to raise some important questions specifically about geospatial technologies, their use and effectiveness in the classroom, and the challenges that may arise with implementation of these technologies in education. Enhancing student learning opportunities in the digital age is partially dependent on the quality of teacher professional development. A variety of models have been proposed for successful professional development in utilizing geospatial technologies to improve spatial thinking. Yet, there remains a disconnect between providing teacher professional development and actually seeing long-term classroom implementation. The chapter concludes with an exploration of some of the necessary elements required for the sustained use of geospatial technologies in the classroom and offers recommendations for transformation in teacher practice such as pre-service intervention, continuous follow-up and coaching, and curriculum modifications which include the direct instruction of both spatial thinking and geospatial technologies.

LITERATURE REVIEW

A universal mode of cognitive processing used in everyday life, spatial thinking is a distinctive form of thinking centered around the concept of space. The body of knowledge around when and how spatial thinking develops is growing. This form of thinking reached a level of prominence with the publication from the National Research Committee (NRC) report, *Learning to Think Spatially* (2006). The NRC defines spatial thinking as the knowledge, skills, and habits of mind to use concepts of space (such as distance, orientation, distribution, and association), tools of representation (such as maps, graphs, and diagrams), and processes of reasoning (such as cognitive strategies to facilitate problem solving and decision making) to structure problems, find answers, and express solutions to these problems (2006). Put simply, spatial thinking is the ability to visualize space and solve problems spatially.

Challenging traditional beliefs about intelligence in the fields of both education and cognitive science at the time, Gardner (1983) developed the Theory of Multiple Intelligences by identifying eight distinctive intelligences or ways of thinking that provide insight on how students process and learn information. He originally identified spatial intelligence as one of these intelligences in which he defined as an object-based intelligence comprising the ability to visualize, rotate, transform and manipulate objects and their location in the world (1983). Typically, spatial intelligence is closely tied to the visual modality, however, Gardner explains that in much the same manner that the linguistic intelligence is not completely dependent on the auditory modality, spatial intelligence can be developed in both visually-impaired and sighted individuals (1983).

It is important to note that methods of spatial thinking are broadly applicable and are not restricted to information that is inherently spatial. The ability to spatialize information allows for the examination of patterns and trends that would otherwise not have been readily apparent from the raw data. For example, showing the number of malaria cases by country would certainly disclose that certain countries have higher amounts of malaria cases than other countries. However, when this data is spatially represented, it will show that the number of malaria cases is highest in countries located in the tropics. While spatial thinking is often linked to visual modes of representation, it also extends to other sensory systems including olfactory, tactile, and auditory. One example is the ability to know where to look for a bird after hearing its call if the bird is not visually apparent; another example is being able to identify change in location or land use by noting texture of the ground surface (e.g., pavement vs. brick vs. grass).

A number of spatial thinking skills or core concepts have been developed, but little consensus exists among scholars as to how these skills are separately distinguished from one another. The complexity of spatial thinking is evident in the differing in number and range of terminology utilized by the structures and hierarchies proposed by Gersmehl (2008); Golledge, Marsh, and Battersby (2008); and Janelle and Goodchild (2009). The basis of spatial thinking is understandably location, without which identifying and assessing spatial relationships and patterns across space cannot occur. Gersmehl (2008) identified eight spatial thinking skills that can foster problem-solving and analytical skills in the classroom: comparing one place with another (comparison), describing the influence that a place can have on neighboring locations (aura), drawing a line around all places that have similar characteristics or are linked together in some way (region), describing what happens between two places with known conditions (transition), finding places that have similar positions and therefore have similar conditions (analogy), identifying a spatial hierarchy or how "nested" features relate to one another, describing the arrangement of features or conditions in an area (pattern), and identifying the extent to which features have the same map pattern (association).

Spatial thinking skills develop in a cumulative nature, with each additional skill serving as a building block to understand new concepts (Golledge, Marsh, & Battersby, 2008). The ability to think spatially varies greatly, but these abilities can be improved through education and training. Mastery of these basic skills early in life provides a solid foundation for continued development throughout life. There is also a correlation between thinking spatially and thinking geographically. Intellectual knowledge about space, or geospatial thinking is defined as the "application of spatial thinking to address complex geographic concepts or problems" (Metoyer & Bednarz, 2017, 21). Having the ability to read and create visual representations is vital, but having the visual-spatial thinking skills needed to interpret patterns and processes shown in these visualizations is also essential (Collins, 2018a).

Researchers are concerned that the lack of clearly defined terminology surrounding not only spatial thinking as a term, but individual spatial thinking skills themselves could act as a roadblock to deeper understanding and growth in the field of spatial intelligence (Jadallah et al., 2017 & Collins, 2018a). Often shifting or overlapping among different researchers, these terms should be developed into a commonly defined language within which clarity and consensus among researchers can be reached. Furthermore, it is essential that valid and reliable assessments designed to measure specific geospatial thinking skills for students in all age groups be developed so that these skills may be accurately assessed and better understood in educational research.

Although there has been a growing amount of recent research in the context of spatial thinking, there has not been a significant amount of research and development of instruments to assess student spatial thinking skills. Downs (1994) argued that geography education research would benefit from producing an instrument to assess student performance. However, despite the importance and universality of spatial thinking, the National Research Council (2006) reported that there are few instruments that have been tested for reliability and validity to measure spatial thinking skills within the discipline of geography. Spatial thinking has been predominantly researched and tested in the disciplines of psychology

Creating Geospatial Thinkers

and geography. A variety of instruments have been used such as psychometric scales and intelligence tests (Gardner, 1983; Liben, 2002), cognitive ability tests (Golledge, Marsh, & Battersby, 2008; Lee & Bednarz, 2009), a paper-pencil test involving visual manipulation (Newcombe, 2010), and a geospatial thinking test (Huynh & Sharpe, 2013). Out of these developed assessments, only one serves as a standardized instrument integrating both geography content knowledge and spatial skills that have been tested for reliability and validity. The Spatial Thinking Ability Test (STAT) developed by Lee and Bednarz (2009) was created to assess individual's growth in spatial thinking skills. It was designed to specifically assess many of the spatial thinking skills and geospatial concepts identified in the structures and hierarchies of Gersmehl (2008) and Golledge, Marsh, and Battersby (2008). Two different but equivalent forms of the test were created so that change in spatial thinking could be measured and evaluated over time through a pre- and posttest setting. While serving as a pioneer in assessments on spatial thinking that have been tested for reliability and validity, it was primarily designed for undergraduate students. Modifications could be made to make it more age appropriate for multiple ages to participate and thus more user friendly in the K-12 environment.

Meaningful assessment of any intelligence (spatial or otherwise) is not possible if students have little or no experience with a particular way of thinking. Spatial thinking helps us to identify, remember, understand, and make decisions about the relationships between objects represented in space and the spatiotemporal and thematic attributes of natural and human features and events occurring there (Montello, 2009; Kulo & Bodzin, 2011). By using this set of skills, people are able to survive in a complex environment, however, they may not be functioning at their highest capability if they have not developed further than a basic, naïve understanding of spatial relationships. As with all types of intelligences, individuals possess different ranges in ability levels of specific intelligences due to both hereditary and environmental reasons. Existing spatial thinking skills can be improved and new skills can be developed through practice. One way to develop the ability to think spatially is with the use of digital technologies such as geospatial technologies.

Digital technologies are impacting the way that classroom instruction is taking place. Over the past decade there have been a rapidly increasing number of digital technologies available, in large part a consequence of the substantial growth and accessibility of geospatial data, commonly referred to as the geospatial revolution. Geospatial data are data that have a geographic component to them tied to them. These data have locational information tied to them such as geographic coordinates, address, city, or zip code. As increasing amounts of geospatial data are becoming more readily available throughout society, the use of geospatial technologies as a tool to understand the world and engage in problem solving has grown into a necessity (Kulo & Bodzin, 2011). Geospatial technologies are a specialized subset of information technologies that handle geo-referenced data. Geospatial technology uses in education include, but are not limited to smartphone and tablet applications, global positioning systems (GPS), geographic information systems (GIS), remote sensing, photogrammetry, and virtual globes such as Google Earth. There are a multitude of digital technologies available in each of these categories and many are available online at no cost. Additionally, these technologies are available to students and teachers in all disciplines across the curriculum.

While geospatial technologies have become increasingly popular and widely used, the integration of these technologies into the curriculum has been startlingly slow. Some of the reasons that have been speculated as the reasons for this slow adoption of geospatial technologies include research on its effectiveness, a shortage of related curricula, software complexities, school technology limitations, scarce teacher training opportunities, and lack of teacher comfort in teaching with geospatial technologies (Kerski, 2008, Kulo & Bodzin, 2011). This lack of comfort certainly translates into a lack of confidence to incorporate these tools in the classroom. There are limited opportunities for pre-service and in-service teachers to participate in training where they have the chance to develop confidence ultimately leading to competence. Furthermore, even if a higher percentage of teachers did possess enough knowledge to ensure the confidence needed to implement these technologies, the era of standardized testing often prohibits teachers from allowing time into the curriculum for the inclusion.

Another possible barrier that can limit the use of geospatial technologies in the classroom is the issue of lack of student focus while using these technologies. If students are utilizing technologies that exist on the internet, a smartphone, or a tablet, there are many distractions that can lure them away from the task at hand. Students who do know how to properly navigate the technology seldom stay on task and do not follow instructions. This situation not only limits the amount of learning taking place on the objectives of the lesson, but can also lead to other students in the classroom being tempted to lose focus as well. As an instructor, it can be difficult to manage and maintain group focus for any age group when it comes to technology.

Additionally, there are school-based and district-based issues that can create barriers for the incorporation of geospatial technologies. Often the most immediate hurdles are related to hardware, software, and networking issues that may frequently occur. Many schools or districts limit the amount of data that can be downloaded onto school computers, thus preventing use of these technologies in some areas. Furthermore, a major issue in K-12 schools is that teachers must compete for time in the computer lab so that each student or group of several students may work individually on a computer. Often times, language arts teachers occupy the majority of this scheduled time leaving science and social studies teachers without an abundance of time to utilize in the labs. In some cases, there may be only one computer lab in the entire school building. This is not necessarily an issue with geospatial technologies themselves, but it can greatly limit access to them. However, this issue is slowly being alleviated as more schools move to the one-to-one model with each student possessing their own laptop computer or tablet.

Although challenges may certainly arise with implementation of these technologies in education, using tools of representation such as maps and GIS is essential for competency in spatial thinking. These tools of representation can be analyzed to further understand spatial patterns and spatial relationships. Following is a discussion about the methods best suited for delivering content that fosters the improvement of these spatial thinking skills. Specifically, the discussion focuses on research evidence that supports a framework for including GIS into professional development activities. Models and approaches for utilizing geospatial technologies to improve spatial thinking will also be discussed.

EVIDENCE OF A FRAMEWORK

Geospatial technologies such as virtual globes and GIS support and facilitate the acquisition of spatial thinking (NRC, 2006). Many researchers suggest that geospatial technologies are superior tools for teaching and learning spatial thinking skills. For example, Goldstein and Alibrandi (2013) found that student learning and student achievement on standardized test scores in reading as well as final course grades in science and social studies are enhanced in middle-school classrooms with the inclusion of GIS in the curriculum. Kulo and Bodzin (2011) assert that geospatial technologies provide more optimal learning experiences in middle-school classrooms when investigating spatial data than the use of static maps.

Jadallah et al. (2017) explored whether elementary-school students receiving GIS instruction would exhibit more growth in spatial thinking and spatial abilities than those students who did not receive GIS instruction. Researchers in this study suggest that while students who received GIS instruction did demonstrate greater gains in spatial ability, map-reading skills and map-analysis skills than students who did not receive the same instruction, GIS is not the only means of producing these results. Jadallah et al. also contend not only that spatial thinking skills may improve through use of GIS in the classroom, but also that elementary-age students are capable of using GIS for meaningful classroom activities (2017).

However, in a study involving high-school students, Metoyer and Bednarz (2017) found that the instructional use of geospatial technologies did not improve students' spatial thinking skills. Students in this study who used geospatial technologies did however demonstrate greater gains in content knowledge than students using traditional paper maps. Although the use of geospatial technologies was a more effective teaching method than the use of paper maps in this study, the use of geospatial technologies had no effect on improving students' spatial thinking skills. Additionally, students with high levels of spatial skill prior to instruction were found to be better prepared to learn spatially dependent concepts (Metoyer & Bednarz, 2017). The same students possessing higher levels of spatial skills initially also performed better when using geospatial technologies than when using paper maps therefore suggesting that there is a correlation between higher levels of spatial thinking and superior geographic thinking (Metoyer & Bednarz, 2017). As geography is broadly defined as the study of the location, distribution, and relationships of things on Earth or more simply, the study of space, it is fitting that the discipline of geography is a suitable home for teaching students the ability to think spatially.

A similar study aimed to determine if spatial thinking skill development among middle-school students differs between paper or digital map instruction. Ultimately, this study determined that students taught by both paper and digital media showed improvements in spatial thinking skills and that it is highly likely that different spatial thinking skills are best taught by different media (Collins, 2018a). Both paper and digital media have their own strengths and weaknesses; some skills may be best developed when taught with paper maps while others may be best taught with digital maps. Therefore, it may be more advantageous for student learning to focus on which specific spatial thinking skills to teach and how best to teach them rather than solely on which media to use. Qualitative findings were also explored in this study through interviews from participatory students and teachers. Most students reported enjoying the novelty of this type of thinking and learning regardless of the media utilized in their instruction while teachers in the study offered that digital map instruction is interactive and entertaining, but student attention and focus was more difficult to maintain with multiple computer distractions than with those students taught with paper maps (Collins, 2018b). An increase in exposure to maps and spatial thinking activities regardless of media not only increase student awareness of space, but improve student spatial thinking skills. Based on evidence from these studies and the reality that these technologies are increasingly ubiquitous, geospatial technologies should be utilized in instruction to teach students to think spatially. Nevertheless, these technologies are simply tools to help aid in the teaching of spatial thinking and should not necessarily be used alone or in replacement of traditional, non-technical tools of representation such as paper maps.

The Significance of Teacher Training

Although geospatial technologies are increasingly widespread, this accessibility does not imply that teachers can teach effectively with these technologies or that students can use them competently. Enhancing student learning opportunities in the digital age is largely dependent on the quality of teacher professional development. A variety of models have been proposed for successful professional development in utilizing geospatial technologies to improve spatial thinking. Yet, there remains a disconnect between providing teacher professional development and actually seeing long-term classroom implementation.

In order to be an effective teacher, teachers must be educated and trained in the content knowledge of their discipline of choice. Although much of the school curriculum is decided by state policy-makers and school district officials, teachers do have some autonomy in making professional decisions about what specific content is provided in their classrooms and what methods of instruction to utilize in delivering that content. One aspect that influences teacher decision on choosing specific content and the instructional methods with which to employ that content is teacher familiarity and comfort level with both the content and the instructional method. If teachers do not feel confident in teaching the content, they are unlikely to teach it (Collins, 2018b; Shin, Milson, & Smith, 2016).

While it is understood that greater attention to spatial thinking in K-12 education is necessary, this devotion requires that teachers themselves are also equipped with the skills to think spatially. One study set out to examine the spatial thinking skills and attitudes of undergraduate students majoring in elementary education and secondary social studies education (Shin, Milson & Smith, 2016). Data was also collected from geography majors as a comparison group against which to assess the level of performance revealed by both sets of education majors. This study found that future elementary teachers possess weaker spatial thinking skills than future secondary social studies teachers and future secondary social studies teachers possess weaker spatial thinking skills than geography majors. These findings suggest that these future teachers may struggle when required to teach students to think spatially or may even be reluctant to design and teach lessons that cultivate spatial thinking (Shin, Milson & Smith, 2016). Explicit instruction of spatial thinking is needed in pre-service teacher development programs.

In an effort to develop pre-service teachers' confidence and competencies in incorporating geospatial technologies into their teaching practice, one study targeted teacher education programs in which pre-service teachers were immersed in collaborative learning environments that provided opportunities to develop knowledge of geospatial technologies, build confidence in designing learning experiences utilizing geospatial technologies, and formulate implementation strategies to incorporate geospatial technologies into their teaching practice (Harte, 20117). Harte found that through deliberate instruction on geospatial technologies, pre-service teacher confidence in the incorporation and likelihood of using geospatial technologies in the classroom increased over the instructional period. Additionally, pre-service teachers who did not yet have the opportunity to experiment with putting their learning into practice in the classroom may still lack confidence (Harte, 2017).

The inclusion of spatial thinking and geospatial technologies, particularly GIS, is not yet commonplace in pre-service teacher training nor is it part of in-service teacher professional development. This absence presents an obstacle to implementing the skills and technologies into the K-12 curriculum. Millsaps and Harrington (2017) have developed a time-sensitive framework for including GIS into professional development activities by identifying relevant GIS content recommendations which are reproducible (with minor local adaptations) to fit professional development in other states. This framework was designed to introduce educators to the use of GIS in the classroom for all content areas and grade-levels. The decision of how much GIS content to include and the context in which to include the GIS material is often directly related to the amount of time available in professional development opportunities. Millsaps and Harrington assert that although teachers are certainly capable of jumping right into GIS, they receive more benefit from beginning initial training with learning to teach with maps and simply being introduced to current online mapping resources such as Esri Story Maps and ArcGIS Online (2017). If more time is available, teachers then learn to create a map to support an existing lesson. This extension obviously offers hands-on practice and time to interact with and learn the software being utilized thus building teacher confidence in geospatial technologies. Another extension of the professional development has teachers report out and share their lesson along with ideas of how to implement the lesson which stimulates discussion and offers perhaps the most worthwhile aspect of the professional development.

Using the same sequential process of professional development, Collins and Mitchell (2018) extended the professional development over the course of a year-long period. Participating teachers were then assessed on the effectiveness of this long-term teacher training by interviewing participating teachers over a full year after they completed training to determine if they were continuing to teach with GIS and of so, how. Despite following the suggested components of effective teacher training in GIS, providing multiple incentives, only two of eighteen participants continued long-term GIS use in their classrooms. Although teachers unanimously enjoyed and found value in the professional development, true behavioral change in teacher practice was very minimal. Multiple teachers conveyed that they observed increased student engagement as a result of teaching with maps more often. However, teachers collectively cited the main reason for discontinuing the use of GIS in the classroom as too time consuming. When asked to elaborate, teachers explained that GIS lessons were not only too time consuming to create, but also finding time in the curriculum to implement them was difficult.

Another possible reason for this disconnect between teacher development and teacher practice is that many teachers are struggling to teach a population of students who speak an entirely different digital language than them. Presnky (2001) identifies many teachers as Digital Immigrants while most students he classifies as Digital Natives. Digital Immigrants are defined as people who were not born into the digital world, but at some point later in life have adopted many aspects of new technologies. Digital Natives are conversely defined as people who were born in the digital age and are thus 'native' to the digital language of computers, video games, and the internet. Ensuring quality professional development for both pre-service and in-service teachers in the utilization of geospatial technologies to improve spatial thinking skills might lessen this digital language barrier. The following section concludes with a reflection of some of the necessary elements required for the sustained use of geospatial technologies in the classroom and offers recommendations for transformation in teacher practice such as pre-service intervention, continuous follow-up and coaching, and curriculum modifications which include the direct instruction of both spatial thinking and geospatial technologies.

FUTURE RESEARCH AND CONCLUSION

Spatial thinking and geospatial technologies have emerged as an increasingly indispensable part of contemporary life in the 21st century. An increasing interconnectedness in the modern world demands an unprecedented need for geographic literacy. Creating geospatial thinkers prepares students to understand and address economic, political, and environmental issues at the local, state, national, and global levels. However, the development of spatial knowledge and the direct teaching and learning of spatial thinking skills is severely underrepresented in the classroom. Ultimately, direct instruction through the use of both paper map and digital map instruction best fosters the improvement of spatial thinking skills. Teachers must be deliberate about including instruction that allows students opportunities to think spatially and thus develop stronger skills in this way of thinking. There is not a one-size fits all model to best cultivate spatial thinking skills among students. As previously discussed, both digital and non-digital technologies have their strengths and weaknesses in the classroom in general as well as with fostering spatial thinking skills. Nevertheless, in our increasingly digital world, it is imperative that geospatial technologies become mainstream in education.

In order to implement spatial thinking skills and geospatial technologies that are so critical to possess throughout society into sustainable classroom instruction, changes must be made to achieve improved student outcomes. Collins and Mitchell (2018) suggest three recommendations for measurable and sustainable change: increased pre-service teacher preparation in geography and GIS, continuous follow-up with teachers, and the inclusion of GIS in academic standards. It all begins with pre-service teachers. If exposure to spatial thinking and the use of geospatial technologies as a means to improve these skills begins in teacher preparation programs in colleges and universities, then these practices will be seamlessly utilized by teachers as they begin their teaching practice rather than becoming add-ons after their teaching careers begin. Continuous follow-up for teachers is warranted as GIS is so very technical in nature. Teachers need coaching in both technical GIS use as well as pedagogic strategies to employ in the classroom. As with any technology, this continual follow-up and training allows teachers to maintain competency. Finally, if GIS is deliberately included in academic standards from the local to the national level, then it is therefore mandated to be taught in classrooms and the time-constraints that were cited earlier as the main reason for unsustainable GIS use becomes an unacceptable excuse.

REFERENCES

Collins, L. (2018a). The impact of paper versus digital map technology on students' spatial thinking skill acquisition. *The Journal of Geography*, *117*(4), 137–152. doi:10.1080/00221341.2017.1374990

Collins, L. (2018b). Student and teacher response to use of different media in spatial thinking skill development. *International Journal of Geospatial and Environmental Research*, *5*, 1–16.

Collins, L., & Mitchell, J. (2018). Teacher training in GIS: What is needed for long-term success? *International Research in Geographical and Environmental Education*. doi:10.1080/10382046.2018.1497119

Downs, R. (1994). The need for research in geography education: It would be nice to have some data. *The Journal of Geography*, *93*(1), 57–60. doi:10.1080/00221349408979690

Gardner, H. (1983). *Frames of mind: the theory of multiple intelligences*. New York: Basic Books.

Gersmehl, P. (2008). *Teaching geography*. New York: The Guilford Press.

Goldstein, D., & Alibrandi, M. (2013). Integrating GIS in the middle school curriculum: Impacts on diverse students' standardized test scores. *The Journal of Geography, 112*(2), 68–74. doi:10.1080/00221341.2012.692703

Golledge, R. M., Marsh, M., & Battersby, S. (2008). A conceptual framework for facilitating geospatial thinking. *Annals of the Association of American Geographers, 98*(2), 285–308. doi:10.1080/00045600701851093

Harte, W. (2017). Preparing preservice teachers to incorporate geospatial technologies in geography teaching. *The Journal of Geography, 116*(5), 226–236. doi:10.1080/00221341.2017.1310274

Huynh, N. T., & Sharpe, B. (2013). An assessment instrument to measure geospatial thinking expertise. *The Journal of Geography, 112*(1), 3–17. doi:10.1080/00221341.2012.682227

Jadallah, M., Hund, A. M., Thayn, J., Studebaker, J. G., Roman, Z. J., & Kirby, E. (2017). Integrating geospatial technologies in fifth-grade curriculum: Impact on spatial ability and map-analysis skills. *The Journal of Geography, 116*(4), 139–151. doi:10.1080/00221341.2017.1285339

Janelle, D. G., & Goodchild, M. F. (2009). Location across disciplines reflections of the CSISS experience. In H. J. Scholten, N. van Manen, & R. V. D. Velde (Eds.), *Geospatial technology and the role of location in science* (pp. 15–29). Dordrecht, The Netherlands: Springer. doi:10.1007/978-90-481-2620-0_2

Kerski, J. J. (2008). The world at the students' fingertips. In *Digital geography: geospatial technologies in the social studies classroom*. Charlotte, NC: Information Age Publishing.

Kulo, V. A., & Bodzin, A. M. (2011). Integrating geospatial technologies in an energy unit. *The Journal of Geography, 110*(6), 239–251. doi:10.1080/00221341.2011.566344

Lee, J., & Bednarz, R. (2009). Effects of GIS learning on spatial thinking. *Journal of Geography in Higher Education, 33*(2), 183–198. doi:10.1080/03098260802276714

Liben, L. S. (2002). Where are we know? In U. C. Goswami (Ed.), *Blackwell Handbook of Childhood Cognitive Development* (pp. 326–348). Malden, MA: Blackwell Publishers. doi:10.1002/9780470996652.ch15

Metoyer, S., & Bednarz, R. (2017). Spatial thinking assists geographic thinking: Evidence from a study exploring the effects of geospatial technology. *The Journal of Geography, 116*(1), 20–33. doi:10.1080/00221341.2016.1175495

Millsaps, L. T., & Harrington, J. A. (2017). A time-sensitive framework for including geographic information systems (GIS) in professional development activities for classroom teachers. *The Journal of Geography, 116*(4), 152–164. doi:10.1080/00221341.2017.1294611

Montello, D. R. (2009). Cognitive science. In K. K. Kemp (Ed.), *Encyclopedia of geographic information science* (pp. 40–43). Thousand Oaks, CA: Sage Publications.

National Research Council. (2006). *Learning to think spatially: GIS as a support system in the K-12 curriculum*. Washington, DC: National Research Council and National Academic Press.

Newcombe, N. (2010). Picture this: Increasing math and science learning by improving spatial thinking. *American Educator*, *32*, 29–43.

Presnky, M. (2001). Digital natives, digital immigrants. *On the Horizon*, *9*, 1–6.

Shin, E. E., Milson, A. J., & Smith, T. J. (2016). Future teachers' spatial thinking skills and attitudes. *The Journal of Geography*, *115*(4), 139–146. doi:10.1080/00221341.2015.1100654

ADDITIONAL READING

Baker, T. (2005). Internet-Based GIS Mapping in Support of K-12 Education. *The Professional Geographer*, *57*, 44–50.

Baker, T., Kerski, J., Huynh, N., Viehrig, K., & Bednarz, S. (2012). Call for an Agenda and Center for GIS Education Research. *Review of International Geographical Education Online*, *2*, 254–288.

Bednarz, S., & Audet, R. (1999). The Status of GIS Technology in Teacher Preparation Programs. *The Journal of Geography*, *98*(2), 60–67. doi:10.1080/00221349908978861

Bednarz, S., & van der Schee, J. (2006). Europe and the United States: The implementation of geographic information systems in secondary education in two contexts. *Technology, Pedagogy and Education*, *15*(2), 191–205. doi:10.1080/14759390600769573

Bourke, T., & Lidstone, J. (2015). Mapping geographical knowledge and skills needed for pre-service teachers in teacher education. *SAGE Open*, 1–13.

Gersmehl, P. J., & Gersmehl, C. A. (2007). Spatial thinking by young children: Neurological evidence for early development and "educability.". *The Journal of Geography*, *106*(5), 181–191. doi:10.1080/00221340701809108

Goodchild, M. F., & Janelle, D. (2010). Toward critical spatial thinking in the sciences and humanities. *GeoJournal*, *75*(1), 3–13. doi:10.100710708-010-9340-3 PMID:20454588

Henry, P., & Semple, H. (2012). Integrating Online GIS into the K-12 Curricula: Lessons from the Development of a Collaborative GIS in Michigan. *The Journal of Geography*, *111*(1), 3–14. doi:10.1080/00221341.2011.549237

Höhnle, S., Fögele, J., Mehren, R., & Schubert, J. (2016). GIS teacher training: Empirically-Based indicators of effectiveness. *The Journal of Geography*, *115*(1), 12–23. doi:10.1080/00221341.2015.1016546

Höhnle, S., Schubert, J., & Uphues, R. (2013). What are the constraints to GIS usage? Selected results of a teacher survey about constraints in the school context. *International Research in Geographical and Environmental Education*, *22*(3), 226–240. doi:10.1080/10382046.2013.817662

Hong, J. (2014). Promoting Teacher Adoption of GIS Using Teacher-Centered and Teacher-Friendly Design. *The Journal of Geography*, *113*(4), 139–150. doi:10.1080/00221341.2013.872171

Hong, J., & Stonier, F. (2015). GIS In-Service Teaching Training Based on TPACK. *The Journal of Geography, 114*(3), 108–117. doi:10.1080/00221341.2014.947381

Ishikawa, T. (2016). Spatial thinking in geographic science: Student's geospatial conceptions, map-based reasoning, and spatial visualization ability. *Annals of the Association of American Geographers, 106*(1), 76–95. doi:10.1080/00045608.2015.1064342

Jo, I., Bednarz, S., & Metoyer, S. (2010). Selecting and designing questions to facilitate spatial thinking. *Geography Teacher, 7*(2), 49–55. doi:10.1080/19338341.2010.510779

Mishra, P., & Koehler, M. J. (2006). Technological pedagogical content knowledge: A framework of teacher knowledge. *Teachers College Record, 108*(6), 1017–1054. doi:10.1111/j.1467-9620.2006.00684.x

KEY TERMS AND DEFINITIONS

Digital Immigrant: People who were not born into the digital world, but at some point later in life have adopted many aspects of new technologies.

Digital Native: People who were born in the digital world and thus are "native" to the digital languages of computers, video games, and the internet.

Geospatial Data: Data that have a geographic component to them tied to them such as geographic coordinates, address, city, or zip code.

Geospatial Technologies: A specialized subset of information technologies that handle geo-referenced data such as global positioning systems (GPS), geographic information systems (GIS), and remote sensing.

Geospatial Thinking: Application of spatial thinking to address complex geographic concepts or problems.

Spatial Thinking: The knowledge, skills, and habits of mind to use concepts of space (such as distance, orientation, distribution, and association), tools of representation (such as maps, graphs, and diagrams), and processes of reasoning (such as cognitive strategies to facilitate problem solving and decision making) to structure problems, find answers, and express solutions to these problems.

Visual-Spatial Intelligence: An object-based intelligence comprising the ability to visualize, rotate, transform, and manipulate objects and their location in the world.

Chapter 7
Stimulating Multiple Intelligences in Infant Education From an Augmented Didactic Itinerary

María del Rosario Neira-Piñeiro
https://orcid.org/0000-0003-2355-4682
University of Oviedo, Spain

M. Esther Del-Moral
University of Oviedo, Spain

Inés Fombella-Coto
https://orcid.org/0000-0001-6908-9697
University of Oviedo, Spain

ABSTRACT

This chapter investigates the contributions made by augmented reality (AR) to develop multiple intelligences in infant education, along with the opportunities offered by augmented didactic itineraries (ADI) as a suitable formula for the global activation of different intelligences by means of AR resources. The methodological guidelines followed to prepare an ADI are explained, and the case study method is adopted for the purpose of describing a model aimed at infant education schoolchildren—used in teacher training—in which are specified the activities included, together with the AR resources and applications that it comprises. More precisely, this ADI takes children's literature as a starting point and especially activates naturalistic, spatial, and bodily kinesthetic intelligence. Likewise, its training potential is analyzed from a didactic, digital and creative dimension so that it can serve as a model for future teachers to design their own aids.

DOI: 10.4018/978-1-7998-0249-5.ch007

Stimulating Multiple Intelligences in Infant Education From an Augmented Didactic Itinerary

INTRODUCTION

The concept of mind offered by the Theory of Multiple Intelligences (MIs) (Gardner, 2011) groups together subjects' skills around eight intelligences —linguistic; musical; logical-mathematical; spatial; bodily-kinesthetic; interpersonal; intrapersonal; and naturalistic— stressing their interdependence relationship as well as their potential development throughout people's life. According to this theory, the acquisition and qualitative improvement of intelligences is related to the opportunities provided by stimulus-rich educational contexts (Armstrong, 2009) when it comes to promoting the overall training of subjects, incorporating didactic strategies and activities supported on motivating resources which facilitate conscious and systematic training, particularly in the earliest ages (Delgoshaei & Delavari, 2012).

The key to success in educational proposals oriented to increase MIs includes a planning and systematization of didactic activities, suited to the educational goals, and aimed to stimulate intelligences at a global level. Some research works suggest using digital games (Armor, 2017; Beauchamp, 2016; Valente & Marchetti, 2015), videogames or serious games (Kasemsap, 2017), or gamified practices (Landers & Callan, 2011; Lim & Leong, 2017) in order to activate MIs. More recently, the emergence of technologies such as Augmented Reality (AR) has resulted in the publication of studies dedicated to examine its contribution to MI development (Campos, Pessanha, & Pires, 2010; Green, Lea, & McNair, 2014).

In this sense, the qualification of teachers arises as a critical factor for them to be able to design their own innovative didactic activities and/or resources meant to favor MI development. More specifically, on the basis of the Project ITINER-AR (2018-19) —implemented at the Faculty of Education of the University of Oviedo (Spain)— an effort has been made to enhance teacher training from the creation of Augmented Didactic Itineraries (ADIs), formed by various activities supported on AR resources and applications (Villalustre & Del Moral, 2016), since they are considered to be an ideal formula to activate MIs.

Thus, within the Degree in Infant Education Teacher Training, and after introducing students into the use of several AR applications and into the Theory of Multiple Intelligences, they were asked to develop their own ADI which, in the form of a project, had to fulfil the specified requirements. The Project Based Learning methodology was adopted because it involved the collaborative design of a didactic proposal to activate the different intelligences (Kaldi, Filippatou, & Govaris, 2011; Guven, Yurdatapan, & Sahin, 2014), incorporating AR as a powerful learning catalyst. This methodology enhances the acquisition of significant learning based on previous knowledge (Reyero, 2019), where digital resources turn out to be facilitating tools that boost its scope.

Logically, teachers' didactic-technological training becomes essential to articulate significant activities focused on the collaborative design of projects that encourage students' participation (Chai, Koh, & Tsai, 2010) and explore the educational opportunities offered by AR (Kerawalla, Luckin, Seljeflot, & Woolard, 2006). For that reason, they were offered an example of an ADI which included motivating activities supported on AR resources and applications addressed to infant education students which took children's literature as its starting point and particularly activated linguistic, naturalistic and visual intelligence.

This chapter firstly investigates the opportunities provided by AR to enhance MI development in infant education, carrying out a review of the research studies focused on the utilization of this innovative technology and highlighting the most relevant results and conclusions in this respect. The ADI development process is subsequently described and presented to future teachers as a model to design theirs, to finish with an examination of its training potential from a didactic, creative and digital dimension. It can additionally prove useful both in lifelong training and in the updating of in-service teachers.

MI DEVELOPMENT IN INFANT EDUCATION: CONTRIBUTIONS MADE BY AR

A variety of research works derived from educational experiences performed in the context of infant education with AR resources and applications emphasize the valuable help that this technology provides for learning in the early years (Castellanos & Pérez, 2017; Rasalingam, Muniandy, & Rass, 2014). These works stress the versatility of AR when it comes to favoring the acquisition of learning related to linguistic development, natural sciences and mathematical concepts, amongst other things. Furthermore, AR-based resources destined to infant education, such as flashcards or puzzles, turn out to be especially appealing to children, who perceive the 3D elements generated as something magical and fun (Yilmaz, 2016; Yilmaz, Kucuk, & Goktas, 2017). In turn, Wei, Guo, and Weng (2018) consider that the use of AR in infant education contexts positively impacts learners' learning and is likely to help in the development of multiple intelligences.

More precisely, AR may contribute to boost naturalistic intelligence because it generates three-dimensional representations of various elements belonging to the natural world, facilitating manipulation and interaction with virtual objects. The use of games with AR flashcards and other resources provides learning experiences linked to natural world processes, as well as to the knowledge of the human body (Castellanos & Pérez, 2017), encouraging us to come closer to animals, their classification and their habitat, amongst other contents (Campos, Pessanha, & Jorge, 2010; Cascales, Laguna, Pérez-López, Perona, & Contero, 2013; Rasalingam, Muniandy, & Rasalingam, 2014).

AR activates linguistic intelligence too. For instance, augmented books favor initial literacy by incorporating activities which combine reading and interaction with contents through mobile devices (Dünser & Hornecker, 2007). AR can also be applied to reading-and-writing learning by means of AR Alphabet Books (Rambli, Matcha, & Sulaiman, 2013), or using AR cards and games with AR aimed at letter learning (Castellanos & Pérez, 2017; Bhadra, Brown, Ke, Liu, Shin, Wang, & Kobsa, 2016; Cieza & Luján, 2018). Other research studies explore the application of AR to language learning. Thus, Hsieh and Lin (2010) analyze a proposal to acquire English language vocabulary which combines an augmented book with AR cards.

Similarly, other researchers highlight the importance of AR resources for mathematical learning (e.g. counting or geometric shape discrimination) at early ages, from games (Lee & Lee 2008; Stotz, 2018), cards (Cieza & Luján, 2018) or other activators which generate 3D geometric figures (Castellanos & Pérez, 2017; Gecu-Parmaksiz & Delialioğlu, 2019). It must be added that books also exist which combine literary education with the implementation of interactive games for the development of basic mathematical skills (Tomia & Awang, 2013).

In turn, spatial intelligence may be boosted by comparing the specific characteristics of different objects, including shapes, scales, directions, or spatial orientation, to quote but a few (Utami & Adiati, 2017). In the case of infant education, AR makes it possible to visualize images and objects mentally (Aguilera, 2017), to observe 3D objects from various perspectives, to assimilate three-dimensional concepts such as volume (Huang, Li, & Fong, 2015), to arouse types of learning typical of plastic language (colors and their mixtures) (Ucelli, Conti, Amicis, & Servidio, 2005) and to develop spatial skills (Gecu-Parmaksiz & Delialioğlu, 2018). Moreover, some plastic education experiences use sheet-markers that children color so that they can subsequently interact with the 3D images generated (Castellanos & Pérez, 2017; Huang, Li, & Fong, 2015).

With regard to bodily-kinesthetic intelligence, it becomes evident that the interaction with mobile devices to perform different activities with AR or the implementation of tasks such as the coloring of sheet-markers imply the development of motor skills. Some more specific experiences additionally exist (Han, Jo, Hyun, & So, 2015) which apply this technology to develop motricity in infant education, through the use of a robot, combined with AR resources to favor dramatic game activities at early ages.

Finally, a number of research works suggest the possible contribution made by AR to develop intra- and interpersonal intelligence, emphasizing its positive impact through the encouragement of collaborative behaviors as well as interaction between participants (Campos, Pessanha, & Pires, 2010; Cascales, Laguna, Pérez-López, Perona, & Contero, 2013). The experience carried out by Han et al. (2015) stresses how AR helps activate these intelligences through the promotion of an emotional involvement of participants with a robot designed to recognize different face expressions.

Other studies adopt a holistic approach to activate all intelligences globally. Wei, Guo, and Weng (2018) demonstrated optimal results derived from combining reading and oral tasks (linguistic intelligence), logic problem solving (logical-mathematical intelligence), observation and interaction with images (spatial intelligence), listening to different sounds (musical intelligence), activities which require movement (bodily-kinesthetic intelligence), and exploration of various animals and their environment (naturalistic intelligence). Cooperation with peers (interpersonal intelligence) and self-knowledge (intrapersonal intelligence) are simultaneously encouraged too.

MAIN FOCUS OF THIS CHAPTER

Augmented Didactic Itineraries to Activate MIs in Infant Education

Conventional didactic itineraries are conceived as a strategy to exploit the educational opportunities provided by the different paths —either real or imaginary— to deal with contents linked to a specific context or territory focusing on geographical, historical, literary or artistic aspects, amongst others. They are mainly supported on the formulation of activities around a main topic and often from a globalizing approach, seeking to ensure that both the physical movement and the mental or virtual journey of the student will entail increased motivation and promote significant learning.

AR's immersive capacity undoubtedly helps improve the training potential of some activities, insofar as it immerses schoolchildren in experiences which provide them with new formulas to interact with the real world, activating their desire to explore and to learn through discovery (Del Moral & Villalustre, 2013). Hence why Augmented Didactic Itineraries (ADIs) arise as paths which, thanks to the advantages brought by augmented reality resources and applications, incorporate attractive activities that enrich students' learning through investigation and the interaction with mobile devices to access multimedia information (videos, images, online games, etc.) (Villalustre & Del Moral, 2016).

Nevertheless, the challenge for teachers lies in planning activities and generating learning situations which are not only adapted to the particular characteristics and interests of students (Botella, Fosati, & Canet, 2017) but also oriented to activate all intelligences. That is why the design of an ADI is seen as a suitable formula for this purpose, since it allows us to develop didactic projects focused on various themes which can offer a multidisciplinary and/or global approach where AR will acquire special prominence.

Below can be found the methodological guidelines that guide the process of designing an ADI for infant education.

1. **Selection of the Topic that will be Covered:** The focus is to ensure the sequence of activities with coherence by avoiding isolated exercises that have nothing to do with one another. It is important to choose a topic which infant education students can find appealing and interesting, as this will guarantee schoolchildren's motivation and involvement in the suggested activities, while simultaneously contributing to MI development. The leitmotif could be a book or a literary text, a current issue, a trip, the life of a real or fictional character or a work of art, to quote but a few options, adopting a conceptual, sensorial or time-based approach.
2. **Selection of the Physical Medium**: The role of the physical medium is to host the activators with which schoolchildren will be able to interact using their mobile devices, with the aim of accessing the information linked to different AR elements (e.g. QR codes, markers, etc.). More precisely, a real and tangible artifact enables infant education students to come closer to the itinerary. This makes it easier to understand both the time sequence and the organization of activities because it is done visually, thus being beneficial both in terms of motivation to complete the tasks and regarding the development of spatial skills.

Depending on the educational level, the medium may be: a) a two-dimensional element like a map, a plan, a brochure, a game board, a lap-book or a mural; or b) a three-dimensional object like a box, a model, a book, a sculpture or an art facility. To which must be added that the classroom and other spaces can also be turned into containers where we will be able to distribute AR activators or geolocation.

3. **Selection of AR Applications and Digital Resources:** Teachers must look for AR applications and resources suited to the age of students, to the topic and to the didactic itinerary designed. They will additionally need to choose other digital tools which can help illustrate and complement the contents that they want to cover, such as video or animation editors, image creations and websites, amongst others. And they must also collect online accessible multiformat resources which can enrich the itinerary with further information, which are relevant, and which have aesthetic quality.
4. **Planning of Activities With AR:** The design of activities related to the theme has to be varied and follow a variety of approaches for the purpose of activating the different intelligences of students. Furthermore, the sequencing and timing of activities must show a balanced project adapted to students' learning paces. The formulation of activities often implies a search for resources (AR images, videos or applications), and conversely, some of the resources found favor the development of new activities.

Methodology: Single Case Study

The methodology adopted has a qualitative nature and focuses, on the one hand, on describing the structure of an Augmented Didactic Itinerary (ADI) designed for infant education —utilized in teacher training— and on the other hand, on analyzing its educational potential. The ADI was created by university instructors involved in the ITINER-AR project, with the purpose to be used in teacher training.

This single case study focuses on analyzing the materials created or selected by the instructors, together with the didactic proposal presented to the university students (https://bit.ly/2WiEHPw), which includes the grouping, timing, environment, activators, AR applications used, links to online resources and MI activated. The analysis of the results include:

1. ADI Descriptive study, taking into account:
   a. The resources used: the literary work selected, the elements of the model made as the physical medium for the ADI, the computer software and the applications, and the digital and non-digital resources.
   b. The activities designed, with and without AR.
2. Analysis of the ADI educational potential, paying attention to three dimensions:
   a. *Didactic*, analyzing the activation of MI in each activity.
   b. *Digital*, identifying how the digital resources and AR applications foster digital competence.
   c. *Creative*, considering how the ADI can encourages creativity.

RESULTS

Descriptive Study of the ADI

Seeking to offer a model for future infant education teachers, an ADI was designed taking as a reference the picturebook *Rosie's Walk*, written and illustrated by the British creator Pat Hutchins, widely and highly valued by specialized critics, and addressed to infant education schoolchildren. The picturebook acts as a leitmotif and helps articulate all activities. Despite the discrepancy between the verbal and the visual tale, it develops a straightforward story with a repetitive structure, the main characters of which are a chicken and a fox, where illustrations clearly prevail over the text.

The picturebook makes it possible to deal with a wide range of spatial concepts and is related to centers of interest typically associated with infant education, such as the farm, household plants or animals, etc. The relevance of the visual component, as well as the themes based on the farm and the verbal stimulation provided by its shared reading turn this book into a suitable instrument for the global development of intelligences.

Moreover, a three-dimensional model was chosen as the physical medium for the itinerary because it was considered a highly appreciated educational resource used in different areas (Torres-Porras & Arrebola, 2018) that permits to improve spatial orientation and helps in the development of children's symbolic thinking (Jauck, Maita, Mareovich, & Peralta, 2015). The three-dimensional model designed consequently reproduces the scenario of the story and shows the spatial concepts reflected in the picturebook, such as in front/behind, up/down, around, on, across, and so forth.

The model serves to represent the spatial location of characters and to anchor every activity (Figure 1). It additionally complements the picturebook and makes it easier for students to understand the characters' evolution by recording the time sequence of their journey. It was prepared with lightweight materials, easy to make and to handle, so that every schoolchild could take part in their design. Flat colors, simple shapes and clean volumes predominate in the visual language used, thus encouraging the acquisition of concepts specific to plastic education (e.g. color, textures, geometric shapes, and size) and favoring the development of spatial intelligence.

The applications Quiver and Chromville were selected to incorporate sheet-markers which schoolchildren could color; HP Reveal proved useful to turn some clips into AR markers; and Wallame served to hide texts in the classroom and QR code editors linked to online resources. Digital tools such as PhotoSpeak, Evertoon and Learning Apps were also used to create online videos, animations and microgames which were included in the model to complement the picturebook contents. Therefore, some pieces from the farm universe became AR activators (Figure 2) that build a link to online resources for the introduction of activities (QR codes) or permit to interact with characters who come to life (HP Reveal) (Figure 3).

Likewise, we created a video-animation by means of the application EverToon (https://bit.ly/2X2LYjN) which was activated with a QR code integrated in a letter that the main character of the picturebook— the chicken Rosie— sent to the students and which served to present the tour around the farm. Another three videos were also made animating dolls with the application PhotoSpeak. These dolls, turned into AR activators with the program HP Reveal, were situated in different places of the model, thus helping to present specific activities.

In parallel, traditional games with cards and puzzles were created to strengthen learning through play and the manipulation of tokens with the same images of animals as digital applications. Furthermore, masks made from the synthetic image of the fox which represented the different emotions of the character depending on the situations narrated in the picturebook allowed students to identify them and to work both on intrapersonal and interpersonal intelligence.

The timing for the set of activities included in this ADI was adapted to infant education schoolchildren, envisaging short sessions during a three-week period. Some activities of an individual nature are oriented to the development of intrapersonal intelligence, while others can be performed in small or large groups, thus favoring the stimulation of interpersonal intelligence. Therefore, all elements were

Figure 1. Three-dimensional model designed

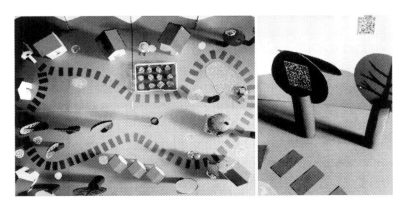

Figure 2. AR interactive sheet and an example of the use of Wallame

Figure 3. Dolls converted into activators with HP Reveal. QR code linked to the initial video

incorporated into the pedagogical proposal, in turn supported on the three-dimensional model created from the picturebook. Table 1 shows the planning of activities without AR:

On the other hand, activities with AR were planned that favor different types of learning, activating MIs to a different extent. Table 2 shows each activity together with the digital and augmented resources used.

Table 1. Description of activities proposed without AR and the resources used

Activities without AR	Resources
1. Shared reading of the picturebook and debate in the assembly.	Picturebook *Rosie's Walk* (by Pat Hutchins).
2. Reading of Rosie's letter in which she invites children to visit her farm.	Letter.
3. Sowing pulse seeds in the school orchard, in a small group.	Seeds.
4. Baking bread in the school kitchen oven, using the ingredients of a recipe.	Ingredients to make bread.
5. Self-expression: representation of a bird with art supplies.	Tempera, brushes, drawing paper, colored pencils, feathers.
6. Recognition game, visual memory and coordination with animal puzzles.	Puzzles of animal figures.
7. Recognition game and expression of emotions with different fox masks.	Fox masks.
8. Relaxation in the gym after a race, listening to music with nature sounds.	Music with nature sounds.

Source: elaborated by the authors

Table 2. Description of AR-supported activities and the resources used

Activities with AR	AR markers and resources
1. Visit to the picturebook author's website	QR code (http://pathutchins.com)
2. Viewing of the musical video clip about the birth of chicks	QR code (https://bit.ly/1jP0fMj)
3. Coloring and scanning a sheet illustrated with a cow converted into a dancing 3D image	Pre-designed sheet-marker (Quiver)
4. Online game to draw geometric shapes	QR code (https://bit.ly/2Puxx3x)
5. Coloring a sheet illustrated with a strawberry field to interact and simulate irrigation and fertilizing	Pre-designed sheet-marker (Chromville Science)
6. Viewing of the video-tale *The apple and the butterfly*	QR code (https://bit.ly/2GZtnBs)
7. Coloring and scanning a sheet illustrated with a tadpole that becomes a frog	Pre-designed sheet-marker (Quiver)
8. Learning the song *The cowboy mouse* and its choreography	QR code (https://bit.ly/2RHMEeV)
9. Online game to make a cake using virtual ingredients	QR code (https://bit.ly/2Rzquvb)
10. Viewing of an animated documentary about the life of bees	QR code (https://bit.ly/2SFdlhf)
11. Listening to Nikolai Rimsky-Korsakov's *Flight of the Bumblebee*, simulating the movement of a swarm	QR code (https://bit.ly/1fHqG3C)
12. Viewing an opera with birds. *The Magic Flute* (W.A. Mozart)	QR code (https://bit.ly/2SGTgay)
13. Online game to identify animal sounds	QR code (https://bit.ly/2Twtohu)
14. Learning Apps game to associate products with the animal that they come from	QR code (https://bit.ly/2VB3Npx)
15. Search for the riddles hidden on the classroom walls	Geolocation application Wallame

Educational Potential of the ADI

The three dimension features portend the educational potential of the Augmented Didactic Itinerary for Infant Education schoolchildren. Specifically, they show pedagogical merits in: a) didactic, analyzing the extent to which the activities comprised activate the development of the different intelligences; b) digital, verifying how the use of digital resources and AR applications favors digital competence; and c) creative, considering the opportunities that it provides to encourage creativity.

Didactic Dimension

The different activities comprised in the ADI -8 without AR (Table 1) and 15 with AR (Table 2)- were subject to expert evaluation seeking to check if they help activate the different intelligences and the extent to which each one of them does. Thus, a score was assigned (1=a little; 2=quite: 3=very much) to each activity, according to the degree to which it boosts each of the 8 intelligences. After this assignment, the scores were added to verify which intelligences are enhanced to a greater extent (Table 3). Figure 4 shows the didactic potential of the ADI from the complementariness between the incorporated activities, either AR-based or without AR, to deal with contents from the different areas in the infant education curriculum and to activate MIs.

Table 3. Activities developed in the ADI and MI activation level

Intelligences	Activity type(*)	Classification of each activity (A) depending on MI activation level (**) 1	2	3	Score (***)	Total
Spatial	W-AR	A1	A3, A6, A12	A4, A5, A7, A8, A9, A11, A14, A15	31	44
	N-AR		A1 & A4	A2, A5, A6	13	
Naturalist	W-AR		A1	A2, A5, A6, A7, A10, A12, A13, A14	26	42
	N-AR		A4, A8	A1, A3, A5, A6	16	
Bodily-kinesthetic	W-AR	A1	A14	A3, A4, A5, A7, A8, A9, A11	23	31
	N-AR		A7	A4, A6	8	
Musical	W-AR	A3		A2, A6, A8, A11, A12, A13	19	22
	N-AR			A8	3	
Linguistic	W-AR		A4	A9, A10, A15	11	17
	N-AR			A1, A4	6	
Interpersonal	W-AR			A8, 11	6	14
	N-AR		A1	A3, A7	8	
Logical-mathematical	W-AR			A9, A14	6	8
	N-AR		A4		2	
Intrapersonal	W-AR			A12	1	9
	N-AR		A1	A3, A7	8	

(*) Type of activity: W-AR (with AR): N-AR (without AR or no AR) (see Table 1 and Table 2).
(**) Level of activation: (1=a little; 2=quite: 3=very much).
(***) Obtained by adding the score of each activity taking into account the level of activation of the MI.

Figure 4. MI activation level with the activities included in the ADI. Source: elaborated by the authors

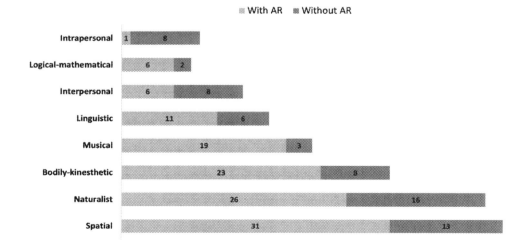

It should be noted that naturalistic and spatial intelligence, together with the bodily-kinesthetic one, are the ones which can benefit to a larger extent from the execution of activities supported on AR applications and through the interaction with mobile devices. In turn, linguistic-verbal intelligence is especially boosted with the reading of the picturebook, the others being simultaneously activated by means of complementary activities (see Table 3).

Digital Dimension

The ADI comprises activities which imply the use of applications to generate different types of AR: QR codes, pre-designed sheet-markers (Quiver or Chromville) which become 3D elements when interacting with them, and objects which behave as AR activators (HP Reveal). A simple geolocation application (Wallame) is then added which permits to discover hidden elements in a classroom. QR codes activate motivating resources such as videos, websites, online games or 3D elements (Table 2) that encourage students to carry out fun activities or provide complementary information, for instance, to acquire and/or consolidate concepts. These practices help students become familiar with AR, insofar as the interaction with mobile devices enables them to observe the elements converted into 3D. Logically, this process implies bringing them closer to the use of both digital resources and AR applications and, accordingly, to the development of their digital competence.

Creative Dimension

Likewise, the utilization of a three-dimensional model (Figure 1) as a medium to host the didactic proposal with AR not only stimulates the understanding of that space, recreating the farm scenarios and showing the characters' journey, but is also original. This resource makes it possible to bring students closer to reality through volume and in a way that differs from the usual one, normally two-dimensional. This scale approach allows infant education students to have a better perception of the relationships between spatial objects or concepts, it permits the manipulation of elements, develops motricity and visual control, giving them autonomy for the individual management of the objects that make up the model (Jiménez, 2018).

The three-dimensional model helps alternate and sequence activities by means of QR codes linked to objects such as a mill, beehives or a granary, made of cardboard and located in the model. Dolls are also included as AR activators to propose new activities. Without a doubt, the design of this ADI has meant a display of creativity to offer a 3D spatial representation of the story contained in the original picturebook. It constitutes an attractive medium — suited to the cognitive development of infant education students — to propose activities which can be adapted to various learning paces and cognitive styles, as well as to promote the global development of all intelligences.

CONCLUSION

The didactic proposal described above highlights the potential offered by AR to develop multiple intelligences in infant education. Starting from a picturebook, and taking the farm as the center of interest, an ADI has been created which includes a wide variety of activities from a globalizing approach. It is also worth highlighting the combination of ICT-based activities with others that lack any technological support, which permits to achieve a balance between the real sphere and the virtual one.

As far as the didactic dimension is concerned, the ADI makes it possible to stimulate every intelligence through the proposed activity sequence, even though it provides greater training in naturalistic intelligence — linked to the center of interest represented by the farm — spatial intelligence and bodily-kinesthetic intelligence. For this reason, it can be considered a versatile as well as motivating resource suited to cover all the areas in the infant education curriculum. Concerning the digital dimension, the ADI comprises different types of AR resources (QR codes, predesigned sheet-markers, 3D objects turned into markers and texts geolocated with Wallame), which give students access to videos, online games or 3D animations, amongst other things. Finally, as for the creative dimension, the use of a three-dimensional model as a suitable and original medium to present the itinerary in the infant education context must be highlighted as well.

In relation to the significance of this study, it should be pointed out that, despite the existence of several research works dedicated to these issues, few of them provide models which jointly activate all intelligences using AR resources. Therefore, this proposal offers an innovative formula to stimulate MIs in infant education by means of AR. The coined term "augmented didactic itinerary" (ADI) is original too and describes its role as a structuring axis for the sequence of activities interspersed in the three-dimensional model from AR resources. Added to this, the ADI is supported on a picturebook, thus stressing the value of children's literature for the presentation of globalizing didactic proposals — that represents another innovation. Likewise, the incorporation and description of the methodological guidelines followed in its design gives the chance to take it as a reference for the elaboration of similar proposals oriented to develop MIs using AR in the early ages.

FUTURE RESEARCH DIRECTIONS

It must be mentioned that this prototype forms part of the project ITINER-AR (financed by the University of Oviedo, Spain) currently in progress and aimed at the training of future teachers in this context. The ADI described is being used as a model for the students enrolled in the Degree in Infant Education Teacher Training to prepare their own proposals with AR, ultimately seeking a balanced global development of MIs. Among the future research lines stands out the analysis of the ADIs designed by university students during this academic year (2018-2019). Similarly, the implementation of the ADIs designed by teacher trainees in infant education classrooms is making it possible to assess their effectiveness.

ACKNOWLEDGMENT

This research was supported by the University of Oviedo (Spain) [project reference: PAPI-18-EMERG.22].

REFERENCES

Aguilera, N. A. (2018). Development of Spatial Skills with Virtual Reality and Augmented Reality. *International Journal on Interactive Design and Manufacturing*, *12*(1), 133–144. doi:10.100712008-017-0388-x

Armor, D. (2017). *Maximizing intelligence*. London: Routledge. doi:10.4324/9780203786000

Armstrong, T. (2009). *Multiple Intelligences in the Classroom*. ASCD.

Beauchamp, G. (2016). *Computing and ICT in the Primary School: From pedagogy to practice*. London: Routledge. doi:10.4324/9781315628042

Bhadra, A., Brown, J., Ke, H., Liu, C., Shin, E. J., Wang, X., & Kobsa, A. (2016, March). ABC3D-Using an Augmented Reality Mobile Game to Enhance Literacy in Early Childhood. In *IEEE International Conference on Pervasive Computing and Communication Workshops (PerCom Workshops)*, (pp. 1-4). Sydney, Australia: IEEE. 10.1109/PERCOMW.2016.7457067

Botella, A. M., Fosati, A., & Canet, R. (2017). Desarrollo emocional y creativo en Educación Infantil mediante las artes visuales y la música [Emotional and creative development in early childhood education though the visual arts and music]. *Creativity and Educational Innovation Review*, *1*, 70–86. doi:10.7203/CREATIVITY.1.12063

Campos, P., Pessanha, S., & Pires, J. (2010). Fostering Collaboration in Kindergarten through an Augmented Reality Game. *International Journal of Virtual Reality*, *5*(3), 1–7.

Cascales, A., Laguna, I., Pérez-López, D., Perona, P., & Contero, M. (2013). An Experience on Natural Sciences Augmented Reality Contents for Preschoolers. In R. Shumaker (Ed.), Lecture Notes in Computer Science: Vol. 8022. *Virtual, Augmented and Mixed Reality. Systems and Applications. VAMR 2013*. Berlin: Springer. doi:10.1007/978-3-642-39420-1_12

Castellanos, A., & Pérez, C. (2017). New Challenge in Education: Enhancing Student's Knowledge through Augmented Reality. In J. M. Ariso (Ed.), *Augmented Reality* (pp. 243–293). Berlin: De Gruyter. doi:10.1515/9783110497656-015

Chai, C. S., Koh, J. H. L., & Tsai, C. C. (2010). Facilitating Preservice Teachers' Development of Technological, Pedagogical, and Content Knowledge (TPACK). *Journal of Educational Technology & Society*, *13*(4), 63–73.

Cieza, E., & Luján, D. (2018). Educational Mobile Application of Augmented Reality Based on Markers to Improve the Learning of Vowel Usage and Numbers for Children of a Kindergarten in Trujillo. *Procedia Computer Science*, *130*, 352–358. doi:10.1016/j.procs.2018.04.051

Del Moral, M. E., & Villalustre, L. (2013). Realidad aumentada: experimentando en el aula en 3D [Augmented reality: experimenting in the classroom in 3D]. In *Smartphones y tablets: ¿enseñan o distraen?* [Smartphones and tablets: do they teach or distract?] (pp. 107–124). Madrid: ESIC Editorial.

Delgoshaei, Y., & Delavari, N. (2012). Applying Multiple-Intelligence Approach to Education and Analyzing its Impact on Cognitive Development Of Pre-School Children. *Procedia: Social and Behavioral Sciences*, *32*, 361–366. doi:10.1016/j.sbspro.2012.01.054

Dünser, A., & Hornecker, E. (2007). An Observational Study of Children Interacting with an Augmented Story Book. In K. Hui, Z. Pan, R.C. Chung, C.C.L. Wang, X. Jin, S. Göbel & E.C.-L. Li (Eds.), *International Conference on Technologies for E-Learning and Digital Entertainment. Proceedings of the Third International Conference, Edutainment 2007* (pp.305-315). New York: Springer. 10.1007/978-3-540-73011-8_31

Gardner, H. (2011). *Frames of mind: The theory of multiple intelligences*. London: Hachette UK.

Gecu-Parmaksiz, Z., & Delialioğlu, O. (2019). Augmented Reality-Based Virtual Manipulatives Versus Physical Manipulatives for Teaching Geometric Shapes to Preschool Children. *British Journal of Educational Technology*, 1–15. doi:10.1111/bjet.12740

Green, M., Lea, J. H., & McNair, C. L. (2014). Reality Check: Augmented Reality for School Libraries. *Teacher Librarian*, *41*(5), 28–34.

Guven, I., Yurdatapan, M., & Sahin, F. (2014). The Effect of Project-Based Educational Applications on the Scientific Literacy of 2nd Grade Elementary School Pupils. *International Journal of Education and Research*, *2*(1), 1–12.

Han, J., Jo, M., Hyun, E., & So, H. J. (2015). Examining Young Children's Perception toward Augmented Reality-Infused Dramatic Play. *Educational Technology Research and Development*, *63*(3), 455–474. doi:10.100711423-015-9374-9

Hsieh, M. C., & Lin, H. C. K. (2010). Interaction Design Based on Augmented Reality Technologies for English Vocabulary Learning. In S.L. Wong et al. (Ed.), *Proceedings of the 18th International Conference on Computers in Education* (vol. 1, pp. 663–666). Putrajaya, Malaysia: Asia-Pacific Society for Computers in Education.

Huang, Y., Li, H., & Fong, R. (2015). Using Augmented Reality in early art education: A case study in Hong Kong kindergarten. *Early Child Development and Care*, *186*(6), 879–894. doi:10.1080/03004430.2015.1067888

Jauck, D. E., Maita, M. D. R., Mareovich, F., & Peralta, O. A. (2015). Maternal teaching of the symbolic function of a scale model [La enseñanza materna de la función simbólica de una maqueta]. *Infancia y Aprendizaje*, *38*(3), 617–646. doi:10.1080/02103702.2015.1054666

Jiménez, J. J. (2018). Expresión Plástica tridimensional: Acercamiento a la realidad en Educación Infantil [Three-dimensional plastic expression. Approach to reality in Children's Education]. *Omnia*, *8*(1), 37–43. doi:10.23882/OM08-1-2018-H

Kaldi, S., Filippatou, D., & Govaris, C. (2011). Project-Based Learning in Primary Schools: Effects on Pupils' Learning and Attitudes. *Education 3-13*, *39*(1), 35-47. doi:10.1080/03004270903179538

Kasemsap, K. (2017). Mastering Educational Computer Games, Educational Video Games, and Serious Games in the Digital Age. In *Gamification-Based E-Learning Strategies for Computer Programming Education* (pp. 30–52). Hershey, PA: IGI Global. doi:10.4018/978-1-5225-1034-5.ch003

Kerawalla, L., Luckin, R., Seljeflot, S., & Woolard, A. (2006). *Making it real:* Exploring the Potential of Augmented Reality for Teaching Primary School Science. *Virtual Reality (Waltham Cross)*, *10*(3-4), 163–174. doi:10.100710055-006-0036-4

Landers, R. N., & Callan, R. C. (2011). Casual social games as serious games: The psychology of gamification in undergraduate education and employee training. In M. Ma, A. Oikonomou, & L. Jain (Eds.), *Serious games and edutainment applications* (pp. 399–423). London: Springer. doi:10.1007/978-1-4471-2161-9_20

Lee, H., & Lee, J. (2008). Mathematical Education Game Based on Augmented Reality. In Z. Pan, X. Zhang, A. El Rhalibi, W. Woo, & Y. Li (Eds.), *Technologies for e-Learning and Digital Entertainment. Proceedings of the Third International Conference, Edutainment 2008* (pp. 442–450). New York: Springer. 10.1007/978-3-540-69736-7_48

Lim, K. C., & Leong, K. E. (2017). A Study of Gamification on GeoGebra for Remedial Pupils in Primary Mathematics. In *Asian Conference on Technology in Mathematics (ATCM)* (pp. 222-228). Chungli, Taiwan: Mathematics and Technology, LLC.

Rambli, D. R. A., Matcha, W., & Sulaiman, S. (2013). Fun Learning with AR Alphabet Book for Preschool Children. *Procedia Computer Science*, *25*, 211–219. doi:10.1016/j.procs.2013.11.026

Rasalingam, R.R., Muniandy, B., & Rass, R. (2014). Exploring the application of Augmented Reality technology in early childhood classroom in Malaysia. *Journal of Research & Method in Education*, *4*(5), 33-40.

Reyero, M. (2019). La educación constructivista en la era digital [Constructivist education in the digital era]. *Revista Tecnología Ciência & Educação (Bauru)*, *12*, 111–127.

Stotz, M. D. (2018). *Creature Counting: The Effects of Augmented Reality on Perseverance and Early Numeracy Skills* (Doctoral thesis). Lehigh University. Retrieved from https://preserve.lehigh.edu/etd/4254

Tomia, A. B., & Awang, R. D. R. (2013). An Interactive Mobile Augmented Reality Magical Playbook: Learning Number with the Thirsty Crow. *Procedia Computer Science*, *25*, 123–130. doi:10.1016/j.procs.2013.11.015

Torres-Porras, J., & Arrebola, J. (2018). Construyendo la ciudad sostenible en el Grado de Educación Primaria [Building the sustainable city in the Primary Education Degree]. *Revista Eureka sobre Enseñanza y Divulgación de las Ciencias*, *15*(2), 1-15 doi:10.25267/Rev_Eureka_ensen_divulg_cienc.2018.v15.i2.2501

Ucelli, G., Conti, G., Amicis, R. D., & Servidio, R. (2005). Learning using augmented reality technology: Multiple means of interaction for teaching children the theory of colours. In M. Maybury, O. Stock, & W. Wahlster (Eds.), *Intelligent Technologies for Interactive Entertainment 2005* (Vol. 3814, pp. 193–202). Heidelberg, Germany: Springer. doi:10.1007/11590323_20

Utami, S. N. A., & Adiarti, W. (2017). Application of Building Playing in the Center of Beams to improve the Visual-Spatial Intelligence of Children at the Age 5-6 Years Old in Mutiara Insan Kindergarten, Sukoharjo Regency. *BELIA: Early Childhood Education Papers*, *6*(1), 27–31.

Valente, A., & Marchetti, E. (2015, July). *Make and Play: Card Games as Tangible and Playable Knowledge Representation Boundary Objects. In 2015 IEEE 15th International Conference on Advanced Learning Technologies (ICALT)* (pp. 137–141). Hualien, Taiwan: IEEE. doi.ieeecomputersociety.org/10.1109/ICALT.2015.31

Villalustre, L., & Del Moral, M. E. (2016). Itinerarios interactivos con geolocalización y realidad aumentada para un aprendizaje ubicuo en la formación inicial de docentes de educación infantil [Interactive itineraries with geolocation and augmented reality for ubiquitous learning in the initial training of early childhood teachers] In L. Villalustre & M.E. Del Moral (Coords.), Experiencias interactivas con realidad aumentada en las aulas [Interactive experiences with augmented reality in the classroom]. Barcelona: Octaedro.

Wei, X., Guo, D., & Weng, D. (2018, April). A Study of Preschool Instructional Design Based on Augmented Reality Games. In *Chinese Conference on Image and Graphics Technologies* (pp. 106-113). Singapore: Springer. 10.1007/978-981-13-1702-6_11

Yilmaz, R. M. (2016). Educational magic toys developed with augmented reality technology for early childhood education. *Computers in Human Behavior*, *54*, 240–248. doi:10.1016/j.chb.2015.07.040

Yilmaz, R. M., Kucuk, S., & Goktas, Y. (2017). Are augmented reality picture books magic or real for preschool children aged five to six? *British Journal of Educational Technology*, *48*(3), 824–841. doi:10.1111/bjet.12452

ADDITIONAL READING

Armstrong, T. (2009). *Multiple Intelligences in the Classroom*. Virginia, USA: ASCD.

Carbonell, C., & Bermejo, L. A. (2017). Augmented reality as a digital teaching environment to develop spatial thinking. *Cartography and Geographic Information Science*, *44*(3), 259–270. doi:10.1080/15230406.2016.1145556

Cawood, S., & Fiala, M. (2008). *Augmented Reality: A Practical Guide*. Denver: Pragmatic Bookshelf.

Del Moral, M. E., Guzmán, A. P., & Fernández, L. C. (2018). Game-Based Learning: Increasing the Logical-Mathematical, Naturalistic, and Linguistic Learning Levels of Primary School Students. *Journal of New Approaches in Educational Research*, *7*(1), 31–39. doi:10.7821/naer.2018.1.248

Gardner, H. (2011). *Frames of mind: The theory of multiple intelligences*. London: Hachette UK.

Huang, Y., Li, H., & Fong, R. (2015). Using Augmented Reality in early art education: A case study in Hong Kong kindergarten. *Early Child Development and Care*, *186*(6), 879–894. doi:10.1080/03004430.2015.1067888

Jiménez, J. J. (2018). Expresión Plástica tridimensional: Acercamiento a la realidad en Educación Infantil [Three-dimensional plastic expression. Approach to reality in Children's Education]. *Omnia*, *8*(1), 37–43. doi:10.23882/OM08-1-2018-H

Koutromanos, G., Sofos, A., & Avraamidou, L. (2015). The use of augmented reality games in education: A review of the literature. *Educational Media International*, *52*(4), 253–271. doi:10.1080/09523987.2015.1125988

Villalustre, L., & Del Moral, M. E. (Coord.) (2016). Experiencias interactivas con realidad aumentada en las aulas. Barcelona: Octaedro.

Wei, X., Guo, D., & Weng, D. (2018, April). A Study of Preschool Instructional Design Based on Augmented Reality Games. In *Chinese Conference on Image and Graphics Technologies* (pp. 106-113). Singapore: Springer. 10.1007/978-981-13-1702-6_11

Yilmaz, R. M., Kucuk, S., & Goktas, Y. (2017). Are augmented reality picture books magic or real for preschool children aged five to six? *British Journal of Educational Technology*, *48*(3), 824–841. doi:10.1111/bjet.12452

Yuen, S., Yaoyuneyong, G., & Johnson, E. (2011). Augmented reality: An overview and five directions for AR in education. *Journal of Educational Technology Development and Exchange*, *4*(1), 119–140. doi:10.18785/jetde.0401.10

KEY TERMS AND DEFINITIONS

3D Model: A scale manual or automated representation of an environment or an object.

ADI: Augmented didactic itinerary, a journey which exploits the educational opportunities offered by a specific context by integrating augmented reality resources.

Augmented Reality: A technology which superimposes virtual information upon a real environment through the use of mobile devices.

Globalizing Approach: A vision that brings together different areas of knowledge.

Infant Education (Second Cycle): A non-compulsory stage of the Spanish Educational System divided into three academic years which goes from the ages of 3 to 6.

Marker: An element from the real world (photograph, object, illustrated sheet) which, after being scanned, allows us to access a superimposed virtual content by means of a computer program or application.

MI Theory: Theory of Multiple Intelligences by H. Gardner (2011) which defines the human mind as a set of eight different intelligences or intellectual capabilities—spatial, bodily kinesthetic, musical, interpersonal, intrapersonal, linguistic, logical-mathematical, and naturalistic—which can be jointly activated throughout life with the appropriate stimuli.

Picturebook: A type of literary and visual work belonging to children's literature. It combines sequenced images and written texts which complement one another to narrate stories. There are also picturebooks without text, where the work is built exclusively from the illustrations.

Chapter 8
Geolocation for the Improvement of Spatial and Naturalist Intelligence in Primary Education

Lourdes Villalustre Martínez
University of Oviedo, Spain

María Belén San Pedro-Veledo
University of Oviedo, Spain

Inés López-Manrique
University of Oviedo, Spain

ABSTRACT

Geolocation provides a new learning model by combining physical and digital content, creating an enriched and interactive universe. This mobile technology offers new opportunities for the promotion of learning inside and outside the classroom, linked to multiple intelligences, in particular, to the spatial and naturalistic intelligences. Taking these premises into account, an analysis of several geolocation applications (N=20) is carried out in order to determine their potential to develop spatial and naturalistic intelligences. To this end, case study methodology is adopted, and an analysis instrument is proposed consisting of 15 indicators grouped into three dimensions: 1) geolocation, 2) spatial intelligence (spatial orientation and spatial representation), and 3) naturalistic intelligence (physical geography and environment). Although the geolocation applications analyzed boost spatial intelligence through the different options they incorporate, the same cannot be said of the naturalist one. It is considered relevant that they include contents oriented to environmental awareness.

DOI: 10.4018/978-1-7998-0249-5.ch008

INTRODUCTION

Augmented reality offers numerous opportunities to promote innovative experiences through the combination of physical and virtual contents in the same space, offering further information about the environment which surrounds us. AR makes it possible to broaden the knowledge and perception of the physical world with three-dimensional images, sounds or animations, among other things, for the purpose of enriching reality with interactive and digital contents (Lee, 2012). The portability that is associated with this technology through the utilization of mobile devices has implications in training processes, insofar as it allows learning to take place anytime and anywhere (Burbules, 2012; Villalustre, 2016). Thus, thanks to geolocation, one can promote new contexts and strategies which influence learning. Bearing this in mind, several experiences have been carried out in different contexts and levels based on using geolocation. Among them stands out the one developed by Villalustre and Del Moral (2016) in the university context, where students enrolled in the degree in teacher training for infant education designed a variety of training proposals to exploit this technology.

Geolocation favors a new learning model by combining physical contents with digital ones, thus creating an enriched and interactive universe. Geolocation is characterized by its customization capacity, its portability and interaction, as well by its ubiquity (Kaufmann & Schmalstieg, 2003). Similarly, the superimposition of information added by means of geolocation makes it possible to view images and videos about the place where we find ourselves when the GPS coordinates are activated, enlarging the experience and favoring —in the words of Mtebe and Raisamo (2014)— a more prominent role of students. Training goes beyond the classroom with geolocation, since the possibility exists to plan activities in spaces open to the environment helping to ensure that learning will be really significant and situated (Paul, 2014). Thus, according to the Horizon 2020 report, collected by Durall, Gros, Maina, Johnson, and Adams (2012), the benefits brought by this technology include the following: 1) the framework of m-learning projects favors territory-linked types of learning and adds experiential value to the work that revolves around specific contents and skills; 2) the geolocated information permits to establish relationships between various types of data and to visualize them, which in turn facilitates the identification of patterns; and 3) the geolocated data allow users to find like-minded people located in a nearby environment and to contact them through location-based social networking services.

This mobile technology consequently offers new opportunities to promote types of learning developed inside and outside the classroom, linked to multiple intelligences, and more precisely, to spatial and naturalist intelligence. Geolocations makes it possible to put together and develop training initiatives associated with the exploration and knowledge of the environment. In this sense, Sharples (2003) considers that it boosts spatial thinking for the representation and manipulation of information, as well as problem solving. The mobility linked to this type of technology helps to bring us closer to the physical elements in the environment combined with virtual elements so that spatial and visual representation can be developed. Geolocation likewise breaks down the physical barriers in the classroom, allowing for the interaction with different natural environment spaces to generate new meanings. All in all, this paper performs an analysis of various geolocation applications to determine their educational potential as precursors of abilities and skills related to spatial and naturalist intelligence.

LITERATURE REVIEW

Multiple Intelligences: Spatial and Naturalist

The Theory of Multiple Intelligences has long been becoming an integral part of the educational context. According to this theory, intelligence is a capacity that the individual has to solve problems and to develop products within a specific cultural context (Gardner, 2011). The model sees intelligence in a three-dimensional manner proposing the existence of diverse intelligences (spatial, naturalist, linguistic, logical-mathematical, musical, body and kinesthetic, intrapersonal and interpersonal) which appear in a unique and multiple way in each person, cognitive aspects being enhanced through the educational and cultural context. The impact of this theory resulted in the development by some schools of a new configuration regarding learning styles, pedagogical strategies and didactic materials (Gardner, 2005). However, the school curricula in the first years tended to focus on developing linguistic and logical-mathematical intelligence, considering that their mastery was equivalent to being intelligent and successful in studies (Batdı, 2017) —obviating the main characteristic of multiplicity.

These experiences have been corrected and the theory continues to be applied at present, with the value corresponding to the individuality of students and their different capacities, which constituted the focus of attention particularly at Infant and Primary Education levels (Ubago, Viciana, Pérez, Martínez, Padial, & Puertas, 2018), and different results were obtained depending on the methodology used to address multiple intelligences (Ali, Soosan, & Hamze, 2013). As for gender, the analysis carried out by Lori (2005) about the preferences of higher education students when it comes to learning activities revealed that men preferred those including logical-mathematical intelligence, whereas women showed a predilection for activities linked to intrapersonal intelligence. Instead, the study with 5-to-6-year-old students carried out by Lizano and Umaña (2008) showed that both boys and girls preferred activities from the logical-mathematical field, perhaps because of the materials used. With respect to the degree of difficulty, boys found it to a greater extent in activities related to interpersonal intelligence such as making friends; instead, girls had more difficulties in developing fine motor skills linked to kinesthetic intelligence.

Nevertheless, this study will examine the possibilities to develop spatial and naturalist intelligence through geolocation applications. Thus, spatial intelligence, also known as visuo-spatial intelligence, refers to the ability to learn visually and to solve spatial problems; and it is present, among other contexts, in the resolution of problems linked to experimental sciences (Samsudyn, Haniza, Abdul-Talib, & Ibrahim, 2015). A key aspect of spatial intelligence is the ability to understand and master the space through the observation and viewing of objects from different perspectives. Its development is supported in activities that revolve around observing elements and their arrangement in space. Observation as well as all the visual aspects are highly present, the same as the representation of symbols by means of writing and drawing, along with the creation of 2D and 3D representations using different materials and representation strategies. Spatial intelligence will sometimes be linked to kinesthetic intelligence, as evidenced in the use of geolocation apps that include the hand manipulation of tablets and devices in interaction with the spatial environment and the elements shaping it.

As for naturalist intelligence, it consists in the ability to observe, recognize and interpret elements of the natural environment such as the natural phenomena of ecosystems. Its development consequently seems typical of open natural spaces, but there are other ways, of course. In the context of primary education, Meyer (2005) suggested the possibility to work on it through field tasks and observation in environments such as the school center premises. This type of intelligence clearly relates to some knowledge areas typically linked to different sciences, e.g. biology, zoology, geography, physics, geology and astronomy. This includes experimenting and interacting with the different materials present in the environment as well as with living beings like animals and plants. Naturalist intelligence is connected to other intelligences, among them the logical-mathematical one in problem solving (Del Moral, Fernández, & Guzmán, 2015). In the field of experimental sciences, kinesthetic and spatial intelligence are linked to each other, sometimes being developed with activities that require the manipulation of objects such as magnifying glasses or maps as well as the drawing of graphs with shapes and colors (Samsudyn, Haniza, Abdul-Talib, & Ibrahim, 2015). In turn, Santos, Gusmão, and Mangueira (2006) have developed research works about its implementation in virtual spaces.

Geolocation to Boost Spatial and Naturalist Intelligence in Ubiquitous Ecosystems

The irruption of mobile devices into training processes has helped to generate a more situated and contextual type of learning, promoting new opportunities and challenges for teachers' professional development. Thus, teacher training should deal with the possibilities offered by ubiquitous learning, where one can access information anytime and anywhere. For Melhuish and Falloon (2010), its potential lies in the flexibility that it provides to access training resources without any time and space limitations, creating an environment enriched thanks to augmented reality and geolocation. Abernathy (2001) in turn considered that these technologies have great potential to optimize training processes. Because of its versatility and portability, ubiquitous learning becomes a powerful ally to enhance multiple intelligences and, particularly, spatial and naturalist intelligence, since it contributes to generate learning experiences closer to the environment, where spatial orientation and representation, as well as contact with the environment, acquire prominence.

Ubiquitous technologies additionally trigger a situated and socially distributed type of learning where educational centers and their teaching staff can benefit from the experiences and knowledge developed in other learning environments to boost the development of multiple intelligences. In this sense, the potential of a ubiquitous resource often lies in the contributions made by numerous teachers, since the creation of learning communities makes it possible to implement a distributed and shared process as a collective good for the educational community (Liao, Huang, Chen, & Huang, 2015). Situated or ubiquitous learning consequently generates a series of opportunities, not only for students, who can play a more active role, but also for teachers, shaping a new teaching ecology linked both to the potential of digital tools and to the motivational factors generated by them. Ubiquitous learning essentially permits to relate learning goals to the educational contexts and purposes associated with experience, as suggested by Pimmer, Mateescu, and Gröhbiel (2016). For their part, Cattaneo, Motta, and Gurtner (2015) highlight the benefits derived from using them in classrooms in terms of usability, effectiveness and student satisfaction, as they help to develop learning linked to multiple intelligences. Instead, Martín-Gutiérrez, Contero, and Alcañiz (2010) believe that the development of spatial and natural intelligence will only be possible through the design of learning experiences which focus the student's attention on the real task.

On another note, Slijepcevic (2013) took the cognitive load theory as a reference to carry out an analysis about the possibilities of augmented reality and of geolocation applications, concluding that the latter still find themselves at an initial stage of development and that further studies will be needed to have a real knowledge of their whole potential when it comes to developing spatial and naturalist intelligence. Nevertheless, Huang, Schmidt, and Gartner (2012) analyzed the influence that the use of geolocation exerts on spatial learning, reaching the conclusion that a positive relationship exists between them. In turn, Joo-Nagata, Abad, Giner, and García-Peñalvo (2017) deduced that the incorporation of geolocation increases the effectiveness of learning and teaching processes linked to spatial and naturalist intelligence among others.

All in all, augmented reality and geolocation enable mobile devices to provide students with an additional multimedia layer of interactive experiences which add a simultaneous flow of information that may result in enriching training activities (Hsu, Chiou, Tseng, & Hwang, 2016; Carbonel & Bernejo, 2017; González, 2014), this being a hugely powerful resource to boost the acquisition and consolidation of multiple intelligences, especially naturalist and spatial intelligence. Therefore, when faced with this new ecosystem, teachers need new strategies able to integrate and exploit the opportunities brought by mobile technologies (Hung et al., 2014; Merino, Pino, Meyer, Garrido, & Gallardo, 2015) to develop these intelligences. In this regard, our paper analyzes a set of geolocation-based applications for the purpose of determining their potential to develop spatial and naturalist intelligence and giving primary education teachers tools and resources able to enhance ubiquitous learning in various contexts.

THE STUDY: ANALYSIS ABOUT GEOLOCATION APPLICATIONS AND THEIR RELATIONSHIP WITH SPATIAL AND NATURALIST INTELLIGENCE

Context and Objectives

The advances experienced by mobile devices have turned geolocation into an accessible and user-friendly tool. The utilization of different technologies which combine real and virtual information has given rise to the emergence of numerous applications which cover all sorts of contents, among them, those related to spatial and naturalist intelligence. Hence why this paper examines a total of 20 geolocation-based applications with the aim of determining their educational potential as precursors of abilities and skills linked to spatial and natural intelligence.

Methodology

The study adopts a methodology based on case studies in which a content analysis is performed about 20 geolocation applications to promote students' acquisition of knowledge linked to spatial and naturalist intelligence. Such geolocation applications characteristically make virtual and real elements converge in an attempt to shape a new environment for learning.

Study Sample

The selection of the 20 cases which constitute the study sample took place late in 2018 and was confined to the search for applications to address contents closely related to the development of abilities and skills linked to spatial and natural intelligence. These were the criteria followed in the selection of cases: 1) applications based on geolocation; 2) free applications; 3) applications a priori focused on spatial and naturalist intelligence; and 4) applications which could be adapted to primary education students. The study sample thus includes the following mobile applications (Table 1):

Table 1. Study sample of the geolocation applications analyzed

Application ID	Platform	Language
Eduloc	IOS and Android	Spanish, Catalan, Basque, English, and Portuguese
WallaMe	IOS and Android	Spanish, German, English, and Italian
Mapstory	PC	English
Pokemon Go	IOS and Android	Spanish, German, traditional Chinese, Korean, French, English, Italian, Japanese, and Portuguese
Geoguessr	IOS and PC	English
GmapGIS	PC	English
Scribble Maps	PC	English
Story maps de arcgis	PC	English, German, Spanish, French, Japanese, Russian, and Chinese
Google Maps	PC, IOS and Android	77 languages
Geocaching	PC, IOS and Android	26 languages
Star Chart	IOS and Android	English, French, German, Italian, Japanese, Korean, Chinese, and Spanish
Google Sky Map	PC	27 languages
Acrossair	IOS	English, Spanish, German, French, Italian, Portuguese, Korean, Japanese, Dutch, and Chinese
AR GPS Compass Map 3D	Android	English
ARCITY	IOS	English
Measure Kit	IOS	English
View Ranger	PC, IOS and Android	English, Czech, French, German, Italian, Russian, Spanish, and Swedish
Horizon Explorer	IOS and Android	English
Yeapp	IOS and Android	English, Spanish, Portuguese, and Catalan
Cuaderno de campo	IOS	English and Spanish

Analysis Tool

The 20 selected applications were analyzed taking into account the contributions made by Burgos & Guatame (2011) and Dziekonski (2012), according to the study dimensions and indicators listed below:

1. Geolocation
   a. It offers the superimposition of virtual objects (augmented digital contents).
   b. It makes interaction with virtual objects possible.
   c. Type of digital information that it offers or which can be added (images; audios; videos; text; 3D objects).
2. Visual-spatial intelligence
   a. Spatial orientation
   b. It identifies the subject's position on the map.
   c. It includes spatial rotation actions (moving, manipulating the map).

d. It incorporates elements of interest to facilitate orientation (monuments, museums…).
   e. Spatial representation
   f. It permits to add several points on the same map.
   g. It provides the possibility to visualize the environment with different types of maps (e.g. satellite maps, geographical maps or street maps).
   h. It identifies and incorporates the scale for measuring distances.
3. Naturalist intelligence
   a. Physical geography
   b. It includes options to identify altitude and latitude
   c. It adds a system to recognize the geographical accidents (e.g. mountains, peaks or valleys) in the environment.
   d. It incorporates information about lakes, lagoons, rivers, etc. in the geolocated space.
   e. Environment
   f. It offers a system to identify the flora and fauna of the geolocated place.
   g. It incorporates resources to raise awareness about the problems that may affect the environment.
   h. It has a system able to offer solutions to environmental problems in the context or which makes it possible to place them at the student's disposal.

THE SIGNIFICANCE OF STUDY: RESULTS

Based on the study of the selected applications and using the instrument created for that purpose, the aim sought is to determine the capacity of geolocation applications to boost abilities and skills closely related to spatial and naturalist intelligence. The results can be found below.

Geolocation

A first block of analysis has as its aim to identify the geolocation resources incorporated by applications. For this purpose, we firstly checked if the latter make it possible to superimpose virtual objects on the physical reality. Thus, Figure 1 reveals that more than half of applications (60%) include this possibility, among them the applications *WallaMe* or *Story Maps de Arcgis* to quote but two. Nevertheless, 40% of them lack mechanisms to add augmented digital contents, such as *Geoguessr* or *GmapGIS*, which in our view limits the didactic opportunities offered by this technology.

Similarly, as shown in Figure 1, a high proportion of the geolocation applications under analysis (80%) does not allow the student to interact with the virtual objects that are incorporated. In other words, they do not permit to move or rotate the objects appearing on the mobile device screen and which are superimposed on the physical reality —examples of this are the applications *Cuaderno de campo* or *Google Maps*. 20% of them offer this option to the student, though, providing a more enriching experience, e.g. *Pokemón Go* or *Acrossair*.

Furthermore, we also examined the type of digital information that the selected applications permit to incorporate (Figure 2). This made it possible to check that images (37%) and textual information (33%) are the most predominant ones, since they usually need fewer technical requirements for their inclusion and visualization, as exemplified by the applications *Scribble Maps* and *Geocaching* among others. A lower proportion corresponds to those which allow for the incorporation of 3D objects (14%), such as

Figure 1. Results obtained after analyzing the capacity of apps to superimpose objects and to make interaction with virtual objects possible

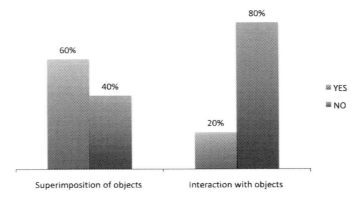

Figure 2. Type of digital information that the apps offer or which can be added

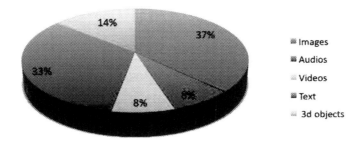

Story Maps de Arcgis and *Pokemon Go*, and which make possible a more attractive experience for the student. And, in final position, we find applications like *Mapstory* and *Eduloc*, which permit the inclusion of videos and audios —among other types of information— with the same percentage in both cases (8%).

Spatial Intelligence

A second block of study has as its aim to verify the extent to which the geolocation applications under examination permit to deal with different elements linked to spatial intelligence, and more precisely, to spatial orientation and representation.

Spatial Orientation

The results obtained provide evidence that 51% of applications identify the student's position on the map, as opposed to 49% which do not offer this possibility. Spatial rotation, an element which may prove relevant to understand spatial issues, is an action included in a high percentage of applications (80%) —only apps such as *WallaMe, Scribble Maps, Acrossair* and *Horizon Explorer* do not incorporate it. The scale for measuring distances is included in a large proportion of cases (90%), which helps the development of activities linked to spatial intelligence —the remaining 10% of applications, among them *WallaMe* and *AR GPS Compass Map3D*, do not include this possibility (Figure 3).

Figure 3. Results obtained in relation to the possibilities that apps offer to facilitate spatial orientation

Spatial Representation

When it comes to spatial representation, only half of the applications develop this indicator properly. Thus, 65% identify and incorporate some type of scale for measuring distances and 50% permit to visualize the environment on the basis of different types of maps with diverse information, as is the case of *Google Maps, Geocaching, GMap* and *Map Story*. In contrast, only 49% of applications —e.g. *Eduloc* or *Cuaderno de campo*— make it possible to add several points on a single map or plan (Figure 4).

Naturalist Intelligence

These third block of analysis seeks to determine the extent to which the applications analyzed try to or can favor the development of naturalist intelligence based on two dimensions: Physical Geography and Environment.

Figure 4. Results obtained in relation to the possibilities that apps offer to facilitate spatial orientation

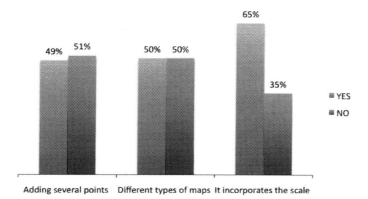

Physical Geography

An initial analysis of the applications, reflected in Figure 5, shows that 50% of them include options to determine the altitude and longitude of a specific point, as illustrated by the apps *Mapstory, Google Maps* or *Geocaching*. The remaining 50%, among them applications such as *Pokemon Go* and others generally utilized in educational contexts such as *Eduloc* and *WallaMe*, do not permit to incorporate any information whatsoever about the recognition of geographical coordinates.

A similar trend becomes visible when analyzing how many of the applications make it possible to recognize different geographical accidents in the environment (Figure 5). Thus, 50% of applications —e.g. *Scribble Maps* or *Story Maps de arcgis*— add a system to recognize mountains, peaks or valleys. Instead, the remaining 50% include no information about these geographical accidents; applications such as *Cuaderno de Campo* or *Geocaching* stand out in this group. It is additionally necessary to highlight that only 30% of applications provide simultaneous data about geographical coordinates and accidents.

The results obtained in the analysis about the information offered with regard to the recognition of waterways, aquifers and lakes reveals that apps pay more attention to this issue if compared to the previous items, with the number of applications that include it growing to 65% (Figure 5). Examples of this can be found in *Horizon Explorer, Yeapp* or *Geoguessr*. However, 35% of applications —including *Measure Kit, Geocaching, Eduloc* or *Wallame*— provide no type of information whatsoever in this respect. This lack acquires more relevance if we take into account that the last three applications mentioned are usually connected to educational environments.

Environment

It can be stated that environmental information is obviated by nearly all the applications examined. None of them permits to consult and identify the flora and fauna in the environment, and only 5% of them incorporate resources meant to raise environmental awareness or to offer solutions for the environmental problems that the user can put into practice —as can be seen in Figure 6. Only the application *Story maps de arcgis* offers information about this, which not only reduces to a huge extent the didactic possibilities

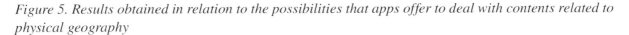

Figure 5. Results obtained in relation to the possibilities that apps offer to deal with contents related to physical geography

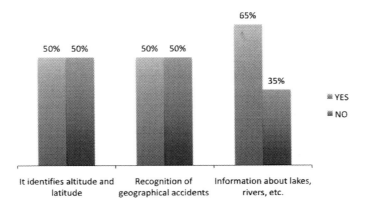

Figure 6. Results obtained in relation to the possibilities that apps offer to deal with contents related to the environment

Category	YES	NO
It identifies flora and fauna	100%	0%
Environmental awareness	5%	95%
Environmental solutions	5%	95%

of these applications when it comes to the knowledge of the environment and the involvement with it but also prevents the development of personal attitudes towards sustainability.

DISCUSSION

Augmented reality and geolocation offer numerous opportunities to facilitate the construction of new types of learning linked to visual and naturalist intelligence among others. Geolocation applications are thus shaping new scenarios to optimize training processes beyond conventional classrooms. However, the latter may determine the training experiences depending on the options that they incorporate. Therefore, after performing an analysis about the 20 selected applications, Table 2 collects those which comply with the established evaluation indicators, i.e. those which superimpose virtual objects on the already existing physical reality, which allow for interaction with digital elements, and which make it possible to incorporate a greater variety of digital information.

We can consequently check the existence of a large number of geolocation applications which combine two realities —the physical and the digital one— within a single space, thus favoring a familiarization and knowledge about the physical elements in the environment, in tune with the suggestions made by Melhuish and Falloon (2010), together with an enriched training experience, as stressed by Cattaneo, Motta, & Gurtner (2015). Nevertheless, only *Pokemon Go, AR GPS Compass Map 3D* and *View Ranger* make it possible to manipulate digital elements, increasing students' interaction with the devices, as

Table 2. Applications which superimpose objects, allow for interaction and incorporate a greater variety of digital information

Apps which superimpose virtual objects	Apps which allow for interaction with digital elements	Apps which incorporate a greater variety of digital information
WallaMe; Pokemon Go; Google Sky Map; Acrossair; AR GPS Compass Map 3D; ARCITY; Measure Kit; View Ranger; Horizon Explorer; Yeapp	Pokemon Go; AR GPS Compass Map 3D; View Ranger	Eduloc; MapStory; Story maps de arcgis.

well as their involvement in educational tasks. In turn, *Eduloc, MapStory* and *Story maps* de Arcgis are the ones which make it possible to incorporate a greater variety of digital information. Along the same lines, the works carried out by Kaufmann & Schmalstieg (2003) reinforce the need to offer immersive multimedia experiences in which these emergent technologies are used to favor the development of competences and skills of different kinds.

On the other hand, the set of indicators related to spatial orientation offer a positive assessment, even though it is necessary to highlight the results corresponding to the applications which include the student's identification in the physical space. The examination of the way in which mobile applications and devices are utilized in educational contexts made by Chiang, Yang and Hwang (2014) revealed that GPS accuracy in learning limited the visualization and location of elements. Somehow, without drawing a comparison with this study, it is considered that the absence of the student's position in applications implies a limitation in the educational experiences which benefits neither spatial orientation nor learning, insofar as the principles of spatial and temporal continuity are restricted, thus making it impossible to provide complete information about the contexts. Half of the applications analyzed offer these possibilities, though, which helps to improve the student's spatial orientation (Table 3).

In turn, Del Cerro and Méndez (2017) examined the benefits derived from using augmented reality and geolocation to develop spatial intelligence —especially in the ability to rotate elements and to visualize them in space— as well as spatial visualization in general. In this respect, applications such as *Eduloc, MapStory, PokemonGo, Geoguessr, GMapGIS, Story maps de arcgis* or *Google Maps* make it easier to improve these skills. However, we consider it advisable for the group of applications to favor spatial orientation through the incorporation of the student's position in the physical space, since that would help to understand geographical and spatial concepts even better, as suggested by Slijepcevic (2013).

In what regards spatial representation, the applications *Google Maps, Geocaching, GMap* and *Map Story* are the most complete when it comes to these indicators (Table 4). In this sense, Huang, Schmidt, and Gartner (2012) claim that geolocation applications for mobile devices should have a pedestrian navigation system which can offer enriching experiences to enhance learning and development of spatial skills by students, perhaps through the design of specific applications for teaching.

If, as explained above, the analysis shows that the use of applications which include geolocation constitutes a good resource to develop spatial intelligence, one cannot say the same about their relationship with naturalist intelligence, even though it is necessary to highlight the differences between the results obtained in the dimensions "Physical Geography" and "Environment". Concerning the former, as can be seen in Table 5, only half of them identify altitude and longitude —basic concepts for training

Table 3. Applications that include the subject's position, incorporate special rotation and facilitate orientation

Apps which include the subject's position	Apps which include spatial rotation	Apps which facilitate orientation
Map story;PokemonGo;GMap GIS;GoogleMaps;Geocaching; AR GPS Compass Map 3D;Measure Kit;View Ranger;Horizon Explorer;Yeapp;Cuaderno de campo.	Eduloc;MapStory;PokemonGo;Geoguessr;GMapGIS;Story maps de arcgis; Google Maps;Geocaching;Star Chat;Google Sky Map;AR GPS Compass;Map 3D;ARCITY;Measure Kit; View Ranger; Yeapp;Cuaderno de campo.	Eduloc;Mapstory; Pokemon Go;Geoguessr;Gmap GIS;Scribble Maps;Story maps de arcgis; Google Maps;Geocaching;Star Chat;Google Sky Map;Acrossair;ARCITY; Measure Kit; View Ranger; Horizon;Explorer; Yeapp;Cuaderno de campo.

Geolocation for the Improvement of Spatial and Naturalist Intelligence in Primary Education

Table 4. Applications which make it easier to add several points, include different types of maps, and incorporate scales

Apps which permit to add several points	Apps with different types of maps	Apps which incorporate the scale
Eduloc; Mapstory; GmapGIS; Scribble Maps; Story maps de arcgis; Google Maps; Geocaching; Yeapp; Cuaderno de campo	Eduloc; Mapstory; Pokemon Go; Geoguessr; GmapGIS; Scribble Maps; Story maps de arcgis; Google Maps; Geocaching; View Ranger;	Mapstory; Geoguessr; GmapGIS; Scribble Maps; Story maps de arcgis; Google Maps; Geocaching; Star Chart; Acrossair; AR GPS Compass Map 3D; ARCITY; Measure Kit; View Ranger; Horizon Explorer.

Table 5. Applications that include information about geographical coordinates, geographical accidents and water elements

Apps which identify altitude and longitude	Apps which add systems for the recognition of geographical accidents	Apps which add information about waterways, aquifers and lakes
Mapstory; GmapGis; Google Maps; Geocaching; Acrossair; Ar GPS Compass Map 3D; ARCITY; Measure Kit; View Ranger; Horizon Explorer	Mapstory; Geoguessr; GmapGis; Scribble Maps; Story maps de arcgis; Google Maps; Geocaching; View Ranger; Horizon Explorer; Yeapp	Mapstory; Geoguessr; GmapGis; Scribble Maps; Story maps de arcgis; Google Maps; Geocaching; Acrossair; AR GPS Compass Map 3D; ARCITY; Measure Kit; View Ranger; Horizon Explorer; Yeapp

in Geography. As pointed out by Hammond, Bozdin, and Stanlick (2014), the educational use of geolocation devices with Global Positioning Systems (GPS) may prove highly useful to provide a practical clarification of these concepts, which are abstract in principle, promoting spatial thinking skills; hence why applications should prioritize their incorporation. However, it is worth mentioning that applications such as *Star Chart* or *Google Sky Map* do not include information about this indicator, because they focus on the visualization of stellar elements outside Planet Earth.

Medzini, Meishar-Tal, and Sneh (2015) pointed out that mobile devices are suited to perform learning activities in the context of Geography outside the classroom, but only 6 of the applications examined add information about coordinates, geographical accidents and water elements in the environment, namely: *Mapstory, GmapsGis, Google Maps, View Ranger, Horizon Explorer* and *Geocaching*. However, although Gros and Forés (2013) referred to the connection existing between geolocation and a closer link with the territory which can facilitate the implementation of projects associated with the community and the environment, the dimension "Environment" reveals that none of the applications permits to recognize the flora and fauna, and only *Story maps de arcgis* includes resources to raise awareness about environmental problems while simultaneously offering possible solutions to them.

Apart from that, in the planning of activities for Primary Education with these aplications is considered appropriate/we consider appropriate as a suggestion:

1. The search for a balance between technological and traditional activities at the curriculum for the develop of all intelligences and skills.
2. The proposals for flexible activities in which the student can self-regulate their learning process.
3. Facilitate a relationship between mobile applications and spaces of cultural and natural heritage (museums, exhibitions, routes through places of artistic and cultural heritage, routes through natural

environments, etc.). It is important that they be places with contents already organized, because they are a very positive educational resource for teachers.
4. Increase the musical and sound resources of the applications to a greater extent.
5. Generate inter-level experiences that favor collaboration between students in schools and the use of applications. In this sense, the Scape´s Room methodology can be a trigger.
6. Use applications without using all their features. With the aim of promoting the autonomy and reasoning of the students.
7. The organization of programs to promote multiple interdisciplinary intelligences that promote human as well as technological aspects.
8. To relate the use of these applications with processes of gamification in the educational field through the realization of track games or treasure hunts that stimulate both the MI and the cognitive abilities of the students, linking the games with the contents taught ordinarily in classroom.

CONCLUSION

Mobile devices currently make it possible for learning to take place anytime and anywhere, which favors a greater knowledge of the surrounding environment and an interaction with it. The use of applications which incorporate augmented reality and geolocation additionally helps in the acquisition and enhancement of multiple intelligences through the enrichment of the educational experience by means of virtual contents and the supply of associated contents. More precisely, utilizing geolocation with augmented contents makes it possible to obtain immediate information in any physical environment, which favors the development of spatial and naturalist intelligence by providing additional contents related either to spatial orientation and representation or to physical geography and the environment.

A total of 20 geolocation applications have thus been analyzed in this study seeking to check the extent to which those apps favor the implementation of spatial and naturalist intelligence based on an *ad-hoc* prepared instrument. After examining the dimensions and indicators linked to geolocation, it can be concluded that only more than half of the applications under study use augmented and superimposed digital contents, preferably together with images and texts, and to a lesser extent audios, videos or 3D objects, which limits the chances of an immersive experience. Nevertheless, 80% permit the interaction with virtual objects and their manipulation, which in principle may benefit the development of the intelligences under examination. Similarly, the applications analyzed make tactile interaction possible and perhaps their improvement in combination with virtual reality will eventually facilitate the complete learning that they mention. The applications under study which permit an interaction with digital elements (*PokemonGo, AR GPS Compass Map 3D* and *View Ranger*) would be close to this manipulative possibility.

Based on the analysis about the potential that the geolocation applications analyzed have when it comes to developing spatial intelligence, it deserves to be pointed out that, although the results suggest that such apps contribute to develop this intelligence, the contents referred to spatial orientation are more present than those associated with representation. Thus, 80% of the applications under study incorporate interest elements to make orientation easier as can be milestones or significant buildings (monuments and museums, to quote but two), and 90% include spatial rotation as a task when it comes to moving or manipulating the map. However, only 51% of applications identify the student's position on the map, which constrains the chances of spatial location according to the teacher's location and perspective. Even though the geolocation applications examined pay quite a lot of attention to orientation, thus developing a basic element of spatial intelligence, the results suggest lacks in terms of the representation possibilities offered by those apps. Only half of them offer the chance to visualize the environment with different types of maps (satellite maps, geographical maps or street maps, among others), bringing together the relationship and understanding of various spatial planes. Likewise, just above half of these applications incorporate the scale, which makes it impossible to relate the real space dimensions to those offered by the application. The fact that almost half of them do not permit to add several points on a single map reinforces the limitation regarding the measurement and representation of distances.

The study at hand allows us to state that the geolocation applications examined have severe lacks in the treatment of naturalist intelligence, much more so in what regards the information supplied with respect to the environment than in that linked to physical geography. More than half of these apps provide information about the water elements in the environment, although only half of them make it possible to recognize geographical accidents of interest, such as mountains or valleys, and supply information about coordinates and GPS positioning. As for the treatment of the environment, it is never possible to identify the associated flora and fauna, and only one application among those examined offers environmental awareness resources and solutions for that purpose which the student can incorporate.

As it has been possible to verify a new field is opened where to develop different research lines. The first way is to measure the improvement of the spatial and naturalistic intelligence with the use of these applications in Primary Education students, through validated instruments referred to MI or the validation of new ones. Also, it would be interesting to carry out research on the use of these applications and their contribution to the development of MI in Secondary Education.

Another way to explore is to produce research studies on the relationship between the use of applications, multiple intelligences, creativity and other internal variables of people. For this it is necessary to establish work programs with students of different ages and also integrate other variables such as academic performance or the learning strategies used. Also could be interesting promote digital platforms for the educational community that collect feedback from teachers and students about its usefulness and functionality.

The advancement of technology and its integration into society is very fast. For this reason, these investigations should be addressed in the short and medium term. It is necessary to expand studies on intelligences in educational environments where virtual reality and artificial intelligence are also used. In this way knowing the development of multiple intelligences in relation to mobile applications, artificial intelligence and virtual reality would help to know which are the best tools for teaching in Primary Education.

In the light of all the above, taking into account that learning with mobile devices fosters educational experiences outside the classroom and in the nearby physical and natural environment, it would be advisable to ensure that the geolocation applications which can be used as potential educational resources include contents oriented to environmental awareness, supplying information about the problems which affect the environment and suggesting possible personal actions, ultimately seeking the improvement of a sustainable milieu.

REFERENCES

Abernathy, D. J. (2001). Get ready for m-learning. *Training & Development*, *55*(2), 10–20.

Ali, A., Soosan, L., & Hamze, A. (2013). The Effect of Teaching Strategy Based on Multiple Intelligences on Students' Academic Achievement in Science Course. *Universal Journal of Educational Research*, *1*(4), 281-284. Retrieved from http://www.hrpub.org

Batdı, V. (2017). The effect of multiple intelligences on academic achievement: A meta-analytic and thematic study. *Educational Sciences: Theory & Practice*, *17*(6). Retrieved of doi:10.12738/estp.2017.6.0104

Burbules, N. C. (2012). Ubiquitous Learning and the Future of Teaching. *Encounters*, *13*, 3–14.

Burgos, B. M. V., & Guatame, A. X. L. (2011). ¿Cómo la estrategia de mapas mentales y conceptuales estimulan el desarrollo de la inteligencia espacial en estudiantes universitarios? *Tabula Rasa*, *15*(15), 221–254. doi:10.25058/20112742.105

Carbonell, C., & Bermejo, L. A. (2017). Landscape interpretation with augmented reality and maps to improve spatial orientation skill. *Journal of Geography in Higher Education*, *41*(1), 119–133. doi:10.1080/03098265.2016.1260530

Cattaneo, A. A., Motta, E., & Gurtner, J. L. (2015). Evaluating a Mobile and Online System for Apprentices' Learning Documentation in Vocational Education: Usability, Effectiveness and Satisfaction. *International Journal of Mobile and Blended Learning*, *7*(3), 40–58. doi:10.4018/IJMBL.2015070103

Chiang, T. H. C., Yang, S. J., & Hwang, G. J. (2014). An augmented reality-based mobile learning system to improve students' learning achievements and motivations in natural science inquiry activities. *Journal of Educational Technology & Society*, *17*(4), 352–365.

Del Cerro, F., & Morales, G. (2017). Realidad Aumentada como herramienta de mejora de la inteligencia espacial en estudiantes de educación secundaria. *Revista de Educación a Distancia*, *54*. doi:10.6018/red/54/5

Del Moral, M. E., Fernández, L. C., & Guzmán, A. P. (2015). Videogames: Multisensorial incentives for strengthening multiple intelligences in primary education. *Electronic Journal of Research in Educational Psychology*, *13*(2), 243–270. doi:10.14204/ejrep.36.14091

Durall, G. E., Gros, S. B., Maina, M. F., Johnson, L., & Adams, S. (2012). *Perspectivas tecnológicas: educación superior en Iberoamérica 2012-2017*. Austin, TX: The New Media Consortium.

Dziekonski, M. (2012). La inteligencia espacial: Una mirada a Howard Gardner. *Revista ArteOficio*, *2*(2), 1–12.

Gardner, H. (2005). *Multiple intelligences and education*. Retrieved from http://www.infed.org/thinkers/gardner.htm

Gardner, H. (2011). *Inteligencias múltiples. La teoría en la práctica*. Barcelona: Paidós.

González, R. D. M. (2014). Aprendizaje por descubrimiento, enseñanza activa y geoinformación: hacia una didáctica de la geografía innovadora. *Didáctica geográfica*, *14*, 17-36.

Gros, B., & Forés, A. (2013). Using geolocation in secondary education to improve situated learning: Analysis of two case studies. *RELATEC, 12*(2), 41–53.

Hammond, T., Bozdin, A., & Stanlick, S. E. (2014). Redefining the Longitude/Latitude Experience with a Scaffolded Geocache. *Social Studies, 105*(5), 237–244. doi:10.1080/00377996.2014.920289

Hsu, T. Y., Chiou, C. K., Tseng, J. C., & Hwang, G. J. (2016). Development and evaluation of an active learning support system for context-aware ubiquitous learning. *IEEE Transactions on Learning Technologies, 9*(1), 37–45. doi:10.1109/TLT.2015.2439683

Huang, H., Schmidt, M., & Gartner, G. (2012). Spatial knowledge acquisition with mobile maps, augmented reality and voice in the context of GPS-based pedestrian navigation: Results from a field test. *Cartography and Geographic Information Science, 39*(2), 107–116. doi:10.1559/15230406392107

Hung, P. H., Hwang, G. J., Lee, Y. H., Wu, T. H., Vogel, B., Milrad, M., & Johansson, E. (2014). A problem-based ubiquitous learning approach to improving the questioning abilities of elementary school students. *Journal of Educational Technology & Society, 17*(4), 316–334.

Joo-Nagata, J., Abad, F. M., Giner, J. G. B., & García-Peñalvo, F. J. (2017). Augmented reality and pedestrian navigation through its implementation in m-learning and e-learning: Evaluation of an educational program in Chile. *Computers & Education, 111*, 1–17. doi:10.1016/j.compedu.2017.04.003

Kaufmann, H., & Schmalstieg, D. (2003). Mathematics and geometry education with collaborative augmented reality. *Computers & Graphics, 27*(3), 339–345. doi:10.1016/S0097-8493(03)00028-1

Lee, K. (2012). Augmented Reality in Education and Training. *TechTrends, 56*(2), 13–21. doi:10.100711528-012-0559-3

Liao, Y. W., Huang, Y. M., Chen, H. C., & Huang, S. H. (2015). Exploring the antecedents of collaborative learning performance over social networking sites in a ubiquitous learning context. *Computers in Human Behavior, 43*, 313–323. doi:10.1016/j.chb.2014.10.028

Lizano, K., & Umaña, M. (2008). La Teoría de las Inteligencias Múltiples en la práctica docente en Educación Preescolar. *Revista Electrónica Educare, 12*(1), 135–149.

Lori, A. A. (2005). Multiple Intelligences: A comparative study between the preferences of males and females. *Social Behavior and Personality, 33*(1), 77–88. doi:10.2224bp.2005.33.1.77

Martín-Gutiérrez, J., Contero, M., & Alcañiz, M. (2010). Evaluating the usability of an augmented reality based educational application. In *International Conference on Intelligent Tutoring Systems* (pp. 296-306). Springer. 10.1007/978-3-642-13388-6_34

Medzini, A., Meishar-Tal, H., & Sneh, Y. (2015). Use of mobile technologies as support tools for geography field trips. *International Research in Geographical and Environmental Education, 24*(1), 13–23. doi:10.1080/10382046.2014.967514

Melhuish, K., & Falloon, G. (2010). Looking to the future: M-learning with the iPad. *Computers in New Zealand Schools: Learning, Leading. Technology (Elmsford, N.Y.), 22*(3), 1–16.

Merino, C., Pino, S., Meyer, E., Garrido, J. M., & Gallardo, F. (2015). Realidad aumentada para el diseño de secuencias de enseñanza-aprendizaje en química. *Educación en la Química, 26*(2), 94–99.

Meyer, M. (1998). Learning and Teaching through the Naturalist Intelligence. *Clearing, 102,* 7–11.

Mtebe, J. S., & Raisamo, R. (2014). Investigating students' behavioural intention to adopt and use mobile learning in higher education in East Africa. *International Journal of Education and Development Using Information and Communication Technology, 10*(3), 4–20.

Paul, T. V. (2014). An Evaluation of the Effectiveness of E-Learning,Mobile Learning, and Instructor-Led Training in Organizational Training and Development. *The Journal of Human Resource and Adult Learning, 10*(2), 1–13.

Pimmer, C., Mateescu, M., & Gröhbiel, U. (2016). Mobile and ubiquitous learning in higher education settings. A systematic review of empirical studies. *Computers in Human Behavior, 63,* 490–501. doi:10.1016/j.chb.2016.05.057

Samsudyn, M. A., Haniza, N. H., Abdul-Talib, C., & Ibrahim, H. M. M. (2015). The relationship between Multiple Intelligences with Preferred Science Teaching and Science Process Skills. *Journal of Education and Learning EduLearn, 1*(9), 53–60. doi:10.11591/edulearn.v9i1.1118

Santos, R., Gusmão, E., & Mangueira, I. (2006). Aplicações interativas como potencializadoras de múltiplas inteligências. *ETD-Educação Temática Digital, 18*(2), 465–484. doi:10.20396/etd.v18i2.8635194

Sharples, M. (2003). Disruptive devices: Mobile technology for conversational learning. *International Journal of Continuing Engineering Education and Lifelong Learning, 12*(5), 504–520.

Slijepcevic, N. (2013). The effect of augmented reality treatment on learning, cognitive load, and spatial visualization abilities. *Theses and Dissertations.* Retrieved from https://uknowledge.uky.edu/edc_etds/4

Ubago-Jiménez, J. L., Viciana-Garófano, V., Pérez-Cortés, A. J., Martínez-Martínez, A., Padial-Ruz, R., & Puertas-Molero, P. (2018). Relación entre la Teoría de las Inteligencias Múltiples y la actividad físico-deportiva. *Sportis Sci J, 4*(1), 144–161. doi:10.17979portis.2018.4.1.2067

Villalustre, L. (2016). Educación Aumentada, una Realidad para favorecer el aprendizaje 3.0. *CIREI, 2016,* 6–12.

Villalustre Martínez, L., & Del Moral Pérez, M. E. (2016). Itinerarios interactivos con geolocalización y realidad aumentada para un aprendizaje ubicuo en la formación inicial de docentes de Educación Infantil. In *Experiencias interactivas con realidad aumentada en las aulas* (pp. 81–100). Barcelona: Ediciones Octaedro.

ADDITIONAL READING

Azuma, R. T. (1997). A survey of augmented reality. *Presence (Cambridge, Mass.), 6*(4), 355–385. doi:10.1162/pres.1997.6.4.355

Billinghurst, M. (2002). Augmented reality in education. *New Horizons for Learning, 12*(5), 1-5.

Bower, M., Howe, C., McCredie, N., Robinson, A., & Grover, D. (2014). Augmented Reality in education–cases, places and potentials. *Educational Media International, 51*(1), 1–15. doi:10.1080/09523987.2014.889400

Furht, B. (Ed.). (2011). *Handbook of augmented reality*. Florida: Springer Science & Business Media. doi:10.1007/978-1-4614-0064-6

Gardner, H. (1992). *Multiple intelligences*. Minnesota: Center for Arts Education.

Gardner, H. (2011). *Frames of mind: The theory of multiple intelligences*. UK: Hachette.

Kaufmann, H., Schmalstieg, D., & Wagner, M. (2000). Construct3D: A virtual reality application for mathematics and geometry education. *Education and Information Technologies, 5*(4), 263–276. doi:10.1023/A:1012049406877

Kaufmann, H., Steinbügl, K., Dünser, A., & Glück, J. (2005). General training of spatial abilities by geometry education in augmented reality. *Annual Review of CyberTherapy and Telemedicine: A Decade of VR, 3*, 65-76.

Koutromanos, G., Sofos, A., & Avraamidou, L. (2015). The use of augmented reality games in education: A review of the literature. *Educational Media International, 52*(4), 253–271. doi:10.1080/09523987.2015.1125988

Lee, K. (2012). Augmented reality in education and training. *TechTrends, 56*(2), 13–21. doi:10.100711528-012-0559-3

McLellan, H. (1994). Virtual reality and multiple intelligences: Potentials for higher education. *Journal of Computing in Higher Education, 5*(2), 33–66. doi:10.1007/BF02948570

Medzini, A., Meishar-Tal, H., & Sneh, Y. (2015). Use of mobile technologies as support tools for geography field trips. *International Research in Geographical and Environmental Education, 24*(1), 13–23. doi:10.1080/10382046.2014.967514

Meyer, M. (1998). Learning and Teaching through the Naturalist Intelligence. *Clearing, 102*, 7–11.

Thornton, T., Ernst, J. V., & Clark, A. C. (2012). Augmented reality as a visual and spatial learning tool in technology education. *Technology and Engineering Teacher, 71*(8), 18–21.

Yuen, S. C. Y., Yaoyuneyong, G., & Johnson, E. (2011). Augmented reality: An overview and five directions for AR in education. *Journal of Educational Technology Development and Exchange, 4*(1), 11. doi:10.18785/jetde.0401.10

KEY TERMS AND DEFINITIONS

Education: Education can be defined as the process to develop the intellectual, moral, and affective capacity of people according to the acquisition of certain knowledge, skills, and attitudes.

Geolocation: Geolocation is the ability to know the geographical position or location of a mobile device: phone, tablet, computer or others. To do this, it makes use of GPS coordinates or global positioning system.

Geolocation Apps: Geolocation applications are those tools designed to be used in mobile devices, where the use of GPS coordinates takes center stage.

Mobile Apps: A mobile application is a program that must be downloaded and accessed directly from the phone or from another mobile device.

Multiple Intelligences: The theory of Multiple Intelligences, developed by Dr. Howard Gardner, psychologist, researcher, and professor at Harvard University, is based on the fact that all people possess at least eight forms of intelligence, and these can be developed through stimulation.

Naturalistic Intelligence: Naturalistic intelligence is the ability to categorize elements of the environment recognizing their differences and the way in which they relate to each other. Similarly, it alludes to the ability to use that information to interact with the environment in a beneficial way.

Spatial Intelligence: This type of intelligence can be defined as the set of mental abilities directly related to navigation and rotation of objects in an abstract way. Thus, in spatial intelligence the person is able to imagine a three-dimensional space that maintains its coherence with the passage of time independent of the angle from which it is mentally visualized.

Section 3

Integrating Digital Technology in Multiple Intelligences–Based Teaching and Learning: Verbal–Linguistic Intelligence

Chapter 9
Influence of Multimedia and Cognitive Strategies in Deep and Surface Verbal Processing:
A Verbal–Linguistic Intelligence Perspective

Robert Z. Zheng
University of Utah, USA

ABSTRACT

The traditional view of linguistic-verbal intelligences focuses on individual linguistic abilities at the levels of phonology, syntax, and semantics. This chapter discusses the individual linguistic abilities from a text-comprehension perspective. The chapter examines the roles of multimedia and cognitive prompts in deep and surface verbal processing. Drawn from research in working memory, multimedia learning, and deep processing, a theoretical framework is proposed to promote learners' deep and surface learning in reading. Evidence from empirical studies are reviewed to support the underlying theoretical assumptions of the framework. The theoretical and practical significance of the theoretical framework is discussed with suggestions for future research.

INTRODUCTION

Learners learn differently due to their individual differences in terms of age, gender, cognitive abilities, intelligence, interest, and personality traits (Colby, Clayards, & Baum, 2018; Kubat, 2018; Zheng, Flygare, Dahl, & Hoffman, 2009). It is believed that individual intelligence can be significantly influenced by a range of factors related to learning and performance (Cifuentes & Hughey, 1998; Iyer, 2006). Previous research has demonstrated the relationship between intelligence and its associated factors like age, working memory capacity, spatial ability, and processing speed (Salthouse, 2012). It was found that changes in working memory capacity, processing speed, and spatial ability can significantly influence learners' performance in verbal information processing (Pazzaglia, Toso, & Cacciamani, 2008; Rast, 2011; Smith

DOI: 10.4018/978-1-7998-0249-5.ch009

et al., 2019). Smith et al. (2019) pointed out that due to cognitive impairments caused by the ageing process, older people experience tremendous challenges when learning new skills like browsing the Internet and engaging in online social communication. In additional to age factor, studies have shown that multimedia play an important role in influencing individuals' cognitive abilities in performances like verbal learning (Pazzaglia et al., 2008; Shadiev, Hwang, Liu, 2018), analytical thinking (Zheng, 2007), and scientific reasoning (Mayer & Anderson, 1992). Given the unique cognitive features in multimedia, Reiser (1994) suggested that educators, trainers, and instructional designers need to take into perspective the relationship between multimedia and cognitive abilities when designing and developing instruction for learners. Despite a growing body of research on multimedia and learning, studies that focus on the relation of age, visual-spatial ability, and multimedia in verbal learning are rare and research in this area is undertheorized. The current chapter therefore seeks to examine the influence of multimedia on cognitive processing ability in verbal learning. By reading the chapter, the readers will be able to:

1. Understand the role of multimedia in verbal-linguistic processing,
2. Explain the age factor in the design of multimedia for verbal learning, and
3. Describe the relationship between working memory capacity and multimedia in verbal learning.

LITERATURE REVIEW

Multiple Dimensions of Intelligences

According to Howard Gardner (2011), intelligence refers to "the ability to solve problems, or to create products, that are valued within one or more cultural settings" (p. xxviii). Gardner argued that the construct of intelligence should be examined in a larger context rather than limited to psychometric testing. This includes understanding the cultural connotations involved in the intelligence-relevant performances. Gardner noted that there is no "pure" intelligence independent of the culture in which one happens to live. In fact, an individual's intelligence is partially defined by one's sensitivity to the varying contents around him/herself (Sternberg, 1985). For example, verbal-linguistic intelligence is associated with an individual's competence to appropriately use and apply a particular language which entails the cultural and social values within the boundary of one's culture. Similarly, there is no pure individual centered visual-spatial intelligence. As a matter of fact, this type of intelligence is always incarnated in culturally rich activities like solving a Taj Mahal jigsaw puzzle problem, making a Japanese paper crane origamis, or creating a 3D object relating to an Egyptian historical artifact. Gardner thus proposed that intelligence should be conceived as something that is contextualized within social and cultural settings and that it should be considered as a process known as socially shared cognition. As Gardner rightly pointed out, intelligence does not stop at one's skin; rather, it goes beyond our biological brain to meaningfully interact with the environment around us such as tools (paper, pencil, and computer) and our network of associates (friends, colleagues, and collaborators). As a matter of fact, the cultural view of intelligence is well aligned with the framework of general world knowledge in language learning in which the learner's ability to encode and decode the verbal information is largely dependent on his/her knowledge about the subject, the context and background information culturally and socially. In other words, an individual's intelligence is related to his/her schema that relates to both subject domain and world knowledge (Cook & Gueraud, 2005; Williams, Cook, & O'Brien, 2018).

In addition to cultural aspects, intelligence is anchored, as mentioned previously, in the knowledge domain that reflects the dimensions of cognitive abilities. Gardner (2011) noted that intelligence is closely related and can be largely explained by the domain it associates with such as music intelligence is associated with the music domain. A person who is musically talented is more likely to appreciate the music and possibly more likely to become a composer, a concert conductor, or a professional musician like a violinist or a pianist, and who may excel in the music domain more than those who are less musically talented. However, becoming a musician requires more than music intelligence. Other intelligences like bodily-kinesthetic, visual-spatial, and verbal-linguistic are essential for someone to be successful in music domain. Gardner thus concluded "nearly all domains require proficiency in a set of intelligences; and any intelligence can be mobilized for use in a wide array of culturally available domains" (Gardner, 2011, p. xxxv). Given the relations between intelligence and knowledge domain, and its associations with other types of intelligences, the current study uses the intelligence-domain framework to examine the relationship between verbal-linguistic intelligence and domain knowledge.

Verbal-Linguistic Intelligence

A person who is linguistically talented often demonstrates "considerable command of the linguistic tetrad of phonology, syntax, semantics, and pragmatics" (Gardner, 2011, p. 82). Individuals with such linguistic talents are able to appreciate with nuances the subtlety of language through the musicality of words and decipher the meaning of the text at phonological, syntactic, and semantic levels. Gardner noted that poets are considered linguistically talented and they are particularly sensitive to the sounds, rhythms, inflections, and meters of words. They have "that ability which can make even poetry in a foreign tongue beautiful to hear" (Gardner, 2011, p. 82). Evidently, people who are linguistically talented tend to be more sensitive to the lexicon, semantics and syntax features of language. This linguistic talent or intelligence empowers people to discern the shades of meaning of a word and deliberate on the choice of words as in the case of T.S. Eliot who exerted strenuous efforts deciding on a correct word from a dozen of choices when composing *Four Quartets*. While the construct of verbal-linguistic intelligence certainly encompasses linguistic processing abilities at lexicon, semantics and syntax levels, it also relates to individuals' ability to process verbal information at the text level in terms of comprehension and knowledge transfer (Kintsch, 1988; 2000).

A Review of Literature on Deep and Surface Learning

Studies have shown that humans process information differently: some at deep levels, others at shallow levels (Chi, 2009; Greenberg & Zheng, 2018; Kintsch, 1988; 2000). Deep level processing is often associated with learning activities such as interacting with content, understanding and reasoning with material, along with applying and transferring knowledge to new learning situations; whereas shallow level process is associated with learning activities that are characterized by recalling and rote memorization. The knowledge gained from shallow learning is considered passive and static, and is thus often considered less transferrable to new knowledge domain.

Marton and Säljö's Study

Marton and Säljö (1976) investigated human cognitive processes in text processing, in particularly the process of deep and surface learning. They studied the learners who performed a reading task (a 1500-word article). Later, the researchers interviewed the learners to understand how they approached the reading text when studying the material. During the interviews the learners were asked to report what they remembered, how they felt about the task, and how they had approached the task. The results showed that those who took the surface approach (i.e., reproducing factual information) focused on memorizing the parts of the article they thought they might be questioned about later. Those who took the deep approach (i.e., generating new understanding) engaged in active searching for meaning. They found that students who took deep learning approach tended to engage in "knowledge-making" by searching for the underlying structure, exploring the implications, and relating the meaning to themselves. Marton and Säljö concluded that learners who took the deep learning approach internalized the information and applied them effectively to new problem solving. For these learners, as Marton and Säljö argued, the content of the learning materials was processed at a deep level because the learner applied new knowledge to solution development. On the other hand, those who focused on reproducing the factual information through memorization and recall processed the content at a surface level by limiting to shallow reasoning and rote memorization.

Kintsch's Comprehension Construction-Integration Model

Kintsch and colleagues (Kintsch, 1994; Kintsch & Van Dijk, 1978) proposed that knowledge can be represented at three levels: surface, text-base, and situation levels. According to Kintsch (1994), surface level representation limits to comprehension at the lexicon level like words. Therefore, the cognitive processes at the lexicon unit level involve shallow learning activities like rote memorization without going deep to understand the relationship between the words. An example of surface level comprehensions involves recalling the individual words like book, read, and student. The cognitive process involved at the surface is limited to the understanding of the lexicon meaning of individual words. Differing from the surface level representation, text-base representation goes beyond the lexicon units and involves the semantic meaning of words and phrases. It focuses on the relationship between words and their meanings at the sentence level. For instance, the sentence "Henry is writing a novel" can be analyzed by the grammatical relations among the components of the sentence, i.e., subject, object, predicator, etc. or by understanding the meaning of the sentence through an identification of the abstract nature of the proposition. For example, the underlying abstract nature of the proposition for "Henry is writing a novel" can be represented in the forms of:

A novel is written by Henry.

The writing of a novel by Henry.

Henry's writing of a novel.

Kintsch pointed out that readers encode information faithfully from the learning materials at the surface and text-base representations and therefore both levels represent a shallow learning process. It is believed that the encoded information tends to be short lived with surface and text-base representations and can fade relatively quickly from learners' long-term memory. Different from the previous levels of text comprehension, Kintsch believes that a third level exists which is by far the most powerful in text processing which he called situation representation, known as situation model. Within the situation model, prior knowledge or schema plays an important role.

According to Kintsch (1994), a schema provides a context in which inferences can be made to complete the meaning of a text. The schema provides a structure within which both implicit and explicit propositions become meaningful. For example, with the proposition "Jacob's birthday party" one may generate the inference of "Jacob gets presents and gifts" since the schema of birthday party is usually associated with concepts like cakes, balloons, gifts, presents, etc. Based on Kintsch's situation model, deep learning occurs through the activation of schema where the learner sees the connection between new information and schema and where he/she develops a personalized experience in making inferences through the connection between new information and schema.

Chi's Active-Constructive-Interactive Framework

As Marton and Säljö (1976) point out, deep learning is related to vigorous interaction with the text, while shallow learning is associated with passive behavior in text processing. Chi (2009) further examined the active interaction behavior in learning and proposed an active-constructive-interactive framework for deep learning. According to Chi, active learning means *doing something* while learning. Active learning activities include searching a term in the Internet, underlying a sentence in the textbook, repeating verbatim a line from a play, copying and pasting a paragraph into a composition, pointing to a 3D object in a multimedia math tutorial, and so forth. By actively doing something, the learner becomes engaged in the content he/she is learning. However, as Chi points out, being active in learning does not necessarily guarantee that the learner is processing information deeply. This view is in consistent with Engelkamp's (1998) research in which acting on action words enhanced learners' encoding process resulting in a longer retention of the words but did not necessarily improve learners' deep understanding of the words. In other words, active learning is not equivalent to deep learning. One can repeat verbatim lines from a play but it does not indicate that one understands the lines. Thus, Chi argues that being active in learning is necessary but not sufficient enough to guarantee deep cognitive learning to occur. Chi contended that for deep learning to occur, learners must engage in constructive and interactive activities in which the learners analyze, compare, categorize, classify, hypothesize and make predictions about the learning problem. For example, if a learner wants to know which social system is better in terms of enabling its citizens to exercise their individual rights, he/she would have to propose hypotheses, collect data, compare the structures of different societies in terms of political system, economy, social infrastructure based on the data collected, analyze the unique features of different social systems and draw conclusions. According to Chi (2009), *being constructive* is different from *being active*. The former involves producing "new content-relevant ideas that go beyond the information given" (p. 78) whereas the latter just shows the learner is doing something to being active.

Influence of Multimedia and Cognitive Strategies in Deep and Surface Verbal Processing

Summary

The traditional definition of verbal-linguistic intelligence focuses on specific learners' linguistic abilities such as the abilities to process verbal information lexically, semantically and syntacticaly. However, as was previously discussed, verbal linguistic intelligence also involves the ability to process verbal information at deep and surface levels. The Marton and Säljö's study (1976) and Kintsch's Comprehension Construction-Integration Model both demonstrate that verbal processing -- an important aspect in verbal-linguistic intelligence -- can be categorized into deep and surface processes which reflect individual differences in verbal skills and abilities. Similar to Gardner's (2011) view that intelligence reflects the social and cultural aspects of cognitive activities and that it is tied to domain specific knowledge, both Marton and Säljö's study (1976) and Kintsch's model emphasize the important role of domain knowledge and schema in intelligences. Particularly, the deep learning processing (i.e., situation model) in Kintsch's C-I model accentuates the relationship between schema and meaningful cognitive processing. This is further supported by Chi's framework in which prior knowledge and schema play a key role in deep processing through interactive and constructive learning. Thus, it becomes apparent that the ability to process verbal information at both deep and surface levels should be considered within the framework of verbal-linguistic intelligence traits, that is, the influence of cultural and schema factors in verbal processing. In this chapter, the deep-surface framework is adopted to guide the discussion on linguistic-verbal processing.

Working Memory Theory

One of the important factors that significantly impacts linguistic-verbal processing at deep and surface level is working memory. Research has shown that the effectiveness of human cognitive activities regarding information processing is influenced and oftentimes determined by the individual's capacity in working memory (Kalish, Newell, & Dunn, 2017; Greenberg & Zheng, 2019; Zheng & Gardner, 2019). Our discussion in the following section focuses on the relationship between working memory and verbal information processing.

Human Cognitive Architecture

Human cognitive architecture consists of two major processing systems: long-term memory and short-term memory. The short-term memory holds the information in an active and readily manner for a short period of time such as remembering a list of things when shopping in a super market. According to Miller (1956), the short-term memory is limited in capacity and can only hold about seven, plus or minus two information at one time. Recently, researchers found that short-term memory is actually more limited than it was thought to be: it holds about four, plus or minus one information (Cowan, 2001). Apparently, the short-term memory is limited. This limitation can certainly affect human's ability to process information, especially when the processing of information contains large amount of information with high element interactivity (Braddeley, 1992; Sweller & Chandler, 1994). Related to short-term memory is the construct of working memory which is considered part of short-term memory, but it is different from short-term memory in that working memory holds and *manipulates* the information in a limited memory space in a short period of time.

Working Memory

According to Braddeley (1992), input information such as auditory, visual, and kinesthetic information is processed through temporary storage before it is coded into the long-term memory (Baddeley & Logie, 1992; Logie, 1995). This temporary storage, also known as working memory, is characterized by a central executive function which has two sub-systems: phonological loop and visuo-spatial sketchpad. The phonological loop stores phonological information and prevents its decay by silently articulating its contents, thereby refreshing the information in a rehearsal loop. The visuo-spatial sketchpad (VSS) is believed to process and manipulate visuo-spatial images (Logie, 1995; Pearson & Logie, 2000). For example, the ability to mentally manipulate 3D images by rotating them in the mind is largely determined by the VSS function. The central executive function carries out the cognitive activities such as reasoning and problem-solving by coordinating information from phonological loop and visuo-spatial skethpad. Studies show that the working memory is very limited in both duration and capacity (Bollaert, 2000; Mayer & Moreno, 2003). Van Merrienboer and Sweller (2005) observed that the working memory stores about seven elements but normally operates on only two or three elements. When the working memory becomes overloaded with information, learning can be adversely affected (Marcus, Cooper, & Sweller, 1996; Sweller & Chandler, 1994). Zheng (2007) asserted that the learner's ability to learn and solve problems can be affected by the amount of cognitive load occurred during learning. When the learner becomes cognitively overloaded which means there is little room for thinking and information processing, his/her ability to learn and solve problems can be impaired. Researchers have been studying ways to reduce the cognitive load in learning (Castro-Alonso, Wong, Ayres, & Paas, 2018; Sweller & Chandler, 1994). One of the approaches is to employ multimedia to support learning. The following section discusses the effects of multimedia on verbal learning.

Effects of Multimedia on Verbal Learning

Research has demonstrated the benefits of multimedia learning (Reed, 2006; Zheng, Miller, Snelbecker, & Cohen, 2006). The cognitive theory of multimedia learning (CTML) (Mayer, 2001; Mayer & Moreno, 2003) posits that incoming information that is presented visually and auditorily improves learners' cognitive performance as information processed through dual channels (i.e., visual and auditory) is likely to ease the pressure on working memory and makes cognitive resources available for learning (see also Paivio, 1986; Pearson & Logie, 2000; Ploetzner, Bodemer, & Feuerlein, 2001). Imagine learning how to assemble a laptop. If the information is delivered in text only, the learner will have a hard time understanding the relationship among the motherboard, video card, sound card, and external ports. If instead of learning the material in text form only, the information is delivered through image and narration. The learner is able to examine the process of putting together different parts of the laptop by looking at the pictures while listening to the steps of assembling the parts. The latter approach would help the learner better process the information. This is because the same amount of information gets processed through separate sensory input: visual and sound which alleviate the processing load and provides more working memory space for learning.

Despite the benefits of multimedia, researchers find that improperly designed multimedia can actually hurt learning. Mayer (2001) studied the multimedia design and the cognitive consequences associated with the design. He found that improper design in multimedia can distract people from learning due to redundancy or split attention effect. Mayer has identified a range of design issues in multimedia from spatial design to visual redundancy. For the purpose this chapter, the focus will be on redundancy effect in the context of linguistic information acquisition by putting in perspective the age factor in multimedia-based processing.

Redundancy Effect

Redundancy effect in multimedia learning refers to a state of learning caused by improper design in multimedia (Mayer, 2001; Zheng, 2007). With redundant design, unnecessary media elements (visual, or auditory) are added to the multimedia learning which causes additional cognitive processes, therefore additional cognitive resources are needed to handle the process in learning which as Sweller and Chandler (1994) pointed out, can impose extra cognitive load on working memory. Mayer, Heiser, and Lonn (2001) studied the redundancy effect by including redundant visual elements in learning material. The study included redundancy and non-redundancy conditions. The learners in redundancy condition were asked to watch an animation video that had animation, narration and on-screen text that matched the exact narration in the video. The learners in non-redundancy condition were asked to watch the same video except it contained only animation and narration without on-screen text this time. Mayer and colleagues hypothesized that the on-screen text could cause some redundancy effect when learners processed the information in the video as they had to listen to the narration and read the text at the same while watching the animated video. Such process could overload the working memory and affect the outcomes of learning. As expected, a redundancy effect was found in Mayer et al.'s study showing the learners in non-redundancy condition outperformed these in the redundancy condition as measured by retention and transfer quizzes. The redundancy effect principle has been widely used to guide the design of multimedia in teaching and learning (Dousay, 2016; McNeill, Doolittle, & Hicks, 2009).

Contrary to the findings above, Samur (2012) found adding on-screen text to a multimedia presentation with animation and narration helped students to learn new vocabulary in a previously unfamiliar foreign language. Samur's study involved a foreign language learning where the learners had little or no schemas of the language. It was possible that the narration and redundant identical text both could aid learners' comprehension and mental representation of new information if they lacked a schema to begin with. That is, lacking schemas may deter learners from comprehending the narration meaningfully. In such case, adding on-screen text identical to the narration may not be redundant and could actually compensate the decreased ability in information processing.

Compensatory Hypothesis

Initial evidence has shown that the diminishing function of primary sensory process may be compensated by adding a secondary sensory process in learning (Samur, 2012). This is particularly true for older people. For example, Anstey et al. (2001) study the older people's sensory functioning in relation to their cognitive processes. It is found that the memory which is an important indicator in older people's cognitive processing is heavily loaded onto sensory functions. This means older people's abilities to process information can be significantly affected by their sensory functioning. In a cross-sectional-age study Bates and Lindenberger (1997) compare the older people with young population (age range: 25–103 years) in terms of sensory functioning and intellectual abilities. Of five different intellectual abilities (e.g., memory, reasoning, processing speed), two of major sensory functions (i.e., vision and hearing) are found to be strong predictors for intellectual abilities with 31% of the total variances for the older sample (age range: 70–103 years) compared to 11% of the total variances for the younger sample (age range: 25–69 years). What this means is that when processing information older people tend to rely on more sensory inputs in order to make sense of the new content. Researchers thus hypothesize that given the association between older persons' cognition and sensory functions, the diminishing cognitive abilities in older people, like working memory deficits, can be compensated by extra sensory support, which is known as the Compensatory Hypothesis (Bates & Lindenberger; 1997; Anstey et al., 2001; Christensen, H., Mackinnon, Korten, & Jorm, 2001). The significance of compensatory hypothesis lies in (1) explaining the role of redundant visuals from the perspective of aging process, and (2) modifying redundancy hypothesis by showing that redundant visuals may not necessarily be detrimental to older learners due to a compensatory effect.

Summary

In this part of the chapter we review the mechanism of working memory and how working memory affects people's learning. From Baddeley's working memory theory we learn that incoming information is processed differently in the working memory. The sound information is processed in a sub-system called phonological loop and the visual information is processed in a sub-system called visual-spatial sketchpad. When the information is presented in one format only, say text, the working memory can become overloaded, thus affecting the outcomes of learning. Multimedia has been used to address the working memory issue in learning. That is, instead of presenting the information in a single format, the same amount of information is presented through multiple sensory inputs which alleviate the processing load in working memory. However, too many sensory inputs (text, image, sound) at one time can render the working memory less functionally due to a redundancy effect. That is, the learner would have to spend extra cognitive resources to coordinate different sources of information (e.g., narration and identical on-screen text) in order to understand the content. The redundancy effect hypothesis is however challenged when putting the age and schema factors in perspective. Studies have shown that redundant multimedia can be beneficial to learners who do not have adequate schemas and who experience a cognitive impairment due to aging.

Cognitive Prompts as a Strategy to Support Deep and Surface Learning

While the research on multimedia has shown that making multiple sensory inputs available during learning results in improved performance in learning in terms of deep and surface learning. The rationale behind that is: with multimedia, learners will be able to reduce the cognitive load and make cognitive resources available in working memory during learning. However, achieving deep and surface learning relies more than on making cognitive resources available in working memory. It depends on the kinds of mental representations the learner has formed in relation to new information, schema, and cultural and social factors. Cognitive scientists have found that strategies like cognitive prompts can significantly influence the way the mental representations are formed and they can connect learners' schemas with new information.

Cognitive prompts are learning questions placed throughout an educational presentation – be they in person or through multimedia – that aim at activating prior knowledge or focusing on the learners' attention during learning. Cognitive prompts can support both cognitive processes – including memory retrieval - and metacognitive development in learning (Berthold, Nuckles, & Renkl, 2007). Studies show that cognitive prompts can improve knowledge transfer significantly by directing learners' attention to structural features that are related to previously learned information (Monks, Robinson, & Kotiadis, 2016). Preliminary evidence suggests that cognitive prompts help activate learners' prior knowledge/schemas, thus improving learners' abilities to comprehend the content and apply the knowledge to new learning (Berthold et al, 2007; Hsu, Wang, & Zhang, 2017). Wolfson, Cavanagh, and Kraiger (2014) indicated that technology-based training may benefit from cognitive prompts by directing learners' attention to key information to avoid unnecessary processing in learning. This view is shared by Colombo and Antonietti (2017), who found that cognitive prompts help the learners relate previously learned information to the present task through prior knowledge/schema activation.

A FRAMEWORK TO PROMOTE DEEP AND SURFACE LANGUAGE PROCESSING

The previous discussion suggests that learners' learning can be supported by multimedia which, as Mayer (Mayer & Moreno, 2003) pointed out, can alleviate the processing load in learning. The review also indicates overly developed multimedia learning, i.e., redundant visuals, can hurt learning. However, the redundancy principle in multimedia learning is modified by the compensatory hypothesis suggesting redundancy can vary dependent on individual differences. The supporters of multimedia argued that multiple sensory inputs in multimedia lead to a reduction of cognitive load in working memory and therefore increase cognitive resources during learning. This assumption becomes questionable when considering the mechanism that promotes deep and surface learning, particularly in linguistically related verbal information acquisition. Research in cognitive thinking process tells us that the individual's deep learning is related to one's prior knowledge or schema, social and cultural background, and strategies in both cognitive and metacognitive processes. Evidently, making cognitive resources available through multimedia is sufficient but not the necessary condition for attaining deep learning. We propose that in a multimedia learning environment, the appropriate design of multimedia to make cognitive resources available is important, but more importantly, the cognitive strategies that can be used to activate learners' schemas so the extra cognitive resources are well used to serve the meaningful learning is the key to the success of deep learning. Since the goal of this chapter is on deep and surface verbal processing in light of linguistic-verbal intelligence, we predict that embedding cognitive strategies in multimedia would improve learners' deep and surface learning in verbal information acquisition. We also predict that since the effects of multimedia can be affected by the age factor, redundant information should be avoided for the younger learners but can be considered for the older learners due to a compensatory effect in learning. Based on the above predictions, a theoretical framework with two models is presented as follows.

Figure 1. Model 1 redundancy and compensatory effects in multimedia

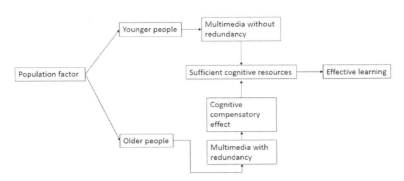

Model 1: Design of Multimedia Based on Age Factor

Model 1 delineates the relationship among age factor, multimedia design, cognitive resources and learning outcomes. In this model, the factor which has two levels (younger vs. older population) affects the design of multimedia which also has two levels (with vs. without redundancy). The multimedia design relevant to the age population results in sufficient cognitive resources in working memory which in turn leads to effective learning. The model hypothesizes that the learners of different age group would be more efficient in processing verbal information if the multimedia is designed in ways that fit their cognitive processing abilities.

Model 2: Cognitive Prompts to Optimize Cognitive Resources in Verbal Information Processing

Model 2 is based on Model 1 to further hypothesize that by utilizing the extra cognitive resources to activate learners' schemas, learners would be able to engage in deep level thinking and thus achieving deep learning. Notice that the difference of learning outcomes between Model 1 and Model 2: Model 1 suggests that multimedia makes cognitive resources available and thus learners are able to process information more effectively but not necessary in the sense of deep processing. Model 2 suggests that multimedia makes cognitive resources available, therefore it provides space for making connection between new information and schemas through cognitive prompts. This process of connecting with schemas generates (1) meaningful learning and (2) deep understanding of the content. Thus, Model 2 argues that deep learning occurs when cognitive strategies like cognitive promotes are used in multimedia learning.

Figure 2. Model 2 cognitive prompts in multimedia learning

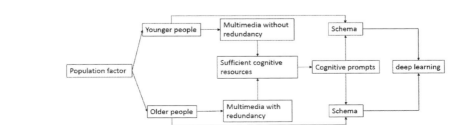

Empirical Evidence to Support Models 1 And 2 in Verbal Learning

In this section we will discuss both models with initial empirical evidences to support the hypothesis regarding multimedia learning and deep learning with cognitive promotes. The empirical studies demonstrate that the individual's linguistic-verbal intelligence can be potentially brought to full play with multimedia and cognitive strategies.

Study 1. Modality Effects in Multimedia-Based Reading for Early Readers

As suggested by research, modes of learning provide the opportunity for learners to engage in learning with multiple sensory stimuli (Mayer, 2001; Mayer & Anderson, 1991). Research in reading also confirms the modality effect on learners' achievements in reading performance (Robinson, 1985; Zheng & Smarkola, 2003). Zheng and Smarkola (2003) studied the multimedia learning environments for early readers ($N=42$). The study consisted of three conditions: traditional (control group), structured multimedia learning (experimental group 1) and unstructured multimedia learning (experimental group 2). In the traditional learning group, students were taught within a direct instructional environment that had a strong emphasis on phonics. The instruction was focused on the level of questioning and practice in language patterns and drills. In the structured multimedia learning group, students used the selected basal reader text and multimedia reading package accompanied by a study guide, an advanced organizer for content, and collaborative learning activities. In the unstructured multimedia learning group, students were allowed to explore the multimedia content, self-define goals and objectives, and self-pace through the learning content without formal instructional support. The reading comprehension test was administered at the end of learning. The comprehension test consisted of 25 questions with 13 questions targeting the low level factual knowledge and 12 questions on high level causal relationship. The results showed that the structure multimedia learning group ($M=123.71$, $SD=11.27$) outperformed both the traditional learning group ($M=108.07$, $SD=8.33$) and the unstructured multimedia learning group ($M=104.29$, $SD=7.66$) and that the traditional learning group ($M=108.07$, $SD=8.33$) performed better than the unstructured multimedia learning group ($M=104.29$, $SD=7.66$). The study confirmed the multimedia effect in reading, demonstrating a relationship between students' linguistic-verbal ability and multimedia learning. However, the outcomes of the study also call for attention to the instructional strategies involved in multimedia-based learning in reading. That is, students' ability to comprehend and answer both lower-level (factual knowledge) and higher-level (causal relationship) questions seemed to be influenced by the instructional strategies in reading education, for example, the structured multimedia learning included instructional support that guided students' reading along with reinforcement activities.

Study 2. Aspects of Multimedia-Based Reading in Caregiving Learning: Age Factor, Redundancy Effect and Compensatory Hypothesis

The literature shows that multimedia learning can be adversely affected if it is not designed properly by including redundant visuals (Mayer & Anderson, 1992; Mayer et al., 2001). The redundancy hypothesis was challenged by the compensatory hypothesis when studying the multimedia-based reading in the context of aging (Zheng et al., 2016). Based on Mayer's (2001) redundancy hypothesis, Zheng et al. (2016) carried out a cross-sectional study ($N=92$) to test both redundancy and compensatory hypotheses in reading. The study consisted of 44 older adults ($M_{age}=69.93$, $SD=7.29$) and 48 young adults

(M_{age}=23.84, SD=5.94). Participants learned the caregiving topics with multimedia. Two conditions were created: one had video, narration and on-screen text identical to narration (redundant) and other had video and narration only (non-redundant). The results showed that older adults performed better in redundant condition (text+video+narration) than in non-redundant condition (video+narration) in terms of deep and surface learning as measured by knowledge transfer and information recall. In contrast, young adults performed better in non-redundant condition (video+narration) than in redundant condition (text+video+narration). The findings support the compensatory hypothesis which posits that older adults may need extra sensory support in information processing. It was found that as older adults learned verbal based information such as the facts, concepts, and procedures in caregiving, redundant sensory input (e.g., text) compensated their diminishing ability in hearing. Even with narration and video, they had a hard time processing the verbal information, memorizing and encoding the concepts. With extra visual support, their performance in reading improved. On the other hand, the study confirmed the redundancy hypothesis with young population. The results showed that redundant information can be detrimental to young people's information processing in learning which is consistent with the research by Mayer and colleagues (Mayer, 2001; Mayer et al., 2001).

Studies 1 and 2 provide initial evidence to *Model 1: redundancy and compensatory effects in multimedia* in terms of identifying the modality effect in learning (Study 1) and the relationship between design of multimedia and age factor (Study 2). Several questions arise with regard to the outcomes of both studies. First, although Study 1 confirmed the modality effect in multimedia learning, the findings can be potentially confounded as structured multimedia learning and traditional learning (non-multimedia) both contained instructional strategies whereas non-structured multimedia did not. The results showed that when multimedia learning did not contain instructional strategies, it performed less well than traditional and structured multimedia, both of which employed instructional strategies to support students' learning. This suggests that instructional strategy could play a role in influencing learners' outcomes. Second, although Study2 sheds light on the relationship between redundancy effect and compensatory hypothesis with respect to age factor, the study primarily focuses on the functional role of sensory stimuli and the influence on cognitive resources in working memory. There is a lack of explanation how deep learning occurs. It remains unclear whether it is due to the manipulation of multimedia or something else. Nonetheless, in Study 2 prior knowledge which is often interpreted as schema, was found to be a significant covariate for learning outcome. This suggests that learners' schemas, other than multimedia, may influence their cognitive processes in learning.

Study 3. Cognitive Prompts as an Instructional Strategy to Activate Prior Knowledge in Multimedia-Based Reading in Caregiving Learning

As was discussed above, the instructional strategies in Study1 and significance of prior knowledge as a covariate may be responsible for learner performance with respect to deep and surface processing in reading. To that end, a third study was conducted to investigate the role of cognitive prompts in multimedia learning pertaining to caregiving information acquisition (Smith et al., 2019). The goal of Study 3 was to find out whether individuals who face working memory loss can learn with multimedia through cognitive prompts strategy. Thus, the target population chosen for Study 3 were older adults (N=60) who have experienced at various levels diminishing capacity in working memory functioning. It was hypothesized that with multimedia, older people would be able to have more cognitive resources available when reading caregiving materials, and be able to gain deep understanding by activating their prior knowledge

Influence of Multimedia and Cognitive Strategies in Deep and Surface Verbal Processing

through cognitive prompts. Sixty older adults (M_{age}=69.47, SD=9.22) were recruited from three senior centers in a mid-size city in western United States. The participants watched two videos: dementia and incontinence. Two conditions were created for the study: cognitive prompts vs. non-cognitive prompts in multimedia-based reading. In cognitive prompt condition, prompts were embedded in the video. The following is an example cognitive prompts in dementia video.

STAGES OF DEMENTIA: (Prompts approx. 16 sec)

Doctor says, "Socializing is good for you"

PROMPT: Imagine ways that socializing can improve quality of life for someone with dementia.

Doctor says, "Stick with hobbies you've enjoyed all your life; anything that stimulates the brain helps"

PROMPT: Imagine activities that can improve quality of life for someone with dementia

Doctor says, "Hoarding, repetitive movements, paranoia, emotional - even physical outbursts..."

PROMPT: Think of other unusual behaviors that dementia patients may show at a moderate or severe stage.

To determine the effects of cognitive prompts on prior knowledge, the crystalized knowledge, which represents individual cumulative knowledge, was measured using the Vocabulary subtest from WAIS-R. The recall and transfer tests were administered at the end of each video. The recall test consisted of 10 items assessing factual knowledge about the learning video. The transfer test consisted of three short answers. Here is an example of transfer question relating to incontinence: "Walter had incontinence one night and was upset. Even though Sarah tried her best to comfort him, Walter still felt embarrassed. He could not help thinking that everyone knew. He was losing his temper when Sarah took him to the bathroom. What is the best way for Sarah to help make Walter's incontinence less upsetting? Why?" The participant responded to each transfer question with a short answer. A rubric was developed for scoring the transfer short answers, with a total of four points possible. The answers were coded independently by two research assistants based on the criteria of depth of knowledge, detail, and quality of knowledge. The interrater reliability for transfer tests was .99 indicating a high reliability for the scoring rubric.

The path analysis was used to analyze the data. The results showed that cognitive prompts significantly influenced learners' surface and deep learning in reading as measured by recall and knowledge transfer, respectively. It was found that the effects of cognitive prompts on surface and deep learning were moderated by prior knowledge measured in crystalized knowledge (Carroll, 1997). It was found that when older people experience a decline in working memory, multimedia can improve their information processing by making cognitive resources available in working memory. With cognitive resources available, older adult learners were able to process complex materials through cognitive strategies like cognitive prompts, which in turn help them gain deep understanding with prior knowledge activation. In sum, Study 3 provides initial evidence to *Model 2: cognitive prompts in multimedia learning.*

DISCUSSION

The purpose of this chapter is to study the influence of multimedia and cognitive strategies in deep and surface verbal processing from the perspective of linguistic-verbal intelligence. Gardner's views on intelligences are taken as theoretical underpinning to guide the current studies. Essentially, we take the views that human intelligences are intertwined with their social and cultural background and grounded in the content domain where they develop their schemas. Based on Gardner's social-cultural aspect in intelligence, we extend our theoretical framework to include research in cognitive science, specifically in working memory research, multimedia learning, and human individual factors like age difference. Both working memory theory and multimedia learning help shape our research framework which posits that learning becomes effective when incoming information is processed through multiple sensory channels, and that redundant sensory stimuli may hurt young people's learning but can benefit older people if the redundant stimuli can compensate their declining sensory processing. By studying human cognitive processing and strategies, we conclude that strategies like cognitive prompts can activate learners' schemas and evoke meaningful learning process.

Informed by above theories and theoretical framework we develop a theoretical research framework focusing on multimedia and cognitive learning in reading. Two models are developed from this research framework to test different aspects of multimedia learning in verbal processing. The first model called *redundancy and compensatory effects in multimedia* examines the modality effect in multimedia and also the differential roles of redundancy effect in multimedia learning. By putting age factor in perspective, the model distinguishes the instructional consequences of redundancy effect between young and older adults. It explicates how compensatory effect plays a role in older adults' multimedia learning when the redundant stimuli are included. The second model called *cognitive prompts in multimedia learning* expands on the first model to further investigate the role of cognitive prompts in multimedia learning, particularly by investigating the relationship between multimedia and cognitive resources in working memory. Based on schema research, the model specifies the role of cognitive prompts in prior knowledge activation and deep learning.

To support the proposed theoretical framework and the models associated, evidence from three empirical studies were reviewed. Study 1 identifies the modality effect in multimedia learning showing the benefits of multimedia in reading. Study 2 further examined the design of multimedia in reading by testing the redundancy and compensatory hypotheses. Study 3 examined the relationship between prior knowledge and cognitive prompts in multimedia-based reading process. All three studies support well the proposed framework and contribute to the understanding of multimedia and cognitive prompts in deep and surface verbal processing. The studies raise the awareness that the learner's linguistic-verbal intelligence can be influenced by the multimedia and relevant cognitive strategies in terms of developing their abilities in deep and surface processing in reading.

FUTURE RESEARCH

Although initial empirical evidence has supported the proposed framework and models, future research is warranted to understand how different cognitive strategies may be used to support the connection between schema and learning. For example, when the learner lacks or has low prior knowledge, what cognitive strategies can be used to develop his/her prior knowledge so a meaningful learning can be attained? Next, future efforts should be directed toward understanding the relationship between the cognitive resources in working memory and the cognitive strategies in using cognitive resources to attain deep learning. It has been argued that the availability of cognitive resources in working memory does not guarantee deep learning. Investigation on strategies that optimize the use of cognitive resources to promote deep learning is needed. Finally, studies that investigate the relationship between multimedia and cognitive strategies in terms of types of processing load are essential for future research. For example, schema activation with cognitive prompts in multimedia may support the reduction of intrinsic cognitive load, that is, the load that relates to the difficult level of the materials. However, in situation where text and image are placed far from each other (e.g., text on one page and image on the next), the strategy may involve reducing different type of cognitive load – extraneous cognitive load, meaning the load caused by an improper design rather than the difficulty of the content.

CONCLUSION

This chapter examines one of the most important intelligences defined in Gardner's theory of multiple intelligences, that is, the linguistic-verbal intelligence. Drawing from research in working memory, multimedia, schema, and cognitive strategy in learning, the author proposes that the effective process of linguistic-verbal information depends largely on the availability of cognitive resources in the working memory, and that cognitive resources may be obtained through an optimal design of multimedia in learning. The author also proposes that the available cognitive resource must be actively accessed to serve deep learning which can be achieved through a connection with learners' schemas using cognitive prompts. A theoretical framework is proposed with initial evidences from empirical studies supporting the underlying assumptions of the framework. The chapter is significant at both theoretical and practical levels. Theoretically, it contributes to the research community the understanding of the relations among various variables that influence the deep and surface learning in verbal processing. It also reveals the roles of multimedia and cognitive strategies in influencing individuals' linguistic-verbal intelligence by going beyond the lexicon, semantic and syntax levels to focus on the level of comprehension, that is, deep and surface learning on reading. At the practical level, the current chapter provides practical guidance in verbal learning by showing the functional role of multimedia and how strategies like cognitive prompts can support deep and meaningful learning. As mentioned above, future research is warranted to understand the roles of multimedia and cognitive strategies in verbal processing and their influence on learners' linguistic-verbal intelligence.

REFERENCES

Baddeley, A. D. (1992). Working memory. *Science*, *255*(5044), 556–559. doi:10.1126cience.1736359 PMID:1736359

Baddeley, A. D., & Logie, R. H. (1992). Auditory imagery and working memory. In D. Reisberg (Ed.), *Auditory imagery* (pp. 179–197). Hillsdale, NJ: Lawrence Erlbaum Associates.

Berthold, K., Nuckles, M., & Renkl, A. (2007). Do learning protocols support learning strategies and outcomes? The role of cognitive and metacognitive prompts. *Learning and Instruction*, *17*(5), 564–577. doi:10.1016/j.learninstruc.2007.09.007

Bollaert, M. (2000). A connectionist model of the processes involved in generating and exploring visual mental images. In S. O. Nuallian (Ed.), *Spatial cognition: Foundations and applications* (pp. 329–346). Amsterdam: Joint Benjamins Publishing. doi:10.1075/aicr.26.26bol

Carroll, J. B. (1997). Psychometrics, intelligence, and public perception. *Intelligence*, *24*(1), 25–52. doi:10.1016/S0160-2896(97)90012-X

Castro-Alonso, J. C., Wong, A., Ayres, P., & Paas, F. (2018). Memorizing symbols from static and dynamic presentations: Don't overplay the hand. *Computers & Education*, *116*, 1–13. doi:10.1016/j.compedu.2017.08.011

Chi, M. (2009). Active-constructive-interactive: A conceptual framework for differentiating learning activities. *Topics in Cognitive Science*, *1*(1), 73–105. doi:10.1111/j.1756-8765.2008.01005.x PMID:25164801

Christensen, H., Mackinnon, A. J., Korten, A., & Jorm, A. F. (2001). The common cause hypothesis of cognitive aging: Evidence for not only a common factor but also specific associations of age with vision and grip strength in a cross-sectional analysis. *Psychology and Aging*, *16*(4), 588–599. doi:10.1037/0882-7974.16.4.588 PMID:11766914

Cifuentes, L., & Hughey, J. (1998). *Computer conferencing and multiple intelligences: Effects on expository writing.* Paper presented at 20th Association for Educational Communications and Technology Conference, St. Louis, MO.

Colby, S., Clayards, M., & Baum, S. (2018). The role of lexical status and individual differences for perceptual learning in younger and older adults. *Journal of Speech, Language, and Hearing Research: JSLHR*, *61*(8), 1855–1874. doi:10.1044/2018_JSLHR-S-17-0392 PMID:30003232

Colombo, B., & Antonietti, A. (2017). The role of metacognitive strategies in learning music: A multiple case study. *British Journal of Music Education*, *34*(1), 95–113. doi:10.1017/S0265051716000267

Cook, A. E. & Gueraud, S. (2005). What have we been missing? The role of general world knowledge in discourse processing. *Discourse Processes: A Multidisciplinary Journal, 39*(2&3), 265-278.

Cowan, N. (2001). The magical number 4 in short-term memory: A reconsideration of mental storage capacity. *Behavioral and Brain Sciences*, *24*(1), 1–185. doi:10.1017/S0140525X01003922 PMID:11515286

Dousay, T. A. (2016). Effects of redundancy and modality on the situational interest of adult learners in multimedia learning. *Educational Technology Research and Development*, *64*(6), 1251–1271. doi:10.100711423-016-9456-3

Engelkamp, J. (1998). *Memory for actions.* East Sussex, UK: Psychology Press.

Gardner, H. (2011). *Frames of mind: Theory of multiple intelligences.* New York, NY: Basic books.

Greenberg, K., & Zheng, R. (2018). A study on deep learning and mental reasoning in digital technology in relation to cognitive load. In R. Zheng (Ed.), *Strategies for deep learning with digital technology: Theories and practices in education* (pp. 331–354). Hauppauge, NY: NOVA Science Publishers.

Greenberg, K., & Zheng, R. (2019). *Working memory capacity and the modality effect in the cognitive load theory*. Paper presented at Society for Information Technology and Teacher Education (SITE) 30th International Conference, Las Vegas, NV.

Hsu, Y.-S., Wang, C.-Y., & Zhang, W.-X. (2017). Supporting technology-enhanced inquiry through metacognitive and cognitive prompts: Sequential analysis of metacognitive actions in response to mixed prompts. *Computers in Human Behavior*, *72*, 701–712. doi:10.1016/j.chb.2016.10.004

Iyer, N. (2006). *Instructional practices of teachers in schools that use multiple intelligences theory (SUMIT)* (Unpublished doctoral dissertation). University of Cincinnati.

Kalish, M. L., Newell, B. R., & Dunn, J. C. (2017). More is generally better: Higher working memory capacity does not impair perceptual category learning. *Journal of Experimental Psychology. Learning, Memory, and Cognition*, *43*(4), 503–514. doi:10.1037/xlm0000323 PMID:27656872

Kintsch, W. (1988). The role of knowledge in discourse comprehension construction-integration model. *Psychological Review*, *95*(2), 163–182. doi:10.1037/0033-295X.95.2.163 PMID:3375398

Kintsch, W. (1994). Text comprehension, memory, and learning. *The American Psychologist*, *49*(1), 294–303. doi:10.1037/0003-066X.49.4.294 PMID:8203801

Kintsch, W. (2000). Metaphor comprehension: A computational theory. *Psychonomic Bulletin & Review*, *7*(2), 237–266. doi:10.3758/BF03212981 PMID:10909133

Kintsch, W., & Van Dijk, T. A. (1978). Toward a model of text comprehension and production. *Psychological Review*, *85*(5), 363–394. doi:10.1037/0033-295X.85.5.363

Kubat, U. (2018). Identifying the individual differences among students during learning and teaching process by science teachers. *International Journal of Research in Educational and Science*, *4*(1), 30–38. doi:10.21890/ijres.369746

Logie, R. H. (1995). *Visuo-spatial working memory*. Hove, UK: Lawrence Erlbaum Associates.

Marcus, N., Cooper, M., & Sweller, J. (1996). Understanding instructions. *Journal of Educational Psychology*, *88*(1), 49–63. doi:10.1037/0022-0663.88.1.49

Mayer, R. E. (2001). *Multimedia learning*. Cambridge, UK: Cambridge Press. doi:10.1017/CBO9781139164603

Mayer, R. E., & Anderson, R. B. (1992). The instructive animation: Helping students build connections between words and pictures in multimedia learning. *Journal of Educational Psychology*, *84*(4), 444–452. doi:10.1037/0022-0663.84.4.444

Mayer, R. E., Heiser, J., & Lonn, S. (2001). Cognitive constraints on multimedia learning: When presenting more material results in less understanding. *Journal of Educational Psychology*, *93*(1), 187–198. doi:10.1037/0022-0663.93.1.187

Mayer, R. E., & Moreno, R. (2003). Nine ways to reduce cognitive load in multimedia learning. *Educational Psychologist*, *38*(1), 43–52. doi:10.1207/S15326985EP3801_6

McNeill, A. L., Doolittle, P. E., & Hicks, D. (2009). The effects of training, modality, and redundancy on the development of a historical inquiry strategy in a multimedia learning environment. *Journal of Interactive Online Learning*, *8*(3), 255–269.

Miller, G. A. (1956). The magical number seven, plus or minus two: Some limits on our capacity for processing information. *Psychological Review*, *63*(2), 81–97. doi:10.1037/h0043158 PMID:13310704

Monks, T., Robinson, S., & Kotiadis, K. (2016). Can involving clients in simulation studies help them solve their future problems? A transfer of learning experiment. *European Journal of Operational Research*, *249*(3), 919–930. doi:10.1016/j.ejor.2015.08.037

Paivio, A. (1986). *Mental representations: A dual coding approach*. Oxford, UK: Oxford University Press.

Pazzaglia, F., Toso, C., & Cacciamani, S. (2008). The specific involvement of verbal and visuospatial working memory in hypermedia learning. *British Journal of Educational Technology*, *39*(1), 110–124.

Pearson, D. G., & Logie, R. H. (2000). Working memory and mental synthesis: A dual task approach. In S. O. Nuallian (Ed.), *Spatial cognition: Foundations and applications* (pp. 347–359). Amsterdam: Joint Benjamins Publishing. doi:10.1075/aicr.26.27pea

Ploetzner, R., Bodemer, D., & Feuerlein, I. (2001). *Facilitating the mental integration of multiple sources of information in multimedia learning environments*. Paper presented at ED-Media 2001 World Conference on Educational Multimedia, Hypermedia & Telecommunications, Tampere, Finland.

Rast, P. (2011). Verbal knowledge, working memory, and processing speed as predictors of verbal learning in older adults. *Developmental Psychology*, *47*(5), 1490–1498. doi:10.1037/a0023422 PMID:21574701

Reed, S. K. (2006). Cognitive architectures for multimedia learning. *Educational Psychologist*, *41*(2), 87–98. doi:10.120715326985ep4102_2

Reiser, R. A. (1994). Clark's invitation to the dance: An instructional designer's response. *Educational Technology Research and Development*, *42*(2), 45–48. doi:10.1007/BF02299091

Robinson, K. (1985). *Visual and auditory modalities and reading recall: A review of the research*. ERIC Document Reproduction Service. (No. ED272840)

Salthouse, T. A. (2012). Consequences of age-related cognitive declines. *Annual Review of Psychology*, *63*(1), 201–226. doi:10.1146/annurev-psych-120710-100328 PMID:21740223

Samur, Y. (2012). Redundancy effect on retention of vocabulary words using multimedia presentation. *British Journal of Educational Technology*, *43*(6), 166–170. doi:10.1111/j.1467-8535.2012.01320.x

Shadiev, R., Hwang, W.-Y., & Liu, T.-Y. (2018). Investigating the effectiveness of a learning activity supported by a mobile multimedia learning system to enhance autonomous EFL learning in authentic contexts. *Educational Technology Research and Development*, *66*(4), 893–912. doi:10.100711423-018-9590-1

Smith, D., Zheng, R., Metz, A. J., Morrow, S., Pompa, J., Hill, J., & Rupper, R. (2019). Role of cognitive prompts in video caregiving training for older adults: Optimizing deep and surface learning. *Educational Gerontology*.

Sternberg, R. (1985). *Beyond IQ*. New York, NY: Cambridge University Press.

Sweller, J., & Chandler, P. (1994). Why some material is difficult to learn. *Cognition and Instruction*, *12*(3), 185–233. doi:10.12071532690xci1203_1

Van Merrienboer, J. J. G., & Sweller, J. (2005). Cognitive load theory and complex learning: Recent developments and future directions. *Educational Psychology Review*, *17*(2), 147–177. doi:10.100710648-005-3951-0

Williams, C. R., Cook, A. E., & O'Brien, E. J. (2018). Validating semantic illusions: Competition between context and general world knowledge. *Journal of Experimental Psychology. Learning, Memory, and Cognition*, *44*(9), 1414–1429. doi:10.1037/xlm0000526 PMID:29672121

Wolfson, N. E., Cavanagh, T. M., & Kraiger, K. (2014). Older adults and technology-based instruction: Optimizing learning outcomes and transfer. *Academy of Management Learning & Education*, *13*(1), 26–44. doi:10.5465/amle.2012.0056

Zheng, R. (2007). Cognitive functionality of multimedia in problem solving. In T. Kidd & H. Song (Eds.), *Handbook of Research on Instructional Systems and Technology* (pp. 230–246). Hershey, PA: Information Science Reference/IGI Global Publishing. doi:10.4018/978-1-59904-865-9.ch017

Zheng, R., Flygare, J., Dahl, L., & Hoffman, R. (2009). The impact of individual differences on social communication pattern in online learning. In C. Mourlas, N. Tsianos, & P. Germanakos (Eds.), *Cognitive and emotional processes in web-based education: integrating human factors and personalization* (pp. 321–342). Hershey, PA: Information Science Reference/IGI Global Publishing. doi:10.4018/978-1-60566-392-0.ch015

Zheng, R., & Gardner, M. (2019). *Memory in education*. New York, NY: Routledge.

Zheng, R., Miller, S., Snelbecker, G., & Cohen, I. (2006). Use of multimedia for problem-solving tasks. *Journal of Technology, Instruction. Cognition and Learning*, *3*(1-2), 135–143.

Zheng, R., & Smarkola, C. (2003). Multimedia learning environments for early readers. *Academic Exchange Quarterly*, *7*(4), 229–232.

Zheng, R., Smith, D., Luptak, M., Hill, R., Hill, J., & Rupper, R. (2016). Does visual redundancy inhibit older persons' information processing in learning? *Educational Gerontology*, *42*(9), 635–645. doi:10.1080/03601277.2016.1205365

ADDITIONAL READING

DeSchryver, M. D., & Yadav, A. (2015). Creative and computational thinking in the context of new literacies: Working with teachers to scaffold complex technology-mediated approaches to teaching and learning. *Journal of Technology and Teacher Education, 23*(3), 411–431.

Hyerle, D. (1996). *Visual tools for constructing knowledge (ERIC Document Reproduction Service No. ED399257)*. Alexandria, VA: Association for Supervision and Curriculum Development.

Jamet, E., & Le Bohec, O. (2007). The effect of redundant text in multimedia instruction. *Contemporary Educational Psychology, 32*(4), 588–598. doi:10.1016/j.cedpsych.2006.07.001

Logan, G. D. (1991). Automaticity and memory. In W. E. Hockley and S. Lewandowsky (Eds), Relating theory and data: Essays on human memory in honor of Bennet B. Murdock (pp. 347-366). Mahwah, NJ: Lawrence Erlbaum Associates.

Mayer, R. E., & Johnson, C. I. (2008). Revising the redundancy principle in multimedia learning. *Journal of Educational Psychology, 100*(2), 380–386. doi:10.1037/0022-0663.100.2.380

Moreno, R., & Mayer, R. E. (1999). Cognitive principles of multimedia learning: The role of modality and contiguity. *Journal of Educational Psychology, 91*(2), 358–368. doi:10.1037/0022-0663.91.2.358

Neo, M., & Neo, T.-K. (2013). Exploring students' creativity and design skills through a multimedia project: A constructivist approach in a Malaysian classroom. *Journal of Design and Technology Education, 18*(3), 48–59.

Statham, M. (2014). Change the way your pupils learn by practicing creative thinking and visualization. *Primary Science, 134*, 13–16.

Sweller, J., & Chandler, P. (1991). Evidence of cognitive load theory. *Cognition and Instruction, 8*(4), 351–362. doi:10.12071532690xci0804_5

Zheng, R., McAlack, M., Wilmes, B., Kohler-Evans, P., & Williamson, J. (2009). Effects of multimedia on cognitive load, self-efficacy, and multiple rule-based problem solving. *British Journal of Educational Technology, 40*(5), 790–803. doi:10.1111/j.1467-8535.2008.00859.x

Zheng, R., Miller, S., Snelbecker, G., & Cohen, I. (2006). Use of multimedia for problem-solving tasks. *Journal of Technology, Instruction. Cognition and Learning, 3*(1-2), 135–143.

KEY TERMS AND DEFINITIONS

Cognitive Prompts: Cognitive prompts are learning questions placed throughout an educational presentation—be they in person or through multimedia—that aim at activating prior knowledge or focusing on the learners' attention during learning. Cognitive prompts can support both cognitive processes—including memory retrieval—and metacognitive development in learning.

Compensatory Hypothesis: Compensatory hypothesis states the diminishing function of one sensory process (e.g., auditory) may be compensated by adding a second sensory process (e.g., visual).

Deep Learning: Deep learning refers to learning activities that the learner interacts with the content, engages in understanding and reasoning the material, and applies and transfers knowledge to new learning situations.

Executive Function: Executive function refers to the subsystem in working memory which controls and coordinates the information from phonological loop and visuo-spatial sketchpad. The phonological loop stores phonological information and prevents its decay by silently articulating its contents, thereby refreshing the information in a rehearsal loop. The visuo-spatial sketchpad (VSS) is believed to process and manipulate visuo-spatial images

Redundancy Effect: Redundancy effect in multimedia learning refers to a state of learning caused by improper design in multimedia. With redundant design, unnecessary media elements (visual, or auditory) are added to the multimedia learning which causes additional cognitive processes, therefore additional cognitive resources are needed to handle the process in learning which can impose extra cognitive load on working memory.

Schema: Schema refers an organized body of knowledge in human mind. It can be a mental structure of preconceived ideas and concepts, a framework representing aspects of a domain, or a system of organizing and perceiving new information or procedures. Schema influences learners' attention and process of new knowledge.

Working Memory: Working memory refers to the temporary storage in human brain. It is characterized by a central executive function which has two sub-systems: phonological loop and visuo-spatial sketchpad.

Chapter 10
Concepts of Propaganda:
Educating Responsible Citizens by Integrating Multiple Intelligences and Learning Styles Into a Smart Learning Environment

Anastasia D. Vakaloudi
Greek Ministry of Education, Greece

ABSTRACT

Propaganda represents the communication of information or ideas aimed to influence the audience's view and position on subjects. Forms of propaganda have permeated society for centuries and have evolved to become a common tool of warfare. Through the study of propagandistic posters from the two World Wars-era in the proposed project, students assess the powers of words and images in communication and learn to evaluate the messages they encounter, particularly when those messages urge action. The project is designed as a smart learning environment with the use of open educational resources that focuses on the strengths of all types of learners and the improvement of their weaknesses by integrating learner-centered theories and multiple intelligences and learning styles strategies with various combinations and by enhancing the efforts for self-discovery. This aims to promote students' cognitive engagement, which enables them to immerse themselves in in-depth reflective learning processes that are situated in realistic problem-solving tasks.

INTRODUCTION

Encouraging historical thinking in students is not a new idea in history education. Since the turn of the 20th century, many historians and history educators have argued that history consists of not only facts, but also historians' interpretation of those facts, commonly known as the process of historical thinking, or how to analyze and interpret historical evidence, make historical arguments, and engage in historical debates (Holt, 1990; Wineburg, 2001; Bain, 2005; Suh, 2013, p. 135). An important goal of teaching history is to enable students to acquire the habits of mind that characterize what it means to think historically.

DOI: 10.4018/978-1-7998-0249-5.ch010

Learning history subject requires students to master historical thinking skills which are vital elements for improving academic attainment. The crux of thinking historically is that in order for students to be interested in and truly learn history, they must be involved in it. Research has shown that when students have a low level of learning motivation, this is due to the lack of external motivations to encourage them to be more committed in learning academic subjects (Ahmad et al., 2015).

H. Gardner (1998, p. 23; 2003, p. 9) suggested that classroom instructors can find diverse ways to arouse students' interest in history. He claimed that a historical topic can be introduced to students through a variety of entry points drawing on several intelligences, a historical subject can be made more familiar through the use of analogies and metaphors drawn from diverse domains, and the core ideas of a historical topic can be captured not merely through a single symbolic language but rather through a number of complementary model languages or representations (Gardner, 1998, p. 23). Nowadays, given the means of Information and Communication Technologies (ICT), it is more possible to develop critical/historical thinking in students – to see how they can argue, debate, look at data, evaluate sources, study works of art, and so on. Gardner has often used history to illustrate the potential of his model of multiple intelligences, remarking that there is no reason why everyone has to learn history in the same way (Gardner, 1993; Lambert, 1997, p. 52; Cantu, 1999). According to Gardner:

...if you approach a topic from different perspectives, you get a much richer view... (Gardner, 1998) (P. 23).

Gardner proposed a theory of Multiple Intelligences (MI) in his book, "Frames of Mind: The Theory of Multiple Intelligences" (1983/2003). This book was a direct challenge to the classical view of intelligence. Gardner proposed that there is no single 'intelligence,' but a cluster of eight intellectual abilities, or multiple intelligences and has suggested the possible addition of a ninth known as "existential intelligence." Gardner's theory of Multiple Intelligences certainly provides one approach that at least attempts to address the multiple ways of learning and understanding that students bring with them to the history classroom. Gardner's theory suggests that individuals may possess many different kinds of intelligence. The intelligences are, Verbal/Linguistic, Logical/Mathematical, Visual/Spatial, Bodily-Kinesthetic, Musical, Interpersonal, Intrapersonal, Naturalistic, and Existential. Because each student possesses different strengths and weaknesses, according to Gardner, it is recommended that teachers present content in ways that capitalize on as many different intelligences as possible and help students understand their strengths and weaknesses in each (Gardner, 1995, pp. 16-17; Brahams, 1997, p. 7; Cantu, 1999; Armstrong, 2009, pp. 6-7; Giles et al., 2010; Foster, 2013, p. 1). Gardner defined intelligence as:

The ability to solve problems or to create products that are valued within one or more cultural settings (Gardner, 1983/2003) (P. x).

According to Gardner, nearly all major scholars in the area of human cognitive development have agreed on what it means to be 'well developed' adult. Today's studies have not been looking only at the estimate of overall intelligence, but also at the different combination of intelligences (Erkan & Üster, 2012, p. 274). Multiple Intelligences theory seeks to describe how individuals use their intelligences to solve problems and fashion projects. Due to this, Multiple Intelligences theory has been described as:

A philosophy of education, an attitude toward learning, or even a meta-model of education in the spirit of John Dewey's idea on progressive education rather than a set of programs of fixed techniques and strategies (Brahams, 1997) (P. 23).

Accordingly, this study aims to present a project which includes artwork, a smart learning environment with the use of open educational resources and multiple intelligences strategies and activities with various combinations of intelligences. The aim is to help learners to get the maximum benefit from the lesson at knowledge level as well as to gain a sense of art, interpretation and aesthetic value and learn through more than one style.

One potential tool to help students learn both historical thinking and factual knowledge is art. H. Gardner himself (2000, p. 247) supports the effort to demystify the arts, to construe them as involving the same kinds of skills and capacities as are involved in other domains and other disciplines. Gardner's theory of Multiple Intelligences helps students of all strengths and weaknesses explore the arts, not simply the creatively inclined (Foster, 2013, p. 1).

Researchers have argued that art can be a powerful pedagogical vehicle for engaging students in the process of historical inquiry and to develop their historical thinking (Holt, 1990; Christensen, 2006; Crawford et al., 2010; Suh, 2013, p. 135). Others have claimed that when art is used, students can grasp more vividly what the past signifies (Gabella, 1994; 1996; 1998; Suh, 2013, p. 135). Some researchers also argue that when art is used, students acquire a wider range of background knowledge and become more interested in learning about history (Levstik, 1990; Barton, 2001; Suh, 2013, p. 135). The use of historical visual materials opens an avenue for students to develop a new range of skills – the skills of "visual literacy" – 'reading' pictures to find data, make inferences, and locate meaning (Felton & Allen, 1990, p. 84). In order to use the arts to promote students' historical thinking, teachers should be more thoughtful about how they use art to teach history: what artwork they use, when, and how. The growth of online archives of primary sources has made rich documentary materials widely available, and provided an extensive laboratory for teacher and curriculum development.

Moreover, teaching must involve creating multiple intelligences activities that coincide with the reading curriculum content, and allotting time for successful completion of such activities by the students (Reidel et al., 2003, p. ii). On this basis, Information and Communication Technologies (ICT) as a tool for teaching history can substantially alter the way that students access, gather, analyse, reconstruct, present and convey information (Engeström, 1987; Duffy & Cunningham, 1996; Poole, 1997; Vakaloudi & Dagdilelis, 2016, p. 152).

LITERATURE REVIEW/THEORETICAL BACKGROUND

Theoretical Framework

The proposed project suggests that if primary source documents are going to significantly enhance secondary school students' understanding of the content of history, students need to be both cognitively active and emotionally engaged when working with them. In particular, some of the things that students need to do are: i) closely observe the documents' features, ii) bring prior knowledge to bear, iii) speculate about causes and consequences, iv) make personal connections, and v) use evidence to support their speculations. Indeed, the centrality of these skills is a key reason why digital archives of primary sources have important roles to play in improving elementary, middle, and secondary teaching and learning across the curriculum (Tally & Goldenberg, 2005, p. 1).

Over the course of twenty teaching hours of the proposed project, students analyze primary sources in the form of propaganda posters produced to support the involved countries' war efforts during World War I and II-era and documentary secondary sources. Students closely analyze both the primary source artwork and the secondary sources with the purpose of not only understanding the literal meaning but also inferring the more subtle messages. Students use textual and visual evidence to draw their conclusions and present arguments as directed in each lesson (Bailey, 2013, p. 1). Historical images, in particular, are a useful point of entry for many students, for unlike historical texts – which often present archaic language that children must decode before they can begin to construct meaning – photos, lithographs, cartoons and maps present instantly recognizable features and information, and easily evoke background knowledge that students can begin using in building an interpretation (Tally & Goldenberg, 2005, p. 3).

The proposed project is designed as an environment that will engage secondary school students with history through activities that utilize multiple intelligences based on Gardner's theory that there are a number of intellectual strengths, as opposed to a singular dominant ability, and that students demonstrate preferences for one or more of these defined areas. Teachers have always known that students had different strengths and weaknesses in the classroom. Gardner's research on multiple intelligences was able to articulate that and provide direction as to how to improve a student's ability in any given intelligence. Hence teachers were encouraged to begin to think of lesson planning in terms of meeting the needs of a variety of the intelligences (Giles et al., 2010). Although the intelligences are anatomically separated from each other, Gardner claims that the various intelligences very rarely operate independently. Rather, the intelligences are used concurrently and typically complement each other as individuals develop skills or solve problems. The theory of Multiple Intelligences implies that educators should recognize and teach to a broader range of talents and skills (Brualdi, 1996, pp. 2-3).

Gardner's theory of Multiple Intelligences is an excellent framework for finding the strength in all students, including gifted areas and different learning styles. The term "learning style" is commonly used throughout various educational fields and therefore, has many connotations. In general, it refers to the uniqueness of how each learner receives and processes new information through their senses. Research has identified four basic perceptual style preferences: visual, auditory, reading/writing, and kinesthetic/tactile. To these J. M. Reid (1987) added the dimensions of group versus individual learning (Fasha, 2016). Most individuals utilize multiple learning styles when acquiring new knowledge, but have a predisposed preference toward one based on culture, experience, and developmental influence. The National Association of Secondary School Principals (NASSP) defines learning style as the composite of characteristic cognitive, affective, and physiological factors that serve as relatively stable indicators of how a learner perceives, interacts with, and responds to the learning environment (Keefe, 1979).

Other phrases are used interchangeably with learning styles. Some include perceptual styles, learning modalities, and learning preferences (Silver et al., 2000; Giles et al., 2010; Leonard et al., 2010; Smith, n.d., p. 14).

The difference between the nine intelligences identified by Gardner, and the learning styles is subtle, but critical: intelligence is a cognitive faculty which explains how an individual orders and classifies information, while a learning style refers to the way that an individual prefers to be instructed or shown new information (Smith, n.d., p. 14).

Whether we call them intelligences, learning styles, talents, skills or human attributes, everyone uses them to construct their own meaning (Brahams, 1997, p. 8).

Based on the above, the proposed project creates a multiple intelligences framework which seems ideal for history teachers who can provide students learning opportunities that involve maps, documents, posters, political cartoons, broadsides, videos, and other forms of primary and secondary resources. In addition, computer technology and the Internet seem to only enhance the opportunity to combine these resources into a comprehensive multiple intelligences educational project that can potentially address each of the nine student capacities for learning (Cantu, 1999). Gardner himself refers to this 'marriage' between technology and his Multiple Intelligences theory as he mentions that:

Happily, versatile technologies are being developed, and these should eventually make it much easier to personalize education. "Multiple intelligences" fits comfortably with an open approach to education, and such a stance hungers for continuing renewal, rather than premature closure (Gardner, 1997) (P. 21).

The proposed project is implemented in a learning environment that combines real-world contexts and digital-world resources with the use of ICT to provide students with direct experiences of the real world with sufficient learning support. This aims to promote students' cognitive engagement which enables them to immerse themselves in in-depth reflective learning processes that are situated in realistic problem-solving tasks (Minami et al., 2004; Wu et al., 2013; Wu, Hwang, & Chai, 2013; Hwang, 2014, p. 4; Hwang et al., 2014). The basic precept of constructivism is that learning is achieved via the mediation of tools and interaction. In particular, ICT can substantially contribute to the teaching of history because: a) it can provide access to primary and secondary sources; b) it can cultivate a kind of experience in students, with audio visual material, simulations etc., which makes the understanding of historical terms, concepts and facts feasible; c) it favors the creation of an exploratory and collaborative learning environment; d) it offers rich material to the teacher to transform learning into a social process, collaborative, evolving and informed by a process of self-paced development that happens at a time and place of the learner's choosing (Sutherland et al., 2004; Winters et al., 2005, p. 74; Mikulecký, 2012, p. 217; Vakaloudi, 2016, p. 152; Vakaloudi & Dagdilelis, 2015, p. 78; 2016, p. 152). Accordingly, the proposed project includes theories, strategies and methods which meet the unique needs of all students. The Information and Communication Technologies (ICT) provide both an ideal resource and platform for applying the Multiple Intelligences theory. This kind of teaching not only excites students about learning, but it also allows a teacher to reinforce the same material in a variety of ways by activating a wide assortment of intelligences. Teaching in this manner can facilitate a deeper understanding of the subject material (Brualdi, 1996, pp. 3-4).

Art as Primary Source Material

Besides the purely pedagogical advantages, works of art merit study for their own historical worth. Art teaches history for us not only by supplying the historical details, but also by reflecting the attitudes and human intellectual and emotional responses of people to the events of their times. Finally, incorporating art into our overall scheme of teaching world history enables us to teach critical analytical skills. Just as our students must learn that studying history is an act of interpretation in which we must practice a method of investigation (figuring out what questions to ask, how to approach finding answers to those questions, and determining connections between those questions and answers), they can also learn those

Concepts of Propaganda

skills by looking carefully at works of art and distinguishing the content of the work from its style in order to perceive the point of view of the artist. They can easily learn to recognize ways that the painter manipulates us as viewers, shaping our reactions to the content through stylistic devices such as composition, color, size, and contrasts of light and darkness. What we have found is that once our students have mastered this kind of analysis, they rapidly become more comfortable with textual analysis, as well (Russell, n.d., pp. 2-3).

Examining and interpreting visual sources is a critical skill in history. Historical visual sources are often difficult to understand. They may depict or represent people or events we are unfamiliar with. They may use symbols whose meanings are obscure or have changed over time. Some visual sources may use humor, caricature or satire in a way that confuses or clouds their meaning. The history student must wrestle with these problems and others when analyzing visual sources.

Posters are a means of giving a specific message to a specific group for a specific reason. When we look at posters as historical documents, we must consider what the poster implies. In less than a single sentence, and on occasion with no words at all, posters are highly selective in the way that they depict the world. The way that a group, race, class or gender is portrayed in a poster can be very biased or skewed to fit the needs of the creator or to raise the desired reaction from viewers. Famous images and slogans that originated on posters of past wars are still recognized today. Some of the same techniques that were used to invoke emotion are used today in advertisements, something students will be able to understand. Posters attract our attention and often immediately appeal to some type of emotional reaction ("The Art of War", n.d., p. 1).

THE STUDY

The Role of Propagandistic Posters in War

Propaganda represents the communication of information or ideas aimed to influence the audience's view and position on subjects. Forms of propaganda have permeated society for centuries and have evolved to become a common tool of warfare. L. Finch (2000) defined propaganda as:

The management of opinions and attitudes by the direct manipulation of social suggestion (P. 368).

In other words, propaganda is used to influence people psychologically in order to alter social perceptions (Miles, 2012, p. 2). Propaganda usually produces an emotional response within the audience, rather than rational response; therefore, it is not aimed to appeal to intellect. Propaganda posters are commonly used by governments all around the world during war eras to gain support and communicate ideas to their people.

In view of the above, the proposed project aims to make secondary school students understand that through observation and study of the sources we can verify the historical information, but we can also learn how the opposite sides of a conflict use propaganda to shape international opinion.

Through the study of propagandistic posters from the two World Wars-era students come to realize that propaganda – the spreading of ideas or beliefs to further a particular cause or damage an opposing cause – uses very similar tools and methods with advertising. For instance, the purpose of advertising is generally to get people to buy a product or use a service. Likewise, the purpose of propaganda is to manipulate how people feel, think, or act. Also, advertisers and the creators of propaganda use many of the same tools – such as humor, catchy slogans, emotional images or language, caricatures, and visual symbols – to make their work effective (Cooke, 2014; Fields, n.d., p. 2).

Duration of the Project

The project lasts for twenty lessons/teaching hours (Table 1).

THE SIGNIFICANCE OF THE STUDY

Integrating Learner-Centered Theories and Strategies into a Smart Learning Environment

Contemporary teaching highlights, as the primary objective of history, historical understanding which is based on knowledge of the content of history, the methods of approaching historical fact and the understanding of concepts (evidence, cause, explanation, empathy, etc.) that seem to play a crucial role in historical understanding (Ashby & Lee, 1987; Levstik & Barton, 2001, pp. 246-261; Limón, 2002; Peck, 2005; Vakaloudi, 2016, pp. 151-152). In the proposed project, which incorporates innovative learner-centered approaches, secondary school students analyze World War I and II posters, chosen from online collections, and the secondary information about the era from which they come, to explore argument, persuasion, and propaganda. Furthermore, students discuss and develop an understanding of the techniques used to create effective propaganda. Then students present their findings to the class.

The project is based on *personality learning theories* (they define the influences of basic personality on preferences to acquiring and integrating information), *information processing theories* (they encompass individuals' preferred intellectual approach to assimilating information), *social learning theories* (they determine how students interact in the classroom), and *multidimensional and instructional theories* (they address the student's environmental preference for learning and include the *Learning Style Model* of Dunn and Dunn and the *Multiple Intelligences theory* of Howard Gardner) (Giles et al., 2010; Dybvig & Church, n.d.). Research on the importance of metacognitive thinking supports the notion that instructional approaches that help students reflect on their own learning processes are highly beneficial to their overall learning and tend to stimulate motivation to improve as learners (Marzano et al., 1988; Silver et al., 2000).

Table 1. Duration of the Educational Program

Educational Project		
Duration	**Thematic Units**	**Educator/s**
• Twenty teaching hours • Students work as partners, or in small groups and as a whole class	• Presentation of the project (Theoretical framework) • Two Interactive workshops (related to World War I and II): Research, Discussion and Feedback • Students work and collaborate either in the classroom or at home via online tools • Conclusion – Evaluation	

Concepts of Propaganda

The project is also based on the learning theories of *constructivism* and the *socio-cultural dimensions of knowledge*, in effect *socio-cultural constructivism,* that allow the students to interface with the digital teaching environment and determine the issues of investigation according to their needs and potential (Smith, 2010, pp. 94-95; Vakaloudi & Dagdilelis, 2013, p. 477). The project's teaching and learning activities are combined with free and easy-to-use ICT tools needed to bring open educational resources into the classroom, to enhance teaching and learning and support a student-centered learning environment (promoting problem solving, knowledge construction, critical thinking evaluation, interactivity, and collaboration skills among students) (Mikulecký, 2012, p. 217; Price, 2015, pp. 4, 5, 13; Kennah, 2016; Vakaloudi, 2016, p. 152; Vakaloudi & Dagdilelis, 2013, pp. 476-477; 2016, p. 152).

Just as there are nine intelligences and certain characteristics germane to each of these nine intelligences, so too are there specific teaching strategies that address each of these student ways of learning. According to Gardner everyone is born possessing multiple intelligences. Nevertheless, all students will come into the classroom with different sets of developed intelligences. This means that each child will have his own unique set of intellectual strengths and weaknesses. These sets determine how easy (or difficult) it is for a student to learn information when it is presented in a particular manner. Furthermore, Gardner suggested that specific functions come from different regions in the brain and the mind's problem-solving capacities are multifaceted and can work independently or together. Students possess all intelligences in varying amounts, but each student has a different intellectual composition. Therefore, the introduction of multiple intelligences activities into the classrooms of history teachers must be accompanied with a change in how educators view student thinking (Cantu, 1999).

Accordingly, the proposed project, by structuring material in a way that engages most of the intelligences, can show students how to use their more developed intelligences to assist in the understanding of a subject (Lazear, 1992; Brualdi, 1996, p. 4). More specifically, the proposed project contains various teaching strategies to stimulate motivation, study skills, learning skills, thinking skills, critical thinking to secondary school students. These strategies develop each student's talents and apply the theory of Multiple Intelligences in ways appropriate for students. By improving and identifying various intelligence strengths and weaknesses through the proposed project, students acquire the capability to ask researchable questions, identify varied resources, create realistic timelines, bring closure to learning activities and, through metacognition, create solutions to problems in real aspects of life (Reidel et al., 2003, pp. 15-17).

The strategy of "teaching history through inquiry" helps students move toward knowledge by engaging with the primary documents of the past. Our world is saturated with media and students need to form the habit of taking a stance of healthy skepticism toward the information they receive. They need the tools to distinguish the truth, to evaluate the information they encounter, based on where it comes from, who is producing it and when, its use of evidence, and its intended audience (Lazar, 2011, pp. 1-2)

In the proposed project the author also uses the strategy of "historical empathy" in order to succeed students' cognitive and affective engagement with historical figures to better understand and contextualize their lived experiences, decisions, or actions (Lee & Ashby, 2001; Barton & Levstik, 2004; Brooks, 2008; Endacott & Brooks, 2013, pp. 41, 43; Vakaloudi, 2017, pp. 120, 121). When we teach world history, it is helpful to structure lesson plans aiming not only to educate students about particular topics such as the World Wars and global mass atrocities but to help them prevent possible future atrocities. Through the historical analysis we should be engaged to the moral and anti-racist education (Layman & Harris, 2013, p. 4; Vakaloudi, 2017, p. 121). In light of the above, students study how propaganda manipulates emotional responses of people to the events of their times (Nokes et al., 2007; Yilmaz, 2007, pp. 333-334).

Through the study of propagandistic posters from the two World Wars-era this project also aims to make students recognize the stereotypes and understand why stereotypes is an important part of understanding the use of anti-symbols and the portrayal of the enemy in propaganda (e.g. caricatures, monsters, demons, beasts, etc.) intending to dehumanize the enemy. This dehumanization could turn to a precursor of discrimination, racism, isolation, and violence (Grobman, 1990; Schniedewind & Davidson, 2006, pp. 117-119; Friedman, 2008; Renz, 2010, pp. 124, 130-131).

The author also uses the teaching strategy of "project-based learning," (PBL) an overall approach to the design of learning environments (Blumenfeld et al., 1991; Stepien & Gallagher, 1993; Krajcik et al., 1994; Marx et. al., 1994, p. 518; Barron et al., 1998, p. 274; Thomas, 2000, pp. 1, 3; Krajcik et al., 2002; Helle et al., 2006, p. 288; Krajcik & Blumenfeld, 2006, p. 318; Coffey, 2008, p. 1). On this basis, the principal aim of the proposed project is to explore secondary school students' knowledge/understanding of debating ideas, collecting and analyzing data, drawing conclusions, communicating ideas and findings to others, asking new questions, making predictions, etc. However, the author is also interested in examining how knowledge/understanding is related to other issues, such as students' attitudes towards out-groups or their beliefs in a 'just world' (Barron et al., 1998, p. 285; Krajcik & Blumenfeld, 2006, pp. 321, 324; Vakaloudi, 2017, p. 121).

The author also uses the teaching strategies of "visual literacy," "multimodal literacy," and "analyzing visual images and stereotyping" in order to lead students in a critical analysis of an image, and to help students develop and enhance observational, interpretive, and critical thinking skills. The exploration of World War I and II posters and their multimodal messages enable students to deal constructively with complex modes of delivering information, multisensory tactics for persuasion, and technology-based art forms (Sullivan, 2007, pp. 174-176; Wright, 2017).

As it was mentioned, students prefer different learning styles in which they receive information, which are directly related to Gardner's multiple intelligences. The proposed project is engaged in learning-style based instruction since all the aforementioned strategies are also learning strategies for the learning styles. Replacing words with symbols and vice versa, turning visuals into words, creating key information with words and symbols/images support Visual Learning Style. Discussing topics or solving problems with the instructor and other students focus on Auditory Learning Style. Writing out important information, organizing data into statements helps the Reading/Writing Learning Style. Copying key points using interactive white board, word processing software, or presentation software, seeing and listening to videos, taking in information through collections, putting real life examples into notes summary, using pictures and photographs that illustrate an idea support Kinesthetic/Tactile Learning Style (Giles et al., 2010).

Finally, using a systematic approach to pursue questions about students' thinking and collecting, analyzing, and sharing the data is a form of informal teacher classroom research, often described as "action research." Action research deepens teachers' understanding of teaching (Roberts et al., 2007, p. ix; Keeley, 2014, pp. 85-86).

The Project's Teaching Methods

1. Students engage in historical issues-analysis, interpretation, and decision-making (they analyze, and interpret historical events, conditions, trends, and issues to develop historical perspective; they observe, analyze, and interpret human behaviors, social groupings, and institutions to better understand people and the relationships among individuals and among groups; they describe various forms of interactions – compromise, cooperation, conflict – that occurred between diverse

groups during WW I and II-era; they describe significant historical events and explain cause and effect relationships. Challenging questions or problems are used, which involve students in various activities. Questions serve to organize and drive activities of the project, provide a context in which students can use and explore learning goals and provide continuity and coherence to the full range of project activities. As students pursue solutions to the questions, they develop understandings of key concepts (Levstik & Barton, 2001, pp. 246-261; Peck, 2005; Vakaloudi, 2016, p. 151; 2017, p. 123). During the process students comprehend the essential difference between *primary* and *secondary* sources ("Distinguish between primary and secondary sources", 2016, p. 2; "Distinguish between primary and secondary sources", n.d.).

2. Students design and conduct investigations working in teams. They discuss the questions which encourage reflection. During this time, teachers should be moving between stations, prompting conversations, pointing out important details, and doing 'mid-workshop interruptions' to point out clever student observations and useful strategies. To encourage students to not rush, teachers could set a timer so students will know when to move to the next stop (Elms, 2014, p. 4). Co-operative activities and exercises prevent conflicts and discrimination and achieve discipline. They also help collaboration among students and teachers, so that participants can learn from one another and the use of cognitive tools that help learners represent their ideas. Students hold each other responsible for learning and the completion of tasks as 'self-managers' (Coffey, 2008, pp. 1-3; "Cooperation and Participation", n.d.).

3. Students access, add and modify knowledge using different technology tools. They work in the classroom and at home as part of a blended-learning strategy. The technologies are used in creative ways to support learning, engaging the learner in a dialogue or facilitating group dialogue on a relevant topic or problem and providing meaningful and timely feedback to a learner based on the learner's progress and profile and the learning task at hand (Ehlers, 2011, p. 5; Hwang, 2014; Spector 2014; Zhu et al., 2016; Singh & Hassan, 2017, pp. 5, 9-12).

4. The project specifically aims at supporting students with learning difficulties. These students usually have difficulty with comprehending the spoken or written language. When visual sources of the proposed project are used, good reading skills are not necessary for successful learning, and, at the same time, the visual provides meaning-centered, language-sharing techniques. Teachers utilize many of the techniques of verbal language analysis when they use the visual sources. Furthermore, students experience the important sense of language control (and self-power) that may occur when they intentionally combine pictures with spoken and written language in the project's activities (Fransecky & Debes, 1972, pp. 7, 13; Felton & Allen, 1990, p. 84). The main points of the topic are highlighted as comprehension exercises; topics are dealt with by asking questions. Web based education and the accessibility of ICT based resources facilitates engagement within education and social participation. Students use alternative ways, e.g. they do their writing on the computer, which has been proven to help children with learning difficulties. They use assistive technology (e.g. spelling checkers, grammar and style checkers, online dictionaries, and multimedia applications), record their notes online; the method of recording notes teaches them to reorganize information into a more understandable and useful format. Note-taking is also a cognitive skill of active learning. Skills are cultivated for collaborative learning and the value of group collaboration and teaching among peers (peer teaching) emerges, engagement in interaction is organized inside and outside the classroom (MacArthur, 1996; Istenic Starcic & Kerr, 2014, p. 521; Vakaloudi, 2016, pp. 342-345; Vakaloudi & Dagdilelis, 2015, p. 80; 2016, p. 165).

The Integration of Information and Communication Technologies in the Teaching and Learning Process

The students are divided into groups, with the teachers' guidance. The project is conducted either in the classroom with students' laptops, or in computer lab and the process consists of the handling of objects and tools, both material (e.g. hardware, software, Internet, technology tools, worksheets) and symbolic (language, communication, interaction, cooperation of educators – students, and students amongst themselves). A role-playing game, which engages the imagination and empathy of the students, is put into practice. Each group chooses its coordinator who coordinates the processes, the manager of the computer, the timekeeper, etc. (Vakaloudi, 2016, p. 339; Vakaloudi & Dagdilelis, 2013, pp. 477-478; 2016, p. 166).

As a warm up, the teacher uses a free Web tool, e.g. a *padlet*, to create a collaborative interactive white board and to share it with his/her students. He/she writes on the white board the word "propaganda" and asks students as a class to brainstorm what this word means. He/she encourages students to think about the definition, examples, situations in which it is used, etc., and write their thoughts on the white board. The aforementioned Web tool provides a shared 'dialogic space' for reasoned discussion, within which students are able to jointly access relevant information, share different points of view and achieve collective solutions (Mercer et al., 2010, p. 367). After the discussion, students should understand that propaganda refers to a type of message aimed at influencing opinions and/or behavior of people. Many governments, especially the Nazis during World War II, use propaganda effectively. Propaganda may provide only partial information or be deliberately misleading. Propaganda techniques are often found on television and radio, as well as magazines, newspapers, posters, etc.

Teacher poses the following questions to the class:

- Why do you think governments would use propaganda, especially during wartime?
- How strongly do you think propaganda influences people's opinions?
- Do you think that people can recognize propaganda as soon as they see it?
- Can you think of any propaganda you have seen recently? Summarize what you saw and where you saw it ("Decoding World War II Propaganda", n.d., p. 2).

Teacher has the class ensure that they identify the attributes of propaganda: i) spreading ideas, information, or rumor; ii) intention of helping or injuring; iii) focus is on an institution, cause, or person ("Propaganda and World War II", n.d., p. 2).

Then, students discuss the similarities and differences between argument, persuasion, and propaganda after studying the relative information ("Read, Write, Think", 2005) and watching the instructional film, "Propaganda Techniques," 1949, 10 minutes, from https://archive.org/details/PropagandaTechniques ("Analyzing Propaganda", n.d., p. 2).

Next, teacher provides students with a World War I and II Poster Art historical overview on the white board for their preparation and lets them share their ideas and comments. This way, every student can see what others think and the whole class discusses the given answers. Teacher can use any kind of online resource platform to share relevant historical details about the posters, as well as instructions, resources, assignments, worksheets, rubrics of evaluation, answers to technical questions, etc. (in the form of documents, Power Point files, PDF files, texts, links, audio files, videos, etc.).

Consequently, students as pares or groups engage with various tasks and activities with online media:

Concepts of Propaganda

- They surf the Internet, assess a variety of WW I and II propaganda posters (from online collections, e.g. British Library, Library of Congress, the National Archives, and countless universities, museums, and libraries), interpret them, and identify their persuasive messages. They also gather information about the key issues from primary documents (e.g. The World War I Document Archive: https://wwi.lib.byu.edu/index.php/Main_Page), from Cybraries (e.g. http://remember.org and https://www.ushmm.org, about the Holocaust) from Eyewitness accounts such as Robert Lindsay Mackay WW I Diary (http://www.firstworldwar.com/diaries/rlm.htm), etc. If students select a source, they must briefly explain why they chose the particular source focusing on relevance and credibility (Shea & Stockford, 2015, p. 24; Eisenberg et al., 2016, p. 51).
- Students watch videos (e.g. as an introduction to the WW II, the History Channel offers a broad overview of the causes of WW II: http://www.history.com/topics/world-war-ii/world-war-ii-history). Using videos (moving images and sound) to communicate a topic can be used to promote 'active viewing' approaches with students (Galbraith, 2004). They also study historical maps and secondary sources found on the Internet and then they create timelines with online tools about the most important events of the two World Wars. The representation of the concept of time and place in conjunction with the consideration of sources helps the students to better interpret the historical material that they have at their disposal and to structure their historical thinking (Donovan & Bransford, 2005; Vakaloudi, 2016, pp. 78-79, 184, 329-331; Vakaloudi & Dagdilelis, 2016, p. 159).
- Students create various gallery collections of WW I and WW II posters, specifying the fields that they want to include from the data sources by setting certain criteria. They organize and categorize the posters' data into tables (e.g. Images and Text – Facts – Emotions) on free online *databases*. Then they analyze the data, identify certain characteristics, discover relationships, techniques, strategies, trends, patterns and publish the search results on the Web.
- Among the visual sources students are assigned to collect two German propaganda poster-maps (e.g. "German Propaganda Archive", nr. 22: http://www.bytwerk.com/gpa/posters3.htm and nr. 15: http://www.bytwerk.com/gpa/posters2.htm) and compare them with common historical maps. Students know that usually maps give an idea of the place in which the events occurred. The assignment is to trace elements of the Nazi propaganda that intend to glorify Germany, justify territorial expansion, and decrease support for the U.S.A., France, and Britain (Jacobs, 2017, p. 1), and to explain their purpose. Thus, they realize that in this case the poster-maps are used as an interpretation of reality that is influenced by the political and cultural views of their creators. The manipulation finds expression in the information chosen to appear on the map, in the means of representing it and in the decision as to what information to feature and underscore and what to merely hint at or understate. In this case the maps depict worldviews, and they serve as tools for shaping consciousness (Hoepper, 2009; Medzini, 2012, pp. 23-24; Vakaloudi, 2016, pp. 104-105, 195 ff., 324-325; Vakaloudi & Dagdilelis, 2016, p. 156). Students can even create their own "propagandistic maps" with a presentation program or with various free *Map Tools* on Web using information from the timelines and the sources.
  - Students combine posters and information from a variety of sources to create multimedia presentations (with *MS Power Point, Windows Movie Maker,* and online tools). They present in their works poster themes and the intentions of the artists and the governments, based on various criteria.

- "Does each poster tell a story? Use your imagination and briefly narrate the story": Students choose posters and create and share multimedia stories inspired by images, slogans, and their interpretation. They can even create online a graphic novel, i.e. a comic in a more literary form, combining images and text. Comics can engage students in multiple literacies and the use of graphic novels is seen as one strategy that encourages literacy and literate practices (Jacobs, 2007, p. 20).

For this assignment students use free Digital Storytelling Tools such as *Photo Story 3*, *iMovie*, etc., adding poster-images and text from documents, books, magazines or newspapers. They can touch-up, crop, or rotate pictures, add special effects, music, and their own narration to the photo stories.

- Students create online two Propaganda Posters related to WW I and WW II-era and an issue/event/condition during that time, remembering to focus on one of the key reasons for why propaganda posters were produced (Rudiger, 2003; "Posters: World War I Posters", n.d.).
- The groups study how the posters try to persuade, mainly through words, visuals, or both equally. They also notice how the stylistic devices such as language, composition, colors, size, space, and contrasts of light and darkness support the message in the posters. Then, students create their own posters with free online tools which allow them to display images, text, to include a quick video, links to all the sources, and to allow others to quickly add and comment.

The above activities establish cross-curricular collaboration and work because they involve history, literature, linguistics, music, technology, etc. (Schrag, n.d., p. 1).

- Students use discussion groups/lists (e.g. *Google Groups*), to exchange opinions about posters' themes. In this case the synchronous discussion is preferred as teachers are able to instantly understand students' learning attitudes. In collaborative learning, the real-time coordination between members influences the quality of group discussions, facilitates learners' group decision-making and brainstorming skills and enhances the understanding of fellow group members' learning attitudes in an online community. Furthermore, the teacher must ensure that a high-quality discussion is conducted, with 'completeness,' which includes the length and richness, and 'depth,' which is the level of focus and contribution towards the discussion topics (Hou & Wu, 2011, p. 1460).
- Students use *Wikis* to write essays sharing and collaborating with others. The use of wikis in group projects is predicted to encourage a more equal participation from all team members, since on a wiki a record is kept of every contribution to every Web page, when it was made and who made it, allowing the teacher to judge both the quantity and quality of contributions by different team members. Wikis also permit both interaction and simultaneous work on the conjoined result, thereby removing the boundaries between the active author and the passive user of content (Parker & Chao, 2007; Elgort et al., 2008, pp. 197-199).
- Groups create *Blogs* where they discuss and comment various topics. Educational blogging is an effective tool for user centered, participatory learning and it contributes vitally to a reconceptualization of students as critical, collaborative, and creative participants in the social construction of knowledge (Farmer et al., 2008, p. 124).

Concepts of Propaganda

The students-authors write, as their reflexion on the given subject evolves, their opinions, impressions, etc., so as to make them public and receive reactions and comments about them.

- Students can also be assigned to create a digital journal using online tools like *Penzu*. Writing a journal challenges students to reflect on past situations, as well as consider how they might perform differently should similar situations arise in the future.

  Examples:
  - After studying various posters with different themes, students compose journal entries from the perspective of common people describing the effect of each poster (according to its theme) on their feelings and reactions (as men, women, and children). They can express their point of view with texts, diaries, poetry, songs, etc. (Wallace, 2003, p. 98).
  - "Living in Lidice in 1942…": Students, inspired by the poster of "The Lidice massacre" in "National Archives and Records Administration", section "This is Nazi Brutality" (https://www.archives.gov/exhibits/powers_of_persuasion/this_is_nazi_brutality/this_is_nazi_brutality.html) and the "Lidice" (also known as "Fall of the Innocent" in the U.K.) Czech drama film, impersonate a habitant of the village Lidice and create a Diary. Lidice was a Czech mining village that was obliterated by the Nazis in retaliation for the 1942 shooting of a Nazi official by two Czechs. All men of the village were killed in a 10-hour massacre; the women and children were sent to concentration camps; a few children considered racially suitable for Germanisation were handed over to SS families and the rest were sent to the Chełmno extermination camp where they were gassed to death. The destruction of Lidice became a symbol for the brutality of Nazi occupation during World War II. Students create journal entries and depict, in the first person, the facts, the thoughts and the feelings of a villager (man, woman, or child) during this era. They can add photos, music and videos to their posts to make them more interesting.
- A journal like *Penzu* can also engage teachers and students in a dynamic discussion about the project. At regular intervals students create journal entries, to write in their journal about their tasks, their thoughts, observations, comments, problems, and their interactions with the other members of their group. Then students use the "share" feature on Penzu to allow teacher to see their work in the journal and give the necessary feedback or evaluation based on their needs.

All the aforementioned free technology tools enable the groups of students to work together to complete the project. They have the advantage that anyone can contribute anytime, anywhere. Students evaluate and add recourses, add and edit text, post posters, as well as links to the references they used. They work collaboratively add/delete/modify content directly from the Web browser. Thus, collaborative skills, skills in negotiation and organization, critical writing skills, and a sense of responsibility and ownership are developed. This way students are helped to reach Bloom's higher order skills, e.g. creating, evaluation, etc. (Richardson, 2005; Kurt, 2017).

Final Stage

Students compare posters, subjects, techniques of propaganda between World War I and World War II, they pinpoint similarities and differences and make some final conclusions about the effectiveness of the techniques and methods of persuasion in an Overall Reflection and Evaluation Worksheet (Cf. "Analyzing a World War II Poster", n.d.). The groups either orally support their perspectives (using their online notes) in relation to the topic in the open plenary session of the class, or compose, using their findings, conclusive arguments with a word processor or presentation software, which they present in the open plenary session of the class, with commentary and discussion (Vakaloudi, 2016, p. 153; Vakaloudi & Dagdilelis, 2016, p. 153).

FUTURE RESEARCH DIRECTIONS

Students Apply the Gained Knowledge to Contemporary Era and Their Lives

- Students create a *Wiki* to compare the techniques in the world wars' posters and modern propaganda posters about contemporary issues such as drinking and driving, smoking, or environmental concerns. An interesting topic for such a study is that the American Propaganda ads and protest art from the WW I-era portray the same themes that we still see in today's political climate (Boyd, 2017).
- Inspired by the WW I and WW II posters students create *propaganda posters* online about contemporary issues.
  Examples:
    - Study the World Wars posters which impose the terror and the feeling of personified danger and create a similar one to point out the risks from smoking (like cigarette packaging which contains labels disclosing the risks of smoking).
    - Think about how the WW I and II posters' messages can be updated and made relevant for our current fight to address global climate change and achieve energy independence. Is recycled paper the new scrap metal? Is investment in renewable energy the new war bond? ("Green Patriot Posters", n.d.).
    - Study the "Four Freedoms" WW II American posters ("National Archives and Records Administration": https://www.archives.gov/exhibits/powers_of_persuasion/four_freedoms/four_freedoms.html) and connect the *freedom of speech and expression - everywhere in the world* poster with contemporary issues of free speech ("War of the future", 2011).
    - Create an anti-war poster like the one of 1972 in which the Uncle Sam in James Flagg's WW I recruiting poster is supplanted by a symbol of death (Lester, 2013, p. 85).

Teachers put the posters on display and they have students vote on which poster is most effective.

- Each group creates a *Blog* where the members define the origin of the term "scapegoat," and how this term is used today. Then they describe processes in their environment by which a stereotype is created. Where they see materials that they would consider propaganda in their daily lives. They post examples for discussion and analysis. Thus, students identify problematic propaganda messages or hate speech in their community and become empowered to respond.

Concepts of Propaganda

Furthermore, they can search on the Web case studies of youth who opposed to hate speech and stereotypes. This provides concrete role models and action steps ("Analyzing Propaganda", n.d., p. 6; "United States Holocaust Memorial Museum", 2013; "United States Holocaust Memorial Museum", n.d.b.; Vakaloudi, 2017, pp. 129-132).

CONCLUSION

The evaluation of the project takes place in the end with the evaluative reports from the participants about the achievement of the project's objectives and the success of the activities (based on how well the students have incorporated the concepts discussed in class).

The theory of Multiple Intelligences' greatest contribution to assessment is that it allows for multiple ways to evaluate students. The traditional methods of assessment which require students to show what they know or have learned through standardized tests that focus narrowly on verbal or logical domains are not aligned with the Multiple Intelligences philosophy (Brahams, 1997, pp. 26-27). H. Gardner talks about assessment of the intelligences in terms of constructing an "intelligence profile" on students. This means that the teacher will figure out what makes each student 'tick' in terms of how they best know, understand, perceive, and learn. Gardner believes that careful observation of students involved in various activities and learning tasks, can give a fairly accurate intelligence profile of them. We then can use this information to help them master their studies and deal with everyday problems and challenges (Lazear, 1992, pp. 36 ff.; Gardner, 1995, p. 17; Brahams, 1997, p. 27; Gardner, 1999; Almeida et al., 2010).

Significant benefits can result from the proposed type of multiple intelligences teaching project. First it is a learner-centered approach in which students actually create a variety of different materials that demonstrate their understanding of the subject matter. This learner-centered approach allows students to actively use their varied forms of intelligence. Activities involving all nine intelligences are presented as options for the class, and each student participates in the tasks by choice.

More specifically, using the Internet for research and then presenting their findings is an excellent project for linguistic learners. In the proposed project, ICT facilitate these students' self-expression, because they can use their verbal skills to express themselves in many ways. Using the interactive white board to accent important points or providing outlines of the lesson material, composing essays, poetry, journals, logs, articles, storytelling, debates, PowerPoint presentations, etc. are used to provide an opportunity for students to exercise Verbal/Linguistic Intelligence.

Story problems, categorizing facts in databases, creating timelines, strategizing, problem-solving, reasoning, interpretation are used for Logical/Mathematical Intelligence.

The timeline and map assignments are student-centered activities that are designed to enhance students' Logical/Mathematical Intelligence and Visual/Spatial Intelligence. Students must collect and organize information from the timelines, the maps and other sources therefore using their Logical/Mathematical intelligence. In creating these items, students must think visually as well.

Studying and designing maps encourage Naturalistic Intelligence.

Teaching others, leading, cooperative learning groups, environmental, social, and political issues, blogs, wikis encourage the growth of Interpersonal Intelligence.

The databases and spreadsheets of the project facilitate the logical and interpersonal learners, because they allow them to organize data. The project's activities offer these students a problem and then given resources to solve it.

Exploratory, interactive and cooperative activities of the project exercise the communication and creative strengths of the interpersonal learners.

Copying key points onto interactive white board, cooperative Web searches, role playing activities that incorporate Web resources, using ICT tools, classroom presentations, simulations are used for Kinesthetic Intelligence.

The visual aspects and texts of the project offer spatial learners the creativity they need. Once their research is complete, they can share their work with the use of multiple presentation means. Art, maps, videos, graphs, imagining things, creating posters, illustrating graphic novels, filmmaking foster Visual/Spatial Intelligence.

The computer-based concept mapping, and Internet research of the project are good technology options for the intrapersonal learners. Blogs are also a great resource for these learners. Self-assessment, goal setting, emotional processing, self-directed / reflective individual activities such as a diary are also used to awaken students' Intrapersonal Intelligence.

Designing and publishing presentations or videos which incorporate music and visual elements, writing songs, composing music encourage Musical Intelligence.

Finally, the project's communication and problem-solving applications are ideal for the existentialist learners. Philosophical discussions, creating art that questions life and reality, discussion of good and evil, suffering, and death etc., in a way that can shake up students' personal belief system and cause them to think in new ways about human existence, encourage Existential Intelligence (McKenzie, 2005, pp. 47, 53-55; MacCoog, 2007, pp. 26-27; Armstrong, 2009, p. 187; Giles et al., 2010).

The project is also designed to address all learning styles. Visual learners process information most effectively when the information is seen. They also remember best what they see – pictures, diagrams, flow charts, timelines, films, videos, presentations, etc. Aural learners process information most effectively when spoken or heard and they are excellent listeners. These learners respond well to discussions, debates and arguments. They are effective in putting forward a case – for and against. They also like to talk and enjoy music and dramas. Reading/Writing learners learn preferentially through interaction with textual materials and they process information most effectively when presented in a written language format. Kinesthetic/Tactile learners prefer learning experiences that emphasize doing and they process information actively through experience, interaction, role playing, or simulation (Giles et al., 2010; Vakaloudi & Dagdilelis, 2015, p. 80).

In view of the above, it is concluded that using the proposed Multiple Intelligences theory project in the classroom as a teacher and learner someone can realize that there are many ways to be 'smart.' All forms of intelligence have equal importance. A sense of increased self-worth may be seen as students build on their strengths and work towards becoming an expert in certain areas. Students may develop strong problem-solving skills that they can use in real life situations (Cantu, 1999; Giles et al., 2010).

Furthermore, in this project, the students learn to analyze some basic propaganda techniques and they notice that many times the posters have more than one technique ("Propaganda Techniques", 1979; "Propaganda Techniques to Recognize", n.d.). Students develop criteria about what makes an effective piece of propaganda, and use these criteria to look critically at a collection of posters from the two World Wars-era. Students look at the way images and words are combined to create effective propaganda messages. Moreover, the *doing of history* is where students pose questions, collect and analyze sources, struggle with issues of significance, and ultimately build their own historical interpretations (Levstik, 1996, p. 394).

Concepts of Propaganda

Accordingly, during the project, students use their skills of inquiry, research, and communication in working through this project while also learning from it. Students are engaged in historical inquiry, in order to develop an understanding of the broad picture of the past in a cyclical process: *historical questions — historical sources — historical evidence* (Lee, 2005, p. 58; "Distinguish between primary and secondary sources", 2016, p. 2; "Distinguish between primary and secondary sources", n.d.; "SCIM-C: Historical Inquiry", n.d.).

By studying primary and secondary sources through historical questions, students contextualize people's thoughts, decisions and actions in the past and they try to understand and interpret them. Thus, students develop an understanding of the social and/or political implications of propaganda and the ability to understand propaganda within the context of the two World Wars in the involved countries (Barton, 2012; Elms, 2014, p. 8; Huang, 2015).

Students also discuss how someone differentiates "propaganda" from "persuasion." In the proposed project students discover that most of the negativity associated with the word "propaganda" stems from wartime propaganda historically used by 'us' and 'them.' Finally, students study how and why the late nineteenth and early twentieth centuries were periods of great expansion of propaganda activities ("The Techniques of Propaganda", n.d., p. 2).

It is essential that the students can identify the critical differences between, for example, propaganda and debate or propaganda and advertising. Thus, through the study of the posters, students identify and prove that: Propaganda is, first and foremost, ideological. It tries to sell a belief system or dogma. Propaganda can be religious, political, or economic; propaganda uses mass media (e.g. posters); propaganda seeks commonality in the beliefs, attitudes, and behaviors of its receivers; usually, appeals to the hearts and not the minds of the audience; propaganda uses stereotyping. Through powerful descriptive language, the out-group is characterized with negative attributes and quality ("The Techniques of Propaganda", n.d., pp. 1-2, 4, 12).

Students assess the powers of words and images in communication. Today we are exposed to greater amounts of information from more sources than ever before. Students, as future citizens, have a responsibility as consumers of that information to thoughtfully evaluate the messages they encounter, particularly when those messages urge action ("United States Holocaust Memorial Museum", n.d.a.).

Connective writing in various online tools is a form that forces those who do it to read carefully and critically, that demands clarity and cogency in its construction, that is done for a wide audience, and that links to the sources of the ideas expressed (Richardson, 2006). Moreover, the implemented technologies help students to become not only readers and writers, but editors and collaborators. Research findings demonstrate that the encouragement of active learning, cooperation and collaboration among students promotes and improves learning, and it is an important factor in academic achievement, personal development and student satisfaction (Winters et al., 2005, p. 74; Elgort et al., 2008, p. 197; Zhu et al., 2016).

Teachers evaluate students', understanding of the concepts of propaganda; ability to relate these concepts to the images and text in their posters; ability to situate the posters and their messages within the context of the WW I and II; ability to determine the central ideas or information of a primary or secondary source and provide an accurate summary that makes clear the relationships among the key details and ideas; ability to evaluate various explanations for actions or events; ability to determine the meaning of words and images as they are used in a poster, including analyzing how an artist uses and refines the meaning of a key word or image. Also, teachers check for the: clarity with which the argument is presented; ability of the students to cite specific examples to support their analysis; active participation of all students (as group members and individually) ("Analyzing Propaganda", n.d., p. 5).

All the components of the proposed project – connecting different open educational resources and making a composite whole – are an effort to cultivate and develop the abilities, skills, attitudes and behaviours of students and teachers by constructing knowledge assets, sharing them with others, and receiving feedback and reviews in an environment in which knowledge is co-created and facilitated through mutual interaction and reflection. Also established is the development of a variety of linguistic and multimodal forms of expression, which arise in a natural and cooperative way, in cross-thematic combination with the processing of questions (Smith, 2007, p. 81; Spector & Merrill, 2008; Smith, 2010, pp. 94-95; Daniels, 2011, p. 4; Ehlers, 2011, p. 4; Merrill, 2013; Spector, 2014; Kanwar & Uvalić-Trumbić, 2015, p. 13; Spector, 2016, p. 2731; Zhu et. al., 2016; Singh & Hassan, 2017, p. 15).

REFERENCES

Ahmad, R. A., Seman, A. A., Awang, M. M., & Sulaiman, F. (2015). Application of Multiple Intelligence Theory to Increase Student Motivation in Learning History. *Asian Culture and History*, *7*(1), 210–219.

Almeida, L. S., Prieto, M. D., Ferreira, A. I., Bermejo, M. R., Ferrando, M., & Ferrándiz, C. (2010). Intelligence assessment: Gardner multiple intelligence theory as an alternative. *Learning and Individual Differences*, *20*(3), 225–230. doi:10.1016/j.lindif.2009.12.010

Analyzing a World War II Poster. (n.d.). Retrieved May 24, 2019, from http://www.readwritethink.org/files/resources/AnalyzingWorldWarII-Poster.htm

Armstrong, T. (2009). *Multiple Intelligences in the Classroom* (3rd ed.). Alexandria, VA: ASCD.

Ashby, R., & Lee, P. (1987). Discussing the evidence. *Teaching History*, *48*, 13–17.

Bailey, T. (2013). *World War II. Posters and propaganda*. Retrieved January 22, 2019, from https://www.gilderlehrman.org/history-by-era/world-war-ii/resources/world-war-ii-posters-and-propaganda

Bain, R. (2005). 'They thought the world was flat?': Applying the principles of How People Learn in teaching high school history. In J. Bransford & S. Donovan (Eds.), *How students learn history, mathematics and science in the classroom* (pp. 179–215). Washington, DC: National Academics Press.

Barron, B. J. S., Schwartz, D. L., Vye, N. J., Moore, A., Petrosino, A., Zech, L., Bransford, J. D. (1998). Doing with understanding: Lessons from research on problem and project-based learning. *The Journal of the Learning Sciences: Learning through Problem Solving, 7*(3/4), 271-311.

Barton, K. (2001). A picture's worth: Analyzing historical photographs in the elementary grades. *Social Education*, *65*(5), 278–283.

Barton, K. (2012, April). Agency, choice and historical action: How history teaching can help students think about democratic decision making. *Citizenship Teaching & Learning*, *7*(2), 131–142. doi:10.1386/ctl.7.2.131_1

Barton, K., & Levstik, L. (2004). *Teaching history for the common good*. Mahwah, NJ: Lawrence Erlbaum Associates. doi:10.4324/9781410610508

Blumenfeld, P. C., Soloway, E., Marx, R. W., Krajcik, J. S., Guzdial, M., & Palincsar, A. (1991). Motivating project-based learning: Sustaining the doing, supporting the learning. *Educational Psychologist, 26*(3&4), 369–398. doi:10.120715326985ep2603&4_8

Boyd, N. (2017, February). Now and Then: American Propaganda and Protest Posters. *20th Century Typographers.* Retrieved January 3, 2019, from http://www.printmag.com/design-education/online-design-courses/now-then-american-propaganda-posters

Brahams, Y. R. (1997). *Development of a social studies curriculum reflecting Howard Gardner's theory of multiple intelligences.* Theses Digitization Project. 1424. Retrieved May 22, 2019, from http://scholarworks.lib.csusb.edu/etd-project/1424

Brooks, S. (2008). Displaying historical empathy: What impact can a writing assignment have? *Social Studies Research & Practice, 3*(2), 130–146.

Brualdi, A. C. (1996). *Multiple Intelligences: Gardner's Theory. ERIC Digest.* Washington, DC: ERIC Clearinghouse on Assessment and Evaluation. Retrieved May 19, 2019, from https://files.eric.ed.gov/fulltext/ED410226.pdf

Cantu, A. D. (1999, November). An Internet Based Multiple Intelligences Model for Teaching High School History. *Journal of the Association for History and Computing, 2*(3). Retrieved from http://hdl.handle.net/2027/spo.3310410.0002.305

Christensen, L. M. (2006). Using art to teach history to young learners. *Social Education, 70*(5), 312–315.

Coffey, H. (2008). *Project-based learning.* Learn NC.

Cooke, I. (2014, January). *Propaganda as a weapon? Influencing international opinion.* World War One. British Library. Retrieved January 7, 2019, from https://www.bl.uk/world-war-one/articles/propaganda-as-a-weapon#sthash.RdLggEDT.dpuf

Council of Europe. (n.d.). *Cooperation and Participation. Transversal attitudes, skills and knowledge for democracy.* Retrieved May 24, 2019, from http://www.coe.int/t/dg4/education/pestalozzi/Source/Documentation/Module/Tasks/Cooperation%20and%20participation.pdf

Crawford, B. S., Hicks, D., & Doherty, N. (2009). Worth the wait: Engaging social studies students with art in a digital age. *Social Education, 73*(3), 136–139.

NC Civic Education Consortium. (n.d.). *Decoding World War II Propaganda.* Retrieved January 10, 2019, from http://civics.sites.unc.edu/files/2012/05/DecodingWWIIPropaganda9.pdf

Santa Cruz University of California. (n.d.). *Distinguish Between Primary and Secondary Sources.* Retrieved May 23, 2019, from https://guides.library.ucsc.edu/primarysecondary

Cengage Learning. (2016). *Distinguish between primary and secondary sources.* Retrieved May 23, 2019, from https://www.cengage.com/english/book_content/wadsworth_9781428277427/questia_conducting_research_distinguish_primary_secondary_sources.pdf

Donovan, S. M., & Bransford, J. D. (2005). Introduction. In S. M. Donovan & J. D. Bransford (Eds.), *How Students Learn: History in the Classroom* (pp. 1–28). Washington, DC: The National Academies Press.

Duffy, T. M., & Cunningham, D. J. (1996). Constructivism: Implications for the design and delivery of instruction. In D. H. Jonassen (Ed.), *Educational communications and technology* (pp. 170–199). New York, NY: Simon & Schuster Macmillan.

Dybvig, T., & Church, S. (n.d.). *Learning Styles.* Retrieved May 31, 2019, from http://www.teresadybvig.com/learnsty.htm

Ehlers, U.-D. (2011). Extending the territory: From open educational resources to open educational practices. *Journal of Open. Flexible and Distance Learning, 15*(2), 1–10.

Eisenberg, M. B., Murray, J., & Bartow, C. (2016). *The Big 6 Curriculum. Comprehensive Information and Communication Technology (ICT) Literacy for All Students.* Santa Barbara, CA: ABC-CLIO, LLC.

Elgort, I., Smith, A. G., & Toland, J. (2008). Is wiki an effective platform for group course work? *Australasian Journal of Educational Technology, 24*(2), 195–210. doi:10.14742/ajet.1222

Elms, M. D. (2014). *Propaganda Posters of World War I: Analyzing the Methods Behind the Images.* NHD. Retrieved January 26, 2019, from https://nhd.org/sites/default/files/1REVISED-Elms-LM-1-Propaganda.pdf

Endacott, J., & Brooks, S. (2013, Spring). An Updated Theoretical and Practical Model for Promoting Historical Empathy. *Social Studies Research & Practice, 8*(1), 41–58.

Engeström, Y. (1987). *Learning by expanding an activity-theoretical approach to developmental research.* Helsinki: Orienta-Konsultit.

Erkan, T., & Üster, S. (2012, May). Application of Multiple Intelligences Theory in Art History Instruction. *Journal of Social Sciences, 25,* 273-297. Retrieved May 18, 2019, from https://dergipark.org.tr/download/article-file/117869

Farmer, B., Yue, A., & Brooks, C. (2008). Using blogging for higher order learning in large cohort university teaching: A case study. *Australasian Journal of Educational Technology, 24*(2), 123–136. doi:10.14742/ajet.1215

Fasha, S. D. (2016). *Chapter Report Summaries Learning Styles and Good Language Learners.* University of Education. Retrieved January 9, 2019, from https://www.academia.edu

Felton, R. G., & Allen, R. F. (1990, March/April). Using Visual Materials as Historical Sources. *Social Studies, 81*(2), 84–87. doi:10.1080/00377996.1990.9957501

Fields, S. (n.d.). *World War I Propaganda Posters.* McKeel Academy. Retrieved May 23, 2019, from https://www.polk-fl.net/staff/teachers/tah/documents/turningpoints/lessons/f-worldwar1posters.pdf

Finch, L. (2000, Spring). Psychological Propaganda: The War of Ideas on Ideas During the First Half of the Twentieth Century. *Armed Forces and Society, 26*(3), 367–386. doi:10.1177/0095327X0002600302

Foster, J. (2013). *Howard Gardner's Theory of Multiple Intelligences in Relation to Art Education.* Retrieved May 18, 2019, from https://cpb-us-w2.wpmucdn.com/sites.stedwards.edu/dist/0/696/files/2013/01/Educ2331-ContentConnection4-HowardGardner-1rnkvvk.pdf

Fransecky, R. B., & Debes, J. L. (1972). *Visual Literacy: A Way to Learn - A Way to Teach*. Washington, DC: Association for Educational Communications and Technology. Retrieved January 9, 2019, from https://files.eric.ed.gov/fulltext/ED064884.pdf

Friedman, H. A. (2008, December). *Race as a Military Propaganda Theme*. psywar.org. Retrieved May 28, 2019, from: https://www.psywar.org/race.php

Gabella, M. S. (1994). Beyond the looking glass: Bringing students into the conversation of historical inquiry. *Theory and Research in Social Education, 22*(3), 340–363. doi:10.1080/00933104.1994.10505728

Gabella, M. S. (1996). The art(s) of historical sense. *Journal of Curriculum Studies, 27*(2), 139–163. doi:10.1080/0022027950270202

Gabella, M. S. (1998). Formal fascinations and nagging excerpts: The challenge of the arts to curriculum and inquiry. *Curriculum Inquiry, 28*(1), 27–56. doi:10.1111/0362-6784.00074

Galbraith, M. W. (2004). *Adult Learning Methods: A Guide for Effective. Instruction* (3rd ed.). Malabar, FL: Krieger Publishing Company.

Gardner, H. (1983/2003). *Frames of Mind: The Theory of Multiple Intelligences*. New York, NY: Basic Books.

Gardner, H. (1993, July). Educating for Understanding. *The American School Board Journal, 180*(7), 20–24.

Gardner, H. (1995, December). "Multiple Intelligences" as a Catalyst. *English Journal, 84*(8), 16–18. doi:10.2307/821182

Gardner, H. (1997, September). Multiple Intelligences as a Partner in School Improvements. *Educational Leadership, 55*(1), 20–21.

Gardner, H. (1998). A Multiplicity of Intelligences. *Scientific American*, 19–23.

Gardner, H. (1999). *The disciplined mind: What all students should understand by Howard Gardner*. New York, NY: Simon & Schuster.

Gardner, H. (2000, Summer). Project Zero: Nelson Goodman's Legacy in Arts Education. *The. The Journal of Aesthetics and Art Criticism, 58*(3), 245–249. doi:10.2307/432107

Gardner, H. (2003, April). *Multiple Intelligences After Twenty Years*. Paper presented at the American Educational Research Association, Chicago, IL. Retrieved May 21, 2019, from http://ocw.metu.edu.tr/pluginfile.php/9274/mod_resource/content/1/Gardner_multiple_intelligent.pdf

Giles, E., Pitre, S., & Womack, S. (2010). Multiple Intelligences and Learning Styles. In M. Orey (Ed.), *Emerging perspectives on learning, teaching, and technology* (pp. 77-92). Zurich, Switzerland: Jacobs Foundation. Retrieved May 30, 2019, from https://www.academia.edu

Green Patriot Posters. (n.d.). Retrieved May 21, 2019, from http://www.greenpatriotposters.org/inspire.php

Grobman, G. M. (1990). *Stereotypes and Prejudices*. Remember.org. Retrieved May 24, 2019, from http://remember.org/guide/history-root-stereotypes

Helle, L., Tynjälä, P., & Olkinuora, E. (2006). Project-based learning in post-secondary education – theory, practice and rubber sling shots. *Higher Education*, *51*(2), 287–314. doi:10.100710734-004-6386-5

Hoepper, B. (2009). Stand inside my shoes: developing historical empathy. *QHistory*, 34-39. Retrieved January 29, 2019, from https://www.academia.edu

Holt, T. (1990). *Thinking historically: Narrative, imagination, and understanding*. New York, NY: The College Board.

Hou, H.-T., & Wu, S.-Y. (2011). Analyzing the social knowledge construction behavioral patterns of an online synchronous collaborative discussion instructional activity using an instant messaging tool: A case study. *Computers & Education*, *57*(2), 1459–1468. doi:10.1016/j.compedu.2011.02.012

Huang, H. (2015, July). Propaganda as Signaling. *Comparative Politics*, *47*(4), 419–437. doi:10.5129/001041515816103220

Hwang, G.-J. (2014, November). Definition, framework and research issues of smart learning environments - a context-aware ubiquitous learning perspective. *Smart Learning Environments*, *1*(4). Retrieved January 17, 2019, from https://slejournal.springeropen.com/articles/10.1186/s40561-014-0004-5

Hwang, G. J., Hung, P. H., Chen, N. S., & Liu, G. Z. (2014). Mindtool-Assisted In-Field Learning (MAIL): An advanced ubiquitous learning project in Taiwan. *Journal of Educational Technology & Society*, *17*(2), 4–16.

Istenic Starcic, A., & Kerr, S. (2014). Learning Environments – Not Just Smart for Some! In K. Miesenberger, D. Fels, D. Archambault, P. Peňáz, & W. Zagler (Eds.), Lecture Notes in Computer Science: Vol. 8548. *Computers Helping People with Special Needs. ICCHP 2014* (pp. 520–527). Cham: Springer. doi:10.1007/978-3-319-08599-9_77

Jacobs, D. (2007, January). More Than Words: Comics as a Means of Teaching Multiple Literacies. *English Journal*, *96*(3), 19–25. doi:10.2307/30047289

Jacobs, J. (2017, March). *Propaganda Maps*. ThoughtCo. Retrieved January 25, 2019, from https://www.thoughtco.com/propaganda-maps-overview-1435683

Kanwar, A., & Uvalić-Trumbić, S. (Eds.). (2015). *A Basic Guide to Open Educational Resources (OER)*. Paris: UNESCO and Commonwealth of Learning.

Keefe, J. W. (1979). Learning Style: An overview. In *NASSP's Student learning styles: Diagnosing and prescribing programs* (pp. 1–17). Reston, VA: National Association of Secondary School.

Keeley, P. (2014). *What Are They Thinking?: Promoting Elementary Learning Through Formative Assessment*. Arlington, VA: NSTA Press.

Kennah, M. R. (2016). *The Use of ICT in the Teaching and Learning Process in Secondary Schools: A Case Study of Two Cameroonian schools* (Master's Thesis). Department of Education Institute of Educational Leadership, University of Jyväskylä.

Krajcik, J. S., & Blumenfeld, P. C. (2006). Project-based learning. In R. K. Sawyer (Ed.), *The Cambridge Handbook of the Learning Sciences* (pp. 317–334). Cambridge, UK: Cambridge University Press.

Krajcik, J. S., Blumenfeld, P. C., Marx, R. W., & Soloway, E. (1994). A collaborative model for helping middle grade teachers learn project-based instruction. *The Elementary School Journal, 94*(5), 483–497. doi:10.1086/461779

Krajcik, J. S., Czerniak, C. M., & Berger, C. M. (2002). *Teaching science in elementary and middle school classrooms: A project-based approach* (2nd ed.). New York, NY: McGraw Hill.

Kurt, S. (2017, September). Wikis in Education: How Wikis are Being Used in the Classroom. *Educational Technology*. Retrieved May 24, 2019, from https://educationaltechnology.net/wikis-in-education

Lambert, W. E. (1997, September). From Crockett to Tubman: Investigating Historical Perspectives. *Educational Leadership, 55*(1), 51–54.

Layman, T., & Harris, R. (2013, January). Connecting the dots: Helping Year 9 to debate the purposes of Holocaust and genocide education. *Teaching History, 153*, 4–10.

Lazar, S. (2011, November). Teaching History Through Inquiry. *Education Week Teacher*. Retrieved January 6, 2019, from http://www.edweek.org/tm/articles/2011/10/31/tln_lazar.html

Lazear, D. (1992). *Teaching for Multiple Intelligences. Fastback 342*. Bloomington, IN: Phi Delta Kappan Educational Foundation. Retrieved May 21, 2019, from https://files.eric.ed.gov/fulltext/ED356227.pdf

Lee, P. (2005). Putting principles into practice: understanding history. In M. S. Donovan & J. D. Bransford (Eds.), *How Students Learn: History in the Classroom. Committee on How People Learn: A Targeted Report for Teachers. National Research Council* (pp. 31–77). Washington, DC: National Academy Press.

Lee, P., & Ashby, R. (2001). Empathy, perspective taking, and rational understanding. In O. L. Davis, E. Yeager, & S. Foster (Eds.), *Historical empathy and perspective taking in the social studies* (pp. 21–50). New York, NY: Rowman and Littlefield.

Leonard, K., Noh, E. K., & Orey, M. (2010). Introduction to Emerging Perspectives on Learning, Teaching, and Technology. In M. Orey (Ed.), *Emerging perspectives on learning, teaching, and technology* (pp. 8-24). Zurich, Switzerland: Jacobs Foundation. Retrieved May 30, 2019, from https://www.academia.edu

Lester, P. M. (2013). *Visual Communication: Images with Messages* (6th ed.). Belmont, CA: Wadsworth Publishing Company.

Levstik, L. (1990). From the outside in: American children's literature from 1920-1940. *Theory and Research in Social Education, 18*(4), 327–343. doi:10.1080/00933104.1990.10505620

Levstik, L. S. (1996). Negotiating the historical landscape. *Theory and Research in Social Education, 24*, 393–397.

Levstik, L. S., & Barton, K. (2001). *Doing history: Investigating with children in elementary and middle schools*. Mahwah, NJ: Lawrence Erlbaum Associates.

Limón, M. (2002). Conceptual Change in History. In M. Limón & S. Mason (Eds.), *Reconsidering Conceptual Change: Issues in Theory and Practice* (pp. 259–289). Dordrecht: Kluwer Academic Publishers. doi:10.1007/0-306-47637-1_14

MacArthur, C. A. (1996, July). Using Technology to Enhance the Writing Processes of Students with Learning Disabilities. *Journal of Learning Disabilities, 29*(4), 344–354. doi:10.1177/002221949602900403 PMID:8763550

MacCoog, I. J. (2007). Integrated Instruction: Multiple Intelligences and Technology. *The Clearing House: A Journal of Educational Strategies, Issues and Ideas, 81*(1), 25–28. doi:10.3200/TCHS.81.1.25-28

Marx, R. W., Blumenfeld, P. C., Krajcik, J. S., Blunk, M., Crawford, B., Kelley, B., & Meyer, K. M. (1994). Enacting project-based science: Experiences of four middle grade teachers. *The Elementary School Journal, 94*(5), 517–538. doi:10.1086/461781

Marzano, R. J. (1988). *Dimensions of Thinking: A Framework for Curriculum and Instruction*. Alexandria, VA: Association for Supervision and Curriculum Development.

McKenzie, W. (2005). *Multiple Intelligences and Instructional Technology* (2nd ed.). Eugene, OR: ISTE Publications.

Medzini, A. (2012, March). The war of the maps: The political use of maps and atlases to shape national consciousness – Israel versus the Palestinian authority. *European Journal of Geography, 3*(1), 23–40.

Mercer, N., Warwick, P., Kershner, R., & Kleine Staarman, J. (2010, March). Can the interactive whiteboard help to provide 'dialogic space' for children's collaborative activity? *Language and Education, 24*(5), 367–384. doi:10.1080/09500781003642460

Merrill, M. D. (2013). *First principles of instruction: Identifying and designing effective, efficient and engaging instruction*. San Francisco, CA: Wiley.

Mikulecký, P. (2012). Smart Environments for Smart Learning. In *Proceedings of 9th International Scientific Conference on Distance Learning in Applied Informatics* (pp. 213-222). Divai. Retrieved January 13, 2019, from https://conferences.ukf.sk/index.php/divai/divai2012/paper/view/873

Miles, H. (2012, March). *WWII Propaganda: The Influence of Racism.* Artifacts 6. University of Missouri. Retrieved January 18, 2019, from https://artifactsjournal.missouri.edu/2012/03/wwii-propaganda-the-influence-of-racism

Minami, M., Morikawa, H., & Aoyama, T. (2004). The Design Of Naming-Based Service Composition System For Ubiquitous Computing Applications. In *Proceedings of the 2004 International Symposium on Applications and the Internet Workshops (SAINTW'04)* (pp. 304–312). Washington, DC: IEEE Computer Society. 10.1109/SAINTW.2004.1268652

Nokes, J. D., Dole, J. A., & Hacker, D. J. (2007). Teaching high school students to use heuristics while reading historical texts. *Journal of Educational Psychology, 99*(3), 492–504. doi:10.1037/0022-0663.99.3.492

Parker, K. R., & Chao, J. T. (2007). Wiki as a Teaching Tool. *Interdisciplinary Journal of Knowledge and Learning Objects, 3*, 57–78.

Peck, C. (2005, Winter). Introduction to the Special Edition of Canadian Social Studies. *Canadian Social Studies, 39*(2). Retrieved January 20, 2019, from http://www.educ.ualberta.ca/css/Css_39_2/Editorial_39_2.htm

Canadian War Museum (n.d.). *Plan APPL*. Retrieved January 7, 2019, from http://www.warmuseum.ca/firstworldwar/wp-content/mcme-uploads/2014/07/4-a-4-all_e.pdf

Poole, B. J. (1997). *Education for an information age. Teaching in the computerized classroom*. Boston: McGrow Hill.

Library of Congress. (n.d.). *Posters: World War I Posters*. Retrieved May 27, 2019, from http://www.loc.gov/pictures/collection/wwipos/background.html

Price, J. K. (2015). Transforming learning for the smart learning environment: Lessons learned from the Intel education initiatives. *Smart Learning Environments*, 2(16), 1–16.

Propaganda and World War II. (n.d.). Retrieved May 21, 2019, from http://www.flyingheritage.com/FHCAM/media/Docs/Lesson3_Propaganda.pdf

Propaganda Techniques to Recognize. (n.d.). Retrieved January 22, 2019, from https://www.uvm.edu/~jleonard/AGRI183/propoaganda.html

NCTE/IRA. (2005). *Read, write, think*. Retrieved January 19, 2019, from http://www.readwritethink.org/files/resources/lesson_images/lesson829/Argument-Propaganda.pdf

Reid, J. M. (1987, March). The Learning Style Preferences of ESL Students. *TESOL Quarterly*, 21(1), 87–110. doi:10.2307/3586356

Reidel, J., Tomaszewski, T., & Weaver, D. (2003, May). *Improving Student Academic Reading Achievement Through the Use of Multiple Intelligence Teaching Strategies*. Field-Based Master's Program. Chicago, IL: Saint Xavier University & SkyLight. Retrieved January 25, 2019, from https://files.eric.ed.gov/fulltext/ED479204.pdf

Renz, B. B. (2010). Our Own Worst Enemy as Protector of Ourselves: Stereotypes, Schemas, and Typifications as Integral Elements in the Persuasive Process. Lanham, MD: University Press of America.

Richardson, W. (2005). What's a wiki? A powerful collaborative tool for teaching and learning. That's What! *Multimedia & Internet@schools*, 12(6), 17-21.

Richardson, W. (2006). *Blogs, wikis, podcasts and other powerful web tools for classrooms*. Thousand Oaks, CA: Corwin Press.

Roberts, D., Bove, C., & van Zee, E. (2007). *Teacher research: Stories of learning and growing*. Arlington, VA: NSTA Press.

Rudiger, C. (2003, Spring). *World War II and Propaganda*. Research Paper. Stanford University. Retrieved May 27, 2019, from https://web.stanford.edu/class/e297a/World%20War%20II%20and%20Propaganda.htm

Russell, M. K. (n.d.). *Using Art in Teaching World History*. Retrieved January 7, 2019, from http://www.phschool.com/eteach/social_studies/2000_10/essay.html

Schniedewind, N., & Davidson, E. (2006). *Open Minds to Equality* (3rd ed.). Milwaukee, WI: Rethinking Schools, Ltd.

Schrag, V. (n.d.). *World War I Lesson Plan*. Harry S. Truman Presidential Library & Museum. Retrieved January 28, 2019, from https://www.trumanlibrary.org/wwi/valerieschraglesson1.doc

Historical Inquiry. (n.d.). *SCIM-C*. Retrieved May 26, 2019, from http://historicalinquiry.com

Shea, J., & Stockford, A. (2015). *Inspiring the Secondary Curriculum with Technology*. New York, NY: Routledge.

Silver, H. F., Strong, R. W., & Perini, M. J. (2000). *So Each May Learn: Integrating Learning Styles and Multiple Intelligences*. Alexandria, VA: ASCD. Retrieved May 22, 2019, from http://www.ascd.org/publications/books/100058/chapters/Teaching-Learning-Styles-and-Multiple-Intelligences-to-Students.aspx

Singh, A. D., & Hassan, M. H. (2017, July). In Pursuit of Smart Learning Environments for the 21st Century. *Current and Critical Issues in Curriculum, Learning and Assessment, 12*(28). Retrieved January 13, 2019, from http://unesdoc.unesco.org/images/0025/002523/252335E.pdf

Smith, B. (2007). Using presentation technology. In M. Hunt (Ed.), *A Practical Guide to Teaching History in the Secondary School* (pp. 81–89). New York, NY: Routledge.

Smith, J. (n.d.). *Free-form assessment: A Multiple Intelligences approach to History at Key Stage 4* (Master's dissertation). University of Lancaster. Retrieved May 18, 2019, from https://portal.stir.ac.uk/api/research/entities/get/file/17331

Smith, N. (2010). *The History Teacher's Handbook*. New York, NY: Continuum International Publishing Group.

Spector, J. M. (2014). Conceptualizing the emerging field of smart learning environments. *Smart Learning Environments, 1*(2). Retrieved January 14, 2019, from http://www.slejournal.com/content/1/1/2

Spector, J. M. (2016). Smart Learning Environments: Concepts and Issues. In G. Chamblee & L. Langub (Eds.), *Proceedings of Society for Information Technology & Teacher Education International Conference* (pp. 2728-2737). Savannah, GA: Association for the Advancement of Computing in Education (AACE). Retrieved January 22, 2019, from https://www.researchgate.net/publication/301612985_Smart_Learning_Environments_Concepts_and_Issues

Spector, J. M., & Merrill, M. D. (Eds.). (2008, August). Effective, Efficient and Engaging (E3) Learning in the Digital Age. Distance Education, 29(2).

Stepien, W., & Gallagher, S. (1993). Problem-based learning: As authentic as it gets. *Educational Leadership, 51*, 25–28.

Suh, Y. (2013, Spring). Past Looking: Using Arts as Historical Evidence in Teaching History. *Social Studies Research & Practice, 8*(1), 135–159.

Sullivan, S. (2007). Media and Persuasion: Techniques, Forms, and Construction. In M. Christel & S. Sullivan (Eds.), *Lesson Plans for Creating Media-Rich Classrooms* (pp. 173–176). Urbana, IL: NCTE.

Sutherland, R., Armstrong, V., Barnes, S., Brawn, R., Breeze, N., Gall, M., ... John, P. (2004). Transforming teaching and learning: Embedding ICT into everyday classroom practices. *Journal of Computer Assisted Learning, 20*(6), 413–425. doi:10.1111/j.1365-2729.2004.00104.x

Tally, B., & Goldenberg, L. B. (2005). Fostering Historical Thinking With Digitized Primary Sources. *Journal of Research on Technology in Education, 38*(1), 1–21. doi:10.1080/15391523.2005.10782447

Propoganda Techniques. (1979, August). Washington, DC: Department of the Army. Retrieved January 22, 2019, from http://www.constitution.org/col/propaganda_army.htm

Eastern Illinois University. (n.d.). *The Art of War. WWI and WWII Posters.* Retrieved January 30, 2019, from http://www.eiu.edu/eiutps/art_of_war.php

The Techniques of Propaganda. (n.d.). Retrieved May 22, 2019, from http://www.cengage.com/resource_uploads/downloads/0534619029_19636.pdf

Thomas, J. (2000, March). *A Review of the Research on Project-Based Learning.* San Rafael, CA: The Autodesk Foundation. Retrieved January 23, 2019, from https://dl.icdst.org/pdfs/files1/aac48826d-9652cb154e2dbf0033376fa.pdf

United States Holocaust Memorial Museum. (2013). Are you more powerful than propaganda? Propaganda Techniques. *Mind over Media* [For Teachers]. Retrieved May 27, 2019, from http://mindovermedia.ushmm.org/teachers

United States Holocaust Memorial Museum. (n.d.a). *State of Deception. The Power of Nazi Propaganda. Redefining How We Teach Propaganda. Lesson 2.* Retrieved May 23, 2019, from https://www.ushmm.org/m/pdfs/20150703-propaganda-2-0_LESSON-2.pdf

United States Holocaust Memorial Museum. (n.d.b). *Extension 1.8 Diagram Worksheet State of Deception.* Retrieved May 23, 2019, from https://www.ushmm.org/m/pdfs/20150703-propaganda-1EXT-1-8_Diagram_Worksheets.pdf

Vakaloudi, A. D. (2016). *The Teaching of History with the Use of Information and Communication Technologies.* Thessaloniki: K. & M. Ant. Stamoulis.

Vakaloudi, A. D. (2017, Spring-Summer). From the holocaust to recent mass murders and refugees. What does history teach us? *International Journal of Historical Learning, Teaching and Research, 14*(2), 119–149.

Vakaloudi, A. D., & Dagdilelis, V. (2013, October). Differentiation in the teaching of Social Sciences with the development of Information and Communication Technologies. In *Proceedings of the 3rd International Conference on Cognitonics, The Science about the Human Being in the Digital World, a subconference of the 16th International Multiconference Information Society 2013* (*vol. A*, pp. 476-479). Ljubljana: Institut "Jožef Stefan".

Vakaloudi, A. D., & Dagdilelis, V. (2015, October). The Role of Information and Communication Technologies in the Teaching and Learning of History. In *Proceedings of the 5th International Conference on Cognitonics, The Science about the Human Being in the Digital World, a subconference of the 18th International Multiconference Information Society 2015* (*vol. F*, pp. 78-81). Ljubljana: Institut "Jožef Stefan".

Vakaloudi, A. D., & Dagdilelis, V. (2016, Spring-Summer). The Transformation of History Teaching Methods in Secondary Education Through the Use of Information and Communication Technology (ICT). *International Journal of Historical Learning, Teaching and Research, 13*(2), 150–174.

Wallace, B. (2003). *Using History to Develop Problem Solving and Thinking Skills at Key Stage 2*. New York, NY: David Fulton Publishers.

War of the future: Brian Moore's WWIII propaganda posters. (2011). Retrieved January 19, 2019, from https://www.theguardian.com/artanddesign/gallery/2011/jan/22/brian-moore-wwiii-propaganda-posters

Wineburg, S. (2001). *Historical thinking and other unnatural act: Charting the future of teaching the past*. Philadelphia, PA: Temple University Press.

Winters, N., Walker, K., & Rousos, D. (2005). Facilitating Learning in an Intelligent Environment. In *The IEE International Workshop on Intelligent Environments* (pp. 74-79). Colchester, UK: IET. 10.1049/ic:20050219

Wright, J. (2017). Propaganda Techniques in Literature and Online Political Ads. *Read, Write, Think*. Retrieved January 15, 2019, from http://www.readwritethink.org/classroom-resources/lesson-plans/propaganda-techniques-literature-online-405.html

Wu, H. K., Lee, S. W. Y., Chang, H. Y., & Liang, J. C. (2013). Current status, opportunities and challenges of augmented reality in education. *Computers & Education, 62*, 41–49. doi:10.1016/j.compedu.2012.10.024

Wu, P. H., Hwang, G. J., & Chai, W. H. (2013, October). An expert system-based context-aware ubiquitous learning approach for conducting science learning activities. *Journal of Educational Technology & Society, 16*(4), 217–230.

Yilmaz, K. (2007, May). Historical Empathy and Its Implications for Classroom Practices in Schools. *The History Teacher, 40*(3), 331–337.

Zhu, Z. T., Yu, M. H., & Riezebos, P. (2016, March). A research framework of smart education. *Smart Learning Environments, 3*(4), 1-17. Retrieved January 3, 2019, from https://slejournal.springeropen.com/articles/10.1186/s40561-016-0026-2

ADDITIONAL READING

Barrington, E. (2004). Teaching to student diversity in higher education: How Multiple Intelligence Theory can help. *Teaching in Higher Education, 9*(4), 421–434. doi:10.1080/1356251042000252363

Cowgill, D. A. II, & Waring, S. M. (2017). Historical Thinking: An Evaluation of Student and Teacher Ability to Analyze Sources. *Journal of Social Studies Education Research, 8*(1), 115–145.

Davies, P., & Davies, R. (2003/2012). *Enlivening Secondary History. Abingdon, OX*. New York, NY: RoutledgeFalmer/Routledge.

Dunn, R. (2000). Learning styles: Theory, research, and practice. *National Forum of Applied Educational Research Journal, 13*(1), 3-22.

Duraisingh, L. D., & Mansilla, V. B. (2007, December). Interdisciplinary forays within the history classroom: How the visual arts can enhance (or hinder) historical understanding. *Teaching History, 129*, 22–30.

Hopper, B., & Hurry, P. (2000, December). Learning the MI Way: The Effects on Students' Learning of Using the Theory of Multiple Intelligences. *Pastoral Care in Education. An International Journal of Personal. Social and Emotional Development, 18*(4), 26–32.

McClaskey, J. (1995, December). Assessing Student Learning through Multiple Intelligences. *English Journal, 84*(8), 56–59. doi:10.2307/821191

McCombs, B. L., & Whisler, J. S. (1997). *The Learner-Centered Classroom and School Strategies for Increasing Student Motivation and Achievement.* San Francisco, CA: Jossey-Bass Publishers.

Nelson, K. (2001). *Teaching in the Cyberage: Linking the Internet and brain theory.* Thousand Oaks, CA: Corwin Press.

Phillips, R. (2002, March). Historical significance - the forgotten "key element"? *Teaching History, 106*, 14–19.

Pritchard, A. (2008). *Ways of Learning. Learning Theories and Learning Styles in the Classroom* (2nd ed.). London: Routledge. doi:10.4324/9780203887240

Schmeck, R. R. (1988). *Learning Strategies and Learning Styles.* New York: Springer Science & Business Media. doi:10.1007/978-1-4899-2118-5

Tamilselvi, B., & Geetha, D. (2015, September - November). Efficacy in Teaching through "Multiple Intelligence" Instructional Strategies. *Journal of Science Education and Technology, 11*(2), 1–10.

KEY TERMS AND DEFINITIONS

Cognition: Cognition refers to the mental action or process of acquiring knowledge and understanding through thought, experience, and the senses.

Historical Thinking: A set of critical literacy skills for evaluating and analyzing primary source documents to construct a meaningful account of the past.

Information and Communication Technology (ICT): The infrastructure and components that enable modern computing.

Metacognition: Includes the learner's knowledge of their own cognitive abilities and of different strategies including when to use these strategies.

Multimodal Literacy: A term that originates in social semiotics and refers to the study of language that combines two or more modes of meaning.

Open Educational Resources (OER): Freely accessible, openly licensed text, media, and other digital assets that are useful for teaching, learning, and assessing as well as for research purposes.

Smart Learning Environment: It is a more learner-centered learning environment which features the use of innovative technologies and elements that allow greater flexibility, adaptation, engagement, and feedback for the learner.

Visual Literacy: The ability to interpret, negotiate, and make meaning from information presented in the form of an image.

Section 4

Integrating Digital Technology in Multiple Intelligences–Based Teaching and Learning: Logical–Mathematical Intelligence

Chapter 11
How Can Digital Technology Enhance Mathematics Teaching and Learning?

Monika Dockendorff
https://orcid.org/0000-0002-4957-0245
Pontificia Universidad Católica de Chile, Chile

ABSTRACT

As digital technology becomes more ubiquitous in society and education, mathematics teachers are expected to design and integrate technology-enriched learning environments effectively. This task encompasses many challenges, but primarily, it entails the identification of how technology may produce insights. This study examines several categories of core mathematical processes that can be enhanced by the integration of dynamic interactive software such as identifying properties, connecting multiple representations, and solving problems, among others. The process of visualization appears at the center of dynamic and interactive mathematics learning environments. Evidence of its functionality and the benefits it reports to the teaching and learning process for each category is presented. Further discussion on the challenges that mathematics teacher education programs and teachers face—not only in their digital competences but also in the role they play—are outlined.

INTRODUCTION

Since the rise of digital technologies in society, schools have been attempting to integrate them for learning and communicating purposes, but according to Cuban (2001) the process of embedding technology in classrooms has been slow and complex. For several decades now, games and simulations have been introduced in schools as tools used for science learning. But there are many cases reported in which digital technology has ultimately made little impact in meaningful learning. These tools should serve a purpose, otherwise their integration would lack real relevance: "tools are just tools until they are applied to some end" (Clark, Nelson, Sengupta, & D´Angelo, 2009, p. 52).

DOI: 10.4018/978-1-7998-0249-5.ch011

How Can Digital Technology Enhance Mathematics Teaching and Learning?

In the mathematics curricula, where major benefits can be obtained, ICT has been integrated to a diverse extent, unequally throughout the world. ICT integration in mathematics teaching and learning serves many purposes and goals. There are several perspectives that justify the use of digital technology in mathematics education such as practical reasons (easy-fast-exact), student motivation and interest, and the cognitive benefits it entails for better understanding abstract mathematical entities (Hoyles, 2018). Creating a conceptual image of a mathematical object is a complex process given its abstract nature. Therefore, visualizing and manipulating virtual entities that represent these objects facilitates a deeper understanding, both procedural and conceptual. "Visual forms of representation can be important, not only as a heuristic and pedagogical tools, but as legitimate elements of mathematical proof"(Barwise & Etchemendy, 1991, p. 9). Technology offers multiple representations of mathematical objects that are related dynamically, elucidating the interplay between different registers of representations. These features elevate the dynamic-graphic register to a new status, supporting reasoning and proof (Novembre, Nicodemo, & Coll, 2015). Because these dynamic visual environments became so important for the representation of complex concepts and communication of ideas, design principles that assure their educational effectiveness have been validated. These principles encompass two dimensions: visual and interactive (Plass, Homer, & Hayward, 2009).

Many teachers are not fully prepared to integrate ICT into the mathematics curriculum, and many teacher training approaches tend to focus on the available digital resources and their use rather than focusing on their pedagogical purposes (Hamilton, Rosenberg, & Akcaoglu, 2016). Therefore, the framework used for integrating digital technology and the prominence of the pedagogical dimension, is key to create effective digital learning environments.

Several models offer ways to inform and guide K-12 teachers' understanding and uses of technology in teaching. For example, Beaudin and Bowers (1997) *Play, Use, Recommend, Incorporate and Assess* (PURIA) model structures the process as consecutive stages, as Puentedura's (2006) *Substitution, Augmentation, Modification, and Redefinition* (SAMR) model describes how technology may transform or enhance learning. But, the most commonly used theoretical framework that describes how technology is integrated into mathematics teaching and learning is TPACK: Mishra & Koehler's (2006) Technological Pedagogical Content Knowledge includes the teacher's understanding of how to represent concepts using technologies; pedagogically addressing the use of technological resources to teach, and constructively promoting student learning on the curricular concepts – in this case, mathematics concepts. History and experience, however, have taught us that this integration should have an emphasis: pedagogy. We should not forget that the whole purpose is learning, this is, learner's knowledge construction.

It is important that pre-service and in-service teachers are capable to question, evaluate and assess the validity and relevance of digital technology integration and its impact in teaching and learning mathematics. International standards for preparing high school teachers of mathematics consider this ability a key aspect regarding ICT integration. In particular the new AMTE's standards (2017): part one describes the *Candidate's Knowledge, Skills, and Dispositions* where the *Use of Tools and Technology to Teach High School Mathematics* is one of four indicators in this category. One fundamental idea regarding this ability is that teachers should have the knowledge needed to "make sound decisions regarding when such tools enhance teaching and learning, recognizing both the insights to be gained and possible limitations of such tools" (NCTM, 2012, p. 3). Naturally, the development of this competence involves, as a prerequisite, a positive attitude and disposition towards the use of technology for teaching and learning mathematics, and the knowledge of specialized mathematical tools such as: platforms, programs, software, simulators, applets, digital manipulatives, accompanied by the expertise in their instrumental use (Gómez-Chacón & Prieto, 2010).

LITERATURE REVIEW

The literature describes many concrete examples and case studies in which digital technology enhances mathematics teaching and learning for specific contents or concepts. One can find examples in a range of different contents such as: fractions (Poon, 2018), similar triangles (Poon & Wong, 2017), Euler´s line (Amado, Sanchez, & Pinto, 2015), isometric transformations (Morera, 2011), linear equations (Cervantes et al., 2012), functions (Attorps, Radic, & Viirman, 2011; Berger & Bowie, 2012), inequalities (Kabaca, 2013), the derivative (Asprilla & Antioquia, 2014; Verhoef, Coenders, Pieters, van Smaalen, & Tall, 2015), Viviani´s theorem (Contreras, 2014), Euclid's theorem (Dockendorff & Solar, 2018), free fall motion (Rubio, Prieto, & Ortiz, 2016), ellipse (León & Flores, 2015), limit of a sequence (Cheng & Leung, 2015), iterations (Bertone & Barbosa, 2015), fractals (Alfieri, 2017), complex numbers (Gülseçen, Karataş, & Koçoğlu, 2012), loci (Abánades et al., 2016), polynomial approximations (Attorps, Björk, & Radic, 2016), calculus (del Río, 2017), exponential and logarithm functions (Gómez-Chacón & Prieto, 2010), among others.

Other studies are more broad in their scope, and offer more general conclusions regarding the use of technology in certain mathematical topics like: proving and proof (Zengin, 2017), mathematical reasoning (Mithalal, 2010), multiple representations (Cervantes et al., 2012; De Simone, 2017; Juan & Dawson, 2015), dynamic geometry (Arzarello, Bairral, & Dané, 2014; Tran et al., 2014), Van Hiele's levels of understanding (Kutluca, 2013), and connections between graphical representations and formal definitions (Cheng & Leung, 2015). Additionally, extensive research has been conducted regarding attitudes, beliefs, and views of student teachers and teachers when using dynamic mathematics software (Ertmer et al., 2012; Koparan, 2017; Yorgancı, 2018). Further readings on this issue are proposed below.

Regardless of the specificity or scope of the study, there are several mathematical topics where these tools appear suitable to enhance teaching and learning, where visualization becomes a key process for deeper understanding. For example, exploring patterns, shapes, transformations and sequences, making connections between multiple representations, boosting students' conceptual understanding of mathematical concepts, building computational models of mathematical objects, and performing mathematical experiments.

MULTIPLE INTELLIGENCES THEORY

Howard Gardner´s seven distinct types of intelligences described in 1983, have been successfully used in classroom environments, demonstrating that learners can benefit from multiple entry points and multiple representations of material (Dara-Abrams, 2002). The integration of digital technology in mathematics education fosters and connects directly two of these intelligences: logical-mathematical and visual-spatial learning. On the one hand logical-mathematical intelligence is associated with processes such as: problem-solving, deductive reasoning, pattern detection, sequencing, logical thinking, cause-effect relationship recognition and the understanding of complex and abstract ideas. Traditionally these abilities are exercised and acquired in the mathematics secondary classroom mainly by means of symbolic and algebraic language (Strausova & Hasek, 2013). On the other hand, digital technology integration allows to add dynamic-graphic representations of these mathematical processes, incorporating and exploiting visual-spatial abilities as well. These are understood as the capacity to think in images and pictures, to visualize accurately and abstractly, with a sharp sense of space, distance and measurement. Therefore, the effective use of learning technology can optimize both logical-mathematical and visual-spatial intelligences, nurturing and complementing each other.

This is central to mathematics teaching and learning because mathematical objects are abstract in nature, therefore according to Raymond Duval (1999) the only way to access and understand them is to incorporate the multiple registers of representation used in mathematics. In the last 20 years technologies took a turn towards representational pluralism; we are no longer limited to work with text-based forms of representation (Zimmermann & Cunningham, 1991). Today we have access to dynamic-graphic visual forms of representation that are simultaneously linked to the symbolic expressions of the mathematical object under analysis, thus helping the learner to connect them and translate from one register to the other.

Therefore, the key concept that will be used and displayed throughout the rest of the chapter is the concept of visualization. In the context of mathematics education and the integration of digital technology, visualization refers to the ability of learning by graphically representing mathematical concepts, principles or problems, manually or using the computer; visualization lies in the connection that an individual makes between an internal construction and an image; be it mental, drawn or digital (Zazkis, Dubinsky, & Dautermann, 1996). The new characteristic of visualization is its dynamic feature: on the one hand dynamism allows to faithfully represent the dynamic nature of certain mathematical concepts and to observe the behavior of particular mathematical objects. On the other hand, the dynamic feature provides learners with many different alternative heuristic strategies to address mathematical activity and problem solving, as will be described later.

THE STUDY

In order to guide and illustrate the decisions mathematics teachers are expected to make, it is necessary to organize and structure a body of categories in which mathematics teaching and learning may be enhanced by the use of technology. *"Recognizing the insights to be gained"* is not a trivial ability to develop; it requires certain orientations, evidence, experience, and models to follow.

Therefore, this chapter presents a classification of eleven categories of mathematical activities, offering strong evidence of how digital technology enhances teaching and learning mathematics for each one of them. These categories encompass the following mathematical processes: identifying properties, discovering patterns and relationships, verifying and rejecting conjectures, connecting multiple representations, simulating physical and random phenomena, providing meaning to mathematical objects, solving problems, graphing in a 3D register, dynamizing representations, accessing complex mathematical concepts and learning mathematics trough exploration. All these categories, associated to the logical-mathematical intelligence, correspond to activities that are at the very core of doing mathematics and central in secondary mathematics education, which is the main focus of this study. Each case will reveal how visualization triggers the achievement of the corresponding mathematical process, and how the representation´s dynamic feature is key to that achievement. Their descriptions are a result of a thorough revision of research in the field and have been modified and constantly updated in the light of newer evidence.

As the reader advances through the text, she/he will realize that most of the examples, case studies, research and experiments selected to illustrate how these mathematical categories benefit from the integration of digital technologies, use the GeoGebra[1] software. This is not a coincidence but a very deliberate decision. GeoGebra is a free and opensource educational mathematics software tool, with millions of users worldwide. It is a multi-platform and easy to use software, offering interactive digital environments that nurture students' motivation and active participation. The integration of CAS -computer algebra system- and DGS -dynamic geometry system-, among other features, facilitates student discovery and experimental learning through visualization.

The interactive use of this software can be carried out not only by handling a usual PC – where manipulation is produced with the help of a mouse, but also making use of touch screen devices, where students can use their fingers in order to move figures (Bairral, Arzarello, & Assis, 2017). Thus, the integration of digital technology by means of touch-screen devices may enhance learning opportunities for tactile or kinesthetic learners, who rely on touch as a means of comprehending a given concept. Body-kinesthetic intelligence is related to the ability to process information physically through hand and body movement, control, and expression, seeking to touch and manipulate objects (or their representations) when learning about them. This way, GeoGebra-Touch caters to the visual and kinesthetic learners who want to visualize and manipulate diagrams on the screen with their own hands (Saylor, 2004 as cited in Juan & Dawson, 2015).

The impact of dynamic visualization will be revealed throughout the descriptions of the 11 categories proposed. To help the reader identify each incidence, these concepts will appear highlighted trough the text.

Identifying Properties

In mathematics, a property is any characteristic or feature that applies to a given set and holds true. At school students learn number, geometric and algebraic properties throughout the years. In particular, DGS -Dynamic Geometry Software, allow students to identify geometric properties easily instead of having them transmitted by the teacher. This helps to learn them meaningfully by promoting the protagonism of the student´s own construction of knowledge.

The main mechanism to identify these properties visually using DGS is dragging: vertexes of geometric shapes can be dragged freely by students, modifying the size, position and orientation of the figure, while the properties remain unchanged, "making explicit that which is implicit, and drawing attention to that which is often left unnoticed" (Hoyles, 2018, p. 4). The purpose is that students transit from a perceptive notion of geometric shapes (drawings) to a constructive notion of these shapes based on their properties (figures) (Acosta & Fiallo, 2017). For example, Figure 1 shows a dynamic sketch of a house representation, both in its final version and its construction properties. Only the two inferior points can be dragged. All other elements depend on them by construction. Under dragging, the complete house will hold its shape, this is, angles and relative proportion of segments will remain unchanged; it will only modify its size and orientation (it could rotate around one of the inferior points).

Figure 1. Sketch of a house representation: final version and construction properties

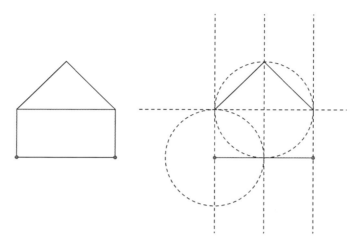

In other words, when the representation is based on geometric properties -*hard* geometric construction- "technology allows a variety of possibilities to manipulate and transform iconic representations, so that students can investigate which properties remain invariant in all positions and therefore are characteristic of a mathematical concept" (Hohenwarter, 2014, p. 3). The principles of dynamic geometry (movement, deformation and conservation of the properties of the figures) are at stake in this identification process.

What characterizes dynamic sketches is their capacity to be modified by a continuous movement of its components, granting the invariance of their geometric properties. This means that every geometric property translates into a visual phenomenon which takes place under dragging, where dragging becomes the means of recognition and verification of the geometric properties of the dynamic sketch (Amman & González, 2012, p. 20).

Discovering Patterns and Relationships

Patterns are everywhere in our world and expressing them mathematically helps learners to understand how these regularities apply to many real-life situations. As early as third grade, patterns and regularities appear as basic mathematical notions to address in order to develop the ability to discuss mathematically, by convincing others of the validity of patterns and regularities discovered in natural and mathematical systems.

Identifying patterns in numbers, images, sequences, geometry, and measurement that present regularities, and representing them in concrete, pictorial or symbolic ways, will foster the mathematical thinking and reasoning that constitute the foundations for the development of more abstract concepts and ideas for later grades, like algebraic thinking. This includes, for high school level, recognizing and analyzing patterns, studying and representing relationships, making generalizations, and analyzing how things change.

One feature of dynamic mathematics software DGS is that it allows learners to visualize relations between objects, posing and investigating "what-if" questions, by identifying what varies and what remains unchanged. "Visualization should not be reduced to vision, that is to say: visualization makes visible all that is not accessible to vision. A semiotic representation shows relations, or better, organization between relations between representational units" (Raymond Duval, 1999, p. 7). For example, discovering the relationship between the position of point P (located in the interior of an equilateral triangle as shown in Figure 2), and the sum of the distances from P to the sides of the triangle -Viviani´s Theorem-, requires learners to drag the point around and observe its effect. By means of the dynamic text which presents the changing length of the segments and their sum, as P takes different positions, students discover that the sum of distances remains constant (Contreras, 2014). Naturally, this becomes possible only in a digital environment, in which the elements involved are related dynamically and experience simultaneous modifications.

The mechanism to discover this pattern is covering "all possible" positions of the analyzed points or objects and verifying whether the found relationship holds true for all cases. Therefore, further dragging of point P is necessary to confirm that the sum of the segments remains invariant, for any position it takes in the interior of an equilateral triangle.

Hopefully, many other inquiries will emerge after this finding. Inquisitive learners will wonder if this relationship is valid for points on the triangle, outside of it or for other types of triangles. DGS facilitates investigating these questions, modifying the conditions of the problem effortlessly (dragging the point to extreme positions, within and outside the triangle and verifying the validity of the pattern for scalene triangles, for example). In saying this, the author does not mean this process replaces formal proof or proving. On the contrary, demonstrations for these early empirical finding are necessary, but the benefit of giving students more agency on their knowledge construction is transforming and helps students achieve a higher level of understanding.

Verifying and Rejecting Conjectures

A conjecture is a statement that is believed to be true but has not yet been proven. The process of students making mathematical conjectures about predictable outcomes, and then testing these conjectures can impact student learning by engaging students as they become invested in learning. Regardless of whether their conjectures are correct or not, stimulating them to think and reason, giving them a chance

Figure 2. PD+PE+PF is invariant

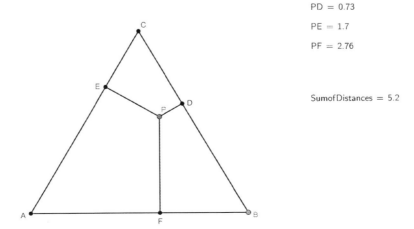

How Can Digital Technology Enhance Mathematics Teaching and Learning?

to confront their misconceptions or faulty ideas then helps them construct their knowledge in a way that leads to deeper understanding and reasoning abilities (Digital Chalkboard, n.d.).

For example, 11th graders in Barcelona where challenged to generalize the result of the composition of two axial symmetries in terms of an equivalent transformation. The case in which the axes are two parallel lines as shown, is presented in Figure 3. By means of GeoGebra, students construct the problematic situation and formulate a conjecture which is tested and verified using the dynamic features of the software.

Learners reached a valid conclusion and generalized that the composition of two axial symmetries, with parallel lines, is equivalent to a translation using a vector of twice the distance between the parallel axes. In this case, the mechanism to verify the conjecture implied sketching the situation, selecting an object to reflect, drawing the two parallel lines and applying consecutively axial symmetries about both lines (*reflect about a line* tool). To test the conjecture, learners can apply a translation to the original image to verify it yields the same result. To corroborate the generalization, one can modify the distance between both axes. The availability of these kind of tools, makes this complex and laborious double procedure, more accessible and fruitful for students, allowing learners to acquire new knowledge that otherwise would hardly be reachable for them due to the high level of abstraction involved when lacking testing and experimental means like GeoGebra. The researchers who conducted this experiment in Barcelona stated that by visualizing the exact representation of a certain mathematical problem, learners could easily raise conjectures and reject the false ones with counterexamples dynamically (Morera, 2011). Therefore, the dynamic feature of digital environments like GeoGebra, constitutes a qualitative

Figure 3. Visual demonstration of the conjecture

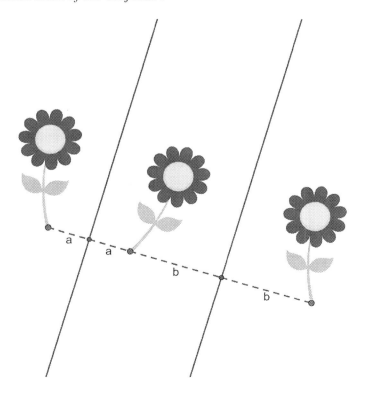

enhancement and a major benefit for mathematics teaching and learning by allowing figures to move while holding their properties unchanged, becoming a particularly rich scenario for raising conjectures and the basis for new proof (Amado et al., 2015).

Connecting Multiple Representations

The principle of interaction of multiple representations states that mathematical knowledge is retained more easily if it was acquired using multiple representations: enactive, iconic and symbolic (Bruner, 1966). In this sense, dynamic mathematics software offer two different registers of representation: a simultaneous graphic (iconic) and algebraic (symbolic) representation of the same abstract mathematical object, supporting visualization and the principle of interaction of representations (Hohenwarter, 2014). Raymond Duval states that mathematical objects are only accessible through representations: "There is no true understanding in mathematics for students who do not incorporate into their cognitive architecture the various registers of semiotic representations used to do mathematics" (1999, p. 15). But the incorporation of these various registers of representation implies the coordination among them, this is, translating from one register to another in both ways. In High School, this ability involves normally the conversion form the symbolic register to the iconic register and vice versa. With the support of the synchronic algebraic and graphic views that DGS offer, students are able to link these two different representation registers fluently.

For example, linear equations is a mathematical topic that is very interesting to analyze in terms of the coordination among different representation registers, especially using digital technologies (De Simone, 2017). A proposal for a meaningful understanding of the geometric effects that the modification of parameters produces on the graphic representation of the $f(x) = ax + b$ function, contributes to a more transparent conversion among registers. The line experiences two kinds of geometric modifications: rotation and vertical translation. Figure 4 shows the visualization of the change of slope for linear functions by means of GeoGebra (Cervantes et al., 2012).

The mechanism to explore the geometric effect upon the line, due to the modification of the parameters a and b of its symbolic expression, is defining these parameters as sliders. Sliders can take any value in their range of configuration and can be defined as integers or real numbers. In figure 4 (left) the slope slider takes values bigger than 1, where the family of lines defines angles between 45° and 90° with the X axis. Figure 4 (center) depicts the family of lines with slopes ranging from 0 to 1, defining

Figure 4. Slope changes produced by the modification of parameter a

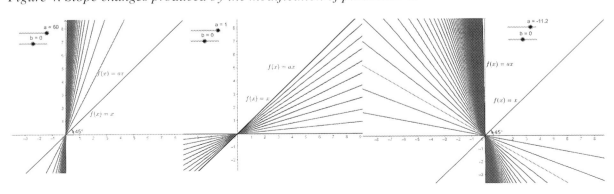

angles between 0° and 45° with the X axis. Figure 4 (right) shows negative slopes. The trace activation of the line, allows to visualize many lines at once, contributing to a better understanding of the behavior and characterization of the function. As Juan and Dawson (2015) point out, "GeoGebra provides such a visual platform, as students can manipulate the graphical representations and alter the algebraic functions to visually observe the changes on the graphs" (p. 16)

Unfortunately, conventional teaching's approaches to functions focuses on applying formulas directly and solving common problems. Consequently, students are often unable to properly characterize and describe functions' behavior from their symbolic expression (Darmawan & Iwan, 2011 as cited in Cervantes et al., 2012, p. 1). Using ICT assists students to easily relate their symbolic and graphic registers and realize the role parameters play in their behavior.

Simulating Physical and Random Phenomena

Simulations are computational models of real or hypothesized situations or natural phenomena that allow users to explore the implications of manipulating or modifying parameters within them (Clark et al., 2009 as cited in National Research Council, 2011, p. 9). Simulations favor the use of mathematics as a tool to approach situations and events of the world, enabling learners to link the facts and ideas of physical and random phenomena with theoretical frameworks.

Simulations can allow learners to visualize, explore, and formulate scientific explanations for scientific phenomena that would otherwise be impossible to observe and manipulate. They can help learners to mentally link abstract representations of a scientific phenomenon (for example, equations) with the invisible processes underlying it and the learner's own observations (Linn et al., 2010 as cited in National Research Council, 2011).

Regarding random phenomena, probability in middle and high school has been mainly taught from a classic and axiomatic approach. This means that counting techniques and formal concepts have sometimes been used excessively. This approach does not help to develop an adequate probabilistic reasoning due to its focus on procedures and probability computations (Inzunsa, 2014). On the other hand, the relative frequency approach has proved to be more successful in mathematics education, especially when combined with digital technology. This frequentist approach reveals the importance of graphic representation, helping to visualize probability distributions properties such as: central tendency, distribution and variability. Graphically learners can easily identify which regions are more or less probable, the effect of the parameters and the distinction between theoretical and frequentist probability. Figure 5 illustrates a dice roll simulation generated by means of GeoGebra, using its spreadsheet and graphic view. *Random (1,6)* was used to generate the possible results of the dice, and *Conditional IF* to identify and accumulate the result 6. The graph shows an intuitive idea of the law of large numbers, whereas the relative frequency of a particular result converges to its theoretical probability as the number of experiments increases.

Please note that students can simultaneously access to the raw results of each dice roll (column B), the absolute and accumulated frequency of result 6, and its relative accumulated frequency. These data are concurrently presented with its graphic representation, helping students understand and interpret the experiment and translate its results from a tabular to a graphic register. Additionally, by pressing F9, random numbers are recalculated and the whole experiment depicts again. This may scaffold the underlying idea of the law of large numbers: even though the behavior will be different each time, the tendency towards the theoretical probability will remain unchanged.

Figure 5. Dice roll simulation generated by means of GeoGebra

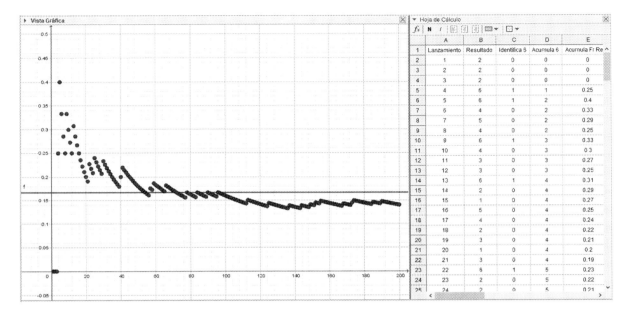

In this case, the mechanism to simulate a rolling dice was generating random numbers that follow a certain distribution, linking them dynamically to the spreadsheet and graphing the accumulated relative frequency of an event, with respect to the experiment number. In general, for probability teaching and learning using GeoGebra, the spreadsheet, the graphic view, the probability calculator and sliders become relevant. The latter occurs when the increasing number of experiments is configured by means of a slider.

Providing Meaning to Mathematical Objects

The idea of meaningful learning is that new concepts are completely understood and can be used to make connections with other previous known knowledge, aiding in further understanding. *Promoting transfer,* i.e. the ability to use what was learned to solve new problems, and answer new questions- is the key to achieve meaningful learning (Mayer, 2002).

When related to digital technology, meaningful and effective learning of mathematics in the computer-based learning environment created by GeoGebra is achieved by "representations of the content with visual and concrete elements" (Yorgancı, 2018, p. 71). Some mathematical concepts and definitions are very abstract and complex in their nature and are to some extent inaccessible for students when presented in conventional manners. For example, the concept of locus, a set of points in the plane that verify a property, is usually introduced at school studying the perpendicular bisector of a segment, the circumference first and the other conics afterwards. It remains a difficult topic to understand for students, and teachers quite often do not go into its details. Nevertheless, it is very important that the concept of locus is properly understood by the students, not only because of its cross-cutting nature, but also because it is an example of typically mathematical methodological rigor, good to establish reasoning about the properties of mathematical objects (Ferrarello, Mammana, Pennisi, & Taranto, 2017).

How Can Digital Technology Enhance Mathematics Teaching and Learning?

Due to the permanent algebraic predominance in introductory stages of the study of loci, researchers have recognized the necessity of promoting geometric constructions during the teaching and learning process of geometric places. For example, the conventional connection between locus and the cartesian coordinate system explains that students conceptualize the ellipse as a curve dependent on that system, whereas in other reference contexts, its properties would not be considered invariant (León & Flores, 2015).

The use of GeoGebra, as a dynamic geometrical environment was fundamental for León & Flores´ analyzed pedagogical proposal, allowing students to integrate concepts and interact with the ellipse to better understand its properties. For example, **visualizing** the trace of the set of points that satisfy the ellipse as locus, i.e. *all points the sum of whose distances from two fixed points is a constant*, was crucial for the ellipse to cease being an abstract artifact for students (Figure 6).

The mechanism used to provide meaning to the locus definition of the ellipse was primarily activating the trace of point A that draws the ellipse while P travels through the circumference. This was possible because the construction was based on the curve´s properties, including a circumference, an isosceles triangle and the perpendicular bisector of its base, that assured the sum of distances from both fixed points be a constant.

Solving Problems

According to the Chilean mathematics curriculum, the four abilities students should develop in high school are: solving problems, representing, modeling and argumentation. Problem solving is seen both as a means and an end, due to the relevance of the process and its results. Solving problems gives the opportunity to connect with other areas and offers evidence of math´s utility in real life; as a process it implies creativity and applying different strategies to obtain answers (Ministerio de Educación, 2015). Research has shown that dynamic software provides support for problem solving; not only visual support but algebraic and conceptual as well (Moreno & Llinares, 2018).

This is the case study concerning the diverse strategies that different types of 15-year-old Spaniard students apply to solve geometric problems in both, pencil and paper and DGS environments. As shown in Figure 7, given the coordinates of two vertices and the perimeter of a rhombus, students had to find the remaining two vertexes and the figure´s area[2]. The strategies used by learners produced four categories of students: autonomous, instrumental, procedural, and naïve, from higher to lower levels of performance (Iranzo & Fortuny, 2009).

Autonomous: drawing the other diagonal, perpendicular to the segment PQ in its midpoint, draws a circumference of radius 5, finding the other vertices, in the intersections.

Figure 6. Construction of Ellipse as locus

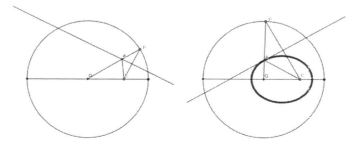

Figure 7. Autonomous and instrumental student´s strategies

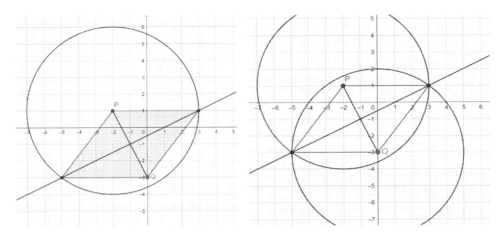

Instrumental: finds the remaining vertices by drawing two circumferences of radius 5 with center in P and Q.

Procedural: drawing the other diagonal, perpendicular to the segment PQ in its midpoint, places point A on it, and obtains it symmetric A´ by reflection about PQ. Then drags point A until all sides measure 5 cm.

Naïve: drawing the other diagonal, perpendicular to the segment PQ in its midpoint, places point A and B on it, dragging each one trying to obtain the same length sides. The figure does not pass the *dragging test* (properties do not hold true)

Regardless of the students´ level of performance -to a greater or lesser extent- all learners benefited from the use of DGS. This kind of technology-enriched learning environments promote a deeper geometrical thinking and helps avoiding algebraic obstacles. It is interesting to notice that there are more strategies available with DGS and some of them have no clear transference to a method with pen and pencil, for example the dynamic procedural strategy. According to Zimmermann and Cunningham (1991), students who use representations and graphs as part of their problem-solving strategies tend to be more successful in obtaining results. This means more opportunities for all students to engage in problem solving, providing more equitable access to mathematics.

Figure 8. Procedural and naïve student´s strategies

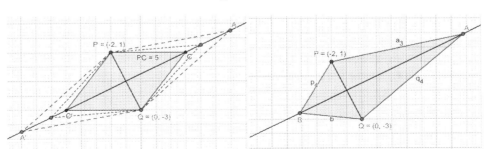

Enabling 3D Graphical Register

In the last two decades, a considerable body of literature has argued that working on three-dimensional shapes helps learners develop spatial awareness, the ability to visualize, geometrical intuition and the capability to understand geometrical theorems, axioms and propositions (Jones, Fujita, & Ding, 2006). Its complexity is attributed to the fact that three-dimensional thinking is a visuospatial ability that comprises several elements, i.e. spatial orientation and spatial visualization (Saralar, 2017).

Raymond Duval´s theory of semiotic registers of representation was mentioned before regarding multiple representations. When addressing 3D mathematical entities, the articulation between these registers becomes harder because of the complexity involved in representing objects in a tridimensional space by means of models or plane projections. Both types have constraints: models are too restrictive and time-consuming; figures with pencil and paper require a 3D perspective drawing in the plane but their visual information is not reliable. For instance, due to perspective, two parallel lines look like they will intersect; regarding the position of a point in space, in 3D it is not possible to know its exact position without further data. In space geometry, it seems to be much harder for students to be certain of a visual noticing, and they may need new tools to study representations and to solve problems (Mithalal, 2010).

Consequently, visualizing and creating mental images of three-dimensional space objects is not trivial. Therefore, teachers and learners often chose not to work with the 3D graphic register, restricting and limiting their work to the algebraic register (del Río, 2017). Currently, we can easily represent complex 3D mathematical objects by means of specialized 3D software. This can enhance students' spatial abilities because digital 3D constructions are richer than 2D perspective representations of 3D objects in the plane, due to the dynamic features the software offers, but also because of the possibility to rotate the view: providing depth to 3D digital images helps learners to achieve a deeper understanding of the represented object. In fact, GeoGebra's 3D view has a tool for 3D projection using anaglyph glasses that result in a tridimensional effect.

Mathematical topics that can benefit from the use of 3D dynamic software are logically contents of space geometry but also differential and integral calculus i.e. solids of revolution, relative maximum and minimum (for two variables functions) and limits of two variables functions. For example, Figure 9 shows a GeoGebra-based applet[3] representing a solid of revolution generated by the rotation of a function around X axis. This type of dynamic 3D representation promotes students´ spatial geometrical intuition due to possibility of analyzing the object from different angles, views and projections.

The mechanism used to enable this 3D graphic representation is the *rotate around axis* tool from the 3D view, and a slider that determines the angle of rotation dynamically. The reader can recognize that the 2D graphic view from the left side corresponds to the XY plane of the 3D view. The function $f(x) = x$ (identity function) is the object which is rotated around the X axis. The rotation of the function gradually generates the cone depicted in the 3D view from the right, by completing the surface of the solid. This dynamic process enables the visualization of both, the generation of the solid and the complete cone.

Figure 9. A GeoGebra-based applet representing a solid of revolution generated by the rotation of a function around X axis

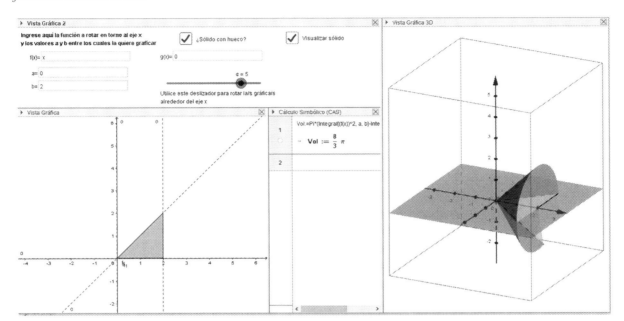

Dynamizing Representations

According to Danckwerts and Vogel (2003, as cited in Hohenwarter, 2014) static representations can only illustrate fixed realities, as opposed to dynamic representations that allow transformation and interactivity, helping learners create an internal image of the object under study. In other words, static geometry creates a barrier for learning, because students are unable to visualize geometric transformations and movements in order to understand the mathematics concepts that are being displayed pictorially (Juan & Dawson, 2015). In the words of Laborde (2007) diagrams in DGS are no longer static. Instead of representing an instance of a geometrical object, they signify a class of drawings, representing the same relationships among variable elements. This gives learners the possibility to generalize geometric patterns and regularities. In some cases, dynamizing figures serves the purpose of characterizing shapes based on their properties. The common didactic obstacle students face when studying certain figures like squares and rhombuses, is the standard orientation these shapes are presented to them: conventionally squares are drawn horizontally and rhombuses vertically, so when students see them in different orientations, they get confused (Figure 10).

By means of DGS these prototype images are easily modified, manipulating their orientation and size. This way, student internalize figures rather than drawings; hard constructions based on properties that pass the *dragging test*.

In other scenarios visualizing dynamic figures allows to expand on certain problematic situations. Dynamic software environments allow the "creation of a family of related problems that share characteristics but, at the same time, provoke new directions of exploration caused by the changing constraints"

How Can Digital Technology Enhance Mathematics Teaching and Learning?

Figure 10. Square and rhombus in different orientations

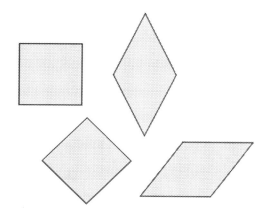

(Gentile & Mattei, 2017, p. 208). To illustrate the difference between using static and dynamic representations for exploring mathematical situations, the author selected Gentile and Mattei's school activity aimed at twelve-year-old students in Italy. It was initially addressed with pen and pencil, then with static use of GeoGebra and finally with dynamic use of GeoGebra. This problem is called the "Street Lamp Problem", which is an open-ended situation. Students are asked to determine the best location to install a lamp in a triangular pedestrian area in order to illuminate the whole surface. This problem leads students to find the centers of the triangle and determine which location better satisfies the conditions, based on their geometrical properties.

Figure 11 shows how students analyzed the differences between the incentre and the circumcenter -with static use of GeoGebra- and decided the latter satisfied better the constraints. Then, based on the circumcenter properties, students formulated the instructions the technician should follow to reach the point in order to install the lamp.

Figure 11. Analysis and comparison between incentre and circumcenter as possible solutions

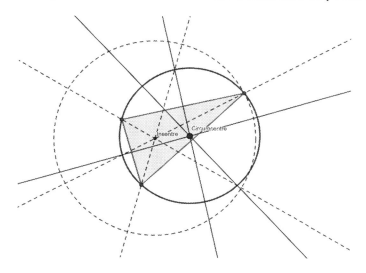

Later, they dragged the vertices of the triangle -dynamic use of GeoGebra- exploring different situations impossible otherwise. Students claimed that with the original triangle, the lamp was inside the park, but "changing the shape of the triangle we saw that the circumcenter is outside" (Gentile & Mattei, 2017, p. 211). Learners realized that the shape of the triangle determined the location of the circumcenter (interior, exterior or on the triangle), impacting the provided solution.

Accessing Complex Mathematical Concepts

In calculus, traditionally inscribed within an axiomatic-deductive approach, we can find many concepts that are difficult to understand and inaccessible to grasp easily. Due to the complex logical structure of their rigorous definitions, conceptual understanding fails, and students often resort to rote memorization and are inclined to use symbolic operations without conceptual understanding. Procedures, algorithms and rules are applied to solve standard exercises, but no deeper meaning comes along. Examples of these complex topics are the limit of a sequence or a function and the derivative. These mathematical concepts are difficult to learn because their understanding implies dealing with notions like infinity (Asprilla & Antioquia, 2014, p. 2).

Visual-geometric teaching proposes that include ICT have proved to be more effective in this field. Making connections between the graphical representation and the formal definition of its core components helps students to achieve conceptual understanding and coordination between the diverse registers of representation (Cheng & Leung, 2015). The notion of infinitesimal change is the core idea when finding the gradient of a curve. We are looking at a secant line that approaches the tangent at a point; when the distance between both points is small enough, one visualizes local straightness. But in order to gain a sense of this approach it is necessary to zoom in the graph around that point. DGS allows this zooming-in and out in order to examine these curves, lines and points in the scale needed to apply the local straightness approach to better understand the concept of derivative (Verhoef et al., 2015). One of the participating teachers in Verhoef´s study thus stated: "Contrary to my previous experience I am now convinced that starting with local straightness is better" (p. 124). This approach promotes a better conceptual understanding of the derivative before solving problems with operational symbolism later in the course. Figure 12 illustrates a GeoGebra-based dynamic applet[4] designed to visualize local straightness. The graph in the left shows the plotted curve of the function

$$f(x) = \sin(4x) + \sin(2x) + \sin(x),$$

next to the zoomed-in area at the right. Clearly the curve looks "locally straight" between the two points. As h approaches to zero -by means of a slider- we visualize how the gradient of the secant line approximates the gradient of the tangent line.

Learning Mathematics Through Exploration

Allowing real experimentation, conjecturing, collective and productive discussions, promoting arguments and counterarguments and letting each student experience the knowledge construction as its protagonist, are the real goals for education in the XXI century. Students need to experience a glimpse of real mathematics by making discoveries, and developing mathematical arguments, which are all activities

How Can Digital Technology Enhance Mathematics Teaching and Learning?

Figure 12. A GeoGebra-based dynamic applet designed to visualize local straightness

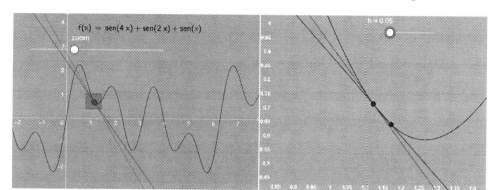

that are at the very core of our discipline. It is important to distinguish this type of "real" exploration from the very commonly performed, that sometimes uses digital technology in the classroom for *verification* or *corroboration* purposes only. For example, teaching first the results of the Thales' theorem or Laplace rule, and then *verifying* them by means of digital technology, is inverting the sense of teaching, according to Freudenthal (as cited in Barra & Vidal, 2018). This way, the magic of experimentation and discovery is lost, as are deduction, reasoning, motivation, curiosity and the appropriation of knowledge construction by students. Therefore, it is key that experimentation occurs before formal instruction, letting students´ conjectures and hypothesis become part of the theoretical knowledge construction later. Mathematics should become *necessary* for students in order to formalize the relationships, patterns and properties found in the experimental phase.

One example of learning mathematics through exploration is a case study conducted from the view point of phenomeography, where experiencing the world is central to constituting the internal relation between the subjective and real world. This observation was implemented in a Swede high school, 9th grade, where the following mathematical challenge was posed: *What is the formula for a circle with its midpoint on the line $y = 3x$ and with a tangent point at $(0,2)$?*

Figure 13 (left) shows the construction made by students in order to addres the challenge. Looking at the symbolic expresion of the circunference they realized that $0,67$ is an aproximation of $2/3$ and therfore the expresion corresponded to

$$\left(x - \frac{2}{3}\right)^2 + (y-2)^2 = 0,44.$$

They wondered why all left hand terms were squared while the right term was not. One student solves their doubt arguing that $\left(\frac{2}{3}\right)^2 = \frac{4}{9}$ and $0,44$ is its decimal aproximation. Learners were happy to discover they were able to solve the problem: the ecuation is

How Can Digital Technology Enhance Mathematics Teaching and Learning?

Figure 13. Construction made by students to solve the ecuation challenge

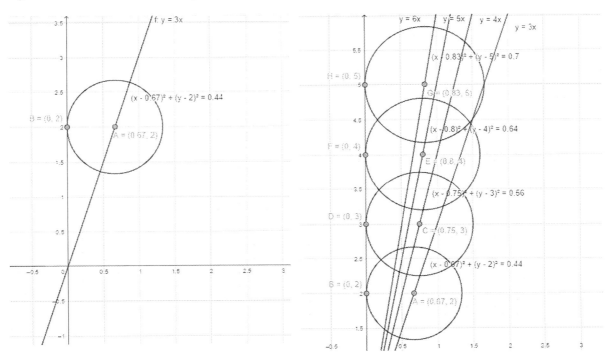

$$\left(x - \frac{2}{3}\right)^2 + \left(y - 2\right)^2 = \left(\frac{2}{3}\right)^2.$$

But afterwards, students wanted to check whether their findings hold true for other circles, lines and tangent points. They added a slider that modified the slope of the line and created the construction shown in Figure 13 (right). Students analyzed the symbolic expressions[5] of the objects in their construction and started to write in paper a generalization of their findings. "We´ll call the line $y = kx$, where k is the slope. Then we´ll place a point A on the line. Construct a circle with center in A and adjust it so that the circle is tangent to $(0, y_1)$. The circle's equation will be

$$\left(x - \frac{y_1}{k}\right)^2 + \left(y - y_1\right)^2 = \left(\frac{y_1}{k}\right)^2,$$

(Lingefjärd, 2012, p. 389). This example shows that activities of experimental nature in the mathematics classroom can be very interesting and gratifying for students. Learners were able to establish complex relationships between algebra and geometry by generalizing the equation of the circle.

The mechanism to obtain the general equation was based on the possibility to modify the lines´ slope and the tangent point and simultaneously visualizing the changes experienced by the algebraic expressions, so they could discover patterns and relationships that hold true. As this example shows, exploring and investigation as mathematics activities have a huge potential to create knowledge.

THE SIGNIFICANCE OF THE STUDY

As stated at the beginning, the purpose of this chapter was offering pre-service and in-service teachers a notion of how digital technology can enhance mathematics teaching and learning trough a systematization of categories that have proved the potential to produce insights. Each category is associated to the logical-mathematical type of intelligence and fostered by visualization, a core ability of visual-spatial intelligence. This synergetic combination of approaches strengthens and validates the theory of semiotic registers of representation, which lies at the foundations of mathematics teaching and learning. The pedagogical emphasis in each category's description is intended to illustrate and guide the decision-making process of mathematics teachers when introducing digital technology in their daily schoolwork.

Nevertheless, the proposed classification does not produce excluding categories that work independently from one another. On the contrary, sometimes these categories overlap, happen simultaneously or appear consecutively. Some of them are very specific, such as *discovering properties* and others are very broad and transversal like *learning mathematics trough exploration*. One could say some of them are a natural continuation of others, like *discovering patterns and relationships* and *verifying or rejecting conjectures*. In other cases, certain categories could appear to be nested within others; for example, *dynamizing representations* within *solving problems*. Decomposing the pedagogical and technological knowledge involved in each category serves the purpose of better understanding how each of these processes unfold and occur, and how technology plays a role in fostering them, but certainly, while teaching, these knowledge blend and some of these processes could occur in a compound and intertwined way. In other words, the natural complexity of the teaching and learning process does not get simpler by using technology or by relying on illustrative categories like the ones proposed in this study. Despite the apparent growing complexity, one should not lose sight of the benefits of its effective use: students' appropriation of a deep and active knowledge construction.

It is expected that the outcomes associated with an effective and meaningful integration of digital technology will become stronger and clearer in the near future, and that 20 or more years of lessons learned by a vast amount of research and studies in the field will bear their fruits.

FUTURE RESEARCH DIRECTIONS AND CONCLUSION

Integration of digital technology into teaching and learning mathematics poses multiple challenges for teachers. Besides the technical, operational and infrastructural difficulties, teachers face a fundamental transformation which is the role they play in teaching. In order to take advantage of the possibilities digital technology offers for enhancing teaching and learning mathematics, teachers should transit from an *instructional* role to a *mediator* or *facilitator* role where guiding, leading, coaching and orienting students becomes their major task; consequently, the direct transmission of contents ceases to be central in the classroom. In this new scenario, class planning, sequencing, designing activities, and preparing material becomes especially important in order to create meaningful learning opportunities for all students. This new configuration and its focus on designing learning opportunities for students, should take into consideration all types of intelligences learners exhibit; at least in secondary mathematics education the conventional logical-mathematical intelligence and the visual-spatial one should be intertwined purposefully.

This transformation should not be taken lightly: it constitutes a major change of paradigm that involves the whole educational system. Teacher educators and teachers' programs should be the first ones to promote this change. It is not reasonable to expect that pre-service and in-service teachers will spontaneously adopt this new role if they were trained conventionally and, moreover, if they experienced a conventional type of teaching at school as learners. It is known that early experiences become strong foundations of future behavior and are very hard to transform and modify.

On the other hand, parents and schools should encourage effective and meaningful uses of technology in their classrooms and should offer the technical and infrastructural support needed to ensure a successful implementation of these innovative teaching strategies. A key aspect in technology integration at school is avoiding teachers´ and students´ frustration caused by device malfunction, which is the main reason for teachers not persevering in its use.

On top of the whole structure lie governments and educational ministries that provide guidelines and orientations for the development of education at all levels and the means to implement it. Unfortunately, the ideas and beliefs of policy elites who frame the problems and select the solutions for improving public schools, include errors and mistakes that could explain the low impact of school structural changes and reforms (Cuban, 2013, p. 110). Therefore, an active and engaged participation of mathematics education organizations, academics, schools, teachers and the greater community in the decision-making process, is crucial to achieve an effective and meaningful integration of digital technology for teaching and learning mathematics globally.

REFERENCES

Abánades, M., Botana, F., Kovács, Z., Recio, T., & Sólyom-Gecse, C. (2016). Development of automatic reasoning tools in GeoGebra in ISSAC 2016 Software Presentations Communicated by Roman Pearce. *ACM Communications in Computer Algebra*, *50*(197), 85–88.

Acosta, M., & Fiallo, J. (2017). Enseñando Geometría con tecnología Digital: una propuesta desde la Teoría de las Situaciones Didácticas (Universidad Distrital Francisco José de Caldas, Ed.). Bogotá, Colombia: Énfasis.

Alfieri, A. (2017). L-System Fractals as Geometric Patterns: A Case Study. In *Mathematics and Technology* (pp. 313–333). Cham: Springer; doi:10.1007/978-3-319-51380-5_14.

Amado, N., Sanchez, J., & Pinto, J. (2015). A Utilização do Geogebra na Demonstração Matemática em Sala de Aula: o estudo da reta de Euler. Bolema - Mathematics Education Bulletin, 29(52), 637–657. doi:10.1590/1980-4415v29n52a11

Amman, S., & González, C. (2012). Construcción de triángulos: del dibujo a la figura. In R. Ferragina (Ed.), *GeoGebra entra al aula de matemática*. Buenos Aires: Miño y Dávila; Retrieved from www.minoydavila.com

Arzarello, F., Bairral, M. A., & Dané, C. (2014). Moving from dragging to touchscreen: Geometrical learning with geometric dynamic software. *Teaching Mathematics and Its Applications*, *33*(1), 39–51. doi:10.1093/teamat/hru002

Asprilla, Y. C., & De Antioquia, U. (2014). La comprensión del concepto de Derivada Mediante El Uso De Geogebra como propuesta didáctica. In *Congreso Iberoamericano de Ciencia* (pp. 1–22). Buenos Aires: Tecnologia y Educación.

Association of Mathematics Teacher Educators. (2017). Standards for preparing teachers of mathematics. Retrieved from amte.net/standards

Attorps, I., Björk, K., & Radic, M. (2016). Generating the patterns of variation with GeoGebra: The case of polynomial approximations. *International Journal of Mathematical Education in Science and Technology, 47*(1), 45–57. doi:10.1080/0020739X.2015.1046961

Attorps, I., Radic, M., & Viirman, O. (2011). Teaching inverse functions at tertiary level. In *Proceedings of the Eighth Conference of the European Society for Research in Mathematics Education* (pp. 2524–2533). Academic Press.

Bairral, M., Arzarello, F., & Assis, A. (2017). Domains of Manipulation in Touchscreen Devices and Some Didactic, Cognitive, and Epistemological Implications for Improving Geometric Thinking. In G. Aldon, F. Hitt, L. Bazzini, & U. Gellert (Eds.), *Mathematics and Technology* (pp. 113–142). Cham: Springer; doi:10.1007/978-3-319-51380-5_7.

Barra, M., & Vidal, R. (2018). De una Formación Matemática Normativa a una Educación Matemática Inclusiva. Algunos ejemplos para la reflexión sobre la práctica docente. Cuaderno de Educación, UAH, 81.

Barwise, J., & Etchemendy, J. (1991). Visual information and valid reasoning. In W. Zimmermann & S. & Cunningham (Eds.), Visualization in Mathematics (pp. 9–24). Washington, DC: Mathematical Association of America. Retrieved from https://ci.nii.ac.jp/naid/10006844948/

Beaudin, M., & Bowers, D. (1997). *Logistics for facilitating CAS instruction.* Lancashire, UK: Chartwell-York; Retrieved from https://scholar.google.es/scholar?hl=es&as_sdt=0%2C5&q=Beaudin%2C+M+and+Bowers%2C+D.+%281997%29.+Logistics+for+facilitating+CAS+instruction.+In+J.+Berry%2C+J.+Monaghan%2C+M.+Kronfellner%2C+and+B.+Kutzler+%28Eds.%29%2C+The+state+of+computer+algebra+in+math

Berger, M., & Bowie, L. (2012). A course on functions for in-service mathematics teachers: Changing the discourse. *Education as Change, 16*(2), 217–229. doi:10.1080/16823206.2012.745751

Bertone, A. M., & Barbosa, L. M. (2015). Geogebra y los sistemas de funciones iteradas: Socios en la creación de un árbol de sakura. *Revista Do Instituto GeoGebra Internacional de São Paulo, 4*(2), 78–87.

Bruner, J. S. (1966). Toward a theory of instruction. Cambridge, MA: Belknap Press of Harvard University. Retrieved from https://buscador.bibliotecas.uc.cl/primo-explore/fulldisplay?docid=puc_alma2156343420003396&context=L&vid=56PUC_INST&lang=es_CL&search_scope=alma_scope&adaptor=Local SearchEngine&isFrbr=true&tab=libros_tab&query=any,contains

Cervantes, A., López, N., Luque, R., & Prieto, J. (2012). Relaciones entre la variación de parámetros y los efectos geométricos en la función afín: una propuesta de análisis con GeoGebra. In *Conferencia Latinoamericana de GeoGebra Uruguay 2012* (pp. 468–475). Montevideo: Academic Press.

Cheng, K., & Leung, A. (2015). A dynamic applet for the exploration of the concept of the limit of a sequence. *International Journal of Mathematical Education in Science and Technology, 46*(2), 187–204. doi:10.1080/0020739X.2014.951007

Clark, D., Nelson, B., Sengupta, P., & D'Angelo, C. (2009). Rethinking Science Learning Through Digital Games and Simulations: Genres, Examples, and Evidence. Learning science: Computer games, simulations, and education workshop sponsored by the National Academy of Sciences. Retrieved from https://sites.nationalacademies.org/cs/groups/dbassesite/documents/webpage/dbasse_080068.pdf

Contreras, J. N. (2014). Discovering and Extending Viviani's Theorem with GeoGebra. *GeoGebra International Journal of Romania, 3*(1), 1–14.

Cuban, L. (2001). *Oversold and underused : computers in the classroom*. Cambridge, MA: Harvard University Press.

Cuban, L. (2013). Why so many structural changes in schools and so little reform in teaching practice? *Journal of Educational Administration, 51*(2), 109–125. doi:10.1108/09578231311304661

Dara-Abrams, B. (2002). Applying Multi-Intelligent Adaptive Hypermedia to Online Learning. In E-Learn: World Conference on E-Learning in Corporate, Government, Healthcare, and Higher Education (pp. 1382–1385). Montreal, Canada: Association for the Advancement of Computing in Education (AACE).

De Simone, M. (2017). Disclosing the "Ræmotionality" of a Mathematics Teacher Using Technology in Her Classroom Activity. In G. Aldon, F. Hitt, L. Bazzini, & U. Gellert (Eds.), *Mathematics and Technology* (pp. 255–284). Cham: Springer; doi:10.1007/978-3-319-51380-5_12.

del Río, L. S. (2017). Enseñar y aprender cálculo con ayuda de la vista gráfica 3D de GeoGebra. Revista Digital Matemática. *Educación e Internet., 17*(1), 13. doi:10.18845/rdmei.v17i1.2739

Digital Chalkboard. (n.d.). 3.1.3 Introduction to Conjectures : CCSS Mathematics: K-12 Standards for Mathematical Practice. Retrieved February 18, 2019, from https://www.mydigitalchalkboard.org/portal/default/Content/Viewer/Content?action=2&scId=306591&sciId=12796

Dockendorff, M., & Solar, H. (2018). ICT integration in mathematics initial teacher training and its impact on visualization: The case of GeoGebra. *International Journal of Mathematical Education in Science and Technology, 49*(1), 66–84. doi:10.1080/0020739X.2017.1341060

Duval, R. (1999). Representation, Vision and Visualization: Cognitive Functions in Mathematical Thinking. Basic Issues for Learning. Retrieved from http://pat-thompson.net/PDFversions/1999Duval.pdf

Ertmer, P. A., Ottenbreit-Leftwich, A. T., Sadik, O., Sendurur, E., & Sendurur, P. (2012). Teacher beliefs and technology integration practices: A critical relationship. *Computers & Education, 59*(2), 423–435. doi:10.1016/j.compedu.2012.02.001

Ferrarello, D., Mammana, M. F., Pennisi, M., & Taranto, E. (2017). Teaching Intriguing Geometric Loci with DGS. In G. Aldon, F. Hitt, L. Bazzini, & U. Gellert (Eds.), *Mathematics and Technology* (pp. 579–605). Cham: Springer; doi:10.1007/978-3-319-51380-5_26.

Gentile, E., & Mattei, M. (2017). The Street Lamp Problem: Technologies and Meaningful Situations in Class. In G. Aldon, F. Hitt, L. Bazzini, & U. Gellert (Eds.), *Mathematics and Technology* (pp. 197–223). Cham: Springer; doi:10.1007/978-3-319-51380-5_10.

Gómez-Chacón, I. M., & Prieto, N. (2010). Developing Competencies to Teach Exponential and Logarithmic Functions using GeoGebra from a Holistic Approach. *Educação Matemática Pesquisa, 12*(3), 485–513.

Gülseçen, S., Karataş, R., & Koçoğlu, R. (2012). Can GeoGebra Make Easier The Understanding of Cartesian Co-Ordinates? A Quantitative Study In Turkey. International Journal on New.

Hamilton, E. R., Rosenberg, J. M., & Akcaoglu, M. (2016). The Substitution Augmentation Modification Redefinition (SAMR) Model: A Critical Review and Suggestions for its Use. *TechTrends, 60*(5), 433–441. doi:10.1007/s11528-016-0091-y

Hohenwarter, M. (2014). Multiple representations and GeoGebra-based learning environments. Union. *Revista Iberoamericana de Educación Matemática, 39*, 11–18.

Hoyles, C. (2018). Transforming the mathematical practices of learners and teachers through digital technology*. *Research in Mathematics Education, 20*(3), 209–228. doi:10.1080/14794802.2018.1484799

Inzunsa, S. (2014). GeoGebra: Una herramienta cognitiva para la enseñanza de la probabilidad. In Congreso Iberoamericano de Ciencia, Tecnología, Innovación y Educación. Retrieved from https://www.oei.es/historico/congreso2014/memoriactei/104.pdf

Iranzo, N., & Fortuny, J. (2009). La influencia conjunta del uso de GeoGebra y lápiz y papel en la adquisición de comeptencias del alumnado. *Ensenañza de las Ciencias, 27*(3), 433–446. Retrieved from www.geogebra.org

Jones, K., Fujita, T., & Ding, L. (2006). Informing the pedagogy for geometry: Learning from teaching approaches in China and Japan. *Proceedings of the British Society for Research into Learning Mathematics, 26*(2), 109–114. Retrieved from https://eprints.soton.ac.uk/41852/

Juan, K., & Dawson, K. (2015). Effects of interactive software on student achievement and engagement in four secondary school geometry classes, compared to two classes with no technology integration. University of Florida. ProQuest Dissertations Publishing. Retrieved from https://search-proquest-com.pucdechile.idm.oclc.org/docview/1815189905?pq-origsite=primo

Kabaca, T. (2013). Software to Teach One-Variable Inequalities by the View of Semiotic. Eurasia Journal of Mathematics. *Science & Technology Education, 9*(1), 73–81.

Koparan, T. (2017). Analysis of Teaching Materials Developed by Prospective Mathematics Teachers and Their Views on Material Development. Malaysian Online Journal of Educational Technology, 5(4), 8–28. Retrieved from http://ezproxy.lib.uconn.edu/login?url=https://search.ebscohost.com/login.aspx?direct=true&db=eric&AN=EJ1156942&site=ehost-live

Kutluca, T. (2013). The Effect of Geometry Instruction with Dynamic Geometry Software; GeoGebra on Van Hiele Geometry Understanding Levels of Students. *Educational Research Review, 8*(17), 1509–1518. doi:10.5897/ERR2013.1554

Laborde, C. (2007). The role and uses of technologies in mathematics classrooms: Between challenge and modus vivendi. Canadian Journal of Science, Mathematics and Technology Education, 7(1), 68–92. doi:10.1080/14926150709556721

León, J., & Flores, J. (2015). Instrumentalización de la elipse utilizando Geogebra. In Conferencia Interamericana de Educación Matemática (pp. 1–9). Chiapas.

Lingefjärd, T. (2012). A Kaiserin of mathematics education. In Mathematikunterricht im Kontext von Realität, Kultur und Lehrerprofessionalität (pp. 385–390). Vieweg + Teubner Verlag. doi:10.1007/978-3-8348-2389-2_40

Mayer, R. E. (2002). Rote Versus Meaningful Learning. *Theory into Practice*, *41*(4), 226–232. doi:10.1207/s15430421tip4104_4

Ministerio de Educación. (2015). Bases Curriculares 7o básico a 2o medio. Santiago, Gobierno de Chile: Unidad de Currículum y Evaluación.

Mishra, P., & Koehler, M. J. (2006). Technological Pedagogical Content Knowledge: A Framework for Teacher Knowledge. *Teachers College Record*, *108*(6), 1017–1054. doi:10.1111/j.1467-9620.2006.00684.x

Mithalal, J. (2010). 3D Geometry and Learning of Mathematical Reasoning. In *Proceedings of CERME* (pp. 796–805). Academic Press.

Moreno, M., & Llinares, S. (2018). Prospective Mathematics Teachers' Perspectives on Technology. In *Educating Prospective Secondary Mathematics Teachers* (pp. 125–142). Cham: Springer; doi:10.1007/978-3-319-91059-8_8.

Morera, L. (2011). Uso del Geogebra en la enseñanza de las Transformaciones. Uno: Revista de Didáctica de Las Matematicas, 56, 95–104. Retrieved from https://es.slideshare.net/mcnavarr1/el-uso-del-geogebra-en-la-enseanza-de-la-geometra

National Research Council. (2011). *Learning Science Through Computer Games and Simulations* (2nd ed.). Bioinformatics and Functional Genomics; doi:10.1080/00498250110091767

NCTM. (2012). NCTM CAEP Standards -Elementary Mathematics Specialist (Advanced Preparation). Retrieved from https://cehd.gmu.edu/assets/docs/MathEducation/nctm-caep-elementary-math-advanced.pdf

Novembre, A., Nicodemo, M., & Coll, P. (2015). Matemática y TIC Orientaciones para la enseñanza. *CABA: ANSES*, *91*, 399–404.

Plass, J. L., Homer, B. D., & Hayward, E. O. (2009). Design factors for educationally effective animations and simulations. *Journal of Computing in Higher Education*, *21*(1), 31–61. doi:10.1007/s12528-009-9011-x

Poon, K. K. (2018). Learning Fraction comparison by using a dynamic mathematics software - GeoGebra. *International Journal of Mathematical Education in Science and Technology*, *49*(3), 469–479. doi:10.1080/0020739X.2017.1404649

Poon, K. K., & Wong, K. L. (2017). Pre-constructed dynamic geometry materials in the classroom–how do they facilitate the learning of 'Similar Triangles'? *International Journal of Mathematical Education in Science and Technology*, 48(5), 735–755. doi:10.1080/0020739X.2016.1264636

Puentedura, R. (2006). Transformation, technology, and education [Blog post]. Retrieved February 18, 2019, from https://scholar.google.es/scholar?hl=es&as_sdt=0%2C5&q=Puentedura%2C+R.+%282006%29.+Transformation%2C+technology%2C+and+education+%5BBlog+post%5D.+Retrieved+from+http%3A%2F%2Fhippasus.com%2Fresources%2Ftte%2F.&btnG=

Raymond Duval. (1999). Representation, Vision and Visualization: Cognitive Functions in Mathematical Thinking. Basic Issues for Learning. Retrieved from https://files.eric.ed.gov/fulltext/ED466379.pdf

Rubio, L., Prieto, J. L., & Ortiz, J. (2016). La matemática en la simulación con GeoGebra. Una experiencia con el movimiento en caída libre. *International Journal of Educational Research and Innovation*, 2, 90–111.

Saralar, I. (2017). An exploration of middle school mathematics teachers' beliefs and goals regarding GeoGebra: Four cases from the Turkish Republic. In European Conferance on Educatioal Research 2017: Reforming Education and the Imperative of Constant Change: Ambivalent Roles of Policy and Educational Research. University College Copenhagen (pp. 2012–2014). Copenhagen, Denmark: EERA ECER. Retrieved from https://www.academia.edu/38303474/An_exploration_of_middle_school_mathematics_teachers_beliefs_and_goals_regarding_GeoGebra_Four_cases_from_the_Turkish_Republic?email_work_card=title

Strausova, I., & Hasek, R. (2013). *"Dynamic visual proofs" using DGS*. Electronic Journal of Mathematics and Technology.

Tran, T., Nguyen, N., Bui, M., & Phan, A. (2014). Discovery learning with the help of the geoGebra dynamic deometry software. International Journal of Learning, Teaching and Educational Research, 7(1).

Verhoef, N. C., Coenders, F., Pieters, J. M., van Smaalen, D., & Tall, D. O. (2015). Professional development through lesson study: Teaching the derivative using GeoGebra. Professional Development in Education, 41(1), 109–126. doi:10.1080/19415257.2014.886285

Yorgancı, S. (2018). A study on the views of graduate students on the use of GeoGebra in mathematics teaching. *European Journal of Education Studies*, 4. doi:10.5281/zenodo.1272935

Zazkis, R., Dubinsky, E., & Dautermann, J. (1996). Coordinating Visual and Analytic Strategies: A Study of Students' Understanding of the. Source. *Journal for Research in Mathematics Education*, 27, •••. Retrieved from https://www-jstor-org.pucdechile.idm.oclc.org/stable/pdf/749876.pdf?refreqid=excelsior%3A8682c126bb55b92ec0c3279ba2c90068

Zengin, Y. (2017). The effects of GeoGebra software on pre-service mathematics teachers' attitudes and views toward proof and proving. *International Journal of Mathematical Education in Science and Technology*, 48(7), 1002–1022. doi:10.1080/0020739X.2017.1298855

Zimmermann, W., & Cunningham, S. (1991). What is mathematical visualization? In W. Zimmermann & S. Cunningham (Eds.), Visualization in teaching and learning mathematics (Vol. 19, pp. 1–8). Washington, DC: Series, MAA. Retrieved from https://www.semanticscholar.org/paper/Editors'-introduction%3A-What-is-mathematical-Zimmermann-Cunningham/46339bd5e52c9f6785b70ef1e62812f5f02b1ec7

ADDITIONAL READING

Alacacı, C., & McDonald, G. (2012). The Impact of Technology on High School Mathematics Curriculum. *Turkish Journal of Computer and Mathematics Education*, *3*(1), 21–34. Retrieved from http://dergipark.gov.tr/download/article-file/201353%0Ahttp://www.ceeol.com/aspx/getdocument.aspx?logid=5&id=1eb1053f3c7e40c191ceb666d32e7ca7

Amman, S., Bifano, F., Cicala, R., González, C., & Lupinacci, L. (2012). *GeoGebra entra al aula de matemática*. Retrieved from www.minoydavila.com

Botana, F., Hohenwarter, M., Janičić, P., Kovács, Z., Petrović, I., Recio, T., & Weitzhofer, S. (2015). Automated Theorem Proving in GeoGebra: Current Achievements. *Journal of Automated Reasoning*, *55*(1), 39–59. doi:10.100710817-015-9326-4

Bray, A., & Tangney, B. (2017). Technology usage in mathematics education research – A systematic review of recent trends. *Computers & Education*, *114*, 255–273. doi:10.1016/j.compedu.2017.07.004

Cuban, L., & Jandrić, P. (2015). The dubious promise of educational technologies: Historical patterns and future challenges. *E-Learning and Digital Media*, *12*(3-4), 425–439. doi:10.1177/2042753015579978

Fabian, K., Topping, K. J., & Barron, I. G. (2016). Mobile technology and mathematics: Effects on students' attitudes, engagement, and achievement. *Journal of Computers in Education*, *3*(1), 77–104. doi:10.100740692-015-0048-8

Kadijevich, D. (2018). Mathematics teachers as multimedia lesson designers. *International Journal of Scientific and University Research Publication*, *704*(13).

Smith, R. C., Shin, D., & Kim, S. (2016). Prospective and current secondary mathematics teachers' criteria for evaluating mathematical cognitive technologies. *International Journal of Mathematical Education in Science and Technology*, *48*(5), 659–681. doi:10.1080/0020739X.2016.1264635

Strutchens, M. E. (2018). *Educating Prospective Secondary Mathematics Teachers*. doi:10.1007/978-3-319-91059-8

Sutherland, R. (2018). Education in the 21st century. In Education and social justice in a digital age. doi:10.2307/j.ctt9qgszm.12

Tatar, E. (2013). The Effect of Dynamic Software on Prospective Mathematics Teachers' Perceptions Regarding Information and Communication Technology. *Australian Journal of Teacher Education*, *38*(12). doi:10.14221/ajte.2013v38n12.6

KEY TERMS AND DEFINITIONS

Dragging Test: Changing a geometrical object without changing the significant properties of the object. Normally the dragging test is performed by dragging one or more vertices of geometric figures.

GeoGebra-Based Dynamic Applet: Is a digital tool generated by means of GeoGebra software with extension *ggb*. It is used to teach and learn mathematics in an exploratory way due to its interactive and dynamic features. Given the software opensource nature, shared applets can be modified and further used by other learners around the world.

Hard Construction: As opposed to *soft construction* or drawing. Geometric construction based on the object´s properties. If correctly drawn the shape of the figure will remain unchanged under dragging.

Simultaneous Dynamic Representations: Software capability to depict simultaneously the symbolic and graphic representation of a mathematical entity. Combined with the dynamic interactive feature -that enables the user to modify either the symbolic or the graphic representation and observe the corresponding modification in the other register of representation- allows deep access to mathematical objects.

Stages of Cognitive Representation: Three stages are usually described regarding levels of abstraction. Enactive, which is the representation of knowledge through actions. Iconic, which is the visual summarization of images. Symbolic representation, which is the use of words and other symbols to describe experiences.

Technology-Enriched Learning Environment: Classrooms, in which open-ended, rich information tasks and resources are available, most of which use a range of technologies or digital tools in interactive, multi-media and inter-disciplinary formats, constantly challenging students and teachers.

Visualization: Visualization is the ability, the process and the product of creation, interpretation, use of and reflection upon pictures, images, diagrams, in our minds, on paper, or with technological tools, with the purpose of depicting and communicating information, thinking about and developing previously unknown ideas and advancing understandings.

ENDNOTES

[1] www.geogebra.org
[2] A rhombus has 2 vertices P=(-2,1) and Q=(0,-3) that constitute one of its diagonals. The perimeter is 20 cm. Find the remaining vertices and its area.
[3] http://www.geogebra.org/material/simple/id/15095493
[4] https://www.geogebra.org/m/qbdxhjcu
[5] Originally at the algebraic view. For image quality purposes the labels have been included in the graphics view.

Chapter 12
Game Development-Based Learning:
A New Paradigm for Teaching Computer and Object-Oriented Programming

Alaa Khalaf Al-Makhzoomy
Yarmouk University, Jordan

Ke Zhang
Wayne State University, USA

Timothy Spannaus
Wayne State University, USA

ABSTRACT

This chapter presents the findings from a quasi-experimental study analyzing the effect of Game Development-Based Learning on students' academic performance in programming courses in Jordan. The study tested an argument proposing a positive significant association between GDBL instruction and students' performance. The analysis of variance results investigating the effect of enrollment and completion of a concurrent GDBL course to normal courses found that the treatment group outperformed two other groups: the control and the comparison group. The positive gains in the post-assessment scores, were consistent across the two programming courses: C++ and Object-Oriented Programming. This finding confirms the earlier results across countries and contexts documenting the salubrious effect of GDBL on students' academic performance in Computer Science and Information Technology courses. Findings also support the overarching constructionist approach where the use of scaffolding and technology in instruction and assessment yield better academic outcomes for learners.

DOI: 10.4018/978-1-7998-0249-5.ch012

INTRODUCTION

Computer Science (CS) jobs are expected to grow at the highest rate compared to any other occupation in the next decade according to the Bureau of Labor Statistics of the United States. An average annual increase of 13% between 2016 and 2026 is projected yielding an addition of 557,100 openings to the marketplace, the best choice for any uncertain student looking for job security (Bureau of Labor Statistics, 2019). All such jobs feature the rudimentary or advanced use of programming from coding to data analytics. Therefore, mastering programming knowledge, skills and abilities (KSAs) proves essential in obtaining, retaining and advancing in a CS or information technology (IT) job.

Empirical evidence on passing rates of programming courses is conflicting. Two quantitative studies based on low response rates and available secondary data, mostly surveys-based, indicate that passing rates of programming is about 67%, a figure contradicting the popular claim that most students fail programming (Watson & Li, 2014; Porter, Guzdial, McDowell, & Simon, 2013). Other studies have concluded that students' dropout rates from computer science are the highest among college majors and such a trend is plausibly due to the difficult learning curve faced in programming courses (Baytak, Land & Smith, 2011; Wu & Wang, 2012; Ismail, Ngah, & Umar, 2010). This is evident in the lower rates of conferred degrees in CS and IT compared to other fields like Engineering or Biological Sciences. No matter what the truth is, whether passing rates are high or low in programming, instructors need to improve their instruction and assessment of programming, providing students with the best available education for them to succeed (Ernst & Clark, 2012; Alkhawaldeh & Menchaca, 2014).

Game Development-Based Learning (GDBL) is an emerging educational strategy where students design and build their games as learning activities aimed at mastering programming content (Charlier, & De Fraine, 2012). GDBL is based on the constructivist learning approach where learners engage in experiential and interactive learning with the instructor and peers, thereby increasing their involvement and motivation for taking part in the learning process (Overmars, 2004). The use of GameMaker® in teaching programming across countries and courses has demonstrated a steady improvement in students' outcomes and skills (Papastergiou, 2009). Mathematical-Logical Intelligence plays a crucial role in computer programming where learners think conceptually and abstractly dealing with numbers, memory and statements. It also plays a role in GDBL especially when using GameMaker® alongside with the Visual-Spatial Intelligence. The learner will design and develop games using their ability to visualize the objects and their actions.

This chapter outlines the results of an experiment that took place at a public university in the north of Jordan where GameMaker® was introduced in two courses, C++ and Object-Oriented Programming, and was found to positively and significantly improve students' motivation, performance and retention in CS and IT (Eagle & Barnes, 2009; Yarmouk University, 2017b). The findings recommend CS instructors to incorporate GDBL learning strategies in their classes and advocates that such a practice should be embedded in departmental curricula (Doman, Sleigh & Garrison, 2015).

BACKGROUND

Previous research has noted the wide array of benefits gained through the use of GameMaker® for teaching programming at all educational levels. First, students' motivation and interest in CS and IT improves with game authoring and design as part of programming courses (Johnson, 2017). GameMaker® can be introduced as early as middle school as an effective tool introducing students to programming and CS where their attitudes towards the field could potentially change the negative perceptions surrounding IT fields (Jenson & Droumeva, 2015). GDBL has been employed in Object-Oriented Programming and introductory to C++ with the overarching finding that it serves as a complementary pedagogical tool to the formal programming instruction increasing the potential for programming learning for students (Dalal, Kak & Sohoni, 2012).

Game Development-Based Learning has been linked with many positive attitudes and behaviors improving the educational outcomes for students. First, it is said to increase interest and motivation of CS and IT students in learning programming and mastering its content (Wu & Wang, 2012). GDBL is likely to also improve learners' engagement with the materials and assessments utilized in programming courses (Marlow, 2012). GDBL has also been shown to positively correlate with learners' autonomy and independent thinking abilities where he or she inserts the customized preferences into the game being created (Patton, 2011). Most importantly, GDBL is linked to the evolution of learning tolerance for their own mistakes (Majgaard, 2014). Learners develop the sense of graceful failure where they do not beat themselves up over failing in one or more standard in their learning journey (Hamari, Shernoff, Rowe, Coller, Asbell-Clarke, & Edwards, 2016).

Learning theories explaining GDBL span a single framework to engage numerous models that include not only constructivist approaches, but also social learning theories (Ismail, Ngah & Umar, 2010). Therefore, a better theoretical approach is to utilize a model that features the common characteristics of all digital game environments like GameMaker® (Kindler & Krivy, 2011; Dalal, Kak, & Sohoni, 2012). Figure 1 presents the three shared elements across all games: challenge, response and feedback. This model posits that every game will feature a varying theoretical approach contingent upon the challenges it purports, responses it solicits and feedback it targets. For instance, a programming game will present students with a challenge that activates problem solving skills, and secure responses based on the process and documentation of problem solving (Pretelín-ricárdez & Sacristán, 2015). Feedback by peers and instructors are provided and the loop continues to increase the learning ability of the learner.

GDBL places the learner at the center of the educational process (Jong, Shang & Lee, 2010). It differs from traditional approach where it considers the cognitive, behavioral, social and emotional dimensions of the learners' personality and environment. This points to the significance of design and usability from a learning design perspective of GDBL. Figure 2 presents the overall framework researchers and practitioners should approach GDBL in any setting including CS and IT educational outcomes. Research has demonstrated that a small portion of academic performance is explained by school characteristics (Kunkle & Allen, 2016). This emphasize the importance of cognitive, behavioral and social characteristics that games need to be designed to address. This logic also applies to programming GDBL frameworks such as the one tested in the current case study.

Research Problem and Research Design

This research aims to assess the effects of Game Development-Based Learning on students' performance in programming courses. More specifically, the study examined the effects of GDBL on students' achievement in two courses, C++ and Object-Oriented Programming. Based on the literature review, it is hypothesized that the use of GDBL improves students' performance in programming courses at the undergraduate level.

Game Development-Based Learning

Figure 1. Model of Game-Based Learning (Plass, Homer, & Kinzer, 2015)

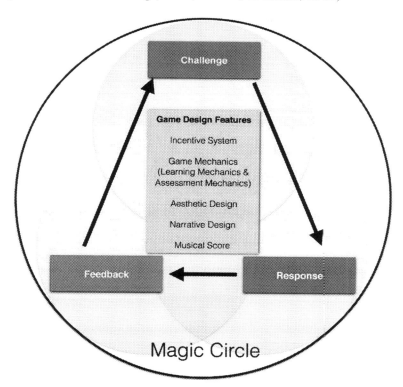

This study utilized the non-equivalent control group quasi-experimental, pre-and post- design to test the proposed hypothesis. Participants were recruited from an urban public university in Jordan in 2018. The treatment of the study was an online course housed on Moodle where enrolled students were expected to create their own games using the GameMaker® Platform. The course ran concurrently with two programming courses students: CS110 and CS210 (C++ and Objected-Oriented Programming). The group of students who enrolled and completed the course online was the experimental group and those who did not participate in the online course were the control group. A third group was introduced for comparison, with students who enrolled but did not complete the entire online course. The online course lasted eight weeks throughout the winter semester of 2018. Table 1 presents the structure of the GDBL course over 8 weeks.

Measurement

The dependent variable academic performance was measured by test scores obtained from courses instructors. Two courses were used in the study, C++ and Object-Oriented Programming. The pre-test for the quasi-experimental study was measured by taking the scores of the first examination in both courses, administered in the first three weeks of the semester. The post-assessment was the final examination at the concluding week of the semester. The independent variable used in the analysis is the treatment,

Figure 2. Integrated design framework of game-based and playful learning (Plass, Homer, & Kinzer, 2015)

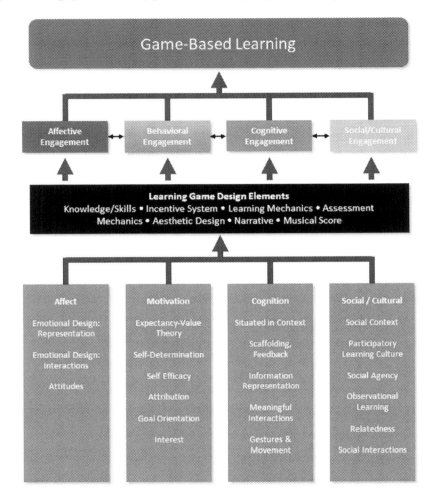

whether students took part in the online game development course or not. Three values were assigned, one per group. Those were students who fully participated, students who enrolled but did not complete the course and students who did not participate.

Data Analysis

To analyze the effect of the game development course on academic performance, a One-Way Analysis of Variance was used. This tested the effect of a single factor on a single outcome. The means' differences obtained from the dependent variable, final examination across the three groups, is evaluated. The criteria of assessing whether the difference is significant or not was through the examination of the observed significance level obtained from the ANOVA test.

Game Development-Based Learning

Table 1. Game development course weekly schedule

Week	Topic	Assignments
1	• Introduction to GameMaker® • Installing and Discovering GameMaker® 8.1	• Description of GameMaker® 8.1 environment
2	• Your First Game: Devilishly Easy	• ClickBall Game Tutorial - V1 • ClickBall Game Tutorial - V2
3	• More Actions • Target the Player	• Space Invaders Game Tutorial – V1 • Space Invaders Game Tutorial – V2 • Space Invaders Game Tutorial – V3
4	• Fixing problems. • Getting it together.	• Normal Distribution Curve Game
5	• Design your own game	• Lumosity Game
6	• Fixing problems. • Getting it together.	• Mind Reader Game
7	• Fixing problems. • Getting it together.	• Memory Game
8	• Become a Programmer (Introduction to programming in GML)	• Reflection on Learning

Results

A total of 250 students participated in this study. Table 2 summarizes the d the relationship between gender and academic performance, as well as residence area type and academic performance. In C++, females did better compared to males both in the first, pre-test, and final, post-test, examinations. On the other hand, rural residents did similar compared to urban residents rendering an absence of association between residence type and academic performance in C++. Gender also mattered in differentiating the scores in Object-Oriented Programming where females received higher scores compared males on both assessments. There was no significant difference between rural and urban students in the same subject. This result is consistent with previous research on gender and academic performance where females have been found repeatedly to score higher compared to males on academic assessments at the undergraduate level (Belland, B. R., Walker, Kim & Lefler. 2017).

Tables 3 and 4 display the three groups, control, treatment and comparison, performance on both the first and final examinations in both courses. The means' difference is in favor of the treatment group,

Table 2. Pre- and post- results by gender and area type

Assessment	First Exam C++ (Pre-test)	Final Exam C++ (Post-Test)	First Exam OOP (OOP)	Second Exam OOP (Post-Test)
Male	10.26 (92)	27.10 (78)	12.52 (58)	27.92 (83)
Female	12.13 (48)	33.30 (46)	12.65 (48)	34.75 (18)
Urban	10.79 (42)	29.13 (38)	14.19 (16)	30.87 (17)
Rural	11.17 (98)	30.03 (86)	12.28 (88)	28.75 (84)

n = the number between the parentheses. Note that OOP Second Exam original score was multiplied by 2.5 to make it out of 50 to ease comparisons.

Table 3. Performance in pre-test and post-test assessments for C++ groups

Group		First Exam	Final Exam
Partial Participation	Mean	11.32	30.59
	n	41	37
	Std. Deviation	3.467	12.417
Full Participation	Mean	12.64	34.30
	n	33	33
	Std. Deviation	4.022	11.876
No Participation	Mean	9.77	25.59
	n	66	54
	Std. Deviation	4.285	11.331
Total	Mean	10.90	29.40
	n	140	124
	Std. Deviation	4.140	12.263

Table 4. Performance in pre-test and post-test assessments for OOP groups

Group		First Exam	Second Exam * 2.5
Partial Participation	Mean	12.95	24.47
	n	20	19
	Std. Deviation	5.052	7.664
Full Participation	Mean	15.06	44.72
	n	18	19
	Std. Deviation	3.298	6.341
No Participation	Mean	11.79	25.80
	n	66	63
	Std. Deviation	3.936	7.634
Total	Mean	12.58	29.10
	n	104	101
	Std. Deviation	4.217	7.946

Table 5. ANOVA results for C++ final exam by group

ANOVA					
Final Exam					
	Sum of Squares	df	Mean Square	F	Sig.
Between Groups	1628.913	2	814.457	5.842	.004
Within Groups	16868.926	121	139.413		
Total	18497.839	123			

Table 6. ANOVA means' comparison for groups on C++ final exam

<td colspan="6" align="center">**Multiple Comparisons**</td>
<td colspan="6" align="center">**Dependent Variable: Final Exam**</td>
<td colspan="6" align="center">**Tukey HSD**</td>
Group	**Group**	**Mean Difference (I-J)**	**Std. Error**	**Sig.**	**95% Confidence Interval**	
					Lower Bound	**Upper Bound**
Partial Participation (0)	1	-3.708	2.827	.391	-10.42	3.00
	2	5.002	2.520	.120	-.98	10.98
Full Participation (1)	0	3.708	2.827	.391	-3.00	10.42
	2	8.710*	2.609	.003	2.52	14.90
No Participation (2)	0	-5.002	2.520	.120	-10.98	.98
	1	-8.710*	2.609	.003	-14.90	-2.52

*. The mean difference is significant at the 0.05 level.

the students who completed the courses. Those students scored higher than the control group, students who did not participate in the research, and the comparison group, the group who partially completed the courses. Results also confirm the expectation of the study where the comparison group, those students who expressed a modicum of motivation and passion for Game Development by signing up and never completing the courses, scored better than the control group, those students who did not do anything with Game Development.

To statistically test the effect of taking part in the online GDBL course, an Analysis of Variance (ANOVA) was performed with participation as the factor and performance in the final exam, post-test, as the outcome. The coefficients generated lead to the conclusion that participation improves academic performance, F= 5.84 (2), P= 0.004. To better understand the differences between groups, in the C++ setting, a post-hoc analysis was carried out confirming the earlier recovered descriptive evidence, the best group is that who fully participated and completed the course. The post-hoc test found that all the differences in means among the fully participating group and the two other groups were significant with the fully participating group, the treatment, at the top trailed by those who expressed some interest and lastly is the control. On the other hand, there was no statistical significance detected between the group who partially participated and that who did not take any part in the research.

Similar to the C++ setting, another ANOVA was carried out to detect the effect of participating in the online game development course on academic performance measured in the Object-Oriented Programming final examination scores. Findings from the analysis indicate that taking an active role in the online course improved students' performance in the course, F= 8.34 (2), P= 0.001. Table 7 demonstrates a post-hoc test comparing statistical significance among the three different groups. Consistent with the results for the C++, the analysis showed that the fully participating group mean is statistically different from the two other means. Also, the mean of the group who expressed interest in completing part of the course did not statistically differ from that of the control group. Results of the Analysis of Variance supports the overarching conclusion that participating in game development courses improve students' abilities, skills and knowledge in programming languages.

Table 7. ANOVA results for OOP second exam by group

ANOVA						
Transformed Second Exam OOP						
	Sum of Squares	df	Mean Square	F	Sig.
Between Groups	5741.063	2	2870.532	8.344	.000
Within Groups	33716.239	98	344.043		
Total	39457.302	100			

Table 8. Post-Hoc comparison between groups

Multiple Comparisons						
Dependent Variable: Transformed Second Exam						
Tukey HSD						
Group	Group	Mean Difference (I-J)	Std. Error	Sig.	95% Confidence Interval	
					Lower Bound	Upper Bound
Partial Participation (0)	1	-20.26316*	6.01790	.003	-34.5848	-5.9415
	2	-1.31997	4.85474	.960	-12.8735	10.2336
Full Participation (1)	0	20.26316*	6.01790	.003	5.9415	34.5848
	2	18.94319*	4.85474	.001	7.3897	30.4967
No Participation (2)	0	1.31997	4.85474	.960	-10.2336	12.8735
	1	-18.94319*	4.85474	.001	-30.4967	-7.3897

*. The mean difference is significant at the 0.05 level.

DISCUSSION

This research corroborates a steady line of scholarship establishing a robust significant positive relationship between the uses of GameMaker® in improving undergraduate students' KSAs in programming. It also proves a strong relationship between Mathematical-Logical Intelligence and computer programming using any computer programming language. In addition, it proves a strong relationship between GDBL with the Visual-Spatial Intelligence, where learners design and develop games using their ability to visualize the objects and their actions.

Table 9 presents synthesized literature on the utilization of GameMaker® across many programming courses, universities and countries. The result is consistent: the platform improves students' interest, ability and mastery of programming languages. This study marks one of the first experiments testing the effect of GameMaker® on students' academic performance in programming courses in Jordan confirming the already established knowledge gained from other researchers as presented in the table.

The research at hand supports the ideas and educational delineations put forward by Papert and his advocates through the constructionist approach (Papert & Harel, 1991). Social learning theory and experiential learning both emphasize the constructionist idea that learners better master the content if they apply it to specified tasks within reasonable time and supportive environments (Piaget, 1976; Vygotskiĭ & Cole, 1978). Learning programming by seeing how peers and instructors design games through cod-

Game Development-Based Learning

Table 9. Literature review main findings

Author	Country	Main Findings
Papastergiou (2009).	Greece	Gaming approach is better than non-gaming approach in improving students' understanding of computer-memory concepts. Gender was not a statistically significant variable in the experiment.
Hamari, Shernoff, Rowe, Coller, Asbell-Clarke & Edwards (2016).	The United States	Gaming was found to a good predictor of learning outcomes. The challenge of the game positively improved learning outcomes for participants across different types of games.
Eagle & Barnes (2009)	The United States	Assignments conducted through gaming environments improve the attitudes and ability of students in introductory computer science courses. Students who perform programming assignments in a gaming environment spend less time and master the material more than students who program without a gaming environment. All students preferred to program in a gaming environment.
Doman, Sleigh & Garrison (2015)	The United States	The use of GameMaker® in computer science courses improve students' attitudes towards programming. It also improves their perceptions of the instructor on the short-term and the long-term.
Jenson & Droumeva (2015)	Canada	GameMaker® use in classrooms improved students' learning outcomes. This finding generalizes over high-school, as well as undergraduate students in multiple disciplines including mathematics and computer science.
Johnson (2017)	The United Kingdom	The use of GameMaker® in undergraduate computer science curriculum improved students' programming skills. Further, the incorporation of GameMaker® into programming courses improved students' engagement and enjoyment of programming-oriented courses.

ing proves to be a great instructional strategy. This finding calls for more integration of technology and applied implementation of learned skills through doing live examples on software or applications. This also encourages instructors whether in the K-12 system or higher education sector to introduce more applied technical skills in their pedagogy and andragogy.

An ancillary, yet important, findings of this research is that the use of computers and tasks to be completed on them improves students' performance. This is especially when instructors apply scaffolding instruction and assessment using computers. This is very important for courses in the STEM fields. A review of the literature by education experts for studies involving computer based scaffolding strategies indicate that "computer-based scaffolding showed a consistently positive ($\bar{g} = 0.46$) effect on cognitive outcomes across various contexts of use, scaffolding characteristics, and levels of assessment" (Belland, Walker, Kim, & Lefler, 2017, p.309).

One of the most important observations to note during the experiment is the high interactivity rating of the GDBL course. The instructor responded to requests and inquiries quickly and supported the learning of students through administering tutorials on how to program. The e-learning literature has established a significant positive relationship between interactive instruction and academic performance, something that this study has confirmed.

The research results also support the argument for the use of blended learning. Students who participated in an online course and an on-campus course outperformed the other two groups who were instructed with one stand-alone technique. Academic performance has improved with the use of structured pre-recorded lessons and assessment exemplars available to students by the online course. This helped them better understand and engage in the learning process they are exposed to in their classrooms.

RECOMMENDATIONS

The implementation of GameMaker® on a multitude of programming courses, including C++, object-oriented programming, and other courses, in educational setting seems to be important to better generate invariant findings and enhance programming skills of students. This is important for researchers and stakeholders to be able to determine whether GameMaker® or any similar technology for the same purpose holds tantamount impact on students' performance. This will, in return, lead to changes to the existing curriculums and the creation of new curriculums which are more robust, valid, and reliable, presenting best-practice research.

Furthermore, other parties than researchers should also conduct experiments on the use of computer-aided design. This means that class instructors teaching such courses would have better assessed the effectiveness of GameMaker® than computer scientists who do not teach the courses since it will reduce the potential internal validity biases to the experimental design and increase objectivity bringing the research closer to real-world arrangements.

One of the main recommendations of this research is the offer of GameMaker® as a 1-credit course given for information technology majors in a lab-course format for several reasons. This is mainly due to the fact that the course is perceived to be difficult not only by student, but also by faculty members. In Jordanian Universities, C++ is a required course for students. In the United States, however, Python replaced C++ programming in many universities. The logic behind this move is to keep students motivated on computer science, given the fact that many students drop out of computer science fearing from C++ programming. Thus, a 1-credit GameMaker® course in the first semester would provide a cushion for many students who are not yet very confident about their courses

FUTURE RESEARCH

One of the weaknesses of the existing literature on computer-based learning is the absence of action-based research. While much research has been devoted to explaining how certain predictors, whether theory- or practice-based, influence students' outcome, other great information resources covering researchers' and students' potential contributions have largely remained unexplored. Researcher may use instruments or tools which are ready for implementation in research settings without worrying about changing them in more beneficial ways to teaching. For instance, researchers could improve GameMaker® by suggesting new theoretically and structurally new lesson plans alongside the inquiry-based assignments delivered to students. Students, on the other hand, could offer feedback for researchers on the practicality, simplicity, and challenges of given assignments or technology. This will provide a rich qualitative information with the active involvement of all participants, allowing for the refinement of course experiment and generations of observational studies with more confident results (Creswell, 2013). Future research examining computer-based technology should make use of action-based research to develop and assess new curriculums for STEM undergraduate education.

Future studies examining the use of technology in STEM education should devote more attention to instructors as an important source to increase explanatory power of the research to understand educational outcomes. This is of great importance since the perspective of instructors has been neglected in the extant literature while much attention has been given to the issues such as, type of technology, content, duration, and perceptions of students. Also, there is a need for more experimental work on the effect of

Game Development-Based Learning

different interactivity levels displayed by instructors. This is also in line with the general assumption in educational leadership that teachers` leadership styles are associated with educational outcomes (Beck, 2010). Furthermore, by doing so, more effective learning environment can be developed where students benefit from both the constructionist educational methods and educational leadership practice, which is believed to produce an increased combined effect improving educational outcomes.

Although non-equivalent experimental research designs have their strengths, they fail to produce analogous results to classical experiments. The absence of random assignments of participants into groups provides more insights into the confounding variables including income, education level, stress level, income, and home environment. Contextual factors could still hold potential threats to the internal validity of experiments although students enrolled in the same class no matter where they came from. Thus, future research should rely on random assignment for experimental design in order to produce more confident findings.

Future research might also consider providing more refined measurements of educational outcomes other than overall test scores. Although test scores provide a fair measurement of students` academic achievements as a general performance assessment, future research can definitely benefit from more fine-grained assessments such as codes` creation, evaluation, and/or validation exercises. This way, future research will contribute to the understanding of best practices in undergraduate classrooms. In that regard, a moderation analysis testing the influence of participating in a specific instructional technique on several tasks constituting a general assessment will provide a detailed understanding of the extent which the new instructional method contributes to the given task.

Last, future research might consider using mediation analysis testing the relationship between computer-based instruction and performance on STEM assessments in colleges since it has shown that that students perform higher on mathematics and computer science course when they are instructed by constructionist methods, such as GameMaker®. However, it is still a debate why such relationship exists. Therefore, more research is needed to explore how two variables are linked. There is no doubt that such knowledge linking the relationship between instructional methods and performance measures will greatly enhance the quality of learning environments and learning outcomes, by improving instructors` ability, the depth of content in class, and students` performance on courses. This is also believed and desired to build up to the expectation that graduate students secure meaningful positions with their gained knowledge and skill in colleges.

CONCLUSION

This chapter explored the influence of using game development on academic performance in programming courses at the undergraduate level in Jordanian universities. The main outcome of the study was that the use of game development learning improved students' academic achievement in C++ and Object-Oriented Programming at a public university in the northern of Jordan. This result is consistent with previous studies documenting the statistical significance of computer-based learning on students' outcomes at the college level. The study utilized original data obtained from a field experiment conducted by the researcher in 2018. The researcher recruited three groups of students, those who took an online course using GDBL, those who completed part of the course and those who did not participate.

Across all assessments, C++ and OOP, students who completed the course performed better than the two other groups. This research urges computer science departments to incorporate game development as a mandatory part in programming courses to improve students' motivation and academic outcomes.

REFERENCES

Alkhawaldeh, N., & Menchaca, M. (2014). Barriers to Utilizing ICT in Education in Jordan. *International Journal on E-Learning, 13*(2), 127–155.

Baytak, A., Land, S. M., & Smith, B. K. (2011). Children as Educational Computer Game Designers: An Exploratory Study. *TOJET: The Turkish Online Journal of Educational Technology, 10*(4).

Beck, M. (2010). *Civic Participation and Local Development: Building Effective Communities in Jordan*. Publications, Jordan Office. Retrieved from http://www.kas.de/jordanien/en/publications/19795/

Belland, B. R., Walker, A. E., Kim, N. J., & Lefler, M. (2017). Synthesizing results from empirical research on computer-based scaffolding in STEM education: A meta-analysis. *Review of Educational Research, 87*(2), 309–344. doi:10.3102/0034654316670999 PMID:28344365

Bureau of Labor Statistics. (2019). *Occupational Outlook Handbook*. Retrieved from https://www.bls.gov/ooh/computer-and-information-technology/computer-and-information-research-scientists.htm

Charlier, N., & De Fraine, B. (2012). Game-Based Learning in Teacher Education: A Strategy to Integrate Digital Games into Secondary Schools. *International Journal of Game-Based Learning, 2*(2), 1–12. doi:10.4018/ijgbl.2012040101

Creswell, J. W. (2013). *Qualitative inquiry and research design: choosing among five approaches* (3rd ed.). Los Angeles, CA: SAGE Publications.

Dalal, N., Kak, S., & Sohoni, S. (2012). Rapid digital game creation for learning object-oriented concepts. In *Proceedings of Informing Science* (pp. 22–27). Montreal, Canada: IT Education Conference. doi:10.28945/1653

Doman, M., Sleigh, M., & Garrison, C. (2015). Effect of GameMaker® on Student Attitudes and Perceptions of Instructors. *International Journal of Modern Education and Computer Science, 7*(9), 1–13. doi:10.5815/ijmecs.2015.09.01

Eagle, M., & Barnes, T. (2009). Experimental evaluation of an educational game for improved learning in introductory computing. *ACM SIGCSE Bulletin, 41*(1), 321–325. doi:10.1145/1539024.1508980

Ernst, J. V., & Clark, A. C. (2012). Fundamental Computer Science Conceptual Understandings for High School Students Using Original Computer Game Design. *Journal of STEM Education: Innovations and Research, 13*(5), 40.

Hamari, J., Shernoff, D. J., Rowe, E., Coller, B., Asbell-Clarke, J., & Edwards, T. (2016). Challenging games help students learn: An empirical study on engagement, flow and immersion in game-based learning. *Computers in Human Behavior, 54*, 170–179. doi:10.1016/j.chb.2015.07.045

Ismail, M. N., Ngah, N. A., & Umar, I. N. (2010). Instructional Strategy in the Teaching of Computer Programming: A Need Assessment Analyses. *TOJET: The Turkish Online Journal of Educational Technology, 9*(2).

Jenson, J., & Droumeva, M. (2015). Making games with Game Maker: A computational thinking curriculum case study. In *ECGBL2015-9th European Conference on Games Based Learning: ECGBL2015* (p. 260). Academic Conferences and Publishing Limited.

Johnson, C. (2017). Learning to Program with Game Maker. *Online Submission, 1*(2).

Jong, M. S., Shang, J., & Lee, F. (2010). Constructivist Learning Through Computer Gaming. In M. Syed (Ed.), Technologies Shaping Instruction and Distance Education: New Studies and Utilizations (pp. 207–222). Hershey, PA: Academic Press. doi:10.4018/978-1-60566-934-2.ch014

Kindler, E., & Krivy, I. (2011). Object-oriented simulation of systems with sophisticated control. *International Journal of General Systems, 40*(3), 313–343. doi:10.1080/03081079.2010.539975

Kunkle, W. M., & Allen, R. B. (2016). The Impact of Different Teaching Approaches and Languages on Student Learning of Introductory Programming Concepts. *ACM Transactions on Computing Education, 16*(1), 3:1–3:26.

Majgaard, G. (2014). The Playful and Reflective Game Designer. *Electronic Journal of E-Learning, 12*(3), 271–280.

Marlow, C. M. (2012). Making Games for Environmental Design Education: Revealing Landscape Architecture. *International Journal of Gaming and Computer-Mediated Simulations, 4*(2), 60–83. doi:10.4018/jgcms.2012040104

Overmars, M. (2004). *Game design in education*. Academic Press.

Papastergiou, M. (2009). Digital Game-Based Learning in high school Computer Science education: Impact on educational effectiveness and student motivation. *Computers & Education, 52*(1), 1–12. doi:10.1016/j.compedu.2008.06.004

Papert, S., & Harel, I. (1991). Situating constructionism. *Constructionism, 36*, 1–11.

Patton, R. M. (2011). *Games as artistic medium: Interfacing complexity theory in game-based art pedagogy*. Academic Press.

Piaget, J. (1976). Piaget's Theory. In B. Inhelder, H. H. Chipman, & C. Zwingmann (Eds.), *Piaget and His School: A Reader in Developmental Psychology* (pp. 11–23). Berlin: Springer Berlin Heidelberg. doi:10.1007/978-3-642-46323-5_2

Plass, J. L., Homer, B. D., & Kinzer, C. K. (2015). Foundations of game-based learning. *Educational Psychologist, 50*(4), 258–283. doi:10.1080/00461520.2015.1122533

Porter, L., Guzdial, M., McDowell, C., & Simon, B. (2013). Success in introductory programming: What works? *Communications of the ACM, 56*(8), 34–36. doi:10.1145/2492007.2492020

Pretelín-ricárdez, A., & Sacristán, A. I. (2015). Videogame Construction by Engineering Students for Understanding Modelling Processes: The Case of Simulating Water Behaviour. *Informatics in Education - An International Journal, 14*(2), 265–277.

The Ministry of Higher Education of Jordan. (2015). *The Annual Statistical Report on higher Education in Jordan for the year 2015 – 2016*. Retrieved from http://www.mohe.gov.jo/en/pages/Statistics.aspx

Vygotskiĭ, L. S., & Cole, M. (1978). *Mind in society: the development of higher psychological processes*. Cambridge, MA: Harvard University Press.

Watson, C., & Li, F. W. (2014). Failure rates in introductory programming revisited. In *Proceedings of the 2014 conference on Innovation & technology in computer science education* (pp. 39-44). ACM.

Wu, B., & Wang, A. I. (2012). A Guideline for Game Development-Based Learning: A Literature Review. *International Journal of Computer Games Technology*.

Yarmouk University. (2017a). *Academic Departments*. Retrieved from http://www.yu.edu.jo/index.php

Yarmouk University. (2017b). *Admission & Registration Department*. Retrieved from http://admreg.yu.edu.jo/index.php?option=com_docman&task=cat_view&gid=154&Itemid=159

ADDITIONAL READING

Brandenburger, A. M., & Nalebuff, B. J. (1995). *The right game: Use game theory to shape strategy* (Vol. 76). Harvard Business Review Chicago.

Bruder, P. (2015). Game on: Gamification in the classroom. *Education Digest, 80*(7), 56.

Jenson, J., & Droumeva, M. (2015). Making games with Game Maker: A computational thinking curriculum case study. *ECGBL2015-9th European Conference on Games Based Learning: ECGBL2015*, 260. Academic Conferences and publishing limited.

Jenson, J., & Droumeva, M. (2016). Exploring Media Literacy and Computational Thinking: A Game Maker Curriculum Study. *Electronic Journal of E-Learning, 14*(2), 111–121.

Salen, K. (2007). Gaming literacies: A game design study in action. *Journal of Educational Multimedia and Hypermedia, 16*(3), 301–322.

Van Eck, R. (2006). Digital game-based learning: It's not just the digital natives who are restless. *EDUCAUSE Review, 41*(2), 16.

Wu, B., & Wang, A. I. (2012). A Guideline for Game Development-Based Learning: A Literature Review. *International Journal of Computer Games Technology*.

KEY TERMS AND DEFINITIONS

Academic Performance: Learner's, educator's, or educational institution's achievement of short or long-term educational goals.

Game Development: The process of creating computer games that starts with conception and storyline to computer programming.

Learning Design: The educational process in which a pedagogical model is applied to design instruction and the employment of emergent technologies in variety of settings.

Learning Management System (LMS): A cloud-based software platform that enables learners and educators experience the learning process in an asynchronous or synchronous online setting.

Moodle: An open-source learning management system used by many educational institutions around the world to provide online learning experience to their learners. MOODLE stands for "Modular Object-Oriented Dynamic Learning Environment."

Object-Oriented Programming (OOP): A computer programming approach where the programmer perceives the problem to be solved as objects. It is the matter of defining data not the process.

Programming Courses: Courses provided by educational institutions for learners to learn the fundamentals of computer programming using selected computer programming languages.

Scaffolding: An instructional approach that helps learners acquire knowledge and skill to elevate to a better understanding and independence in the learning process.

Section 5

Integrating Digital Technology in Multiple Intelligences–Based Teaching and Learning: Intra- and Inter-Personal Intelligences

Chapter 13
Multiple Intelligences Analysis and Emotional Implications in STEM Education for Students up to K–12

Esperanza Rosiña
University of Extremadura, Spain

M. Luisa Bermejo
University of Extremadura, Spain

Miriam del Barco
University of Extremadura, Spain

Florentina Cañada
University of Extremadura, Spain

Jesus Sanchez-Martin
University of Extremadura, Spain

ABSTRACT

This chapter investigates whether there is a relationship between emotional management and the prevailing intelligence profile of a sample of pupils in the last year of primary education and two years of lower secondary education with respect to their learning in STEM subjects. A questionnaire was designed to collect information on multiple intelligences and the emotional factor. The sample comprised 143 pupils from the 6th of primary education and 2nd and 4th of secondary education classes in a state school. It was found that the pupils with a predominantly logical-mathematical and/or visual-spatial intelligence also scored better on the items related to the emotional and adaptation factor in science classes.

DOI: 10.4018/978-1-7998-0249-5.ch013

INTRODUCTION

In the last 40 years, we have been witnessing a steady decline in scientific vocations. Fewer and fewer students are choosing to pursue degree courses related to STEM (Science Technology Engineering Mathematics) subjects (Vázquez & Manassero, 2011, 2008; Ardies, De Maeyer & Gijbels, 2015). Studies show that while pupils' interest in science is present in primary education, it decreases as they progress to compulsory secondary education. At this latter level, a progressive attitudinal depression is detected towards science content, with pupils pointing to them as being difficult and of no use for their everyday lives (Osborne, Simon & Collins, 2003). In any given class, there are pupils who have different ways of learning, and, as the teaching goes deeper into more abstract content, this separation grows. In part, this is because the teaching methods tend to be homogeneous, so that many pupils are left out with their interests or "other way" of learning not taken into account. According to Sánchez-Martín, Álvarez, Dávila & Mellado (2017a), awareness of pupils' emotions in face of the knowledge and practices in the classroom favours the teacher's control and direction of the teaching and learning process.

Until relatively recently, the pupils' emotional environment was not the competence of formal education which instead focused on teaching knowledge and social rules without taking into account the pupils' characteristics, individual skills, motivations, etc (Mellado et al., 2014). The present work revolves around two concepts of great relevance in recent years in the field of education: the affective domain and "multiple intelligences", both related to the learner's integral cognitive and affective development.

The objectives that we set for the study were: (1) to determine the attitudes of pupils (ages 11 to 15 years) in 6th of primary and 2nd and 4th of lower secondary (denoted ESO in Spain) through their stress management, adaptability, and general mood in relation to learning STEM content; (2) to analyse the relationship of these affective factors with the different intelligences that the pupils present; and (3) to compare the results found between the different school years.

THEORETICAL BACKGROUND

Emotions in the Teaching and Learning of Science

The emphasis of science teaching research has been on the cognitive factors involved in teaching and learning different science subjects. Enrolment in different science degree courses has declined in recent years perhaps due to an adverse emotional scenario being developed concerning learning in general, in which the cognitive is perceived as predominating and its concepts as being irrelevant for life outside school (Vázquez & Manassero, 2011; Ardies, De Maeyer & Gijbels, 2015). Given also that positive attitudinal and affective factors decrease with age from the primary to the secondary education stages (Pérez & de Pro, 2013; Vázquez & Manassero, 2008, 2011), these factors should be even more strongly worked on during secondary since this is the educational stage with the greatest failure rate. Affectivity not only has a very positive influence on learning, but also should itself be taken into account as a result of learning (Koballa & Glynn, 2007).

In recent years, the study of emotions in the teaching and learning of science and technology has been a major subject of research in education in these subjects (Mellado et al., 2014). Different studies have found that university students have a very positive emotional memory of science subjects during their primary education (Brígido, 2014). However, their memory of their emotions as secondary pupils depends on the content: positive for Biology and Geology, and negative for Physics and Chemistry (Brígido et al., 2010, 2013a,b). The causal attributions of these emotions are related to the content, the teacher, and the pupil themself, with boys and girls differing depending on the content (Borrachero, Brígido, Mellado, Costillo & Mellado, 2014), with the emotions being generally more intense in girls (Hazari, Tai & Sadler, 2007). Tomas, Rigano & Ritchie (2016) found a relationship between class activities and the regulation of the emotions of secondary pupils when they were learning science. Emotions influence the pupils' motivation, interest, and commitment when they are learning. The results of the study of Da Silva, Rico, Souza, and Losch (2015) on the influence of the introduction of inquiry activities in a secondary science class on the pupils' emotions are in the same line.

One tries harder and works harder in what one feels one is most effective and competent at (Huinker & Madison, 1997). One therefore should not avoid being aware of the concept of self-efficacy in learning. Indeed, beliefs about self-efficacy and emotions are related (Pajares, 1992). But not only can one's own abilities be enabled or suppressed by emotions, but conceptions can also play an important role in this process (Wood & Bandura, 1989). Self-efficacy is the belief in one's competence to perform a task (Bandura, 1986). If a pupil considers him/herself to be competent in learning a subject they will have more motivation and commitment. They will regard challenges as stimulants, and their expectations of success will be heightened.

Self-efficacy is closely related to self-regulation, and is an important predictor variable for student achievement (Cakiroglu & Isiksal 2009). Thus self-efficacy and self-regulation are aspects which are essential for learning and for achieving possibilities in learning (Pintrich & De Groot, 1990). A person's concept of security, challenges, and expectations will have a positive influence in facing the difficulties that they will encounter in the teaching and learning process. According to Brigido et al. (2013a), there is a correlation between the negative emotions that pupils have of a subject and their self-efficacy. Negative self-efficacy is correlated with a negative emotion. It is therefore necessary to know what the pupil's profile is so as to be able to define strategies for each subject, and this knowledge would also be interesting in making vocational decisions (Pérez & Beltrán, 2006). Kurbanoğlu and Akin (2012) related self-efficacy specifically with attitudes and emotions in learning Chemistry.

Pupils' Profile and Theory of Multiple Intelligences

The studies contributed by Gardner (1983, 1989, 2005) represented a great advance in theories of education, including their introduction of the theory of multiple intelligences. This noted how intelligence has traditionally been focused on mathematical or linguistic skills and abilities as measured with an IQ. For Gardner (2005, p.27): *"Intelligence is the ability to solve problems, or to elaborate products that are of great value for a specific community or cultural context."*

Gardner's theory includes eight types of intelligence. These are detailed in Table 1, together with the characteristics of the pupils' who stand out in them, what they like, and how they learn best depending on their type of intelligence.

For Gardner (2005), IQ tests exclusively measure linguistic and logical-mathematical skills. They can predict academic success, which is primarily based on the resolution of problems of this type, but not professional, social, or personal success. The application of multiple intelligences can help to improve the learning and integration of different pupils (Barrington, 2004). Koifman (1998), for example, studied the relationships between emotional intelligence and creativity and life satisfaction. Loori (2005) applied the theory to compare the learning of boys and girls in secondary education, and concluded that boys

Table 1. Multiple intelligences (Adapted from Gardner, 1983)

Type of intelligence	Outstanding in ...	Likes to ...	Learns best ...
Linguistic-verbal	Reading, writing, storytelling, memorizing dates, think of words	Read, write, tell stories, speak, memorize, do jigsaw puzzles	Reading, listening to and seeing words, speaking, writing, discussing and debating
Logical-mathematical	Maths, reasoning, logic, problem solving, patterns	Solve problems, question, work with numbers, experiment	Using patterns and relationships, classifying, working with the abstract
Visual-spatial	Using patterns and relationships, classifying, working with the abstract	Design, draw, build, create, daydream, look at drawings	Working with drawings and colours, visualizing, seeing with the mind's eye, drawing
Bodily-kinæsthetic	Athletics, dance, dramatic art, handicrafts, use of tools	Move about, touch and speak, body language	Touching, moving about, processing information through bodily sensations
Musical	Singing, recognizing sounds, remembering melodies, rhythms	Sing, hum, play an instrument, listen to music	Rhythm, melody, singing, listening to music and melodies
Interpersonal	Understanding people, leading, organizing, communicating, resolving conflicts, selling	Have friends, talk with people, get together with people	Sharing, comparing, relating, interviewing, cooperating
Intrapersonal	Self-awareness, recognizing your strengths and weaknesses, setting goals	Work alone, reflect, follow their interests	Working alone, doing projects at your own pace, giving yourself room, reflecting
Naturalistic	Understanding nature, making distinctions, identifying flora and fauna	Participate in nature, make distinctions	Working in the natural environment, exploring living beings, learning about plants and topics of nature

prefer activities related to logical-mathematical intelligence and girls prefer those related to intrapersonal intelligence. Recent studies by Sosa and Ortega (2011) indicate that, in addition to arithmetic and linguistic intelligences, lower secondary education pupils have developed musical, interpersonal, and bodily intelligences. Fernández, Bermejo, Sainz, Ferrando, and Prieto (2008) analysed the development of logical-mathematical intelligence in pre-primary and primary education pupils.

One particularly strong point of Gardner's theory of multiple intelligences is its direct applicability to educational practice (Sánchez & Llera, 2006). But traditional education has forgotten that there are other types of intelligences, and that these have already evolved in the pupils but have been given no methodological coverage – intellectual skills that pupils already have but are not taken advantage of. This abandonment has led to the pupils' discouragement and distancing themselves from learning Science and Technology. Gardner (2005) rejects a uniform school, and defends a school focused on the individual. He considers that "the objective of the school should be to develop intelligences and help people achieve vocational goals and hobbies that are appropriate to their particular spectrum of intelligences" (Gardner, 2005, p.30). According to Gardner's theory of multiple intelligences (2005), these should be used as a tool in the class for the teacher to adapt the content to the characteristics of the pupils, as this will generate experiences that are more satisfactory for them and therefore more positive emotions that favour meaningful learning. Gardner (2005) considered that any topic can be approached in various ways related to the different intelligences, and that a competent teacher should address each

Multiple Intelligences Analysis and Emotional Implications in STEM Education

topic using strategies that are adapted to the different pupil profiles. "*A skilful teacher is a person who can open many different windows to the same concept*" (Gardner, 2005, p.269).

There are antecedents of research on learning which are based on multiple intelligences (Bower, Highfield, Furney & Mowbray, 2013; Escamilla, 2014; Mokhtar, Majid, & Foo, 2008). In the subjects of Science and Technology, methods based on multiple intelligences encourage pupil-centred classes (Goodnough, 2001), pupil creativity (Cheng, 2004), and a greater variety of activities (Karamustafaoglu, 2010).

Gallegos, Sagaz, Sánchez, Huerto, & Sánchez (2013) combined Science and Art with the aim of promoting intelligence and creativity in 2nd of primary pupils. The results show the process in which scientific concepts are understood through communication using sound and movement, and through how an orchestra or a dance is organized, and, above all, through the resolution of problems related to Science and Art. Sánchez-Martín et al. (2017a) noted the importance of knowing the types of intelligence pupils have in order to be able to offer them various learning techniques. Together with the ability to interpret the emotional events that occur within the individual, this will provide us as teachers with the control and direction of the teaching and learning process, and increase the chances of success. Sánchez-Martín, Gragera, Dávila & Mellado (2017b) studied the emotions of secondary education pupils in the subject of Technology depending on their types of intelligence. Among their conclusions, those authors noted the strong relationship between the pupils' intellectual profiles and the emotions generated depending on the contents of the subject. In the same line, authors such as Olitsky & Milne (2012) and Vázquez & Manassero (2007) are in agreement that positive emotional states favour the learning of science and pupils' commitment as active learners, while negative states limit the ability to learn.

THE STUDY

A non-experimental or ex post facto quantitative method was applied for this study. There was no intervention on the part of the researcher, who was limited to analysing and describing the data collected. In addition, this was a causal-correlational experimental study since, through this design, the data were acquired at a given moment and then analysed to establish relationships among them. The selection of the study sample was by non-probabilistic convenience or accidental sampling. The reason for this choice was the limitation in the availability of cases.

The sample comprised 143 pupils, corresponding to three course years – 6th of primary education, and 2nd and 4th of secondary – in a state school in the city of Badajoz (Spain) during the 2017/2018 academic year (Table 2).

Table 2. Distribution of the sample by year

Year	N° of pupils	Percentage
6th of primary	44	31%
2nd of secondary	55	38%
4th of secondary	44	31%
Total	**143**	**100%**

We chose to acquire the data for the study using a questionnaire as instrument. Some of the advantages offered by questionnaires when collecting data are their ease of execution and evaluation, and the possibility of directly comparing groups and individuals (Hopkins, 1989).

Given the objectives of the study, we designed a conjoint questionnaire based on that of Bar-On (1997) on the emotional factor and adaptability in STEM content classes, and that of Armstrong (2006) on multiple intelligences (Annexes I and II). The teachers responsible for the different courses were asked to hand out the questionnaires. It took the pupils approximately 25 minutes to complete the questionnaire.

Firstly, the "*Bar-On Emotional Intelligence Inventory for Young People (EQi-YV)*" is a questionnaire developed and structured around the analysis of five components including those of adaptability, general mood, and stress management which, together with other aspects, form the emotional coefficient. In these three sections, the original questionnaire formulated items about emotions in a general way. In our case, we drafted items that contextualized these same aspects for STEM subjects (Annex II). Each item is measured on a 4-point Likert scale, with 1 being "*Never*" and 4 "*Always*".

Secondly, we adapted Thomas Armstrong's multiple intelligences questionnaire to the characteristics of our sample. This adaptation was made on the basis of Sánchez-Martín et al (2017a, b), simply rewriting the specific questions related to Secondary Education to Primary Education. This questionnaire measures the different intelligences that may be present in pupils through their responses to simple items centred on Logical-mathematical I., Linguistic I., Visual-spatial I., Musical I., Interpersonal I., Intrapersonal I., Bodily-kinæsthetic I., and Naturalistic I. Each item is measured on a 4-point Likert scale with 0 being "*Never*" and 3 "*Always*".

For the data analysis, we used the Microsoft Office 2016 statistical program, making a descriptive analysis, constructing frequency tables and bar graphs, and calculating such descriptive statistics as the percentages. In the inferential analysis, we worked with a confidence level of 95%.

The following tests were used:

- A single-factor ANOVA to analyse the variance and check whether there are significant differences between the means.
- Student's t test for two independent samples to know whether there are significant differences between the means.
- Pearson's correlations to find whether there are significant relationships or associations between two quantitative variables.

The Significance of Study

Regarding the pupils' sociodemographic characteristics, 58% of the sample were girls and the remaining 42% boys. By year, 31% were in 6th of primary, 38% in 2nd of secondary, and 31% in 4th of secondary. Figure 1 shows the results for the mean values of the multiple intelligences scores depending on the year.

As can be seen in the figure (bearing in mind that the minimum score was 0 and the maximum 3), the means obtained by the pupils for each of the intelligences were between 1.5 and 2 points. For 6th of primary, the lowest score corresponded to Intrapersonal Intelligence, and the highest to Bodily-kinæsthetic I. followed by Interpersonal I. and Naturalistic I. For 2nd of secondary, the highest score corresponded to Interpersonal I. followed by Bodily-kinæsthetic I, while the lowest scores were in Naturalistic I. and

Multiple Intelligences Analysis and Emotional Implications in STEM Education

Figure 1. Multiple intelligences by year (PE: primary education; SE: Secondary education)

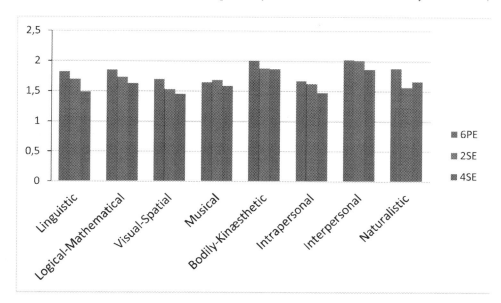

Visual-spatial I. Finally, for 4th of secondary, the mean of the pupils' scores for the different intelligences was lower than in the previous years. The lowest values of around 1.5 points corresponded to Linguistic I., Visual-spatial I., Musical I., and Intrapersonal I. The highest scores corresponded to Bodily-kinæsthetic I. and Interpersonal I., although they did not reach 2 points.

Table 3 presents the results of the single-factor ANOVA carried out to check if there were significant differences between the mean values found for each intelligence in the different years, giving the F-statistic and the significance (Sig.) for a confidence level of 95%. One observes that there were significant differences ($p<0.05$) in the mean values obtained for the Linguistic and Naturalistic Intelligences. However, the norm was that all the different intelligences were found in each year with there being no significant differences.

In the following, we shall describe the results corresponding to the sections of adaptability, stress management, and general mood in sciences for each of the years. Figure 2 shows the mean values that

Table 3. Single-factor ANOVA by year for the scores obtained for the multiple intelligences (MI)

MI	F	Sig.
Linguistic	3.743	0.026*
Logical-mathematical	1.311	0.273
Visual-spatial	2.491	0.086
Musical	0.274	0.761
Bodily-kinæsthetic	1.094	0.337
Intrapersonal	1.959	0.145
Interpersonal	1.646	0.196
Naturalistic	3.186	0.044*

Figure 2. Mean value of adaptability by year (PE: Primary Education; SE: Secondary Education)

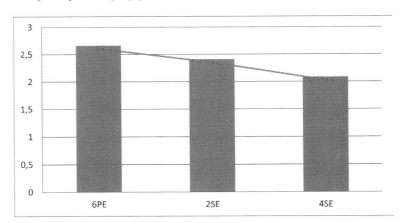

the pupils obtained in the aspect of adaptability, differentiated by year. As can be seen, the pupils with the highest scores belonged to 6th of primary followed by those in 2nd of secondary, with those in 4th of secondary being last. The line drawn indicates that the trend in this case is decreasing. In order to determine the degree of significance of these differences, Student's t test for two independent samples was performed at a 95% confidence level. The result showed that there were significant differences ($p<0.05$) between the means for each of the years.

Figure 3 shows the means of the pupils' results for stress management depending on the year.

As can be seen in the figure, the pupils with the most positive results were those belonging to 6th of primary, with a mean of 2.75 points. The lowest scores were those for the 2nd of secondary education, with a mean of 2.36 points. As in the previous case, the trend line indicates a decrease with year. We performed a Student's t test for two independent samples at a 95% confidence level in order to check whether the differences were significant. The result showed there to be significant differences between the mean values for 6th of primary and 2nd of secondary ($p=0.0012$) and between 6th of primary and 4th of secondary ($p=0.014$).

Figure 3. Mean value of stress management by year

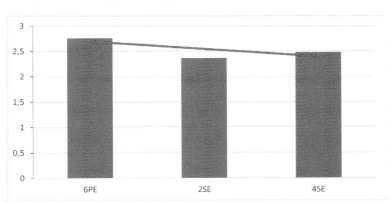

Finally, Figure 4 shows the mean values obtained for general mood depending on the years that were studied.

The 6th of primary pupils presented the highest values for general mood in sciences, with a mean of 3.21 points, as can be seen in the figure. One observes the decreasing trend as the educational level increases: in 2nd of secondary the mean for general mood in sciences was 3.01, and in 4th of secondary it dropped to 2.67 points.

To check whether the differences were significant, as in the previous cases we applied Student's t test. For a confidence level of 95%, the results showed there to be significant differences between 6th of primary and 4th of secondary, and between the 2nd and 4th years of secondary, with $p<0.05$ in both cases.

The results obtained by the 6th of primary pupils for stress management, adaptability, and general mood were positive, exceeding the overall mean in each section analysed. In all the sections, the mean for these pupils surpassed 2.5 points (bearing in mind that the minimum score was 1 and the maximum 4). The aspect of adaptability had the lowest score, behind that for stress management. General mood in sciences was the highest scoring section, obtaining a mean of 3.21 points, indicating that the pupils had good attitudes and positive emotions towards the study of STEM subjects.

The aspect for which the 2nd of secondary pupils obtained the lowest scores was stress management with a mean value of 2.36 points, only slightly surpassed by adaptability. The general mood in sciences was the section with the highest mean value for these pupils, reaching 3 points.

The mean scores of the 4th of secondary pupils for the three sections analysed were between 2 and 3 points. The aspect with the lowest mean value was that of adaptability (2.08 points). The mean value for stress management was 2.47 points, and for general mood in sciences 2.67 points, this being the lowest mean value of the three years studied in this aspect.

In view of the results found for the different comparisons, we can affirm that there were significant differences in adaptability, stress management, and general mood in sciences depending on the year the pupils were in, and that, in the line of the studies of Vázquez & Manassero (2011), there were better results for primary than for secondary pupils, with a progressive descent as the educational level increased. In particular, the present results for the general mood in sciences are concordant with those reported by Dávila, Borrachero, Cañada & Sánchez-Martín (2016) in a study of the emotions of 2nd, 3rd, and 4th

Figure 4. Mean value of general mood by year

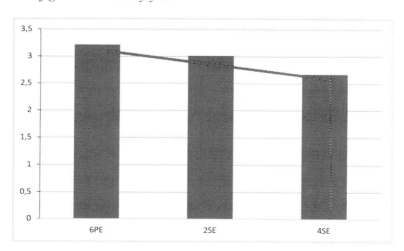

of secondary education pupils regarding their learning of Physics and Chemistry which found positive emotions to decrease as the educational level increased.

We studied the relationship between each pupil's score in the different intelligences and those they assigned to the affective factors (general mood in sciences, adaptability, and stress management). The purpose was to see if there was any relationship between the score obtained in each intelligence and the score given to each of the above factors. In particular, we looked at whether the pupils whose predominant intelligence was logical-mathematical, visual-spatial, or naturalistic showed higher levels of stress management, adaptability, and mood towards STEM content subjects. The comparison was made using Pearson's correlation test. Table 4 lists the correlation coefficients found in each case.

The strongest correlations in all the years were obtained for logical-mathematical intelligence followed by visual-spatial intelligence with both the general mood in sciences and adaptability. This means that the pupils in whom these intelligences predominate usually scored highly on items related to the mood in sciences and to adaptability, and vice versa. In addition, the trend was similar in the three years, increasing in the 2nd and 4th of secondary relative to 6th of primary education. Therefore, we can say that those pupils who have a high logical-mathematical and/or visual-spatial intelligence will also have more positive attitudes and emotions towards the study of STEM subjects. These intelligences predominate in individuals who have more facility for mathematics, abstract operations, and problem solving, as well as in activities where they are required to visualize objects, to make models, etc. All of these are activities that are linked to the contexts of science in general, mathematics, technology, and engineering.

FUTURE RESEARCH AND CONCLUSION

In relation to the objectives proposed at the beginning of the study, we have been able to determine the different intelligences presented by pupils of the 6th year of primary education, and the 2nd and 4th years of secondary education. Sánchez-Martín et al. (2017a) note the importance of knowing the different types of intelligence that pupils have and their management of emotions. This is why we have sought to determine the intelligences present in the subjects of our sample.

Table 4. Pearson correlation (r) between the different types of intelligences and the affective factors studied

Type of Intelligence	Mood in Science (r) 6PE	2SE	4 SE	Adaptability (r) 6PE	2SE	4SE	Stress management (r) 6PE	2SE	4SE
Linguistic	0.401	0.069	0.217	0.379	0.102	0.188	0.390	0.217	0.154
Logical-mathematical	0.373	0.422	0.401	0.392	0.548	0.564	0.086	0.380	0.077
Visual-spatial	0.383	0.293	0.176	0.319	0.348	0.321	0.044	0.109	-0.152
Musical	0.223	0.139	0.189	0.172	0.333	0.072	0.088	-0.071	-0.066
Bodily-kinæsthetic	0.220	0.148	0.145	0.336	0.125	0.085	0.240	0.067	-0.162
Intrapersonal	0.107	0.106	0.219	0.262	0.192	0.133	-0.003	-0.183	0.039
Interpersonal	0.266	0.177	0.274	0.365	0.174	0.260	0.095	-0.036	0.069
Naturalistic	0.204	0.289	0.158	0.100	0.409	0.106	-0.017	0.146	-0.193

Multiple Intelligences Analysis and Emotional Implications in STEM Education

With respect to the pupils' emotional management through how they deal with stress, their adaptability, and their general mood in STEM subjects, this was found to vary according to their course year. This variation followed the line reported in other studies which have found the presence of negative emotions towards the sciences and a worrying increase of these emotions as the pupils advance in level, this being especially visible in secondary education (Solbes, 2011; Vázquez & Manassero, 2011; Dávila et al., 2016). Sánchez-Martín et al. (2017b) describe a strong relationship between pupils' intellectual profiles and the emotional management that they show in a given subject. Those authors point out that the teacher's awareness of this situation can help improve the teaching and learning process as such awareness will guide the adaptation of the content to their pupils' profile. This will enhance the pupils' educational performance and success, and consequently foster positive emotions towards the subject in question.

We studied the relationship between the scores each pupil obtained in the different intelligences and the scores they assigned to the affective factors (general mood in science, adaptability, and stress management). In all three years, the strongest correlations were found between logical-mathematical followed by visual-spatial intelligence and both adaptability and the general mood in sciences. This means that the pupils in whom these intelligences predominate usually scored highly on items related to the mood in sciences and to adaptability, and vice versa. In addition, the trend was similar in the three years, increasing in the 2nd and 4th of secondary relative to 6th of primary education. Therefore, we can say that those pupils who have a high logical-mathematical and/or visual-spatial intelligence will also have more positive attitudes and emotions towards the study of the sciences. These intelligences predominate in individuals who have more facility for mathematics, abstract operations, and problem solving, as well as in activities where they are required to visualize objects, to make models, etc. All of these are activities that are linked to the contexts of science in general, mathematics, technology, and engineering.

The data obtained are in agreement with those obtained by Brigido et al. (2013a) in a study with prospective teachers. They found that, in the subjects of Physics and Chemistry, the students who showed high self-efficacy also had more emotions that were positive towards those subjects. These data were corroborated by Borrachero (2015) in a study with students in the first years of various degree courses in the University of Extremadura, in which they were surveyed about their recall of the emotions they had experienced in their Secondary Education. The most positive emotions in the subjects of science, mathematics, and technology were recalled by those students who were from degree courses linked to scientific and technological disciplines.

With respect to naturalistic intelligence (which is the intelligence most closely related to the study of Biology or Geology content), we found no clear trend in either the general mood in sciences or adaptability. I.e., a pupil with high naturalistic intelligence does not necessarily tend to show positive attitudes and/or emotions towards the sciences in general. Results with prospective teachers (Brígido et al., 2013a) indicate that, for the teaching of biology, self-efficacy has no influence on their emotions.

The correlation data between the three emotional aspects studied and the intelligences other than logical-mathematical, visual-spatial, and naturalistic showed no clear trend.

On the other hand, increased science attitudes in our students are linked with engages to pupils in learning activities in the classroom such as science workshop, socio-scientific issues in the local community, etc. (Olsen, Prenzel & Martin, 2011). This idea was also referenced by Martínez Borreguero, Naranjo-Correa, Mateos-Núñez & Sánchez-Martín (2018) when recreational experiences were put in relationship with curricular contents of Primary Education, such as density and pressure.

Finally, this study has allowed a diagnosis to be made of primary and secondary education pupils' emotional management in the science classroom, and its relationship with the intelligences they present. As a future line of work, following Sánchez-Martín et al. (2017a), we would like to include a program of teaching and learning intervention in the science classroom taking into account the pupils' intellectual and emotional profiles. Such a program will foster more satisfactory experiences in this area, and therefore more positive emotions. In addition, bearing in mind the results of the research carried out by Vázquez & Manassero (2011), we want to include an analysis of the variables by gender in our study.

ACKNOWLEDGMENT

This work was funded through Research Project EDU2016-77007-R (AEI/FEDER, EU), Grant *GR18004* and Project IB16068 (Govern of Extremadura / European Fund for Regional Development). Miriam Hernández-Barco thanks to Spain's Ministry of Science, Innovation and Universities by pre-doctoral Grant (BES-2017-081566).

REFERENCES

Ardies, J., De Maeyer, S., & Gijbels, D. (2015). A longitudinal study on boys' and girls' career aspirations and interest in technology. *Research in Science & Technological Education*, *33*(3), 366–386. doi: 10.1080/02635143.2015.1060412

Armstrong, T. (2006). *Inteligencias múltiples en el aula: guía práctica para educadores*. Barcelona: Paidós.

Bandura, A. (1986). *Social foundations of thought and action: A social cognitive theory*. Prentice-Hall.

BarOn, R. (1997). BarOn Emotional Quotient Inventory. Technical manual. Toronto: Multi-Health Systems Inc.

Barrington, E. (2004). Teaching to student diversity in higher education: How Multiple Intelligence Theory can help. *Teaching in Higher Education*, *9*(4), 421–434. doi:10.1080/1356251042000252363

Bath, J. L., Lang, K. E., Roger, K. R., & Neton, K. J. (2016). Using EEG to understand student learning in algebra: The role of examples. *Learning and Instruction*, *25*, 24–34.

Bisquerra, R. (2003). Educación emocional y competencias básicas para la vida. *Revista de Investigación Educacional*, *21*(1), 7–43.

Borrachero, A. B., Brígido, M., Mellado, L., Costillo, E., & Mellado, V. (2014). Emotions in prospective secondary teachers when teaching science content, distinguishing by gender. *Research in Science & Technological Education*, *32*(2), 182–215. doi:10.1080/02635143.2014.909800

Borrachero Cortés, A. B. (2015). *Las emociones en la enseñanza y el aprendizaje de las ciencias en Educación Secundaria* (Doctoral Thesis). Universidad de Extremadura.

Bower, M., Highfield, K., Furney, P., & Mowbray, L. (2013). Supporting pre-service teachers' technology-enabled learning design thinking through whole of programme transformation. *Educational Media International, 50*(1), 39–50. doi:10.1080/09523987.2013.777183

Brígido, M. (2014). *Programa metacognitivo de intervención emocional en la enseñanza de las ciencias experimentales para maestros de primaria en formación inicial* (Doctoral Thesis). Universidad de Extremadura.

Brígido, M., Bermejo, M. L., Conde, M. C., & Mellado, V. (2010). The emotions in teaching and learning Nature Sciences and Physics/Chemistry in pre-service primary teachers. *US-China Education Review, 7*(12), 25–32.

Brígido, M., Borrachero, A. B., Bermejo, M. L., & Mellado, V. (2013a). Prospective primary teachers' self-efficacy and emotions in science teaching. *European Journal of Teacher Education, 36*(2), 200–217. doi:10.1080/02619768.2012.686993

Brígido, M., Couso, D., Gutiérrez, C., & Mellado, V. (2013b). The Emotions about Teaching and Learning Science: A Study of Prospective Primary Teachers in Three Spanish Universities. *Journal of Baltic Science Education, 12*(3), 299–311.

Cakiroglu, E., & Isiksal, M. (2009). Pre-service elementary teachers' attitudes and self-efficacy beliefs toward mathematics. *Education in Science, 34*(151), 132–139.

Cheng, V. M. (2004). Developing physics learning activities for fostering student creativity in Hong Kong context. *Asia-Pacific Forum on Science Learning and Teaching, 5*(2), 1–33.

Da Silva, V., Rico, E., Souza, D., & Losch de Oliveira, D. (2015). Impacto do uso de estratégias investigativas sobre as emoções e a motivação dos alunos e as suas concepções de ciência e cientista. *Revista Electrónica de Enseñanza de las Ciencias, 14*(1), 17–34.

Dávila Acedo, M. A., Borrachero, A. B., Cañada, F., & Sánchez-Martín, J. (2016). Evolution of emotion in learning physics and chemistry in secondary education. In E. Harvey (Ed.), *Secondary education: Perspectives, global issues and challenges* (pp. 115–132). New York: Nova Science Publisher.

Escamilla, K. (2014). Struggling reader or emerging biliterate student? Reevaluating the criteria for labeling emerging bilingual students as low achieving. *Journal of Literacy Research, 46*(1), 68–89. doi:10.1177/1086296X13504869

Fernández, C., Bermejo, R., Sainz, M., Ferrando, M., & Prieto, M. D. (2008). Estudio del razonamiento lógico-matemático desde el modelo de las inteligencias múltiples. *Anales de Psicología, 24*(2), 213–222.

Gallegos, C., Sagaz, M. A., Sánchez, A., Huerto, M. L. & Sánchez, M. A. (2013). Desarrollo de un proyecto de ciencia basado en el uso de diversas inteligencias. *Revista Eureka sobre Enseñanza y Divulgación de la Ciencia, 10*(1), 100-109.

Gardner, H. (1983). *Frames of Mind: The Theory of Multiple Intelligences*. London: Basic Books.

Gardner, H. (1989). Educational implications of the Theory of Multiple Intelligences. *Educational Researcher, 18*(8), 4–10.

Gardner, H. (2005). *Inteligencias múltiples. La teoría en la práctica*. Madrid: Paidós.

Goodnough, K. (2001). Multiple Intelligences Theory: A Framework for Personalizing Science Curricula. *School Science and Mathematics*, *101*(4), 180–193. doi:10.1111/j.1949-8594.2001.tb18021.x

Hazari, Z., Tai, R. H., & Sadler, P. M. (2007). Gender Differences in Introductory University Physics Performance: The Influence of High School Physics Preparation and Affective Factors. *Science Education*, *91*(6), 847–876. doi:10.1002ce.20223

Hopkins, D. (1989). *Investigación en el aula. Guía del profesor*. Barcelona: PPU.

Huinker, D., & Madison, S. K. (1997). Preparing efficacious elementary teachers in science and mathematics: The influence of methods course. *Journal of Science Teacher Education*, *8*(2), 107–126. doi:10.1023/A:1009466323843

Karamustafaoglu, S. (2010). Evaluating the Science Activities Based On Multiple Intelligence Theory. *Journal of Turkish Science Education*, *7*(1).

Koballa, T. R., & Glynn, S. M. (2007). Attitudinal and Motivational constructs in science learning. In S. K. Abell & N. G. Lederman (Eds.), *Handbook of Research on Science Education* (pp. 75–102). Mahwah, NJ: Erlbaum.

Koifman, R. (1998). *The Relationship between EQ, IQ, and Creativity*. Ontario: University Windsor.

Kurbanoglu, N. I., & Akin, A. (2012). The relationships between university studentsí organic chemistry anxiety, chemistry attitudes, and self-efficacy: A structural equation model. *Journal of Baltic Science Education*, *11*(4), 347–356.

Loori, A. A. (2005). Multiple intelligences: A comparative study between the preferences of males and females. *Social Behavior and Personality*, *33*(1), 77–88. doi:10.2224bp.2005.33.1.77

Martínez Borreguero, M.G., Naranjo-Correa, F.L., & Mateos-Núñez, M. & Sánchez-Martín. (2018). Recreational experiences for teaching basic scientific concepts in Primary Education: The case of density and pressure. *Eurasia Journal of Mathematics. Science and Technology Education*, *14*(12), 1–16.

Mellado, V., Borrachero, A. B., Brígido, M., Melo, L. V., Dávila, M. A., Cañada, F., ... Bermejo, M. L. (2014). Las Emociones en la Enseñanza de las Ciencias. *Enseñanza de las Ciencias*, *32*(3), 11–36.

Mokhtar, I. A., Majid, S., & Foo, S. (2008). Information literacy education: Applications of mediated learning and multiple intelligences. *Library & Information Science Research*, *30*(3), 195–206. doi:10.1016/j.lisr.2007.12.004

Molero, C., Saiz, E., & Esteban, C. (1998). Revisión histórica del concepto de inteligencia: Una aproximación a la inteligencia emocional. *Revista Latinoamericana de Psicología*, *30*, 11–30.

Olitski, S., & Milne, C. (2012). Understanding engagement in science education: The psychological and the social. In B. J. Fraser, K. G. Tobin, & C. J. McRobbie (Eds.), *Second International Handbook of Science Education* (pp. 19–33). Dordrecht: Springer. doi:10.1007/978-1-4020-9041-7_2

Olsen, R. V., Prenzel, M., & Martin, R. (2011). Interest in Science: A many-faceted picture painted by data from the OECD PISA study. *International Journal of Science Education, 33*(1), 1–6. doi:10.1080/09500693.2010.518639

Osborne, J., Simon, S., & Collins, S. (2003). Attitudes towards science: A review of the literature and its implications. *International Journal of Science Education, 25*(9), 1049–1079. doi:10.1080/0950069032000032199

Pajares, F. (1992). Teachers' beliefs and educational research: Cleaning up a messy construct. *Review of Educational Research, 62*(3), 307–332. doi:10.3102/00346543062003307

Pérez, L., & Beltrán, J. (2006). Dos décadas de Inteligencias Múltiples: Implicaciones para la psicología de la educación. *Papeles del Psicólogo, 3*, 147–164.

Pintrich, P. R., & De Groot, E. V. (1990). Motivational and self-regulated learning components of classroom academic performance. *Journal of Educational Psychology, 82*(1), 33–40. doi:10.1037/0022-0663.82.1.33

Sánchez, L., & Llera, J. (2006). Dos décadas de inteligencias múltiples: Implicaciones para la psicología de la educación. *Papeles del Psicólogo, 27*(3), 147–164.

Sánchez-Martín, J., Álvarez Gragera, G. J., Dávila Acedo, M. A., & Mellado, V. (2017a). Teaching technology: From knowing to feeling enhancing emotional and content acquisition performance through Gardner's multiple intelligences theory in technology and design lessons. *Journal of Technology and Science Education, 7*(1), 58–79. doi:10.3926/jotse.238

Sánchez-Martín, J., Álvarez Gragera, G. J., Dávila Acedo, M. A., & Mellado, V. (2017b). What do K-12 students feel when dealing with technology and engineering issues? Gardner's multiple intelligence theory implications in technology lessons for motivating engineering vocations at Spanish Secondary School. *European Journal of Engineering Education, 42*(6), 1330–1343. doi:10.1080/03043797.2017.1292216

Solbes, J. (2011). ¿Por qué disminuye el alumnado de ciencias? *Alambique: Didáctica de las ciencias experimentales, 17*(67), 53-61.

Sosa & Ortega (2011). Análisis sobre los tipos de inteligencias en estudiantes de educación secundaria y universidad. *Revista Iberoamericana de educación matemática, 26*, 89-102.

Tomas, L., Rigano, D., & Ritchie, S. M. (2016). Students' Regulation of Their Emotions in a Science Classroom. *Journal of Research in Science Teaching, 53*(2), 234–260. doi:10.1002/tea.21304

Vázquez, A. & Manassero, M. (2007). En defensa de las actitudes y emociones en la educación científica (I): Evidencias y argumentos generales. *Revista Eureka sobre Enseñanza y Divulgación de las Ciencias, 4*(2), 247-271.

Vázquez, A. & Manassero, M.A. (2008). El declive de las actitudes hacia la ciencia de los estudiantes: un indicador inquietante para la educación científica. *Revista Eureka sobre Enseñanza y Divulgación de las Ciencias, 5*(3), 274-292.

Vázquez, A., & Manassero, M. A. (2011). El descenso de las actitudes hacia la ciencia de chicos y chicas en la Educación Obligatoria. *Ciência & Educação (Bauru), 17*(2), 249–268. doi:10.1590/S1516-73132011000200001

Wood, R., & Bandura, A. (1989). Social Cognitive Theory of organizational management. *Academy of Management Review, 14*(3), 361–384. doi:10.5465/amr.1989.4279067

ADDITIONAL READING

Abdi1, A., Laei, S. & Ahmadyan, H. (2013). The Effect of Teaching Strategy Based on Multiple Intelligences on Students' Academic Achievement in Science Course. *Universal Journal of Educational Research, 1*(4), 281-284.

Ahvan, Y. R., & Pour, H. Z. (2016). The correlation of multiple intelligences for the achievements of secondary students. *Educational Research Review, 11*(4), 141–145. doi:10.5897/ERR2015.2532

Akkuzu, N., & Akçay, H. (2011). The design of a learning environment based on the theory of multiple intelligence and the study its effectiveness on the achievements, attitudes and retention of students. *Procedia Computer Science, 3*(0), 1003–1008. doi:10.1016/j.procs.2010.12.165

Armstrong, T. (2009). *Multiple Intelligences in the Classroom*. Alexandria, VA: Association of Supervision and Curriculum Development.

Choliz, M. (2005). *Emotion psychology. The emotional process*. Available online at: http://goo.gl/3ZBptJ

Díaz-Posada, L. D., Varela-Londoño, S. P., & Rodríguez-Burgos, L. P. (2017). Multiple Intelligences and Curriculum Implementation: Progress, Trends and Opportunities. *Journal of Psychodidactics, 22*(1), 69–83.

Furnham, A., Wytykowska, A., & Petrides, K. V. (2005). Estimates of Multiple Intelligences: A Study in Poland. *European Psychologist, 10*(1), 51–59. doi:10.1027/1016-9040.10.1.51

Gardner, H. (1995). Reflections on multiple Intelligences: Myths and Messages. *Phi Delta Capan, 77*, 200–209.

Giorgis, N. (2007). Multiple Intelligences Profiles. *Electronic Bulletin 'Engineering First', 5*.

Goleman, D. (1996). *Emotional Intelligence*. NewYork: Bantam Books.

Karamikabir, N. (2012). Gardner's Multiple Intelligence and Mathematics Education. *Procedia: Social and Behavioral Sciences, 31*(0), 778–781. doi:10.1016/j.sbspro.2011.12.140

Lavonen, J., Gedrovics, J., Byman, F., Meisalo, V., Juuti, K., & Uitto, A. (2008). Students' motivational orientations and career choice in science and technology: A comparative investigation in Finland and Latvia. *Journal of Baltic Science Education, 7*(2), 86–102.

Otero, M. R. (2006). Emotions, feelings and reasoning in science education. *Electronic Journal of Science Education, 1*(1), 24–53.

Prieto, M. D., Ferrandiz, C., & Ballester, P. (2001). Cognitive skill evaluation under the Multiple Intelligences Theory. *Ensenañza de las Ciencias*, *19*, 91–111.

Sulaiman, T., Abdurahman, A. R., & Rahim, S. S. A. (2010). Teaching Strategies Based on Multiple Intelligences Theory among Science and Mathematics Secondary School Teachers. *Procedia: Social and Behavioral Sciences*, *8*(0), 512–518. doi:10.1016/j.sbspro.2010.12.070

KEY TERMS AND DEFINITIONS

Adaptability: The characteristic, and the degree, of being adaptable. In sociology, it is applied to a person's capacity to adapt or adjust to a new environment, new situation, different condition, etc.

Multiple Intelligences: The theory of multiple intelligences is a model of conception of the mind. It was proposed in 1983 by the US psychologist Howard Gardner who later taught at Harvard University. In this model, intelligence is not a unitary set of different specific capacities but is rather like a network of interrelated autonomous sets. Gardner proposed that for the development of life one needs more than one type of intelligence.

Self-Efficacy: Confidence in one's own ability to achieve the intended results.

APPENDIX 1

Multiple Intelligences Questionnaire

Except from the questionnaire prepared by Thomas Armstrong (Armstrong, 2006).

Each item will be responded to on a scale of 0 to 3 in accordance to how much we identify with the statement: 0 – Never and 3 – Always.

Table 5.

Question	Score
1. I am the type of person whom others ask for an opinion and advice	
2. I habitually spend time thinking, meditating, or reflecting about important life issues	
3. I practice at least one sport or some type of physical activity on a regular basis	
4. I perceive when a musical note is off key	
5. When I close my eyes I see clear visual images	
6. I have no trouble calculating operations in my head	
7. Books are very important to me	
8. I like to go on excursions, hiking, or simply walking in nature	
9. I prefer team sports to individual sports	
10. I am capable of facing setbacks with moral strength	
11. I like to work with my hands in specific activities – sewing, weaving, carving, carpentry, or building models	
12. I am always listening to music	
13. I like jigsaw puzzles, labyrinths, and other visual games	
14. Mathematics and/or natural sciences are some of my favourite school subjects	
15. I like word games like Scrabble, Anagram Scramble, or Stop the Pencil	
16. I am quite good at writing down the differences between different types of trees, dogs, birds, or other kinds of flora or fauna	
17. I like sociable games like Monopoly or cards more than activities that are done on your own, like video games	
18. I have a realistic view of my strengths and weaknesses (confirmed by contrast then with other sources)	
19. I like to spend my free time outdoors	
20. I play a musical instrument	
21. In general, I am able to orient myself in an unknown place	
22. Scientific advances interest me	
23. When I am reading, speaking, or writing, I hear the words in my head	
24. I like to read books or magazines, or watch films or TV programmes in which nature is present	
25. I have at least three close friends	
26. I consider myself to be a strong-willed or independent person	
27. I tend to gesticulate a lot or use other forms of bodily language when I am talking with someone	
28. I can easily follow the rhythm of a musical theme with a percussion instrument	
29. What I like most about Mathematics is geometry	

continued on following page

Table 5. Continued

Question	Score
30. I like games or riddles that require logical thinking	
31. In school, I assimilate Language and Literature, Social Sciences, and History better than Mathematics and Natural Sciences	
32. I love visiting zoos, aquariums, and other places where the natural world is studied	
33. I feel comfortable in a crowd	
34. I keep a personal diary in which I collect my thoughts related to my inner life	
35. I believe that I am a person with good coordination	
36. I know the melodies of many songs or pieces of music	
37. I have no trouble imagining what things would look like seen from above	
38. My mind looks for patterns, regularity, or logical sequences in things	
39. For me, learning to speak or read in other languages (English, French, …) is relatively easy	
40. I have a hobby that is related to nature in some way (for example, bird watching)	

APPENDIX 2

Questionnaire of Stress Management, Adaptability, and General Mood for pupils in the Sciences

Adaptation of the questionnaire elaborated by Bar-On (1997).

Each item will be responded to on a scale of 1 to 4 in accordance to how much we identify with the statement: 1 – Never and 4 – Always.

Table 6.

Question				
1. I like to have fun	1	2	3	4
2. I can be calm when I have to solve science problems	1	2	3	4
3. I am happy when we are doing science experiments	1	2	3	4
4. I feel sure of myself in science classes	1	2	3	4
5. It is easy for me to relax in the science class	1	2	3	4
6. When I am asked hard questions in science, I try to answer in different ways	1	2	3	4
7. I think that most of the activities or tasks I do in science come out well	1	2	3	4
8. Some science topics put me in a bad mood	1	2	3	4
9. It is easy for me to understand science	1	2	3	4
10. In the science class, I generally hope for the best	1	2	3	4
11. I fight with my classmates when we do group activities in science classes	1	2	3	4
12. I can understand difficult questions in science	1	2	3	4
13. I like to smile	1	2	3	4
14. I keep working on a science problem until I solve it	1	2	3	4
15. I am generally in a bad mood in the science class	1	2	3	4
16. I give good answers to difficult questions in science	1	2	3	4
17. I know how to have a good time	1	2	3	4
18. I get angry easily when I do science activities	1	2	3	4
19. I can solve science problems in different ways	1	2	3	4
20. A lot has to happen to make me angry	1	2	3	4
21. I feel good about the work I do in the science class	1	2	3	4
22. When I get angry with someone I get angry for a long time	1	2	3	4
23. I am good at solving problems in science	1	2	3	4
24. I find it hard to wait my turn when we are doing science activities	1	2	3	4
25. The sciences surprise me	1	2	3	4
26. I do not give up in science problems, even when things get difficult	1	2	3	4
27. When I get angry, I act without thinking	1	2	3	4
28. I like the subject of sciences	1	2	3	4

Chapter 14
A Framework for Human-Technology Social Systems:
The Role of Inter-Personal Interactions

Monika Lohani
University of Utah, USA

Eric G. Poitras
University of Utah, USA

Charlene Stokes
The MITRE Corporation, USA

ABSTRACT

Advancements in semi- and fully-autonomous systems have made human-technology interaction a dynamic and social process. In this chapter, the authors highlight the importance of interpersonal interactions between human and technology and how they can be modeled, tracked, and fostered in the context of adaptive instructional systems. They will first introduce a human-technology social systems framework, which integrates individual factors (human and technology), situational factors (e.g., stress), and team interaction-relevant factors (e.g., communication and team cognition) that contribute to various team-related outcomes (e.g., learning and performance). Using examples from interactive virtual agents and educational technology, they discuss attributes of technology that should be considered to optimize joint learning and performance in applied contexts. The proposed framework points to novel research directions and is likely to offer an understanding of mechanisms that could enhance learning opportunities in diverse socioemotional contexts.

INTRODUCTION

Technological advancements in semi and fully-autonomous machines have created an opportunity for humans and technology to work dynamically as teammates in complex and high-stakes environments, making it essential to identify factors that can optimize human-technology interaction for better perfor-

DOI: 10.4018/978-1-7998-0249-5.ch014

mance and learning outcomes. In this chapter, we focus on the importance of interpersonal interactions between human and technology, which may be conceptualized in terms of several measurable components grounded in accounts of information processing and other contemporary approaches, as defined in the proposed framework of human-technology social systems. The main contributions of this chapter can be summarized as follows: First, we present a framework that integrates individual and human-technology interaction related processes that may impact their functioning together. We focus on the importance of fostering critical non-technical factors, namely, a set of cognitive, social, and emotional abilities that promote human-technology interaction. Next, as preliminary supporting evidence, a case study is presented that examined the impact of facilitating non-technical skills while experienced military intelligence analysts work with a virtual agent technology as a team in a real-world environment. This case study (based on focus groups) provides a proof-of-concept of our framework and shows how non-technical skills can be developed and evaluated during human and technology interactions in applied contexts. Finally, we discuss application of this framework to an enhanced technology and socio-emotional learning context, where optimizing human-technology interaction may improve academic and social life outcomes. The broader implication of this work is that interpersonal abilities outlined in the proposed framework can be tracked, modeled, and fostered in the context of adaptive instructional systems.

AN OVERVIEW OF THE HUMAN-TECHNOLOGY SOCIAL SYSTEMS FRAMEWORK

Human-technology interactions are dynamic and complex. With everyday interactive technologies on the rise, it has become increasingly important to understand how human-technology relationships can be shaped to improve effective use of technology through an integration of technical and non-technical factors. We define *technical factors* as task-relevant abilities and *non-technical factors* as cognitive, social, and emotional abilities that are crucial for successful interactions with humans (Anderson, Jensen, Lippert, & Østergaard, 2010; Buljac-Samardzic, Dekker-van Doorn, van Wijngaarden, & van Wijk, 2010; Flin and Maran 2004; Mathieu, Maynard, Rapp, & Gilson, 2008; Salas et al., 2008). A lack of consideration of non-technical factors can lead to poor performance, accidents, and error (Flin, Glavin, & Patey, 2003; Hancock et al., 2011; Schaefer et al., 2016). While much progress has been made in building technical capabilities in technologies, development of non-technical skills is still in its infancy. Little is known about *how* non-technical skills could be effectively embedded in technology. Seminal work on interpersonal intelligence can inform a way to embed non-technical skills in technology. Interpersonal intelligence is an ability to understand, interact, and relate to other people (Gardner, 1983; Gardner & Moran, 2006). It is considered essential for social functioning, including working with others to meet shared goals (e.g., Connell, Sheridan, & Garner, 2004). Lessons learned from interpersonal intelligence can inform and build non-technical capabilities in human-technology interactions, as we discuss further.

While trying to develop interactive technology, several elements could be considered including team dynamics (Cannon-Bowers, Salas, Tannenbaum, & Mathieu, 1995; Cooke, Gorman, & Winner, 2007; Hinds & Weisband, 2003; Kozlowski & Ilgen, 2006; Salas, Cooke, & Rosen, 2008; Salas, Dickinson, Converse, & Tannenbaum, 1992), coordination (Shah, 2011), communication (Harbers, Jonker, & Riemsdijk, 2012), rapport (Gratch et al., 2007), cognitive-affective processes (Breazeal, 2004; Lisetti

A Framework for Human-Technology Social Systems

& Hudlicka, 2014), shared mental models (Borst, 2016) and perspective-taking (Trafton et al., 2005). However, there is a need for an integrative framework to provide guidelines on potential elements to consider when trying to delineate interactions between new technologies and human users (Hart & Proctor, 2016) as well as its implications for instructional research and practice. What are the antecedents and effects of non-technical skills applied in the context of human-technology interactions? How can these skills be measured and are they amenable to instructional interventions? The human-technology social systems (HTSS) framework is based on the premise that individual learner characteristics and design guidelines for training systems are central to interpersonal processes and outcomes, represented in terms of *input-process-outcome* reciprocal linkages. Corollaries of the theory pertain to the conceptualization of interpersonal intelligence as multiple elements that specifically inform inter-personal interactions in human-technology and is based on an initial effort to understand how humans may interact with machines (Lohani et al., 2017).

The HTSS framework adopts an input-process-outcome approach (McGrath, 1962) to examine how human-technology teams perform together (see Figure 1). *Inputs* are member/team, task, and situational factors that bound the potential human-technology interaction space. Example *inputs* include, individual characteristics (e.g., the technology's and human's physical features and personality) and technical capabilities (e.g., the technology's and human's technical expertise, task-management ability, situation awareness, decision-making ability). The framework has a few typical individual-level characteristics and capabilities for humans and technology that can be further developed based on the goals of the technology. Shaped by the inputs, various *team-processes* emerge dynamically in the team (e.g., human-technology team's communication and rapport, team cognition, and emotion regulation), which lead to related and cascading *outputs* (e.g., trust, stress reduction, learning, and performance). In addition, contextual factors may also significantly influence and define team-process factors (e.g., settings in which the human-technology are working together, environmental complexity and uncertainties). Non-technical team dynamics have been shown to be an essential part of (human only) team effectiveness models (Buljac-Samardzic et al., 2010; Flin et al., 2003; Paulus and Brown, 2007; Salas et al., 1992) and we believe these models have important insights to inform successful human-technology interactions as well.

Figure 1. Human-Technology social systems framework

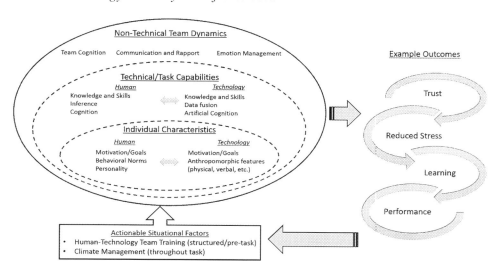

In fact, seminal work from Nass and colleagues (Nass, Fogg, & Moon, 1996; Nass, Moon, & Green, 1997a; Nass, Moon, & Morkes, Kim, & Fogg,1997b; Nass, Moon, & Carney, 1999; Nass & Moon, 2000) have shown that social characteristics randomly attributed to desktop computers can influence human behavior and human-computer interaction. For instance, humans extend overlearned social behavior to computers, such as politeness (Nass et al., 1999; Nass & Moon, 2000). Similarly, social cues, personality and ethnicity assigned to a computer can also evoke social behavior and preferences towards computers (Nass et al., 1997a; 1997b; 1999; Nass & Moon, 2000). Others have extended social behaviors of humans to other technologies, such as digital assistants. Past research (Large, Clark, Quandt, Burnett, & Skrypchuk, 2017) has shown that humans engaged in social interactions and actions (e.g., affording equal social status to the digital assistant, turn taking, mitigating requests, and politeness and praise). In a similar manner, virtual tutors communicate with learners using animated talking heads to mimic natural language, enabling tutoring discourse related to express and communicate domain knowledge, implement strategies, and generate inferences (Nye, Graesser, & Hu, 2014). Such technological advancements in embodied pedagogical agents have been found to improve performance outcomes and affective detection and responses towards interactions with learners (D'Mello, Picard, & Graesser, 2007; Moreno, Mayer, Spires, & Lester, 2001; Graesser & McNamara, 2010). These findings suggest that human-technology interactions can benefit from the existing team-building literature and the inclusion of social aspects of working with others. The HTSS framework is based on the premise that team processes (including antecedent factors such as, team cognition, rapport, and emotion management) are central to attaining desirable outcomes experienced in human-technology interactions (such as, trust, learning, and performance).

STRUCTURE OF THE FRAMEWORK: OVERVIEW OF THE DIMENSIONS AND ASSUMPTIONS

Team Cognition

Team cognition is critical for team effectiveness (Salas and Fiore, 2004). *Team cognition* is defined as cognitive activity that takes place when team members interact together (Cooke et al., 2007). Such team-level interaction can include, but is not limited to, team situation awareness, transparency, and coordination (e.g., Chen & Joyner, 2014; Demir et al., 2016; Salmon et al., 2008). Numerous studies have shown an absence or degradation of such elements to adversely influence team performance (Demir, McNeese, & Cooke, 2016, 2018; Harbers et al., 2012; Wilson, Priest, & Andrews, 2007). Team cognition also applies to human-technology interaction contexts and we discuss below two important elements that have been found to be most relevant.

Coordination

Coordination between team members involves activities that help maintain shared mental models of the task they are performing together and the role and responsibilities of each member to accomplish the task. Effective coordination requires several activities to meet a team's goals, including establishing a mutual understanding of who is proceeding with which task and when, or who needs help, and also who can handle unexpected situations as they come up. In order to improve coordination, team members should interact regularly to update each other about their mutual tasks and assess needs of the group (Entin &

A Framework for Human-Technology Social Systems

Serfaty, 1999). In addition, coordination can benefit from planning around the needs and capabilities of each member, which in turn can lead to a more efficient generation of plans of action that can effectively meet the teams' goals (Sebanz, Bekkering, & Knoblich, 2006). Needless to say, coordinating the timing of each team member's tasks is important to successfully meet task requirements.

In human-technology interactions, coordination of tasks can be challenging yet critical. Instructional systems can track actions taken by team members and devise ways to react in real time, for example, on the basis of messages sent between team members in shared virtual battlespace simulations (Sinatra et al., 2018). Technology may also support the delivery of feedback related to communication skills by supporting role playing scenarios, reviewing video playback, and discussing amongst team members for simulated scenarios such as communicating bad news to patients (Lee, Lajoie, Poitras, Nkangu, & Doleck, 2017) and treatment of combat trauma injuries (Lajoie & Poitras, 2014). Lack of coordination between human and technology can lead to time idling, repetition of same tasks, or execution of unnecessary tasks. Timely coordination can lead to effective human as well as joint learning and performance. Shah's (2011) framework of coordination provides a set of algorithms that could be used to develop fluid coordination between human and technology coordination. This framework is effective in reducing idle time and task allocation over time based on the needs of a team, which can help with fluid coordination and effective decision making.

Perspective Taking

An important ability that helps with coordination is perspective taking. Perspective taking is the ability to be able to view a scenario from another person's mental or visuospatial point of view. While humans are able to do it moderately well, it is a challenging human ability to model in human-technology interactions. Perspective taking has been successfully implemented in human-technology interaction, such as joint assembly task (Trafton et al., 2005). Perspective taking helps humans and technology to perform together by resolving ambiguities (Lemaignan, Warnier, Sisbot, Clodic, & Alami, 2017) and improving communication (Pandey, Ali, & Alami, 2013).

While human teamwork studies provide valuable insights, some work has shown ways that humans can treat technology differently than other humans (Demir & Cooke, 2014; Mou & Xu, 2017). For example, when individuals thought they were interfacing with interactive technology instead of humans (but in reality, they were interacting with humans), individuals were found to exert more control over the functioning of the technology (Demir & Cooke, 2014). Moreover, recent work has also shown that mere perceptions of working with non-human member can lead to reduced team performance (Demir et al., 2018). Inclusion of social cues and human-like behavior can help overcome negative team performance due to perceptions of working with non-humans (Demir et al., 2016). Similarly, placement of virtual pedagogical agents in an interface can reduce cognitive demands (Goldberg, 2015).

Another promising approach may consist of augmented reality devices to ensure immersive training in authentic settings to circumvent traditional limitations associated with desktop tutoring systems, as evidenced by the use of human instructors with realistic renditions of physical environments to conduct training scenarios for physical tasks (LaViola et al., 2015). This highlights the importance of developing proper interactions between humans and technology to override any presumptions related to working with non-humans that may lead to poor human-technology joint learning and performance. Inclusion of subtle behaviors similar to a good human team member can promote learning and performance with technology. The next two sections provide more approaches that can help interactions with technology to overcome such presumptions.

Communication and Rapport

Communication can be referred to as an observable exchange of information and sentiments. Several verbal and non-verbal techniques to promote communication between human and technology are available (Mavridis, 2015). Communication has been found to improve contextual and situation awareness and thereby reduce errors (Schaefer et al., 2016; Lucas et al., 2018). Ineffective communication leads to poor human-technology performance (Demir et al., 2016). In human-technology interactions, it is helpful to establish preferences for timing of communications, such as when and how to assist a human to maximize productive collaborative work (Cummings & Guerlain, 2007; Chen & Barnes, 2014; Chen & Joyner, 2009; Hayes & Scassellati, 2013). Transparency in communication is an important determinant of trust in technology (Hancock et al., 2011; Schaefer et al., 2016). Communication can be critical in development and maintenance of trust in technology.

Communication and rapport go hand-in-hand. *Rapport* is a feeling of being "in sync" with a teammate (Gratch et al., 2007). Good rapport with a technology improves its acceptance and influence on human decision making, e.g., improved acceptance of medical advice and successful negotiations (Gratch et al., 2007; Pecune, Chen, Matsuyama, & Cassell, 2018). Past research has found a few ways to develop rapport between humans and an interactive technology. For instance, head nods, gaze, and gesture mimicking have been quite effective in building rapport while interacting with human users (Gratch et al., 2007). Mimicking posture change and head movement is another way to develop rapport (DeCarlo, Stone, Revilla, & Venditti, 2004; Huang, Morency, & Gratch, 2011). While developing rapport, a technology not only has to convey information to the human user, but it is also essential that a technology appears to respond to the human in a timely manner. A tight sense-act loop (i.e., sensing the need for a response followed by a prompt response) has been suggested to be most effective in developing rapport (Gratch et al., 2006). For instance, posture and head movements should be timely in response to an action by human teammates. Other examples include, a head nod in response to a sentence completion by a human right when s/he lowers their pitch (signaling an intended end of speaking turn) or in response to prosodic emphasis expressed in a sentence (Huang et al., 2011; Lubold, Walker, & Pon-Barry, 2015). Past work has also adopted pitch adaptation to mimic voice pitch and quality of human speaker to build rapport (Lubold et al., 2015; Maatman, Gratch, & Marsella, 2005). Similarly, mimicking emotional expressions and behavior of humans (Bickmore & Cassell, 2005; Woolf et al., 2009) has been shown to result in a stronger bond between humans and technology.

Embedding conversational agents with good communication and rapport capabilities has been possible through social signals (Pecune et al., 2018). This has been the motivation of the newly developing field of Social Signal Processing, a "computing domain aimed at modeling, analysis and synthesis of social signals in human-human and human-machine interactions" (Vinciarelli & Pentland, 2015). Advanced and affordable technology has led the field of social signal processing to adopt non-verbal cues during

A Framework for Human-Technology Social Systems

human-technology interactions (such as, verbal cues and facial expressions, head movement, eye gazing, nodding, or body movements in form of gestures and postures) to be automatically detected, interpreted, and conveyed as social signals. For example, in a recent study, temporal sequences of non-verbal behavioral patterns were examined to automatically predict high and low interpersonal rapport (Zhao, Sinha, Black, & Cassell, 2016). Real-time detection and response systems (e.g. based on facial expression, body posture and movement, acoustic and linguistic patterns) that are sensitive to task context will be useful to further improve on communication systems in human-technology interactions. This area of research is critical for embodied pedagogical agents as acceptance of the virtual agent is related to acceptance of the learning environment as a whole, suggesting that acceptance may influence future trainee resistance to the utilization of training systems (Holden & Goldberg, 2011).

Emotion Management

While rapport helps build mutual harmony between team members, situation-based emotion management skills are also critical for developing non-technical team dynamics. *Emotion management* is needed to provide leadership, plan and anticipate conflict, solve problems, give critical judgment, and ensure team success. Emotion management skills are not mutually exclusive from other components. For instance, they are implicit in effective rapport, communication, rapport building, and coordination. Enhancing emotion regulation skills provides individuals with a capacity to lead self and others toward collaborative and goal-focused action (Gross & Thompson, 2007; Prati, Douglas, Ferris, Ammerter, & Buckley, 2003) and enhance personal growth, performance, problem solving, and relationships (Lerner, Liben, & Mueller, 2015; Salovey & Mayer, 1990). Past research has shown that technology can be used to facilitate emotion regulation (e.g., Hadley et al., 2018; Gebhard, Schneeberger, Baur, & André, 2018).

Technology could be designed to utilize effective emotion regulation strategies to manage team interactions and modulate the emotional climate. Depending upon the context, technology can be a manager and a trainer to facilitate team management and ensure team success. For instance, a recent study used virtual reality to teach emotion regulation strategies to adolescents (Hadley et al., 2018). Likewise, motivational messages could be used by technology to regulate emotions in the user. Human-technology interaction could be structured such that it can regulate inter-personal dialogue (Gebhard et al., 2018). Such regulation can help maintain a stable emotional state that is most conducive to meeting the goals of a human-technology team. Depending upon the context, given emotions' implicit and explicit influence on other team process and outcome factors, further research is needed to develop emotion management skills through targeted joint-training where the human and technology jointly develop optimal emotion regulation skills and shared climate management techniques.

Social-interaction related benefits share a significant overlap with emotion management. Social dialogue can be used to create a social bond between a team such that its members can empathize, reassure, motivate, and support their team (Breazeal, 2004; Breazeal, Kidd, Thomaz, Hoffman, & Berlin, 2005). For instance, preliminary work has shown that social agents can be developed who can engage in empathetic dialogues with human users (Gebhard et al., 2018). Social dialogues developed between humans and technology can also positively influence engagement levels (Devillers et al., 2018). Moreover, technologies that present social qualities (e.g., expression and gestures) have been found to be more accepted as conversational partners than their non-social counterparts (de Melo, Marsella, & Gratch, 2018; Heerink, Krose, Evers, & Wielinga, 2006; Mutlu, 2011; Pecune et al., 2018; Sidner et al., 2015). Similarly, social robots that display social cues can impact knowledge transfer through their interactions

(Dang & Tapus, 2007; Lallée et al., 2015). Furthermore, the degree of presented social cues matters too as shown in a recent study where extrovert agents with more exaggerated non-verbal cues elicited more behavioral involvement from its users (Sajjadi, Hoffmann, Cimiano, & Kopp, 2018). In fact, a systematic review found that social cues can be successfully adopted to develop feelings of a "social being" in a virtual agent (Oh, Bailenson, & Welch, 2018).

On a related note, technological advancements have also enabled proactive help to support human needs. For instance, robots can be programmed to provide help to a human it is interacting with when the human asks for help, or even when it notices that the human may need help (Baraglia, Cakmak, Nagai, Rao, & Asada, 2016). Recent work has developed state-of-the art interactive technologies that can adopt capabilities to detect and display relevant social signals in a real-time fashion (Glas, Satake, Kanda, & Hagita, 2012; Hartholt et al., 2014; Vinciarelli & Pentland, 2015). A few models provide promising approaches to establish social signal processing and build socially intelligent technology, such as the architectural framework for components of affective and non-affective processes (Scheutz, 2012), the interaction design framework for social robots (Glas et al., 2012), and a computational framework to analyze human social behaviors during face-to-face interactions (Morency, 2010). Training systems have implemented machine-learned models to detect affective states, either through sensor-based physiological or posture measurements (Brawner & Gonzalez, 2016) or sensor-free approaches that leverage behavior logs or tutorial dialogues with embodied pedagogical agents (Paquette et al., 2015). These emerging technologies enable virtual avatars to improve training by becoming more adaptive to learner behaviors, engaging, and motivating them to perform better (Sottilare & Hart, 2012).

In high-stress scenarios, non-technical support provided by a technology may help humans cope with stress better and also assist in managing workload (Chen & Barnes, 2014; Lohani et al., 2016a). Although more promising evidence exists for stress management in humans, there is limited evidence that has directly tested the influence of non-technical skills on stress management in a human-technology team context. In a study (Lohani et al., 2016a), we manipulated the framing of a simulated automated decision aid as a teammate versus tool with an associated socioemotional dialog and assessed stress appraisals using a standard measure (Schneider, 2008). We found that social interactions with a virtual agent lead to greater stress coping abilities (Lohani et al., 2016a). Other work has also utilized virtual characters in interventions for stress resilience and stress therapy (e.g., Rizzo et al., 2012). For example, one study showed that an agent can be programmed to provide different kinds of support to its human interaction partner based on personality characteristics of the human in ways that effectively manage stress (Tapus, 2013). These findings suggest that creating deeper team dynamics with a technology that is considerate of contextual factors can facilitate effective interactions and the ability to cope with stress-evoking scenarios.

APPLICATION OF THE FRAMEWORK: LINKAGES BETWEEN INDIVIDUAL/ TECHNICAL FACTORS, NON-TECHNICAL TEAM DYNAMICS, AND OUTCOMES

Thus, a growing number of promising studies illustrate that technology can be designed to provide non-technical support to their human users. Past research has shown that climate-management training focused on non-technical skills is effective in improving human-technology team dynamics and outcomes in humans (Anderson et al., 2010; Buljac-Samardzic et al., 2010; Flin & Maran, 2004; Flin et al., 2003; Mathieu et al, 2008). Non-technical skills are a fundamental aspect of human teams, and we

A Framework for Human-Technology Social Systems

believe that they play a critical role in human-technology interaction as well. Our framework on human-technology social systems presents essential elements of non-technical skills that have been consistently found to impact human team outcomes. These elements can be fostered through collective learning (joint training) to include team building exercises and performance feedback on individual and group goals (Cannon-Bowers et al., 1995; Kozlowski & Ilgen, 2006). As with human teams, it may be beneficial for team functioning and performance if these non-technical skills are fostered early on, such as in introductory training, as well as continually (externally or internally) throughout the life cycle of the team. We now turn to a practical case example taken from a real-world context to discuss the applications of the framework to characterize linkages between inputs, processes, and outcomes that underlie effective human-technology interactions.

Here we present an example case study in which four military intelligence analysts interacted with a virtual agent technology to complete an intelligence, surveillance and reconnaissance task together, which was conducted in a mock environment as a field exercise for training purposes only. This required the human-technology team to work together and learn about the unpredictable environment together, monitor any suspicious activity, create reports of observed activity, and disseminate information to relevant personnel. A more complete treatment of the training scenario is beyond the scope of the present chapter, rather we illustrate elements of the proposed HTSS framework, including team interactions in an experimental team as compared to those of a control team (i.e., without any non-technical interactions). According to the framework, assumptions related to linkages between team cognition, rapport and communication, and emotion management towards the joint-performance of the team as a whole were implemented into the design of human-technology interactions, see Table 1.

Participant Sample

The intelligence analysts specialized in integrated, predictive intelligence in the air, space, and cyberspace domains, enabling military operations. They had on average four years of experience with intelligence, surveillance and reconnaissance missions, similar to the team exercise they performed in this study. Both the experimental and control teams were introduced and helped by the virtual technology, Sgt. Rivers. It provided technical skills to support the ongoing mission, including threat analysis, threat recognition, assisting with call-outs and creation of intelligence products, and providing situational awareness of the mission. In addition to the technical skills emulated in the control team, the virtual agent was designed to emulate non-technical skills focused on inter-personal interactions in the experimental team.

Virtual Analyst Setup

The virtual analyst ("Sgt. Rivers") was presented on a screen between the two analysts, as shown in the experimental setup illustrated in Figure 2. A Wizard of Oz experimental design (Kelley, 1984) was used for prototyping purposes, where a human is tasked to operate some (or most) of the functioning of the virtual agent, without the knowledge of the other human participants in the study. The methodology enables empirical evaluation of a prototype as team members think they are interacting with a fully automated virtual agent. In this study, an experienced intelligence analyst served as a confederate, acting out the behaviors (verbal and non-verbal) of the virtual agent. FaceWare software converted these facial actions in real-time so that the participants could see these expressions mirrored by the virtual agent. FaceWare uses motion-capture that gets transformed into facial animations that can be used to drive 3D

Figure 2. Case study setup
Note. *The right image shows the confederate analyst (performer) whose video is being converted to an animated virtual analyst in real-time (visible on the laptop screen). In the left image, the intelligence analysts are seen performing the mission with the virtual analyst ("Sgt. Rivers") on the screen between the two analysts*

avatars. This enabled us to present a virtual analyst who had the physical and emotional characteristics and technical expertise of an experienced analyst. The analysts were unaware that the virtual analyst was enacted by another human and not technology.

The live virtual analyst was presented on a monitor by converting the confederate's video in real-time and mapping it into animation data for an avatar using FaceWare software. The avatar looked like an intelligence analyst who was wearing a similar uniform as the human intelligence analysts. The model still needed to be slightly calibrated to the confederate performer's face. This allows for a performer to precisely author emotional expressions for use in a simulation with a virtual agent. Importantly, we were also able to pre-select the FaceWare settings to ensure differences between the experiment and the control conditions were maintained (see Table 1 for differences between experimental and control teams). For instance, the FaceWare software allowed us to restrict head nods and emotive expressions in the virtual analyst's display during the control condition, regardless of the confederate's actions. In addition, the voice of the confederate was slightly modified using voice-changing software so that the virtual agent's voice did not exactly sound like a natural human voice. This was done to ensure that the experience was more realistic, as an actual automated virtual agent would interact with team members.

Measures of the Quality of Human-Technology Team Interaction

To evaluate the quality of human-technology inter-personal interaction (non-technical team dynamics), the following self-report measures assessed several components of the framework: team cognition (Gallagher et al., 2014; Nass et al., 1996), rapport (Kang & Gratch, 2012) and emotion management (Schneider, 2008). An example item of team cognition is, "I think Sgt. Rivers and I were collaborative," and "I think of Sgt. Rivers as a partner." An example item of rapport is, "I felt I had a connection with Sgt. Rivers." An example of emotional management is "how threatening did you find this task to be." All these items were on a 5-point Likert scale (1 = strongly disagree to 5 = strongly agree). All of the items were focused on assessing non-technical interactions with the virtual agent named, Sgt. Rivers.

Procedure and Design

Before the teams started working together, they were introduced to the mission and the software platform that they would use to execute the intelligence, surveillance and reconnaissance mission. The virtual

A Framework for Human-Technology Social Systems

Table 1. Comparison between experiment and control teams

Virtual agent's attributes	Experiment agent: Technical + non-technical [a]	Control agent: Technical only
Team cognition	*Yes:* Establishing roles and responsibilities and shared understanding	*No*
Rapport	*Yes:* Head nods as gestures Slightly positive expressions when applicable; stable and calm demeanor	*No:* No head nods Neutral expressions Neutral
Emotion management	*Yes:* Social interactions [b]	*No*

Note: [a] Non-technical skills were established during pre-mission interaction and followed up throughout the mission. [b] Social content included: previous experiences, day-to-day activities, hobbies. Only mission environment suitable interactions were initiated by the agent.

semi-automated intelligent system, Sgt. Rivers, and had a brief meet-and-greet session with them. Sgt. Rivers presented itself as a geospatial intelligence analyst who was there to be the two intelligence analysts' third teammate. In order to illustrate the linkages assumed in our framework, we implemented design guidelines grounded in the research literature related to non-technical team dynamics (e.g., Flin & Maran, 2004; Flin et al. 2003; Gratch et al., 2007). By close consultations with a senior intelligence analyst who served as the subject matter expert, a protocol was then developed to facilitate non-technical interactions between the virtual technology and human analysts. While interacting with the experimental team, Sgt. Rivers followed scripted prompts to build inter-personal interactions. Specifically, the protocol targeted building rapport and establish effective team communication and social interaction between the team members. Based on previous research, to build rapport, the agent utilized head nods, facial expressions, and social interactions (e.g., Bickmore & Cassell, 2005; Bickmore & Picard. 2005; Cassell & Thorisson, 1999; DeCarlo et al., 2004, Gratch et al., 2006; 2007; Huang et al., 2011; Lisetti & Hudlicka, 2015; Zheng, Glas, Kanda, Ishiguro, & Hagita, 2013). Examples of social interactions that were initiated by the virtual agent included previous experiences, day-to-day activities, and hobbies. It is important to note that only interactions suitable to have in an intelligence, surveillance and reconnaissance mission context were initiated by the agent to maintain cultural-sensitivity. For instance, the facial and verbal expressions of the virtual agent were intentionally kept low to moderately high intensity only to match the acceptable social context in an intelligence, surveillance and reconnaissance environment.

For effective communication that is not disruptive to the mission, the virtual agent checked in with the human analysts if the analyst had any preferences for the team to work together. For example, the agent prompted team members to consider how frequently they should communicate, and how they would like to be communicated with, as part of a team. For better coordination, the virtual agent brought clarity in terms of responsibilities of each team member (two human analysts and one virtual agent) so that everyone knew what each member was responsible for to maximize performance outcomes. Such discussions took place during the introduction phase and any established preferences were implemented during the course of the surveillance task.

Once the analysts had introduced each other and covered the ground rules on how and when to interact with each other, the teams started working as a team on the surveillance mission for around eight hours over the course of two days. Upon completion of the mission, the human analysts filled out surveys to assess their perceptions of the virtual technology. Once the teams had completed their mission, via a focus group interview, their experiences with the virtual technology were also captured.

Descriptive Results

Because the sample size did not allow for parametric analytic methods, we used descriptive methods to understand the pattern of findings in this field study sample. Our goal was to examine if the pattern across variables to assess the quality of human-technology inter-personal interaction was more positive for the experimental team versus the control team. Effect sizes were calculated as mean differences between experiment and control teams. That is, the percentage score for each team was calculated, then a difference in percentage score between the experiment team and control team was calculated. A positive value would imply the experiment team's ratings (e.g., for rapport) were higher than the control team's ratings.

The percentage-point differences between the two teams on team cognition and rapport were compared. The experimental team reported a 9-percentage point higher score on team cognition compared to the control team, see Figure 3. In addition, the experimental team reported a 6.2 percentage point higher rapport with the virtual agent than the control team (range). Based on these differences between experimental and control teams, we can say that embedding non-technical skills in the virtual agent positively impacted human-technology interactions in the experimental group.

Percentage-point differences in perceived threat were also examined. If human-technology interactions were helpful in emotion management, the experimental team would report lower threat relative to the control group that did not receive team support while interacting with the virtual technology. Strikingly, the experimental group reported a 17.1 percentage point lower threat reactivity compared to the control group. This finding suggests that non-technical interactions with virtual agent helped with emotion management.

Qualitative Results

Furthermore, the qualitative data collected from post-mission interviews were integrated to interpret the pattern of findings. During the final focus team interviews, the analysts from the experiment team reported that the communication with the virtual agent was very good. On the other hand, the control

Figure 3. Non-technical skills experienced by members assigned to the experiment team differed from those in the control team. The data are plotted in the form of a percentage difference plot. A higher percentage is evident in both team cognition as well as communication and rapport in the experimental team, suggesting superior interpersonal skills use across team members. A lower percentage for threat reactivity implies superior emotional management in the experimental team.

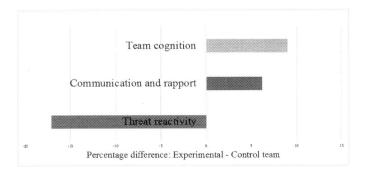

A Framework for Human-Technology Social Systems

team mentioned that, *"I was initially concerned about the agent to interfere with the mission."* This suggests that the experiment team also benefited from a discussion of communication preferences during the first interactions. In addition, we interviewed the experiment team about their feelings associated with interacting socially with a virtual agent. The experiment team did not find these interactions to be odd. *"The social interaction was not odd, in fact liked it..."*. Rather they were the normal kind of conversations they may have in low-stress situations. *"I have been in the exact situation doing very boring missions, it is nice to have someone to chat with... I have had the same kind of interaction in previous missions... When there is downtime, we could respond via chat (we could not speak)."* On being asked if they would like an automated agent with an ability to have social dialogue, the experiment team said that *"It is obviously more engaging to talk to someone rather than just answer questions"* ... *"I have been in 12 hours long missions. It is nice to have someone to respond during downtime."* Furthermore, analysts from both the experimental and control teams liked working with the virtual agent and found the agent was a helpful member, as suggested by comments like these during the interview, *"It was fun to work with the technology"* and called it *"a helpful addition."*

These findings provide preliminary evidence that integrating non-technical skills, such as the team process variables targeted in this study, into social technologies is feasible, non-intrusive and non-disruptive to real-world activities, and may be positively perceived by actual analysts operating in real-world simulated training environment. Indeed, as with human teams, non-technical factors provide untapped benefits for improving human-technology team effectiveness and performance. The results from the case study further illustrate and support the assumptions pertaining to the linkages described in the framework, consistent with other research which have found evidence for the importance of non-technical skills in human-technology interactions (Demir et al., 2016; Harbers et al., 2012; Wilson et al., 2007). In the next section, we situate these findings in our conceptualization of the different components for interpersonal intelligence at a social level. Next, the applications of the framework to inform the design of adaptive training systems that implement embodied pedagogical agents are discussed.

COROLLARIES WITH EMPIRICAL STUDIES AND EXTENSIONS TO THE HTSS FRAMEWORK

Interpersonal Intelligence in Teams

Human analysts did not find the social interactions with the virtual analyst to be odd, but rather they reported the conversations to be natural conversations between team members during low workload scenarios. Consistent with past research (Large et al., 2017; Nass et al., 1999; Moon and Nass, 1998; von der Pütten, Krämer, Gratch, & Kang, 2010), we found that the analysts in experimental and control teams used social norms such as affording the virtual analyst equal social status, turn-taking, and politeness. Analysts also agreed that there is value in a conversational agent during long shifts, which is an encouraging feedback. This is consistent with past studies, such as complex interactions with a socially competent robot (Lallée et al., 2015) has also found that social cues can influence knowledge transfer during human-robot interaction. These findings show that inclusion of social interactions can facilitate non-technical team processes that may promote team outcomes.

One explanation for these findings is that non-technical interactions may have led to a change in the affective state of the experimental team compared to the control team that only discussed task-specific content. For instance, facial expressions could signal emotional cues and lead to perceptions of trustworthiness (Krumhuber et al., 2007; Todorov, 2008). During non-technical interactions, such emotional cues may lead to changes in affective state of the perceiver, thereby leading to lower perceived threat levels. In previous work we have also reported that non-technical human-technology team interactions from the beginning of the relationship can impact trust and trustworthiness (Lohani et al., 2017). Inclusions of non-technical interactions initiated by the virtual agent technology in the experiment team on average were associated with higher trust levels (Lohani et al., 2017). These results are also consistent with our past findings that the socioemotional interactions of a virtual agent as a teammate (versus a tool) led to higher reports in the ability to cope with stress, acceptance of physiological assessment sensors, and moderate the relationship between trust and reliance (Lohani et al., 2016a, 2016b). Thus, non-technical interactions may lead to perceived social support from a conversational agent that may facilitate joint learning and performance improve stress and trust appraisals.

While these findings are encouraging, there are important limitations to address in future work. First, we did not have a fully autonomous agent that interacted with the human analysts. A Wizard-of-Oz approach was used to facilitate non-technical team processes and avoid unrealistic agent capabilities. This was a logistical decision that was made because our primary interest was to test the impact of non-technical skills integration and the case study environment was very unpredictable, which did not allow designing a scripted agent. The rich context-sensitive dialogues that we have gained from this case study will help add relevant conversational features to our automated agent in follow-up studies. In future work, we plan to adopt state-of-the-art automated communication capabilities that allow detection and display social signals (Glas et al., 2012; Hartholt et al., 2014; Vinciarelli & Pentland 2015). Second, it is difficult to tease out the effect that additional communication (in order to establish non-technical interactions) may have had on the measured variables. On a related note, non-technical skills have been discussed as shared processes of individual factors (rapport, team cognition, etc.), but it is hard to specify exactly what processes are involved to what extent. Third, this is a very preliminary focus group-based case study. A randomized study with an appropriate sample size will need to be conducted to make reliable interpretations. Fourth, we did not directly examine the influence of specific emotion regulation strategies and benefits of incorporating additional relevant components (such as transparency). Using an iterative testing approach, additional elements may be assimilated to the HTSS framework. In future work, the levels of team dynamics should be formally measured. For instance, new approaches to optimize coordination (Farinelli, Boscolo, Zanotto, & Pagello, 2017) and measure of collaboration (Pan & Bolton, 2016) and conflicts in task-oriented dialogue (Yang & Heeman, 2010) between team-members could be assessed.

The virtual simulation of human-technology interactions provided a proof-of-concept of impact of non-technical skills on outcome variables of interest. This allowed us to avoid the problems in making the virtual agent display non-verbal behaviors. At the same time, technological capabilities are not error free. Trust hinges on judgments of vulnerability in an effort to reduce risk. Misperceptions of technology's decisions making process can lower trust and even cause disuse of the technology's capabilities (Schaefer et al., 2016). It is critical to align the subjective trust attitudes with the objective reliability and trustworthiness of the system. Even with the most advanced state-of-the-art capabilities, there will be many technical mishaps that will have an effect on building non-technical skills. For example, issues

A Framework for Human-Technology Social Systems

with timely communication and coordination can substantially challenges team effectiveness (Demir et al., 2015; Lucas et al., 2018).

Such limitations need future work to better maintain positive team dynamics that could eventually be automated during human-technology interactions. In further research we plan to directly test trust calibration and trust repair strategies in a less reliable automated technology. Adopting strategies to repair non-technical skills and trust could be a helpful approach to recover from any capability mishaps, but this is another challenge that needs to be understood and implemented. Also, building rapport and team cognition may improve intent error. Trust calibration can be improved by communicating technology's intention to the human teammates (Schaefer et al., 2016). A recent study has shown that multimodal trackers could be used to predict objective trustworthiness (Lucas et al., 2017) and such predictors could be further automated for a technology to predict trustworthiness during human-technology interaction.

Team Training Systems with Embodied Pedagogical Agents

The past thirty years have seen rapid advances in the field of adaptive training systems that implement embodied pedagogical agents (Guo & Goh, 2015; Nye, Graesser, & Hu, 2014). It is now well established from a variety of studies, that virtual agents can serve as effective learning companions, not only in the professional domains, but also in the classroom (Mayer & DaPra, 2012). Until recently, research has focused on individual learning during one-to-one training scenarios. A systematic understanding of how virtual agents contribute to joint team outcomes such as learning, performance, and motivation is still lacking (Mousavinasab et al., 2018). Researchers have begun to explore how pedagogical agents may influence team learning (Sottilare & Roessingh, 2014), and outline methodological concerns specific to this type of training system (Burke, Feitosa, & Salas, 2015; Sottilare, Holden, Brawner, & Goldberg, 2011).

The HTSS framework outlined in this chapter provides the conceptual grounding for the antecedents and effects that mediate the interdependencies across individual team members involved in learning and performance. The members of the team work collectively towards attaining a joint learning or task objective, therefore their efforts are interdependent. In their seminal work, Salas and colleagues (Salas, Shuffler, Thayer, Bedwell, & Lazzara, 2014) conceptualize these skills as coordinating mechanisms, including facets that characterize how team members work together, their mutual understanding of a task, the resources available, teammate's capabilities, and their mutual trust. The proposed framework builds on these notions in terms of linkages between these processes, their individual and technological antecedents, and their effects on learning and performance. What roles can a virtual pedagogical agent play as a working and cooperative member of a group? How can embodied pedagogical agent track, diagnose, and foster specific knowledge and roles that are lacking across team members? How can agents adaptively facilitate information sharing and coordination? We postulate several design guidelines in accordance with the proposed framework that enhance social emotional learning in teams.

At an *individual* level, learners are susceptible to look for and apply social behavior and norms to technology (e.g., Nass and Moon, 2000; von der Pütten et al., 2010). Designing embodied pedagogical agents with anthropomorphic features and behavior can help acceptance by learners (Demir et al., 2016; DeCarlo et al., 2004; Huang et al., 2011; Mou and Xu, 2017). Anthropomorphic features also prompt politeness (Hoffmann, Birnbaum, Vanunu, Sass, & Reis, 2014) and personable responses from humans (Jung & Kopp, 2003). Past work has shown that personality traits displayed by technology can also impact the decision-making process. For instance, a technology with an enthusiastic extrovert personality was able to influence the decisions of humans (López, Peñaloza, & Cuéllar, 2016). The interactive technology could also be given a personality that compliments the personality of the student user. In addition, the conversational style of virtual tutor may be designed to maintain engagement because humans are more personable and open to conversation with and trusting of embodied conversational agents (Sabanovic, Michalowski, & Simmons, 2006; Shamekhi, Czerwinski, Mark, Novotny, & Bennett, 2016). Displays of trustworthiness in technology (via facial expressions and gestures) can be a strong social signal that can help develop human-technology interactions (Lucas et al., 2017). Based on this past research, it is preferred that a virtual tutor has human-like features and embodies a supportive and engaging demeanor. In case, this technology is limited to auditory modality only, then at least the voice could be human-like. In the case of text-based interactions, the messages could be phrased to embody language used by a supportive tutor (informed by social emotional learning methods). Careful consideration of individual-level characteristics of a technology can help meet the goals of a technology to develop socio-emotional competence.

At a *technological level*, the development and improvement of team models in training systems for adaptive virtual tutors require insights into both the team and the learners. While the relevant states that mediate team performance are stipulated in the proposed framework as well as in past research (Sottilare et al., 2016), much less is known regarding best practices to allow machine recognition of these states. An important challenge for collaborative team learning is to distill interactions in a modality that is amenable for automated assessment (Sottilare, Holden, Brawner, & Goldberg, 2011). Although desktop training systems such as virtual environments, serious games, and simulations are amenable to sensor-based or sensor-free detection of social emotional states, training scenarios in authentic environments remain a significant challenge. Multi-sensory data can help inform systems to keep a track of cognitive states (for a review see Lohani, Payne, & Strayer, 2019). Through data fusion, "aware" systems can have artificial cognition (Lemaignan et al., 2017) by assimilating multi-modal data to predict and manage students' cognitive states. The proposed framework contributes to this emerging area through the identification of relevant *team-processes* that emerge dynamically in the team (e.g., human-technology team's communication and rapport, team cognition, and emotion regulation) as a first step towards enabling the classification of those states.

CONCLUSION

In this chapter, we provided an overview of the dimensions and assumptions of the HTSS framework, as well as some of its implications for research on interpersonal intelligence in human-technology teams. The framework tries to synthesize several elements that are critical to meaningful interactions between humans and technology and for the design of training systems with embodied pedagogical agents. Many facets point to novel avenues for future research and is likely to offer an understanding of factors that could enhance learning opportunities in diverse socioemotional contexts. Empirically, many facets of the theory have consistently been corroborated in past research, while the linkages postulated in the framework were illustrated in a case example of a training scenario. The evidence collected so far is preliminary, but perhaps more importantly, the assumptions provided by the theory provides practical guidelines for fostering team cognition, rapport, and emotion management in humans-technology interactions.

The broader implications of conceptualizing interpersonal intelligence in terms of its social dimensions has several applications for training with embodied pedagogical agents. Such non-technical team processes will help technology to mirror social cues (Belpaeme et al., 2012; Mutlu, 2011; Sabanovic et al., 2006) and promote acceptance (Pecune et al., 2018). Emotion management will be a critical component to develop in this technology and will be informed by evidence-based techniques (Hedley et al., 2019; Gebhard et al., 2018; Lohani & Isaacowitz, 2014, Lohani, Payne, & Isaacowitz, 2017) to guide learners in using real-time regulation strategies to manage their cognitive and affective states. Complex human cognition, including persuasion (André et al., 2011) and negotiation (Mell, Lucas, & Gratch, 2017; de Melo, Marsella, & Gratch, 2018) can be successfully initiated by intelligent systems. Similarly, social emotional learning technology can be designed to give feedback to students on emotion regulation strategies that may be effective in managing challenging concepts. It is expected that there are significant individual differences in students' cognitive-affective behavior, and with significant data collection it may be possible in the future to identify customized profiles depending upon the individual characteristics of students. The proposed framework is still is a working model and further iterative testing and validation in specific contexts is needed to integrate components that are critical for developing human-technology joint learning and performance. Interdisciplinary collaborations between education, learning sciences, human factors, affective sciences, and computer sciences will be needed to advance the development of this new genre of technology to support digital learning and optimal performance.

REFERENCES

Andersen, P. O., Jensen, M. K., Lippert, A., & Østergaard, D. (2010). Identifying non-technical skills and barriers for improvement of teamwork in cardiac arrest teams. *Resuscitation*, *81*(6), 695–702. doi:10.1016/j.resuscitation.2010.01.024 PMID:20304547

André, E., Bevacqua, E., Heylen, D., Niewiadomski, R., Pelachaud, C., Peters, C., ... Rehm, M. (2011). Nonverbal Persuasion and Communication in an Affective Agent. In P. Petta, C. Pelachaud, & R. Cowie (Eds.), *Emotion-Oriented Systems: The Humaine Handbook* (pp. 585–608). Springer. doi:10.1007/978-3-642-15184-2_30

Baraglia, J., Cakmak, M., Nagai, Y., Rao, R., & Asada, M. (2016). Initiative in robot assistance during collaborative task execution. *2016 11th ACM/IEEE International Conference on Human-Robot Interaction (HRI)*, 67-74.

Belpaeme, T., Baxter, P. E., Read, R., Wood, R., Cuayáhuitl, H., Kiefer, B., & ... . (2012). Multimodal child-robot interaction: Building social bonds. *Journal of Human-Robot Interaction*, *1*(2), 33–53.

Bickmore, T., & Cassell, J. (2005). Social dialogue with embodied conversational agents. In Advances in natural multimodal dialogue systems. Springer.

Bickmore, T., & Picard, R. W. (2005). Establishing and maintaining long-term human-computer relationships. *ACM Transactions on Computer-Human Interaction*, *12*(2), 293–327. doi:10.1145/1067860.1067867

Borst, C. (2016). Shared mental models in human-machine systems. *IFAC-PapersOnLine*, *49*(19), 195–200. doi:10.1016/j.ifacol.2016.10.517

Brawner, K. W., & Gonzalez, A. J. (2016). Modelling a learner's affective state in real time to improve intelligent tutoring effectiveness. *Theoretical Issues in Ergonomics Science*, *17*(2), 183–210. doi:10.1080/1463922X.2015.1111463

Breazeal, C. (2004). Function meets style: Insights from emotion theory applied to HRI. *IEEE Transactions on Systems, Man and Cybernetics. Part C, Applications and Reviews, 34*(2), 187–194. doi:10.1109/TSMCC.2004.826270

Breazeal, C., Kidd, C. D., Thomaz, A. L., Hoffman, G., & Berlin, M. (2005). Effects of nonverbal communication on efficiency and robustness in human-robot teamwork. *2005 IEEE/RSJ International Conference on Intelligent Robots and Systems*, 708-713. 10.1109/IROS.2005.1545011

Buljac-Samardzic, M., Dekker-van Doorn, C. M., van Wijngaarden, J. D. H., & van Wijk, K. P. (2010). Interventions to improve team effectiveness: A systematic review. *Health Policy (Amsterdam), 94*(3), 183–195. doi:10.1016/j.healthpol.2009.09.015 PMID:19857910

Burke, S., Feitosa, J., & Salas, E. (2015). The unpacking of team models in GIFT. In *Proceedings of the 3rd Annual GIFT Users Symposium (GIFTSym3); 2015 June 17-18; Orlando, FL*. Aberdeen Proving Ground, MD: Army Research Laboratory.

Cannon-Bowers, J.A., Salas, E., Tannenbaum, S.I., & Mathieu, J.E. (1995). Toward theoretically based principles of training effectiveness: A model and initial empirical investigation. *Military Psychology, 7*(3), 141.

Cassell, J. & Thorisson, K.R. (1999). The power of a nod and a glance: Envelope vs. emotional feedback in animated conversational agents. *Applied Artificial Intelligence, 13*(4-5), 519-538.

Chen, J. Y. C., & Barnes, M. J. (2014). Human–agent teaming for multirobot control: A review of human factors issues. *IEEE Transactions on Human-Machine Systems, 44*(1), 13–29. doi:10.1109/THMS.2013.2293535

Chen, J.Y.C. & Joyner C.T. (2009). Concurrent performance of gunner's and robotics operator's tasks in a multitasking environment. *Military Psychology, 21*(1), 98.

Connell, M., Sheridan, K., & Gardner, H. (2004). Experts, generalists, and expert generalists: On the relation between general competence and expertise in a domain. In R. Sternberg & E. Grigorenko (Eds.), *Perspectives on the psychology of abilities, competencies, and expertise* (pp. 126–155). New York: Cambridge University Press.

Cooke, N. J., Gorman, J. C., & Winner, J. L. (2007). Team cognition. Handbook of Applied Cognition, 239-268.

Cummings, M. L., & Guerlain, S. (2007). Developing operator capacity estimates for supervisory control of autonomous vehicles. *Human Factors: The Journal of the Human Factors and Ergonomics Society, 49*(1), 1–15. doi:10.1518/001872007779598109 PMID:17315838

D'Mello, S., Picard, R., & Graesser, A. (2007). Towards an affect –sensitive autotutor. *IEEE Intelligent Systems, 22*(4), 53–61. doi:10.1109/MIS.2007.79

Dang, T. H. H., & Tapus, A. (2007). Coping with Stress Using Social Robots as Emotion-Orientated Tool: Potential Factors Discovered from Stress Game Experiment. In G. Hermann, M. J. Pearson, A. Lenz, P. Bremner, A. Spiers, & U. Leonards (Eds.), *Social Robots. LNAI* (Vol. 8239, pp. 160–169). Heidelberg, Germany: Springer. doi:10.1007/978-3-319-02675-6_16 de Melo, C. M., Marsella, S., & Gratch, J. (2018). Social decisions and fairness change when people's interests are represented by autonomous agents. *Autonomous Agents and Multi-Agent Systems*, *32*(1), 163–187. doi:10.100710458-017-9376-6

DeCarlo, D., Stone, M., Revilla, C., & Venditti, J. J. (2004). Specifying and animating facial signals for discourse in embodied conversational agents. *Computer Animation and Virtual Worlds*, *15*(1), 27–38. doi:10.1002/cav.5

Demir, M., & Cooke, N. J. (2014). Human teaming changes driven by expectations of a synthetic teammate. *Proceedings of the Human Factors and Ergonomics Society Annual Meeting*, *58*(1), 1. doi:10.1177/1541931214581004

Demir, M., McNeese, N. J., & Cooke, N. J. (2016). Team communication behaviors of the human-automation teaming. In *Cognitive Methods in Situation Awareness and Decision Support (CogSIMA), 2016 IEEE International Multi-Disciplinary Conference on*. IEEE.

Demir, M., McNeese, N. J., & Cooke, N. J. (2018). The Impact of Perceived Autonomous Agents on Dynamic Team Behaviors. *IEEE Transactions on Emerging Topics in Computational Intelligence*, *2*(4), 258–267. doi:10.1109/TETCI.2018.2829985

Demir, M., McNeese, N. J., Cooke, N. J., Ball, J. T., Myers, C., & Frieman, M. (2015, September). Synthetic teammate communication and coordination with humans. *Proceedings of the Human Factors and Ergonomics Society Annual Meeting*, *59*(1), 951–955. doi:10.1177/1541931215591275

Devillers, L., Rosset, S., Duplessis, G. D., Bechade, L., Yemez, Y., Turker, B. B., . . . Deléglise, P. (2018, May). Multifaceted Engagement in Social Interaction with a Machine: The JOKER Project. In *2018 13th IEEE International Conference on Automatic Face & Gesture Recognition (FG 2018)* (pp. 697-701). IEEE.

Entin, E. E., & Serfaty, D. (1999). Adaptive team coordination. *Human Factors: The Journal of the Human Factors and Ergonomics Society*, *41*(2), 312–325. doi:10.1518/001872099779591196

Farinelli, A., Zanotto, E., & Pagello, E. (2017). Advanced approaches for multi-robot coordination in logistic scenarios. *Robotics and Autonomous Systems*, *90*, 34–44. doi:10.1016/j.robot.2016.08.010

Flin, R., Glavin, R., & Patey, R. (2003). *Framework for observing and rating anaesthetists' non-technical skills. Anaesthetists' non-technical skills (ANTS) system handbook v1. 0*. University of Aberdeen and Scottish Clinical Simulation Centre.

Flin, R., & Maran, N. (2004). Identifying and training non-technical skills for teams in acute medicine. *Quality & Safety in Health Care*, *13*(1), i80–i84. doi:10.1136/qshc.2004.009993 PMID:15465960

Gallagher, M.E., Tasca, G.A., Ritchie, K., Balfour, L., Maxwell, H., & Bissada, H. (2014). Interpersonal learning is associated with improved self-esteem in group psychotherapy for women with binge eating disorder. *Psychotherapy*, *51*(1), 66.

Gardner, H. (1987). The theory of multiple intelligences. *Annals of Dyslexia*, *37*(1), 19–35. doi:10.1007/BF02648057 PMID:24234985

Gardner, H., & Moran, S. (2006). The science of multiple intelligences theory: A response to Lynn Waterhouse. *Educational Psychologist, 41*(4), 227–232. doi:10.120715326985ep4104_2

Gebhard, P., Schneeberger, T., Baur, T., & André, E. (2018, July). MARSSI: Model of Appraisal, Regulation, and Social Signal Interpretation. In *Proceedings of the 17th International Conference on Autonomous Agents and MultiAgent Systems* (pp. 497-506). International Foundation for Autonomous Agents and Multiagent Systems.

Glas, D., Satake, S., Kanda, T., & Hagita, N. (2012). An interaction design framework for social robots. *Robotics: Science and Systems, 7*, 89.

Goldberg, B. (2015, September). Feedback source modality effects in game-based training: A trade-off analysis. *Proceedings of the Human Factors and Ergonomics Society Annual Meeting, 59*(1), 1858–1862. doi:10.1177/1541931215591401

Graesser, A., & McNamara, D. (2010). Self-regulated learning in learning environments with pedagogical agents that interact in natural language. *Educational Psychologist, 45*(4), 234–244. doi:10.1080/00461520.2010.515933

Gratch, J., Okhmatovskaia, A., Lamothe, F., Marsella, S., Morales, M., van der Werf, R. J., & Morency, L. (2006). Virtual rapport. In *International Workshop on Intelligent Virtual Agents*. Springer Berlin Heidelberg. 10.1007/11821830_2

Gratch, J., Wang, N., Gerten, J., Fast, E., & Duffy, R. (2007). Creating rapport with virtual agents. In *International Workshop on Intelligent Virtual Agents*. Springer Berlin Heidelberg. 10.1007/978-3-540-74997-4_12

Gross, J. J., & Thompson, R. A. (2007). Emotion Regulation: Conceptual Foundations. In J. J. Gross (Ed.), *Handbook of emotion regulation* (pp. 3–24). New York, NY: The Guilford Press.

Guo, Y. R., & Goh, D. H. L. (2015). Affect in Embodied Pedagogical Agents: Meta-Analytic Review. *Journal of Educational Computing Research, 53*(1), 124–149. doi:10.1177/0735633115588774

Hadley, W., Houck, C., Brown, L. K., Spitalnick, J. S., Ferrer, M., & Barker, D. (2018). Moving beyond role-play: Evaluating the use of virtual reality to teach emotion regulation for the prevention of adolescent risk behavior within a randomized pilot trial. *Journal of Pediatric Psychology, 44*(4), 425–435. doi:10.1093/jpepsy/jsy092 PMID:30551157

Hancock, P. A., Billings, D. R., Schaefer, K. E., Chen, J. Y. C., De Visser, E. J., & Parasuraman, R. (2011). A meta-analysis of factors affecting trust in human-robot interaction. *Human Factors: The Journal of the Human Factors and Ergonomics Society, 53*(5), 517–527. doi:10.1177/0018720811417254 PMID:22046724

Harbers, M., Jonker, C., & Van Riemsdijk, B. (2012). Enhancing team performance through effective communication. *Proceedings of the 4th Annual Human-Agent-Robot Teamwork Workshop*, 1-2.

Hart, J. L., & Proctor, M. D. (2016). Framework and assessment of conversational virtual humans as role-players in simulated social encounters with people. *Journal of the International Association of Advanced Technology and Science, 2*, 24–33.

Hartholt, A., Traum, D., Marsella, S., Morency, L. P., Shapiro, A., & Gratch, J. (2014). A Shared, Modular Architecture for Developing Virtual Humans. *Architectures and Standards for Intelligent Virtual Agents at IVA*, 4.

Hayes, B. & Scassellati, B. (2013). Challenges in shared-environment human-robot collaboration. *Learning, 8,* 9.

Heerink, M., Krose, B., Evers, V., & Wielinga, B. (2006). The influence of a robot's social abilities on acceptance by elderly users. *ROMAN 2006-The 15th IEEE International Symposium on Robot and Human Interactive Communication,* 521-526. 10.1109/ROMAN.2006.314442

Hinds, P.J. & Weisband, S.P. (2003). Knowledge sharing and shared understanding in virtual teams. *Virtual teams that work: Creating conditions for virtual team effectiveness,* 21-36.

Hoffman, G., Birnbaum, G. E., Vanunu, K., Sass, O., & Reis, H. T. (2014). Robot responsiveness to human disclosure affects social impression and appeal. In *Proceedings of the 2014 ACM/IEEE international conference on Human-robot interaction.* ACM. 10.1145/2559636.2559660

Holden, H. K., & Goldberg, B. (2011). *The impact of student expectations and tutor acceptance on computer-based learning environment acceptance and future usage intentions. International Defense & Homeland Security Simulation (DHSS) Workshop.*

Huang, L., Morency, L., & Gratch, J. (2011). Virtual Rapport 2.0. In *International Workshop on Intelligent Virtual Agents.* Springer Berlin Heidelberg. 10.1007/978-3-642-23974-8_8

Jung, B., & Kopp, S. (2003, September). Flurmax: An interactive virtual agent for entertaining visitors in a hallway. In *International Workshop on Intelligent Virtual Agents* (pp. 23-26). Springer. 10.1007/978-3-540-39396-2_5

Kang, S., & Gratch, J. (2012). Socially anxious people reveal more personal information with virtual counselors that talk about themselves using intimate human back stories. *Annual Review of Cybertherapy and Telemedicine, 181,* 202–207. PMID:22954856

Kelley, J. F. (1984). An iterative design methodology for user-friendly natural language office information applications. *ACM Transactions on Information Systems, 2*(1), 26–41. doi:10.1145/357417.357420

Kozlowski, S. W., & Ilgen, D. R. (2006). Enhancing the effectiveness of work groups and teams. *Psychological Science in the Public Interest, 7*(3), 77–124. doi:10.1111/j.1529-1006.2006.00030.x PMID:26158912

Krumhuber, E., Manstead, A. S., Cosker, D., Marshall, D., Rosin, P. L., & Kappas, A. (2007). Facial dynamics as indicators of trustworthiness and cooperative behavior. *Emotion (Washington, D.C.), 7*(4), 730–735. doi:10.1037/1528-3542.7.4.730 PMID:18039040

Lajoie, S. P., & Poitras, E. (2014). Macro and micro-strategies in for metacognition and co-regulation in the medical tutoring domain. In R. Sottilare, A. Graesser, X. Hu, & B. Goldberg (Eds.), *Design Recommendations for Adaptive Intelligent Tutoring Systems: Adaptive Instructional Management* (Vol. 2, pp. 151–168). Orlando, FL: U.S. Army Research Laboratory.

Lallée, S., Vouloutsi, V., Munoz, M. B., Grechuta, K., Llobet, J. Y. P., Sarda, M., & Verschure, P. F. (2015). Towards the synthetic self: Making others perceive me as an other. *Paladyn: Journal of Behavioral Robotics*, 6(1). doi:10.1515/pjbr-2015-0010

Large, D. R., Clark, L., Quandt, A., Burnett, G., & Skrypchuk, L. (2017). Steering the conversation: A linguistic exploration of natural language interactions with a digital assistant during simulated driving. *Applied Ergonomics*, 63, 53–61. doi:10.1016/j.apergo.2017.04.003 PMID:28502406

LaViola, J., Williamson, B., Brooks, C., Veazanchin, S., Sottilare, R., & Garrity, P. (2015, December). Using augmented reality to tutor military tasks in the wild. *Proceedings of the Interservice/Industry Training Simulation & Education Conference*.

Lee, J. D., & See, K. A. (2004). Trust in automation: Designing for appropriate reliance. *Human Factors: The Journal of the Human Factors and Ergonomics Society*, 46(1), 50–80. doi:10.1518/hfes.46.1.50.30392 PMID:15151155

Lee, L., Lajoie, S., Poitras, E., Nkangu, M., & Doleck, T. (2017). Co-regulation and knowledge construction in an online synchronous problem based learning setting. *Education and Information Technologies*, 22(4), 1623–1650. doi:10.100710639-016-9509-6

Lemaignan, S., Warnier, M., Sisbot, E. A., Clodic, A., & Alami, R. (2017). Artificial cognition for social human–robot interaction: An implementation. *Artificial Intelligence*, 247, 45–69. doi:10.1016/j.artint.2016.07.002

Lerner, R. M., Liben, L. S., & Mueller, U. (2015). *Handbook of Child Psychology and Developmental Science, Cognitive Processes* (Vol. 2). John Wiley & Sons. doi:10.1002/9781118963418

Lisetti, C., & Hudlicka, E. (2015). Why and how to build emotion-based agent architectures. In *The Oxford Handbook of Affective Computing* (p. 94). Oxford Library of Psychology.

Lohani, M., & Isaacowitz, D. M. (2014). Age differences in managing response to sadness elicitors using attentional deployment, positive reappraisal and suppression. *Cognition and Emotion*, 28(4), 678–697. doi:10.1080/02699931.2013.853648 PMID:24206128

Lohani, M., Payne, B. R., & Isaacowitz, D. (2018). Emotional Coherence in Early and Later Adulthood During Sadness Reactivity and Regulation. *Emotion (Washington, D.C.)*, 18(6), 789–804. doi:10.1037/emo0000345 PMID:28682087

Lohani, M., Payne, B. R., & Strayer, D. L. (2019). A Review of Psychophysiological Measures to Assess Cognitive States in Real-World Driving. *Frontiers in Human Neuroscience*, 13. PMID:30941023

Lohani, M., Stokes, C., Dashan, N., McCoy, M., Bailey, C. A., & Rivers, S. E. (2017). A Framework for Human-Agent Social Systems: The Role of Non-technical Factors in Operation Success. In *Advances in Human Factors in Robots and Unmanned Systems* (pp. 137–148). Springer International Publishing. doi:10.1007/978-3-319-41959-6_12

Lohani, M., Stokes, C., McCoy, M., Bailey, C. A., Joshi, A., & Rivers, S. E. (2016b). Perceived role of physiological sensors impacts trust and reliance on robots. In *Robot and Human Interactive Communication (RO-MAN), 2016 25th IEEE International Symposium on*. IEEE. 10.1109/ROMAN.2016.7745166

Lohani, M., Stokes, C., McCoy, M., Bailey, C. A., & Rivers, S. E. (2016a). Social Interaction Moderates Human-Robot Trust-Reliance Relationship and Improves Stress Coping. In *The Eleventh ACM/IEEE International Conference on Human Robot Interaction*. IEEE Press. 10.1109/HRI.2016.7451811

Lohani, M., Stokes, C. K., Oden, K. B., Frazier, S. J., Landers, K. J., Craven, P. L., . . . Macannuco, D. J. (2017). The Impact of Non-Technical skills on Trust and Stress. In *Proceedings of the Companion of the 2017 ACM/IEEE International Conference on Human-Robot Interaction* (pp. 191-192). ACM. 10.1145/3029798.3038321

López, A., Peñaloza, C., & Cuéllar, F. (2016). Influence of a Humanoid Robot in Human Decision-Making When Using Direct & Indirect Requests. In *The Eleventh ACM/IEEE International Conference on Human Robot Interaction*. IEEE Press. 10.1109/HRI.2016.7451812

Lubold, N., Walker, E., & Pon-Barry, H. (2015). Relating Entrainment, Grounding, and Topic of Discussion in Collaborative Learning Dialogues. Proceedings of Computer Supported Collaborative Learning.

Lucas, G. M., Boberg, J., Traum, D., Artstein, R., Gratch, J., Gainer, A., ... Nakano, M. (2017, October). The role of social dialogue and errors in robots. In *Proceedings of the 5th International Conference on Human Agent Interaction* (pp. 431-433). ACM. 10.1145/3125739.3132617

Lucas, G. M., Boberg, J., Traum, D., Artstein, R., Gratch, J., Gainer, A., ... Nakano, M. (2018, February). Getting to know each other: The role of social dialogue in recovery from errors in social robots. In *Proceedings of the 2018 ACM/IEEE International Conference on Human-Robot Interaction* (pp. 344-351). ACM. 10.1145/3171221.3171258

Maatman, R. M., Gratch, J., & Marsella, S. (2005). Natural behavior of a listening agent. In *International Workshop on Intelligent Virtual Agents*. Springer Berlin Heidelberg. 10.1007/11550617_3

Mathieu, J., Maynard, M. T., Rapp, T., & Gilson, L. (2008). Team effectiveness 1997-2007: A review of recent advancements and a glimpse into the future. *Journal of Management*, *34*(3), 410–476. doi:10.1177/0149206308316061

Mavridis, N. (2015). A review of verbal and non-verbal human–robot interactive communication. *Robotics and Autonomous Systems*, *63*, 22–35. doi:10.1016/j.robot.2014.09.031

Mayer, R. C., Davis, J. H., & Schoorman, F. D. (1995). An integrative model of organizational trust. *Academy of Management Review*, *20*(3), 709–734. doi:10.5465/amr.1995.9508080335

Mayer, R. E., & DaPra, C. S. (2012). An embodiment effect in computer-based learning with animated pedagogical agents. *Journal of Experimental Psychology. Applied*, *18*(3), 239–252. doi:10.1037/a0028616 PMID:22642688

McGrath, J. E. (1962). Leadership behavior: some requirements for leadership training. Washington, DC: US Civil Service Commission.

Mell, J., Lucas, G. M., & Gratch, J. (2018, July). Welcome to the real world: How agent strategy increases human willingness to deceive. In *Proceedings of the 17th International Conference on Autonomous Agents and MultiAgent Systems* (pp. 1250-1257). International Foundation for Autonomous Agents and Multiagent Systems.

Moon, Y., & Nass, C. (1998). Are computers scapegoats? Attributions of responsibility in human–computer interaction. *International Journal of Human-Computer Studies*, *49*(1), 79–94. doi:10.1006/ijhc.1998.0199

Morency, L. (2010). Modeling human communication dynamics. *IEEE Signal Processing Magazine*, *27*(5), 112–116. doi:10.1109/MSP.2010.937500

Moreno, R., Mayer, R. E., Spires, H. A., & Lester, J. C. (2001). The case for social agency in computer-based teaching: Do students learn more deeply when they interact with animated pedagogical agents? *Cognition and Instruction*, *19*(2), 177–213. doi:10.1207/S1532690XCI1902_02

Mou, Y., & Xu, K. (2017). The media inequality: Comparing the initial human-human and human-AI social interactions. *Computers in Human Behavior*, *72*, 432–440. doi:10.1016/j.chb.2017.02.067

Mousavinasab, E., Zarifsanaiey, N., & Niakan Kalhori, S., Rakhshan, M., Keikha, L., & Ghazi Saeedi, M. (2018). Intelligent tutoring systems: A systematic review of characteristics, applications, and evaluation methods. *Interactive Learning Environments*, 1–22. doi:10.1080/10494820.2018.1558257

Mutlu, B. (2011). Designing embodied cues for dialog with robots. *AI Magazine*, *32*(4), 17–30. doi:10.1609/aimag.v32i4.2376

Nass, C., Fogg, B. J., & Moon, Y. (1996). Can computers be teammates? *International Journal of Human-Computer Studies*, *45*(6), 669–678. doi:10.1006/ijhc.1996.0073

Nass, C., & Moon, Y. (2000). Machines and mindlessness: Social responses to computers. *The Journal of Social Issues*, *56*(1), 81–103. doi:10.1111/0022-4537.00153

Nass, C., Moon, Y., & Carney, P. (1999). Are respondents polite to computers? Social desirability and direct responses to computers. *Journal of Applied Social Psychology*, *29*(5), 1093–1110. doi:10.1111/j.1559-1816.1999.tb00142.x

Nass, C., Moon, Y., & Green, N. (1997a). Are computers gender-neutral? Social desirability and direct responses to computers. *Journal of Applied Social Psychology*, *27*(10), 864–876. doi:10.1111/j.1559-1816.1997.tb00275.x

Nass, C., Moon, Y., Morkes, J., Kim, E.-Y., & Fogg, B. J. (1997b). Computers are social actors: A review of current research. In B. Friedman (Ed.), *Moral and ethical issues in human-computer interaction* (pp. 137–162). Stanford, CA: CSLI Press.

Nye, B. D., Graesser, A. C., & Hu, X. (2014). AutoTutor and family: A review of 17 years of natural language tutoring. *International Journal of Artificial Intelligence in Education*, *24*(4), 427–469. doi:10.100740593-014-0029-5

Oh, C. S., Bailenson, J. N., & Welch, G. F. (2018). A Systematic Review of Social Presence: Definition, Antecedents, and Implications. *Front. Robot. AI*, *5*, 114. doi:10.3389/frobt.2018.00114

Pan, D., & Bolton, M. L. (2018). Properties for formally assessing the performance level of human-human collaborative procedures with miscommunications and erroneous human behavior. *International Journal of Industrial Ergonomics*, *63*, 75–88. doi:10.1016/j.ergon.2016.04.001

Pandey, A. K., Ali, M., & Alami, R. (2013). Towards a task-aware proactive sociable robot based on multi-state perspective-taking. *International Journal of Social Robotics*, *5*(2), 215–236. doi:10.100712369-013-0181-3

Paquette, L., Rowe, J., Baker, R. S., Mott, B., Lester, J., DeFalco, J., ... Georgoulas, V. (2015). Sensor-Free or Sensor-Full: A Comparison of Data Modalities in Multi-Channel Affect Detection. *Proceedings of the 8th International Conference on Educational Data Mining*, 93-100.

Paulus, P. B., & Brown, V. R. (2007). Toward more creative and innovative group idea generation: A cognitive-social-motivational perspective of brainstorming. *Social and Personality Psychology Compass*, *1*(1), 248–265. doi:10.1111/j.1751-9004.2007.00006.x

Pecune, F., Chen, J., Matsuyama, Y., & Cassell, J. (2018, July). Field Trial Analysis of Socially Aware Robot Assistant. *Proceedings of the 17th International Conference on Autonomous Agents and MultiAgent Systems*, 1241-1249.

Prati, L. M., Douglas, C., Ferris, G. R., Ammeter, A. P., & Buckley, M. R. (2003). Emotional intelligence, leadership effectiveness, and team outcomes. *The International Journal of Organizational Analysis*, *11*(1), 21–40. doi:10.1108/eb028961

Rizzo, A., John, B., Newman, B., Williams, J., Hartholt, A., Lethin, C., & Buckwalter, J. G. (2013). Virtual reality as a tool for delivering PTSD exposure therapy and stress resilience training. *Military Behavioral Health*, *1*(1), 52–58. doi:10.1080/21635781.2012.721064

Sabanovic, S., Michalowski, M. P., & Simmons, R. (2006). Robots in the wild: Observing human-robot social interaction outside the lab. In *9th IEEE International Workshop on Advanced Motion Control*. IEEE. 10.1109/AMC.2006.1631758

Sajjadi, P., Hoffmann, L., Cimiano, P., & Kopp, S. (2018, September). On the Effect of a Personality-Driven ECA on Perceived Social Presence and Game Experience in VR. In *2018 10th International Conference on Virtual Worlds and Games for Serious Applications (VS-Games)* (pp. 1-8). IEEE. 10.1109/VS-Games.2018.8493436

Salas, E., Cooke, N. J., & Rosen, M. A. (2008). On teams, teamwork, and team performance: Discoveries and developments. *Human Factors*, *50*(3), 540–547. doi:10.1518/001872008X288457 PMID:18689065

Salas, E., Dickinson, T. L., Converse, S. A., & Tannenbaum, S. I. (1992). Toward an understanding of team performance and training. In R. W. Swezey & E. Salas (Eds.), *Teams: Their Training and Performance* (pp. 3–29). Ablex.

Salas, E., Shuffler, M. L., Thayer, A. L., Bedwell, W., & Lazzara, E. (2014). Understanding and improving teamwork in organizations: A scientifically based practical guide. *Human Resource Management*, *54*(4), 599–622. doi:10.1002/hrm.21628

Salas, E. E., & Fiore, S. M. (2004). *Team cognition: Understanding the factors that drive process and performance*. American Psychological Association. doi:10.1037/10690-000

Salmon, P. M., Stanton, N. A., Walker, G. H., Baber, C., Jenkins, D. P., McMaster, R., & Young, M. S. (2008). What really is going on? Review of situation awareness models for individuals and teams. *Theoretical Issues in Ergonomics Science*, 9(4), 297–323. doi:10.1080/14639220701561775

Salovey, P., & Mayer, J. D. (1990). Emotional intelligence. *Imagination, Cognition and Personality*, 9(3), 185–211. doi:10.2190/DUGG-P24E-52WK-6CDG

Schaefer, K. E., Chen, J. Y., Szalma, J. L., & Hancock, P. A. (2016). A meta-analysis of factors influencing the development of trust in automation: Implications for understanding autonomy in future systems. *Human Factors*, 58(3), 377–400. doi:10.1177/0018720816634228 PMID:27005902

Schneider, T. R. (2008). Evaluations of stressful transactions: What's in an appraisal? *Stress and Health*, 24(2), 151–158. doi:10.1002mi.1176

Sebanz, N., Bekkering, H., & Knoblich, G. (2006). Joint action: Bodies and minds moving together. *Trends in Cognitive Sciences*, 10(2), 70–76. doi:10.1016/j.tics.2005.12.009 PMID:16406326

Shah, J. A. (2011). *Fluid coordination of human-robot teams* (PhD diss.). Massachusetts Institute of Technology.

Shamekhi, A., Czerwinski, M., Mark, G., Novotny, M., & Bennett, G. A. (2016, September). An exploratory study toward the preferred conversational style for compatible virtual agents. In *International Conference on Intelligent Virtual Agents* (pp. 40-50). Springer. 10.1007/978-3-319-47665-0_4

Sidner, C. L., Rich, C., Shayganfar, M., Bickmore, T. W., Ring, L., & Zhang, Z. (2015). A Robotic Companion for Social Support of Isolated Older Adults. HRI (Extended Abstracts), 289. doi:10.1145/2701973.2702103

Sinatra, A., Gilbert, S., Dorneich, M., Winer, E., Ostrander, A., Ouverson, K., . . . Sottilare, R. (2018, June). Considerations for Dealing with Real-Time Communications in an Intelligent Team Tutoring System Experiment. *The Team Tutoring Workshop of the 19th International Conference of the Artificial Intelligence in Education (AIED) Conference*.

Sottilare, R. & Hart, J. (2012). Cognitive and affective modeling in intelligent virtual humans for training and tutoring applications. *Advances in Applied Human Modeling and Simulation*, 113.

Sottilare, R., Holden, H., Brawner, K., & Goldberg, B. (2011). Challenges and Emerging Concepts in the Development of Adaptive, Computer-based Tutoring Systems for Team Training. *Proceedings of the Interservice/Industry Training Simulation & Education Conference*.

Sottilare, R., & Roessingh, J. J. (2014). Application of Intelligent Agents in Embedded Virtual Simulations. In *NATO Technical Report: Improving Human Effectiveness through Embedded Virtual Simulation: Findings of Task Group HFM-165*. NATO Science & Technology Organization.

Sottilare, R. A., Burke, C. S., Salas, E., Sinatra, A. M., Johnston, J. H., & Gilbert, S. B. (2018). Designing adaptive instruction for teams: A meta-analysis. *International Journal of Artificial Intelligence in Education*, 28(2), 225–264. doi:10.100740593-017-0146-z

Tapus, A. (2013). Coping with Stress Using Social Robots as Emotion-Oriented Tool: Potential Factors Discovered from Stress Game Experiment. In *International Conference on Social Robotics*. Springer International Publishing.

Todorov, A. (2008). Evaluating faces on trustworthiness. *Annals of the New York Academy of Sciences, 1124*(1), 208–224. doi:10.1196/annals.1440.012 PMID:18400932

Trafton, G. J., Cassimatis, N. L., Bugajska, M. D., Brock, D. P., Mintz, F. E., & Schultz, A. C. (2005). Enabling effective human-robot interaction using perspective-taking in robots. *IEEE Transactions on Systems, Man, and Cybernetics. Part A, Systems and Humans, 35*(4), 460–470. doi:10.1109/TSMCA.2005.850592

Vinciarelli, A., & Pentland, A. S. (2015). New social signals in a new interaction world: The next frontier for social signal processing. *IEEE Systems, Man, and Cybernetics Magazine, 1*(2), 10–17. doi:10.1109/MSMC.2015.2441992

Von der Puetten, A. M., Krämer, N. C., Gratch, J., & Kang, S. H. (2010). It doesn't matter what you are! Explaining social effects of agents and avatars. *Computers in Human Behavior, 26*(6), 1641–1650. doi:10.1016/j.chb.2010.06.012

Wilson, K., Salas, E., Priest, H., & Andrews, D. (2007). Errors in the heat of battle: Taking a closer look at shared cognition breakdowns through teamwork. *Human Factors, 49*(2), 243–256. doi:10.1518/001872007X312478 PMID:17447666

Woolf, B., Burleson, W., Arroyo, I., Dragon, T., Cooper, D., & Picard, R. (2009). Affect-aware tutors: Recognising and responding to student affect. *International Journal of Learning Technology, 4*(3/4), 3–4, 129–164. doi:10.1504/IJLT.2009.028804

Yang, F., & Heeman, P. A. (2010). Initiative conflicts in task-oriented dialogue. *Computer Speech & Language, 24*(2), 175–189. doi:10.1016/j.csl.2009.04.003

Zhao, R., Sinha, T., Black, A. W., & Cassell, J. (2016, September). Socially-aware virtual agents: Automatically assessing dyadic rapport from temporal patterns of behavior. In *International Conference on Intelligent Virtual Agents* (pp. 218-233). Springer International Publishing. 10.1007/978-3-319-47665-0_20

Zheng, K., Glas, D. F., Kanda, T., Ishiguro, H., & Hagita, N. (2013). Designing and implementing a human–robot team for social interactions. *IEEE Transactions on Systems, Man, and Cybernetics. Systems, 43*(4), 843–859. doi:10.1109/TSMCA.2012.2216870

ADDITIONAL READING

Azevedo, R., & Aleven, V. (2013). *International handbook of metacognition and learning technologies* (Vol. 26). Amsterdam, The Netherlands: Springer. doi:10.1007/978-1-4419-5546-3

Badizadegan, P., & Butcher, K. R. (2015). *Understanding and evaluating effective technology integration in the classroom.* Undergraduate Research Journal.

Belpaeme, T., Kennedy, J., Ramachandran, A., Scassellati, B., & Tanaka, F. (2018). Social robots for education: A review. *Science Robotics, 3*(21), eaat5954.

Butcher, K. R., & Jameson, J. M. (2016). Computer-based instruction (CBI) within special education. In J. K. Luiselli & A. J. Fischer (Eds.), *Computer-Assisted and Web-Based Innovations in Psychology, Special Education, and Health. Elsevier. Published, 01/2016.* doi:10.1016/B978-0-12-802075-3.00009-7

Butcher, K. R., Runburg, M., & Altizer, R. (2017). Dino Lab: Designing and Developing an Educational Game for Critical Thinking. In Handbook of Research on Serious Games for Educational Applications (pp. 115-148). IGI Global.

Lajoie, S. P., & Poitras, E. (2014). Macro and micro strategies for metacognition and socially shared regulation in the medical tutoring domain. In R. Sottilare, A. Graesser, X. Hu, & B. Goldberg (Eds.), *Design Recommendations for Adaptive Intelligent Tutoring Systems: Adaptive Instructional Management* (Vol. 2). Orlando, FL: U.S. Army Research Laboratory.

Lajoie, S. P., & Poitras, E. (2017). Crossing disciplinary boundaries to improve technology rich learning environments. *Teachers College Record, 119*(3), 1–30.

Leite, I., McCoy, M., Lohani, M., Ullman, D., Salomons, N., Stokes, C., ... Scassellati, B. (2017). Narratives with robots: The impact of interaction context and individual differences on story recall and emotional understanding. *Frontiers in Robotics and AI, 4*, 29. doi:10.3389/frobt.2017.00029

Leyzberg, D., Ramachandran, A., & Scassellati, B. (2018). The Effect of Personalization in Longer-Term Robot Tutoring. *ACM Transactions on Human-Robot Interaction, 7*(3), 19. doi:10.1145/3283453

Poitras, E., Fazeli, N., & Mayne, Z. (2018). Modeling Student Teachers' Information-Seeking Behaviors while Learning with Network-Based Tutors. *Journal of Educational Technology Systems, 47*(2), 227–247. doi:10.1177/0047239518797086

Ramachandran, A., Huang, C. M., & Scassellati, B. (2019). Toward Effective Robot--Child Tutoring: Internal Motivation, Behavioral Intervention, and Learning Outcomes. *ACM Transactions on Interactive Intelligent Systems, 9*(1), 2. doi:10.1145/3213768

Ranellucci, J., Rosenberg, J., & Poitras, E. (accepted). Exploring pre-service teachers' use of technology: The technology acceptance model and expectancy-value theory. *Journal of Computer Assisted Learning.*

Sottilare, R. A., Graesser, A., Hu, X., & Holden, H. (Eds.). (2013). Design recommendations for intelligent tutoring systems: Volume 1-learner modeling (Vol. 1). US Army Research Laboratory

Waterhouse, L. (2006). Inadequate evidence for multiple intelligences, Mozart effect, and emotional intelligence theories. *Educational Psychologist, 41*(4), 247–255. doi:10.120715326985ep4104_5

Zheng, R. (2018). Personalization with digital technology: A deep cognitive process perspective. In R. Zheng (Ed.), *Digital technologies and instructional design for personalized learning* (pp. 1–27). Hershey, PA: Information Science Reference/IGI Global Publishing. doi:10.4018/978-1-5225-3940-7.ch001

Zheng, R., & Greenberg, K. (2018). Effective design in human and machine learning: A cognitive perspective. In F. Chen & J. Zhou (Eds.), *Human and machine learning: Visible, explainable, trustworthy and transparent* (pp. 55–74). New York, NY: Springer. doi:10.1007/978-3-319-90403-0_4

KEY TERMS AND DEFINITIONS

Human-Technology Team: A set of two or more members who interact dynamically, interdependently, and adaptively toward a common and valued goal. Inherent in this definition is the assumption that at least one of the team members will be technology-based and that this technology is intelligent or autonomous to a sufficient degree for a dynamic interaction with human team member(s).

Non-Technical Skills: Non-technical skills are cognitive, social, and emotional abilities that are fundamental in human interaction. From an educational technology perspective, an example would be the socioemotional learning methods that a technology may adopt to help students manage their emotional reactions (e.g., frustration).

Technical Skills: Technical skills are generally referred to any task-specific skills that an individual or technology was trained to execute. An example of technical skills from automation industry would be to have skills to drive a vehicle. From an educational technology perspective, an example is capability of a technology designed to teach coding. The technology would need to have the technical skills to know how to introduce the concept of coding to a student, use helpful examples and visuals so that a student can learn to code.

Compilation of References

Abánades, M., Botana, F., Kovács, Z., Recio, T., & Sólyom-Gecse, C. (2016). Development of automatic reasoning tools in GeoGebra in ISSAC 2016 Software Presentations Communicated by Roman Pearce. *ACM Communications in Computer Algebra*, *50*(197), 85–88.

Abernathy, D. J. (2001). Get ready for m-learning. *Training & Development*, *55*(2), 10–20.

Acosta, M., & Fiallo, J. (2017). Enseñando Geometría con tecnología Digital: una propuesta desde la Teoría de las Situaciones Didácticas (Universidad Distrital Francisco José de Caldas, Ed.). Bogotá, Colombia: Énfasis.

Acuna, S. R., Lopez-Aymes, C., & Acuna-Castillo, S. T. (2018). How does the type of task influence the performance and social regulation of collaborative learning? *International Journal of Higher Education*, *7*(2), 28–29. doi:10.5430/ijhe.v7n2p28

Adcock, P. (2014). The longevity of multiple intelligence theory in education. *The Delta Kappa Gamma Bulletin*, 50-57.

Aguilera, N. A. (2018). Development of Spatial Skills with Virtual Reality and Augmented Reality. *International Journal on Interactive Design and Manufacturing*, *12*(1), 133–144. doi:10.100712008-017-0388-x

Ahmad, R. A., Seman, A. A., Awang, M. M., & Sulaiman, F. (2015). Application of Multiple Intelligence Theory to Increase Student Motivation in Learning History. *Asian Culture and History*, *7*(1), 210–219.

Aksoy, E., & Narlı, S. (2015). An Examination of Mathematically Gifted Students' Learning Styles by Decision Trees. *Turkish Journal of Giftedness & Education*, *5*(2).

Aksoy, E., Narli, S., & Aksoy, M. A. (2018). Examination of Mathematically Gifted Students Using Data Mining Techniques in Terms of Some Variables. *International Journal of Research in Education and Science*, *4*(2), 471–485. doi:10.21890/ijres.428280

Alfieri, A. (2017). L-System Fractals as Geometric Patterns: A Case Study. In *Mathematics and Technology* (pp. 313–333). Cham: Springer; doi:10.1007/978-3-319-51380-5_14.

Ali, A., Soosan, L., & Hamze, A. (2013). The Effect of Teaching Strategy Based on Multiple Intelligences on Students' Academic Achievement in Science Course. *Universal Journal of Educational Research*, *1*(4), 281-284. Retrieved from http://www.hrpub.org

Alkhawaldeh, N., & Menchaca, M. (2014). Barriers to Utilizing ICT in Education in Jordan. *International Journal on E-Learning*, *13*(2), 127–155.

Almeida, L. S., Prieto, M. D., Ferreira, A. I., Bermejo, M. R., Ferrando, M., & Ferrándiz, C. (2010). Intelligence assessment: Gardner multiple intelligence theory as an alternative. *Learning and Individual Differences*, *20*(3), 225–230. doi:10.1016/j.lindif.2009.12.010

Compilation of References

Amado, N., Sanchez, J., & Pinto, J. (2015). A Utilização do Geogebra na Demonstração Matemática em Sala de Aula: o estudo da reta de Euler. Bolema - Mathematics Education Bulletin, 29(52), 637–657. doi:10.1590/1980-4415v29n52a11

Amman, S., & González, C. (2012). Construcción de triángulos: del dibujo a la figura. In R. Ferragina (Ed.), *GeoGebra entra al aula de matemática*. Buenos Aires: Miño y Dávila; Retrieved from www.minoydavila.com

Analyzing a World War II Poster. (n.d.). Retrieved May 24, 2019, from http://www.readwritethink.org/files/resources/AnalyzingWorldWarII-Poster.htm

Andersen, P. O., Jensen, M. K., Lippert, A., & Østergaard, D. (2010). Identifying non-technical skills and barriers for improvement of teamwork in cardiac arrest teams. *Resuscitation*, 81(6), 695–702. doi:10.1016/j.resuscitation.2010.01.024 PMID:20304547

André, E., Bevacqua, E., Heylen, D., Niewiadomski, R., Pelachaud, C., Peters, C., ... Rehm, M. (2011). Nonverbal Persuasion and Communication in an Affective Agent. In P. Petta, C. Pelachaud, & R. Cowie (Eds.), *Emotion-Oriented Systems: The Humaine Handbook* (pp. 585–608). Springer. doi:10.1007/978-3-642-15184-2_30

Angeli, C., Howard, S. K., Ma, J., Yang, J., & Kirschner, P. A. (2017). Data mining in educational technology classroom research: Can it make a contribution? *Computers & Education*, 113, 226–242. doi:10.1016/j.compedu.2017.05.021

Ang, R., Tan, J. L., Goh, D. H., Huan, V. S., Ooi, Y. P., Boon, J. S. T., & Fung, D. S. S. (2017). A game-based approach to teaching social problem-solving skills. In R. Zheng & M. Gardner (Eds.), *Serious game for educational applications* (pp. 168–195). Hershey, PA: IGI Publishing. doi:10.4018/978-1-5225-0513-6.ch008

Annamalai, N., & Jaganathan, P. (2017). Exploring students' reflective writing on Facebook. *The EUROCALL Review*, 25(2), 3–17. doi:10.4995/eurocall.2017.7750

Arce, P. (2006). Learning futures: Using multiple intelligence theory for adult learners. *Futurics*, 30(3/4), 89–90.

Ardies, J., De Maeyer, S., & Gijbels, D. (2015). A longitudinal study on boys' and girls' career aspirations and interest in technology. *Research in Science & Technological Education*, 33(3), 366–386. doi:10.1080/02635143.2015.1060412

Armor, D. (2017). *Maximizing intelligence*. London: Routledge. doi:10.4324/9780203786000

Armstrong, T. (2006). *Inteligencias múltiples en el aula: guía práctica para educadores*. Barcelona: Paidós.

Armstrong, T. (2009). *Multiple intelligences in the classroom*. Alexander, VA: ASCD.

Armstrong, T. (2009). *Multiple Intelligences in the Classroom*. ASCD.

Arzarello, F., Bairral, M. A., & Dané, C. (2014). Moving from dragging to touchscreen: Geometrical learning with geometric dynamic software. *Teaching Mathematics and Its Applications*, 33(1), 39–51. doi:10.1093/teamat/hru002

Ashby, R., & Lee, P. (1987). Discussing the evidence. *Teaching History*, 48, 13–17.

Asif, R., Merceron, A., Ali, S. A., & Haider, N. G. (2017). Analyzing undergraduate students' performance using educational data mining. *Computers & Education*, 113, 177–194. doi:10.1016/j.compedu.2017.05.007

Asprilla, Y. C., & De Antioquia, U. (2014). La comprensión del concepto de Derivada Mediante El Uso De Geogebra como propuesta didáctica. In *Congreso Iberoamericano de Ciencia* (pp. 1–22). Buenos Aires: Tecnologia y Educación.

Association of Mathematics Teacher Educators. (2017). Standards for preparing teachers of mathematics. Retrieved from amte.net/standards

Attorps, I., Björk, K., & Radic, M. (2016). Generating the patterns of variation with GeoGebra: The case of polynomial approximations. *International Journal of Mathematical Education in Science and Technology, 47*(1), 45–57. doi:10.1080/0020739X.2015.1046961

Attorps, I., Radic, M., & Viirman, O. (2011). Teaching inverse functions at tertiary level. In *Proceedings of the Eighth Conference of the European Society for Research in Mathematics Education* (pp. 2524–2533). Academic Press.

Attwell, G. (2007). The personal learning environments - the future of eLearning? *eLearn. Pap., 2*(1).

Baddeley, A. D. (1992). Working memory. *Science, 255*(5044), 556–559. doi:10.1126cience.1736359 PMID:1736359

Baddeley, A. D., & Logie, R. H. (1992). Auditory imagery and working memory. In D. Reisberg (Ed.), *Auditory imagery* (pp. 179–197). Hillsdale, NJ: Lawrence Erlbaum Associates.

Bahn, D. (2001). Social learning theory: Its application in the context of nurse education. *Nurse Education Today, 21*(2), 110–117. doi:10.1054/nedt.2000.0522 PMID:11170797

Bailey, T. (2013). *World War II. Posters and propaganda.* Retrieved January 22, 2019, from https://www.gilderlehrman.org/history-by-era/world-war-ii/resources/world-war-ii-posters-and-propaganda

Bain, R. (2005). 'They thought the world was flat?': Applying the principles of How People Learn in teaching high school history. In J. Bransford & S. Donovan (Eds.), *How students learn history, mathematics and science in the classroom* (pp. 179–215). Washington, DC: National Academics Press.

Bairral, M., Arzarello, F., & Assis, A. (2017). Domains of Manipulation in Touchscreen Devices and Some Didactic, Cognitive, and Epistemological Implications for Improving Geometric Thinking. In G. Aldon, F. Hitt, L. Bazzini, & U. Gellert (Eds.), *Mathematics and Technology* (pp. 113–142). Cham: Springer; doi:10.1007/978-3-319-51380-5_7.

Baker, R. S., & Yacef, K. (2009). The state of educational data mining in 2009: A review and future visions. *Journal of Educational Data Mining, 1*(1), 3-17.

Bakhshinategh, B., Zaiane, O. R., ElAtia, S., & Ipperciel, D. (2018). Educational data mining applications and tasks: A survey of the last 10 years. *Education and Information Technologies, 23*(1), 537–553. doi:10.100710639-017-9616-z

Bandura, A. (1977). *Social learning theory.* New York: General Learning Press.

Bandura, A. (1986). *Social foundations of thought and action: A social cognitive theory.* Prentice-Hall.

Bandura, A., & Walters, R. (1963). *Social learning and personality development.* New York: Holt, Rinehart & Winston.

Bano, M., Zowghi, D., Kearney, M., Schuck, S., & Aubusson, P. (2018). Mobile learning for science and mathematics school education: A systematic review of empirical evidence. *Computers & Education, 121*, 30–58. doi:10.1016/j.compedu.2018.02.006

Baraglia, J., Cakmak, M., Nagai, Y., Rao, R., & Asada, M. (2016). Initiative in robot assistance during collaborative task execution. *2016 11th ACM/IEEE International Conference on Human-Robot Interaction (HRI),* 67-74.

BarOn, R. (1997). BarOn Emotional Quotient Inventory. Technical manual. Toronto: Multi-Health Systems Inc.

Barra, M., & Vidal, R. (2018). De una Formación Matemática Normativa a una Educación Matemática Inclusiva. Algunos ejemplos para la reflexión sobre la práctica docente. Cuaderno de Educación, UAH, 81.

Barrington, E. (2004). Teaching to student diversity in higher education: How Multiple Intelligence Theory can help. *Teaching in Higher Education, 9*(4), 421–434. doi:10.1080/1356251042000252363

Compilation of References

Barron, B. J. S., Schwartz, D. L., Vye, N. J., Moore, A., Petrosino, A., Zech, L., Bransford, J. D. (1998). Doing with understanding: Lessons from research on problem and project-based learning. *The Journal of the Learning Sciences: Learning through Problem Solving, 7*(3/4), 271-311.

Barton, K. (2001). A picture's worth: Analyzing historical photographs in the elementary grades. *Social Education, 65*(5), 278–283.

Barton, K. (2012, April). Agency, choice and historical action: How history teaching can help students think about democratic decision making. *Citizenship Teaching & Learning, 7*(2), 131–142. doi:10.1386/ctl.7.2.131_1

Barton, K., & Levstik, L. (2004). *Teaching history for the common good*. Mahwah, NJ: Lawrence Erlbaum Associates. doi:10.4324/9781410610508

Barwise, J., & Etchemendy, J. (1991). Visual information and valid reasoning. In W. Zimmermann & S. & Cunningham (Eds.), Visualization in Mathematics (pp. 9–24). Washington, DC: Mathematical Association of America. Retrieved from https://ci.nii.ac.jp/naid/10006844948/

Bas, G. (2016). The effect of multiple intelligences theory-based education on academic achievement: A meta-analytic review. *Educational Sciences: Theory & Research, 16*(6), 1833–1864.

Bas, G. (2016). The Effect of Multiple Intelligences Theory-Based Education on Academic Achievement: A Meta-Analytic Review. *Educational Sciences: Theory and Practice, 16*(6), 1833–1864. doi:10.12738/estp.2016.6.0015

Baş, G., & Beyhab, Ö. (2017). Effects of multiple intelligences supported project-based learning on students' achievement levels and attitudes towards English lesson. *International Electronic Journal of Elementary Education, 2*(3), 365–386.

Batdı, V. (2017). The effect of multiple intelligences on academic achievement: A meta-analytic and thematic study. *Educational Sciences: Theory & Practice, 17*(6). Retrieved of doi:10.12738/estp.2017.6.0104

Bath, J. L., Lang, K. E., Roger, K. R., & Neton, K. J. (2016). Using EEG to understand student learning in algebra: The role of examples. *Learning and Instruction, 25*, 24–34.

Bava Harji, M., & Gheitanchian, M. (2017). Effects of multimedia task-based teaching and learning approach on EFL learners' accuracy, fluency and complexity of oral production. *Turkish Online Journal of Educational Technology, 16*(2), 25–34.

Baytak, A., Land, S. M., & Smith, B. K. (2011). Children as Educational Computer Game Designers: An Exploratory Study. *TOJET: The Turkish Online Journal of Educational Technology, 10*(4).

Beauchamp, G. (2016). *Computing and ICT in the Primary School: From pedagogy to practice*. London: Routledge. doi:10.4324/9781315628042

Beaudin, M., & Bowers, D. (1997). *Logistics for facilitating CAS instruction*. Lancashire, UK: Chartwell-York; Retrieved from https://scholar.google.es/scholar?hl=es&as_sdt=0%2C5&q=Beaudin%2C+M+and+Bowers%2C+D.+%281997%29.+Logistics+for+facilitating+CAS+instruction.+In+J.+Berry%2C+J.+Monaghan%2C+M.+Kronfellner%2C+and+B.+Kutzler+%28Eds.%29%2C+The+state+of+computer+algebra+in+math

Beck, M. (2010). *Civic Participation and Local Development: Building Effective Communities in Jordan*. Publications, Jordan Office. Retrieved from http://www.kas.de/jordanien/en/publications/19795/

Becker, K. (2007). *Pedagogy in commercial video games. In Games and Simulations in Online Learning: Research and Development Frameworks*. Hershey, PA: Information Science Publishing.

Beetham, H., & Sharpe, R. (Eds.). (2013). *Rethinking pedagogy for a digital age: Designing for 21st century learning*. Routledge.

Beldagli, B., & Adiguzel, T. (2010). Illustrating an ideal adaptive e-learning: A conceptual framework. *Procedia: Social and Behavioral Sciences*, *2*(2), 5755–5761. doi:10.1016/j.sbspro.2010.03.939

Belland, B. R., Walker, A. E., Kim, N. J., & Lefler, M. (2017). Synthesizing results from empirical research on computer-based scaffolding in STEM education: A meta-analysis. *Review of Educational Research*, *87*(2), 309–344. doi:10.3102/0034654316670999 PMID:28344365

Belpaeme, T., Baxter, P. E., Read, R., Wood, R., Cuayáhuitl, H., Kiefer, B., & ... . (2012). Multimodal child-robot interaction: Building social bonds. *Journal of Human-Robot Interaction*, *1*(2), 33–53.

Berger, M., & Bowie, L. (2012). A course on functions for in-service mathematics teachers: Changing the discourse. *Education as Change*, *16*(2), 217–229. doi:10.1080/16823206.2012.745751

Berthold, K., Nuckles, M., & Renkl, A. (2007). Do learning protocols support learning strategies and outcomes? The role of cognitive and metacognitive prompts. *Learning and Instruction*, *17*(5), 564–577. doi:10.1016/j.learninstruc.2007.09.007

Berthold, M., & Hand, D. I. (2000). Intelligent data analysis. *Technometrics*, *42*(4), 442–442. doi:10.1080/00401706.2000.10485739

Bertone, A. M., & Barbosa, L. M. (2015). Geogebra y los sistemas de funciones iteradas: Socios en la creación de un árbol de sakura. *Revista Do Instituto GeoGebra Internacional de São Paulo*, *4*(2), 78–87.

Bhadra, A., Brown, J., Ke, H., Liu, C., Shin, E. J., Wang, X., & Kobsa, A. (2016, March). ABC3D-Using an Augmented Reality Mobile Game to Enhance Literacy in Early Childhood. In *IEEE International Conference on Pervasive Computing and Communication Workshops (PerCom Workshops)*, (pp. 1-4). Sydney, Australia: IEEE. 10.1109/PERCOMW.2016.7457067

Bickmore, T., & Cassell, J. (2005). Social dialogue with embodied conversational agents. In Advances in natural multimodal dialogue systems. Springer.

Bickmore, T., & Picard, R. W. (2005). Establishing and maintaining long-term human-computer relationships. *ACM Transactions on Computer-Human Interaction*, *12*(2), 293–327. doi:10.1145/1067860.1067867

Binet, A., & Simon, T. (1916). *The development of intelligence in children*. Baltimore, MD: Williams & Wilkins.

Bisquerra, R. (2003). Educación emocional y competencias básicas para la vida. *Revista de Investigación Educacional*, *21*(1), 7–43.

Bloom, B. S. (1956). *Taxonomy of Educational Objectives*. New York: Academic Press.

Blumenfeld, P. C., Soloway, E., Marx, R. W., Krajcik, J. S., Guzdial, M., & Palincsar, A. (1991). Motivating project-based learning: Sustaining the doing, supporting the learning. *Educational Psychologist*, *26*(3&4), 369–398. doi:10.120715326985ep2603&4_8

Bollaert, M. (2000). A connectionist model of the processes involved in generating and exploring visual mental images. In S. O. Nuallian (Ed.), *Spatial cognition: Foundations and applications* (pp. 329–346). Amsterdam: Joint Benjamins Publishing. doi:10.1075/aicr.26.26bol

Borenstein, M., Hedges, L. V., Higgins, J. P., & Rothstein, H. R. (2010). A basic introduction to fixed-effect and random-effects models for meta-analysis. *Research Synthesis Methods*, *1*(2), 97–111. doi:10.1002/jrsm.12 PMID:26061376

Boring, E. G. (1950). *A history of experimental psychology*. New York, NY: Appleton-Century-Crofts.

Compilation of References

Borrachero Cortés, A. B. (2015). *Las emociones en la enseñanza y el aprendizaje de las ciencias en Educación Secundaria* (Doctoral Thesis). Universidad de Extremadura.

Borrachero, A. B., Brígido, M., Mellado, L., Costillo, E., & Mellado, V. (2014). Emotions in prospective secondary teachers when teaching science content, distinguishing by gender. *Research in Science & Technological Education*, *32*(2), 182–215. doi:10.1080/02635143.2014.909800

Borst, C. (2016). Shared mental models in human-machine systems. *IFAC-PapersOnLine*, *49*(19), 195–200. doi:10.1016/j.ifacol.2016.10.517

Botella, A. M., Fosati, A., & Canet, R. (2017). Desarrollo emocional y creativo en Educación Infantil mediante las artes visuales y la música [Emotional and creative development in early childhood education though the visual arts and music]. *Creativity and Educational Innovation Review*, *1*, 70–86. doi:10.7203/CREATIVITY.1.12063

Bottino, R. M., Ferlino, L., Ott, M., & Tavella, M. (2007). Developing strategies and reasoning abilities with computer games at primary school level. *Computers & Education*, *49*(4), 1272–1286. doi:10.1016/j.compedu.2006.02.003

Bower, M., Highfield, K., Furney, P., & Mowbray, L. (2013). Supporting pre-service teachers' technology-enabled learning design thinking through whole of programme transformation. *Educational Media International*, *50*(1), 39–50. doi:10.1080/09523987.2013.777183

Boyd, N. (2017, February). Now and Then: American Propaganda and Protest Posters. *20th Century Typographers*. Retrieved January 3, 2019, from http://www.printmag.com/design-education/online-design-courses/now-then-american-propaganda-posters

Brahams, Y. R. (1997). *Development of a social studies curriculum reflecting Howard Gardner's theory of multiple intelligences*. Theses Digitization Project. 1424. Retrieved May 22, 2019, from http://scholarworks.lib.csusb.edu/etd-project/1424

Brawner, K. W., & Gonzalez, A. J. (2016). Modelling a learner's affective state in real time to improve intelligent tutoring effectiveness. *Theoretical Issues in Ergonomics Science*, *17*(2), 183–210. doi:10.1080/1463922X.2015.1111463

Breazeal, C. (2004). Function meets style: Insights from emotion theory applied to HRI. *IEEE Transactions on Systems, Man and Cybernetics. Part C, Applications and Reviews*, *34*(2), 187–194. doi:10.1109/TSMCC.2004.826270

Breazeal, C., Kidd, C. D., Thomaz, A. L., Hoffman, G., & Berlin, M. (2005). Effects of nonverbal communication on efficiency and robustness in human-robot teamwork. *2005 IEEE/RSJ International Conference on Intelligent Robots and Systems*, 708-713. 10.1109/IROS.2005.1545011

Brígido, M. (2014). *Programa metacognitivo de intervención emocional en la enseñanza de las ciencias experimentales para maestros de primaria en formación inicial* (Doctoral Thesis). Universidad de Extremadura.

Brígido, M., Bermejo, M. L., Conde, M. C., & Mellado, V. (2010). The emotions in teaching and learning Nature Sciences and Physics/Chemistry in pre-service primary teachers. *US-China Education Review*, *7*(12), 25–32.

Brígido, M., Borrachero, A. B., Bermejo, M. L., & Mellado, V. (2013a). Prospective primary teachers' self-efficacy and emotions in science teaching. *European Journal of Teacher Education*, *36*(2), 200–217. doi:10.1080/02619768.2012.686993

Brígido, M., Couso, D., Gutiérrez, C., & Mellado, V. (2013b). The Emotions about Teaching and Learning Science: A Study of Prospective Primary Teachers in Three Spanish Universities. *Journal of Baltic Science Education*, *12*(3), 299–311.

Brooks, S. (2008). Displaying historical empathy: What impact can a writing assignment have? *Social Studies Research & Practice*, *3*(2), 130–146.

Brualdi, A. C. (1996). *Multiple Intelligences: Gardner's Theory. ERIC Digest.* Washington, DC: ERIC Clearinghouse on Assessment and Evaluation. Retrieved May 19, 2019, from https://files.eric.ed.gov/fulltext/ED410226.pdf

Bruner, J. S. (1966). Toward a theory of instruction. Cambridge, MA: Belknap Press of Harvard University. Retrieved from https://buscador.bibliotecas.uc.cl/primo-explore/fulldisplay?docid=puc_alma2156343420003396&context=L&vid=56PUC_INST&lang=es_CL&search_scope=alma_scope&adaptor=Local SearchEngine&isFrbr=true&tab=libros_tab&query=any,contains

Brusilovsky, P. (1996). Methods and Techniques of Adaptive Hypermedia. *User Modeling and User-Adapted Interaction: The Journal of Personalization Research, 6*(2–3), 87–129. doi:10.1007/BF00143964

Brusilovsky, P. (2001). *User Modeling and User-Adapted Interaction.* Kluwer Academic Publishers.

Buljac-Samardzic, M., Dekker-van Doorn, C. M., van Wijngaarden, J. D. H., & van Wijk, K. P. (2010). Interventions to improve team effectiveness: A systematic review. *Health Policy (Amsterdam), 94*(3), 183–195. doi:10.1016/j.healthpol.2009.09.015 PMID:19857910

Burbules, N. C. (2012). Ubiquitous Learning and the Future of Teaching. *Encounters, 13*, 3–14.

Bureau of Labor Statistics. (2019). *Occupational Outlook Handbook.* Retrieved from https://www.bls.gov/ooh/computer-and-information-technology/computer-and-information-research-scientists.htm

Burgos, B. M. V., & Guatame, A. X. L. (2011). ¿Cómo la estrategia de mapas mentales y conceptuales estimulan el desarrollo de la inteligencia espacial en estudiantes universitarios? *Tabula Rasa, 15*(15), 221–254. doi:10.25058/20112742.105

Burgos, C., Campanario, M. L., de la Pena, D., Lara, J. A., Lizcano, D., & Martínez, M. A. (2018). Data mining for modeling students' performance: A tutoring action plan to prevent academic dropout. *Computers & Electrical Engineering, 66*, 541–556. doi:10.1016/j.compeleceng.2017.03.005

Burke, S., Feitosa, J., & Salas, E. (2015). The unpacking of team models in GIFT. In *Proceedings of the 3rd Annual GIFT Users Symposium (GIFTSym3); 2015 June 17-18; Orlando, FL.* Aberdeen Proving Ground, MD: Army Research Laboratory.

Cakiroglu, E., & Isiksal, M. (2009). Pre-service elementary teachers' attitudes and self-efficacy beliefs toward mathematics. *Education in Science, 34*(151), 132–139.

Campos, P., Pessanha, S., & Pires, J. (2010). Fostering Collaboration in Kindergarten through an Augmented Reality Game. *International Journal of Virtual Reality, 5*(3), 1–7.

Canadian War Museum (n.d.). *Plan APPL.* Retrieved January 7, 2019, from http://www.warmuseum.ca/firstworldwar/wp-content/mcme-uploads/2014/07/4-a-4-all_e.pdf

Cannon-Bowers, J.A., Salas, E., Tannenbaum, S.I., & Mathieu, J.E. (1995). Toward theoretically based principles of training effectiveness: A model and initial empirical investigation. *Military Psychology, 7*(3), 141.

Cantu, A. D. (1999, November). An Internet Based Multiple Intelligences Model for Teaching High School History. *Journal of the Association for History and Computing, 2*(3). Retrieved from http://hdl.handle.net/2027/spo.3310410.0002.305

Carbonell, C., & Bermejo, L. A. (2017). Landscape interpretation with augmented reality and maps to improve spatial orientation skill. *Journal of Geography in Higher Education, 41*(1), 119–133. doi:10.1080/03098265.2016.1260530

Carroll, J. B. (1997). Psychometrics, intelligence, and public perception. *Intelligence, 24*(1), 25–52. doi:10.1016/S0160-2896(97)90012-X

Cascales, A., Laguna, I., Pérez-López, D., Perona, P., & Contero, M. (2013). An Experience on Natural Sciences Augmented Reality Contents for Preschoolers. In R. Shumaker (Ed.), Lecture Notes in Computer Science: Vol. 8022. *Virtual, Augmented and Mixed Reality. Systems and Applications. VAMR 2013*. Berlin: Springer. doi:10.1007/978-3-642-39420-1_12

Cassell, J. & Thorisson, K.R. (1999). The power of a nod and a glance: Envelope vs. emotional feedback in animated conversational agents. *Applied Artificial Intelligence, 13*(4-5), 519-538.

Castellanos, A., & Pérez, C. (2017). New Challenge in Education: Enhancing Student's Knowledge through Augmented Reality. In J. M. Ariso (Ed.), *Augmented Reality* (pp. 243–293). Berlin: De Gruyter. doi:10.1515/9783110497656-015

Castro-Alonso, J. C., Wong, A., Ayres, P., & Paas, F. (2018). Memorizing symbols from static and dynamic presentations: Don't overplay the hand. *Computers & Education, 116*, 1–13. doi:10.1016/j.compedu.2017.08.011

Cattaneo, A. A., Motta, E., & Gurtner, J. L. (2015). Evaluating a Mobile and Online System for Apprentices' Learning Documentation in Vocational Education: Usability, Effectiveness and Satisfaction. *International Journal of Mobile and Blended Learning, 7*(3), 40–58. doi:10.4018/IJMBL.2015070103

Cengage Learning. (2016). *Distinguish between primary and secondary sources*. Retrieved May 23, 2019, from https://www.cengage.com/english/book_content/wadsworth_9781428277427/questia_conducting_research_distinguish_primary_secondary_sources.pdf

Cervantes, A., López, N., Luque, R., & Prieto, J. (2012). Relaciones entre la variación de parámetros y los efectos geométricos en la función afín: una propuesta de análisis con GeoGebra. In *Conferencia Latinoamericana de GeoGebra Uruguay 2012* (pp. 468–475). Montevideo: Academic Press.

Chai, C. S., Koh, J. H. L., & Tsai, C. C. (2010). Facilitating Preservice Teachers' Development of Technological, Pedagogical, and Content Knowledge (TPACK). *Journal of Educational Technology & Society, 13*(4), 63–73.

Chai, C. S., & Kong, S. C. (2017). Professional learning for 21st century education. *Journal of Computers in Education, 4*(1), 1–4. doi:10.100740692-016-0069-y

Chan, D. W. (2006). Perceived multiple intelligences among male and female Chinese gifted students in Hong Kong: The structure of the student multiple intelligences profile. *Gifted Child Quarterly, 50*(4), 325–338. doi:10.1177/001698620605000405

Chan, D. W. (2008). Giftedness of Chinese students in Hong Kong: Perspectives from different conceptions of intelligences. *Gifted Child Quarterly, 52*(1), 40–54. doi:10.1177/0016986207311058

Chanel, G., Rebetez, C., Bétrancourt, M., & Pun, T. (2008). Boredom, engagement and anxiety as indicators for adaptation to difficulty in games. *Proceedings of the 12th International Conference on Entertainment and Media in the Ubiquitous Era - MindTrek '08*, 13. 10.1145/1457199.1457203

Charles, D., Kerr, A., & McNeill, M. (2005). Player-centred game design: Player modelling and adaptive digital games. *Proceedings of the Digital Games Research Conference, 285*(6), 285–298.

Charles, D., & Black, M. (2004). Dynamic Player Modelling: A Framework for Player-centred Digital Games. *Proceedings of 5th International Conference on Computer Games: Artificial Intelligence, Design and Education (CGAIDE'04), Microsoft*, 29–35.

Charlier, N., & De Fraine, B. (2012). Game-Based Learning in Teacher Education: A Strategy to Integrate Digital Games into Secondary Schools. *International Journal of Game-Based Learning, 2*(2), 1–12. doi:10.4018/ijgbl.2012040101

Charteris, J., Quinn, F., Parkes, M., Fletcher, P., & Reyes, V. (2016). e-Assessement for learning. *Australasian Journal of Educational Technology, 32*(3), 112–122.

Chen, J.Y.C. & Joyner C.T. (2009). Concurrent performance of gunner's and robotics operator's tasks in a multitasking environment. *Military Psychology*, *21*(1), 98.

Chen, C.-M., & Sun, Y.-C. (2012). Assessing the effects of different multimedia materials on emotions and learning performance for visual and verbal style learners. *Computers & Education*, *59*(4), 1273–1285. doi:10.1016/j.compedu.2012.05.006

Cheng, G., & Chau, J. (2009). Digital video for fostering self-reflection in an ePortfolio environment. *Learning, Media and Technology*, *34*(4), 337–350. doi:10.1080/17439880903338614

Cheng, K., & Leung, A. (2015). A dynamic applet for the exploration of the concept of the limit of a sequence. *International Journal of Mathematical Education in Science and Technology*, *46*(2), 187–204. doi:10.1080/0020739X.2014.951007

Cheng, V. M. (2004). Developing physics learning activities for fostering student creativity in Hong Kong context. *Asia-Pacific Forum on Science Learning and Teaching*, *5*(2), 1–33.

Chen, J. Y. C., & Barnes, M. J. (2014). Human–agent teaming for multirobot control: A review of human factors issues. *IEEE Transactions on Human-Machine Systems*, *44*(1), 13–29. doi:10.1109/THMS.2013.2293535

Chiang, T. H. C., Yang, S. J., & Hwang, G. J. (2014). An augmented reality-based mobile learning system to improve students' learning achievements and motivations in natural science inquiry activities. *Journal of Educational Technology & Society*, *17*(4), 352–365.

Chi, M. (2009). Active-constructive-interactive: A conceptual framework for differentiating learning activities. *Topics in Cognitive Science*, *1*(1), 73–105. doi:10.1111/j.1756-8765.2008.01005.x PMID:25164801

Chorianopoulos, K., & Lekakos, G. (2008). Introduction to social TV: Enhancing the shared experience with interactive TV. *International Journal of Human-Computer Interaction*, *24*(2), 113–120. doi:10.1080/10447310701821574

Christensen, H., Mackinnon, A. J., Korten, A., & Jorm, A. F. (2001). The common cause hypothesis of cognitive aging: Evidence for not only a common factor but also specific associations of age with vision and grip strength in a cross-sectional analysis. *Psychology and Aging*, *16*(4), 588–599. doi:10.1037/0882-7974.16.4.588 PMID:11766914

Christensen, L. M. (2006). Using art to teach history to young learners. *Social Education*, *70*(5), 312–315.

Chuang, T.-Y., & Sheng-Hsiung, S. (2012). Using mobile console games for multiple intelligences and education. *International Journal of Mobile Learning and Organisation*, *6*(3–4), 204–217. doi:10.1504/IJMLO.2012.050047

Cieza, E., & Luján, D. (2018). Educational Mobile Application of Augmented Reality Based on Markers to Improve the Learning of Vowel Usage and Numbers for Children of a Kindergarten in Trujillo. *Procedia Computer Science*, *130*, 352–358. doi:10.1016/j.procs.2018.04.051

Cifuentes, L., & Hughey, J. (1998). *Computer conferencing and multiple intelligences: Effects on expository writing*. Paper presented at 20th Association for Educational Communications and Technology Conference, St. Louis, MO.

Clark, D., Nelson, B., Sengupta, P., & D'Angelo, C. (2009). Rethinking Science Learning Through Digital Games and Simulations: Genres, Examples, and Evidence. Learning science: Computer games, simulations, and education workshop sponsored by the National Academy of Sciences. Retrieved from https://sites.nationalacademies.org/cs/groups/dbassesite/documents/webpage/dbasse_080068.pdf

Clark, D. B., Sampson, V., Weinberger, A., & Erkens, G. (2007). Analytic frameworks for assessing dialogic argumentation in online learning environments. *Educational Psychology Review*, *19*(3), 343–374. doi:10.100710648-007-9050-7

Clark, R. (1983). Reconsidering research on learning from media. *Review of Educational Research*, *53*(4), 445–459. doi:10.3102/00346543053004445

Compilation of References

Coffey, H. (2008). *Project-based learning*. Learn NC.

Coffield, F., Moseley, D., Hall, E., & Ecclestone, K. (2004). *Learning styles and pedagogy in post-16 learning: A systematic and critical review*. Academic Press.

Coil, R. A. (1998). *Multiple intelligences and computer assisted learning with adult learners* (Ph.D. diss.). Union Institute. Retrieved from Dissertation Abstracts International, 58, no. 12, 4523A, UMI. (No. AAT 98-17952)

Colby, S., Clayards, M., & Baum, S. (2018). The role of lexical status and individual differences for perceptual learning in younger and older adults. *Journal of Speech, Language, and Hearing Research: JSLHR*, *61*(8), 1855–1874. doi:10.1044/2018_JSLHR-S-17-0392 PMID:30003232

Collins, L. (2018a). The impact of paper versus digital map technology on students' spatial thinking skill acquisition. *The Journal of Geography*, *117*(4), 137–152. doi:10.1080/00221341.2017.1374990

Collins, L. (2018b). Student and teacher response to use of different media in spatial thinking skill development. *International Journal of Geospatial and Environmental Research*, *5*, 1–16.

Collins, L., & Mitchell, J. (2018). Teacher training in GIS: What is needed for long-term success? *International Research in Geographical and Environmental Education*. doi:10.1080/10382046.2018.1497119

Colombo, B., & Antonietti, A. (2017). The role of metacognitive strategies in learning music: A multiple case study. *British Journal of Music Education*, *34*(1), 95–113. doi:10.1017/S0265051716000267

Connell, M., Sheridan, K., & Gardner, H. (2004). Experts, generalists, and expert generalists: On the relation between general competence and expertise in a domain. In R. Sternberg & E. Grigorenko (Eds.), *Perspectives on the psychology of abilities, competencies, and expertise* (pp. 126–155). New York: Cambridge University Press.

Contreras, J. N. (2014). Discovering and Extending Viviani's Theorem with GeoGebra. *GeoGebra International Journal of Romania*, *3*(1), 1–14.

Cook, A. E. & Gueraud, S. (2005). What have we been missing? The role of general world knowledge in discourse processing. *Discourse Processes: A Multidisciplinary Journal, 39*(2&3), 265-278.

Cook, A., Zheng, R., & Blaz, J. W. (2009). Measurement of cognitive load during multimedia learning activities. In R. Zheng (Ed.), *Cognitive effectives of multimedia learning* (pp. 34–50). Hershey, PA: Information Science Reference/IGI Global Publishing. doi:10.4018/978-1-60566-158-2.ch003

Cooke, I. (2014, January). *Propaganda as a weapon? Influencing international opinion*. World War One. British Library. Retrieved January 7, 2019, from https://www.bl.uk/world-war-one/articles/propaganda-as-a-weapon#sthash.RdLggEDT.dpuf

Cooke, N. J., Gorman, J. C., & Winner, J. L. (2007). Team cognition. Handbook of Applied Cognition, 239-268.

Costa, E. B., Fonseca, B., Santana, M. A., de Araújo, F. F., & Rego, J. (2017). Evaluating the effectiveness of educational data mining techniques for early prediction of students' academic failure in introductory programming courses. *Computers in Human Behavior*, *73*, 247–256. doi:10.1016/j.chb.2017.01.047

Council of Europe. (n.d.). *Cooperation and Participation. Transversal attitudes, skills and knowledge for democracy.* Retrieved May 24, 2019, from http://www.coe.int/t/dg4/education/pestalozzi/Source/Documentation/Module/Tasks/Cooperation%20and%20participation.pdf

Covacevich, J. A. (2013). A naturalist born, made or both? *Queensland Naturalist, 51*(1/2/3), 3-4.

Cowan, N. (2001). The magical number 4 in short-term memory: A reconsideration of mental storage capacity. *Behavioral and Brain Sciences*, *24*(1), 1–185. doi:10.1017/S0140525X01003922 PMID:11515286

Cowley, B., Charles, D., Black, M., & Hickey, R. (2008). Toward an understanding of flow in video games. *Computers in Entertainment*, *6*(2), 1. doi:10.1145/1371216.1371223

Crawford, B. S., Hicks, D., & Doherty, N. (2009). Worth the wait: Engaging social studies students with art in a digital age. *Social Education*, *73*(3), 136–139.

Crescenzi-Lanna, L., & Grané-Oró, M. (2016). An Analysis of the Interaction Design of the Best Educational Apps for Children Aged Zero to Eight. *Comunicar*, *24*(46), 77–85. doi:10.3916/C46-2016-08

Creswell, J. W. (2013). *Qualitative inquiry and research design: choosing among five approaches* (3rd ed.). Los Angeles, CA: SAGE Publications.

Csikszentmihalyi, M., & Csikszentmihalyi, I. S. (1992). *Optimal experience: Psychological studies of flow in consciousness*. Cambridge University Press.

Cuban, L. (2001). *Oversold and underused : computers in the classroom*. Cambridge, MA: Harvard University Press.

Cuban, L. (2013). Why so many structural changes in schools and so little reform in teaching practice? *Journal of Educational Administration*, *51*(2), 109–125. doi:10.1108/09578231311304661

Cummings, M. L., & Guerlain, S. (2007). Developing operator capacity estimates for supervisory control of autonomous vehicles. *Human Factors: The Journal of the Human Factors and Ergonomics Society*, *49*(1), 1–15. doi:10.1518/001872007779598109 PMID:17315838

D'Mello, S., Picard, R., & Graesser, A. (2007). Towards an affect –sensitive autotutor. *IEEE Intelligent Systems*, *22*(4), 53–61. doi:10.1109/MIS.2007.79

Da Silva, V., Rico, E., Souza, D., & Losch de Oliveira, D. (2015). Impacto do uso de estratégias investigativas sobre as emoções e a motivação dos alunos e as suas concepções de ciência e cientista. *Revista Electrónica de Enseñanza de las Ciencias*, *14*(1), 17–34.

Dabbagh, N., & Kitsantas, A. (2018). Fostering self-regulated learning with digital technologies. In R. Zheng (Ed.), Strategies for deep learning with digital technology (pp. 51-69). New York, NY: Nova Science Publishers.

Dabbagh, N., & Kitsantas, A. (2012). Personal Learning Environments, social media, and self regulated learning: A natural formula for connecting formal and informal learning. *Internet High. Educ.*, *15*(1), 3–8. doi:10.1016/j.iheduc.2011.06.002

Dalal, N., Kak, S., & Sohoni, S. (2012). Rapid digital game creation for learning object-oriented concepts. In *Proceedings of Informing Science* (pp. 22–27). Montreal, Canada: IT Education Conference. doi:10.28945/1653

Dang, T. H. H., & Tapus, A. (2007). Coping with Stress Using Social Robots as Emotion-Orientated Tool: Potential Factors Discovered from Stress Game Experiment. In G. Hermann, M. J. Pearson, A. Lenz, P. Bremner, A. Spiers, & U. Leonards (Eds.), *Social Robots. LNAI* (Vol. 8239, pp. 160–169). Heidelberg, Germany: Springer. doi:10.1007/978-3-319-02675-6_16

Daniels, D. & Price V. (2004). *Essential Enneagram the Definitive Personality Test and Self Discovery Guide* (S. Çiftçi, Trans.). İstanbul Kaknüs. (Original work published 2000)

Daniels, D., & Price, V. (2000/2009). *The Essential Enneagram: The Definitive Personality Test and Self-Discovery Guide--Revised & Updated*. Harper Collins.

Compilation of References

Dara-Abrams, B. (2002). Applying Multi-Intelligent Adaptive Hypermedia to Online Learning. In *E-Learn: World Conference on E-Learning in Corporate, Government, Healthcare, and Higher Education* (pp. 1382–1385). Montreal, Canada: Association for the Advancement of Computing in Education (AACE).

Dávila Acedo, M. A., Borrachero, A. B., Cañada, F., & Sánchez-Martín, J. (2016). Evolution of emotion in learning physics and chemistry in secondary education. In E. Harvey (Ed.), *Secondary education: Perspectives, global issues and challenges* (pp. 115–132). New York: Nova Science Publisher.

DCMI. (2014). *Dublin Core Metadata Initiative*. Retrieved from http://www.dublincore.org/documents/dcmi-terms/

de Melo, C. M., Marsella, S., & Gratch, J. (2018). Social decisions and fairness change when people's interests are represented by autonomous agents. *Autonomous Agents and Multi-Agent Systems*, *32*(1), 163–187. doi:10.100710458-017-9376-6

De Simone, M. (2017). Disclosing the "Ræmotionality" of a Mathematics Teacher Using Technology in Her Classroom Activity. In G. Aldon, F. Hitt, L. Bazzini, & U. Gellert (Eds.), *Mathematics and Technology* (pp. 255–284). Cham: Springer; doi:10.1007/978-3-319-51380-5_12.

DeCarlo, D., Stone, M., Revilla, C., & Venditti, J. J. (2004). Specifying and animating facial signals for discourse in embodied conversational agents. *Computer Animation and Virtual Worlds*, *15*(1), 27–38. doi:10.1002/cav.5

Dede, C. (2009). Immersive Interfaces for Engagement and Learning. *Science*, *323*(5910), 66–69. doi:10.1126cience.1167311 PMID:19119219

Del Cerro, F., & Morales, G. (2017). Realidad Aumentada como herramienta de mejora de la inteligencia espacial en estudiantes de educación secundaria. *Revista de Educación a Distancia*, *54*. doi:10.6018/red/54/5

Del Moral, M. E., Fernández, L. C., & Guzmán, A. P. (2015). Videogames: Multisensorial incentives for strengthening multiple intelligences in primary education. *Electronic Journal of Research in Educational Psychology*, *13*(2), 243–270. doi:10.14204/ejrep.36.14091

Del Moral, M. E., & Villalustre, L. (2013). Realidad aumentada: experimentando en el aula en 3D [Augmented reality: experimenting in the classroom in 3D]. In *Smartphones y tablets: ¿enseñan o distraen?* [Smartphones and tablets: do they teach or distract?] (pp. 107–124). Madrid: ESIC Editorial.

del Río, L. S. (2017). Enseñar y aprender cálculo con ayuda de la vista gráfica 3D de GeoGebra. Revista Digital Matemática. *Educación e Internet.*, *17*(1), 13. doi:10.18845/rdmei.v17i1.2739

Delgoshaei, Y., & Delavari, N. (2012). Applying Multiple-Intelligence Approach to Education and Analyzing its Impact on Cognitive Development Of Pre-School Children. *Procedia: Social and Behavioral Sciences*, *32*, 361–366. doi:10.1016/j.sbspro.2012.01.054

DeLorenzo, R. A., Battino, W., Schreiber, R., & Carrio, B. (2009). *Delivering on the promise*. Solution Tree Press.

Demir, M., McNeese, N. J., & Cooke, N. J. (2016). Team communication behaviors of the human-automation teaming. In *Cognitive Methods in Situation Awareness and Decision Support (CogSIMA), 2016 IEEE International Multi-Disciplinary Conference on*. IEEE.

Demir, M., & Cooke, N. J. (2014). Human teaming changes driven by expectations of a synthetic teammate. *Proceedings of the Human Factors and Ergonomics Society Annual Meeting*, *58*(1), 1. doi:10.1177/1541931214581004

Demir, M., McNeese, N. J., & Cooke, N. J. (2018). The Impact of Perceived Autonomous Agents on Dynamic Team Behaviors. *IEEE Transactions on Emerging Topics in Computational Intelligence*, *2*(4), 258–267. doi:10.1109/TET-CI.2018.2829985

Demir, M., McNeese, N. J., Cooke, N. J., Ball, J. T., Myers, C., & Frieman, M. (2015, September). Synthetic teammate communication and coordination with humans. *Proceedings of the Human Factors and Ergonomics Society Annual Meeting, 59*(1), 951–955. doi:10.1177/1541931215591275

Denig, S. J. (2004). Multiple intelligences and learning styles: Two complementary dimensions. *Teachers College Record, 106*(1), 96–111. doi:10.1111/j.1467-9620.2004.00322.x

Devillers, L., Rosset, S., Duplessis, G. D., Bechade, L., Yemez, Y., Turker, B. B., . . . Deléglise, P. (2018, May). Multifaceted Engagement in Social Interaction with a Machine: The JOKER Project. In *2018 13th IEEE International Conference on Automatic Face & Gesture Recognition (FG 2018)* (pp. 697-701). IEEE.

Dickinson, D. (1998). *How Technology Enhances Howard Gardner's Eight Intelligences*. New Horizons for Learning and America Tomorrow. Retrieved from https://www.yumpu.com/en/document/view/44874093/how-technology-enhances-howard-gardners-eight-intelligences

Digital Chalkboard. (n.d.). 3.1.3 Introduction to Conjectures : CCSS Mathematics: K-12 Standards for Mathematical Practice. Retrieved February 18, 2019, from https://www.mydigitalchalkboard.org/portal/default/Content/Viewer/Content?action=2&scId=306591&sciId=12796

Digitalisierung, H. (2017). *The digital turn À pathways for higher education in the digital age*. Hochschulforum Digitalisierung, Arbeitspap.

Dillenbourg, P. (1999). *Collaborative learning: Cognitive and computational approaches*. New York, NY: Elsevier.

Dishon, G. (2017). New data, old tensions: Big data, personalized learning, and the challenges of progressive education. *Theory and Research in Education, 15*(3), 272–289. doi:10.1177/1477878517735233

Dockendorff, M., & Solar, H. (2018). ICT integration in mathematics initial teacher training and its impact on visualization: The case of GeoGebra. *International Journal of Mathematical Education in Science and Technology, 49*(1), 66–84. doi:10.1080/0020739X.2017.1341060

Doman, M., Sleigh, M., & Garrison, C. (2015). Effect of GameMaker® on Student Attitudes and Perceptions of Instructors. *International Journal of Modern Education and Computer Science, 7*(9), 1–13. doi:10.5815/ijmecs.2015.09.01

Dondlinger, M. J. (2007). Educational video game design: A review of the literature. *Journal of Applied Educational Technology, 4*(1), 21–31. doi:10.1108/10748120410540463

Donovan, S. M., & Bransford, J. D. (2005). Introduction. In S. M. Donovan & J. D. Bransford (Eds.), *How Students Learn: History in the Classroom* (pp. 1–28). Washington, DC: The National Academies Press.

Dorfeld, N. M. (2016). Being heard: Motivating millennials through multiple intelligences. *Journal on Excellence in College Teaching, 27*(4), 65–75.

Dousay, T. A. (2016). Effects of redundancy and modality on the situational interest of adult learners in multimedia learning. *Educational Technology Research and Development, 64*(6), 1251–1271. doi:10.100711423-016-9456-3

Downs, R. (1994). The need for research in geography education: It would be nice to have some data. *The Journal of Geography, 93*(1), 57–60. doi:10.1080/00221349408979690

Duffy, T. M., & Cunningham, D. J. (1996). Constructivism: Implications for the design and delivery of instruction. In D. H. Jonassen (Ed.), *Educational communications and technology* (pp. 170–199). New York, NY: Simon & Schuster Macmillan.

Dunn, R. (1984). Learning style: State of the science. *Theory into Practice, 23*(1), 10–19. doi:10.1080/00405848409543084

Compilation of References

Dünser, A., & Hornecker, E. (2007). An Observational Study of Children Interacting with an Augmented Story Book. In K. Hui, Z. Pan, R.C. Chung, C.C.L. Wang, X. Jin, S. Göbel & E.C.-L. Li (Eds.), *International Conference on Technologies for E-Learning and Digital Entertainment. Proceedings of the Third International Conference, Edutainment 2007* (pp.305-315). New York: Springer. 10.1007/978-3-540-73011-8_31

Durall, G. E., Gros, S. B., Maina, M. F., Johnson, L., & Adams, S. (2012). *Perspectivas tecnológicas: educación superior en Iberoamérica 2012-2017*. Austin, TX: The New Media Consortium.

Duval, R. (1999). Representation, Vision and Visualization: Cognitive Functions in Mathematical Thinking. Basic Issues for Learning. Retrieved from http://pat-thompson.net/PDFversions/1999Duval.pdf

Duval, S., & Tweedie, R. (2000). Trim and fill: A simple funnel-plot–based method of testing and adjusting for publication bias in meta-analysis. *Biometrics, 56*(2), 455–463. doi:10.1111/j.0006-341X.2000.00455.x PMID:10877304

Dybvig, T., & Church, S. (n.d.). *Learning Styles*. Retrieved May 31, 2019, from http://www.teresadybvig.com/learnsty.htm

Dziekonski, M. (2012). La inteligencia espacial: Una mirada a Howard Gardner. *Revista ArteOficio, 2*(2), 1–12.

Eagle, M., & Barnes, T. (2009). Experimental evaluation of an educational game for improved learning in introductory computing. *ACM SIGCSE Bulletin, 41*(1), 321–325. doi:10.1145/1539024.1508980

Eastern Illinois University. (n.d.). *The Art of War. WWI and WWII Posters*. Retrieved January 30, 2019, from http://www.eiu.edu/eiutps/art_of_war.php

Ehlers, U.-D. (2011). Extending the territory: From open educational resources to open educational practices. *Journal of Open. Flexible and Distance Learning, 15*(2), 1–10.

Eisenberg, M. B., Murray, J., & Bartow, C. (2016). *The Big 6 Curriculum. Comprehensive Information and Communication Technology (ICT) Literacy for All Students*. Santa Barbara, CA: ABC-CLIO, LLC.

Elgort, I., Smith, A. G., & Toland, J. (2008). Is wiki an effective platform for group course work? *Australasian Journal of Educational Technology, 24*(2), 195–210. doi:10.14742/ajet.1222

Elms, M. D. (2014). *Propaganda Posters of World War I: Analyzing the Methods Behind the Images*. NHD. Retrieved January 26, 2019, from https://nhd.org/sites/default/files/1REVISED-Elms-LM-1-Propaganda.pdf

Endacott, J., & Brooks, S. (2013, Spring). An Updated Theoretical and Practical Model for Promoting Historical Empathy. *Social Studies Research & Practice, 8*(1), 41–58.

Engelkamp, J. (1998). *Memory for actions*. East Sussex, UK: Psychology Press.

Engeström, Y. (1987). *Learning by expanding an activity-theoretical approach to developmental research*. Helsinki: Orienta-Konsultit.

Entin, E. E., & Serfaty, D. (1999). Adaptive team coordination. *Human Factors: The Journal of the Human Factors and Ergonomics Society, 41*(2), 312–325. doi:10.1518/001872099779591196

Erfanian Mohammadi, J., Elahi Shirvan, M., & Akbari, O. (2018). Systemic functional multimodal discourse analysis of teaching students developing classroom materials. *Teaching in Higher Education*, 1–23. doi:10.1080/13562517.2018.1527763

Eris Fose, L. (2005). *Exploring technology to address student multiple intelligences & learning styles*. Retrieved from https://www.calpoly.edu/~lfose/articles/Exploring_Technology.pdf

Erkan, T., & Üster, S. (2012, May). Application of Multiple Intelligences Theory in Art History Instruction. *Journal of Social Sciences, 25,* 273-297. Retrieved May 18, 2019, from https://dergipark.org.tr/download/article-file/117869

Ernst, J. V., & Clark, A. C. (2012). Fundamental Computer Science Conceptual Understandings for High School Students Using Original Computer Game Design. *Journal of STEM Education: Innovations and Research, 13*(5), 40.

Ertmer, P. A., Ottenbreit-Leftwich, A. T., Sadik, O., Sendurur, E., & Sendurur, P. (2012). Teacher beliefs and technology integration practices: A critical relationship. *Computers & Education, 59*(2), 423–435. doi:10.1016/j.compedu.2012.02.001

Escamilla, K. (2014). Struggling reader or emerging biliterate student? Reevaluating the criteria for labeling emerging bilingual students as low achieving. *Journal of Literacy Research, 46*(1), 68–89. doi:10.1177/1086296X13504869

Fabricatore, C. (2007). Gameplay and game mechanics design: a key to quality in video games. *Proceedings of the OECD-CERI Expert Meeting on Videogames and Education,* 1–18. Retrieved from http://www.oecd.org/dataoecd/44/17/39414829.pdf

Fallon, C., & Brown, S. (2000). *e-Learning Standards: A Guide to Purchasing, Developing and Deploying Standards-Conformant E-Learning.* St Lucie Press.

Farinelli, A., Zanotto, E., & Pagello, E. (2017). Advanced approaches for multi-robot coordination in logistic scenarios. *Robotics and Autonomous Systems, 90,* 34–44. doi:10.1016/j.robot.2016.08.010

Farmer, B., Yue, A., & Brooks, C. (2008). Using blogging for higher order learning in large cohort university teaching: A case study. *Australasian Journal of Educational Technology, 24*(2), 123–136. doi:10.14742/ajet.1215

Fasha, S. D. (2016). *Chapter Report Summaries Learning Styles and Good Language Learners.* University of Education. Retrieved January 9, 2019, from https://www.academia.edu

Felton, R. G., & Allen, R. F. (1990, March/April). Using Visual Materials as Historical Sources. *Social Studies, 81*(2), 84–87. doi:10.1080/00377996.1990.9957501

Fernandes, E., Holanda, M., Victorino, M., Borges, V., Carvalho, R., & Van Erven, G. (2019). Educational data mining: Predictive analysis of academic performance of public school students in the capital of Brazil. *Journal of Business Research, 94,* 335–343. doi:10.1016/j.jbusres.2018.02.012

Fernández, C., Bermejo, R., Sainz, M., Ferrando, M., & Prieto, M. D. (2008). Estudio del razonamiento lógico-matemático desde el modelo de las inteligencias múltiples. *Anales de Psicología, 24*(2), 213–222.

Ferrarello, D., Mammana, M. F., Pennisi, M., & Taranto, E. (2017). Teaching Intriguing Geometric Loci with DGS. In G. Aldon, F. Hitt, L. Bazzini, & U. Gellert (Eds.), *Mathematics and Technology* (pp. 579–605). Cham: Springer; doi:10.1007/978-3-319-51380-5_26.

Ferrer, L. M. (2004). Developing understanding and social skills through cooperative learning. *Journal of Science and Mathematics Education in Southeast Asia, 27*(2), 45–61.

Field, A. P., & Gillett, R. (2010). How to do a meta-analysis. *British Journal of Mathematical & Statistical Psychology, 63*(3), 665–694. doi:10.1348/000711010X502733 PMID:20497626

Fields, S. (n.d.). *World War I Propaganda Posters.* McKeel Academy. Retrieved May 23, 2019, from https://www.polk-fl.net/staff/teachers/tah/documents/turningpoints/lessons/f-worldwar1posters.pdf

Finch, L. (2000, Spring). Psychological Propaganda: The War of Ideas on Ideas During the First Half of the Twentieth Century. *Armed Forces and Society, 26*(3), 367–386. doi:10.1177/0095327X0002600302

Compilation of References

Fleiss, J. L., & Gross, A. J. (1991). Meta-analysis in epidemiology, with special reference to studies of the association between exposure to environmental tobacco smoke and lung cancer: A critique. *Journal of Clinical Epidemiology, 44*(2), 127–139. doi:10.1016/0895-4356(91)90261-7 PMID:1995774

Flin, R., Glavin, R., & Patey, R. (2003). *Framework for observing and rating anaesthetists' non-technical skills. Anaesthetists' non-technical skills (ANTS) system handbook v1. 0.* University of Aberdeen and Scottish Clinical Simulation Centre.

Flin, R., & Maran, N. (2004). Identifying and training non-technical skills for teams in acute medicine. *Quality & Safety in Health Care, 13*(1), i80–i84. doi:10.1136/qshc.2004.009993 PMID:15465960

Foster, J. (2013). *Howard Gardner's Theory of Multiple Intelligences in Relation to Art Education.* Retrieved May 18, 2019, from https://cpb-us-w2.wpmucdn.com/sites.stedwards.edu/dist/0/696/files/2013/01/Educ2331-ContentConnection4-HowardGardner-1rnkvvk.pdf

Fransecky, R. B., & Debes, J. L. (1972). *Visual Literacy: A Way to Learn - A Way to Teach.* Washington, DC: Association for Educational Communications and Technology. Retrieved January 9, 2019, from https://files.eric.ed.gov/fulltext/ED064884.pdf

Friedman, H. A. (2008, December). *Race as a Military Propaganda Theme.* psywar.org. Retrieved May 28, 2019, from: https://www.psywar.org/race.php

Gabella, M. S. (1994). Beyond the looking glass: Bringing students into the conversation of historical inquiry. *Theory and Research in Social Education, 22*(3), 340–363. doi:10.1080/00933104.1994.10505728

Gabella, M. S. (1996). The art(s) of historical sense. *Journal of Curriculum Studies, 27*(2), 139–163. doi:10.1080/0022027950270202

Gabella, M. S. (1998). Formal fascinations and nagging excerpts: The challenge of the arts to curriculum and inquiry. *Curriculum Inquiry, 28*(1), 27–56. doi:10.1111/0362-6784.00074

Gagne, R., Briggs, L., & Wager, W. (1992). *Principles of instructional design.* Fort Worth, TX: Harcourt Brace Jovanovich College Publishers.

Galbraith, M. W. (2004). *Adult Learning Methods: A Guide for Effective. Instruction* (3rd ed.). Malabar, FL: Krieger Publishing Company.

Gallagher, M.E., Tasca, G.A., Ritchie, K., Balfour, L., Maxwell, H., & Bissada, H. (2014). Interpersonal learning is associated with improved self-esteem in group psychotherapy for women with binge eating disorder. *Psychotherapy, 51*(1), 66.

Gallegos, C., Sagaz, M. A., Sánchez, A., Huerto, M. L. & Sánchez, M. A. (2013). Desarrollo de un proyecto de ciencia basado en el uso de diversas inteligencias. *Revista Eureka sobre Enseñanza y Divulgación de la Ciencia, 10*(1), 100-109.

Ganz, J. B., Simpson, R. L., & Lund, E. M. (2012). The picture exchange communication system (PECS): A promising method for improving communication skills of learners with autism spectrum disorders. *Education and Training in Autism and Developmental Disabilities, 47*(2), 176–186.

Gardner, H. (1999). Are there additional intelligences? The case for naturalist, spiritual, and existential intelligences. In Education, information and transformation. Englewood Cliffs, NJ: Prentice Hall.

Gardner, H. (2003, April). *Multiple Intelligences After Twenty Years.* Paper presented at the American Educational Research Association, Chicago, IL. Retrieved May 21, 2019, from http://ocw.metu.edu.tr/pluginfile.php/9274/mod_resource/content/1/Gardner_multiple_intelligent.pdf

Gardner, H. (2005). *Multiple intelligences and education.* Retrieved from http://www.infed.org/ thinkers/gardner.htm

Gardner, H. (1983). *Frames of mind: the theory of multiple intelligences*. New York: Basic Books.

Gardner, H. (1983a). *Frames of Mind: The Theory of Multiple Intelligences*. New York: Basic Books.

Gardner, H. (1983b). *Multiple Intelligences: The Theory in Practice*. New York: Basic Books.

Gardner, H. (1987). The theory of multiple intelligences. *Annals of Dyslexia*, *37*(1), 19–35. doi:10.1007/BF02648057 PMID:24234985

Gardner, H. (1989). Educational implications of the Theory of Multiple Intelligences. *Educational Researcher*, *18*(8), 4–10.

Gardner, H. (1993). *Frames of mind: The theory of multiple intelligences* (2nd ed.). London: Fontana Press.

Gardner, H. (1993). *Multiple intelligences: The theory in practice*. Basic books.

Gardner, H. (1993, July). Educating for Understanding. *The American School Board Journal*, *180*(7), 20–24.

Gardner, H. (1995). Reflections on multiple Intelligences: Myths and Messages. *Phi Delta Capan*, *77*, 200–209.

Gardner, H. (1995, December). "Multiple Intelligences" as a Catalyst. *English Journal*, *84*(8), 16–18. doi:10.2307/821182

Gardner, H. (1997, September). Multiple Intelligences as a Partner in School Improvements. *Educational Leadership*, *55*(1), 20–21.

Gardner, H. (1998). A multiplicity of intelligences. *Scientific American Presents: Exploring Intelligence*, *9*(4), 18–23.

Gardner, H. (1998). A Multiplicity of Intelligences. *Scientific American*, 19–23.

Gardner, H. (1999). *Intelligence Reframed. Multiple intelligences for the 21st century*. New York: Basic Books.

Gardner, H. (1999). *Intelligence Reframed: Multiple Intelligences for the 21st Century*. New York: Basic Books.

Gardner, H. (1999). *Intelligences reframed: Multiple intelligences for the 21st century*. New York: Basic Books.

Gardner, H. (1999). *The disciplined mind: What all students should understand by Howard Gardner*. New York, NY: Simon & Schuster.

Gardner, H. (2000, Summer). Project Zero: Nelson Goodman's Legacy in Arts Education. *The. The Journal of Aesthetics and Art Criticism*, *58*(3), 245–249. doi:10.2307/432107

Gardner, H. (2011). *Frames of mind: Theory of multiple intelligences*. New York, NY: Basic books.

Gardner, H. (2011). *Inteligencias múltiples. La teoría en la práctica*. Barcelona: Paidós.

Gardner, H., & Moran, S. (2006). The science of multiple intelligences theory: A response to Lynn Waterhouse. *Educational Psychologist*, *41*(4), 227–232. doi:10.120715326985ep4104_2

Garg, A. (n.d.). *Spirograph*. Retrieved from http://www.wordsmith.org/~anu/java/spirograph.html

Garrison, D. R. (2011). *E-learning in the 21st century: A framework for research and practice*. Taylor & Francis.

Gebhard, P., Schneeberger, T., Baur, T., & André, E. (2018, July). MARSSI: Model of Appraisal, Regulation, and Social Signal Interpretation. In *Proceedings of the 17th International Conference on Autonomous Agents and MultiAgent Systems* (pp. 497-506). International Foundation for Autonomous Agents and Multiagent Systems.

Gecu-Parmaksiz, Z., & Delialioğlu, O. (2019). Augmented Reality-Based Virtual Manipulatives Versus Physical Manipulatives for Teaching Geometric Shapes to Preschool Children. *British Journal of Educational Technology*, 1–15. doi:10.1111/bjet.12740

Gee, J. P. (2004). *Situated language and learning: A critique of traditional schooling*. Psychology Press. doi:10.1111/j.1467-9345.2006.02802_1.x

Gencel, İ. E. (2007). Kolb'un Deneyimsel Öğrenme Kuramına Dayalı Öğrenme Stilleri Envanteri-III'ü Türkçeye Uyarlama Çalışması. *Dokuz Eylül Üniversitesi Sosyal Bilimler Enstitüsü Dergisi, 9*(2), 120–139.

Gentile, E., & Mattei, M. (2017). The Street Lamp Problem: Technologies and Meaningful Situations in Class. In G. Aldon, F. Hitt, L. Bazzini, & U. Gellert (Eds.), *Mathematics and Technology* (pp. 197–223). Cham: Springer; doi:10.1007/978-3-319-51380-5_10.

Gersmehl, P. (2008). *Teaching geography*. New York: The Guilford Press.

Ghufron, M. A., & Ermawati, S. (2018). The strengths and weaknesses of cooperative learning and problem-based learning in EFL writing class: Teachers' and students' perspectives. *International Journal of Instruction, 11*(4), 657–672. doi:10.12973/iji.2018.11441a

Giles, E., Pitre, S., & Womack, S. (2010). Multiple Intelligences and Learning Styles. In M. Orey (Ed.), *Emerging perspectives on learning, teaching, and technology* (pp. 77-92). Zurich, Switzerland: Jacobs Foundation. Retrieved May 30, 2019, from https://www.academia.edu

Glas, D., Satake, S., Kanda, T., & Hagita, N. (2012). An interaction design framework for social robots. *Robotics: Science and Systems, 7*, 89.

Göbel, S., Hardy, S., & Wendel, V. (2010). Serious Games for Health - Personalized Exergames. *Proceedings of the 18th ACM International Conference on Multimedia*, 1663–1666. 10.1145/1873951.1874316

Goldberg, B. (2015, September). Feedback source modality effects in game-based training: A trade-off analysis. *Proceedings of the Human Factors and Ergonomics Society Annual Meeting, 59*(1), 1858–1862. doi:10.1177/1541931215591401

Goldstein, D., & Alibrandi, M. (2013). Integrating GIS in the middle school curriculum: Impacts on diverse students' standardized test scores. *The Journal of Geography, 112*(2), 68–74. doi:10.1080/00221341.2012.692703

Golledge, R. M., Marsh, M., & Battersby, S. (2008). A conceptual framework for facilitating geospatial thinking. *Annals of the Association of American Geographers, 98*(2), 285–308. doi:10.1080/00045600701851093

Gómez-Chacón, I. M., & Prieto, N. (2010). Developing Competencies to Teach Exponential and Logarithmic Functions using GeoGebra from a Holistic Approach. *Educação Matemática Pesquisa, 12*(3), 485–513.

González, R. D. M. (2014). Aprendizaje por descubrimiento, enseñanza activa y geoinformación: hacia una didáctica de la geografía innovadora. *Didáctica geográfica, 14*, 17-36.

Goodnough, K. (2001). Multiple Intelligences Theory: A Framework for Personalizing Science Curricula. *School Science and Mathematics, 101*(4), 180–193. doi:10.1111/j.1949-8594.2001.tb18021.x

Gouws, E., & Dicker, A. M. (2011). Teaching mathematics that addresses learners' multiple intelligences. *Africa Education Review, 8*(3), 568–587. doi:10.1080/18146627.2011.618721

Gracious, F. L. A, & Shyla, F. L. J. A. (2012). Multiple intelligence and digital learning awareness of prospective B. Ed. teachers. *Turkish Online Journal of Distance Education, 3*.

Graesser, A., & McNamara, D. (2010). Self-regulated learning in learning environments with pedagogical agents that interact in natural language. *Educational Psychologist, 45*(4), 234–244. doi:10.1080/00461520.2010.515933

Gratch, J., Okhmatovskaia, A., Lamothe, F., Marsella, S., Morales, M., van der Werf, R. J., & Morency, L. (2006). Virtual rapport. In *International Workshop on Intelligent Virtual Agents*. Springer Berlin Heidelberg. 10.1007/11821830_2

Gratch, J., Wang, N., Gerten, J., Fast, E., & Duffy, R. (2007). Creating rapport with virtual agents. In *International Workshop on Intelligent Virtual Agents*. Springer Berlin Heidelberg. 10.1007/978-3-540-74997-4_12

Green Patriot Posters. (n.d.). Retrieved May 21, 2019, from http://www.greenpatriotposters.org/inspire.php

Greenberg, K., & Zheng, R. (2019). *Working memory capacity and the modality effect in the cognitive load theory*. Paper presented at Society for Information Technology and Teacher Education (SITE) 30th International Conference, Las Vegas, NV.

Greenberg, K., & Zheng, R. (2018). A study on deep learning and mental reasoning in digital technology in relation to cognitive load. In R. Zheng (Ed.), *Strategies for deep learning with digital technology: Theories and practices in education* (pp. 331–354). Hauppauge, NY: NOVA Science Publishers.

Green, M., Lea, J. H., & McNair, C. L. (2014). Reality Check: Augmented Reality for School Libraries. *Teacher Librarian*, *41*(5), 28–34.

Grobman, G. M. (1990). *Stereotypes and Prejudices*. Remember.org. Retrieved May 24, 2019, from http://remember.org/guide/history-root-stereotypes

Groff, J. (2013). Expanding our "frames" of mind for education and the arts. *Harvard Educational Review*, *83*(1), 15–39. doi:10.17763/haer.83.1.kk34802147665819

Gros, B., & Forés, A. (2013). Using geolocation in secondary education to improve situated learning: Analysis of two case studies. *RELATEC*, *12*(2), 41–53.

Gross, J. J., & Thompson, R. A. (2007). Emotion Regulation: Conceptual Foundations. In J. J. Gross (Ed.), *Handbook of emotion regulation* (pp. 3–24). New York, NY: The Guilford Press.

Gülen, Ö., & Özdemir, S. (2013). Veri Madenciliği Teknikleri İle Üstün Yetenekli Öğrencilerin İlgi Alanlarının Analizi. *Journal of Gifted Education Research*, *1*(3), 215–226.

Gülseçen, S., Karataş, R., & Koçoğlu, R. (2012). Can GeoGebra Make Easier The Understanding of Cartesian Co-Ordinates? A Quantitative Study In Turkey. International Journal on New.

Guo, Y. R., & Goh, D. H. L. (2015). Affect in Embodied Pedagogical Agents: Meta-Analytic Review. *Journal of Educational Computing Research*, *53*(1), 124–149. doi:10.1177/0735633115588774

Guven, I., Yurdatapan, M., & Sahin, F. (2014). The Effect of Project-Based Educational Applications on the Scientific Literacy of 2nd Grade Elementary School Pupils. *International Journal of Education and Research*, *2*(1), 1–12.

Gyselinck, V., Meneghetti, G., De Beni, R., & Pazzaglia, F. (2009). The role of working memory in spatial text processing: What benefit of imagery strategy and visuospatial abilities? *Learning and Individual Differences*, *19*(1), 12–20. doi:10.1016/j.lindif.2008.08.002

Hacker, D. J., & Niederhauser, D. S. (2000). Promoting deep and durable learning in the online classroom. *New Dimensions for Teaching and Learning*, *84*(84), 53–63. doi:10.1002/tl.848

Hadley, W., Houck, C., Brown, L. K., Spitalnick, J. S., Ferrer, M., & Barker, D. (2018). Moving beyond role-play: Evaluating the use of virtual reality to teach emotion regulation for the prevention of adolescent risk behavior within a randomized pilot trial. *Journal of Pediatric Psychology*, *44*(4), 425–435. doi:10.1093/jpepsy/jsy092 PMID:30551157

Hamari, J., Shernoff, D. J., Rowe, E., Coller, B., Asbell-Clarke, J., & Edwards, T. (2016). Challenging games help students learn: An empirical study on engagement, flow and immersion in game-based learning. *Computers in Human Behavior*, *54*, 170–179. doi:10.1016/j.chb.2015.07.045

Compilation of References

Hamilton, E. R., Rosenberg, J. M., & Akcaoglu, M. (2016). The Substitution Augmentation Modification Redefinition (SAMR) Model: A Critical Review and Suggestions for its Use. *TechTrends*, *60*(5). 433–441. doi:10.1007/s11528-016-0091-y

Hammond, T., Bozdin, A., & Stanlick, S. E. (2014). Redefining the Longitude/Latitude Experience with a Scaffolded Geocache. *Social Studies*, *105*(5), 237–244. doi:10.1080/00377996.2014.920289

Hancock, P. A., Billings, D. R., Schaefer, K. E., Chen, J. Y. C., De Visser, E. J., & Parasuraman, R. (2011). A meta-analysis of factors affecting trust in human-robot interaction. *Human Factors: The Journal of the Human Factors and Ergonomics Society*, *53*(5), 517–527. doi:10.1177/0018720811417254 PMID:22046724

Han, J., Jo, M., Hyun, E., & So, H. J. (2015). Examining Young Children's Perception toward Augmented Reality-Infused Dramatic Play. *Educational Technology Research and Development*, *63*(3), 455–474. doi:10.100711423-015-9374-9

Han, J., & Kamber, M. (2006). *Data mining: concepts and techniques* (2nd ed.). Morgan Kaufmann.

Hansen, N., Koudenburg, N., Hiersemann, R., Tellegen, P. J., Kocsev, M., & Postmes, T. (2012). Laptop usage affects abstract reasoning of children in the developing world. *Computers & Education*, *59*(3), 989–1000. doi:10.1016/j.compedu.2012.04.013

Harbers, M., Jonker, C., & Van Riemsdijk, B. (2012). Enhancing team performance through effective communication. *Proceedings of the 4th Annual Human-Agent-Robot Teamwork Workshop*, 1-2.

Harte, W. (2017). Preparing preservice teachers to incorporate geospatial technologies in geography teaching. *The Journal of Geography*, *116*(5), 226–236. doi:10.1080/00221341.2017.1310274

Hartholt, A., Traum, D., Marsella, S., Morency, L. P., Shapiro, A., & Gratch, J. (2014). A Shared, Modular Architecture for Developing Virtual Humans. *Architectures and Standards for Intelligent Virtual Agents at IVA*, 4.

Hart, J. L., & Proctor, M. D. (2016). Framework and assessment of conversational virtual humans as role-players in simulated social encounters with people. *Journal of the International Association of Advanced Technology and Science*, *2*, 24–33.

Havard, B. (2018). Online discussion structure and instructor roles for the promotion of deep learning. In R. Zheng (Ed.), Strategies for deep learning with digital technology (pp. 71-89). New York, NY: Nova Science Publishers.

Hayden, S. (2011). *Enabling Curricula: The Development of a Teaching Observation Protocol to Address Students' Diverse Learning Needs*. ProQuest LLC.

Haydon, T., Musti-Rao, S., McCune, A., Clouse, D., McCoy, D., Kalra, H., & Hawkins, R. (2017). Using video modeling and mobile technology to teach social skills. *Intervention in School and Clinic*, *52*(3), 154–162. doi:10.1177/1053451216644828

Hayes, B. & Scassellati, B. (2013). Challenges in shared-environment human-robot collaboration. *Learning*, *8*, 9.

Hazari, Z., Tai, R. H., & Sadler, P. M. (2007). Gender Differences in Introductory University Physics Performance: The Influence of High School Physics Preparation and Affective Factors. *Science Education*, *91*(6), 847–876. doi:10.1002ce.20223

Heerink, M., Krose, B., Evers, V., & Wielinga, B. (2006). The influence of a robot's social abilities on acceptance by elderly users. *ROMAN 2006-The 15th IEEE International Symposium on Robot and Human Interactive Communication*, 521-526. 10.1109/ROMAN.2006.314442

Helle, L., Tynjälä, P., & Olkinuora, E. (2006). Project-based learning in post-secondary education – theory, practice and rubber sling shots. *Higher Education*, *51*(2), 287–314. doi:10.100710734-004-6386-5

Henriccson, L., & Rydell, A. M. (2004). Elementary school children with behavior problems: Teacher-child relations and self-perception: A prospective study. *Merrill-Palmer Quarterly, 50*(2), 111–138. doi:10.1353/mpq.2004.0012

Hernández-Torrano, D., Prieto, M. D., Ferrándiz, C., Bermejo, R., & Sáinz, M. (2013). Characteristics leading teachers to nominate secondary students as gifted in Spain. *Gifted Child Quarterly, 57*(3), 181–196. doi:10.1177/0016986213490197

Higgins, J. P., Thompson, S. G., Deeks, J. J., & Altman, D. G. (2003). Measuring inconsistency in meta-analyses. *BMJ (Clinical Research Ed.), 327*(7414), 557–560. doi:10.1136/bmj.327.7414.557 PMID:12958120

Hinds, P.J. & Weisband, S.P. (2003). Knowledge sharing and shared understanding in virtual teams. *Virtual teams that work: Creating conditions for virtual team effectiveness*, 21-36.

Historical Inquiry. (n.d.). *SCIM-C*. Retrieved May 26, 2019, from http://historicalinquiry.com

Hoepper, B. (2009). Stand inside my shoes: developing historical empathy. *QHistory*, 34-39. Retrieved January 29, 2019, from https://www.academia.edu

Hoffman, G., Birnbaum, G. E., Vanunu, K., Sass, O., & Reis, H. T. (2014). Robot responsiveness to human disclosure affects social impression and appeal. In *Proceedings of the 2014 ACM/IEEE international conference on Human-robot interaction*. ACM. 10.1145/2559636.2559660

Hohenwarter, M. (2014). Multiple representations and GeoGebra-based learning environments. Union. *Revista Iberoamericana de Educación Matemática, 39*, 11–18.

Holden, H. K., & Goldberg, B. (2011). *The impact of student expectations and tutor acceptance on computer-based learning environment acceptance and future usage intentions. International Defense & Homeland Security Simulation (DHSS) Workshop.*

Holt, T. (1990). *Thinking historically: Narrative, imagination, and understanding*. New York, NY: The College Board.

Hopkins, D. (1989). *Investigación en el aula. Guía del profesor*. Barcelona: PPU.

Hou, H.-T., & Wu, S.-Y. (2011). Analyzing the social knowledge construction behavioral patterns of an online synchronous collaborative discussion instructional activity using an instant messaging tool: A case study. *Computers & Education, 57*(2), 1459–1468. doi:10.1016/j.compedu.2011.02.012

Hoyles, C. (2018). Transforming the mathematical practices of learners and teachers through digital technology*. *Research in Mathematics Education, 20*(3), 209–228. doi:10.1080/14794802.2018.1484799

Hsieh, M. C., & Lin, H. C. K. (2010). Interaction Design Based on Augmented Reality Technologies for English Vocabulary Learning. In S.L. Wong et al. (Ed.), *Proceedings of the 18th International Conference on Computers in Education* (vol. 1, pp. 663–666). Putrajaya, Malaysia: Asia-Pacific Society for Computers in Education.

Hsu, T. Y., Chiou, C. K., Tseng, J. C., & Hwang, G. J. (2016). Development and evaluation of an active learning support system for context-aware ubiquitous learning. *IEEE Transactions on Learning Technologies, 9*(1), 37–45. doi:10.1109/TLT.2015.2439683

Hsu, Y.-S., Wang, C.-Y., & Zhang, W.-X. (2017). Supporting technology-enhanced inquiry through metacognitive and cognitive prompts: Sequential analysis of metacognitive actions in response to mixed prompts. *Computers in Human Behavior, 72*, 701–712. doi:10.1016/j.chb.2016.10.004

Huang, L., Morency, L., & Gratch, J. (2011). Virtual Rapport 2.0. In *International Workshop on Intelligent Virtual Agents*. Springer Berlin Heidelberg. 10.1007/978-3-642-23974-8_8

Huang, H. (2015, July). Propaganda as Signaling. *Comparative Politics, 47*(4), 419–437. doi:10.5129/001041515816103220

Huang, H., Schmidt, M., & Gartner, G. (2012). Spatial knowledge acquisition with mobile maps, augmented reality and voice in the context of GPS-based pedestrian navigation: Results from a field test. *Cartography and Geographic Information Science, 39*(2), 107–116. doi:10.1559/15230406392107

Huang, Y., Li, H., & Fong, R. (2015). Using Augmented Reality in early art education: A case study in Hong Kong kindergarten. *Early Child Development and Care, 186*(6), 879–894. doi:10.1080/03004430.2015.1067888

Huinker, D., & Madison, S. K. (1997). Preparing efficacious elementary teachers in science and mathematics: The influence of methods course. *Journal of Science Teacher Education, 8*(2), 107–125. doi:10.1023/A:1009466323843

Hung, P. H., Hwang, G. J., Lee, Y. H., Wu, T. H., Vogel, B., Milrad, M., & Johansson, E. (2014). A problem-based ubiquitous learning approach to improving the questioning abilities of elementary school students. *Journal of Educational Technology & Society, 17*(4), 316–334.

Hunt, B. (2009). Teaching and learning through music centers. *Musicien Educateur AU Canada, 50*(4), 51–53.

Husmann, P. R., & O'loughlin, V. D. (2019). Another nail in the coffin for learning styles? disparities among undergraduate anatomy students' study strategies, class performance, and reported vark learning styles. *Anatomical Sciences Education, 12*(1), 6–19. doi:10.1002/ase.1777 PMID:29533532

Hutchins, E. (1995). *Cognition in the wild*. Cambridge, MA: MIT Press.

Huynh, N. T., & Sharpe, B. (2013). An assessment instrument to measure geospatial thinking expertise. *The Journal of Geography, 112*(1), 3–17. doi:10.1080/00221341.2012.682227

Hwang, G.-J. (2014, November). Definition, framework and research issues of smart learning environments - a context-aware ubiquitous learning perspective. *Smart Learning Environments, 1*(4). Retrieved January 17, 2019, from https://slejournal.springeropen.com/articles/10.1186/s40561-014-0004-5

Hwang, G. J., Hung, P. H., Chen, N. S., & Liu, G. Z. (2014). Mindtool-Assisted In-Field Learning (MAIL): An advanced ubiquitous learning project in Taiwan. *Journal of Educational Technology & Society, 17*(2), 4–16.

IBM. (n.d.). Retrieved from http://www-01.ibm.com/

IEEE. (1990). *IEEE Standard computer dictionary: A compilation of IEEE standard computer glossaries*. New York: IEEE.

IEEE. (2002). *Learning Object Metadata*. Retrieved from https://standards.ieee.org/standard/1484_12_1-2002.html

Im, K. H., Kim, T. H., Bae, S., & Park, S. C. (2005). Conceptual modeling with neural network for giftedness identification and education. In *Advances in Natural Computation* (pp. 530–538). Springer Berlin Heidelberg. doi:10.1007/11539117_76

IMS. (2001). *IMS Learning Resource Meta-Data Information Model*. Retrieved from https://www.imsglobal.org/metadata/imsmdv1p2p1/imsmd_infov1p2p1.html

International Educational Data Mining Society. (2011). Available: http://www.educationaldatamining.org/

Inzunsa, S. (2014). GeoGebra: Una herramienta cognitiva para la enseñanza de la probabilidad. In Congreso Iberoamericano de Ciencia, Tecnología, Innovación y Educación. Retrieved from https://www.oei.es/historico/congreso2014/memoriactei/104.pdf

Iranzo, N., & Fortuny, J. (2009). La influencia conjunta del uso de GeoGebra y lápiz y papel en la adquisición de comeptencias del alumnado. *Enseñanza de las Ciencias, 27*(3), 433–446. Retrieved from www.geogebra.org

Ismail, M. N., Ngah, N. A., & Umar, I. N. (2010). Instructional Strategy in the Teaching of Computer Programming: A Need Assessment Analyses. *TOJET: The Turkish Online Journal of Educational Technology, 9*(2).

Istenic Starcic, A., & Kerr, S. (2014). Learning Environments – Not Just Smart for Some! In K. Miesenberger, D. Fels, D. Archambault, P. Peňáz, & W. Zagler (Eds.), Lecture Notes in Computer Science: Vol. 8548. *Computers Helping People with Special Needs. ICCHP 2014* (pp. 520–527). Cham: Springer. doi:10.1007/978-3-319-08599-9_77

Iyer, N. (2006). *Instructional practices of teachers in schools that use multiple intelligences theory (SUMIT)* (Unpublished doctoral dissertation). University of Cincinnati.

Jackson, A., Gaudet, L., McDaniel, L., & Brammer, D. (2009). Curriculum integration: The use of technology to support learning. *Journal of College Teaching and Learning*, *6*(7), 71–78.

Jacobs, J. (2017, March). *Propaganda Maps*. ThoughtCo. Retrieved January 25, 2019, from https://www.thoughtco.com/propaganda-maps-overview-1435683

Jacobs, D. (2007, January). More Than Words: Comics as a Means of Teaching Multiple Literacies. *English Journal*, *96*(3), 19–25. doi:10.2307/30047289

Jadallah, M., Hund, A. M., Thayn, J., Studebaker, J. G., Roman, Z. J., & Kirby, E. (2017). Integrating geospatial technologies in fifth-grade curriculum: Impact on spatial ability and map-analysis skills. *The Journal of Geography*, *116*(4), 139–151. doi:10.1080/00221341.2017.1285339

Janelle, D. G., & Goodchild, M. F. (2009). Location across disciplines reflections of the CSISS experience. In H. J. Scholten, N. van Manen, & R. V. D. Velde (Eds.), *Geospatial technology and the role of location in science* (pp. 15–29). Dordrecht, The Netherlands: Springer. doi:10.1007/978-90-481-2620-0_2

Järvinen, A. (2008a). *Games without frontiers: Theories and methods for game studies and design. Game Studies*. Tampere University Press.

Järvinen, A. (2008b). *Games without Frontiers: Theories and Methods for Game Studies and Design*. Game Studies.

Jarvis, P. (2006). *Towards a comprehensive theory of human learning*. London: Routledge.

Jauck, D. E., Maita, M. D. R., Mareovich, F., & Peralta, O. A. (2015). Maternal teaching of the symbolic function of a scale model [La enseñanza materna de la función simbólica de una maqueta]. *Infancia y Aprendizaje*, *38*(3), 617–646. doi:10.1080/02103702.2015.1054666

Jenson, J., & Droumeva, M. (2015). Making games with Game Maker: A computational thinking curriculum case study. In *ECGBL2015-9th European Conference on Games Based Learning: ECGBL2015* (p. 260). Academic Conferences and Publishing Limited.

Jewitt, C. (2006). *Technology, literacy and learning: A multimodal approach*. London: Routledge.

Jiménez, J. J. (2018). Expresión Plástica tridimensional: Acercamiento a la realidad en Educación Infantil [Three-dimensional plastic expression. Approach to reality in Children's Education]. *Omnia*, *8*(1), 37–43. doi:10.23882/OM08-1-2018-H

Jing, L., Sujuan, M., & Linqing, M. (2012). The Study on the Effect of Educational Games for the Development of Students' Logic-Mathematics of Multiple Intelligence. *Physics Procedia*, *33*, 1749–1752. doi:10.1016/j.phpro.2012.05.280

Johnson, C. (2017). Learning to Program with Game Maker. *Online Submission*, *1*(2).

Johnson, D. W., & Johnson, R. (1989). *Cooperation and competition: Theory and research*. Edina, MN: Interaction Book Company.

Johnson, D. W., & Johnson, R. (2009). An educational psychology success story: Social interdependence theory and cooperative learning. *Educational Researcher*, *38*(5), 365–379. doi:10.3102/0013189X09339057

Jones, C., & Shao, B. (2011). The net generation and digital natives. *Higher Education Academy*. Retrieved from https://www.heacademy.ac.uk/system/files/next-generation-and-digital-natives.pdf

Jones, K., Fujita, T., & Ding, L. (2006). Informing the pedagogy for geometry: Learning from teaching approaches in China and Japan. *Proceedings of the British Society for Research into Learning Mathematics*, *26*(2), 109–114. Retrieved from https://eprints.soton.ac.uk/41852/

Jong, M. S., Shang, J., & Lee, F. (2010). Constructivist Learning Through Computer Gaming. In M. Syed (Ed.), Technologies Shaping Instruction and Distance Education: New Studies and Utilizations (pp. 207–222). Hershey, PA: Academic Press. doi:10.4018/978-1-60566-934-2.ch014

Joo-Nagata, J., Abad, F. M., Giner, J. G. B., & García-Peñalvo, F. J. (2017). Augmented reality and pedestrian navigation through its implementation in m-learning and e-learning: Evaluation of an educational program in Chile. *Computers & Education*, *111*, 1–17. doi:10.1016/j.compedu.2017.04.003

Juan, K., & Dawson, K. (2015). Effects of interactive software on student achievement and engagement in four secondary school geometry classes, compared to two classes with no technology integration. University of Florida. ProQuest Dissertations Publishing. Retrieved from https://search-proquest-com.pucdechile.idm.oclc.org/docview/1815189905?pq-origsite=primo

Jung, B., & Kopp, S. (2003, September). Flurmax: An interactive virtual agent for entertaining visitors in a hallway. In *International Workshop on Intelligent Virtual Agents* (pp. 23-26). Springer. 10.1007/978-3-540-39396-2_5

Kabaca, T. (2013). Software to Teach One-Variable Inequalities by the View of Semiotic. Eurasia Journal of Mathematics. *Science & Technology Education*, *9*(1), 73–81.

Kaldi, S., Filippatou, D., & Govaris, C. (2011). Project-Based Learning in Primary Schools: Effects on Pupils' Learning and Attitudes. *Education 3-13*, *39*(1), 35-47. doi:10.1080/03004270903179538

Kalish, M. L., Newell, B. R., & Dunn, J. C. (2017). More is generally better: Higher working memory capacity does not impair perceptual category learning. *Journal of Experimental Psychology. Learning, Memory, and Cognition*, *43*(4), 503–514. doi:10.1037/xlm0000323 PMID:27656872

Kang, S., & Gratch, J. (2012). Socially anxious people reveal more personal information with virtual counselors that talk about themselves using intimate human back stories. *Annual Review of Cybertherapy and Telemedicine*, *181*, 202–207. PMID:22954856

Kanwar, A., & Uvalić-Trumbić, S. (Eds.). (2015). *A Basic Guide to Open Educational Resources (OER)*. Paris: UNESCO and Commonwealth of Learning.

Karagiannidis, C., & Sampson, D. (2004). Adaptation Rules Relating Learning Styles Research and Learning Objects Meta-data. *Workshop on Individual Differences in Adaptive Hypermedia. 3rd International Conference on Adaptive Hypermedia and Adaptive Web-based Systems (AH2004)*.

Karamustafaoglu, S. (2010). Evaluating the Science Activities Based On Multiple Intelligence Theory. *Journal of Turkish Science Education*, *7*(1).

Kardefelf-Winther, D. (2017). How does the time children spend using digital technology impact their mental well-being, social relationships and physical activity? *UNICEF*. Retrieved from https://www.unicef-irc.org/publications/pdf/Children-digital-technology-wellbeing.pdf

Kasemsap, K. (2017). Mastering Educational Computer Games, Educational Video Games, and Serious Games in the Digital Age. In *Gamification-Based E-Learning Strategies for Computer Programming Education* (pp. 30–52). Hershey, PA: IGI Global. doi:10.4018/978-1-5225-1034-5.ch003

Kaufmann, H., & Schmalstieg, D. (2003). Mathematics and geometry education with collaborative augmented reality. *Computers & Graphics*, *27*(3), 339–345. doi:10.1016/S0097-8493(03)00028-1

Keefe, J. W. (1979). Learning Style: An overview. In *NASSP's Student learning styles: Diagnosing and prescribing programs* (pp. 1–17). Reston, VA: National Association of Secondary School.

Keeley, P. (2014). *What Are They Thinking?: Promoting Elementary Learning Through Formative Assessment*. Arlington, VA: NSTA Press.

Kelchen, R. (2015). *The landscape of competency-based education*. Washington, DC: American Enterprise Institute.

Kelley, J. F. (1984). An iterative design methodology for user-friendly natural language office information applications. *ACM Transactions on Information Systems*, *2*(1), 26–41. doi:10.1145/357417.357420

Kennah, M. R. (2016). *The Use of ICT in the Teaching and Learning Process in Secondary Schools: A Case Study of Two Cameroonian schools* (Master's Thesis). Department of Education Institute of Educational Leadership, University of Jyväskylä.

Kerawalla, L., Luckin, R., Seljeflot, S., & Woolard, A. (2006). *Making it real:* Exploring the Potential of Augmented Reality for Teaching Primary School Science. *Virtual Reality (Waltham Cross)*, *10*(3-4), 163–174. doi:10.100710055-006-0036-4

Kerski, J. J. (2008). The world at the students' fingertips. In *Digital geography: geospatial technologies in the social studies classroom*. Charlotte, NC: Information Age Publishing.

Kezar, A. (2001). Theory of Multiple Intelligences: Implications for Higher Education. *Innovative Higher Education*, *26*(2), 141–154. doi:10.1023/A:1012292522528

Kickmeier-Rust, M. D., & Albert, D. (2010). Micro-adaptivity: Protecting immersion in didactically adaptive digital educational games. *Journal of Computer Assisted Learning*, *26*(2), 95–105. doi:10.1111/j.1365-2729.2009.00332.x

Kickmeier-Rust, M. D., Mattheiss, E., Steiner, C., & Albert, D. (2012). A Psycho-Pedagogical Framework for Multi-Adaptive Educational Games. *International Journal of Game-Based Learning*, *1*(1), 45–58. doi:10.4018/ijgbl.2011010104

Kiili, K. (2005). Digital game-based learning: Towards an experiential gaming model. *The Internet and Higher Education*, *8*(1), 13–24. doi:10.1016/j.iheduc.2004.12.001

Kindler, E., & Krivy, I. (2011). Object-oriented simulation of systems with sophisticated control. *International Journal of General Systems*, *40*(3), 313–343. doi:10.1080/03081079.2010.539975

Kintsch, W. (1988). The role of knowledge in discourse comprehension construction-integration model. *Psychological Review*, *95*(2), 163–182. doi:10.1037/0033-295X.95.2.163 PMID:3375398

Kintsch, W. (1994). Text comprehension, memory, and learning. *The American Psychologist*, *49*(1), 294–303. doi:10.1037/0003-066X.49.4.294 PMID:8203801

Kintsch, W. (2000). Metaphor comprehension: A computational theory. *Psychonomic Bulletin & Review*, *7*(2), 237–266. doi:10.3758/BF03212981 PMID:10909133

Kintsch, W., & Van Dijk, T. A. (1978). Toward a model of text comprehension and production. *Psychological Review*, *85*(5), 363–394. doi:10.1037/0033-295X.85.5.363

Compilation of References

Kirschner, P. A., & Stoyanov, S. (2018). Educating Youth for Nonexistent/Not Yet Existing Professions. *Educational Policy*.

Kitsantas, A., & Dabbagh, N. (2011). The role of web 2.0 technologies in self-regulated learning. *New Directions for Teaching and Learning, 126*(126), 99–106. doi:10.1002/tl.448

Klein, P. D. (2003). Rethinking the multiplicity of cognitive resources and curricular representations: Alternatives to 'learning styles' and 'multiple intelligences'. *Journal of Curriculum Studies, 35*(1), 45–81. doi:10.1080/00220270210141891

Koback, R., Little, M., Race, E., & Acosta, M. C. (2001). Attachment disruptions in seriously emotionally disturbed children: Implications for treatment. *Attachment & Human Development, 3*(3), 243–258. doi:10.1080/14616730110096861 PMID:11885812

Koballa, T. R., & Glynn, S. M. (2007). Attitudinal and Motivational constructs in science learning. In S. K. Abell & N. G. Lederman (Eds.), *Handbook of Research on Science Education* (pp. 75–102). Mahwah, NJ: Erlbaum.

Koehler, M. J., & Mishra, P. (2009). What is Technological Pedagogical Content Knowledge (TPACK)? *Contemporary Issues in Technology & Teacher Education, 9*(1), 60–70. doi:10.1016/j.compedu.2010.07.009

Koifman, R. (1998). *The Relationship between EQ, IQ, and Creativity*. Ontario: University Windsor.

Kolb, A. Y. (2005). *The Kolb Learning Style İnventory–Version 3.1 2005 Technical Specifications*. Boston, MA: Hay Resource Direct.

Kolb, D. A. (1984). *Experiential learning: Experience as the source of learning and development*. Prentice-Hall.

Koparan, T. (2017). Analysis of Teaching Materials Developed by Prospective Mathematics Teachers and Their Views on Material Development. Malaysian Online Journal of Educational Technology, 5(4), 8–28. Retrieved from http://ezproxy.lib.uconn.edu/login?url=https://search.ebscohost.com/login.aspx?direct=true&db=eric&AN=EJ1156942&site=ehost-live

Kozlowski, S. W., & Ilgen, D. R. (2006). Enhancing the effectiveness of work groups and teams. *Psychological Science in the Public Interest, 7*(3), 77–124. doi:10.1111/j.1529-1006.2006.00030.x PMID:26158912

Kozma, R. (1994). Will media influence learning? Reframing the debate. *Educational Technology Research and Development, 42*(2), 7–19. doi:10.1007/BF02299087

Krajcik, J. S., & Blumenfeld, P. C. (2006). Project-based learning. In R. K. Sawyer (Ed.), *The Cambridge Handbook of the Learning Sciences* (pp. 317–334). Cambridge, UK: Cambridge University Press.

Krajcik, J. S., Blumenfeld, P. C., Marx, R. W., & Soloway, E. (1994). A collaborative model for helping middle grade teachers learn project-based instruction. *The Elementary School Journal, 94*(5), 483–497. doi:10.1086/461779

Krajcik, J. S., Czerniak, C. M., & Berger, C. M. (2002). *Teaching science in elementary and middle school classrooms: A project-based approach* (2nd ed.). New York, NY: McGraw Hill.

Krumhuber, E., Manstead, A. S., Cosker, D., Marshall, D., Rosin, P. L., & Kappas, A. (2007). Facial dynamics as indicators of trustworthiness and cooperative behavior. *Emotion (Washington, D.C.), 7*(4), 730–735. doi:10.1037/1528-3542.7.4.730 PMID:18039040

Kubat, U. (2018). Identifying the individual differences among students during learning and teaching process by science teachers. *International Journal of Research in Educational and Science, 4*(1), 30–38. doi:10.21890/ijres.369746

Kuder, J. S. (2017). Vocabulary instruction for secondary students with reading disabilities: An updated research review. *Learning Disability Quarterly, 40*(3), 155–164. doi:10.1177/0731948717690113

Kulo, V. A., & Bodzin, A. M. (2011). Integrating geospatial technologies in an energy unit. *The Journal of Geography*, *110*(6), 239–251. doi:10.1080/00221341.2011.566344

Kumar, S. A., & Vijayalakshmi, M. N. (2011, July). Efficiency of decision trees in predicting student's academic performance. *First International Conference On Computer Science*, Engineering And Applications, India.

Kunkle, W. M., & Allen, R. B. (2016). The Impact of Different Teaching Approaches and Languages on Student Learning of Introductory Programming Concepts. *ACM Transactions on Computing Education, 16*(1), 3:1–3:26.

Kurbanoglu, N. I., & Akin, A. (2012). The relationships between university studentsí organic chemistry anxiety, chemistry attitudes, and self-efficacy: A structural equation model. *Journal of Baltic Science Education, 11*(4), 347–356.

Kurilovas, E., Kurilova, J., & Andruskevic, T. (2016). On suitability index to create optimal personalised learning packages. In *International Conference on Information and Software Technologies* (pp. 479-490). Springer. 10.1007/978-3-319-46254-7_38

Kurt, S. (2017, September). Wikis in Education: How Wikis are Being Used in the Classroom. *Educational Technology*. Retrieved May 24, 2019, from https://educationaltechnology.net/wikis-in-education

Kutluca, T. (2013). The Effect of Geometry Instruction with Dynamic Geometry Software; GeoGebra on Van Hiele Geometry Understanding Levels of Students. *Educational Research Review, 8*(17), 1509–1518. doi:10.5897/ERR2013.1554

Laborde, C. (2007). The role and uses of technologies in mathematics classrooms: Between challenge and modus vivendi. Canadian Journal of Science, Mathematics and Technology Education, 7(1), 68–92. doi:10.1080/14926150709556721

Lajoie, S. P., & Poitras, E. (2014). Macro and micro-strategies in for metacognition and co-regulation in the medical tutoring domain. In R. Sottilare, A. Graesser, X. Hu, & B. Goldberg (Eds.), *Design Recommendations for Adaptive Intelligent Tutoring Systems: Adaptive Instructional Management* (Vol. 2, pp. 151–168). Orlando, FL: U.S. Army Research Laboratory.

Lallée, S., Vouloutsi, V., Munoz, M. B., Grechuta, K., Llobet, J. Y. P., Sarda, M., & Verschure, P. F. (2015). Towards the synthetic self: Making others perceive me as an other. *Paladyn: Journal of Behavioral Robotics, 6*(1). doi:10.1515/pjbr-2015-0010

Lambert, W. E. (1997, September). From Crockett to Tubman: Investigating Historical Perspectives. *Educational Leadership, 55*(1), 51–54.

Landers, R. N., & Callan, R. C. (2011). Casual social games as serious games: The psychology of gamification in undergraduate education and employee training. In M. Ma, A. Oikonomou, & L. Jain (Eds.), *Serious games and edutainment applications* (pp. 399–423). London: Springer. doi:10.1007/978-1-4471-2161-9_20

Large, D. R., Clark, L., Quandt, A., Burnett, G., & Skrypchuk, L. (2017). Steering the conversation: A linguistic exploration of natural language interactions with a digital assistant during simulated driving. *Applied Ergonomics, 63*, 53–61. doi:10.1016/j.apergo.2017.04.003 PMID:28502406

Laurillard, D. (2002). *Rethinking university teaching: A conversational framework for the effective use of learning technologies*. New York: Routledge. doi:10.4324/9780203160329

LaViola, J., Williamson, B., Brooks, C., Veazanchin, S., Sottilare, R., & Garrity, P. (2015, December). Using augmented reality to tutor military tasks in the wild. *Proceedings of the Interservice/Industry Training Simulation & Education Conference*.

Lawrence, E. (1970). *The Origins and Growth of Modern Education*. London: Penguin Books.

Compilation of References

Layman, T., & Harris, R. (2013, January). Connecting the dots: Helping Year 9 to debate the purposes of Holocaust and genocide education. *Teaching History, 153*, 4–10.

Lazar, S. (2011, November). Teaching History Through Inquiry. *Education Week Teacher*. Retrieved January 6, 2019, from http://www.edweek.org/tm/articles/2011/10/31/tln_lazar.html

Lazear, D. (1992). *Teaching for Multiple Intelligences. Fastback 342*. Bloomington, IN: Phi Delta Kappan Educational Foundation. Retrieved May 21, 2019, from https://files.eric.ed.gov/fulltext/ED356227.pdf

Le, C., Wolfe, R., & Steinberg, A. (2014). *The past and the promise: Today's competency education movement. Students at the Center: Competency Education Research Series*. Boston, MA: Jobs for the Future.

Lee, H., & Lee, J. (2008). Mathematical Education Game Based on Augmented Reality. In Z. Pan, X. Zhang, A. El Rhalibi, W. Woo, & Y. Li (Eds.), *Technologies for e-Learning and Digital Entertainment. Proceedings of the Third International Conference, Edutainment 2008* (pp. 442–450). New York: Springer. 10.1007/978-3-540-69736-7_48

Lee, C. S. (2007). Diagnostic, predictive and compositional modeling with data mining in integrated learning environments. *Computers & Education, 49*(3), 562–580. doi:10.1016/j.compedu.2005.10.010

Lee, J. D., & See, K. A. (2004). Trust in automation: Designing for appropriate reliance. *Human Factors: The Journal of the Human Factors and Ergonomics Society, 46*(1), 50–80. doi:10.1518/hfes.46.1.50.30392 PMID:15151155

Lee, J., & Bednarz, R. (2009). Effects of GIS learning on spatial thinking. *Journal of Geography in Higher Education, 33*(2), 183–198. doi:10.1080/03098260802276714

Lee, K. (2012). Augmented Reality in Education and Training. *TechTrends, 56*(2), 13–21. doi:10.100711528-012-0559-3

Lee, L., Lajoie, S., Poitras, E., Nkangu, M., & Doleck, T. (2017). Co-regulation and knowledge construction in an online synchronous problem based learning setting. *Education and Information Technologies, 22*(4), 1623–1650. doi:10.100710639-016-9509-6

Lee, P. (2005). Putting principles into practice: understanding history. In M. S. Donovan & J. D. Bransford (Eds.), *How Students Learn: History in the Classroom. Committee on How People Learn: A Targeted Report for Teachers. National Research Council* (pp. 31–77). Washington, DC: National Academy Press.

Lee, P., & Ashby, R. (2001). Empathy, perspective taking, and rational understanding. In O. L. Davis, E. Yeager, & S. Foster (Eds.), *Historical empathy and perspective taking in the social studies* (pp. 21–50). New York, NY: Rowman and Littlefield.

Lemaignan, S., Warnier, M., Sisbot, E. A., Clodic, A., & Alami, R. (2017). Artificial cognition for social human–robot interaction: An implementation. *Artificial Intelligence, 247*, 45–69. doi:10.1016/j.artint.2016.07.002

León, J., & Flores, J. (2015). Instrumentalización de la elipse utilizando Geogebra. In Conferencia Interamericana de Educación Matemática (pp. 1–9). Chiapas.

Leonard, K., Noh, E. K., & Orey, M. (2010). Introduction to Emerging Perspectives on Learning, Teaching, and Technology. In M. Orey (Ed.), *Emerging perspectives on learning, teaching, and technology* (pp. 8-24). Zurich, Switzerland: Jacobs Foundation. Retrieved May 30, 2019, from https://www.academia.edu

Leow, F. T., & Neo, M. (2015). Collaborative learning with Web 2.0 tools: Analyzing Malaysian students' perceptions and peer interaction. *Educational Media International, 52*(4), 308–327. doi:10.1080/09523987.2015.1100392

Lerner, R. M., Liben, L. S., & Mueller, U. (2015). *Handbook of Child Psychology and Developmental Science, Cognitive Processes* (Vol. 2). John Wiley & Sons. doi:10.1002/9781118963418

Leshkovska, E. A., & Spaseva, S. M. (2016). John Dewey's educational theory and educational implications of Howard Gardner's multiple intelligence theory. *International Journal of Cognitive Research in Science, Engineering and Education, 4*(2), 57–66.

Lester, P. M. (2013). *Visual Communication: Images with Messages* (6th ed.). Belmont, CA: Wadsworth Publishing Company.

Levstik, L. (1990). From the outside in: American children's literature from 1920-1940. *Theory and Research in Social Education, 18*(4), 327–343. doi:10.1080/00933104.1990.10505620

Levstik, L. S. (1996). Negotiating the historical landscape. *Theory and Research in Social Education, 24,* 393–397.

Levstik, L. S., & Barton, K. (2001). *Doing history: Investigating with children in elementary and middle schools.* Mahwah, NJ: Lawrence Erlbaum Associates.

Liao, Y. W., Huang, Y. M., Chen, H. C., & Huang, S. H. (2015). Exploring the antecedents of collaborative learning performance over social networking sites in a ubiquitous learning context. *Computers in Human Behavior, 43,* 313–323. doi:10.1016/j.chb.2014.10.028

Liben, L. S. (2002). Where are we know? In U. C. Goswami (Ed.), *Blackwell Handbook of Childhood Cognitive Development* (pp. 326–348). Malden, MA: Blackwell Publishers. doi:10.1002/9780470996652.ch15

Library of Congress. (n.d.). *Posters: World War I Posters.* Retrieved May 27, 2019, from http://www.loc.gov/pictures/collection/wwipos/background.html

Lim, K. C., & Leong, K. E. (2017). A Study of Gamification on GeoGebra for Remedial Pupils in Primary Mathematics. In *Asian Conference on Technology in Mathematics (ATCM)* (pp. 222-228). Chungli, Taiwan: Mathematics and Technology, LLC.

Limón, M. (2002). Conceptual Change in History. In M. Limón & S. Mason (Eds.), *Reconsidering Conceptual Change: Issues in Theory and Practice* (pp. 259–289). Dordrecht: Kluwer Academic Publishers. doi:10.1007/0-306-47637-1_14

Lin, C.-H., & Chen, C.-M. (2016). Developing spatial visualization and mental rotation with a digital puzzle game at primary school level. *Computers in Human Behavior, 57,* 23–30. doi:10.1016/j.chb.2015.12.026

Lingefjärd, T. (2012). A Kaiserin of mathematics education. In Mathematikunterricht im Kontext von Realität, Kultur und Lehrerprofessionalität (pp. 385–390). Vieweg + Teubner Verlag. doi:10.1007/978-3-8348-2389-2_40

Linssen, J. (2011). *Adaptive Learning in an Educational Game-Adapting Game Complexity to Gameplay Increases Efficiency of Learning.* Academic Press.

Lipsey, M. W. (2003). Those confounded moderators in meta-analysis: Good, bad, and ugly. *The Annals of the American Academy of Political and Social Science, 587*(1), 69–81. doi:10.1177/0002716202250791

Li, Q., Zhang, T., Wang, B., & Wang, N. (2013). Effects of RPG on middle school players intrapersonal intelligence. In *Transactions on Edutainment IX* (pp. 160–175). Springer. doi:10.1007/978-3-642-37042-7_10

Lisetti, C., & Hudlicka, E. (2015). Why and how to build emotion-based agent architectures. In *The Oxford Handbook of Affective Computing* (p. 94). Oxford Library of Psychology.

Liu, X., & Ruiz, M. E. (2008). Using data mining to predict K–12 students' performance on large-scale assessment items related to energy. *Journal of Research in Science Teaching, 45*(5), 554–573. doi:10.1002/tea.20232

Lizano, K., & Umaña, M. (2008). La Teoría de las Inteligencias Múltiples en la práctica docente en Educación Preescolar. *Revista Electrónica Educare, 12*(1), 135–149.

Logie, R. H. (1995). *Visuo-spatial working memory*. Hove, UK: Lawrence Erlbaum Associates.

Lohani, M., Stokes, C. K., Oden, K. B., Frazier, S. J., Landers, K. J., Craven, P. L., . . . Macannuco, D. J. (2017). The Impact of Non-Technical skills on Trust and Stress. In *Proceedings of the Companion of the 2017 ACM/IEEE International Conference on Human-Robot Interaction* (pp. 191-192). ACM. 10.1145/3029798.3038321

Lohani, M., Stokes, C., McCoy, M., Bailey, C. A., Joshi, A., & Rivers, S. E. (2016b). Perceived role of physiological sensors impacts trust and reliance on robots. In *Robot and Human Interactive Communication (RO-MAN), 2016 25th IEEE International Symposium on*. IEEE. 10.1109/ROMAN.2016.7745166

Lohani, M., & Isaacowitz, D. M. (2014). Age differences in managing response to sadness elicitors using attentional deployment, positive reappraisal and suppression. *Cognition and Emotion*, 28(4), 678–697. doi:10.1080/02699931.2013.853648 PMID:24206128

Lohani, M., Payne, B. R., & Isaacowitz, D. (2018). Emotional Coherence in Early and Later Adulthood During Sadness Reactivity and Regulation. *Emotion (Washington, D.C.)*, 18(6), 789–804. doi:10.1037/emo0000345 PMID:28682087

Lohani, M., Payne, B. R., & Strayer, D. L. (2019). A Review of Psychophysiological Measures to Assess Cognitive States in Real-World Driving. *Frontiers in Human Neuroscience*, 13. PMID:30941023

Lohani, M., Stokes, C., Dashan, N., McCoy, M., Bailey, C. A., & Rivers, S. E. (2017). A Framework for Human-Agent Social Systems: The Role of Non-technical Factors in Operation Success. In *Advances in Human Factors in Robots and Unmanned Systems* (pp. 137–148). Springer International Publishing. doi:10.1007/978-3-319-41959-6_12

Lohani, M., Stokes, C., McCoy, M., Bailey, C. A., & Rivers, S. E. (2016a). Social Interaction Moderates Human-Robot Trust-Reliance Relationship and Improves Stress Coping. In *The Eleventh ACM/IEEE International Conference on Human Robot Interaction*. IEEE Press. 10.1109/HRI.2016.7451811

Longman, H., O'Conner, E., & Obst, P. (2009). The effect of social support derived from World of Warcraft on negative psychological symptoms. *Cyberpsychology & Behavior*, 12(5), 563–566. doi:10.1089/cpb.2009.0001 PMID:19817567

Longmire, W. (2000, March). A Primer on Learning Objects. *Learning Circuits*, 6.

Lopes, R., & Bidarra, R. (2011). Adaptivity challenges in games and simulations: A survey. *IEEE Transactions on Computational Intelligence and AI in Games*, 3(2), 85–99. doi:10.1109/TCIAIG.2011.2152841

López, A., Peñaloza, C., & Cuéllar, F. (2016). Influence of a Humanoid Robot in Human Decision-Making When Using Direct & Indirect Requests. In *The Eleventh ACM/IEEE International Conference on Human Robot Interaction*. IEEE Press. 10.1109/HRI.2016.7451812

Lori, A. A. (2005). Multiple Intelligences: A comparative study between the preferences of males and females. *Social Behavior and Personality*, 33(1), 77–88. doi:10.2224bp.2005.33.1.77

Lubold, N., Walker, E., & Pon-Barry, H. (2015). Relating Entrainment, Grounding, and Topic of Discussion in Collaborative Learning Dialogues. Proceedings of Computer Supported Collaborative Learning.

Lucas, G. M., Boberg, J., Traum, D., Artstein, R., Gratch, J., Gainer, A., ... Nakano, M. (2017, October). The role of social dialogue and errors in robots. In *Proceedings of the 5th International Conference on Human Agent Interaction* (pp. 431-433). ACM. 10.1145/3125739.3132617

Lucas, G. M., Boberg, J., Traum, D., Artstein, R., Gratch, J., Gainer, A., ... Nakano, M. (2018, February). Getting to know each other: The role of social dialogue in recovery from errors in social robots. In *Proceedings of the 2018 ACM/IEEE International Conference on Human-Robot Interaction* (pp. 344-351). ACM. 10.1145/3171221.3171258

Lundgren, S., & Bjork, S. (2003). Game mechanics: Describing computer-augmented games in terms of interaction. *Proceedings of TIDSE*.

Maatman, R. M., Gratch, J., & Marsella, S. (2005). Natural behavior of a listening agent. In *International Workshop on Intelligent Virtual Agents*. Springer Berlin Heidelberg. 10.1007/11550617_3

MacArthur, C. A. (1996, July). Using Technology to Enhance the Writing Processes of Students with Learning Disabilities. *Journal of Learning Disabilities*, *29*(4), 344–354. doi:10.1177/002221949602900403 PMID:8763550

MacCoog, I. J. (2007). Integrated Instruction: Multiple Intelligences and Technology. *The Clearing House: A Journal of Educational Strategies, Issues and Ideas*, *81*(1), 25–28. doi:10.3200/TCHS.81.1.25-28

Macedo, F. (2013). Teaching creative music technology in higher education: A phenomenological approach. *Journal of Music, Technology & Education*, *6*(2), 207–219.

Magerko, B. (2009). The Future of Digital Game-Based Learning. Handbook of Research on Effective Electronic Gaming in Education, 3, 1274–1288. doi:10.4018/978-1-59904-808-6

Magna, A. J. (2014). Learning strategies and multimedia techniques for scaffolding size and scale cognition. *Computers & Education*, *72*, 367–377. doi:10.1016/j.compedu.2013.11.012

Majgaard, G. (2014). The Playful and Reflective Game Designer. *Electronic Journal of E-Learning*, *12*(3), 271–280.

Mall, K. (2012). *Are you reaching your digital natives?* Scholastic. Retrieved from https://www.scholastic.com/teachers/blog-posts/kristy-mall/are-you-reaching-your-digital-natives/

Manwaring, K. C., Larsen, R., Graham, C. R., Henrie, C. R., & Halverson, L. R. (2017). Investigating student engagement in blended learning settings using experience sampling and structural equation modeling. *The Internet and Higher Education*, *35*, 21–33. doi:10.1016/j.iheduc.2017.06.002

Marcus, N., Cooper, M., & Sweller, J. (1996). Understanding instructions. *Journal of Educational Psychology*, *88*(1), 49–63. doi:10.1037/0022-0663.88.1.49

Mariano, G. J., Doolittle, P., & Hicks, D. (2009). Fostering transfer in multimedia instructional materials. In R. Zheng (Ed.), *Cognitive effects of multimedia learning* (pp. 237–258). Hershey, PA: Information Science Reference/IGI Global. doi:10.4018/978-1-60566-158-2.ch013

Marlow, C. M. (2012). Making Games for Environmental Design Education: Revealing Landscape Architecture. *International Journal of Gaming and Computer-Mediated Simulations*, *4*(2), 60–83. doi:10.4018/jgcms.2012040104

Marquesz Chisholm, I., & Beckett, E. D. (2003). Teacher preparation for equitable access through the integration of TESOL standards, multiple intelligences and technology. *Technology, Pedagogy and Education*, *12*(2), 249–276. doi:10.1080/14759390300200157

Martínez Borreguero, M.G., Naranjo-Correa, F.L., & Mateos-Núñez, M. & Sánchez-Martín. (2018). Recreational experiences for teaching basic scientific concepts in Primary Education: The case of density and pressure. *Eurasia Journal of Mathematics. Science and Technology Education*, *14*(12), 1–16.

Martín-Gutiérrez, J., Contero, M., & Alcañiz, M. (2010). Evaluating the usability of an augmented reality based educational application. In *International Conference on Intelligent Tutoring Systems* (pp. 296-306). Springer. 10.1007/978-3-642-13388-6_34

Compilation of References

Marx, R. W., Blumenfeld, P. C., Krajcik, J. S., Blunk, M., Crawford, B., Kelley, B., & Meyer, K. M. (1994). Enacting project-based science: Experiences of four middle grade teachers. *The Elementary School Journal*, *94*(5), 517–538. doi:10.1086/461781

Marzano, R. J. (1988). *Dimensions of Thinking: A Framework for Curriculum and Instruction*. Alexandria, VA: Association for Supervision and Curriculum Development.

Mathieu, J., Maynard, M. T., Rapp, T., & Gilson, L. (2008). Team effectiveness 1997-2007: A review of recent advancements and a glimpse into the future. *Journal of Management*, *34*(3), 410–476. doi:10.1177/0149206308316061

Mavridis, N. (2015). A review of verbal and non-verbal human–robot interactive communication. *Robotics and Autonomous Systems*, *63*, 22–35. doi:10.1016/j.robot.2014.09.031

Mayer, R. C., Davis, J. H., & Schoorman, F. D. (1995). An integrative model of organizational trust. *Academy of Management Review*, *20*(3), 709–734. doi:10.5465/amr.1995.9508080335

Mayer, R. E. (1997). Multimedia learning: Are we asking the right questions? *Educational Psychologist*, *32*(1), 1–19. doi:10.120715326985ep3201_1

Mayer, R. E. (2001). *Multimedia learning*. Cambridge, UK: Cambridge University Press. doi:10.1017/CBO9781139164603

Mayer, R. E. (2002). Rote Versus Meaningful Learning. *Theory into Practice*, *41*(4), 226–232. doi:10.1207/s15430421tip4104_4

Mayer, R. E., & Anderson, R. B. (1992). The instructive animation: Helping students build connections between words and pictures in multimedia learning. *Journal of Educational Psychology*, *84*(4), 444–452. doi:10.1037/0022-0663.84.4.444

Mayer, R. E., & DaPra, C. S. (2012). An embodiment effect in computer-based learning with animated pedagogical agents. *Journal of Experimental Psychology. Applied*, *18*(3), 239–252. doi:10.1037/a0028616 PMID:22642688

Mayer, R. E., Heiser, J., & Lonn, S. (2001). Cognitive constraints on multimedia learning: When presenting more material results in less understanding. *Journal of Educational Psychology*, *93*(1), 187–198. doi:10.1037/0022-0663.93.1.187

Mayer, R. E., & Moreno, R. (2003). Nine ways to reduce cognitive load in multimedia learning. *Educational Psychologist*, *38*(1), 43–52. doi:10.1207/S15326985EP3801_6

Mayer, R. E., & Sims, V. K. (1994). For whom is a picture worth a thousand words? Extensions of a dual-coding theory of multimedia learning. *Journal of Educational Psychology*, *86*(3), 389–401. doi:10.1037/0022-0663.86.3.389

McCarthy, M., & Butler, B. (2013). *Universal Design for Learning and Multiple Intelligences Theory and Practice as SoTL Levers*. Academic Press.

McCoog, I. (2010). The existential learner. *The Clearing House: A Journal of Educational Strategies, Issues and Ideas*, *83*(4), 126–128. doi:10.1080/00098651003774828

McGrath, J. E. (1962). Leadership behavior: some requirements for leadership training. Washington, DC: US Civil Service Commission.

McKenzie, W. (2004). *Gardner's eight criteria for identifying an intelligence*. Retrieved January 3, 2018 from http://surfaquarium.com/MI/criteria.htm

McKenzie, W. (2005). *Multiple Intelligences and Instructional Technology* (2nd ed.). Eugene, OR: ISTE Publications.

McNeill, A. L., Doolittle, P. E., & Hicks, D. (2009). The effects of training, modality, and redundancy on the development of a historical inquiry strategy in a multimedia learning environment. *Journal of Interactive Online Learning*, 8(3), 255–269.

Medzini, A. (2012, March). The war of the maps: The political use of maps and atlases to shape national consciousness – Israel versus the Palestinian authority. *European Journal of Geography*, 3(1), 23–40.

Medzini, A., Meishar-Tal, H., & Sneh, Y. (2015). Use of mobile technologies as support tools for geography field trips. *International Research in Geographical and Environmental Education*, 24(1), 13–23. doi:10.1080/10382046.2014.967514

Melhuish, K., & Falloon, G. (2010). Looking to the future: M-learning with the iPad. *Computers in New Zealand Schools: Learning, Leading. Technology (Elmsford, N.Y.)*, 22(3), 1–16.

Mell, J., Lucas, G. M., & Gratch, J. (2018, July). Welcome to the real world: How agent strategy increases human willingness to deceive. In *Proceedings of the 17th International Conference on Autonomous Agents and MultiAgent Systems* (pp. 1250-1257). International Foundation for Autonomous Agents and Multiagent Systems.

Mellado, V., Borrachero, A. B., Brígido, M., Melo, L. V., Dávila, M. A., Cañada, F., ... Bermejo, M. L. (2014). Las Emociones en la Enseñanza de las Ciencias. *Enseñanza de las Ciencias*, 32(3), 11–36.

Mercer, N., Warwick, P., Kershner, R., & Kleine Staarman, J. (2010, March). Can the interactive whiteboard help to provide 'dialogic space' for children's collaborative activity? *Language and Education*, 24(5), 367–384. doi:10.1080/09500781003642460

Merino, C., Pino, S., Meyer, E., Garrido, J. M., & Gallardo, F. (2015). Realidad aumentada para el diseño de secuencias de enseñanza-aprendizaje en química. *Educación en la Química*, 26(2), 94–99.

Merrill, D. (1983). Component Display Theory. In C. Reigeluth (Ed.), *Instructional-design theories and models: an overview of their current status*. Hillsdale, NJ: Lawrence Erlbaum Associates.

Merrill, M. D. (2013). *First principles of instruction: Identifying and designing effective, efficient and engaging instruction*. San Francisco, CA: Wiley.

Metoyer, S., & Bednarz, R. (2017). Spatial thinking assists geographic thinking: Evidence from a study exploring the effects of geospatial technology. *The Journal of Geography*, 116(1), 20–33. doi:10.1080/00221341.2016.1175495

Mettetal, G., Jordan, C., & Harper, S. (1997). Attitudes toward a multiple intelligences curriculum. *The Journal of Educational Research*, 91(2), 115–122. doi:10.1080/00220679709597529

Meyer, A., & Rose, D. H. (2000). Universal Design for Individual Differences. *Educational Leadership*, 58(3), 39–43.

Meyer, M. (1998). Learning and Teaching through the Naturalist Intelligence. *Clearing*, 102, 7–11.

Mikulecký, P. (2012). Smart Environments for Smart Learning. In *Proceedings of 9th International Scientific Conference on Distance Learning in Applied Informatics* (pp. 213-222). Divai. Retrieved January 13, 2019, from https://conferences.ukf.sk/index.php/divai/divai2012/paper/view/873

Miles, H. (2012, March). *WWII Propaganda: The Influence of Racism*. Artifacts 6. University of Missouri. Retrieved January 18, 2019, from https://artifactsjournal.missouri.edu/2012/03/wwii-propaganda-the-influence-of-racism

Miller, G. A. (1956). The magical number seven, plus or minus two: Some limits on our capacity for processing information. *Psychological Review*, 63(2), 81–97. doi:10.1037/h0043158 PMID:13310704

Compilation of References

Millsaps, L. T., & Harrington, J. A. (2017). A time-sensitive framework for including geographic information systems (GIS) in professional development activities for classroom teachers. *The Journal of Geography, 116*(4), 152–164. doi:10.1080/00221341.2017.1294611

Milovanovic, M., Obradovic, J., & Milajic, A. (2013). Application of interactive multimedia tools in teaching mathematics--examples of lessons from geometry. *Turkish Online Journal of Educational Technology, 12*(1), 19–31.

Minami, M., Morikawa, H., & Aoyama, T. (2004). The Design Of Naming-Based Service Composition System For Ubiquitous Computing Applications. In *Proceedings of the 2004 International Symposium on Applications and the Internet Workshops (SAINTW'04)* (pp. 304–312). Washington, DC: IEEE Computer Society. 10.1109/SAINTW.2004.1268652

Ministerio de Educación. (2015). Bases Curriculares 7o básico a 2o medio. Santiago, Gobierno de Chile: Unidad de Currículum y Evaluación.

Mishra, P., & Koehler, M. J. (2006). Technological Pedagogical Content Knowledge: A Framework for Teacher Knowledge. *Teachers College Record, 108*(6), 1017–1054. doi:10.1111/j.1467-9620.2006.00684.x

Mithalal, J. (2010). 3D Geometry and Learning of Mathematical Reasoning. In *Proceedings of CERME* (pp. 796–805). Academic Press.

Mokhtar, I. A., Majid, S., & Foo, S. (2008). Information literacy education: Applications of mediated learning and multiple intelligences. *Library & Information Science Research, 30*(3), 195–206. doi:10.1016/j.lisr.2007.12.004

Molero, C., Saiz, E., & Esteban, C. (1998). Revisión histórica del concepto de inteligencia: Una aproximación a la inteligencia emocional. *Revista Latinoamericana de Psicología, 30*, 11–30.

Mondahl, M., & Razmerita, L. (2014). Social media, collaboration and social learning--A case-study of foreign language learning. *Electronic Journal of e-Learning, 12*(4), 339-352.

Monks, T., Robinson, S., & Kotiadis, K. (2016). Can involving clients in simulation studies help them solve their future problems? A transfer of learning experiment. *European Journal of Operational Research, 249*(3), 919–930. doi:10.1016/j.ejor.2015.08.037

Montello, D. R. (2009). Cognitive science. In K. K. Kemp (Ed.), *Encyclopedia of geographic information science* (pp. 40–43). Thousand Oaks, CA: Sage Publications.

Moon, Y., & Nass, C. (1998). Are computers scapegoats? Attributions of responsibility in human–computer interaction. *International Journal of Human-Computer Studies, 49*(1), 79–94. doi:10.1006/ijhc.1998.0199

Moore, D. J. (1998). Computers and people with autism/Asperger syndrome. *Communication*, 20-21.

Morency, L. (2010). Modeling human communication dynamics. *IEEE Signal Processing Magazine, 27*(5), 112–116. doi:10.1109/MSP.2010.937500

Moreno, M., & Llinares, S. (2018). Prospective Mathematics Teachers' Perspectives on Technology. In *Educating Prospective Secondary Mathematics Teachers* (pp. 125–142). Cham: Springer; doi:10.1007/978-3-319-91059-8_8.

Moreno, R., & Mayer, R. (2007). Interactive Multimodal Learning Environments. *Educational Psychology Review, 19*(3), 309–326. doi:10.100710648-007-9047-2

Moreno, R., & Mayer, R. E. (1999). Cognitive principles of multimedia learning: The role of modality and contiguity. *Journal of Educational Psychology, 91*(2), 358–368. doi:10.1037/0022-0663.91.2.358

Moreno, R., Mayer, R. E., Spires, H. A., & Lester, J. C. (2001). The case for social agency in computer-based teaching: Do students learn more deeply when they interact with animated pedagogical agents? *Cognition and Instruction*, *19*(2), 177–213. doi:10.1207/S1532690XCI1902_02

Morera, L. (2011). Uso del Geogebra en la enseñanza de las Transformaciones. Uno: Revista de Didáctica de Las Matematicas, 56, 95–104. Retrieved from https://es.slideshare.net/mcnavarr1/el-uso-del-geogebra-en-la-enseanza-de-la-geometra

Morgan, J., Higgins, K., Miller, S., Pierce, T., Boone, R., & Tandy, R. (2016). Teaching online social skills to students with emotional and behavioral disorders. *Journal of Special Education Technology*, *31*(2), 109–120. doi:10.1177/0162643416651725

Mousavinasab, E., Zarifsanaiey, N., & Niakan Kalhori, S., Rakhshan, M., Keikha, L., & Ghazi Saeedi, M. (2018). Intelligent tutoring systems: A systematic review of characteristics, applications, and evaluation methods. *Interactive Learning Environments*, 1–22. doi:10.1080/10494820.2018.1558257

Mou, Y., & Xu, K. (2017). The media inequality: Comparing the initial human-human and human-AI social interactions. *Computers in Human Behavior*, *72*, 432–440. doi:10.1016/j.chb.2017.02.067

Mtebe, J. S., & Raisamo, R. (2014). Investigating students'behavioural intention to adopt and use mobile learning in higher education in East Africa. *International Journal of Education and Development Using Information and Communication Technology*, *10*(3), 4–20.

Muir, M., & Conati, C. (2012). An Analysis of Attention to Student–Adaptive Hints in an Educational Game. *Intelligent Tutoring Systems*, 112–122. Retrieved from http://www.springerlink.com/index/4L28G36M16605352.pdf

Munzer, S., Suefert, T., & Brunken, R. (2009). Learning from multimedia presentations: Facilitation function of animations and spatial abilities. *Learning and Individual Differences*, *19*(4), 481–485. doi:10.1016/j.lindif.2009.05.001

Mutlu, B. (2011). Designing embodied cues for dialog with robots. *AI Magazine*, *32*(4), 17–30. doi:10.1609/aimag.v32i4.2376

Nachimuthu, K., & Vijayakumari, G. (2011). Role of educational games improves meaningful learning. *i-Manager's Journal of Educational Technology*, *8*(2).

Narlı, S., Özgen, K., & Alkan, H. (2011). In the context of multiple intelligences theory, intelligent data analysis of learning styles was based on rough set theory. *Learning and Individual Differences*, *21*(5), 613–618. doi:10.1016/j.lindif.2011.07.012

Nass, C., Fogg, B. J., & Moon, Y. (1996). Can computers be teammates? *International Journal of Human-Computer Studies*, *45*(6), 669–678. doi:10.1006/ijhc.1996.0073

Nass, C., & Moon, Y. (2000). Machines and mindlessness: Social responses to computers. *The Journal of Social Issues*, *56*(1), 81–103. doi:10.1111/0022-4537.00153

Nass, C., Moon, Y., & Carney, P. (1999). Are respondents polite to computers? Social desirability and direct responses to computers. *Journal of Applied Social Psychology*, *29*(5), 1093–1110. doi:10.1111/j.1559-1816.1999.tb00142.x

Nass, C., Moon, Y., & Green, N. (1997a). Are computers gender-neutral? Social desirability and direct responses to computers. *Journal of Applied Social Psychology*, *27*(10), 864–876. doi:10.1111/j.1559-1816.1997.tb00275.x

Nass, C., Moon, Y., Morkes, J., Kim, E.-Y., & Fogg, B. J. (1997b). Computers are social actors: A review of current research. In B. Friedman (Ed.), *Moral and ethical issues in human-computer interaction* (pp. 137–162). Stanford, CA: CSLI Press.

Compilation of References

National Research Council. (2006). *Learning to think spatially: GIS as a support system in the K-12 curriculum.* Washington, DC: National Research Council and National Academic Press.

National Research Council. (2011). *Learning Science Through Computer Games and Simulations* (2nd ed.). Bioinformatics and Functional Genomics; doi:10.1080/004982501 10091767

NC Civic Education Consortium. (n.d.). *Decoding World War II Propaganda.* Retrieved January 10, 2019, from http://civics.sites.unc.edu/files/2012/05/DecodingWWIIPropaganda9.pdf

NCTE/IRA. (2005). *Read, write, think.* Retrieved January 19, 2019, from http://www.readwritethink.org/files/resources/lesson_images/lesson829/Argument-Propaganda.pdf

NCTM. (2012). NCTM CAEP Standards -Elementary Mathematics Specialist (Advanced Preparation). Retrieved from https://cehd.gmu.edu/assets/docs/MathEducation/nctm-caep-elementary-math-advanced.pdf

Nelson, G. (1998). Internet/Web-based instruction and multiple intelligences. *Educational Media International, 35*(2), 90–94. doi:10.1080/0952398980350206

Newcombe, N. (2010). Picture this: Increasing math and science learning by improving spatial thinking. *American Educator, 32,* 29–43.

Nguyen, L. T., & Ikeda, M. (2015). The effects of ePortfolio-based learning model on student self-regulated learning. *Active Learning in Higher Education, 16*(3), 197–209. doi:10.1177/1469787415589532

Nisbet, R., Elder, J., & Miner, G. (2009). *Handbook of statistical analysis and data mining applications.* Academic Press.

Nithya, P., Umamaheswari, B., & Umadevi, A. (2016). A survey on educational data mining in field of education. *International Journal of Advanced Research in Computer Engineering & Technology, 5*(1), 69–78.

Nodine, T. R. (2016). How did we get here? A brief history of competency-based higher education in the United States. *The Journal of Competency-Based Education, 1*(1), 5–11. doi:10.1002/cbe2.1004

Nokelainen, P., Tirri, K., & Merenti-Välimäki, H. L. (2007). Investigating the influence of attribution styles on the development of mathematical talent. *Gifted Child Quarterly, 51*(1), 64–81. doi:10.1177/0016986206296659

Nokes, J. D., Dole, J. A., & Hacker, D. J. (2007). Teaching high school students to use heuristics while reading historical texts. *Journal of Educational Psychology, 99*(3), 492–504. doi:10.1037/0022-0663.99.3.492

Novembre, A., Nicodemo, M., & Coll, P. (2015). Matemática y TIC Orientaciones para la enseñanza. *CABA: ANSES, 91,* 399–404.

Núñez Cardenas, F. D. J., Hernández Camacho, J., Mariano, T., Tomas, V., Redondo, F., & María, A. (2015). Application of Data Mining to describe Multiple Intelligences in University Students. *International Journal of Combinatorial Optimization Problems and Informatics, 6*(1), 20–30.

Nye, B. D., Graesser, A. C., & Hu, X. (2014). AutoTutor and family: A review of 17 years of natural language tutoring. *International Journal of Artificial Intelligence in Education, 24*(4), 427–469. doi:10.100740593-014-0029-5

O'Neill, K. E. (2011). Reading pictures: Developing visual literacy for greater comprehension. *The Reading Teacher, 65*(3), 214–223. doi:10.1002/TRTR.01026

Oh, C. S., Bailenson, J. N., & Welch, G. F. (2018). A Systematic Review of Social Presence: Definition, Antecedents, and Implications. *Front. Robot. AI, 5,* 114. doi:10.3389/frobt.2018.00114

Olitski, S., & Milne, C. (2012). Understanding engagement in science education: The psychological and the social. In B. J. Fraser, K. G. Tobin, & C. J. McRobbie (Eds.), *Second International Handbook of Science Education* (pp. 19–33). Dordrecht: Springer. doi:10.1007/978-1-4020-9041-7_2

Olsen, R. V., Prenzel, M., & Martin, R. (2011). Interest in Science: A many-faceted picture painted by data from the OECD PISA study. *International Journal of Science Education*, *33*(1), 1–6. doi:10.1080/09500693.2010.518639

Oprescu, M., Cracium, D., & Banaduc, I. (2011). Multiple intelligences in conventional and student-centered school. *Journal of Educational Sciences & Psychology*, *1*(1), 86–94.

Osborne, J., Simon, S., & Collins, S. (2003). Attitudes towards science: A review of the literature and its implications. *International Journal of Science Education*, *25*(9), 1049–1079. doi:10.1080/0950069032000032199

Overmars, M. (2004). *Game design in education*. Academic Press.

Oxford, R. (1998). Style Analysis Survey (SAS): Assessing your own learning and working styles. In J. M. Reid (Ed.), *Understanding learning styles in the second language classroom* (pp. 179–186). Upper Saddle River, NJ: Prentice Hall Regents.

Paas, F., Renkl, A., & Sweller, J. (2004). Cognitive Load Theory: Instructional Implications of the Interaction between Information Structures and Cognitive Architecture. *Learning and Instruction*, *32*(1/2), 1–8. doi:10.1023/B:TRUC.0000021806.17516.d0

Paek, S., Hoffman, D. L., & Black, J. B. (2016). Perceptual factors and learning in digital environments. *Educational Technology Research and Development*, *64*(3), 435–457. doi:10.100711423-016-9427-8

Paivio, A. (1986). *Mental representations: A dual coding approach*. Oxford, UK: Oxford University Press.

Pajares, F. (1992). Teachers' beliefs and educational research: Cleaning up a messy construct. *Review of Educational Research*, *62*(3), 307–332. doi:10.3102/00346543062003307

Palmer, H. (1991). *The Enneagram: Understanding yourself and the others in your life*. Harper San Francisco.

Pan, D., & Bolton, M. L. (2018). Properties for formally assessing the performance level of human-human collaborative procedures with miscommunications and erroneous human behavior. *International Journal of Industrial Ergonomics*, *63*, 75–88. doi:10.1016/j.ergon.2016.04.001

Pandey, A. K., Ali, M., & Alami, R. (2013). Towards a task-aware proactive sociable robot based on multi-state perspective-taking. *International Journal of Social Robotics*, *5*(2), 215–236. doi:10.100712369-013-0181-3

Papageorgiou, V., & Lameras, P. (2017). *Multimodal Teaching and Learning with the Use of Technology: Meanings, Practices and Discourses*. International Association for Development of the Information Society.

Papastergiou, M. (2009). Digital Game-Based Learning in high school Computer Science education: Impact on educational effectiveness and student motivation. *Computers & Education*, *52*(1), 1–12. doi:10.1016/j.compedu.2008.06.004

Papert, S., & Harel, I. (1991). Situating constructionism. *Constructionism*, *36*, 1–11.

Pappas, I., Giannakos, M., & Sampson, D. (2017). Fuzzy set analysis as a means to understand users of 21st-century learning systems: The case of mobile learning and reflections on learning analytics research. *Computers in Human Behavior*, 1–14.

Paquette, L., Rowe, J., Baker, R. S., Mott, B., Lester, J., DeFalco, J., ... Georgoulas, V. (2015). Sensor-Free or Sensor-Full: A Comparison of Data Modalities in Multi-Channel Affect Detection. *Proceedings of the 8th International Conference on Educational Data Mining*, 93-100.

Compilation of References

Paras, B., & Bizzocchi, J. (2005). *Game, Motivation, and Effective Learning: An Integrated Model for Educational Game Design*. Academic Press.

Parker, K. R., & Chao, J. T. (2007). Wiki as a Teaching Tool. *Interdisciplinary Journal of Knowledge and Learning Objects, 3*, 57–78.

Patterson, C., Stephens, M., Chiang, V., Price, A. M., Work, F., & Snelgrove-Clarke, E. (2017). The significance of personal learning environments (PLEs) in nursing education: Extending current conceptualizations. *Nurse Education Today, 48*, 99–105. doi:10.1016/j.nedt.2016.09.010 PMID:27744138

Patton, R. M. (2011). *Games as artistic medium: Interfacing complexity theory in game-based art pedagogy*. Academic Press.

Paul, T. V. (2014). An Evaluation of the Effectiveness of E-Learning,Mobile Learning, and Instructor-Led Training in Organizational Training and Development. *The Journal of Human Resource and Adult Learning, 10*(2), 1–13.

Paulus, P. B., & Brown, V. R. (2007). Toward more creative and innovative group idea generation: A cognitive-social-motivational perspective of brainstorming. *Social and Personality Psychology Compass, 1*(1), 248–265. doi:10.1111/j.1751-9004.2007.00006.x

Pazzaglia, F., Toso, C., & Cacciamani, S. (2008). The specific involvement of verbal and visuospatial working memory in hypermedia learning. *British Journal of Educational Technology, 39*(1), 110–124.

Pearson, D. G., & Logie, R. H. (2000). Working memory and mental synthesis: A dual task approach. In S. O. Nuallian (Ed.), *Spatial cognition: Foundations and applications* (pp. 347–359). Amsterdam: Joint Benjamins Publishing. doi:10.1075/aicr.26.27pea

Peck, C. (2005, Winter). Introduction to the Special Edition of Canadian Social Studies. *Canadian Social Studies, 39*(2). Retrieved January 20, 2019, from http://www.educ.ualberta.ca/css/Css_39_2/Editorial_39_2.htm

Pecune, F., Chen, J., Matsuyama, Y., & Cassell, J. (2018, July). Field Trial Analysis of Socially Aware Robot Assistant. *Proceedings of the 17th International Conference on Autonomous Agents and MultiAgent Systems*, 1241-1249.

Peña-Ayala, A. (2014). Educational data mining: A survey and a data mining-based analysis of recent works. *Expert Systems with Applications, 41*(4), 1432–1462. doi:10.1016/j.eswa.2013.08.042

Pérez, L., & Beltrán, J. (2006). Dos décadas de Inteligencias Múltiples: Implicaciones para la psicología de la educación. *Papeles del Psicólogo, 3*, 147–164.

Piaget, J. (1976). Piaget's Theory. In B. Inhelder, H. H. Chipman, & C. Zwingmann (Eds.), *Piaget and His School: A Reader in Developmental Psychology* (pp. 11–23). Berlin: Springer Berlin Heidelberg. doi:10.1007/978-3-642-46323-5_2

Pimmer, C., Mateescu, M., & Gröhbiel, U. (2016). Mobile and ubiquitous learning in higher education settings. A systematic review of empirical studies. *Computers in Human Behavior, 63*, 490–501. doi:10.1016/j.chb.2016.05.057

Pintrich, P. R., & De Groot, E. V. (1990). Motivational and self-regulated learning components of classroom academic performance. *Journal of Educational Psychology, 82*(1), 33–40. doi:10.1037/0022-0663.82.1.33

Plass, J. L., Homer, B. D., & Hayward, E. O. (2009). Design factors for educationally effective animations and simulations. *Journal of Computing in Higher Education, 21*(1), 31–61. doi:10.1007/s12528-009-9011-x

Plass, J. L., Homer, B. D., & Kinzer, C. K. (2015). Foundations of game-based learning. *Educational Psychologist, 50*(4), 258–283. doi:10.1080/00461520.2015.1122533

Ploetzner, R., Bodemer, D., & Feuerlein, I. (2001). *Facilitating the mental integration of multiple sources of information in multimedia learning environments*. Paper presented at ED-Media 2001 World Conference on Educational Multimedia, Hypermedia & Telecommunications, Tampere, Finland.

Poole, B. J. (1997). *Education for an information age. Teaching in the computerized classroom*. Boston: McGrow Hill.

Poon, K. K. (2018). Learning Fraction comparison by using a dynamic mathematics software - GeoGebra. *International Journal of Mathematical Education in Science and Technology*, *49*(3), 469–479. doi:10.1080/0020739X.2017.1404649

Poon, K. K., & Wong, K. L. (2017). Pre-constructed dynamic geometry materials in the classroom–how do they facilitate the learning of 'Similar Triangles'? *International Journal of Mathematical Education in Science and Technology*, *48*(5), 735–755. doi:10.1080/0020739X.2016.1264636

Porter, L., Guzdial, M., McDowell, C., & Simon, B. (2013). Success in introductory programming: What works? *Communications of the ACM*, *56*(8), 34–36. doi:10.1145/2492007.2492020

Prati, L. M., Douglas, C., Ferris, G. R., Ammeter, A. P., & Buckley, M. R. (2003). Emotional intelligence, leadership effectiveness, and team outcomes. *The International Journal of Organizational Analysis*, *11*(1), 21–40. doi:10.1108/eb028961

Prensky. (2001). Digital natives, digital immigrants. *On the Horizon, 9*(5). Retrieved from http://marcprensky.com/writing/Prensky%20%20Digital%20Natives%20Digital%20Immigrants%20-%20Part1.pdf

Presnky, M. (2001). Digital natives, digital immigrants. *On the Horizon*, *9*, 1–6.

Pretelín-ricárdez, A., & Sacristán, A. I. (2015). Videogame Construction by Engineering Students for Understanding Modelling Processes: The Case of Simulating Water Behaviour. *Informatics in Education - An International Journal*, *14*(2), 265–277.

Price, J. K. (2015). Transforming learning for the smart learning environment: Lessons learned from the Intel education initiatives. *Smart Learning Environments*, *2*(16), 1–16.

Propaganda and World War II. (n.d.). Retrieved May 21, 2019, from http://www.flyingheritage.com/FHCAM/media/Docs/Lesson3_Propaganda.pdf

Propaganda Techniques to Recognize. (n.d.). Retrieved January 22, 2019, from https://www.uvm.edu/~jleonard/AGRI183/propoaganda.html

Propoganda Techniques. (1979, August). Washington, DC: Department of the Army. Retrieved January 22, 2019, from http://www.constitution.org/col/propaganda_army.htm

Puentedura, R. (2006). Transformation, technology, and education [Blog post]. Retrieved February 18, 2019, from https://scholar.google.es/scholar?hl=es&as_sdt=0%2C5&q=Puentedura%2C+R.+%282006%29.+Transformation%2C+technology%2C+and+education+%5BBlog+post%5D.+Retrieved+from+http%3A%2F%2Fhippasus.com%2Fresources%2Ftte%2F.&btnG=

Putman, M. S. (2005). Computer-based reading technology in the classroom: The affective influence of performance contingent point accumulation on 4th grade students. *Reading Research and Instruction*, *45*(1), 19–37. doi:10.1080/19388070509558440

Qarbon Viewlet. (2018). *Viewlet Gallery*. Retrieved January 5, 2018 from https://www.qarbon.com/presentation-software/viewlet/viewlet_gallery.php

Rambli, D. R. A., Matcha, W., & Sulaiman, S. (2013). Fun Learning with AR Alphabet Book for Preschool Children. *Procedia Computer Science*, *25*, 211–219. doi:10.1016/j.procs.2013.11.026

Rasalingam, R.R., Muniandy, B., & Rass, R. (2014). Exploring the application of Augmented Reality technology in early childhood classroom in Malaysia. *Journal of Research & Method in Education*, *4*(5), 33-40.

Raspopovic, M., Cvetanovic, S., Medan, I., & Ljubojevic, D. (2017). The Effects of Integrating Social Learning Environment with Online Learning. *International Review of Research in Open and Distributed Learning*, *18*(1), 141–160. doi:10.19173/irrodl.v18i1.2645

Rast, P. (2011). Verbal knowledge, working memory, and processing speed as predictors of verbal learning in older adults. *Developmental Psychology*, *47*(5), 1490–1498. doi:10.1037/a0023422 PMID:21574701

Raudenbush, S. W., & Bryk, A. S. (2002). *Hierarchical linear models: Applications and data analysis methods* (Vol. 1). Sage Publications, Inc.

Raymond Duval. (1999). Representation, Vision and Visualization: Cognitive Functions in Mathematical Thinking. Basic Issues for Learning. Retrieved from https://files.eric.ed.gov/fulltext/ED466379.pdf

Redding, S. (2016). Competencies and personalized learning. In M. Murphy, S. Redding, & J. Twyman (Eds.), *Handbook on personalized learning for states, districts, and schools* (pp. 3–18). Philadelphia, PA: Temple University, Center on Innovations in Learning.

Reed, S. K. (2006). Cognitive architectures for multimedia learning. *Educational Psychologist*, *41*(2), 87–98. doi:10.120715326985ep4102_2

Refaeilzadeh, P., Tang, L., & Liu, H. (2009). Cross-validation. In Encyclopedia of database systems (pp. 532-538). Springer US.

Reidel, J., Tomaszewski, T., & Weaver, D. (2003, May). *Improving Student Academic Reading Achievement Through the Use of Multiple Intelligence Teaching Strategies*. Field-Based Master's Program. Chicago, IL: Saint Xavier University & SkyLight. Retrieved January 25, 2019, from https://files.eric.ed.gov/fulltext/ED479204.pdf

Reid, J. M. (1987, March). The Learning Style Preferences of ESL Students. *TESOL Quarterly*, *21*(1), 87–110. doi:10.2307/3586356

Reigeluth, C. (1999). The Elaboration Theory: Guidence for Scope and Sequence Decisions. In C. Reigeluth (Ed.), Instructional Design Theories and Models Volume 2: A new paradigm of Instructional Theory (pp. 428 – 453). Mahwah, NJ: Lawrence Erlbaum.

Reinhardt, J. (2019). Social Media in second and foreign language teaching and learning: Blogs, wikis, and social networking. *Language Teaching*, *52*(1), 1–39. doi:10.1017/S0261444818000356

Reiser, R. (1994). Clark's invitation to the dance: An instructional designer's response. *Educational Technology Research and Development*, *42*(2), 45–48. doi:10.1007/BF02299091

Renz, B. B. (2010). Our Own Worst Enemy as Protector of Ourselves: Stereotypes, Schemas, and Typifications as Integral Elements in the Persuasive Process. Lanham, MD: University Press of America.

Reyero, M. (2019). La educación constructivista en la era digital [Constructivist education in the digital era]. *Revista Tecnología Ciência & Educação (Bauru)*, *12*, 111–127.

Richardson, W. (2005). What's a wiki? A powerful collaborative tool for teaching and learning. That's What! *Multimedia & Internet@schools*, *12*(6), 17-21.

Richardson, W. (2006). *Blogs, wikis, podcasts and other powerful web tools for classrooms*. Thousand Oaks, CA: Corwin Press.

Riso, D. R., & Hudson, R. (1996). *Personality types: Using the Enneagram for self-discovery*. Houghton Mifflin Harcourt.

Riso, D. R., & Hudson, R. (1999). *The wisdom of the Enneagram: The complete guide to psychological and spiritual growth for the nine personality types*. New York: Bantam.

Rizzo, A., John, B., Newman, B., Williams, J., Hartholt, A., Lethin, C., & Buckwalter, J. G. (2013). Virtual reality as a tool for delivering PTSD exposure therapy and stress resilience training. *Military Behavioral Health*, *1*(1), 52–58. doi:10.1080/21635781.2012.721064

Roberts, D., Bove, C., & van Zee, E. (2007). *Teacher research: Stories of learning and growing*. Arlington, VA: NSTA Press.

Roberts, M. (2010). Encounters with existential intelligence: Possibilities for today's effective educator. *The International Journal of Interdisciplinary Social Sciences: Annual Review*, *5*(7), 241–253. doi:10.18848/1833-1882/CGP/v05i07/51794

Robinson, K. (1985). *Visual and auditory modalities and reading recall: A review of the research*. ERIC Document Reproduction Service. (No. ED272840)

Rodrigues, M. W., Zárate, L. E., & Isotani, S. (2018). Educational Data Mining: A review of evaluation process in the e-learning. *Telematics and Informatics*, *35*(6), 1701–1717. doi:10.1016/j.tele.2018.04.015

Romero, C., & Ventura, S. (2007). Educational Data Mining: A Survey from 1995 to 2005. *Expert Systems with Applications*, *33*(1), 135–146. doi:10.1016/j.eswa.2006.04.005

Romero, C., & Ventura, S. (2010). Educational data mining: A review of the state of the art. *IEEE Transactions on Systems, Man and Cybernetics. Part C, Applications and Reviews*, *40*(6), 601–618. doi:10.1109/TSMCC.2010.2053532

Rose, D. H., Harbour, W. S., Johnston, C. S., Daley, S. G., & Abarbanell, L. (2006). Universal design for learning in postsecondary education: Reflections on principles and their application. *Journal of postsecondary education and disability*, *19*(2), 135–151.

Rosenberg, M. J. (2001). *E-learning: Strategies for delivering knowledge in the digital age*. McGraw-Hill.

Rothstein, H. R., Sutton, A. J., & Borenstein, M. (2005). Publication bias in meta-analysis. In R. H. Rothestein, A. J. Sutton, & M. Borenstein (Eds.), Publication bias in meta-analysis (pp. 1-7). Hoboken, NJ: John Wiley & Sons Ltd.

Rubio, L., Prieto, J. L., & Ortiz, J. (2016). La matemática en la simulación con GeoGebra. Una experiencia con el movimiento en caída libre. *International Journal of Educational Research and Innovation*, *2*, 90–111.

Rudiger, C. (2003, Spring). *World War II and Propaganda*. Research Paper. Stanford University. Retrieved May 27, 2019, from https://web.stanford.edu/class/e297a/World%20War%20II%20and%20Propaganda.htm

Russell, M. K. (n.d.). *Using Art in Teaching World History*. Retrieved January 7, 2019, from http://www.phschool.com/eteach/social_studies/2000_10/essay.html

Russo, J. (2016). Using picture story books to discover and explore the concept of equivalence. *Australian Primary Mathematics Classroom*, *21*(2), 26–31.

Saban, A. (2009). Content analysis of Turkish studies about the multiple intelligences theory. *Educational Sciences: Theory and Practice*, *9*, 859–876.

Compilation of References

Saban, A. I. (2011). An evaluation of the teaching activities implemented in the elementary science and technology courses in terms of multiple intelligence theory: A sample from Adana. *Educational Sciences: Theory and Practice*, *11*(3), 1641–1649.

Sabanovic, S., Michalowski, M. P., & Simmons, R. (2006). Robots in the wild: Observing human-robot social interaction outside the lab. In *9th IEEE International Workshop on Advanced Motion Control*. IEEE. 10.1109/AMC.2006.1631758

Sajjadi, P., El Sayed, E., & De Troyer, O. (2016). On the Impact of the Dominant Intelligences of Players on Learning Outcome and Game Experience in Educational Games: The TrueBiters Case. In R. Bottino, J. Jeuring, & R. C. Veltkamp (Eds.), *Games and Learning Alliance: 5th International Conference, GALA 2016, Utrecht, The Netherlands, December 5-7, 2016, Proceedings* (pp. 221–231). Cham: Springer International Publishing. 10.1007/978-3-319-50182-6_20

Sajjadi, P., Hoffmann, L., Cimiano, P., & Kopp, S. (2018, September). On the Effect of a Personality-Driven ECA on Perceived Social Presence and Game Experience in VR. In *2018 10th International Conference on Virtual Worlds and Games for Serious Applications (VS-Games)* (pp. 1-8). IEEE. 10.1109/VS-Games.2018.8493436

Sajjadi, P., Lo-A-Njoe, A., Vlieghe, J., & De Troyer, O. (2016). Exploring the Relation Between Game Experience and Game Mechanics for Bodily-Kinesthetic Players. In R. Bottino, J. Jeuring, & R. C. Veltkamp (Eds.), *Games and Learning Alliance: 5th International Conference, GALA 2016, Utrecht, The Netherlands, December 5-7, 2016, Proceedings* (pp. 354–364). Cham: Springer International Publishing. 10.1007/978-3-319-50182-6_32

Sajjadi, P., Van Broeckhoven, F., & De Troyer, O. (2014). Dynamically Adaptive Educational Games: A New Perspective. In Games for Training, Education, Health and Sports (pp. 71–76). Springer International Publishing. doi:10.1007/978-3-319-05972-3_8

Sajjadi, P., Vlieghe, J., & De Troyer, O. (2016). Relation Between Multiple Intelligences and Game Preferences: an Evidence-Based Approach. In *ECGBL2016-10th European Conference on Games Based Learning: ECGBL2016*.

Sajjadi, P., Vlieghe, J., & De Troyer, O. (2017). Exploring the relation between the theory of multiple intelligences and games for the purpose of play-centered game design. *The Electronic Journal of e-Learning*, *15*(4), 320-334.

Sajjadi, P., Vlieghe, J., & Troyer, O. (2017). *Exploring the Relation between the Theory of Multiple Intelligences and Games For the Purpose of Player-Centred Game Design*. Academic Press.

Salas, E. E., & Fiore, S. M. (2004). *Team cognition: Understanding the factors that drive process and performance*. American Psychological Association. doi:10.1037/10690-000

Salas, E., Cooke, N. J., & Rosen, M. A. (2008). On teams, teamwork, and team performance: Discoveries and developments. *Human Factors*, *50*(3), 540–547. doi:10.1518/001872008X288457 PMID:18689065

Salas, E., Dickinson, T. L., Converse, S. A., & Tannenbaum, S. I. (1992). Toward an understanding of team performance and training. In R. W. Swezey & E. Salas (Eds.), *Teams: Their Training and Performance* (pp. 3–29). Ablex.

Salas, E., Shuffler, M. L., Thayer, A. L., Bedwell, W., & Lazzara, E. (2014). Understanding and improving teamwork in organizations: A scientifically based practical guide. *Human Resource Management*, *54*(4), 599–622. doi:10.1002/hrm.21628

Salay, D. M. (2018). *Walk in their shoes: How picture books and critical literacy instruction can foster empathy in first grade students* (Unpublished Dissertation). Drexel University.

Salen, K., & Zimmerman, E. (2004). *Rules of Play: Game Design Fundamentals*. MIT Press.

Salmon, P. M., Stanton, N. A., Walker, G. H., Baber, C., Jenkins, D. P., McMaster, R., & Young, M. S. (2008). What really is going on? Review of situation awareness models for individuals and teams. *Theoretical Issues in Ergonomics Science*, *9*(4), 297–323. doi:10.1080/14639220701561775

Salomon, G. (1979). *Interaction of media, cognition, and learning*. San Francisco: Jossey-Bass.

Salovey, P., & Mayer, J. D. (1990). Emotional intelligence. *Imagination, Cognition and Personality*, *9*(3), 185–211. doi:10.2190/DUGG-P24E-52WK-6CDG

Salthouse, T. A. (2012). Consequences of age-related cognitive declines. *Annual Review of Psychology*, *63*(1), 201–226. doi:10.1146/annurev-psych-120710-100328 PMID:21740223

Samsudyn, M. A., Haniza, N. H., Abdul-Talib, C., & Ibrahim, H. M. M. (2015). The relationship between Multiple Intelligences with Preferred Science Teaching and Science Process Skills. *Journal of Education and Learning EduLearn*, *1*(9), 53–60. doi:10.11591/edulearn.v9i1.1118

Samur, Y. (2012). Redundancy effect on retention of vocabulary words using multimedia presentation. *British Journal of Educational Technology*, *43*(6), 166–170. doi:10.1111/j.1467-8535.2012.01320.x

Sánchez, L., & Llera, J. (2006). Dos décadas de inteligencias múltiples: Implicaciones para la psicología de la educación. *Papeles del Psicólogo*, *27*(3), 147–164.

Sanchez-Martin, J., Alvaez-Gragera, G. J., Davila-Acedo, M. A., & Mellado, V. (2017). Teaching technology: From knowing to feeling enhancing emotional and content acquisition performance through Gardner's multiple intelligences theory in technology and design lesson. *Journal of Technology and Science Education*, *7*(1), 58–79. doi:10.3926/jotse.238

Sánchez-Martín, J., Álvarez Gragera, G. J., Dávila Acedo, M. A., & Mellado, V. (2017b). What do K-12 students feel when dealing with technology and engineering issues? Gardner's multiple intelligence theory implications in technology lessons for motivating engineering vocations at Spanish Secondary School. *European Journal of Engineering Education*, *42*(6), 1330–1343. doi:10.1080/03043797.2017.1292216

Santa Cruz University of California. (n.d.). *Distinguish Between Primary and Secondary Sources*. Retrieved May 23, 2019, from https://guides.library.ucsc.edu/primarysecondary

Santos, R., Gusmão, E., & Mangueira, I. (2006). Aplicações interativas como potencializadoras de múltiplas inteligências. *ETD-Educação Temática Digital*, *18*(2), 465–484. doi:10.20396/etd.v18i2.8635194

Saralar, I. (2017). An exploration of middle school mathematics teachers' beliefs and goals regarding GeoGebra: Four cases from the Turkish Republic. In European Conferance on Educatioal Research 2017: Reforming Education and the Imperative of Constant Change: Ambivalent Roles of Policy and Educational Research. University College Copenhagen (pp. 2012–2014). Copenhagen, Denmark: EERA ECER. Retrieved from https://www.academia.edu/38303474/An_exploration_of_middle_school_mathematics_teachers_beliefs_and_goals_regarding_GeoGebra_Four_cases_from_the_Turkish_Republic?email_work_card=title

Saxby, D., Matthews, G., Hitchcock, E., & Warm, J. (2007). Development of active and passive fatigue manipulations using a driving simulator. In *Proceedings of the Human Factors and Ergonomics Society Annual Meeting* (pp. 1237–1241). Sage Publications. 10.1177/154193120705101839

Schaefer, K. E., Chen, J. Y., Szalma, J. L., & Hancock, P. A. (2016). A meta-analysis of factors influencing the development of trust in automation: Implications for understanding autonomy in future systems. *Human Factors*, *58*(3), 377–400. doi:10.1177/0018720816634228 PMID:27005902

Compilation of References

Scheiter, K., Wiebe, E., & Holsanova, J. (2009). Theoretical and instructional aspects of learning with visualizations. In R. Zheng (Ed.), Cognitive effects of multimedia learning (pp. 67-88). Hershey, PA: IGI Global. doi:10.4018/978-1-60566-158-2.ch005

Schneider, T. R. (2008). Evaluations of stressful transactions: What's in an appraisal? *Stress and Health*, *24*(2), 151–158. doi:10.1002mi.1176

Schniedewind, N., & Davidson, E. (2006). *Open Minds to Equality* (3rd ed.). Milwaukee, WI: Rethinking Schools, Ltd.

Schrag, V. (n.d.). *World War I Lesson Plan*. Harry S. Truman Presidential Library & Museum. Retrieved January 28, 2019, from https://www.trumanlibrary.org/wwi/valerieschraglesson1.doc

SCORM. (2004). *SCORM 1.2*. Retrieved on 13th May 2019 from https://scorm.com/scorm-explained/technical-scorm/scorm-12-overview-for-developers/

Sebanz, N., Bekkering, H., & Knoblich, G. (2006). Joint action: Bodies and minds moving together. *Trends in Cognitive Sciences*, *10*(2), 70–76. doi:10.1016/j.tics.2005.12.009 PMID:16406326

Selçuk, Z., Kayılı, H., & Okut, L. (2004). *Çoklu zeka uygulamaları*. Ankara: Nobel Yayın Dağıtım.

Serrat, O. (2017). *Knowledge Solutions*. Singapore: Springer. doi:10.1007/978-981-10-0983-9

Shadiev, R., Hwang, W.-Y., & Liu, T.-Y. (2018). Investigating the effectiveness of a learning activity supported by a mobile multimedia learning system to enhance autonomous EFL learning in authentic contexts. *Educational Technology Research and Development*, *66*(4), 893–912. doi:10.100711423-018-9590-1

Shah, J. A. (2011). *Fluid coordination of human-robot teams* (PhD diss.). Massachusetts Institute of Technology.

Shamekhi, A., Czerwinski, M., Mark, G., Novotny, M., & Bennett, G. A. (2016, September). An exploratory study toward the preferred conversational style for compatible virtual agents. In *International Conference on Intelligent Virtual Agents* (pp. 40-50). Springer. 10.1007/978-3-319-47665-0_4

Sharples, M. (2003). Disruptive devices: Mobile technology for conversational learning. *International Journal of Continuing Engineering Education and Lifelong Learning*, *12*(5), 504–520.

Shea, J., & Stockford, A. (2015). *Inspiring the Secondary Curriculum with Technology*. New York, NY: Routledge.

Shearer, C. B. (2004). Using a multiple intelligences assessment to promote teacher development and student achievement. *Teachers College Record*, *106*(1), 147–162. doi:10.1111/j.1467-9620.2004.00325.x

Shernoff, D. J., Csikszentmihalyi, M., Shneider, B., & Shernoff, E. S. (2003). Student engagement in high school classrooms from the perspective of flow theory. *School Psychology Quarterly*, *18*(2), 158–176. doi:10.1521cpq.18.2.158.21860

Shin, E. E., Milson, A. J., & Smith, T. J. (2016). Future teachers' spatial thinking skills and attitudes. *The Journal of Geography*, *115*(4), 139–146. doi:10.1080/00221341.2015.1100654

Shute, V. J. (2011). Stealth Assessment in Computer-Based Games To Support Learning. *Computer Games and Instruction*, 503–524. Retrieved from www.ncbi.nlm.nih.gov

Sicart, M. (2008). Defining game mechanics. *Game Studies*, *8*(2), 1–14.

Sidner, C. L., Rich, C., Shayganfar, M., Bickmore, T. W., Ring, L., & Zhang, Z. (2015). A Robotic Companion for Social Support of Isolated Older Adults. HRI (Extended Abstracts), 289. doi:10.1145/2701973.2702103

Silver, H. F., Strong, R. W., & Perini, M. J. (2000). *So Each May Learn: Integrating Learning Styles and Multiple Intelligences*. Alexandria, VA: ASCD. Retrieved May 22, 2019, from http://www.ascd.org/publications/books/100058/chapters/Teaching-Learning-Styles-and-Multiple-Intelligences-to-Students.aspx

Silver, H., Strong, R., & Perini, M. (1997). Integrating learning styles and multiple intelligences. *Educational Leadership*, *55*(1), 22–27. Retrieved from http://www.ascd.org/publications/educational-leadership/sept97/vol55/num01/Integrating-Learning-Styles-and-Multiple-Intelligences.aspx

Sinatra, A., Gilbert, S., Dorneich, M., Winer, E., Ostrander, A., Ouverson, K., . . . Sottilare, R. (2018, June). Considerations for Dealing with Real-Time Communications in an Intelligent Team Tutoring System Experiment. *The Team Tutoring Workshop of the 19th International Conference of the Artificial Intelligence in Education (AIED) Conference*.

Sinclair, G. (2010). *Exploring Canada's digital future*. Paper presented at the Congress of the Humanities and Social Science, Concordia University, Montreal, Canada.

Singh, A. D., & Hassan, M. H. (2017, July). In Pursuit of Smart Learning Environments for the 21st Century. *Current and Critical Issues in Curriculum, Learning and Assessment*, *12*(28). Retrieved January 13, 2019, from http://unesdoc.unesco.org/images/0025/002523/252335E.pdf

Slijepcevic, N. (2013). The effect of augmented reality treatment on learning, cognitive load, and spatial visualization abilities. *Theses and Dissertations*. Retrieved from https://uknowledge.uky.edu/edc_etds/4

Smith, J. (n.d.). *Free-form assessment: A Multiple Intelligences approach to History at Key Stage 4* (Master's dissertation). University of Lancaster. Retrieved May 18, 2019, from https://portal.stir.ac.uk/api/research/entities/get/file/17331

Smith, B. (2007). Using presentation technology. In M. Hunt (Ed.), *A Practical Guide to Teaching History in the Secondary School* (pp. 81–89). New York, NY: Routledge.

Smith, D., Zheng, R., Metz, A. J., Morrow, S., Pompa, J., Hill, J., & Rupper, R. (2019). Role of cognitive prompts in video caregiving training for older adults: Optimizing deep and surface learning. *Educational Gerontology*.

Smith, G. G. (2012). Compute game play as an imaginary stage for reading: Implicit spatial effects of computer games embedded in hard copy book. *Journal of Research in Reading*, *35*(1), 1–19.

Smith, N. (2010). *The History Teacher's Handbook*. New York, NY: Continuum International Publishing Group.

Smith, S. M., & Woody, P. C. (2000). Interactive effect of multimedia instruction and learning styles. *Teaching of Psychology*, *27*(3), 220–223. doi:10.1207/S15328023TOP2703_10

Snethen, G., & Zook, P. (2016). Utilizing social media to support community integration. *American Journal of Psychiatric Rehabilitation*, *19*(2), 160–174. doi:10.1080/15487768.2016.1171176

Solbes, J. (2011). ¿Por qué disminuye el alumnado de ciencias? *Alambique: Didáctica de las ciencias experimentales*, *17*(67), 53-61.

Soltani, P., Figueiredo, P., Fernandes, R. J., & Vilas-Boas, J. P. (2017). Muscle activation behavior in a swimming exergame: Differences by experience and gaming velocity. *Physiology & Behavior*, *181*, 23–28. doi:10.1016/j.physbeh.2017.09.001 PMID:28882467

Sosa & Ortega (2011). Análisis sobre los tipos de inteligencias en estudiantes de educación secundaria y universidad. *Revista Iberoamericana de educación matemática*, *26*, 89-102.

Sottilare, R. & Hart, J. (2012). Cognitive and affective modeling in intelligent virtual humans for training and tutoring applications. *Advances in Applied Human Modeling and Simulation*, 113.

Sottilare, R., Holden, H., Brawner, K., & Goldberg, B. (2011). Challenges and Emerging Concepts in the Development of Adaptive, Computer-based Tutoring Systems for Team Training. *Proceedings of the Interservice/Industry Training Simulation & Education Conference.*

Sottilare, R. A., Burke, C. S., Salas, E., Sinatra, A. M., Johnston, J. H., & Gilbert, S. B. (2018). Designing adaptive instruction for teams: A meta-analysis. *International Journal of Artificial Intelligence in Education, 28*(2), 225–264. doi:10.100740593-017-0146-z

Sottilare, R., & Roessingh, J. J. (2014). Application of Intelligent Agents in Embedded Virtual Simulations. In *NATO Technical Report: Improving Human Effectiveness through Embedded Virtual Simulation: Findings of Task Group HFM-165*. NATO Science & Technology Organization.

Spector, J. M. (2014). Conceptualizing the emerging field of smart learning environments. *Smart Learning Environments, 1*(2). Retrieved January 14, 2019, from http://www.slejournal.com/content/1/1/2

Spector, J. M. (2016). Smart Learning Environments: Concepts and Issues. In G. Chamblee & L. Langub (Eds.), *Proceedings of Society for Information Technology & Teacher Education International Conference* (pp. 2728-2737). Savannah, GA: Association for the Advancement of Computing in Education (AACE). Retrieved January 22, 2019, from https://www.researchgate.net/publication/301612985_Smart_Learning_Environments_Concepts_and_Issues

Spector, J. M., & Merrill, M. D. (Eds.). (2008, August). Effective, Efficient and Engaging (E3) Learning in the Digital Age. Distance Education, 29(2).

SPSS Inc. (2004). Clementine 10.1 Node Reference. Author.

Stark, K. (2014). Cognitive behavior game design: A unified model for designing serious games. *Frontier in Psychology.* Retrieved on March 11, 2019 from https://www.frontiersin.org/articles/10.3389/fpsyg.2014.00028/full

Starks, K. (2014). Cognitive behavioral game design: A unified model for designing serious games. *Frontiers in Psychology, 5*. doi:10.3389/fpsyg.2014.00028 PMID:24550858

Stepien, W., & Gallagher, S. (1993). Problem-based learning: As authentic as it gets. *Educational Leadership, 51*, 25–28.

Sternberg, R. (1985). *Beyond IQ*. New York, NY: Cambridge University Press.

Stotz, M. D. (2018). *Creature Counting: The Effects of Augmented Reality on Perseverance and Early Numeracy Skills* (Doctoral thesis). Lehigh University. Retrieved from https://preserve.lehigh.edu/etd/4254

Strausova, I., & Hasek, R. (2013). *"Dynamic visual proofs" using DGS*. Electronic Journal of Mathematics and Technology.

Suh, Y. (2013, Spring). Past Looking: Using Arts as Historical Evidence in Teaching History. *Social Studies Research & Practice, 8*(1), 135–159.

Sullivan, S. (2007). Media and Persuasion: Techniques, Forms, and Construction. In M. Christel & S. Sullivan (Eds.), *Lesson Plans for Creating Media-Rich Classrooms* (pp. 173–176). Urbana, IL: NCTE.

Surr, W., & Redding, S. (2017). *Competency-based education: staying shallow or going deep?* Retrieved on June 17, 2019 from https://ccrscenter.org/sites/default/files/CBE_GoingDeep.pdf

Surr, W., & Rasmussen, J. (2015). *Partners in crafting competency-based pathways to college and career readiness*. Washington, DC: Great Lakes and Midwest Regional Deeper Learning Initiative, American Institutes for Research. Retrieved from http://www.deeperlearning-cc.org/

Sutherland, R., Armstrong, V., Barnes, S., Brawn, R., Breeze, N., Gall, M., ... John, P. (2004). Transforming teaching and learning: Embedding ICT into everyday classroom practices. *Journal of Computer Assisted Learning*, *20*(6), 413–425. doi:10.1111/j.1365-2729.2004.00104.x

Sutton, A., Allinson, C., & Williams, H. (2013). Personality type and work-related outcomes: An exploratory application of the Enneagram model. *European Management Journal*, *31*(3), 234–249. doi:10.1016/j.emj.2012.12.004

Sweetser, P., & Wyeth, P. (2005). GameFlow: A model for evaluating player enjoyment in games. *Computers in Entertainment*, *3*(3), 1–24. doi:10.1145/1077246.1077253

Sweller, J., & Chandler, P. (1994). Why some material is difficult to learn. *Cognition and Instruction*, *12*(3), 185–233. doi:10.12071532690xci1203_1

Tally, B., & Goldenberg, L. B. (2005). Fostering Historical Thinking With Digitized Primary Sources. *Journal of Research on Technology in Education*, *38*(1), 1–21. doi:10.1080/15391523.2005.10782447

Tamilselvi, T. & Geetha, D. (2015). Efficacy in teaching through "multiple intelligence" instructional strategies. *i-Manager's Journal on School Educational Technology*, *11*(2), 1-11.

Tapus, A. (2013). Coping with Stress Using Social Robots as Emotion-Oriented Tool: Potential Factors Discovered from Stress Game Experiment. In *International Conference on Social Robotics*. Springer International Publishing.

The Ministry of Higher Education of Jordan. (2015). *The Annual Statistical Report on higher Education in Jordan for the year 2015 – 2016*. Retrieved from http://www.mohe.gov.jo/en/pages/Statistics.aspx

The Techniques of Propaganda. (n.d.). Retrieved May 22, 2019, from http://www.cengage.com/resource_uploads/downloads/0534619029_19636.pdf

Thibeault, M. D. (2011). Learning from looking at sound: Using multimedia spectrograms to explore world music. *General Music Today*, *25*(1), 50–55. doi:10.1177/1048371311414050

Thomas, J. (2000, March). *A Review of the Research on Project-Based Learning*. San Rafael, CA: The Autodesk Foundation. Retrieved January 23, 2019, from https://dl.icdst.org/pdfs/files1/aac48826d9652cb154e2dbf0033376fa.pdf

Tiwari, M., Singh, R., & Vimal, N. (2013). An empirical study of application of dm techniques for predicting student performance. *International Journal of Computer Science and Mobile Computing IJCSMC*, *2*(2), 53–57.

Todorov, A. (2008). Evaluating faces on trustworthiness. *Annals of the New York Academy of Sciences*, *1124*(1), 208–224. doi:10.1196/annals.1440.012 PMID:18400932

Tomas, L., Rigano, D., & Ritchie, S. M. (2016). Students' Regulation of Their Emotions in a Science Classroom. *Journal of Research in Science Teaching*, *53*(2), 234–260. doi:10.1002/tea.21304

Tomia, A. B., & Awang, R. D. R. (2013). An Interactive Mobile Augmented Reality Magical Playbook: Learning Number with the Thirsty Crow. *Procedia Computer Science*, *25*, 123–130. doi:10.1016/j.procs.2013.11.015

Torres-Porras, J., & Arrebola, J. (2018). Construyendo la ciudad sostenible en el Grado de Educación Primaria [Building the sustainable city in the Primary Education Degree]. *Revista Eureka sobre Enseñanza y Divulgación de las Ciencias*, *15*(2), 1-15 doi:10.25267/Rev_Eureka_ensen_divulg_cienc.2018.v15.i2.2501

Trafton, G. J., Cassimatis, N. L., Bugajska, M. D., Brock, D. P., Mintz, F. E., & Schultz, A. C. (2005). Enabling effective human-robot interaction using perspective-taking in robots. *IEEE Transactions on Systems, Man, and Cybernetics. Part A, Systems and Humans*, *35*(4), 460–470. doi:10.1109/TSMCA.2005.850592

Tran, T., Nguyen, N., Bui, M., & Phan, A. (2014). Discovery learning with the help of the geoGebra dynamic deometry software. *International Journal of Learning, Teaching and Educational Research, 7*(1).

Treadwell, S. M., & Taylor, N. (2017). PE in pictures: Using photovoice to promote middle school students' reflections on physical activity during free time. *Journal of Physical Education, Recreation & Dance, 88*(4), 26–33. doi:10.1080/07303084.2017.1280436

Tseng, J. C. R., Chu, H. C., Hwang, G. J., & Tsai, C. C. (2008). Development of an adaptive learning system with two sources of personalization information. *Computers & Education, 51*(2), 776–786. doi:10.1016/j.compedu.2007.08.002

Ubago-Jiménez, J. L., Viciana-Garófano, V., Pérez-Cortés, A. J., Martínez-Martínez, A., Padial-Ruz, R., & Puertas-Molero, P. (2018). Relación entre la Teoría de las Inteligencias Múltiples y la actividad físico-deportiva. *Sportis Sci J, 4*(1), 144–161. doi:10.17979portis.2018.4.1.2067

Ucak, E., Bag, H., Usak, M., & Esra Ucak, H. B. (2006). Enhancing Learning through Multiple Intelligences in Elementary Education. *Journal of Baltic Science Education, 2*(10), 61–69.

Ucelli, G., Conti, G., Amicis, R. D., & Servidio, R. (2005). Learning using augmented reality technology: Multiple means of interaction for teaching children the theory of colours. In M. Maybury, O. Stock, & W. Wahlster (Eds.), *Intelligent Technologies for Interactive Entertainment 2005* (Vol. 3814, pp. 193–202). Heidelberg, Germany: Springer. doi:10.1007/11590323_20

Union, I. (2014). *Communication from the Commission to the European Parliament, the Council, the European Economic and Social Committee and the Committee of the Regions*. Retrieved from http://www.xploit-eu.com/pdfs/Europe,202020,20

United States Holocaust Memorial Museum. (2013). Are you more powerful than propaganda? Propaganda Techniques. *Mind over Media* [For Teachers]. Retrieved May 27, 2019, from http://mindovermedia.ushmm.org/teachers

United States Holocaust Memorial Museum. (n.d.a). *State of Deception. The Power of Nazi Propaganda. Redefining How We Teach Propaganda. Lesson 2*. Retrieved May 23, 2019, from https://www.ushmm.org/m/pdfs/20150703-propaganda-2-0_LESSON-2.pdf

United States Holocaust Memorial Museum. (n.d.b). *Extension 1.8 Diagram Worksheet State of Deception*. Retrieved May 23, 2019, from https://www.ushmm.org/m/pdfs/20150703-propaganda-1EXT-1-8_Diagram_Worksheets.pdf

Urban, S. (2017). Pen-enabled, real-time student engagement for teaching in STEM subjects. *Journal of Chemical Education, 94*(8), 1051–1059. doi:10.1021/acs.jchemed.7b00127

Utami, S. N. A., & Adiarti, W. (2017). Application of Building Playing in the Center of Beams to improve the Visual-Spatial Intelligence of Children at the Age 5-6 Years Old in Mutiara Insan Kindergarten, Sukoharjo Regency. *BELIA: Early Childhood Education Papers, 6*(1), 27–31.

Vakaloudi, A. D., & Dagdilelis, V. (2013, October). Differentiation in the teaching of Social Sciences with the development of Information and Communication Technologies. In *Proceedings of the 3rd International Conference on Cognitonics, The Science about the Human Being in the Digital World, a subconference of the 16th International Multiconference Information Society 2013* (vol. A, pp. 476-479). Ljubljana: Institut "Jožef Stefan".

Vakaloudi, A. D., & Dagdilelis, V. (2015, October). The Role of Information and Communication Technologies in the Teaching and Learning of History. In *Proceedings of the 5th International Conference on Cognitonics, The Science about the Human Being in the Digital World, a subconference of the 18th International Multiconference Information Society 2015* (vol. F, pp. 78-81). Ljubljana: Institut "Jožef Stefan".

Vakaloudi, A. D. (2016). *The Teaching of History with the Use of Information and Communication Technologies*. Thessaloniki: K. & M. Ant. Stamoulis.

Vakaloudi, A. D. (2017, Spring-Summer). From the holocaust to recent mass murders and refugees. What does history teach us? *International Journal of Historical Learning, Teaching and Research*, *14*(2), 119–149.

Vakaloudi, A. D., & Dagdilelis, V. (2016, Spring-Summer). The Transformation of History Teaching Methods in Secondary Education Through the Use of Information and Communication Technology (ICT). *International Journal of Historical Learning, Teaching and Research*, *13*(2), 150–174.

Valente, A., & Marchetti, E. (2015, July). *Make and Play: Card Games as Tangible and Playable Knowledge Representation Boundary Objects. In 2015 IEEE 15th International Conference on Advanced Learning Technologies (ICALT)* (pp. 137–141). Hualien, Taiwan: IEEE. doi.ieeecomputersociety.org/10.1109/ICALT.2015.31

Van Eck, R. (2006). Digital Game-Based Learning: It's Not Just the Digital Natives Who Are Restless. *EDUCAUSE Review*, *41*(2), 16–30. doi:10.1145/950566.950596

Van Merrienboer, J. J. G., & Sweller, J. (2005). Cognitive load theory and complex learning: Recent developments and future directions. *Educational Psychology Review*, *17*(2), 147–177. doi:10.100710648-005-3951-0

Vasciliou, C., Loannou, A., Stylianou-Georgiou, A., & Zaphiris, P. (2017). A glance into social and evolutionary aspects of an artifact ecology for collaborative learning through the lens of distributed cognition. *International Journal of Human-Computer Interaction*, *33*(8), 642–654. doi:10.1080/10447318.2016.1277638

Vázquez, A. & Manassero, M. (2007). En defensa de las actitudes y emociones en la educación científica (I): Evidencias y argumentos generales. *Revista Eureka sobre Enseñanza y Divulgación de las Ciencias, 4*(2), 247-271.

Vázquez, A. & Manassero, M.A. (2008). El declive de las actitudes hacia la ciencia de los estudiantes: un indicador inquietante para la educación científica. *Revista Eureka sobre Enseñanza y Divulgación de las Ciencias, 5*(3), 274-292.

Vazquez, A., & Manassero, M. A. (2007). In defense of attitudes and emotions in the scientific Education (I): Evidences and general arguments (En defensa de las actitudes y emociones en la educacion cientifica (I): Evidencias y argumentos generales). *Eureka Journal of Science Education and Divulgation*, *4*(2), 247–271.

Vázquez, A., & Manassero, M. A. (2011). El descenso de las actitudes hacia la ciencia de chicos y chicas en la Educación Obligatoria. *Ciência & Educação (Bauru)*, *17*(2), 249–268. doi:10.1590/S1516-73132011000200001

Verbert, K., & Duval, E. (2004). Towards a Global Component Architecture for Learning Objects: A Comparative Analysis of Learning Object Content Models. Edmedia 2004, Lugano, Switzerland.

Verhoef, N. C., Coenders, F., Pieters, J. M., van Smaalen, D., & Tall, D. O. (2015). Professional development through lesson study: Teaching the derivative using GeoGebra. Professional Development in Education, 41(1), 109–126. doi:10.1080/19415257.2014.886285

Vermunt, J. D. (1998). The regulation of constructive learning processes. *The British Journal of Educational Psychology*, *68*(2), 149–171. doi:10.1111/j.2044-8279.1998.tb01281.x

Viechtbauer, W., & Cheung, M. W.-L. (2010). Outlier and influence diagnostics for meta-analysis. *Research Synthesis Methods*, *1*(2), 112–125. doi:10.1002/jrsm.11 PMID:26061377

Villalustre Martínez, L., & Del Moral Pérez, M. E. (2016). Itinerarios interactivos con geolocalización y realidad aumentada para un aprendizaje ubicuo en la formación inicial de docentes de Educación Infantil. In *Experiencias interactivas con realidad aumentada en las aulas* (pp. 81–100). Barcelona: Ediciones Octaedro.

Villalustre, L., & Del Moral, M. E. (2016). Itinerarios interactivos con geolocalización y realidad aumentada para un aprendizaje ubicuo en la formación inicial de docentes de educación infantil [Interactive itineraries with geolocation and augmented reality for ubiquitous learning in the initial training of early childhood teachers] In L. Villalustre & M.E. Del Moral (Coords.), Experiencias interactivas con realidad aumentada en las aulas [Interactive experiences with augmented reality in the classroom]. Barcelona: Octaedro.

Villalustre, L. (2016). Educación Aumentada, una Realidad para favorecer el aprendizaje 3.0. *CIREI, 2016*, 6–12.

Vinciarelli, A., & Pentland, A. S. (2015). New social signals in a new interaction world: The next frontier for social signal processing. *IEEE Systems, Man, and Cybernetics Magazine*, *1*(2), 10–17. doi:10.1109/MSMC.2015.2441992

Visser, B. A., Ashton, M. C., & Vernon, P. A. (2006). Beyond g: Putting multiple intelligences theory to the test. *Intelligence*, *34*(5), 487–501. doi:10.1016/j.intell.2006.02.004

Vogel, F., Kollar, I., Ufer, S., Reichersdorfer, E., Reiss, K., & Fischer, F. (2016). Developing argumentation skills in mathematics through computer-supported collaborative learning: The role of transactivity. *Instructional Science*, *44*(5), 477–500. doi:10.100711251-016-9380-2

Von der Puetten, A. M., Krämer, N. C., Gratch, J., & Kang, S. H. (2010). It doesn't matter what you are! Explaining social effects of agents and avatars. *Computers in Human Behavior*, *26*(6), 1641–1650. doi:10.1016/j.chb.2010.06.012

Vygotskiĭ, L. S., & Cole, M. (1978). *Mind in society: the development of higher psychological processes*. Cambridge, MA: Harvard University Press.

Wallace, B. (2003). *Using History to Develop Problem Solving and Thinking Skills at Key Stage 2*. New York, NY: David Fulton Publishers.

Wallet, G., Sauzeon, H., Pala, P. A., Larrue, F., Zheng, X., & N'Kaoua, B. (2011). Virtual/real transfer of spatial knowledge: Benefit from visual fidelity provided in a virtual environment and impact of active navigation. *Cyberpsychology, Behavior, and Social Networking*, *14*(7-8), 417–423. doi:10.1089/cyber.2009.0187 PMID:21288136

War of the future: Brian Moore's WWIII propaganda posters. (2011). Retrieved January 19, 2019, from https://www.theguardian.com/artanddesign/gallery/2011/jan/22/brian-moore-wwiii-propaganda-posters

Watson, C., & Li, F. W. (2014). Failure rates in introductory programming revisited. In *Proceedings of the 2014 conference on Innovation & technology in computer science education* (pp. 39-44). ACM.

Webster, J., Trevino, L. K., & Ryan, L. (1993). The dimensionality and correlates of flow in human-computer interactions. *Computers in Human Behavior*, *9*(4), 411–426. doi:10.1016/0747-5632(93)90032-N

Webster, P. R. (2011). Key research in music technology and music teaching and learning. Journal of Music. *Technology and Education*, *4*(2 & 3), 115–130.

Wei, X., Guo, D., & Weng, D. (2018, April). A Study of Preschool Instructional Design Based on Augmented Reality Games. In *Chinese Conference on Image and Graphics Technologies* (pp. 106-113). Singapore: Springer. 10.1007/978-981-13-1702-6_11

Wiley, D. A. (2000). *Learning Object Design and Sequencing Theory*. Department of Instructional Psychology and Technology, Brigham Young University.

Williams, C. R., Cook, A. E., & O'Brien, E. J. (2018). Validating semantic illusions: Competition between context and general world knowledge. *Journal of Experimental Psychology. Learning, Memory, and Cognition*, *44*(9), 1414–1429. doi:10.1037/xlm0000526 PMID:29672121

Wilson, S., Liber, O., Johnson, M., Beauvoir, P., Sharples, P., & Milligan, C. (2007). Personal learning environments: challenging the dominant design of educational systems. *Journal of e-Learn, 3*, 27–38.

Wilson, K., Salas, E., Priest, H., & Andrews, D. (2007). Errors in the heat of battle: Taking a closer look at shared cognition breakdowns through teamwork. *Human Factors, 49*(2), 243–256. doi:10.1518/001872007X312478 PMID:17447666

Wilson, S. D. (2018). Implementing co-creation and multiple intelligence practices to transform the classroom experience. *Contemporary Issues in Education Research, 11*(4), 127–132. doi:10.19030/cier.v11i4.10206

Wineburg, S. (2001). *Historical thinking and other unnatural act: Charting the future of teaching the past*. Philadelphia, PA: Temple University Press.

Winters, N., Walker, K., & Rousos, D. (2005). Facilitating Learning in an Intelligent Environment. In *The IEE International Workshop on Intelligent Environments* (pp. 74-79). Colchester, UK: IET. 10.1049/ic:20050219

Witmer, B. G., & Singer, M. J. (1998). Measuring Presence in Virtual Environments: A Presence Questionnaire. *Presence: Teleoper. Virtual Environ., 7*(3), 225–240. doi:10.1162/105474698565686

Wolfson, N. E., Cavanagh, T. M., & Kraiger, K. (2014). Older adults and technology-based instruction: Optimizing learning outcomes and transfer. *Academy of Management Learning & Education, 13*(1), 26–44. doi:10.5465/amle.2012.0056

Wood, R., & Bandura, A. (1989). Social Cognitive Theory of organizational management. *Academy of Management Review, 14*(3), 361–384. doi:10.5465/amr.1989.4279067

Woolf, B., Burleson, W., Arroyo, I., Dragon, T., Cooper, D., & Picard, R. (2009). Affect-aware tutors: Recognising and responding to student affect. *International Journal of Learning Technology, 4*(3/4), 3–4, 129–164. doi:10.1504/IJLT.2009.028804

Wouters, P., van der Spek, E. D., & van Oostendorp, H. (2009). Current practices in serious game research: A review from a learning outcomes perspective. *Effective Practices*, 232–250. doi:10.4018/978-1-60566-360-9

Wright, J. (2017). Propaganda Techniques in Literature and Online Political Ads. *Read, Write, Think*. Retrieved January 15, 2019, from http://www.readwritethink.org/classroom-resources/lesson-plans/propaganda-techniques-literature-online-405.html

Wu, B., & Wang, A. I. (2012). A Guideline for Game Development-Based Learning: A Literature Review. *International Journal of Computer Games Technology*.

Wu, H. K., Lee, S. W. Y., Chang, H. Y., & Liang, J. C. (2013). Current status, opportunities and challenges of augmented reality in education. *Computers & Education, 62*, 41–49. doi:10.1016/j.compedu.2012.10.024

Wu, P. H., Hwang, G. J., & Chai, W. H. (2013, October). An expert system-based context-aware ubiquitous learning approach for conducting science learning activities. *Journal of Educational Technology & Society, 16*(4), 217–230.

Wu, S. H., & Alrabah, S. (2009). A cross-cultural study of Taiwanese and Kuwaiti EFL students' learning styles and multiple intelligences. *Innovations in Education and Teaching International, 46*(4), 393–403. doi:10.1080/14703290903301826

Yang, F., & Heeman, P. A. (2010). Initiative conflicts in task-oriented dialogue. *Computer Speech & Language, 24*(2), 175–189. doi:10.1016/j.csl.2009.04.003

Yannakakis, G. N., Togelius, J., Khaled, R., Jhala, A., Karpouzis, K., Paiva, A., & Vasalou, A. (2010). Siren: Towards Adaptive Serious Games for Teaching Conflict Resolution. *4th Europeen Conference on Games Based Learning EC-GBL2010, Copenhagen, Denmark*, 10. Retrieved from http://www.image.ntua.gr/papers/640.pdf

Yarmouk University. (2017a). *Academic Departments*. Retrieved from http://www.yu.edu.jo/index.php

Compilation of References

Yarmouk University. (2017b). *Admission & Registration Department*. Retrieved from http://admreg.yu.edu.jo/index.php?option=com_docman&task=cat_view&gid=154&Itemid=159

Yasir, M., & Sharif, S. (2011). An approach to Adaptive E-Learning Hypermedia System based on Learning Styles (AEHS-LS): Implementation and evaluation. *International Journal of Library and Information Science, 3*(January), 15–28. Retrieved from http://www.academicjournals.org/journal/IJLIS/edition/January_2011

Yilmaz, K. (2007, May). Historical Empathy and Its Implications for Classroom Practices in Schools. *The History Teacher, 40*(3), 331–337.

Yilmaz, R. M. (2016). Educational magic toys developed with augmented reality technology for early childhood education. *Computers in Human Behavior, 54*, 240–248. doi:10.1016/j.chb.2015.07.040

Yilmaz, R. M., Kucuk, S., & Goktas, Y. (2017). Are augmented reality picture books magic or real for preschool children aged five to six? *British Journal of Educational Technology, 48*(3), 824–841. doi:10.1111/bjet.12452

Yorgancı, S. (2018). A study on the views of graduate students on the use of GeoGebra in mathematics teaching. *European Journal of Education Studies, 4*. doi:10.5281/zenodo.1272935

Zahedi, S., & Moghaddam, E. M. (2016). The relationship between multiple intelligence and performance of EFL students in different forms of reading comprehension tests. *Theory and Practice in Language Studies, 6*(10), 1929–2939. doi:10.17507/tpls.0610.06

Zahedi, Z., & Ghabanchi, Z. (2014). The relationship between logical, naturalist intelligences and learning grammar for EFL learners at elementary level. *Theory and Practice in Language Studies, 4*(2), 403–410. doi:10.4304/tpls.4.2.403-410

Zazkis, R., Dubinsky, E., & Dautermann, J. (1996). Coordinating Visual and Analytic Strategies: A Study of Students' Understanding of the. Source. *Journal for Research in Mathematics Education, 27*, •••. Retrieved from https://www-jstor-org.pucdechile.idm.oclc.org/stable/pdf/749876.pdf?refreqid=excelsior%3A8682c126bb55b92ec0c3279ba2c90068

Zengin, Y. (2017). The effects of GeoGebra software on pre-service mathematics teachers' attitudes and views toward proof and proving. *International Journal of Mathematical Education in Science and Technology, 48*(7), 1002–1022. doi:10.1080/0020739X.2017.1298855

Zhao, R., Sinha, T., Black, A. W., & Cassell, J. (2016, September). Socially-aware virtual agents: Automatically assessing dyadic rapport from temporal patterns of behavior. In *International Conference on Intelligent Virtual Agents* (pp. 218-233). Springer International Publishing. 10.1007/978-3-319-47665-0_20

Zheng, K., Glas, D. F., Kanda, T., Ishiguro, H., & Hagita, N. (2013). Designing and implementing a human–robot team for social interactions. *IEEE Transactions on Systems, Man, and Cybernetics. Systems, 43*(4), 843–859. doi:10.1109/TSMCA.2012.2216870

Zheng, R. (2007). Cognitive functionality of multimedia in problem solving. In T. Kidd & H. Song (Eds.), *Handbook of Research on Instructional Systems and Technology* (pp. 230–246). Hershey, PA: Information Science Reference/IGI Global Publishing. doi:10.4018/978-1-59904-865-9.ch017

Zheng, R. (2018). Personalization with digital technology: A deep cognitive process perspective. In R. Zheng (Ed.), *Digital technologies and instructional design for personalized learning* (pp. 1–27). Hershey, PA: Information Science Reference/IGI Global Publishing. doi:10.4018/978-1-5225-3940-7.ch001

Zheng, R. (Ed.). (2008). *Cognitive effectives of multimedia learning*. Hershey, PA: Information Science Reference/IGI Global Publishing.

Zheng, R., Burrow-Sanchez, J., Donnelly, S., Call, M., & Drew, C. (2010). Toward an integrated conceptual framework of research in teen online communication. In R. Zheng, J. Burrow-Sanchez, & C. Drew (Eds.), *Adolescent Online Social Communication and Behavior: Relationship Formation on the Internet* (pp. 1–13). Hershey, PA: Information Science Reference/IGI Global Publishing. doi:10.4018/978-1-60566-926-7.ch001

Zheng, R., Burrow-Sanchez, J., & Drew, C. (Eds.). (2010). *Adolescent online social communication and behavior: Relationship formation on the Internet*. Hershey, PA: Information Science Reference/IGI Global Publishing. doi:10.4018/978-1-60566-926-7

Zheng, R., Flygare, J., Dahl, L., & Hoffman, R. (2009). The impact of individual differences on social communication pattern in online learning. In C. Mourlas, N. Tsianos, & P. Germanakos (Eds.), *Cognitive and emotional processes in web-based education: integrating human factors and personalization* (pp. 321–342). Hershey, PA: Information Science Reference/IGI Global Publishing. doi:10.4018/978-1-60566-392-0.ch015

Zheng, R., & Gardner, M. (2019). *Memory in education*. New York, NY: Routledge.

Zheng, R., Miller, S., Snelbecker, G., & Cohen, I. (2006). Use of multimedia for problem-solving tasks. *Journal of Technology, Instruction. Cognition and Learning*, *3*(1-2), 135–143.

Zheng, R., & Smarkola, C. (2003). Multimedia learning environments for early readers. *Academic Exchange Quarterly*, *7*(4), 229–232.

Zheng, R., Smith, D., Luptak, M., Hill, R., Hill, J., & Rupper, R. (2016). Does visual redundancy inhibit older persons' information processing in learning? *Educational Gerontology*, *42*(9), 635–645. doi:10.1080/03601277.2016.1205365

Zheng, R., & Truong, T. N. (2017). A framework for promoting knowledge transfer in SNS game-based learning. In R. Zheng & M. Gardner (Eds.), *Serious game for educational applications* (pp. 66–91). Hershey, PA: IGI Publishing. doi:10.4018/978-1-5225-0513-6.ch004

Zheng, R., Yang, W., Garcia, D., & McCadden, B. P. (2008). Effects of multimedia on schema induced analogical reasoning in science learning. *Journal of Computer Assisted Learning*, *24*(6), 474–482. doi:10.1111/j.1365-2729.2008.00282.x

Zhu, Z. T., Yu, M. H., & Riezebos, P. (2016, March). A research framework of smart education. *Smart Learning Environments*, *3*(4), 1-17. Retrieved January 3, 2019, from https://slejournal.springeropen.com/articles/10.1186/s40561-016-0026-2

Zimmermann, W., & Cunningham, S. (1991). What is mathematical visualization? In W. Zimmermann & S. Cunningham (Eds.), Visualization in teaching and learning mathematics (Vol. 19, pp. 1–8). Washington, DC: Series, MAA. Retrieved from https://www.semanticscholar.org/paper/Editors'-introduction%3A-What-is-mathematical-Zimmermann-Cunningham/46339bd5e52c9f6785b70ef1e62812f5f02b1ec7

About the Contributors

Robert Zheng is Professor of instructional design and educational technology in the Department of Educational Psychology at the University of Utah. His research area includes multimedia and cognition, instructional design and development, and online learning. He has authored and edited eleven books and published over 70 peer-reviewed journal papers and chapters in the areas of cognitive load, multimedia, web-based instruction, and problem solving in multimedia learning.

* * *

Alaa K. Al-Makhzoomy was raised in Irbid city, north of Jordan, where he received his elementary learning and earned his Second-Secondary certificate (equivalent to High School). He earned his first and second bachelor's degrees in Computer Science and Computer Information Systems in 2004 and 2008,respectively. Alaa earned a master's degree in Computer and Information Science from Cleveland State University in 2010. He also earned a Master of Education with a major in Learning Design and Technology from Wayne State University in Winter 2017. He has been working as an adjunct and tenure faculty teaching many disciplinary subfields of Computer Science and Information Systems since he got his first master's degree at various institutes in Jordan and the U.S. Currently, He is an Assistant Professor of Learning Design and Technology at Yarmouk University of Jordan.

Esra Aksoy, PhD, is a mathematics teacher at a middle school and has doctorate in mathematics education. Her research area includes teaching and learning proof and proving, teaching and learning mathematics at middle school, and educational data mining.

Mehmet Akif Aksoy is a PhD. Student at Econometrics Department. His research area includes mathematics education, optimization, fuzzy logic, data mining, and simulation.

Miriam del Barco is a Ph.D student at the University of Extremadura, Spain. She is carrying out her doctoral research at Science Education during four years (2018-2022) at Department of Science and Mathematics Education, University of Extremadura, Spain. Her research area includes Science teaching, training primary education teacher, instructional design and development and emotion regulation.

About the Contributors

María Luisa Bermejo, PhD, is an associate professor in the Department of Psychology and Anthropology at the University of Extremadura, Spain. Her research area includes Pedagogy and Education, cognitive psychology, emotional competencies, pre-service teacher and emotion regulation, among others. She has published over 70 refereed journal papers and book chapters.

Florentina Cañada, PhD, is an associate professor of science education in the Department of Science and Mathematics Education at the University of Extremadura, Spain. Her research area includes Science teaching, pre-service teacher, instructional design and development and emotion regulation, among others. She has published over 50 refereed journal papers and book chapters at Science education area. Since 2013, she is the head of the research group Professional development of science and mathematics teachers.

Larianne Collins is a Lecturer of Geography in the Department of Geography and Earth Sciences at the University of North Carolina Charlotte, USA. Her research interests include spatial thinking, geospatial technologies, geography education and curriculum and teacher development. She is a former secondary social studies teacher and is a National Geographic Certified Educator. She has recently served as the Education Programs Manager for the South Carolina Geographic Alliance and remains an active member.

Monika Dockendorff is a High School Mathematics Teacher and has worked in several types of schools and contexts successfully integrating digital technology for teaching and learning mathematics. For the last 6 years she has worked as a professor of digital learning environments of the Teaching and Learning Mathematics courses in the Faculty of Education at the Catholic University of Chile. She has imparted workshops for in-service teachers as well. Her research area includes the integration of digital technology and dynamic learning environments for mathematics education, particularly at the secondary level. She has published and presented her work in local and international seminars and conferences. She is a member of the advisor committee for the Observatory of Digital Educational Practices at Catholic University of Chile and a board member of Elige Educar, a non-profit organization working to improve education in Chile.

Inés Fombella-Coto is a lecturer of Didactics in Art Education at the Faculty of Teacher Training and Education at the University of Oviedo, Spain. Her main research interest includes creative processes through contemporary art and architecture in art education, ICT uses in art education and relationship between school architecture and learning process. She is a member of Tecn@ Research Group.

Kevin Greenberg is a doctoral student at the University of Utah. His research pertains to learning and cognition, with the focus of cognitive load theory, reasoning, and working memory in STEM education. More specifically, he has researched what factors contribute to reducing cognitive load, along with how students learn about the physics of climate change. He is interested in examining the aspects of working memory and reasoning that most benefit education, when it comes to STEM. He currently has seven publications. He has presented at the international conference at The Society for Information and Technology & Teacher Education in Washington, D.C. and has also been awarded the Steffenson Cannon Scholarship at the University of Utah, along with the University of Utah Outstanding Honors Thesis award.

About the Contributors

Monika Lohani, PhD, is an assistant professor of learning and cognition in the Department of Educational Psychology at the University of Utah, USA. Her research interests include applied cognition in real-world contexts with the goal to improve performance and health outcomes.

Isabelle Maloy is finishing her first year at the University of Utah with a declared major in psychology as a pre-medical student which she is hoping to later use to pursue a career in neurology. Her interest pertains to how the basic building blocks of life come together and give rise to higher cognitive function. Her interest in psychology was spurred when she read an article about split-brain syndrome two years ago and is now looking more into the field of cognitive psychology. She graduated at eighteen with an Associate's degree and was awarded the New Century Scholarship and Trustee's scholarship at the University of Utah.

Inés López Manrique, PhD, is Assistant Professor in the Faculty of Teacher Training and Education in Education Sciences at the University of Oviedo, Spain. She is currently teaching in the Master's Degree in Secondary Education Teacher Training; in the Master's Degree in Innovation in Pre-School and Primary Education Teacher Training; and in the Bachelor's Degree in Pre-School Education and Primary Education. She has made stays in Spanish universities and abroad, participates in specialized conferences and publishes articles in specialized research magazines.

Lourdes Villalustre Martínez, PhD, is Professor of ICT applied to Education in the Faculty of Teacher Training and Education, Department of Sciences Education at the University of Oviedo, Spain. Dr. Martinez is a member of the Tecn @ research group. She has published in about 70 articles in impact magazine (Scopus and JCR). She is an expert evaluator in more than ten journals. She has collaborated in 30 collective works and she is the co-author of three books. She has participated in several competitive research projects and has collaborated as a guest researcher in several universities: Montreal (Canada); Genoa (Italy); Lisbon (Portugal); Lima (Peru). Research areas: digital storytelling, augmented reality, robotics and programming, videogames.

M. Esther del Moral-Pérez, PhD, is a Professor of Educative Technology at the Faculty of Teacher Training and Education at the University of Oviedo, Spain. Leader of Tecn@ Research Group, her research interests include designing and testing hypermedia learning resources, e-Learning and cognitive styles and the networks and Web applications in the learning technologies, videogames and development of multiple intelligences, media literacy, social media, serious games, app, augmented reality, etc.

Serkan Narlı, PhD, is a professor at Dokuz Eylül University, Turkey and has doctorate in mathematics education. His research area includes teacher education, mathematics education, rough sets, topology and educational data mining.

María del Rosario Neira-Piñeiro is a lecturer at the of Faculty of Teacher Training and Education at the University of Oviedo, Spain. Her research interests are children's literature, literary education and the use ICT and audiovisual media in education. She has authored or co-authored works on picturebooks, reading habits, teacher training, film analysis, and digital technologies in education. She is a member of Tecn@ Research Group

About the Contributors

Emma O'Brien is an Academic Developer in Technology Enhanced Learning (TEL) in Mary Immaculate College, having previously worked as a lecturer and researcher in several Irish HEIs for the past fifteen years. Emma has taught across several different disciplines including Business, Humanities and Computer Science, through blended, online and face-to-face mediums. She has taught on undergraduate, postgraduate and professional programmes including several modules in e-learning and instructional design. Emma has mentored over 125 final year students and twelve masters students. Emma has a PhD in Technology Enhanced Learning and a Masters in Computing in Education. Emma has been awarded over €1 million in funding for her research in technology-enhanced learning and has over 30 publications in this area.

Eric G. Poitras, PhD, is an Assistant Professor of Instructional Design and Educational Technology with specialization in adaptive training systems, educational data mining, and self-regulated learning.

Esperanza Rosiña carried out her Master research in the Department of Science and Mathematics Education, University of Extremadura, Spain.

Pejman Sajjadi obtained his PhD from Vrije Universiteit Brussel for a dissertation on "Individualizing Learning Games: Incorporating the Theory of Multiple Intelligences in Player-Centered Game Design". He is currently a post-doc research fellow at Pennsylvania State University. His primary research interests are digital game-based learning (DGBL) and opportunities for individualization, e-learning, and human computer interaction.

Jesús Sánchez-Martín, PhD, is an associate professor at Faculty of Education, Department of Science and Mathematics Education at the University of Extremadura, Spain. He carried out his doctoral research at Chemical Engineering. Since 2014, his research area includes Science teaching, pre-service teacher, educational gamification and emotion regulation, among others. He has published over 40 refereed journal papers and book chapters at Science education area.

Timothy W. Spannaus, PhD, is Senior Lecturer and Program Coordinator in the Learning Design and Technology program and Director of the Graduate Certificate in University Teaching at Wayne State University, Detroit, USA. His books include Creating Video for Teachers and Trainers published by Wiley & Sons. Research interests include instructional design and the scholarship of teaching and learning.

Aubrey Statti, Ed.D., earned a Bachelor of Arts in Political Science and Spanish from the University of Florida and a Master's of Professional Counseling and a Doctorate of Education from Liberty University. She has worked in higher education for 13 years and has taught at the undergraduate, graduate, and post-graduate levels in areas of psychology, counseling, education, and research. Additionally, she has worked in the Florida public schools as both a high school teacher and a school counselor. Dr. Statti is currently a professor for The Chicago School of Professional Psychology's (TCSPP) Educational Psychology and Technology program, primarily teaching qualitative research and ethics courses. She also serves as a Dissertation Chair and reader on doctoral student's dissertations. Her research interests in the areas of educational technology include K-12 education, online education, digital storytelling, rural

About the Contributors

education, and the impact of mentorship in educational settings. Dr. Statti has served as a reviewer for the Contemporary Issues in Technology and Teacher Education journal and is currently on the development committee of TCSPP's International Journal of Educational Psychology and Technology.

Charlene Stokes, PhD, is the Director of the Human-Machine Social Systems Lab at the MITRE Corporation. Her primary research focus is on the social dynamics of human-machine interaction, with 15 years of experience and numerous publications on the topic of trust in autonomy.

Kelly Torres, Ph.D., earned a Bachelor of Arts in Psychology with a minor in Child Development from Florida State University and two Master's degrees in Learning and Cognition and Curriculum Instruction from Florida State University. She also earned a doctorate of philosophy in Educational Psychology from Florida State University. Dr. Torres has a K-12 Florida teaching certificate in ESOL and ESE. She has taught undergraduate and graduate courses in areas of instructional technology, educational psychology, curriculum development, assessment, linguistics, and teacher education. Dr. Torres currently serves as the Department Chair for the Ed.D. Educational Psychology and Technology program at The Chicago School of Professional Psychology. Her research interests are focused on instructional technology integration, online learning, student motivation, rural education, and language learning. She has served as a reviewer for several journals and is currently overseeing the development of the International Journal of Educational Psychology and Technology.

Olga De Troyer, PhD, is a Full Professor in Computer Science at the Vrije Universiteit Brussel (VUB) in Brussels, Belgium. She holds a Master in Mathematics and a PhD in Computer Science. She has more than 30 years of experience in research in conceptual modeling and design methods for innovative information systems, applied to different areas such as databases, web systems, semantic web, software variability, e-learning, mobile applications, virtual reality, and serious games. She is the head of the research group WISE, which she founded in 1998, where one of the foci is on new human-computer interaction aspects, including Virtual Reality, Augmented Reality, data physicalisation, as well as multimodal and multi-touch interaction. Development of new engineering methodologies, authoring tools and software frameworks for the rapid prototyping and efficient realization of innovative information environments is at the kernel of the research. More information on https://wise.vub.ac.be/olga-de-troyer.

Anastasia D. Vakaloudi has a M.A. and a Ph.D. in History, a M.Ed. in the Didactic and Pedagogical Use of Information and Communication Technologies (ICT) in Education and a Ph.D. in the Didactics of History and the Use of ICT in the Teaching of History. She has also attended a second Master's in History Degree program at Ludwig-Maximilians-Universität in Munich (Germany). She is a Teachers' Supervisor (Inspector) in Secondary Education appointed by the Greek Ministry of Education, Research and Religious Affairs, an Adjunct Professor of the Hellenic Open University, and a Teacher trainer in the Didactic and Pedagogical Use of ICT in Education. She is the author of 13 scientific monographs/books, she has published chapters in nine scientific national and international collective volumes, in six textbooks for teacher training programs and postgraduate specialization studies programs, and over 70 articles of scientific research in History, Literature, ICT, Didactics and Pedagogy in national and international refereed journals and Proceedings of national and international Conferences. Website URL: http://users.sch.gr/avakalou.

María Belén San Pedro Veledo, PhD, is a lecturer in the Faculty of Teacher Training and Education, Department of Sciences Education at the University of Oviedo, Spain. She is currently teaching in the Master's Degree in Secondary Education Teacher Training and in the Bachelor's Degree in Primary Education. Her research areas includes Social Sciences Didactics, History Teaching and ITC in the Teaching of Social Sciences. She has published more tan 20 journal papers and book chapters.

Ke Zhang, PhD, is Professor in the Learning Design and Technology Program at Wayne State University in Detroit, Michigan, USA. Her research focuses on innovative technology and emerging big data methods and applications. Her work is translated into and cited in many languages, and adapted to guide research and practices in various countries and settings. Her collaborative research is supported by federal government and agencies, like the US Department of Health and Human Services and National Institute of Health, with multi-million grants to design, develop and research on emerging technologies for STEM education, professional training, or health information management. Dr. Zhang has also consulted by international organizations, national governments and agencies, corporations, educational institutions and healthcare systems.

Index

21st Century Learning 19, 33-34, 40
3D Model 140

A

academic performance 96, 155, 244, 246-249, 251-253, 255, 259
adaptability 262, 266-271, 277, 280
ADI 124-125, 128-130, 132-135, 140
art 42, 66, 97, 128, 185-186, 188-189, 192, 194, 200, 265, 288
Augmented Didactic Itinerary 124, 129, 132, 135, 140
augmented reality 7, 10, 72, 82, 91, 124-125, 127, 140, 142, 144-145, 151-152, 154, 285

B

bodily kinesthetic intelligence 91, 124

C

case study 33, 35, 51, 124, 129, 141, 227, 233, 246, 282, 289-290, 293-294
cognition 3, 69-70, 163, 170, 213, 281, 283-284, 289-290, 292, 294-297
cognitive prompts 162, 170-172, 174-177, 182
communication 1-2, 46, 67, 70, 73, 163, 184-186, 188-189, 194, 200-201, 213, 217, 265, 281-283, 285-287, 289, 291-296
Compensatory Hypothesis 169-171, 173-174, 182
competency 24, 34-36, 40, 43, 73, 116, 120
Competency based education 24
computer application 72-74, 76, 81-83, 91
Constructivist Teaching Strategies 18

D

decision tree 93, 96-97, 101-106
deep learning 67, 165-167, 171-177, 183

digital age 1, 13-14, 18, 113, 118-119
Digital Game-Based Learning 64
Digital Immigrant 123
digital learning 4, 9, 19-20, 26, 29, 33-34, 40-42, 57, 217, 297
Digital Learning Objects 19-20, 26, 29, 33-34, 40
Digital Native 123
digital technology 6, 12, 65-71, 74-76, 80, 82-83, 216-220, 225-226, 233, 235-236
dragging test 228, 230, 243

E

education 1-3, 5-6, 8-9, 11-14, 19-20, 22, 24-25, 28-29, 36, 41, 65-66, 70, 75, 93-95, 100, 105, 113-116, 118, 120, 124-130, 132, 134-135, 140-143, 145, 153, 155, 160, 173, 184, 186, 188, 191, 216-219, 225, 232, 235-236, 245, 253-255, 261-268, 270-272, 297
educational data mining 93-94, 96-97
emotion management 284, 287, 289-290, 292, 297
emotions 12, 14, 130, 262-266, 269-272, 287
executive function 168, 183

G

game development 248, 251, 255-256, 259
game experience 41, 43-47, 50-52, 57-58, 64
GameMaker® 245-247, 252, 254-255
game mechanic 47, 49-52, 54-56, 64
game mechanics 42-43, 45-47, 49-58, 71
Gardner 2-4, 6-7, 9-11, 20-21, 23, 42, 45, 66, 68, 83, 98, 113, 115, 125, 140, 143, 160, 163-164, 167, 176-177, 185-188, 190-192, 199, 218, 263-265, 277, 282
GeoGebra 220, 223-227, 229, 231, 243
GeoGebra-based dynamic applet 232-233, 243
geolocation 128, 134, 141-145, 147-148, 151-155, 160
Geolocation Apps 143, 160

geospatial data 113, 115, 123
geospatial technologies 112-113, 115-120, 123
geospatial thinking 114-115, 123
globalizing approach 127, 134, 140

H

Hard Construction 243
historical thinking 184-186, 213
human-technology team 283, 287-290, 293-294, 296, 309

I

immersive technology 72, 74, 76, 80-83, 91
individualization 41-46, 57-58, 64
infant education 124-130, 132, 134-135, 140, 142
Infant Education (Second Cycle) 140
Information and Communication Technology (ICT) 213
insights 216-217, 219, 235, 255, 283, 285, 296
interactivity 167, 191, 230, 253, 255

L

Learner-Centered Theories 184, 190
learning design 5, 246, 259
learning games 42-46, 57
Learning Management System (LMS) 29, 67, 259
learning outcome 35, 43, 45, 51-52, 57-58, 174
Learning Styles 1-2, 12, 19-23, 25, 35-36, 43-44, 66, 74, 93-94, 97-98, 101-106, 143, 184, 187-188, 190, 192, 200
Logical-Mathematic Intelligence 91

M

Marker 140
mathematically gifted 93-94, 97, 100, 102-106
mathematical processes 216, 219
meaningful learning 40, 171-172, 176-177, 216, 226, 235, 264
meta-analysis 21, 65-66, 72, 74-79, 82-83
metacognition 34, 191, 213
MI theory 20-21, 33, 71, 140
Mobile Apps 160
Moodle 247, 259
multimedia 5-6, 19, 23, 66-69, 72-74, 76, 79-83, 91, 127, 145, 152, 162-163, 166, 168-177, 182-183
multimedia learning 82, 162, 168-169, 171-176, 183
Multimodal Learning 25, 40
Multimodal Literacy 192, 213

multiple intelligences 1-3, 6, 12-14, 18, 20-21, 40-42, 45, 64-66, 71-76, 80, 82-83, 93-94, 97-98, 101, 103, 105-106, 113, 124-126, 134, 140-145, 154-155, 160, 177, 184-188, 190-192, 199-200, 218, 261-267, 277-278
multiple intelligences strategies 186
Multiple Intelligence Theory 1, 3, 13, 18-20, 185, 188, 190, 200, 218

N

naturalistic intelligence 46, 126-127, 135, 141, 155, 160, 199, 271
non-technical skills 282-283, 288-289, 292-295, 309

O

Object-Oriented Programming (OOP) 244-247, 249, 251, 254-256, 259
online learning 12, 18, 259
Open Educational Resources (OER) 36, 184, 186, 191, 202, 213

P

personality type 99, 101, 103, 105-106
personalized 40, 58, 98, 166
Personalized Learning Environment 40
picturebook 129-131, 134-135, 140
player-centered game design 41-43, 45, 50-51, 57-58, 64
primary education 141, 143, 145, 153, 155, 261-262, 264-268, 270-271
programming courses 244-247, 252, 254-256, 259

R

rapport 4, 7, 282-284, 286-287, 289-292, 294-297
recommendation tool 41, 52, 57, 64
redundancy effect 169-170, 173-174, 176, 183
registers of representation 219, 224, 229, 232, 235

S

scaffolding 67, 244, 253, 259
schema 28, 34, 68, 71, 163, 166-167, 169-171, 174, 176-177, 183
schema activation 68, 171, 177
secondary education 155, 261-268, 270-272
self-efficacy 66, 73, 263, 271, 277
Simultaneous Dynamic Representations 243
Smart Learning Environment 184, 186, 190, 214

Index

spatial intelligence 9-10, 46, 113-114, 126-127, 130, 134-135, 141, 143-145, 148, 152, 154-155, 160, 199-200
spatial thinking 112-120, 123, 142, 153
Stages of Cognitive Representation 243
Stealth Assessment 64
STEM 253-255, 261-262, 266, 269-271
student-centered learning 9, 11, 18, 191

T

team cognition 281, 283-284, 289-290, 292, 294-297
technical skills 253, 289, 309
technological tools 243
technology 1-14, 19-20, 22-25, 33-34, 41, 65-76, 78-83, 91-92, 115-116, 120, 125-127, 140-142, 147, 155, 188, 194, 196-197, 200, 213, 216-221, 225-226, 233, 235-236, 244-245, 253-254, 262, 264-265, 270-271, 281-283, 285-297, 309

Technology-Enriched Learning Environment 243

V

verbal-linguistic intelligence 4, 13, 72, 76, 92, 98, 103, 162-164, 167
visual images 65, 72-74, 76, 80, 82-83, 92, 192
visualization 52-56, 67, 69, 92, 147, 152-153, 216, 218-221, 224, 229, 235, 243
visual literacy 186, 192, 214
visual-spatial intelligence 10, 45, 54, 71-72, 80, 92, 98, 103, 123, 163, 235, 245, 252, 261, 270-271

W

working memory 43, 54, 162, 167-172, 174-177, 183

Purchase Print, E-Book, or Print + E-Book

IGI Global's reference books are available in three unique pricing formats:
Print Only, E-Book Only, or Print + E-Book.
Shipping fees may apply.

www.igi-global.com

Recommended Reference Books

Handbook of Research on Assessment Practices and Pedagogical Models for Immigrant Students

ISBN: 978-1-5225-9348-5
© 2019; 454 pp.
List Price: $255

Preparing the Higher Education Space for Gen Z

ISBN: 978-1-5225-7763-8
© 2019; 253 pp.
List Price: $175

Prevention and Detection of Academic Misconduct in Higher Education

ISBN: 978-1-5225-7531-3
© 2019; 324 pp.
List Price: $185

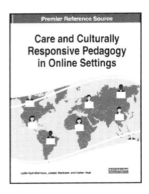

Care and Culturally Responsive Pedagogy in Online Settings

ISBN: 978-1-5225-7802-4
© 2019; 423 pp.
List Price: $195

Handbook of Research on School Violence in American K-12 Education

ISBN: 978-1-5225-6246-7
© 2019; 610 pp.
List Price: $275

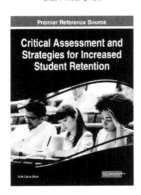

Critical Assessment and Strategies for Increased Student Retention

ISBN: 978-1-5225-2998-9
© 2018; 352 pp.
List Price: $195

Do you want to stay current on the latest research trends, product announcements, news and special offers?
Join IGI Global's mailing list today and start enjoying exclusive perks sent only to IGI Global members.
Add your name to the list at **www.igi-global.com/newsletters**.

Publisher of Peer-Reviewed, Timely, and Innovative Academic Research

IGI Global
DISSEMINATOR OF KNOWLEDGE

Ensure Quality Research is Introduced to the Academic Community

Become an IGI Global Reviewer for Authored Book Projects

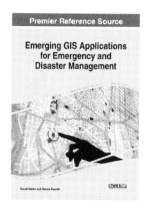
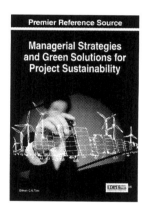

The overall success of an authored book project is dependent on quality and timely reviews.

In this competitive age of scholarly publishing, constructive and timely feedback significantly expedites the turnaround time of manuscripts from submission to acceptance, allowing the publication and discovery of forward-thinking research at a much more expeditious rate. Several IGI Global authored book projects are currently seeking highly-qualified experts in the field to fill vacancies on their respective editorial review boards:

Applications and Inquiries may be sent to:
development@igi-global.com

Applicants must have a doctorate (or an equivalent degree) as well as publishing and reviewing experience. Reviewers are asked to complete the open-ended evaluation questions with as much detail as possible in a timely, collegial, and constructive manner. All reviewers' tenures run for one-year terms on the editorial review boards and are expected to complete at least three reviews per term. Upon successful completion of this term, reviewers can be considered for an additional term.

If you have a colleague that may be interested in this opportunity, we encourage you to share this information with them.

IGI Global Proudly Partners with

eContent Pro International® Publication Services
Committed to Excellent Service, Affordability, and the Highest Quality From Manuscript Development to Publication

Publication Services Provided by eContent Pro International:

Scientific & Scholarly Editing

English Language Copy Editing

Journal Recommendation

Typesetting & Publishing

Figure, Table, Chart & Equation Conversions

Translation

IGI Global Authors Save 25% on eContent Pro International's Services!

Scan the QR Code to Receive Your 25% Discount

The 25% discount is applied directly to your eContent Pro International shopping cart when placing an order through IGI Global's referral link. Use the QR code to access this referral link. eContent Pro International has the right to end or modify any promotion at any time.

Email: customerservice@econtentpro.com

econtentpro.com

www.igi-global.com

Celebrating Over 30 Years of Scholarly Knowledge Creation & Dissemination

InfoSci®-Books

A Database of Over 5,300+ Reference Books Containing Over 100,000+ Chapters Focusing on Emerging Research

GAIN ACCESS TO **THOUSANDS** OF REFERENCE BOOKS AT **A FRACTION** OF THEIR INDIVIDUAL LIST **PRICE**.

InfoSci®-Books Database

The **InfoSci®-Books** database is a collection of over 5,300+ IGI Global single and multi-volume reference books, handbooks of research, and encyclopedias, encompassing groundbreaking research from prominent experts worldwide that span over 350+ topics in 11 core subject areas including business, computer science, education, science and engineering, social sciences and more.

Open Access Fee Waiver (Offset Model) Initiative

For any library that invests in IGI Global's InfoSci-Journals and/or InfoSci-Books databases, IGI Global will match the library's investment with a fund of equal value to go toward **subsidizing the OA article processing charges (APCs) for their students, faculty, and staff** at that institution when their work is submitted and accepted under OA into an IGI Global journal.*

INFOSCI® PLATFORM FEATURES

- No DRM
- No Set-Up or Maintenance Fees
- A Guarantee of No More Than a 5% Annual Increase
- Full-Text HTML and PDF Viewing Options
- Downloadable MARC Records
- Unlimited Simultaneous Access
- COUNTER 5 Compliant Reports
- Formatted Citations With Ability to Export to RefWorks and EasyBib
- No Embargo of Content (Research is Available Months in Advance of the Print Release)

*The fund will be offered on an annual basis and expire at the end of the subscription period. The fund would renew as the subscription is renewed for each year thereafter. The open access fees will be waived after the student, faculty, or staff's paper has been vetted and accepted into an IGI Global journal and the fund can only be used toward publishing OA in an IGI Global journal. Libraries in developing countries will have the match on their investment doubled.

To Learn More or To Purchase This Database:
www.igi-global.com/infosci-books

eresources@igi-global.com • Toll Free: 1-866-342-6657 ext. 100 • Phone: 717-533-8845 x100

www.igi-global.com

Publisher of Peer-Reviewed, Timely, and Innovative Academic Research Since 1988

IGI Global's Transformative Open Access (OA) Model:
How to Turn Your University Library's Database Acquisitions Into a Source of OA Funding

In response to the OA movement and well in advance of Plan S, IGI Global, early last year, unveiled their OA Fee Waiver (Offset Model) Initiative.

Under this initiative, librarians who invest in IGI Global's InfoSci-Books (5,300+ reference books) and/or InfoSci-Journals (185+ scholarly journals) databases will be able to subsidize their patron's OA article processing charges (APC) when their work is submitted and accepted (after the peer review process) into an IGI Global journal.*

How Does it Work?

1. When a library subscribes or perpetually purchases IGI Global's InfoSci-Databases including InfoSci-Books (5,300+ e-books), InfoSci-Journals (185+ e-journals), and/or their discipline/subject-focused subsets, IGI Global will match the library's investment with a fund of equal value to go toward subsidizing the OA article processing charges (APCs) for their patrons.

   Researchers: Be sure to recommend the InfoSci-Books and InfoSci-Journals to take advantage of this initiative.

2. When a student, faculty, or staff member submits a paper and it is accepted (following the peer review) into one of IGI Global's 185+ scholarly journals, the author will have the option to have their paper published under a traditional publishing model or as OA.

3. When the author chooses to have their paper published under OA, IGI Global will notify them of the OA Fee Waiver (Offset Model) Initiative. If the author decides they would like to take advantage of this initiative, IGI Global will deduct the US$ 1,500 APC from the created fund.

4. This fund will be offered on an annual basis and will renew as the subscription is renewed for each year thereafter. IGI Global will manage the fund and award the APC waivers unless the librarian has a preference as to how the funds should be managed.

Hear From the Experts on This Initiative:

"I'm very happy to have been able to make one of my recent research contributions, 'Visualizing the Social Media Conversations of a National Information Technology Professional Association' featured in the *International Journal of Human Capital and Information Technology Professionals*, freely available along with having access to the valuable resources found within IGI Global's InfoSci-Journals database."

– **Prof. Stuart Palmer**, Deakin University, Australia

For More Information, Visit: www.igi-global.com/publish/contributor-resources/open-access or contact IGI Global's Database Team at eresources@igi-global.com.

Are You Ready to Publish Your Research?

IGI Global offers book authorship and editorship opportunities across 11 subject areas, including business, computer science, education, science and engineering, social sciences, and more!

Benefits of Publishing with IGI Global:

- Free one-on-one editorial and promotional support.
- Expedited publishing timelines that can take your book from start to finish in less than one (1) year.
- Choose from a variety of formats including: Edited and Authored References, Handbooks of Research, Encyclopedias, and Research Insights.
- Utilize IGI Global's eEditorial Discovery® submission system in support of conducting the submission and blind review process.

- IGI Global maintains a strict adherence to ethical practices due in part to our full membership with the Committee on Publication Ethics (COPE).
- Indexing potential in prestigious indices such as Scopus®, Web of Science™, PsycINFO®, and ERIC – Education Resources Information Center.
- Ability to connect your ORCID iD to your IGI Global publications.
- Earn royalties on your publication as well as receive complimentary copies and exclusive discounts.

Get Started Today by Contacting the Acquisitions Department at:

acquisition@igi-global.com